Mannerism in Italian Music and Culture, 1530–1630

Mannerism in Italian Music and Culture, 1530–1630

by
Maria Rika Maniates

THE UNIVERSITY OF NORTH CAROLINA PRESS
CHAPEL HILL

© 1979 The University of North Carolina Press
All rights reserved
Manufactured in the United States of America
Library of Congress Catalog Card Number 78-11236
ISBN 0-8078-1319-2

Library of Congress Cataloging in Publication Data

Maniates, Maria Rika, 1937–
    Mannerism in Italian music and culture, 1530–1630.

    Bibliography: p.
    Includes index.
    1. Music—Italy—History and criticism.   2. Style,
Musical.   3. Italy—Intellectual life.   4. Music—
History and criticism—16th century.   5. Music—
History and criticism—17th century.   I. Title.
MI290.2.M36   784'.1   78-11236
ISBN 0-8078-1319-2

To my parents
Sophia and Euripides Maniates

Contents

[vii]

Figures

Music Examples

§❧§❧§❧

Preface

The basic thesis of this study posits the viability of Mannerism as a historic-stylistic concept that arises out of musical patterns evident in the practice of and thought about music between the years 1530 and 1630. An understanding of this concept, in both its broadest and its most narrow relations to musical activity during these years, can help to clarify for us the fundamental changes in musical style that took place between the Renaissance and the Baroque. Indeed, the very notion of "style," or *maniera*, with all its assumptions and problems, lies at the core of mannerist attitudes in the sixteenth century, regardless of whether we assess any of these attitudes to be instinctive or conscious, and regardless of whether we judge the musical results to be successful or misguided in terms of absolute artistic merit. The reader will find that, upon occasion, I inject value judgments of the latter kind. But for the most part, the narrative is restricted to interpreting the value judgments of artists and critics of the time, and for this reason, I try to keep the discussion within the terms of reference used by sixteenth-century thinkers.

Style and style criticism are the primary concerns of musicology. Musical style entails something more than the evolution of musical techniques, even though style criticism cannot be conducted without detailed investigation of such matters. Musical style is the testament of a living art that molds and in its turn bears the imprint of individual personalities and cultural groups. Therefore, style criticism takes its place in the history of the human spirit, the history of ideas and of culture. In my view, Mannerism in the sixteenth century forms an important, but inadequately understood phase of such histories—not only because it represents a major phase in Western European music, but also because during its heyday, the problems entailed in formulating style norms come to the foreground of intellectual preoccupations. Moreover, in spite of concrete aspects having to do with musical techniques and style criticism in sixteenth-century terms—terms which make sense only in their pertinent historical framework—the general picture created by these documents of intellectual history encapsulates for us the perennial conundrum of aesthetics, that branch of philosophy that seeks to synthesize the technical elements of the creative act with the critical elements of value criteria. It is well known that authors, after expending much effort and energy on a project, are wont to stress the importance of their work. Nonetheless, in this case, I do wish to emphasize that during the mannerist period we witness the coming of age of musical aesthetics insofar as many of its issues, some of them contentious in the extreme, survive the historical ambience which gave them birth to remain alive and lively throughout subsequent intellectual history—even to the present day.

Before proceeding to an explanation of specific approaches to the various topics covered in this study, I feel it is necessary to state at the outset that connecting Mannerism and music raises many controversial issues. Aside from legitimate rejection of the thesis posited in this book, the very hypothesis behind it is subject to some debate. Recently, historic-stylistic notions have fallen into disrepute in musicology. Although this is not the place to expose arguments for or against such an approach, it is to the point to indicate here that my thesis relies on a belief in the value of such concepts, and that its entire bias can be dismissed by scholars who disagree with its assumption. I stand by this assumption not only because of its universal validity as an approach to cultural history, but also because of its relevance to the sixteenth century, the period during which historic-stylistic categories first became issues of seminal import.

The three parts of this book embody a broad cultural study. Matters on internal organization are, in the end, idiosyncratic. For this reason, the related arts, intellectual currents, and social conditions are covered without implying that any of these topics is subservient or preparatory to any other topic. But one must begin somewhere, and I have chosen to start with music's sister arts, and then to build my argument by investigating musical theory and musical practice.

In view of the popularity of Mannerism in art history, the existence of many detailed studies devoted to this phenomenon comes as no surprise. Although brief, my chapters on this subject outline a personal view in which I suggest concurrent exploration of a *maniera dolce* and a *maniera grande*—two stylized styles that find appropriate musical embodiments as well. Literary critics, on the other hand, hesitate to connect poetry with Mannerism; and furthermore, their studies often present a somewhat vague picture of poetic trends. This situation is troublesome for the musicologist insofar as parallels between poetry and music are more than mere analogies. The evolution of poetry, in my view, shows a distinct progression from gentle petrarchism to extravagant concettism. And this poetic overview, of course, finds obvious echoes in musical practice. Indeed, the latter art may have had deep repercussions on the former, repercussions largely overlooked by scholars of sixteenth-century literature. As for the background of Mannerism, rather than dwell on opposing interpretations of it, I have drawn together phenomena noted by historians into a network of factors contributing to a mannerist outlook. Because specialists work in isolated fields, few have made such a synthesis and none to my knowledge under the rubric of Mannerism. Although the exposition of relevant data in all these areas depends on pertinent primary and secondary literature, the interpretation of their mannerist aspects is colored by my sense of Mannerism in musical activities contemporary with them. Far from being an apology, this admission indicates that musical research has influenced profoundly the general thesis of the book; and in this sense, then, the application of Mannerism to music is definitely not an appendage of ideas prevalent in the other arts.

In the case of musical theory, one finds many excellent works on individual topics. Yet there exist very few histories written from any point of view. One aspect of this study, therefore, passes in review known data in order to put them into focus as evidence of intellectual history. And because my avowed interest is in Mannerism, I offer new interpretations of technical subjects, interpretations which lead naturally to aesthetic concepts. Taken together, these facets of musical thought aim at projecting a continuum of conservative, progressive, and radical attitudes. It should perhaps be pointed out here that the majority of scholars who examine theoretical writings tend to neglect the aesthetic resonances found in them. By joining technical and aesthetic matters and putting them into a historical narrative, I am convinced that the concept of Mannerism can illuminate how renaissance theory became baroque theory. Referring to only one side of this topic, albeit an important one, research has shown that musical sources pertinent to *maniera* are both numerous and provocative, and they therefore furnish even stronger evidence for the impact of this term and the ideas inherent in it than do the sources customarily mustered by historians of art.

The same situation pertains to the investigation of composition and performance practices. The polyphonic madrigal is the medium through which major style changes were affected. This genre has been studied by many eminent musicologists, but infrequently from the viewpoint of tracing its mannerist elements. And it will become evident that my thesis concerning Mannerism as a major style period differs substantially from the views of those colleagues who admit some validity for this concept in the madrigal. Periodization of any kind, and especially the kind that traces the life cycle of a musical style, can be faulted as a mental construct artificially imposed on the natural and instinctive shaping of a musical language. Even if this criticism rings true, I remind the reader that it can be leveled against sixteenth-century mannerists themselves. Furthermore, there exists strong evidence for self-conscious and deliberate stylization in the musical works as well. Certain dominant characteristics in the madrigal suggest four stages with fluid boundaries between them. In spite of their perilous tendency toward rigidity, the stages thus isolated help us to better grasp the main outlines throughout a period noted for its multifaceted individualism.

The early phase of the madrigal evinces a restrained eclecticism in its amalgamation of current and new features. Exorbitant harmonic audacities mark the second stage. These are eventually absorbed into the arsenal of imitative-affective devices that animate the mosaic madrigal, a stylization that flourishes during the third stage. The final stage shows the ultimate conventionality of madrigalisms as well as the invention of still more novel techniques, the latter pointing to the Baroque. To this last transitional phase belong the newest forms of concerted and solo madrigals. By examining the role of music in the theater, especially in the mannerist intermedio, it is possible to put the earliest essays in staged opera into a meaningful context. And finally, into this exposition of musical events, one must interpolate other factors such as musical academies, printing, humanism, and the influence of the Counter Reformation.

Two parallel chapters investigate concepts of a Renaissance-Mannerism-Baroque continuum—one for the sister arts and one for music. Instead of using them as introductory material, I have chosen to place them at the end of pertinent sections because they gather together detailed strands of a technical or aesthetic nature into broad historic-stylistic concepts. The generalities which come into focus in these concluding chapters can thus be measured against the concrete evidence exposed in the course of earlier discussions.

No doubt, the reader will be struck by several omissions. Instrumental music comprises a separate and complex field with its own theoretical and practical traditions. These are not examined because they deserve their own detailed and focused study, although reference to instrumental music crops up from time to time as a point of reference pertinent to matters of vocal style. I mention as areas of future investigation the notions that the earliest abstract genres are stylizations of vocal *maniere*, and that the appearance of bold harmonies in early seventeenth-century keyboard music derives from madrigalian Mannerism. It is also tempting to suggest that as the madrigal moves closer and closer to rhetorical and dramatic ideals, thus ceding the aesthetic values of abstract logic and coherence, composers turn to exploring instrumental music as a medium in which these precise values can be embodied. This tentative suggestion receives some support from the derogatory evaluation of instrumental music made by champions of the expressive madrigal, monody, and opera. Although I touch on scholarly conceptions of Mannerism that compare the sixteenth century to other periods, notably to the twentieth century, no attempt is made to deal with Mannerism as a recurring phenomenon in Western culture. These omissions should not be construed as a disregard for the usefulness of such investigations. They are simply not germane to my central thesis.

I close these prefatory remarks with two points of a more mundane nature. First, a point of clarification about the consistent use of terms such as Mannerism, mannerist, and mannered is in order. To be sure, the task of this study is to convince the reader that such words are pertinent and useful; their ubiquitous presence should not be construed as an attempt to beguile sympathy. On the contrary, they appear whenever I wish to remind the reader which elements are conceived specifically as belonging to Mannerism rather than to the Renaissance or to the Baroque. The only other solution would be to avoid these admittedly loaded terms until the concluding chapters. But such a subterfuge would render this book like the proverbial German dissertation in which all the verbs are saved for the final pages. Second, a note concerning the footnote apparatus, especially with regard to primary documents, will help those readers wishing to pursue details which may be of interest. Wherever possible, footnotes refer to chapters rather than to specific pages of a given work. Thus, the reader can locate material in the document in question regardless of the format available —original, reprint, reproduction, modern edition, translation. In cases where chapter divisions do not exist, reference to pages is made along with an indication of which specific edition has been used. In the case of short documents, such as letters and prefaces, no specific reference seems necessary. The Bibliography of primary material furnishes pertinent bibliographical information for all documents—literary, artistic, theoretical, and musical.

April 1978   Maria Rika Maniates

ᔆ᙮ᔆ᙮ᔆ᙮

Acknowledgments

I acknowledge with gratitude the generosity of the American Council of Learned Societies, the University of Toronto, and the Canada Council. Their grants supported various phases of the research for this project. In addition, the latter two institutions provided salary funds for three research assistants, Francis Braunlich, Patricia Lake, and Wilfred Renard, whose capable work facilitated certain aspects of the preparation of the book.

My debt to my colleagues and graduate students, friends all, with whom I enjoyed many stimulating discussions, also requires recognition insofar as they acted, inadvertently perhaps, as catalysts for further thought on my part. Special thanks are due to David Mercer, who loaned me his dance material, and to James Haar, who loaned me his set of offprints of the papers given at the conference on Mannerism in Rome long before the papers appeared in *Studi Musicali* 3 (1974). I also note the cooperation of the library staff at Columbia University and the University of Toronto who went out of their way, with unflagging courtesy, to locate elusive primary and secondary material whenever I required it.

The imposition that authors make on friends to peruse and comment on their work can hardly be redressed by mere mention in the course of acknowledgments. Nonetheless, I here express my sincere appreciation to Gregory Butler, and John and Julie Reibetanz, who read portions of an earlier draft of the book, and especially to Howard Smither and Glenn Watkins, whose detailed assessments of the penultimate version were of inestimable value.

To Lewis Bateman, Sandra Eisdorfer, Pamela Morrison, and

[xix]

the copyediting and production staff of The University of North Carolina Press are due many thanks for their limitless patience and good-humored vigilance in supervising the technicalities of turning a complicated manuscript into a book.

The understanding and encouragement of the members of my family helped me overcome what seemed to be insurmountable obstacles throughout the many years during which I was preoccupied with this project.

PART ONE

Mannerism in the Sister Arts

CHAPTER I

ᔓᔓᔓ

Introduction

If writings on Mannerism seem unduly argumentative, their approach is largely a consequence of problems surrounding the term.[1] Because convention imputes derogatory judgments to the meaning of Mannerism, which judgments embody prejudices inherited from art criticism between the seventeenth and nineteenth centuries, we habitually use the word to signify negative criteria of stylistic effeteness. Lately, however, writers have revived the positive value of Mannerism by stressing that its characteristics resemble virile aspects of modern Expressionism and Surrealism.[2] In the sister arts, Mannerism has become a virtual bandwagon, with studies ranging from the scholarly to the popular. Its present-day prevalence can be further gauged from the minting of learned coinage such as antimannerism and even neomannerism.[3] These concepts are not at all absurd; if Classicism can have an "anti" or "neo" phase, the same may be said of Mannerism. This proliferation of terms derives, of course, from the Italian, *maniera*, meaning style or more precisely stylization,[4] a term that first attained prominence in sixteenth-century literature.

In appraising the militant essays of modern scholarship, we must bear in mind that the erstwhile pejorative meanings of labels such as Gothic or Baroque have receded into the annals of the past and are resurrected today as curiosities in the history of taste. Whereas the specialist in the latter epochs uses these epithets with equanimity, his counterpart in Mannerism feels compelled to combat opposition to the term as a valid tool. And yet, many writers within the last decade consider Mannerism to be an emancipated concept and now formulate more rigorous definitions in an effort

[3]

to improve on earlier research. Indeed, it is possible to write a history of the term itself.[5]

One group of scholars focuses on aesthetic premises common to attitudes behind modern art and art between 1530 and 1630. Previously designated as Late Renaissance or Early Baroque, the latter time span is now called the Age of Mannerism—an age that seems to offer alluring parallels to avant-garde art of our own century. The arts of both eras are said to reflect a common disposition. Rather than dismiss their features as instances of sterile decadence, we are asked to examine them as the virile production of a world view.[6] Scholars ascribe the spiritual tension they detect in mannerist art to a cultural situation informed by all sorts of crises. Innate feelings of alienation are aggravated by unstable relationships with a volatile society. Artists therefore emphasize their individual styles in a self-conscious way and rebel against established conventions that they find meaningless. I shall return to the methodological problems posed by this approach in this and future chapters. But in spite of problems, some of the ideas put forward by these scholars are useful, especially when they are tempered by a more historical approach that draws ideas from primary sources. This book attempts just such a synthesis.

Mannerist artworks flaunt formal complexities and through them exhibit deliberate intellectualism. Since difficulty and problem solving are at a premium, each creator strives for his own solution, a strictly personal utterance. When this situation reaches exaggerated proportions, artists turn to distortion. On the one hand, distortion mirrors the grotesque aspects of an irrational world. This type of Mannerism communicates sincere conviction. On the other hand, it also illustrates willful caricaturing of recognized techniques. This type of Mannerism is merely playful and affected. If playfulness has spiritual intensity, it can be bold, pungent, and challenging. After all, *homo ludens* plays many games in deadly seriousness.[7] If it lacks spiritual intensity, playfulness descends to shallow sport in which formal elements are manipulated for the sake of novelty. Then art exhibits caprice and arbitrariness. But the paradox of Mannerism is that it presents a precarious balance between intensity and superficiality. The surface affectation of much mannerist art tends to throw us off balance; but to affect affectation is to reveal an attitude. And when this attitude infects a group, it becomes a cultural symptom.

If paradox is a prominent feature of form, it is an even more salient ingredient of content, for mannerist thought seeks to place extremes in daring apposition. *Discordia concors* functions as an intellectual password. Nicolas Cusanus, a precursor of the neo-platonic school, uses the words *coincidentia oppositorum.* But whereas Cusanus intends the harmonious resolution of opposites into an organic whole, mannerists experiment with attenuated dualities. The opposites never lose their individuality; and the further apart the irreconcilable elements are, the more significant their ingenious combination. Love of paradox is endemic to the mentality of the sixteenth century, as the title of one book on the history of thought indicates—*Paradoxia epidemica.*[8] Paradox aims at revealing hidden meaning by concealing it in enigmatic trappings. Again, this approach can be charged with serious philosophical import or it can be simply frivolous teasing. It also varies from extreme subtlety to coarse fatuity. Thus, paradoxical expression vacillates between illusionistic surprises and impenetrable puzzles.

Above all, Mannerism wants to startle. When the shock value of a device wears off, mannerists move on to yet more startling effects. The canon of the "marvelous" therefore becomes more and more stylized. *Meraviglia* rests on calculated novelty and deliberate stylization addressed to a select audience whose sensibilities appreciate the wit of mannerist play. Perhaps the single most important aesthetic premise of Mannerism is consciousness of style. In stressing this premise, Shearman limits it to refined elegance. But the division between refinement and caprice is tenuous; between caprice and the bizarre it is even more so. When the stylized ideals of graceful beauty are accentuated for the sake of sophisticated variety, restraint cedes to an astonishing luxuriance of ornaments. Variety now functions as a means of avoiding the ordinary and the banal. Hence stylization lifts art above the realm of the commonplace into the rarefied atmosphere of the miracle. When artists begin to stress startling design and content, then the capricious and bizarre move to the forefront of mannerist aesthetics. In short, the qualities of both graceful elegance and monumental deformation can be reduced to one common denominator—novel stylization.

Early mannerists measure the novelty of their art against a classical norm upheld by conservative thinkers. This norm, reputedly representing the perfection of naturalism, can be inspired by antiquity or by the art of the late fifteenth and early sixteenth centuries through which antique ideals are thought to enjoy a renascence. Thus Mannerism can be interpreted as a fruitful trend toward antinatural or anticlassical style. But insofar as it arises out of conscious deviation from a precedent norm, it can also be considered epigonal. Controversy over this problem goes back as far as the sixteenth century. The persistent use of slogans such as *ars perfecta, ars nova, bella/nuova maniera* bespeaks an acute awareness of the issues. For music this situation is crucial. Confronted by a firm theoretical conception of the perfect art, the champions of new music develop into militant avant-gardists. Poggioli believes that the avant-garde movement began after 1875, "born only when art began to contemplate itself from a historical viewpoint."[9] Sixteenth-century mannerists, however, reveal a sense of history inasmuch as they constantly refer in some way to previous conventions. Such retrospective movements are called decadent by Poggioli.[10] But we must try to understand sixteenth-century formulations of the history of style in their proper context. For mannerists, refinement wrought upon established styles is the measure of novelty. And each generation of artists looks back on its predecessors, so that for the most adventuresome, established style itself includes innovative experiments. In the late sixteenth century, certain facets of mannerist novelty do become codified and these herald the incipient academicism of the seventeenth-century arts.

Poggioli lists six aspects of avant-gardism: activism, agonism, futurism, fashion, alienation, and experimentation. Except for futurism, these aspects also pertain to sixteenth-century Mannerism. Obsessed with their personal *maniere*, artists vie for public recognition. But popularization flourishes at the same time as exclusiveness, because everyone measures artistic value by a scale of sophistication. Poggioli further emphasizes the importance of propaganda in modern avant-gardism. And yet, polemics and manifestoes represent a striking element of sixteenth-century debate—witness the vitriolic arguments surrounding Michelangelo, Guarini, Tasso, Vicentino, and Monteverdi.

Insofar as avant-gardism entails an iconoclastic spirit, it easily attracts publicity seekers who exploit the shock tactics of the new. In this way, radical Mannerism descends to a mere fashion, a superficial "stylish" mode based on mechanical dexterity. With reference to modern art, Poggioli puts it this way: "Fashion's task, in brief, is to maintain a continuous process of standardization; putting a rarity or novelty into general and universal use, then passing on to another rarity or novelty when the first has ceased to be such."[11] Although fashions alter more slowly in the sixteenth than in the twentieth century, the development of printing and engraving speeds up the rate of change when compared to that of earlier manuscript culture. The technology of the Gutenberg Galaxy is in a way responsible for the avant-garde dilemma. While seeking to be original, the mannerist also wishes to be popular and a trend setter. Once he has achieved the latter aim, he has lost the former, and to regain it, he must invent other novelties more novel than the previous ones. Virtuosity becomes a necessity and strained exaggeration a virtue. In a fashion-conscious society, novelties have a distressing habit of transforming themselves quickly into stereotypes. Some mannerists slip comfortably into stylized clichés. Others try to transcend prevailing novelties with still more dazzling displays of originality. Artists with sound craft and inventive gift produce works of expressive power, while men of lesser talent seek only to amuse. But since conscious stylization remains the premise of Mannerism, even convincing artworks embody to some degree an element of artificiality. Mannerism is a hothouse flower, rare and exquisite. Even at its best, Mannerism cannot escape its snobbish substratum of fashionable novelty. Baudelaire once said: "The chief task of genius is to invent a stereotype." If this aphorism is true, then one must certainly concede genius to the Age of Mannerism.

It remains to be said that in spite of arguments regarding the interpretation of details, scholarly literature on a general level presents a fairly coherent picture. Quite a few writers concur in using Mannerism as a generic term covering the years between roughly 1530 and 1630. Some, of course, hesitate to employ the term for this purpose. Murray prefers Late Renaissance because she believes that not all artistic phenomena are "manneristic."[12] Battisti chooses Anti-Renaissance to stress the anticlassical spirit of the period.[13] Departing from a narrow definition of *maniera*, Shearman includes only elegance and preciosity, and excludes aggression and tension.[14] The latter, in his opinion, are overemphasized by modern sensitivity to Expressionism and Surrealism. This is certainly true of studies that dwell on northern international Mannerism;[15] but when seen as part of extravagant stylization, the bizarre also forms one aspect of Mannerism. In summation, we may say that most scholars describe the same qualities under different labels, and even Shearman mentions a few grotesqueries in his study.

Many are the problems in paralleling Mannerism in the sixteenth and twentieth centuries. Besides endangering historically viable concepts, this method tends to overplay the serious psychological interpretation of abnormal styles. My approach attempts to balance the facile and deeper aspects of Mannerism, aspects that coexist in various degrees both in the period as a whole and in the works of one artist. What is needed is a flexible definition capable of more precise aesthetic application drawn from specific artworks, and at the same time capable of excluding artworks which do not in any way evince traces of the mannerist outlook.

Since Mannerism stems from *maniera*, the sixteenth century itself provides justification for using the term, provided that we can retain a measure of its original connotations. Reluctance arises from unwarranted uneasiness about its loose definition and its suggestion of effeteness. As Hauser points out, Mannerism must be clearly separated from "mannered."[16] The latter word indicates an aesthetic judgment, while the former is a historic-stylistic category. As suggested here, all mannerist art is to some extent mannered. But when the virile qualities of Mannerism change into academic clichés in the late sixteenth century, then we can speak of a mannered style.[17] Baumgart proposes the term Manneredness for this phase; we could also call it mannered Mannerism. But the original meaning of *maniera* is not equivalent to epigonal Manneredness. In their quest to understand the elusive character of

Mannerism, a period that presents us with some of "the most original, unique and boldest creations of the human spirit,"[18] many scholars turn to sixteenth-century *maniera* as a source for their interpretations. Here too will we begin our detailed study.

CHAPTER II

ℰ☙ℰ☙ℰ☙

Mannerist Theory—
The Visual Arts

Insofar as Mannerism is anything but a naïve style, artistic practice and theory operate through mutual influence.[1] In the theoretical sphere, the meanings of *maniera* evolve in relation to a new idea, *arti del disegno*, that unifies architecture, sculpture, and painting. The primacy of design first emerges in the Renaissance but attains its mature statement in Giorgio Vasari's writings, writings which are considered to be the first important contribution to the aesthetics of *maniera*.[2] Furthermore, *disegno* represents a nucleus concept marshaled as proof that the visual arts should be moved from the classification of *artes mechanicae* to that of *artes liberales*. Any discussion of this controversial issue inevitably involves writers in *paragone*, or comparison among the arts. In early *paragone*, painting is compared to music and poetry. By stressing painting's mathematical laws, its apologists can explain design as a science that can be studied.[3] Although this phase has little to do with Mannerism, it nevertheless places great emphasis on rational and teachable knowledge, and this emphasis, interpreted according to different tastes and for different aims altogether, will eventually become the backbone of mannerist academies in the sixteenth century.

It is well known that the proportional harmony touted by artists, a harmony embodied in all aspects of design, derives its authority from musical theory. A few observations, however, are necessary to put this matter into a focus pertinent to our argument. First, speculative mathematics had long secured for music its revered position in the quadrivium. And although quadrivial studies as such were not popular with renaissance humanists, the science of mathematics retained its dignity—a dignity which artists sought to acquire. Curiously enough, art won its place as a liberal art on the grounds of a justification which was itself fading in importance in musical thought of that time. In other words, the most modern and militant artistic theories of the late fifteenth and early sixteenth centuries were less up to date than their parallels in music. Second, design had both practical and philosophical repercussions, as seen in a reference by Albrecht Dürer to the "secrets of the art of perspective" which he hoped to learn from Luca Pacioli.[4] This humanist's teachings clothed technical matters in neoplatonic effusions on the mysteries of number and divine harmony.[5] Thus even in the Renaissance, design was both a rational discipline and a magic secret of illusion. In the Age of Mannerism, technical mastery of design was taken for granted and interest shifted to the secrets of illusion, and especially to abstruse and surprising secrets. At any rate, the accomplished artist, like the *musicus*, was expected to know both the philosophy and the practical application of number to claim status as a humanist in the quadrivium. His claim in the trivium rested on subject matter, and this brings us to our third point. Leon Battista Alberti's idea that artists must be educated in the *studia humanitatis*, or the modern subjects of history and literature, is repeated by Paolo Pino when he says that "painting is actual poetry, to wit, Invention."[6] Such learning enables artists to depict mythological or allegorical subjects properly, and such themes, of course, become increasingly arcane in the mannerist period.

Whereas renaissance treatises are mainly technical works for a closed circle of professionals, those written in the sixteenth century exhibit a new fascination with criticism. This critical focus has been noted by historians, but its ability to involve lay readers in controversies over aesthetic values has not been sufficiently stressed. The shift is already evident in Leonardo da Vinci's *Paragone*,[7] a work that presages mannerist techniques of comparison. After establishing the superiority of painting over music and poetry (the traditional *paragone*),[8] Leonardo compares painting and sculpture, thus initiating a debate destined to rage well into the sixteenth century. Because painting grapples with the intellectual problem of illusion, a problem that will preoccupy mannerist theory, this art has a scientific basis. Needless to say, mental labor is deemed more becoming to the humanist-artist than the ignoble manual labor of the sculptor.[9] Generally speaking, Leonardo's arguments and the details of his various comparisons all buttress one dominant idea—that painting is the most noble of the liberal arts.

By mid-century, the visual arts are firmly ensconced in the list of the liberal arts.[10] *Paragone* continues, but now in the framework of what we call mannerist issues. The difference between the two climates of *paragone* requires clarification. For example, Hagstrum believes that "this tendency to view various occupations and even ideas and philosophies as competitive is one of the distinguishing marks of Renaissance thought."[11] In my view, it would be more accurate to use "mannerist thought," for the following reasons. The development of academies and printed polemics awakens a wide audience of amateurs who relish debate. These controversies are pursued more for the edification of the public than for professional training, and they have a subtle but pervasive impact on the evolution of mannerist criteria. The change alluded to here can be charted by examining briefly the *paragone* between painting and sculpture. The two rival camps emphasize the necessity for ingenious solutions to self-imposed problems, and after each side has scored a point in its favor, the other side inevitably selects more complex triumphs which it claims for its medium. Although this debate thrives throughout the century, its heyday occurs around 1550,[12] about the same time when certain musical issues reach their most virulent form. While much of the controversy strikes us as trivial quibbling, it nevertheless profiles the centrality of design, particularly its virtuoso variety, in mannerist theory. And the antagonism between design and nature depends on interpretations of *maniera*.

The absolute meaning of *maniera* as good style was used in the Renaissance to praise elegance, poise, and refinement in the deportment of courtiers. This definition influenced the first appearance of *maniera* in connection with music, as we shall see. The same criteria also appeared in relation to art,[13] and they survive in sixteenth-century writings of antimannerist leanings. Thus Raffaele Borghini chastises excessive Mannerism for its lack of *maniera*.[14] We might say that Borghini and similar writers espouse the traditional definition of *maniera*, a definition that harks back to the Renaissance and the renascence of classical ideals. At the same time, the opponents of this view use the same term to advertise their virtuosity, and this fact signals the arrival of mannerist values. *Maniera* becomes a sharply exaggerated canon of aristocratic sophistication and self-conscious elegance. In this sense, *maniera* circulates as a *parola di moda*.[15] Weise's choice of "mode" is especially apt since *maniera* now entails more than just good style; it is the password for artificial stylization, for the affectedly stylish or modish.

In the Renaissance, stylization was leavened by classical norms of harmony and order connected to the imitation of nature. Panofsky states that renaissance thought "consciously elevated it [the direct imitation of reality] to the status of an artistic program."[16] The point I make is that the consciousness of this program becomes self-conscious in the sixteenth century. We must further realize that the seeds of mannerist distortion lie buried in the so-called realism of renaissance art. The rational science of design imposes an artificial order on nature that, in the final analysis, corresponds less to reality than to an internal vision of it created by the artist. For this reason, men such as Alberti and Leonardo were anxious to curb the latent artificiality of design by insisting on natural depiction. Yet renaissance artists also recognized that nature could be surpassed in two ways: by using one's fantasy to alter natural appearance or by selecting the most beautiful elements of nature to produce a beauty never realized in actuality.[17] The *locus classicus* of the latter notion is the story of Zeuxis (from Cicero's *De inventione*), a story that is, significantly, repeated ad nauseam by mannerist writers. For them it functions as the exemplar for subtle and blatant distortion of naturalistic proportions. Whereas the Renaissance demands both realistic imitation and artificial improvement on natural models, and sees no conflict in this dual aesthetic,[18] Mannerism does. And this is the key issue. Such self-conscious awareness manifests itself in the *paragone* between nature and art, a contest eventually won by the antinaturalists. Their view defends two methods. To correct the defects of nature, artists may use an *idea* from their mind as a standard of beauty; to surpass nature and astound the viewer with the originality of their *idea*, they may turn to illusionistic virtuosity and hyperrefinement—in short, the essence of Mannerism. In both cases, *maniera* remains an absolute ideal but one that, in the mannerist case, glorifies exaggerated stylization.

The second facet of Mannerism develops from the relative meanings of *maniera*, meanings that take two forms. In the first, *maniera* refers to individual style. Once a style has been identified, one can imitate it. That this practice extended beyond student exercises, even in the Renaissance, is demonstrated by Leonardo's caution that professionals should guard against copying each other's styles. Both he and Alberti realized that such procedures encouraged superficial conventions. And imitativeness is one of the main criticisms leveled against Mannerism by its detractors. In its second form, *maniera* alludes to historical styles. Here we see the beginnings of stylistic abstraction where the common features of a group can be normalized into concepts of barbaric, ancient, or modern style. In the sixteenth century, stylistic abstraction takes on added significance because it becomes related to notions of progress. To writers of that time, the conquest of illusion represents so recent and novel an achievement (and divides the Renaissance from the Dark Ages) that the history of art is viewed as a successive series of technical advances. When Raphael described three kinds of architecture in Rome,[19] he distinguished antique style (*bella maniera*) from gothic barbarity, which was marked by a lack of grace (*grazia*) and style (*maniera*); he also noted that in his day architects attempted to revive the splendor of their ancient heritage. In Raphael's sketch we discern a historical outline that will inform mannerist aesthetics—an ideal past, a decline, and a renascence of classical perfection. The cyclic rhythm of rise and fall depends on the presence or absence of *maniera*.

As is well known, a similar concept lies at the heart of Vasari's discussion of style.[20] This eminent writer analyzes each artist's work in terms of his teachers, his contemporaries, and his pupils— in other words, his past, present, and future. In this way, individual *maniera* is used to assess the merit and historical significance of its creator who in turn symbolizes the style of an epoch. Vasari in effect merges chronology and style into a causal stream whereby art history emerges as an evolving organism with identifiable stages: birth, youth, maturity, and senility. In Vasari's system, *maniera* forms an indissoluble link with historical self-consciousness that sees style development as a rationally ordered march of progress. The crucial and controversial problem for sixteenth-century criticism concerns the juncture between maturity and senility. When Vasari provides his more detailed description of Raphael's third phase (*rinascità*), he touches on this problem without squarely facing it. Birth, or rebirth, of classical naturalism (1300–1400) leads to youthful vigor (1400–50) and finally to mature and absolute perfection (1500–68). With this overview, Vasari involuntarily hints at the mannerist dilemma: what will happen after 1568? Any concept of stasis goes against the principles of dynamic history. Of course, it may be possible to prolong perfection for a short time, but this does not bar the ultimate onslaught of decline. Later mannerists will combat accusations of decadence by pointing out their novel advances beyond perfection, and their adversaries will consider these novelties to be vacuous technical mannerisms. Gombrich admirably sums up the premises behind these antipodal evaluations when he says, "Fascinating as these discussions are, they frequently suffer from a confusion which we have inherited. The problems of expressive modes are rarely disentangled from that of varying skills. *Thus what looks like progress from the point of view of the mastery of a medium can also be viewed as decline into empty virtuosity.*"[21]

Vasari's position, although ambiguous to some extent, tends toward the former interpretation—that is to say, technical mastery as tantamount to progress. This attitude emerges clearly in his discussion of perfect art where he lists its celebrated five qualities: *regola, ordine, misura, disegno,* and *maniera*. Among the paragons of these virtues, Michelangelo stands out as the unsurpassed master. Nothing is too difficult or strange for his divine talent; in Vasari's words, "the effortless intensity of his graceful style defies comparison."[22] When Vasari boasts that masters like Michelangelo have gone beyond ancient standards, he exacerbates later fears of decadence. His list of desirable qualities raises some interesting points. The first four are technical terms amenable to precise definition; but *maniera* is not. For want of a better definition, we might call it an aesthetic quality. We should also note that Vasari is never content with dry definitions of technical points and always qualifies them with vaguer and suggestive aesthetic attributes of grace, polish, elegance, ornamentation, spontaneity, and the like. Since he proceeds in order from the least to the most important quality, *maniera* leads naturally into a further excursus on perfect style. Here Vasari makes an unequivocable plea for an eclectic approach to representation. Indeed, intellectual idealization is the crux of his definition of *bella maniera*.

If we stop to consider this matter, we can observe that Vasari advocates the mental fabrication of an ideal figure to be used as a model for all human subjects in a painter's work. The consequences of this method are twofold: first, inevitable uniformity and formulaic convention; second, an easily definable personal style. The difference between Vasari's and Alberti's eclecticism relates to the former point. Alberti espouses a reasonable norm chosen by the rational faculty and conforming to nature in a close way. Vasari stresses the operation of individual judgment, instinct, and taste which can create a norm diverging from nature.[23] For this reason, talented artists develop a surprising *maniera* while less gifted ones rely on routine stereotypes. Mannerism can be accused of both failings. Furthermore, eclecticism is by no means restricted to nature as a source of models. Since progress must not be detained—in fact, it needs encouragement at Vasari's time—many mannerists imitate the style of other artists whom they admire. Vasari's system itself implies that future artists who come after the mature phase can do no better than copy and refine the styles of Raphael and Michelangelo. From various comments scattered throughout his book, we gather that Vasari—in a remarkably astute analysis of the contemporary situation—divides younger artists of his own generation into two schools, one based on the *maniera dolce* of Raphael and one on the *maniera grande* of Michelangelo.

In conclusion, we note that Vasari explains *bella maniera* by giving it a series of technical and aesthetic characteristics that easily lend themselves to mannerist exaggeration. Its antipode is defined by opposite characteristics. One slightly different connotation appears in a passage in which he states that sculptors often elaborate hair "more from stylization (*maniera*) than from natural imitation."[24] Here he is recommending a decorative *idea* that has nothing to do with nature. This is the closest Vasari comes to an avowed antinatural notion.[25] The implications of his historical sequence and his definition of *bella maniera*, however, contain within them strong hints of mannerist aesthetics. It matters not that his sucessors may have misunderstood him. What interests us is how they changed his ideals to conform with Mannerism.

Vasari's hints receive thorough codification in the writings of Giovanni Paolo Lomazzo.[26] For one thing, Lomazzo's treatment of proportions and design is far removed from the renaissance ideal, as can be judged from his famous explanation of the *figura serpentinata*.[27] According to this theorist, the term was coined by Michelangelo who taught the design of human figures by means of pyramidal and serpentine shapes. Because he was Michelangelo's pupil, Lomazzo extols the technical dexterity and intellectual ingenuity of the *figura serpentinata* whose violent *contrapposto* embodies the entire mystery of art. In my view, Lomazzo typifies the mannerist delight in distorting natural forms in a stylized manner so that they astonish the viewer with their virtuosity. This idea can be elegant and languorous (precious style) or dynamic and demonic (heroic style). Michelangelo's works contain examples of both, and his style often becomes grotesque in the hands of some of his imitators. Another important point is Lomazzo's belief that the serpentine line symbolizes flames and motion; it can therefore depict vivid emotional states. This novel concept looks forward to the Baroque and illustrates one element of Mannerism that acts as a source for seventeenth-century aesthetics.[28] It is significant that Lomazzo quotes the well-known and often misinterpreted dictum of Horace: *ut pictura poesis*. He gives it a correct reading: "as a picture so is a poem."[29] But unlike literary critics of the time, he cites it to discredit poetry which he relegates to a pale imitation of painting's innate pictorialism.

Although Lomazzo takes cognizance of Venetian coloring technique and tridentine morality,[30] *disegno* and *idea* interest him most. It may seem strange to us that a writer should feel it necessary to expound on perspective at a time when its techniques were practiced with ease. But the perspective that fascinates Lomazzo is a mannerist distortion of the "secrets" of renaissance science. He therefore praises artificial tricks that produce puzzle paintings as well as the ingenuity of Giuseppe Arcimboldo's anamorphotic portraits with their grotesque double meanings.[31] This mannerist bias arises from a bizarre ideal of beauty, a standard of excellence based on the inner unnatural *idea*.[32] Lomazzo's notions about *idea* receive their most extensive treatment in his second tract, a "striking and evocative"[33] study that presents a mixture of astrology and neoplatonism. His philosophy predicates that although beauty possesses many guises in nature and art, in ideal essence it comprises but one single quality, "a certain vivacious and spiritual grace"[34] emanating from God, the primordial *Magus* and Artificer of the universe. Since the *idea* is incorporeal, it exists not in things but in the spirit itself, and as such represents a living inner vision, a flawless and sublime archetype of beauty inspired by the divine *nous*. This concept, combining neoplatonism and gnosticism, in effect confers a new role on art. The artist is no longer a mere artisan; he is an inspired artificer who sees beyond the imperfection of appearance into the perfection of eternal patterns.[35] We must again stress that the patterns Lomazzo has in mind are those that reflect complex and hidden enigmas. In effect, Lomazzo presents the mannerist ideals of visual art as a liberal discipline and of the artist as humanist. In his new role of *magus*, the artist challenges not the poet and musician (as he did of old), but rather the philosopher.

Idea also forms the central focus in the thought of Federico Zuccaro, the last major spokesman for Mannerism during the time limits set in this study.[36] *Maniera* now makes a decisive break with its renaissance origins. Zuccaro denies the primacy of mathematics when he states that students learn proportions to master rudimentary techniques, but that professionals must rely on instinctive judgment and not on mechanical rules. Zuccaro's contention that artists create forms that depart from numerical ratios but "please the eye"[37] finds a striking parallel in the mannerist theory that musicians create sounds that depart from numerical ratios but nevertheless please the ear. The source of this kind of judgment is the *disegno interno*, a phrase used by Zuccaro to designate the *idea*.[38] This abstract faculty even governs sense perception and is instilled by God as a "spark of divinity."[39] Out of the *disegno interno* the artist fashions the *disegno esterno*, or the practical application of the *idea*. According to Zuccaro, there are three kinds of design: natural design (imitation of nature), artificial design (stylized distortion of nature), and fantastic-artificial design (entirely imaginary and unusual images). The first serves as a tool to instruct beginners; the second and third, on the other hand, are most commendable because they permit professional artists to search for astounding and marvelous effects (*effetti meravigliosi*).[40]

From the above discursus, we see that Zuccaro's aesthetic constitutes the first apology of fantasy and free invention as well as the justification for mannerist exaggeration, distortion, and intricate symbolism. Other contemporary theorists propound similar notions but only Zuccaro raises fantastic design to the head of a hierarchy. His philosophy heralds the seventeenth-century viewpoint that divides art into two categories: depiction from *natura* versus depiction from *maniera*. In baroque terms, of course the latter is a derogatory classification of sixteenth-century style while the former indicates the superiority of newer antimannerist style. In the sixteenth century, however, depiction from *natura* is seen as a continuation of renaissance realism (with some refined details), and depiction from *maniera* vindicates mannerist antinaturalism. Both facets are present in Vasari's writings, but they later crystallize into opposing traditions. Good or bad, sixteenth-century *maniera* eventually gives rise to academic routine and even prompts recipe books written for academic amateurs.

From the opposing camp of Venetian naturalism comes the first pejorative evaluation of Mannerism by Lodovico Dolce, a friend of the formidable Pietro Aretino.[41] Like Vasari, Dolce discusses in order of their importance the four cardinal prerequisites of good painting: decorum, design, color, and the raising of the passions and affections.[42] These qualities already tell us about the thrust of Dolce's criticism of *maniera*. Although he admits the relevance of the first two as bases of invention and execution respectively, Dolce singles out the last two as the most important elements, elements that he of course sees only in Venetian style. Dolce makes much of the fact that Michelangelo's works impress people with their *terribilità* solely because they embody unnatural and dazzling design.[43] He also condemns the monotonous representation of nudes drawn from design "which painters today derogatively call *maniera*, or *cattiva pratica*."[44] He alludes specifically to the exaggerated imitation of Michelangelo's manner. The viciousness of Dolce's attack leads one to suspect that Aretino is more than a mouthpiece in this treatise.[45] A great deal of venomous commentary is directed against the *Last Judgment*; its nudes are judged as offensive and its unorthodoxies as shocking.[46] Mannerist aesthetics receive slighting mention when Aretino's interlocutor weakly rejoins that the invention of this fresco is most ingenious and therefore appeals only to a few connoisseurs. After disposing of Michelangelo, Dolce lists the shortcomings of other mannerists. He singles out Parmigianino's penchant for elongating his human figures, but defends Guilio Romano's pornographic drawing engraved by Marcantonio Raimondi.[47] Unlike the public nudes of the *Last Judgment*, these obscenities were meant for private delectation. The treatise closes with a lengthy encomium of Titian who has all the qualities of a good painter and whose "heroic majesty" embodies the peak of Venetian style.

In spite of its pedantry,[48] Dolce's work enjoyed considerable influence on the art world, a world that delighted in its sensational passages and its antimannerist bombast. The champions of Mannerism were quick to respond. Vasari's second edition of the *Vite*, with its enlarged discussion of *disegno* and *bella maniera*, was prompted by Dolce's frontal attack. And Lomazzo's treatise of 1584 represents a rebuttal of Dolce's views in that Lomazzo takes up two of his categories, color and emotion, and unites them with design and an apotheosis of Michelangelo.

When art began its struggle for recognition as a liberal art, its theorists divided their humanistic concept of creation into two categories taken from rhetoric—invention and execution. *Maniera* found its rightful place as style within the second category. The frequent parallels made between *maniera* and *grazia* are more than accidents of diction, for the changing meaning of *grazia* in renaissance and mannerist vocabulary helps to clarify *maniera*. In the Renaissance, *grazia* means beauty, and beauty is the harmony of correct proportions. Thus can beauty be judged by the rational faculty. Vasari intimates the mannerist interpretation of *grazia* when he characterizes it as an undefinable element dependent on the instinctive judgment of the eye. Correct proportions produce beauty but not *grazia*. *Bella maniera*, on the other hand, engenders "a grace that simply cannot be measured." *Grazia* also hinges on facility of execution. The artist must be deft and spontaneous since *grazia* is destroyed by excessive study and diligence. Like Castiglione's *sprezzatura*, Vasari's *grazia* cannot be learned. Facility not only ensures grace, but also encourages freedom and boldness in design.[49] *Bella maniera*, then, is elegant and sweet, with just a hint of graceful deformation and casual virtuosity. This kind of hyperrefined Mannerism delights in surprising the sophisticated art lover. It is still understood and defined in Lomazzo's and Zuccaro's works, but by their time, the tricks of *grazia* are stale; excessive virtuosity renders them studied and affected. Mannerism is now mannered.

As long as virtuosity is tempered with grace, it remains subdued and restrained. But after 1530, as mannerists search for newer novelties, virtuosity takes another road, one that leads to blatant exhibitionism. The more brilliant and unusual the solution to problems of design, the more remarkable the work of art. This type of Mannerism delights in overwhelming the jaded art lover, and its theoretical apology appears in the writings of Lomazzo and Zuccaro. But even as early as 1548, Pino advocates violent foreshortening because connoisseurs value the "forced, mysterious and difficult figure."[50] Just as elegant *maniera* changes into conventional cliché, so heroic *maniera* becomes mannered. Both aspects of Mannerism show the influence of contemporary consciousness of fashion.

In the early stages of *paragone*, renaissance writers stressed the scientific side of execution as well as the learned side of invention. Even Leonardo recognized that painters could draw from an *idea*. He insisted, however, that invention should be founded on natural models. This naturalistic interpretation continued to thrive in the Venetian school which thereby bypassed the radical stream of Mannerism. But in centers profoundly influenced by *disegno*, the *idea* emerges as an independent entity. And thus in mature

Mannerism, the *idea* becomes a preexistent concept independent of nature, perception, and execution. It embodies an innate creative talent which mirrors God's creative power. Because the artist partakes of divinity, he can be called a genius. The concept of genius cannot be understood without the mannerist concept of *idea*, of vision and internal design. In their desire to rise above the banal, mannerists develop a syndrome about their unique gesture or style. At the same time, individual styles somehow reflect a universal, cosmic principle. This paradox of particularity versus universality can be exploited by partisans of both academic stereotypes and daring experiments. It explains the coexistence of routine and innovative manifestations of Mannerism.

꙼꙼꙼

CHAPTER III

Mannerist Theory—Poetry

Practically all the themes found in poetic theory of the sixteenth century entail some sort of comparison, and each *paragone* is shaped by the position allotted to poetry in the liberal arts. Given the widespread influence of aristotelian poetics, it comes as no surprise that the liberal arts should be categorized as arts of imitation. Inasmuch as literary critics in general define poetry as imitative eloquence, a number of them, in particular those with progressive or radical ideas, contribute to theories of poetic style that justify elaborate rhetorical devices.[1] But before examining these theories, we should point out some important aspects of other topics. *Paragone* of a traditional cast centers on the harmony of numbers operative in music and poetry, and we can therefore cite such comparisons as corollaries to the renaissance *paragone* between the visual arts and music. The matter of catharsis, even though it is couched in terms proper to antiquarian scholarship (terms rightly emphasized in secondary studies),[2] nevertheless presents certain issues relevant to the development of Mannerism.

Aristotle's enigmatic remarks furnish the basis for literary speculation that in itself demonstrates the involuted nature of mannerist reasoning. Writers in the earlier part of the century mentioned catharsis only in passing; but around 1550 it becomes a central issue.[3] Hathaway's words, "a toy and a fashion," corroborate my thesis that the surface affectation of much of this dispute grows out of a mannerist ambience. Be that as it may, it is evident that theorists wish to establish that poetic eloquence imitates the passions in the same way as does music. They quote classical authorities without taking into account that in antiquity these two arts were inseparable. At the same time, musical theorists begin to stress catharsis because musical practice verges on dramatic style, and this phenomenon is to some extent a result of the poetic notions we are now outlining. Two arguments can be extracted from the welter of conflicting opinions. In general, homeopathic catharsis is supposed to excite similar passions, whereas allopathic catharsis reputedly moderates passions opposite to those represented. By inference we understand that passions and affections are conceived as static states of mind induced by the four bodily humors. This conception permeates every aspect of the new dramatic tendencies in mannerist music. Such music and the poetry it sets in turn lead to the baroque doctrine of the affections.

Although much of the writing on catharsis embodies academic conjecturing, it has some import for other debates. For example, it functions as a fundamental criterion in assessing the validity of poetic genres. Again, critical sources abound in divergent viewpoints. Some writers limit catharsis to tragedy, some include epic poetry and more rarely comedy, and some connect specific passions to specific genres. Torquato Tasso defends his great epic, *Gerusalemme liberata,* by attributing catharsis to tragedy, comedy, and the epic.[4] In the late sixteenth century, the sovereignty of these genres is challenged by a new mannerist invention, the dramatic pastoral or tragicomedy, whose popularity engenders yet another debate.[5] Angelo Ingegneri places tragedy at the top of his list because it can arouse passions and the pastoral at the bottom because its sole aim is to please.[6] Of course, Giovanni Battista Guarini, the author of *Il pastor fido,* takes the opposite stance. Because music and laughter cure the melancholy passions, he feels that this cathartic effect works especially well in the pastoral.[7] And because the pastoral, even from its inception, was closely related to music and later to opera, the relevance of catharsis to Mannerism emerges in a new light.

Another "burning issue"[8] in sixteenth-century theory is *mimesis,* and this issue also reflects a split between conservative and radical, or renaissance and mannerist, thought. Many of the arguments bring up points already broached in our examination of artistic theory. For example, Giovanni Battista Pigna insists on realistic imitation in poetry,[9] whereas Robortello advocates the fabrication of ideal types, using Zeuxis as his authority. In the opinion of Bernardino Partenio, the poet should imitate other poetic models.[10] He, of course, refers to the refinement of diction and imagery, and therefore heralds the mannerist preoccupation with elegant stylization. Literary critics contemporary with Lomazzo and Zuccaro reflect the current love of capricious and fantastic style. In fact, Giacopo Mazzoni divides poetic imitation into two kinds: icastic (or iconic) imitation of real things and fantastic imitation of images originating in the mind. Although he admits that fantastic imitation lends poetry its "marvelous" quality, Mazzoni remains conservative in that he prefers realistic or naturalistic imitation.[11] Francesco Buonamici outlines a more flexible system that includes fantastic and realistic imitation as well as the ornamenting of nature.[12]

Theories of poetic ornamentation cannot be understood without their concomitant notion of *enargeia*, or the use of rhetorical figures. True to his platonic convictions, Francesco Patrizi discards *mimesis* as the salient definition of poetry. For him, *mimesis* entails icastic imitation, and it therefore relates to matters of content rather than to modes of expression. Patrizi does not define expression as such, but he does suggest that *enargeia* creates striking effects. At the same time, he notes disapprovingly that overemphasis on *enargeia* encourages the development of minor poetry.[13] By minor poetry we are to understand the lyric genres that, in truth, thrive on extravagant rhetoric. Needless to say, *enargeia* and fantasy provide the main points in Guarini's and Tasso's respective defenses of strained imagery and farfetched diction.

Whatever their differences concerning *mimesis*, all conservative writers concur in limiting it to narrative and dramatic poetry. They also take considerable pains to diminish the growing prestige of lyric poetry. Their attitude is important inasmuch as the lyric becomes the central genre for the development of mannerist style. Lyric poetry, of course, is not without its champions, and they justify imitation in this kind of poetry by connecting it to the affections. In mid-century, Benedetto Varchi presents what will become the standard *paragone* between art, which imitates exterior objects, and poetry, which imitates interior objects—that is, "the passions of the mind."[14] This notion is taken up by Agnolo Segni who condemns the limited application of *mimesis* to the imitation of action. This conservative viewpoint in effect ostracizes lyric poetry even though, according to Segni, it imitates character, passion, and thought.[15] Tasso applies such interior imitation to all poetic genres. One cannot deny, however, that lyrical passages prevail in his epic and constitute its controversial aspect. As we might expect, the most militant apology of lyric poetry appears in the writings of the Guarinis. Alessandro Guarini postulates that the lyric imitates the passions and affections better than other types of poetry, and he further comments that a sequence of passions thus imitated forms a *favola*.[16] The dramatic pastoral, often called *favola pastorale*, is just such a series of lyrical moments, and for this reason lends itself to musical settings. Giovanni Battista Guarini reacted to criticism of his famous pastoral by writing a defense in which he stresses the novelty of his invention. And the novelty of *Il pastor fido* consists of the dramatization of lyric sentimentality. If to us this aim seems paradoxical in intent, the result is equally paradoxical in quality. But modern analysts must remember that the pastoral depends on the participation of musical elements. Although musical meter is the initial explanation of lyric *mimesis*, mannerist writers widen their concept to poetic invention (*concetto*) and its rhetorical execution (*enargeia*). And we should note that as the lyric moves toward "musicalization," music is moving toward "literalization." The two meet in madrigal settings of lyric verse.

From the preceding excursus, it is evident that theories interrelating catharsis, passions, and imitation appear relatively early in the history of criticism. Their roots come from antiquity and their evolution parallels that of mannerist poetry. In contrast, writers on conceits await the blossoming of full-scale concettism before formulating a definition of the passionate lyric.[17] Camillo Pellegrino defines the *concetto* thus: "a thought of the intellect, imagined or similar to real things and formed in the fantasy." Its exterior execution entails pungent and recondite language.[18] The poet Giambattista Marino also assesses good poetry as *la maniera del concettare spiritoso* and mentions the "acuity of the conceits" in one of his own poems.[19] Whereas Pelligrino can combine acuity with moderation, later theorists combine it with extravagance. *Bella maniera* in poetry thus becomes an exaggerated ideal.

It is significant that the most thorough treatment of the *concetto* occurs in the seventeenth century, thus showing us one aspect of continuity between Mannerism and the Baroque; Emanuele Tesauro, in particular, refers to sixteenth-century concettism. Baltasar Gracián's explanation of the *concetto*, "an act of understanding that expresses the correspondence which subsists among objects,"[20] has two important implications. First, the *concetto* arises from an instinctive mental *idea*, and second, it discovers hidden relationships. These points mean that ambiguity, double meaning, and poetic anamorphosis become indispensable ingredients of conceptual analogy.[21] Virtuosity is also emphasized by Sforza Pallavicino who calls the *concetto* "a marvelous observation couched in a brief statement."[22] The fusion here of *maniera* and *meraviglia* is unmistakable. Along similar lines, Tesauro compares the startling deceit of the *argomento ingegnoso*, or *concetto*, to the illusionism of art.[23] Indeed, many writers in the baroque period accept violent concettism as an outgrowth of mannerist poetry. These few references to the *concetto* hardly exhaust the available primary literature on the subject, but they are sufficient for us to see that in poetic theory, the *concetto* is the counterpart of the artistic *idea*. We should note, however, that Manneredness comes early to poetry, perhaps because writing ingenious verse is the pastime of so many mannerist poetasters.

Evaluations of *concetti* occur in the context of rhetoric that, in Gracián's opinion, represents an "eloquent flower."[24] As a linguistic ornament, rhetoric enables the poet to put images before his audience in a very vivid way. Now, figurative language entails two styles. It may produce naturalistic imagery, thus reflecting the original meaning of *enargeia*. But it can also be extremely strained, thus tending to artificial stylization and preciosity. The latter tendency, by far the most prominent in mannerist poetry, finds its philosophical definition in the poetic image seen as a radiant personal truth. Such ideas raise poetry to an esoteric level and cast both poet and reader in the role of refined connoisseurs.[25] Because rhetoric operates as an element of *enargeia*, Pigna cites its relevance to realistic imitation; it "makes occult things clear and difficult [things] plain."[26] His rival Giambattista Giraldi Cintio also favors this interpretation,[27] even though his arguments are a little more complicated. Because he discusses the romance, Cintio admits the viability of episodic material featuring monsters, unexpected events, enigmas, and the like. Such fictions demonstrate the poet's ability in invention. However, they must be distributed in an orderly and proportionate way, as secondary decorations, in order to avoid deforming the main structure of the poem.[28] Cintio makes a passing reference to the epic, a genre in which the "marvelous" assumes an important role. To achieve *meraviglia*, the epic poet must stretch the principles of *enargeia* to heroic proportions. Nevertheless, these marvelous inventions should be treated *di maniera* —that is, with stylish grace—and be connected in an orderly way so as not to destroy the primary goal of verisimilitude.[29] The general thrust of Cintio's essay indicates that he is attempting to find a balance between aristotelian restraint and more modern extravagance. The fact that he should feel it his duty to censure overly excessive imagery as early as 1554 suggests that this trend is well under way at the time. It becomes even more pronounced in the lyric style of the later sixteenth century, and Cintio's barb against the frenetic imitation of Petrarch[30] can be taken as a negative augury of things to come.

The artificiality of the stylized lyric cannot be properly judged without its critical framework, and this framework crystallizes rhetoric into an ornament of *maniera*. At first, rhetorical ornamentation functions within gentle ideals, but by mid-century it has been transformed into a vehicle for extravagant style. In a *paragone* between two ancient poets, Sperone Speroni praises Homer whose poetry "consists of redundant and superfluous ornaments"; Virgil may be a greater poet than Homer, but he is less "poetic."[31] Inherent in this comparison is the notion that rhetorical grace arises from artificial *maniera*. For the same reason, Partenio insists that superior diction is very ingenious, almost bizarre, and completely removed from ordinary usage. In his view, the poet must select his words not only for their sense, but also for their sound value (i.e., musicalization).[32] My thesis contends that mannerist criticism stresses fantastic, even grotesque, rhetorical figures as constitutive elements of *enargeia*. Even Pellegrino, who eschews extravagance, is forced to admit the "ardent nature and hyperbolic metaphor of poetic language."[33] And though he means to be critical of Tasso, Pellegrino's comparison of this poet's style to the serpentine figure and violent foreshortening used by painters[34] is a telling illustration of common values in mannerist aesthetics of the various arts. Tasso himself states that novel words, ornaments, and figures are sublime.[35] As Shearman suggests, Tasso casts an oblique glance at Speroni when he intimates that his epic is richer in *meraviglia* than the epics of Homer.[36] In short, Tasso believes that mannerist style not only equals but also surpasses its classical antecedents. And his argument represents a defense both of his unusually eloquent *maniera* and of the marvelous episodes in the *Gerusalemme liberata*, episodes that call forth most of his ingenious inventions.

Just as artists compare themselves to poets, so poets indulge in reciprocal *paragone* rich in ancient authority, mainly from classical writings on rhetoric. These sources are buttressed by the celebrated aphorisms of Horace and Plutarch. The latter's comparison is especially to the point: *Poesia pictura loquens*. According to Pallavicino, pictorial imagery in poetry speaks best through the metaphor, "the queen of figures." Because the metaphor embodies a "tacit comparison" between dissimilar things, he maintains that "the finding of similitudes is a sign of great wit."[37] Proponents of what we call mannerist style admire especially the elliptical metaphor because it arouses wonder. For Tesauro, the metaphor is "the most witty and acute, the most strange and marvelous, the most cheerful and useful, the most eloquent and prolific part of the human intellect."[38] Inasmuch as it represents the highest form of intellectual virtuosity, the metaphor is most striking when the opposites it brings together are most remote from each other. Through its offices, poetic invention and execution are fused into novel *maniera*. Gracián stresses the paradoxical notion of *discordia concors* by elevating the oxymoron to the head of his list of metaphorical figures. He also values the plainer metaphor which he likens to the emblem or *imprese*. Like its visual counterpart, the poetic metaphor expresses startling observations in obscure language.[39] Both Gracián and Pellegrino recognize the emblematic nature of short lyric verse, whose cardinal virtue resides in the witty expansion of a metaphor. And it is precisely this kind of verse that finds favor with composers of mannerist madrigals.

If painting is a mute poem and poetry a speaking picture, then it follows that the emblematic union of both produces the most effective metaphor. This statement appears in Wolfgang Hunger's German translation (1539) of Andrea Alciati's *Emblemata libellus* (1531). And poetry's connection to music induced Caspar Othmayr to bring out his *Symbola* (1547) in which the poetic mottoes are set to music.[40] Here music, poetry, and graphics all contribute to the intellectual metaphor. Although instances of musical iconography in emblem books are relatively rare, it is very important to realize that madrigal settings of lyric poetry comprise a vast repertory of literalized, metaphorical, or emblematic devices. The so-called madrigalisms of this genre indicate the composer's desire to paint in music the flamboyant rhetorical figures of poetry. As the search for novelty progresses, poetic and musical metaphors jointly develop increasingly fantastic and arbitrary characteristics. This kind of mannerist *enargeia* makes occult things obscure and plain things difficult.

The mannerist metaphor, exemplar of rhetorical figures, represents to theorists of concettism the apotheosis of wit, as the title of Gracián's treatise suggests: *Acuity and the Art of Wit*. According to Gracián, *ingenio* creates strange beauty by discovering and expressing hidden correspondences between apparently incompatible images.[41] This mannerist aesthetic also applies to much of the madrigal repertory. Tesauro too discusses wit at great length, and his more ingenious title, *The Aristotelian Perspective-Glass*, appropriately hints at occult scientific secrets. He first posits the existence of mental wit, the archetype, and then divides its communicative forms into three classifications: verbal wit (both vocal and written), mute wit (gestures and painted or sculpted figures), and composite wit (tragedy, scenic spectacles, games, pantomime, ballet).[42] Thus, Tesauro's system extends rhetorical wit to the theater, and this perceptive notion suggests a fascinating insight into dramatic tendencies in music. Quite apart from the role of music in theatrical presentations, a subject that we will examine, the polyphonic madrigal itself owes much of its mannerist novelty to efforts to dramatize poetic conceits. Inherent in Tesauro's and Gracián's thought is the linking of witty invention and genius. This connection occurs in all seventeenth-century writings that discuss Marino's style. In my view, Marino bridges Mannerism and the Baroque, and his works exemplify extravagant, yet superbly controlled illusionism. The latter trait is characteristic of both sixteenth- and seventeenth-century concettism. Mirollo disagrees with the label of Mannerism in the case of Marino. Yet he entitles his study, *The Poet of the Marvelous.* It is precisely in his "marvelous" quality, particularly evident in the *Rime* (a source for musical settings), that Marino represents the culmination of Mannerism in poetry.

Above all other attributes, *meraviglia* is the goal of wit. Mirollo admirably analyzes the classical and the mannerist applications of the "marvelous." From Aristotle's *Poetics*, poets extract the idea of the fabulous that arouses wonder, and therefore utilize supernatural or fantastic imagery with a view to arousing the same reaction. They also cite Aristotle's statements: first, that unusual words raise poetry above low style, and second, that the metaphor should be slightly enigmatic. It goes without saying that poets distort these ideas so that they can justify ingenious and precious *maniera.* This more superficial attitude entails a deeper philosophical position. On the basis of the neoplatonic *idea,* which postulates that the cosmos is full of potential metaphors awaiting revelation, poets can claim that their personal *concetti* embody universal truth in a unique way.[43] The parallels with artistic theory are striking. Although Pigna espouses realistic imitation, he excuses exaggeration on the grounds that it creates marvels for the sake of novelty. Both imitation and the marvelous are mandatory in the epic, but the quintessential element remains *il mirabile* because it originates in the divine enthusiasm of the poet. The poet is "a maker of the marvelous,"[44] a concept echoed by many theorists of mannerist poetry, including Tesauro and Marino who clearly unite rhetorical *concetti* and *meraviglia.* And as we shall see, the same phraseology appears in a surprising number of writings on music.

Controversy over Tasso's epic also centers on the question of *meraviglia.* In general, antimannerist writers level criticism against Tasso's juxtaposition of historical and marvelous episodes. This view is to some extent a result of tridentine morality that rejects such marvelous episodes as improper for a religious theme. But at the same time, stylistic purists untouched by religious concerns condemn the hyperbolic and capricious *maniera* found in these sections of the poem, sections consistently chosen for musical setting. Michelangelo's *Last Judgment* is censured for exactly the same reasons. Since the marvelous effect depends on surprise and astonishment, artistic activity must constantly produce new novelties. One avenue to this end can be described as the inventive manipulation of stereotypes; such an approach rapidly develops into overblown rhetoric. The other avenue, of course, is the invention of entirely new and more bizarre eloquence. And we must remember that the audience is an extremely well-read one, a demanding circle of connoisseurs who expect to be delighted and startled into new awareness. From this situation is born the notion of avant-garde poets whose sensibilities place them, if not above, then at least ahead of ordinary people.[45]

Just as the artist partakes of divine creativity through his *idea*, so the poet does through his *concetto*. Both Gracián and Tesauro intimate that wit is divinely inspired. The doctrine of divine inspiration as the source for intellectual virtuosity in effect merges aristotelian and neoplatonic systems, and this merger becomes a powerful weapon for apologists of Mannerism. Patrizi devotes an entire treatise to the subject of *furor poeticus*, a subject eagerly taken up by many other theorists.[46] The experience of furor raises the poet to the rank of genius and provides the justification for every iconoclastic invention. Giovanni Maria Verdizotti has chosen an apt title for his poem of 1575: *Genius sive de furore poetico*. If poetic furor is a sign of genius, and genius a sign of great wit, then the more pedestrian meaning of *maniera* as external elegance and novel style now emerges as the philosophical manifesto of avant-garde sublimity.

CHAPTER IV

Mannerism in Art

The ensuing discussion of artistic Mannerism, based on selected examples, is presented not with a view to surveying a historical sequence, but rather to provide provocative comparisons to other arts, including music. This approach, therefore, assumes that artists express their mannerist outlook in visual, tactile, and structural values just as musicians express theirs in musical ones. It is fruitless to look for direct analogues between any one musical and artistic technique;[1] however, both may be founded on similar premises, and these will be investigated throughout the book. Within the sphere of art, works created between 1530 and 1630 exhibit a common expressive mode that gathers them into one aesthetic norm, and this in spite of their individual technical differences. Of course, there exist artists and even entire schools that do not come under the rubric of Mannerism, but such exceptions highlight those characteristics which constitute its unique topography.

Although historians usually divide Mannerism into two distinct trends, their terminology differs. Weise suggests that one be called the heroic style, illustrated by the followers of Michelangelo who concentrate on muscular bodies in contorted movements, and the other the graceful style, exemplified by the followers of Raphael who emphasize elegant figures in affected poses.[2] His division relies on historic-stylistic categories untrammeled by intrusive value criteria. Problems arise when such criteria are used in an indiscriminate way. For example, Béguin describes these two trends in terms of pathetic expression versus decorative elegance.[3] But the grand manner can easily be purely decorative while the

[33]

elegant manner can also appear pathetic. Hoffmann conceives
Mannerism as an anticlassical style with two tendencies: one that
refines renaissance norms and one that revolts against classical
ideals.[4] His interpretation has merit in that it points out the link
between the Renaissance and Mannerism. However, it also infers
that the first trend is epigonal and the second is virile and pro-
ductive. His view overemphasizes the expressionistic aspect of
Mannerism. Hauser isolates two psychological phenomena, one
characterized by introverted spiritualism and the other by extro-
verted decorativeness.[5] Many scholars refute his idea because they
find exactly the opposite qualities in the artists cited by Hauser.
Shearman's emphasis on elegant stylization, an assessment that
has already been mentioned, is a notable exception to these dual-
istic theories.[6] My thesis maintains that stylization can be facile
virtuosity of both the elegant and tortured variety, or sincere intensity of both the graceful and dramatic type. *Maniera,* or self-
conscious stylization, underlies all other qualitative values.

As for the history of Mannerism, most writers divide it into
two large phases: ca. 1530–50 and ca. 1550–1630. In the first
phase, activity is centered in Rome and Florence (the schools of
disegno); during the second phase, Mannerism becomes an international style and spreads all over Europe. Friedländer suggests
that this second phase can be properly called mannered since it
copies and exaggerates the creative impetus of early anticlassicism.[7] In his view, the Baroque (Antimannerism) emerges as a
revolt against this conventional artificiality. Following the lead of
Hauser and Baumgart, Hartt attributes Mannerism to social circumstances. In its early phase, Mannerism constitutes a spiritual
crisis, and we therefore observe guilt-ridden art full of "aesthetic
dissonances and poignant lyricism"; in its second phase, the crisis
is resolved by submission to absolutism.[8] Even though we may be
suspicious of social events as effective causes of artistic styles,
Hartt's theory can be put in other terms. The practical and theoretical ambience of academies, as well as of the Counter Reformation, does impose a kind of artistic absolutism. Academic art is
mannered Mannerism at its worst.

Among the artists who can be singled out for their direct
influence on the first generation of mannerists, we mention only

two. The works of the Sienese painter, Il Sodoma, illustrate certain mannerist traits, such as wondrously polished execution and sensuously effeminate male saints.[9] From the early and mature works of Raphael there develops the sweet manner of which Vasari speaks. But some of his later paintings, in which his studio participates to a great extent, demonstrate that Raphael too is moving toward Mannerism. For example, the *Fire in the Borgo* (1512; Figure 1) presents a surprising contrast to the serene and calm style of the frescoes done for the Stanze della Segnatura in the Vatican (1509–12; e.g., *School of Athens*). The former painting is permeated with a sense of dynamic drama built up from a number of elements. For one thing, the crowded figures in the foreground gesticulate wildly in different directions. *Contrapposto* and strained poses are noticeable everywhere; a male nude, staring out at the viewer, hangs precariously from a low unfinished wall. From the aspect of design, we note the disjointed perspective which results from the lack of connection between the background and foreground planes. Thus, the depth of the picture is subtly disturbed by an indeterminate middle ground. Up to this point, we have described formal characteristics imposed on traditional subject matter. Mannerist content makes its appearance in Raphael's *Transfiguration*, commissioned after 1517 and completed by his pupil Giulio Romano, an artist who will become one of the leading mannerists of the next generation. This painting depicts two Biblical episodes with no overt connection between them except that they follow each other in the Gospels.[10] Only those viewers who know their Scriptures well can appreciate the point of this abstruse *idea*.

The first generation of mannerists emanates from Tuscany, particularly Florence and Siena. In Domenico Beccafumi's works we detect the melodramatic side of Mannerism, especially in his use of unusual contrast, of lurid and fiery colors, and the monotonous expression of agony.[11] The latter trait will be repeated by artists until its *maniera* develops into an academic absurdity in baroque manuals devoted to the imitation of the passions. Strange, almost grotesque colors and figures that seem to float in indeterminate space are the most prominent features of Jacopo Pontormo's work. In the *Deposition* (1525–28; Figure 2), flesh tones vary from white, pale pinkish-yellow to pure pink, and the swirling

FIGURE IV-1.   Raphael, *Fire in the Borgo* (1512).
Reproduced by permission of Alinari/Editorial Photocolor Archives.

FIGURE IV-2.   J. Pontormo, *Deposition* (1525–28).
Reproduced by permission of Foto Scala, Florence.

draperies form a riot of primary colors juxtaposed in disturbing proximity to one another. Here color contributes less to molding and realism, and more to abstraction and decorative design. The protagonists of the drama are thrust to the outside flanks of the canvas whereas the central focus of the picture comprises an empty space occupied by four hands. A certain amount of concentration is required to unravel the owners of these hands. From the point of view of design, the predominant structural lines form intersecting curves that whirl about without a primary direction. In a sense, this painting represents an abstract study of line in motion. One repetitive element in the work can be seen in the conventional expression of anguish on all the faces. Pontormo delights in teasing the viewer with illogical perspective and conceptual puzzles.[12] His paintings embody an unmistakable element of willful but graceful distortion that augments the slightly enigmatic quality of his paintings.

The works of Rosso Fiorentino are even more startling than those of Pontormo, perhaps because his mannerist deformation of renaissance norms seems to be a more self-conscious goal. In his famous *Deposition* (1521), Rosso achieves an effect of chaotic imbalance by uniting complicated angular and circular lines as well as natural and abstract treatment of figures. Here Rosso infuses deliberate artificiality with spiritual piquancy, and the resultant *effetto meraviglioso* has emotional depth. It represents an eccentric but telling depiction of a traditional religious scene. However, in this and other religious works, we experience a sense of conscious posing, a cultivation of rare attitudes and grandiloquent gestures. And this facet of his style occasionally descends to superficial virtuosity. A case in point is his *Moses Defending the Daughters of Jethro* (1521; Figure 3). Here subject matter becomes an excuse for the study of the male nude in every unusual position imaginable. In spite of their muscularity, the nudes have a curiously flat quality. The dynamism of the picture arises solely from linear design based on conflicting curves and angles. Various eccentric details surprise the viewer. For example, the head of the foreshortened warrior in the lower right corner is an unfinished spherical shape. This element of abstraction reappears in the two female heads crowded into the upper right corner behind a seminude

FIGURE IV-3.   Rosso Fiorentino, *Moses Defending the Daughters
of Jethro* (1521).
Reproduced by permission of Alinari/Editorial
Photocolor Archives.

woman with a fatuous expression. In sharp contrast to these heads are the ones of the central male figure and the crouching man on the right whose screaming face verges on grotesque caricature. One of Rosso's favorite techniques is to put the most arbitrary, illogical, and unexpected subject matter in the central focus of his design. In the case of the work in question, the focal point emerges in the center of the canvas, and in this center are depicted the male genitalia. This painting serves as an excellent illustration of Rosso's exploitation of the "marvelous," but the superficial tone of this *maniera* can take on a decidedly jarring note when it appears in works on religious themes.[13]

The works of Michelangelo span several generations of Mannerism. As is well known, his grand manner comes to the fore in the controversial *Last Judgment* (1536) and the celebrated *Sistine Ceiling* (1508–12), especially in the Ignudi and Sybils. These works provide the model for the *maniera grande* after 1540. Michelangelo can also be credited with the first major piece of mannerist architecture, the anteroom of the Biblioteca Laurenziana (Florence 1524–55; Figure 4). Its most striking feature is the stairway which spills down from the door as if disgorged by a mysterious force. Now, stairs should have an upward movement, but Michelangelo deliberately reverses the traditional structural significance of this functional element. This reversal holds true for every other unit of the anteroom as well. All lines and masses operate in the opposite manner to the one expected, and the resultant ambiguity puzzles the viewer. Here, the wit of Michelangelo's *idea* represents "a superb wrongness, which, in the hands of a great master, is superbly right. Every element of structure or decoration contradicts its functional purpose with absurd but breathtaking illogicality."[14] In short, this design heralds later mannerist artifices in architecture whose shocking novelty aims at even more marvelous effects.

The sweet style, or *maniera dolce*, of the second generation is well illustrated by the works of two masters. The first, Angelo Bronzino, excels in portraiture.[15] In this genre, he introduces a new manner characterized by studied elegance and refined poise. The "slightly neurotic sensibility"[16] of his sitters, exuding fashionable melancholy, points to a behavioral mode of the day, and

FIGURE IV-4.   Michelangelo, Anteroom of the Biblioteca Laurenziana
(1524–55).
Reproduced by permission of Alinari/Editorial Photocolor
Archives.

Bronzino captures this mode with chilling irony. Particularly striking is the contrast between the detailed treatment given to rich
costumes and the aloof, enigmatic faces. The sitters look out at us,
and yet there seems to be no point of contact between them and
the onlooker. Their mysterious melancholy appears as an affectation, a quality emphasized by Bronzino through the extreme
formalism of his portraiture.

Several religious works by the second painter under discussion, Parmigianino, are famous, or infamous, for their cerebral
eroticism, verging on the immoral. Elongated serpentine forms
and heightened sensuality give ambiguous charm to the Madonna
in the *Madonna of the Long Neck* (ca. 1535; Figure 5). It is not
clear whether this exquisite figure sits or stands as she shows a
languid Christ Child to a group of svelte, adoring angels. Behind

FIGURE IV-5.   Parmigianino, *Madonna of the Long Neck*
(ca. 1535).
Reproduced by permission of Alinari/Mansell
Collection.

her appears an oddly unfinished column supporting nothing, and in the right corner, a tiny figure of St. Jerome distorts the perspective. In Parmigianino's *Madonna of the Rose* (ca. 1530), the Christ Child looks more like a cupid, and the Virgin-Venus paradox tantalizes the imagination. We can conclude that whatever the subject matter, this artist wishes to vaunt his *disegno interno*, his personal *idea* of spiritual beauty. Parmigianino's most sensational embodiment of the *disegno interno* is, of course, the *Self-Portrait in a Convex Mirror* (ca. 1524; Figure 6). Here the artist plays with the notion that his true self can be discerned through a distorted looking-glass, a bizarre game appreciated by those who are familiar with the commonplace symbolism of the mirror. Certainly, his novel self-portrait astonishes us with its marvelous quality.

The foremost exponent of the grand style in the second generation of mannerists is Giulio Romano who, although a pupil of Raphael, falls under the spell of Michelangelo's *terribilità*. Romano takes on the dual role of architect and decorator in the construction of the Palazzo del Tè (Mantua, 1530–34). The building, in all its aspects, demonstrates a self-conscious blending of renaissance and mannerist elements, a blending that goes beyond the vagaries of a prolonged project. As Pevsner states, Romano's manner represents a "deliberate and very subtle attack on the renaissance ideal of architecture."[17] The grotesque violence and theatrical illusionism of the lavish interior decorations show us that the *maniera grande* has already become a rhetorical gesture, a convention of virtuoso eloquence. This development is everywhere evident, but most obvious in the *Sala dei Giganti* (Figure 7). Baldassare Peruzzi's Palazzo Massimo alle Colonne (Rome, ca. 1535) exemplifies a slightly different kind of architectural Mannerism. By curving the façade of the building, Peruzzi creates the impression that the edifice sways away from the street. Although just as virtuoso as Romano's building, Peruzzi's elegant distortion produces playful intensity. We can count his work as illustrative of the *maniera dolce* in architecture.

The third generation of mannerists continues the two conventions established by their predecessors. There also appears at this time a new element of academic formalism and routine imitativeness. Niccolò dell'Abate demonstrates iconographical in-

FIGURE IV-6.   Parmigianino, *Self-Portrait in a Convex Mirror* (ca. 1524).
Reproduced by permission of the Kunsthistorisches Museum, Vienna.

FIGURE IV-7.   G. Romano, *Sala dei Giganti*, Palazzo del Tè (1530–34).
Reproduced by permission of Alinari/Editorial Photocolor Archives.

debtedness to Michelangelo, but he combines this *maniera* with a dramatic tone that presages Italian religious art of the Baroque.[18] But in Pellegrino Tibaldi's palace decorations we can detect a tinge of sterility invading the *maniera grande*. One of his ceiling paintings for the Palazzo Poggi (Bologna, ca. 1555) offers the viewer a scene of *Dancing Spirits* seen from below. As if the unusual perspective of a limitless sky were not enough, Tibaldi exaggerates the theatrical effect through the unusual poses of the male figures. A desire to surpass Michelangelo's Ignudi with more daring effects is clearly the motivation behind this work.

Another aspect of *maniera* at this time entails the delight in variety and in the abundance of exquisite details, an aspect often seen in many of the works already mentioned. This trend inspires a resurgence of the so-called minor arts—metalwork, cameos, jewelry, and the like. Among the many fine practitioners of these arts, Benvenuto Cellini stands out as the undisputed master. Sophisticated elegance and refined preciosity characterize his tiny masterpieces. The *Salt-Cellar of Francis I* (1540–43; Figure 8) also shows the influence of allegorical *tableaux* used in mannerist pageants.

The attenuated grace of Cellini's *Narcissus* (1546–47) admirably embodies the neurotic self-admiration indulged in by many mannerist personalities, Cellini included. This work also exudes a hint of bizarre eroticism. The latter quality, latent in the works of Parmigianino and other earlier mannerists, now becomes overt. We can see this clearly in Francesco Salviati's allegorical and religious paintings, such as *Charity* (1554–58; Figure 9). In addition to dry academicism, the works of Salviati also demonstrate a new trend in depicting deep architectural vistas, a technique borrowed from mannerist stage design, and one destined to become prevalent in baroque theatrical art. I refer especially to his paintings depicting various scenes in the life of Bathsheba (Palazzo Sacchetti, Rome, 1552–54). In many of these works, the frame is a painted one filled with realistic, abstract, and grotesque decorations, thus becoming part of the total illusion. Such tricks reach their zenith in murals where architectural members are painted in and so decorated with objects, including life-size figures, that they deceive the eye. Academicism in its most stilted manifestation appears in the

FIGURE IV-8. B. Cellini, *Salt-Cellar of Francis I* (1540–43).
Reproduced by permission of the Kunsthistorisches Museum, Vienna.

FIGURE IV-9. F. Salviati, *Charity* (1554–58).
Reproduced by permission of Alinari/Mansell Collection.

paintings of Giorgio Vasari. His *Perseus and Andromeda* (1570; Figure 10) belongs to the erotic tradition, but in this case we are chilled by the cold, cerebral sexuality that emerges from Vasari's meticulous treatment of sensual details. It is evident that the *paragone* between art and rhetoric has inspired artists of this generation to produce emblematic works meant to be read like poetry. Unfortunately, Vasari and his colleagues too often sacrifice inventive verve for the sake of learned content. Such is the case with Vasari's *Immaculate Conception* (1540), a symbolic work emulating the Michelangelo manner. Hauser characterizes it as follows: "Though by no means unskilful, the picture is the first boring and 'academically' uninspired picture by a leading mannerist."[19] On the other hand, Vasari's Uffizi Colonnade (Florence, 1560) succeeds with its stylish intention. The top-heavy structure exaggerates the feeling of a narrow corridor leading to the far archway. But this intense rush into space ends abruptly with a view of the Arno River. Very much as in poetry, the summation of the witty *concetto*, the punch line as it were, is saved for a surprising climax.

By and large, Venetian artists remain antimannerists. Yet they flirt with *maniera* in mid-century, influenced largely by the visits of Vasari and Salviati. The sole artist to use mannerist techniques to any great extent is Jacopo Tintoretto. Among such techniques in his *Removal of the Body of St. Mark* (ca. 1562; Figure 11) we can cite the dramatic tone, the stagelike vistas, the many schematic figures, and the muscular nudes in typically virtuoso poses. Nevertheless, Tintoretto's deployment of light and shadow, as well as his painterly technique, must be ascribed to a Venetian tradition. Many scholars consider Tintoretto to be the greatest mannerist of this period because he succeeds in synthesizing variegated details of *maniera* into an organic whole.[20] That Tintoretto uses mannerist devices is self-evident. But his ability to organize them into classical unity arises from Venetian faith in renaissance ideals of structure, a faith passed on to the Baroque. The difference between classical aims and their results in the Renaissance as opposed to similar aims and their results in the Baroque is precisely the advent of Mannerism between the two periods. This observation has great import for the changes in musical styles as well.

Although I stated that the third generation of artists worked

FIGURE IV-10.   G. Vasari, *Perseus and Andromeda* (1570).
Reproduced by permission of Alinari/Editorial Photocolor
Archives.

FIGURE IV-11.   J. Tintoretto, *Removal of the Body of St. Mark*
(ca. 1562).
Reproduced by permission of Alinari/Editorial Photocolor
Archives.

in both the sweet and grand manner, this exposition has been drawn mainly from the latter. To balance the picture I now refer to the sculptures of Giovanni da Bologna, the most polished exponent of the sweet manner in the fourth generation. Both his single figures, such as *Mercury* (ca. 1575), and his group sculptures, such as *The Rape of the Sabines* (1582; Figure 12), exhibit what is perhaps his most famous trademark—the serpentine figure manipulated with stylish and dazzling virtuosity. His works are too well known to require further commentary, except to say that he by no means neglects the monumental style. Bologna's massive *Apennine* (Villa Pratolino, Florence, 1580; Figure 13) symbolizes the mountain range, and in its head there is a tiny room with lights that shine through the eyes at night. Even garden decor has become grotesque and theatrical. Generally speaking, the continuous emphasis placed on refinement and novelty throughout the century inevitably culminates in art whose primary objective is to astound by its bizarre fantasy. Although everyone plays the game of willing disbelief, we can detect a disquieting undercurrent of morbid fascination with the misshapen and the ugly. Such is the case with Vicino Orsini's ideas for the unknown artists who executed the "marvelous" monsters in his Sacred Grove at Bomarzo (Viterbo, ca. 1560–80).[21] We need only compare the expression of some of these monsters with the screaming faces in earlier mannerist art to identify the iconographical tradition; it is a magnified caricature of a caricature.

Architecture in the late sixteenth century is dominated by Andrea Palladio, whose style is the subject of some debate. Several scholars place him in the mannerist stream whereas others believe that his classic functionalism is not mannerist at all.[22] In my view, Palladio's return to the ideals of Alberti, as seen in his Palazzo Chiericati and his more famous Villa Rotunda (Vicenza, 1550), represents a self-conscious stylization of precedent models. Indeed, Palladio's ideals may stem from Alberti, but the mathematical schemes behind his designs are of a more recent vintage.[23] The historical awareness inherent both in Palladio's buildings and in his treatise inspires later neoclassic architecture in the eighteenth century. This well-known fact hardly needs repeating were it not for the striking parallels with music. Like Palestrina in musical

FIGURE IV-12.

G. da Bologna, *The Rape of the Sabines* (1582).

Reproduced by permission of Alinari/Mansell Collection.

FIGURE IV-13. G. da Bologna, *Apennine*, Villa Pratolino (1580).
Reproduced by permission of Foto Scala, Florence.

practice and Zarlino in musical theory, he lifts a historical style into a timeless ideal that lives on after the sixteenth century as a kind of academic *ars perfecta*. When I discuss musical activity, I will explain in some detail how this particular view of music came into being and how it is related to the phenomenon of Mannerism. Furthermore, Palladio's last project, the Teatro Olimpico (Vicenza, 1580–85; Figure 14), combines classical rules with stage design that is a model of ostentatious decorativeness.

Theatricality and excessive ornamentation also characterize the Palazzo Farnese by Giacomo Barozzi da Vignola (Caprarola, 1559–74; Figure 15). Its appropriately grandiose interior decorations were executed by Taddeo Zuccaro. It is worth noting that the optical illusions prevalent in stage scenery for all kinds of mannerist entertainment are the source for the false perspectives that abound in buildings at this time. For example, Bernardo Buontalenti, the famous stage designer, constructed a set of curious altar steps for S. Trinita (Florence, 1574–76). Shearman describes them with these words: "Their most obvious oddity is that the steps on the front face are in fact carved illusionistically in relief; the visitor who has just decided that it is not a staircase finds that, after all, it is, for he can ascend at either end, on the transverse axis."[24] The point of this witty enigma is that the discovery noted by Shearman belies the first impression made by the altar steps. This kind of playful illusionism flourishes particularly during the last phase of Italian Mannerism, although there are some earlier examples. For all their antimannerist leanings, baroque artists cannot resist the blandishments of theatrical illusion. They do, however, eschew that instinct for fantasy that produces the grotesque. An example of the latter, cited by Shearman, is Alessandro Vittoria's fireplace found in Palladio's Palazzo Thiene (Vicenza, 1553).[25]

With Federico Zuccaro we reach the fully mannered phase of Mannerism. His *Allegory of Design* (ca. 1593; Figure 16), which graces the ceiling of the Sala del Disegno in the Palazzo Zuccaro (Rome), is indicative of this state of affairs. He depicts his allegorical theme with mannerist techniques, but the results lack the vitality and verve of earlier Mannerism. *Maniera* and *disegno* in art are waning. The northern phase of international Mannerism stresses only the bizarre features of this style. Thus, Mannerism as

FIGURE IV-14. A. Palladio, *Teatro Olimpico* (1580–85).
Reproduced by permission of Alinari/Editorial Photocolor Archives.

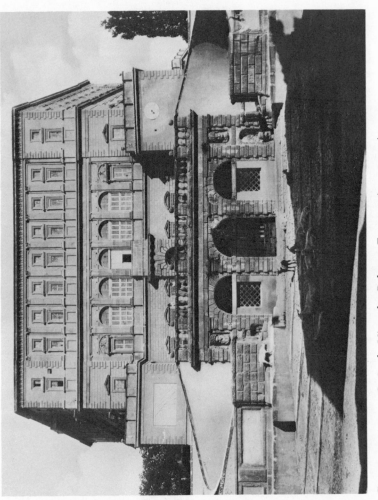

FIGURE IV-15. G. B. da Vignola, Palazzo Farnese (1559–74).
Reproduced by permission of Alinari/Editorial Photocolor Archives.

FIGURE IV-16.   F. Zuccaro, *Allegory of Design*, Palazzo Zuccaro
(ca. 1593).
Reproduced by permission of the director of the Biblioteca
Hertziana.

a virile force begins to decay in art, in contradistinction to its role in music at this time.

To sum up, we easily see that Mannerism between 1530 and 1630 entails two distinct traditions—graceful and heroic *maniere*. The first leads to extreme elegance and preciosity, the second to extreme distortion and monumentality. And we can isolate infinite gradations and subtle mixtures of these two complementary ideals. They are both products of ingenious experimentation and eclectic use of models. Above all, mannerists value abnormal criteria, building on precedent norms. Some of their works impress us with their sincere conviction whereas others exude modish superficiality. And the subject matter ranges from deeply felt religious themes to secular pornography—a bewildering complexity that seems to make it impossible for historians to organize these artworks under one heading.[26] And yet, a current of affectation and stylization runs through them all. Shearman's limitation of *maniera* to elegant stylization excludes too many artists.[27] My thesis is that *maniera* admits both the graceful and the grotesque; these two qualities are sides of the same coin. And both aim to please a very select group of learned and experienced connoisseurs.

The evolution of *maniera* is linked with the constant search for novelty, for the marvelous effect. Shearman maintains that *maniera* is not conceived in historical terms by writers of the sixteenth century. But I insist that it arises in close connection with a historical bias insofar as successions of new novelties are interpreted as equivalent to progress. As stated earlier, novelties tend to congeal into stereotypes, especially when they depend on superficial fashion. And with the advent of artistic academies, bodies that become extremely influential in the later part of the century, there develops a school of convention. In a sense, the academies may be considered as attempts to arrest decline from the heights of virtuosity on which late mannerists find themselves. Academicians see academic style as a contribution to virile *maniera*. They do not realize, as we do, that in stopping the progress of Mannerism, they have ossified it as a style.

Even if we agree with Hartt's view that Mannerism is not a period but rather a tendency, thus taking into account that nonmannerists worked during these years, the fact remains that Mannerism is the dominant tendency. Since modern historians are blessed with hindsight, they can distinguish those elements that connect the Renaissance with Mannerism, and Mannerism with the Baroque. My interpretation—that the years between 1530 and 1630 have a distinctive profile—does not deny the links with Mannerism's past or future. Early mannerists transform their renaissance heritage into *maniere* that they deem innovative. Later mannerists refine these *maniere* until Mannerism loses contact with classical inspiration. At this point, the vitality of artistic Mannerism disappears as a positive factor in style history. But even in its dying stages, it bequeaths features to the Baroque that are in turn transformed into a new and major style after 1630.

CHAPTER V

ᏚᎬᏚᎬᏚᎬ

Mannerism in Poetry

Although the concept of Mannerism is not as widespread in literary criticism as in art history, a significant number of scholars now see some value in it.[1] Among noteworthy exceptions we must count Mirollo's denial that Marino and his followers are mannerists,[2] a denial based on his objection to Sypher's and Friedländer's interpretation of Mannerism. Their notion of anormative, ambiguous, and disruptive anticlassicism does not, in Mirollo's opinion, apply to the polished and highly disciplined art of *marinismo*. But if, as I suggest, *maniera* is defined as sophisticated stylization, then *marinismo* exhibits some features that can be called mannerist.

Like artists, poets cull their models from the past, in this case antiquity and the great lyricist, Francesco Petrarca. The movement known as petrarchism grows from the elaboration of rhetorical devices in Petrarch's *maniera*. These devices crystallize very quickly into one predominant idea—the farfetched, paradoxical *concetto*. Thus, out of petrarchism there subsequently develops another "subtle and artificial"[3] movement called concettism. Studies of these two "isms" often present a rather confused picture. The former term is best limited to poetry that closely reflects stylistic and thematic elements from Petrarch. The latter applies to more extravagant conceits that invade diction, themes, and genres outside the petrarchan canon. In its final phase, concettism exploits all lyric elements in order to vaunt extremely unusual style. By vanquishing difficulty, the poet displays "highly conscious poetic art at the service of acutely refined sensibility."[4] Similar qualities characterize the visual arts that we have included under Mannerism.

Poetic content also presents striking analogues to the visual

[61]

arts. For example, poets deploy the tricks of delicate allusion or overt sexuality in the amorous lyric. Secular style makes inroads into religious subjects, as in *madrigali spirituali*. And religious conceits often tend to neurotic obsession; this trend is exemplified by Luigi Tansillo's *Lagrime di San Pietro* set to music by Orlando di Lasso. In the late sixteenth century, we observe that eccentricities in both style and content produce morbid characterization. Tasso's epic here comes to mind. Generally speaking, abstruse allegory, bizarre topics, and attitudes of affected melancholy all inform the mannerist quality of poetry.

The praise won by *effetti meravigliosi* encourages avidity for novelty in both poets and readers. We must not forget, however, that many images that seem odd today were commonplace in the mannerist period.[5] Extravagant conceits, whether new or old, contribute to conventional *maniera*, and this trait can be divided into two tendencies. The first constitutes the art of miniature delicacy characterized by elegant and languid decorativeness—the *maniera dolce*. The second entails monumentalism in narrative and dramatic forms characterized by emotional impact and heroic dimensions—the *maniera grande*.[6] Of course, both kinds of *maniera* in poetry exude an affectation that stamps them as products of Mannerism. But the theatricality inherent in the grand manner is destined to become a brilliant technique in the Baroque. In short, seventeenth-century poets transform pertinent mannerist criteria into a new style.

The history of mannerist poetry has not been adequately outlined. Many writers stress seventeenth-century literature at the expense of the sixteenth century, and interpretations of Mannerism in this field have been clouded by loose comparative methods that some scholars find objectionable. My analysis takes into account many factors, in particular, the close relationship between lyric poetry and music. I distinguish three stages in the mannerist lyric: in the first, petrarchism appears in tentative form (1500–30); the second marks the maturation of petrarchism on the one hand and the beginning of concettism on the other hand (1530–70); in the third stage, concettism becomes the predominant *maniera* (1570–1630). These rough phases indicate a general change from gentle refinement to rampant distortion of precedent norms of style. They also offer alluring parallels to the evolution of mannerist style in the musical madrigal.

When discussing the mannerist lyric, one cannot overestimate the connection between music and poetry. In the early sixteenth century, solo reciters of Italian verse used fixed forms. When composers set these to music of any artistic pretensions, they tended to impose musical techniques that blurred formal distinctions. By mid-century, music exhibits many rhetorical devices and these highlight literal word painting of tiny details in the text. Poets therefore write free verse—in essence, poetic madrigals written with this kind of musical setting in mind. And as poetic forms become freer, concettism also becomes more prevalent. Unusual imagery inspires and is in turn inspired by the flamboyancy of musical "madrigalisms." Although we are not concerned here with a complete history of these two arts, it is well to recall that musical settings of Italian verse are "literary" in orientation from the start.[7] These poetic-musical creations initiate a twofold tradition that lasts throughout the sixteenth century. The first entails the composition of trivial verse, *poesia per musica*, in imitation of Petrarch's external style. Thus even at this early stage, the uniqueness of Petrarch descends to a convention, but at the same time it takes on "a new independent life as a witty concert performance."[8] Extemporary recitation also influences the second tradition referred to above—singing verse of high literary quality, specifically the sonnets of Petrarch. My point is that composers of polyphonic madrigals continued to use both second- and first-rate poetry. In fact, the popularity of Petrarch's *Rime* can be attributed in part to the numerous settings they receive.[9]

We are concerned only with those elements in Petrarch's *maniera* admired and emulated by mannerist poets. The sampling given below, from the *Rime in vita di Madonna Laura* and *In morte di Madonna Laura*, alerts us to a decided emphasis on striking figures from rhetoric. First, unusual similes and metaphors: *Di cinque perle oriental colore*;[10] second, extravagant puns such as the one on the beloved's name:

L'aura, che'l verde lauro e l'aureo crine
Soavemente sospirando move;[11]

third, witty wordplay:

> Dolce ire, dolci sdegni e dolci paci,
> Dolce mal, dolce affanno e dolce peso,
> Dolce parlare e dolcemente inteso,
> Or di dolce ôra, or pien di dolci faci;[12]

and finally, ingenious *contrapposti verbali*:[13]

> Dolci durezze e placide repulse,
> Piene di casto amore e di pietate;
> Leggiadre sdegni, che le mie infiammate
> Voglie tempraro. . . . [14]

This artful use of conceits turned to polished perfection gives Petrarch's lyrics, to the ears and sensibilities of mannerist poets at least, a tone of self-consciously intense affectation. From this evaluation there develops the *grazia* and *maniera* of petrarchism. As far as musical settings are concerned, it is interesting to note that although individual poems are selected at random, the most striking ones occasion the most unusual music.

The *In vita* cycle contains two outstanding sonnets in which a mood of melancholy is portrayed by antithetical images. In *Ite caldi sospiri* (No. 120), the dramatic tone with which the lover bids his hot sighs to melt the frost of his lady's cold heart and his sweet thoughts to pierce her harsh exterior appeals greatly to musicians. This work contains many paradoxical conceits and evocative words—*caldi, freddo, morte, mercè, dolore, dolci, asprezza*—that provide many opportunities for vivid musical word painting. *Solo e pensoso* (No. 28) represents one of Petrarch's most felicitous expressions of grief, and its magnificent imagery has prompted several very original madrigals. The sonorous epithets of savage nature echo the psychological state of the lover and speaker. Thus, this sonnet fuses the superficial manipulation of conceits with a tone of intense emotion that seems to spark the external *maniera*. When the conceits are represented graphically in music, the combination of words and tones produces a rhetorical style that hints at a baroque aesthetic, one based on the correspondence between natural and human states. It is well known and generally accepted that this aesthetic underlies seventeenth-century dramatic music. It is less well known and not generally accepted that this aesthetic has been explored in the mannerist madrigal of the sixteenth century, albeit in a more affected and mannered way.

The poems of the *In morte* cycle are remarkable for their forceful portrayal of agony. Petrarch's sorrow ranges from serene resignation to furious anger, and his images have a particular acidity that fascinates musicians and induces them to invent novel techniques. The great double sestina, *Mia benigna fortuna/Crudel acerba inesorabil morte,* occasions some of the most unusual music in the literature of the radical madrigal because composers respond to the incredible richness of its vocabulary. The last strophe before the *commiato,* in particular, utters a challenge to the legendary affective power of music, and musicians cannot resist meeting this challenge.

> O voi che sospirate a miglior notti,
> Ch'ascoltate d'Amore o dite in rime,
> Pregate non mi sia più sorda Morte,
> Porto delle miserie e fin del pianto;
> Muti una volta quel suo antico stile,
> Ch'ogni uom attrista e me può far sì lieto.[15]

The general conceit of this strophe is full of evocative resonances, including a series of ambiguous double meanings (*sospirate, notti, sorda Morte, antico stile*). The lover's entreaty to unnamed poet-musicians receives added import from the reference to antique style and the implication that a change or adaptation of ancient style to a modern or contemporary one will gladden the dying lover by making his death an eloquent one. The same interest in verse of extraordinary power prompts composers to choose passages from Dante's *Divine Comedy*; for example *Quivi sospiri, pianti ed alti guai* (*Inferno* III, 22). Significantly, settings of this terrible description of hell appear after 1562 when mannerist composers are engrossed with violent expressivity. The six known settings of this text are exceptional examples of startling techniques. In these cases, excellent verse and audacious music result in mannerist masterpieces for the delectation of both literary and musical connoisseurs.

Although not all petrarchan poetry is manneristic, most mannerist verse, especially in the second stage of poetic development, is petrarchistic. Because Pietro Bembo initiated the fashion of petrarchism, this fashion is sometimes called *bembismo*. And because it flourishes at the same time and in the same centers as does early *maniera* in art, *bembismo* has been linked to Mannerism in poetry.[16] We should further note that *bembismo* also coincides with the first phase of the polyphonic madrigal. Bembo's eclectic approach creates a norm of petrarchan imagery, a canon for imitation.[17] Even though Bembo's aim is to rise above the triviality of previous petrarchism (*poesia per musica*), his emphasis on *maniera* inevitably becomes distorted in the hands of countless imitators. Now, musical settings can raise tawdry verse to a relatively high level of emotional subtlety. But because music is prey to the same trend toward conventionality, routine madrigalisms mirror routine conceits and even debase the force of Petrarch's style. Thus both poetry and music contribute to hyperrefined *maniera* based on melancholy preciosity.[18]

The lyric poetry of Jacopo Sannazaro was quite popular with musicians. But the "progress" of novel poetic style in the late sixteenth century in effect renders his work somewhat old-fashioned, even austere. Luca Marenzio recognizes this fact by including some of his verse in a collection (1588) dedicated to Count Mario Bevilacqua's academy whose members were supposed to appreciate Marenzio's return to serious ideals.

> O fere stelle, homai datemi pace,
> E tu fortuna muta il crudo stile;
> Rendetemi a pastori ed a le selve,
> Al cantar primo, a quelle usate fiamme;
> Ch'io non son forte a sostenar la guerra
> Ch'Amor mi fa co'l suo spietato laccio.[19]

It is evident that Sannazaro's verse deploys conceits similar to those found in the excerpt from Petrarch's double sestina: the idea of the unhappy lover's desire for ancient eloquence and the reference to an altered style—this time, however, connected to that ubiquitous classical and renaissance symbol, Fortuna. Also noteworthy is the pun on Love's proverbial bow; its string can be interpreted as a musical one, thus rounding out the significance of ancient singing. Furthermore, words like *canta* and *guerra* function as cues for onomatopoetic treatment in musical settings. When I discuss specific mannerist madrigals, I shall have occasion to examine Marenzio's settings of both Sannazaro's and Petrarch's verses, for both musical works echo the parallels found in these poems and demonstrate Marenzio's sensitivity to their mannerist ploys. Indeed, these ploys are the inspiration for certain audacious devices in the music.

Lodovico Ariosto's *Orlando furioso* is connected to two kinds of musical settings that have considerable historical importance. Its narrative portions are recited to melodic formulas, or arias, some of which become well-known ostinato patterns in the baroque period. Its lyrical portions receive polyphonic treatment of a special kind. I am referring here to the homophonic and syllabic madrigals that surface in the 1550s. Their *maniera*, interesting in itself, also plays a role in the more drastic innovations of the late sixteenth and early seventeenth centuries.

The poems of Luigi Cassola, one of the most popular petrarchists in mid-century, offer a fecund source for the first generation of madrigalists. His sentimental style becomes so widely known that it is imitated and plagiarized by many later poets. The following example shows us his rather superficial *maniera*, a *maniera* built on the self-conscious "point."

> Altro non è il mio amore che'l proprio inferno,
> Perchè l'inferno è sol vedersi privo,
> Di contemplar in ciel un sol dio vivo,
> Et altro duol non v'è nel foco eterno;
> Adunque il proprio inferno è l'amor mio,
> Ch'in tutto privo di veder son'io
> Quel sol, mio ben, che sol veder desio;
> Ahi, fortezza d'amor, quanto se'forte,
> Se fai provar l'inferno anzi la morte![20]

The poet, in a decidedly playful way, manipulates the antithetical conceits of the eternal fires of dark hell and the sunny climes (of heavenly amorous bliss, we are to understand), both of which states can be produced by his beloved. Her coldness induces an

infernal darkness in her lover who endures it in the hope of some-
day seeing the sun. We note parenthetically the continual punning
on *sol*, and also the witty summation of the lover's problem in the
final rhyming couplet. Cassola's polished elegance presages the
lyric style of Tasso and Guarini.

Two poems in a similar vein by Alfonso d'Avalos, Marquese
di Pescara e del Vasto, achieve immortality because of their musical
settings. *Il bianco e dolce cigno*, set by Jacob Arcadelt, centers on
an ingenious antithesis between the feelings of a dying swan and a
dying lover. The point of this *concetto* lies in the tacit understanding of death as the sexual act. Thus the entire poem represents an
erotic emblem. *Anchor che col partire* gives this emblem a more
overt form.

> Anchor che col partire
> Io mi sento morire;
> Partir vorrei ogn'hor, ogni momento,
> Tant'è il piacer ch'io sento
> De la vita ch'acquista nel ritorno;
> E così mill'e mille volte il giorno
> Partir da voi vorrei,
> Tanto son dolci gli ritorni miei.[21]

Whereas *Il bianco e dolce cigno* expresses the lover's perennial
dilemma through a complex comparison, this poem dispenses with
narrative logic and concentrates instead on three brief statements
of the antithesis. These statements, however, are carefully arranged
in a cumulative fashion so that they intensify the amorous implications of the first aphoristic couplet. In this case, the witty point
comes at the start—a reversal of customary procedure. And the
rest of the poem is nothing more than an extension of an epigram.
Cipriano de Rore's effective setting, one that subtly mirrors the
poetic structure, makes his madrigal the most famous single piece
in the entire repertory.

Although Giovanni della Casa employs the intricate imagery
of petrarchism, his poetry often reaches an impressive level of intensity, as is evident in his celebrated sonnet to Sleep,[22] a work set
to magnificent music by Rore. This poem also furnishes a concrete
example of mannerist conventions and of mannerist delight in

surpassing them. I refer to Marino's O *del Silenzio figlio*, a work closely modeled on della Casa's sonnet.[23]

O Sonno, o della queta, umida, ombrosa
Notte placido figlio; o de'mortali
Egri conforto, oblìo dolce de'mali
Sì gravi, ond'è la vita aspra e noiosa;
Soccorri al core omai, che langue e posa
Non ave; e queste membra stanche e frali
Solleva; a me ten vola, o Sonno, e l'ali
Tue brune sovra me distendi e posa;
Ov'è'l silenzio che'l dì fugge e'lume?
E i lievi sogni che con non secure
Vestigia di seguirti han per costume?
Lasso, ch'invan te chiamo; e queste oscure
E gelide ombre invan lusingo; o piume
D'asprezza colme! O notti acerbe e dure![24]

By now it should not be necessary to list in detail the many evocative adjectives and images used by della Casa. We should, however, isolate two other mannerist characteristics. One of them is quite prominent and pervasive—inverted word order and enjambment. This technique, of course, reinforces the lugubrious and convoluted tone of the poem. In a sense, it helps to dramatize the unspoken context of the first-person lament; we can picture the speaker writhing in bed, unable to sleep. Near the end of the sonnet, where the witty point traditionally appears, della Casa inserts one startling and rather wry concrete image—the harsh feathers of the speaker's bed that seem to conspire against his rest. This surprising image is the first of two brief apostrophes that bring the poem to a climactic close. The last observation to be made concerns della Casa's sonorous diction, a trait that links him directly to Marino.

In addition to excellent poetry, a great deal of conventional verse, often by anonymous authors, appears in musical collections. We limit ourselves to two examples, both of which center on the familiar *concetto* of sweet yet painful love.

Così suav'è'l foco e il nodo
Con che m'incendi Amor, con che mi leghi,
Ch'ars'et preso mi godo;

Ne cercherò giammai s'extingua o sleghi
El foco'l laccio; anzi desio sempre
Si strugge'l cor in sì suave tempre.[25]

Burned by the sweet fire and caught by the sweet knot of love, the poet does not try to extinguish the flames nor untie the string; he rather enjoys the sweet torture of his heart. This slight verse, not without charm, exemplifies the artificial variations played on one theme. An attempt at novelty and virtuosity can be imputed to the five sets of parallel nouns, verbs, and adjectives that appear without logical grammatical connectives. Such a technique is a recognized rhetorical device, and because of its presence, the poem becomes an exercise in petrarchism. This kind of languid lamenting on love often receives tongue-in-cheek treatment, as in the example given below.

Non è lasso martire
Il convenir per voi, donna, morire,
Se la cagion de la mia mort'è tale
Che fa bene ogni male;
Ma quel che mi tormenta
È che del mio morir sete contenta,
E ch'al primo veder d'altr'amadore,
Cangiast'il vostro core;
Non è dunque martire
Il convenir per voi, donna, morire?[26]

The poem begins in a routine way with a lover gallantly offering to die for the pleasure of his lady. But he injects a wry thought on her fickleness, and therefore concludes by turning around the meaning of the opening lines. Thus the witty concluding point is doubly so, because it brings out the irony implied in the opening lines.

In spite of humorous barbs, love laments take on more strained imagery as the century progresses. For example, Carlo Gesualdo's chromatic style fits well with the melancholy doggerel that predominates in his late madrigals. The single most striking feature of these poems is their melodramatic speech, heightened by frequent interjections and short, disjointed phrases.

Mercè grido piangendo,
Ma chi m'ascolta?
Ahi lasso! io vengo meno;
Morrò dunque tacendo;
Deh, per pietade almeno,
Dolce del cor tesoro,
Potessi dirti pria ch'io mora:
"Io moro! Io moro!"[27]

Further commentary on this poem seems hardly necessary, except to point out that the devices found in it are among those that encourage composers to use arresting rhythms and harmonies in a dramatic way. Their success signals the emergence of dramatic ideals, but ones manipulated in a mannered way in both lyric poetry and polyphonic music.

Tansillo's lyrics embody the most extreme form of poetic Mannerism, a form in which many traits previously noted attain their most exaggerated manifestation.

Dolorosi martir, fieri tormenti,
Duri ceppi, empi lacci, aspri catene,
Ov'io la notte, i giorni, hore e momenti,
Misero piango il mio perduto bene;
Triste voci, querele, urli e lamenti,
Lagrime spesse e sempiterne pene,
Son il mio cibo e la quieta cara
Della mia vita, oltr'ogni assenzio amara.[28]

Violent descriptions and sharp conceits are piled one on top of the other in a paroxysm of anguish. One can easily imagine the type of music inspired by such a poem. Tansillo's style belongs to the last phase of concettism as do the masterpieces of Tasso, Guarini, and Marino. Their lyric works depend on startling imagery arising out of wit, point, obscure allusion, and the association of opposites. The paradoxical *concetto*, of course, ripens from the petrarchist tradition. But this tradition itself includes the striving for ever more marvelous effects that make petrarchan style seem mild and conservative by comparison. Although this brief survey cannot go into detail about specific cases of emulation between individual poems, the reader should be aware of the existence of these cases as well as the more general situation of mannerist conventions, conventions that subsume both routine imitativeness and innovative inventions meant to be appreciated by sophisticated connoisseurs.

It remains to be said that concettism can be flippant or sober. The latter quality lends itself easily to adaptation in religious genres such as the spiritual madrigal. Modern scholars usually counter accusations of levity in mannerist wordplay by stressing its serious intent. They talk of psychological unrest and dissociation of sensibility. Although this interpretation may be correct in some cases, we must not forget that much of mannerist concettism amounts to a frolicsome game—though one played with consummate artistry and polish. As Forster suggests, there is such a thing as "good frivolous poetry."[29] Both gay and earnest concettism exist in the works of the three main masters of the late mannerist period.

Tasso, poet and connoisseur of music, chastises excessive *maniera* that threatens to divest music of its lofty quality. Evidently, the convention of sweet and suave devices disturbs him, and he enjoins musicians to abandon these playful mannerisms and to restore to music the ideals of gravity and nobility.[30] This plea is heeded by a number of composers, each in his own way. Tasso's own *maniera* exhibits an abundant compendium of the extreme rhetorical devices characteristic of concettism. His avowed aim is to raise poetry to a high level of spirituality with *concetti* or *acutezze*, to use his own term, that produce astonishing and marvelous effects. The influences on Tasso are many. He himself acknowledges his indebtedness to petrarchism in one instance when he refers to his use of "*contrapposti* in imitation of della Casa." His preference for the more extravagant style of concettism can be adduced from a *paragone* he made between the imagery of Petrarch and Pigna. Tasso favors the graceful obscurity of the latter because he equates it with profundity and the sublime.[31]

However unusual Tasso's techniques may be, they seem singularly appropriate for the evanescent moods he wishes to invoke. Tasso's superior artistry succeeds in "conveying some tiny unit of experience, caught miraculously at the very moment of its dissolution and thus for ever retained."[32] What better words can describe the splendid imagery in the following verse, from the poems dedicated to Laura Peperara.

Ecco mormorar l'onde
E tremolar le fronde,
A l'aura mattutina e gli arboschelli,
E sovra i verdi rami i vaghi augelli
Cantar soavemente,
E rider l'oriente;
Ecco già l'alba appare
E si specchia nel mare,
E rasserena il cielo,
E la campagna imperla il dolce gelo,
E gli alti monti indora;
O bella e vaga Aurora,
L'aura è tua messaggera, e tu de l'aura
Ch'ogni arso cor ristaura.[33]

This work, built on petrarchan punning on Laura's name, is set to magnificent music by Monteverdi, music that captures the gentle rhythm of the asymmetrical lines, the softly sonorous diction, and above all, the active images. *Sovra le verdi chiome,* from the same group, elaborates the Laura pun still further, and its whimsical invitation to love—with onomatopoetic sounds and frequent references to singing birds—inspires composers to match its verbal magic with musical ingenuity.

Tasso's younger contemporary, Guarini, has an even more polished style. Like Tasso, Guarini has intimate connections with musical circles, and his best works, the amorous madrigals written for music, exude a suave and languid tone imbued with pastoral pathos. More than any other poet, Guarini reflects the courtly atmosphere of the *maniera dolce* now carried to new heights of elegant perfection. This achievement can be seen in *A un giro sol,* a charming work that presents a precious study in contrast. It begins with an encomium of a lady couched in the stock metaphors of her influence on nature, and concludes with a piquant point summing up her lover's anguish.

In contrast to this work, Guarini's dramatic style, his *maniera grande,* is illustrated by a most unusual poem that could easily be taken for a speech from *Il pastor fido.*

Non più guerra! Pietade!
Occhi miei belli,
Occhi miei trionfanti, à che v'armate?
Contr'un cor ch'è già prese e vi si rende!
Ancidete i rubelli,
Ancidete chi s'arma e si difende,
Non chi, vinto, v'adora;
Volete voi ch'io mora?
Morrò pur vostro; e del morir l'affanno
Sentirò, sì, ma sarà vostro il danno.[34]

This terse madrigal, free in form and unusual in its extreme agitation (unusual vis-à-vis Guarini's lyric output), contains no similes or metaphors. There are, however, several rhetorical figures—specifically, repetition of words at the start of successive phrases and personification. The entire poem, on the other hand, embodies a single *concetto*—the contrast between the warlike lady and her submissive lover. This antithetical or paradoxical conceit is a commonplace, of course, but Guarini's handling of it is hardly commonplace. In fact, the poem's novelty resides in its extravagant style. Guarini's formal techniques assume a sophisticated guise. For example, the lines have asymmetrical lengths and follow no schematic pattern. And apart from the customary rhyming couplet at the end (which presents the witty point), the rhyme scheme is deployed in such a way as to overlap the logical sequence of thoughts as they unfold. These techniques not only add to the agitated quality of the sentiments, but also contribute to a highly dramatic and virtuoso *maniera*. Among the many musical settings of this poem, that by Monteverdi provides the most ingenious representation. Significantly, Giulio Caccini also set this poem as an accompanied monody; its style suits solo singing eminently well. Before leaving the topic of Guarini's independent lyrics, mention must be made of one of his most famous, if not infamous, dialogues: *Tirsi morir volea*. One scholar calls it obscene, suggestive, and impertinent.[35] The sexual act, described in frank language, takes place between a shepherd and his nymph; thus does mythology offer an excuse for depicting forbidden pleasures. Considering its narrative passages, its direct speech, and its closing moral, the poem is really like the libretto of a miniature cantata, and as such it challenges the imagination of many major composers.

Guarini's witty epigram, *Ardo, sì, ma non t'amo*, and Tasso's *Riposta*, present a contest as to who is going to have the last word in an acidly intellectual game between two angry lovers. These two poems, needless to say, also are the basis of a contest between the two poets; and as a duo as well as separately, they account for the greatest number of musical settings devoted to any single set of poems in the late sixteenth century. In fact, Guarini's work becomes the focal point of a musical publication entitled *Sdegnosi ardori* (1585) in which the poem is graced with twenty-nine different compositions. The finely turned phrases of these two poems represent the apogee of mannerist style, as do the many musical settings that vie to paint their *concetti* with equally polished and witty music.

At the outset of this chapter I implied that the lyric verse of Marino bridges mannerist and baroque styles. And Monteverdi sets a significant number of his poems after 1605, the date that marks the appearance of madrigals that also bridge these two periods. Marino's historical position sheds light on his *maniera*. Both his poems and his writings indicate his awareness of past styles, styles that he tries to surpass by using eclectic and luxuriant ornamentation. Forster places him in the mature phase of petrarchism, a somewhat misleading idea. Mirollo, on the other hand, believes that the sensuality of Marino's style (its "unremitting voluptuousness," to use the words of another writer)[36] is not petrarchan; and this idea is essentially correct. In my view, sensuality counts as a hallmark of concettism, the mannerist outgrowth of petrarchism. Marino's *effetti meravigliosi*, on which he sets great store, must stupefy an elite audience, and therefore the "Poet of the Marvelous" seeks to surpass a formidable tradition.

To illustrate Marino's style, I cite two poems chosen by Monteverdi. The first is cast as a solo madrigal in his seventh book, entitled *Concerto* (1619).

Eccomi pronta ai baci;
Baciami, Ergasto mio, ma bacia in guisa
Che de'denti mordaci

Nota non resti nel mio volto incisa;
Perch'altri non m'additi e in esse poi
Legga le mie vergogne e i baci tuoi;
Ahi! tu mordi e non baci!
Tu mi segnasti, ahi! ahi!
Possa io morir, se più ti bacio mai![37]

This is only one of many poems on the theme of kisses in which "Marino displays thematic virtuosity as he catalogues every conceivable (and inconceivable) type of kiss."[38] Mirollo's characterization of the group can also be extended to its individual members, particularly from the viewpoint of their formal polish, exquisite humor, and daring violence. My second choice is an unusual sonnet, one of six works in Monteverdi's sixth book (1614).

"A Dio, Florida bella, il cor piagato
Nel mio partir ti lascio, e porto meco
La memoria di te, sì come seco
Cervo trafitto suol lo strale alato";

"Caro mio Floro, a Dio, l'amaro stato
Consoli Amor del nostro viver cieco,
Che se'l tuo cor mi resta, il mio vien teco
Come augellin che vola al cibo amato";

Così su'l Tebro, a lo spuntar del sole,
Quinci e quindi confuso un suon s'udio
Di sospir, di baci, e di parole:
"Ben mio, rimanti in pace"; "E tu, ben mio,
Vattene in pace"; "E sia quel che'l ciel vuole,
A Dio Floro!" dicean, "Florida a Dio!"[39]

The poem consists of pathetic speeches by two lovers at dawn and narrative sections for a chorus. Again, Marino's formal virtuosity is truly admirable, inasmuch as he fits the complementary dialogue, choral comment, and final farewells into the form of a sonnet. But this formal structure is obscured by the lyric-dramatic interplay. Mirollo attributes this technique to the influence of the operatic aria that is set off from narrative recitative.[40] This view, however, raises problems because the aria as such is not fully defined in early opera. Marino's idylls belong to the pastoral tradition, a tradition that supplies the affections with either short or long dramatic contexts. There is no doubt that early operatic librettos are modeled on the *favola pastorale*.[41] But the emergence of the full-fledged aria belongs to baroque practice and therefore lies outside this inquiry.

The pastoral erects a sylvan paradise occupied by nymphs and shepherds who declare their amorous sentiments in the stylized language of conceits. Elaborate plots featuring mistaken identities and fortuitous accidents provide the background for passion. Guarini's fame rests equally on his dramatic innovations and on the studied elegance of his *maniera*. These two aspects of his work embody two important paradoxes: lyrical delicacy within grandiose drama, and subjective intensity expressed in external artificiality. For these reasons, the *favola pastorale* enjoyed unprecedented success and best exemplifies Mannerism in sixteenth-century literature.

In the famous *Il pastor fido* (completed in 1583; authoritative edition 1601), Guarini wants his marvelous effects to arouse delight and admiration. Because composers of the time favor texts with vivid imagery and hyperbolic rhetoric, they select the most melodramatic speeches from the poem.[42] Among the most popular are those given to Mirtillo, the unhappy lover. His first soliloquy, *Cruda Amarilli* (1,2) comprises an intricate conceit that works up to an extravagant point: if nature fails to echo Mirtillo's silent lament, his death (the final silence) will eloquently relate his torment to the cruel Amarilli. Parenthetically, we note the punning on *Amarilli, amar,* and *amaramente.*

Act III focuses on Mirtillo and Amarilli. In many ways, it represents the emotional climax of the poem, with the exception of the scene in Act IV where Amarilli is condemned to death. The third act abounds in passionate monologues. For example, Mirtillo comes to join secretly in a blindman's bluff game (*Gioco della cieca*) that Amarilli is going to play with her girl friends (III,1). Alone in the clearing, he voices another melodramatic lament, *O Primavera,* in which he addresses the personification of Spring. Her charming promise of love contrasts sharply with his own despair. He bewails the fact that he has lost the "bitterest sweetnesses of love" (*O dolcezze amarissime d'amore!*—note the echo of the previous pun), even before he has had a chance to enjoy them. In other words, Amarilli's impending marriage to Silvio will rob him of his excuse to wallow in languid longing. Amarilli later dismisses him with the insulting remark that all his talk of dying is pure convention. Mirtillo's reply to this sarcasm is yet another lament (III,3):

> Ah, dolente partita!
> Ah, fin della mia vita!
> Da te parto, e non moro? E pur'i provo
> La pena della morte,
> E sento nel partire
> Un vivace morire
> Che dà vita al dolore,
> Per far che moia immortalmente il core.[43]

Here again Guarini shows his mastery of the pungent epigram. He sums up in piquant fashion the paradoxical conceit of living death that gives life to pain, yet causes the heart to expire but never to rest in the peace of true death.

Amarilli reveals the irony of her situation in a long monologue, O Mirtillo (III,4). The beginning concentrates on one conceit that depicts the secret state of her heart. It closes with a typical concetto contrasting perfidious Love who binds two incompatible people and cruel Destiny who refuses to separate them. Amarilli then begs forgiveness from her absent lover with another powerful conceit: Mirtillo's anguish is really his unknowing revenge on Amarilli; since she loves him but dares not show it, all his sighs, tears, and pain are not his torments but hers. And so the speech ends with a finely turned couplet. Although this lament deploys conceits similar to those found in Mirtillo's speeches, it has a tone of intensity and convincing pathos. She complains in this fashion only once in the poem and her speech is enhanced by the dramatic situation. The audience's sudden comprehension of her unhappiness renders plausible her extravagant passion. Mirtillo's last pathetic outburst, Udite lagrimosi spirti d'Averno (III,6), is a short and conventional lament, containing another twist on mille morte il dì. To sum up, the excessive conceits and dramatized passion in all these excerpts furnish the impetus for extravagant musical settings in both polyphonic and monodic styles. Although these speeches so closely resemble Guarini's independent lyric style that they easily become anonymous, we must not discount the fame of this beloved pastoral. All educated people recognized the excerpts, even out of context. And composers capitalized on this fact.

In comparison with *Il pastor fido*, fewer musical settings of Tasso's *Gerusalemme liberata* exist.[44] But their progressive style is particularly striking. It is clear that the heroic dimensions and serious dramatic tone of this great epic (completed 1575; published 1581) inspire theatrical grandeur and monumentalism, *la maniera grande*, in music. Tasso lavished great care on *maniera* and *meraviglia*. In his view, these two traits furnish proof of progress in the history of literary practice in general terms, and they are as well the vehicles for externalizing his *idea* in personal terms. In effect, Tasso evolves a theory of heroic content and style based on classical references to the sublime. His purpose is to surpass antiquity and his more immediate heritage by exploiting every rhetorical device at his disposal. Hence the *Gerusalemme liberata* abounds in strange words, archaic Latinisms, obscure and unusual word order, hyperboles, metaphors, elipses, sound effects, and personification. In the context of the entire poem, these rhetorical excesses seem to be sparingly employed, especially when compared to the pastoral. However, they are concentrated in the marvelous episodes, at once the most admired and most criticized parts of the epic, and, incidentally, the ones chosen for musical setting.

Four distinct themes occur in these episodes. The first is violence. The longest and most exciting of the many gory battles is the duel between Tancredi and Clorinda. Sonorous descriptions of nature comprise the second theme. These passages are more than ornaments to the poem; they emphasize its emotional tone at strategic points in the narrative. In one brilliant instance, this theme is wedded to supernatural enchantment—the description of Armida's magic garden. Here Tasso reveals his own enchantment with vague mystery and strange but beautiful visions. Thus, he fuses the second and third themes. The latter, the theme of magic, accompanies the theme of love in the case of Armida and Rinaldo. Four pairs of lovers experience their torments and bliss amid the historical events that engulf them. Only the Christian couple,

Olindo and Sofronia, enjoy uncomplicated mutual affection; their problems arise from external complications. In spite of their pathetic situation, they do not capture the imagination of Tasso's contemporaries as much as do the unhappy lovers: Erminia, Tancredi, Clorinda, Rinaldo, and Armida.

After slaying Clorinda, Tancredi wanders about like a madman, possessed by guilt and agony; Tasso devotes the last thirty-three stanzas of Canto XII to his plight. The readers will recall that earlier he killed the woman he loved without knowing her identity. Only when she asked with her dying breath to be baptized did he discover his monstrous deed. Clorinda's request raises some interesting points. On an allegorical level, her act reveals the strength of Christianity. On a more mundane level, it triggers the scene of recognition. But even more important, it allows Tasso to dwell on Tancredi's subsequent despair. His love has been twice frustrated by cruel fate; while Clorinda lived he could not declare his love for this pagan amazon, and when she became a Christian, she died before he could communicate his feelings. Thus is Tancredi reduced to lamenting his love before her tomb in one of the most poignant episodes of the epic.

> Giunto a la tomba, ove al suo spirto vivo
> Dolorosa prigione in Ciel prescrisse,
> Pallido, freddo, muto, e quasi privo
> Di movimento, al marmo gli occhi affisse.
> Al fin, sgorgando un lagrimoso rivo,
> In un languido: "Oimè!" proruppe, e disse:
> "O sasso amato ed onorato tanto,
> Che dentro hai le mie fiamme e fuori il pianto,
>
> Non di morte sei tu, ma di vivaci
> Ceneri albergo, ove è riposto Amore;
> E ben sento io da te l'usate faci,
> Men dolci sì, ma non meno calde al core.
> Deh! prendi i miei sospiri, e questi baci
> Prendi ch'io bagno di doglioso umore;
> E dalli tu, poi ch'io non posso, almeno
> A le amate reliquie c'hai nel seno."[45]

Convoluted word order, unusual diction, extravagant phrases, and sharp conceits characterize this moving passage. What is most interesting is Tasso's use of typically mannerist love conceits that in his hands attain a tone of nobility in spite of their pastoral overtones. His superb concettism inspires many composers.

Taking his cue from amorous complications found in the pastoral, Tasso creates a second pagan princess, Erminia, who is hopelessly in love with Tancredi. On two occasions she pursues him even to the point of endangering her own life. Erminia's unrequited love provides the excuse for two memorable laments. One of these occurs when she goes secretly to find his body on a battlefield. When she sees him lying bloody and motionless, she assumes that he is dead (XIX:106–8). At first she is horrified to realize that the man she found so attractive in life has become loathsome in death. But she then discovers that even in his gory state he is beautiful to her. Begging forgiveness for her audacity, she takes kisses from his lifeless lips as she gives up her breath into his mouth. In spite of the sincerity of Erminia's feelings, the situation is somewhat grotesque. Her sensual longing has morbid overtones considering that she fondles what she thinks is a corpse. And these overtones were not lost on Giaches de Wert when he set this passage to music.

Canto XVI focuses on the dalliance between Rinaldo and Armida on her magic island. As Rinaldo's rescuers approach the castle, they pass through the enchanted garden. The exquisite depiction of nature harkens back to some of Tasso's pastoral lyrics and its imagery challenges many composers. After Rinaldo is brought to his senses, he decides (after some wavering) to abandon his pagan enchantress. His cold speech, *Rimanti in pace*, contrasts sharply with Armida's forceful outbursts. Her speeches contain the most intensely mannered verse in the epic: *Forsennata gridava* and *Vattene pur crudel*. Here the *concetto* reigns supreme.

> "Vattene pur, crudel, con quella pace
> Che lasci a me; vattene, iniquo, omai.
> Me tosto ignudo spirto, ombra seguace
> Indivisibilmente a tergo avrai.
> Nova furia, co'serpi e con le face
> Tanto t'agiterò quanto t'amai.
> E s'è destin ch'esca del mar, che schivi
> Gli scoglie e l'onde e che a la pugna arrivi,

Là tra'l sangue e le morti egro giacente
Mi pagherai le pene, empio guerriero.
Per nome Armida chiamerai sovente
Ne gli ultimi singulti: udir ciò spero."
Or qui mancò lo spirto a la dolente,
Nè quest'ultimo suono espresso intero;
E caddè tramortita e si diffuse
De gelato sudore, e i lumi chiuse.

Chiudeste i lumi, Armida; il Cielo avaro
Invidiò il conforto a i tuoi martiri.
Apri, misera, gli occhi; il pianto amaro
Ne gli occhi al tuo nemico or chè non miri?
Oh s'udir tu'l potessi, oh come caro
T'addolcirebbe il suon de'suoi sospiri!
Dà quanto ei pote, e prende (e tu no'l credi!)
Pietoso in vista gli ultimi congedi.[46]

Antithesis, exaggerated metaphors, paradox, and surprising
thought sequences, tricks all, nonetheless deepen the passion of
Armida's declaration of love, her irrational wrath, and her lurid
vows of revenge. Tasso displays his greatest skill in depicting the
illogical yet very human feelings of this sorceress. This remarkable
passage is extremely popular with musicians, and with good reason. Armida begins in a restrained tone of resignation touched
with irony (*con quella pace*, referring to Rinaldo's speech). But she
suddenly erupts with threats born of her magic powers; her spirit,
transforming her into an infernal Fury (classical reference), will
torment him and impede his journey away from her island. But
Armida senses that Rinaldo will escape and reach the battlefield;
she therefore promises to find him dying on the field (perhaps
implying that she shall engineer his downfall) in order to gloat
over his tormented death. The narrator then describes her fainting
even before she has finished her last words. In the third stanza, the
tone shifts from one of violence to one of pathos as the poet addresses Armida directly and describes Rinaldo's tearful farewells
over her inert body. These stanzas are worthy of a tragic scene on
the stage, and indeed, the Armida-Rinaldo story becomes the basis
for many operatic librettos.

Although Tasso defended the marvelous episodes as ornaments or allegories to this historic-religious theme of the *Gerusalemme liberata*, toward the end of his life he admitted the faults of his *maniera*—the "faults" constituting precisely those elements that we call mannerist. His attempts to ameliorate the epic resulted in a revised version, the *Gerusalemme conquistata*. In the opinion of one scholar, "This process of metrical polish and stylistic clarification is in general an artistic gain, though it tends towards monotony and dullness, and some of the successful originalities of the *Liberata* are jettisoned together with the blemishes."[47] Brand's comments indicate that the revision does not measure up to the boldness of the first version, and this boldness, a kind of learned *sprezzatura*, makes the *Gerusalemme liberata* an effective mannerist epic. Tasso's original intent transforms sentimental effusion, traditionally associated with the genteel pastoral, into dramatic and monumental passion. His achievement is truly personal and novel. Novelty and virtuosity are the main characteristics of Mannerism in poetry,[48] especially when related to mature concettism. This aspect of Tasso's epic is recognized by Galileo Galilei when he disparagingly compares Tasso's style to that of Parmigianino.[49] In view of the sublime tone of Tasso's brilliant verbal straining, one might better compare his style to Michelangelo's *maniera grande*. Even more pertinent is the observation that the heroic dimensions and passionate eloquence of the marvelous episodes inspire composers to experiment with dazzling monumentalism in musical terms. It is no accident that Tasso's epic furnishes both direct and indirect sources for so many operas. The vivid theatrical illusion of his *effetti meravigliosi* begs for dramatic presentation. And the lavish scenery accompanying such productions fits well with the general spirit of the grand manner in text and music. These three arts fuse into one grandiose *concetto* that provides a basis for baroque art. Thus Tasso's work can be taken as an exemplar of the gradual transformation of a timid ideal of stylization into an extravagant ideal of mannerist *maniera*.

CHAPTER VI

Mannerism as
a Cultural Phenomenon

At the outset of the section on the sister arts, I alluded to a view of
Mannerism that was based on a comparison of the sixteenth and
twentieth centuries. This view stresses, above all, one aspect common to both "ages of anxiety"—disruptive social forces that cause
artistic tension.[1] Lowinsky, for example, uses this exegesis to
explain avant-garde elements in sixteenth-century music as does
Poggioli for the modern arts.[2] Political, economic, and religious
events seem to highlight a series of major and minor disasters that
prompted countless jeremiads not only in modern scholarship but
also in contemporary writings. Cultural rebirth in Italy, fostered
by the pride of competitive city states, gradually changed into
absolute and even repressive authoritarianism. To many thinkers
this situation seemed a sorry ending to the glorious promise of the
Renaissance. "Choruses of despair and despondency . . . grew daily
more profound."[3]

Such views support the opinion of those historians who equate
the mannerist aesthetic with that of modern Expressionism. Some
attribute mannerist style to specific events, such as the Sack of
Rome or the so-called copernican revolution, whereas others cite
constellations of events as contributive factors to a prevalent world
view. These methods are problematic in that the impact of such
events is often misinterpreted, and convincing evidence of effective
cause is difficult, if not impossible, to establish. But when carefully
argued, both methods posit one cardinal hypothesis: Mannerism
reflects a real syndrome of spiritual anguish and is therefore not

just a superficial and decadent degeneration of the Renaissance. Those scholars who exclude the bizarre from the qualities attributed to *maniera* also reject what they take to be a "questionable psychoanalytical concept."[4] This concept is indeed questionable, but not because it includes the grotesque. Both bizarre and elegant aspects of Mannerism are due to self-conscious attitudes, and we must therefore search for two kinds of evidence: first, events that have a direct bearing on mannerist aesthetics; and second, mannerist elements in intellectual and social history that develop concurrently with artistic styles.

Aside from connections between Mannerism and crises of a general nature, the phenomenon of eccentric art and outlandish personalities raises a specific criterion. In this regard, scholars discern new patterns in the social role of artists who, being equated with merchant princes and their predatory habits, experienced real problems in handling their role with the same aplomb as their patrons. "Some of these artists sought refuge in various forms of alienation and this in turn helped to foster the idea that artists were by nature a special and odd kind of people."[5] Although this observation is made by the Wittkowers without reference to Mannerism, we can use their analysis to summon several traits as evidence for what we call the mannerist personality. In their work habits, artists vacillated between periods of furious activity and sullen inactivity. They often succumbed to agonizing introspection. And many of them exhibited oddities that ranged from superficial eccentricities such as narcissism or affected melancholy to serious derangements such as manic depression or suicidal tendencies.

In spite of Shearman's objections to explaining Mannerism as a "collective neurosis,"[6] many historians maintain that the notion of the possessed artist, "born under Saturn," first rose to prominence in the sixteenth century. The fact that after 1550 theorists took pains to combat this idea attests to its popularity. Among others, Vasari and Lomazzo promulgated a new image: "the conforming, well-bred, rational philosopher-artist full of grace and virtue."[7] From a historical viewpoint, we can say that the initial phase of Mannerism, which coincided with the decline of the guilds, encouraged an image of the unruly artist. In its later phase, the authoritarian views of academicians promoted the artist as a normal member of society. Such propaganda, arising partly from posttridentine sobriety, was an important factor in taming mannerist style, both artistic and personal.

Commonplaces about the eccentric artist stem from philosophical convictions with more significance than biographical anecdotes, amusing as the latter may be. Like so many other notions in mannerist theory, that of the melancholy genius has its roots in Florentine neoplatonism whose exponents mixed together classical authorities, astrology, and galenic psychology to concoct the salient combination for Mannerism: black bile, earth, Saturn, and melancholy. Now, the talented melancholiac could rise to great heights of achievement or fall to the border of insanity. Medieval scholastics considered melancholy to be a psychic disorder and the Church called it a vice. But for neoplatonists, melancholy was a "heroic disease."[8] In particular, the writings of Marsilio Ficino did much to popularize the doctrine of divine enthusiasm and inspired madness.

As we have seen, this doctrine later came to be called poetic furor, and it was closely connected with the astonishing quality of mannerist art. Cesare Ripa's definition of poetic furor runs thus: "A superabundance of vivacity of the spirit that enriches the soul with numbers and with marvelous conceits, which, because it seems impossible that one may possess them solely by a natural gift, are considered [to be] a particular gift and singular grace from heaven."[9] Generally speaking, then, melancholy temperament and poetic furor were signs of divine genius. Although academies played down madness and melancholy, they glorified the dogma of the marvelous idea, the proof of divine inspiration. And divine inspiration also furnished the justification for ornamenting and deforming nature, and for creating imaginary and utterly fantastic things. Each artwork was a miracle, and miracles could not be priced.[10]

To garner patrons in a competitive and volatile market, independent artists and poets had to cope with a challenging situation. They everywhere encountered "museums" of artworks in libraries, palaces, studios, and gardens—artworks collected less for their practical use than for their stylistic value. The concept of art had shifted imperceptibly from a functional category to an aesthetic luxury.[11] As a result, two ideas arose in the patron-artist relationship, "both central to Mannerism: the concept of the work of art as an enduring virtuoso performance ('something stupendous') and the concept of the 'absolute' work of art."[12] These were the priceless miracles bought by avid patrons. Furthermore, the new social prominence of the creative genius bred a kind of arrogance. In the words of two art historians, "A single work of art was a surer guarantee of immortality than all the deeds of kings and popes."[13] Poets and artists responded to this situation with an unabashed passion for fame. The adulation surrounding creative personalities encouraged eccentric behavior marked by egotism and ambition as well as by unscrupulous intrigue. And because public recognition was necessary for success, artists developed what one scholar calls a "show-window psychology";[14] hence the self-consciousness of mannerists. Artists and poets had to reach a large public, and they therefore capitalized on advertising tactics. Professionals and critics wrote open letters, manifestoes, technical treatises, popular essays, biographies, anecdotal collections, and autobiographies. They also gave lectures and participated in acrid public debates. Artists circulated engraved copies of their works, and poets published authoritative editions of their writings.

Certain cultural aspects of literature and art were closely related to the technology of printing, which attained a high level of financial success in this period. Emblematic block books edified collectors of moral guides and entertained collectors of abstruse curiosities. Through the influence of Albrecht Dürer, whose artistry disseminated the subtle art of design, the high quality of illustrative material transformed books on botany, zoology, and anatomy into artworks. Andreas Vesalius's *De humani corporis fabrica* (1542), for example, was justly prized for the anatomical engravings by Jan Stevenszoon van Calcar. Parenthetically, it is interesting to note that such illustrations provided models for artists interested in the detailed musculature of the human nude. Unlike large paintings and sculptures, wood blocks and engravings were meant for private enjoyment, and they circulated widely and easily. The importance of engraving as a medium for advertising individual styles has been recognized, but its role in both the social and aesthetic background of Mannerism needs to be stressed. In effect, it accentuated current fascination with *maniera*.

It may seem obvious to state that the invention of movable type had deep repercussions on the relationship between writer and public, but the statement is nevertheless made here with a view toward clarifying a mannerist ambience. Every sixteenth-century thinker who aspired to fame (and they all did) published his writings, whether they were commentaries on classical authors or original theories. Intellectual controversies, which previously had animated the sphere of university lectures, now flourished in the arena of the printed word. There can be no doubt that this technology made possible a great body of treatises that has earned the sixteenth century the somewhat disparaging title, The Age of Criticism.[15] Publications popularized styles and influenced attitudes toward art, poetry, philosophy, and science. Also, they certainly helped fan the fires of many an academic debate. We can surmise, however, that these debates had wider ramifications inasmuch as poets and artists willingly entered the fray with writings of their own. Professional prestige was measured not only by public recognition of styles, but also by partisanship in learned arguments. This situation also fostered self-consciousness.

Although the tradition of critisism was an old and venerable one in literature, the humanist revival of classical texts renewed extensive discussion on all sorts of topics. Scholars wrote in the belief that they surpassed the golden age of intellectual discourse, and they easily found controversial subjects. Every thesis and opinion was eagerly dissected by its champions and detractors alike. This vivacious atmosphere of critical debate explains the self-awareness of mannerist poets who sought to conquer a well-educated and discriminating body of readers. To this end they lectured at academic meetings and published apologies of their *maniere*. Although manuscript copies of their works circulated fairly widely, most poets sooner or later felt the need to supervise printed editions. These activities indicate their preoccupation with style in the absolute work of art preserved accurately for all time.

In the visual arts, professional recognition of the popular interest in critical-aesthetic issues is demonstrated by the enthusiastic response to Varchi's *paragone* (except for Michelangelo's surly comments). Indeed, popularization appears most clearly in art, as, for example, in biographies that exploited the cult of creative genius. Also indicative are the many works produced by humanist scholars who must be classed as nonprofessionals in this field. These writings exhibit a broad range in quality, and the worst ones descend to plagiarism or routine recipe books. The latter, moreover, exemplify the connection between humanistic writing and academies. Academic affiliation was also responsible for the treatises of two eminent professionals, Lomazzo and Zuccaro, whose works, as we have seen, provide a theoretical summation of Mannerism.

Before discussing popular writings, we should investigate the other side of the coin—the recipient. Just as artists strove for fame, so did their customers. The wealthy patron thought of himself as a maecenas who attained "an undying reputation through his protégé's dedication."[16] Two aspects concerning cultivated patronage need to be noted. First, the circles of patrons grew considerably in the sixteenth century. And second, the dissemination of humanistic education among these persons colored their approach to the arts. In other words, artists catered to a caste of intellectual art lovers, a "highbrow . . . elite,"[17] that constituted a lively network of consumers. This interaction laid the foundation for the refinement and preciosity of mannerist art and of its theoretico-aesthetic literature. In order to acquire the sophistication necessary for the enjoyment of subtle *maniere*, people read nonprofessional books and participated in pseudo-learned debates. Because most patrons were collectors of famous styles, they provided an avid readership for works that helped them form opinions about *maniera*. And this phenomenon created a new sphere of activity for humanist writers. To this situation we must also ascribe the rise of a new type of writer—the *poligrafi*, adventurers of the pen. These amateurs paid scant attention to professional standards and directed their chatty and sensational remarks to a large audience. As lay critics of society, they deliberately exploited any issues that made good copy. It is significant to our theme that they found it lucrative to pronounce on the liberal arts.

It is well known that the most notorious of the *poligrafi*,

Pietro Aretino, was immortalized by Ariosto as the "scourge of princes." We might add, the "scourge of artists." Aretino's prose style, characterized by pungent wit as well as coarse and convoluted conceits, made him an extremely powerful figure. His career is an amazing document, illustrative of both the most commendable and the most deplorable aspects of the social scene; for Aretino showed how the power of the press could be manipulated to aggrandize a talented but arrogant critic. Aretino's interests were many. We mention here only his self-taught connoisseurship in painting, sculpture, and architecture because this side of his activities had deep repercussions on the world of art criticism. There can be no doubt that his participation in the Venetian triumvirate greatly vitalized the only successful opposition to Florentine-Roman *disegno*, as represented by Vasari and his colleagues. In effect, Aretino founded a school of art theory that aimed at belittling the excesses of *maniera*; both Doni and Dolce were his disciples. And the reputation of Venetian criticism prompted Borghini to publish his work in Florence. Borghini made a point of stating that he was a cultivated amateur writing for other amateurs who wanted to learn how to judge the merit of styles; and the style that we call Mannerism did not rate very highly.

Generally speaking, artworks throughout the sixteenth century were collected and discussed as testimonies of cultural magnificence and intellectual progress. Mannerism flourished as a court art; in this instance, "court" should be interpreted in its widest sense to include the luxurious establishments of royal and papal households, civic enterprises in republican centers, and the entourages of dukes, princes, aristocrats, and wealthy middle-class families. The artificial atmosphere of these courts encouraged *maniera*, a style particularly congenial to an aesthetic steeped in criteria of extravagant elegance, cerebral complexity, and titillating novelty that reputedly raised the art of living to a level of esoteric preciosity.[18] Self-conscious refinement was the watchword of mannerist society.

The academies, which became most influential during the sixteenth century, provided another stimulating but equally artificial meeting ground for artists and patrons. Unlike the informal groups of erudite humanists in the Renaissance, academies in the mannerist period became more formalized in organization and specialized in focus. They concentrated on serious subjects such as literature, law, philosophy, art, science, theater, and medicine as well as on trivial subjects such as courtly behavior, praise of ladies, feasts, and games. Their fantastic rate of multiplication, even in individual cities, offers another indication of mannerist delight in complexities. At the beginning, academies functioned as liberal associations for thinkers who found university systems too constricting. They afforded a more or less official aegis for unorthodox ideas. But as the century progressed, the academies in turn became as authoritarian as the institutions they sought to supersede. Initial academic freedom coincided with the notion of small groups whose main purpose was the advancement of the new humanist education. Mannerist academies, on the other hand, were complex social organizations with wider aims than the mere dissemination of elite scholarship. They became, in a sense, self-conscious ends in themselves and therefore developed a panoply of complicated rules of procedure along with eccentric titles and pseudonyms.

It is true that in some fields, for example, in science, academies in the sixteenth century continued to provide an invigorating milieu for revolutionary thought. But this has more to do with the character of science than with the nature of the academies themselves. For example, Giovanni Battista della Porta founded the Accademia dei Segreti, a body that supported research in astronomy, astrology, experimental mechanics, and natural magic. Religious authorities prohibited the meetings of this society because of its interest in the second and last-mentioned subjects.[19] And yet, it was in the puzzling guise of hermetic magic that the new sciences began. The famous Accademia dei Lincei operated quietly in Rome until it was disbanded because of ecclesiastical disapproval of Galileo Galilei's theories. We shall have more to say about the situation concerning astronomy later in this chapter. Finally, in the field of theater, we can refer to the Accademia Olimpica in Vicenza. The highlight of its program came with the mounting in 1585 of *Edipo tiranno* to inaugurate Palladio's Teatro Olimpico,[20] a production that featured choruses composed by Andrea Gabrieli.

In the field of literature, we should note Varchi's leadership of the Accademia Fiorentina,[21] some of whose members subsequently formed the rival Accademia degli Alterati. But the most important of the Florentine academies was without a doubt the Accademia della Crusca. At first, this group toyed with frivolous literature, but it soon turned to the serious business of codifying Tuscan diction. The fruits of its labor appeared in the famous *Vocabulario* of 1612. Padua, the seat of rhetorical studies in the university, also supported many literary academies, the most influential of which was the Accademia degli Eterei. Guarini and Tasso were both members of this institute. An important point to be kept in mind is that the controversy over Tasso's epic style was largely fomented by academic theorists.[22] And public argument over the pastoral also involved academic sponsorship. The main figures in this case were Iason Denores of the Accademia Pellegrina of Venice (founded by the *poligrafo*, Doni) and of course, Guarini himself.[23]

Academies of art acted not only as teaching bodies but also as humanistic corporations with wide educational objectives. Their activities transformed art from studio craft into a philosophical study accompanied by critical literature on aesthetic problems. The first formal body, an extremely influential one, was the Florentine Accademia del Disegno, begun at the suggestion of Vasari. The aims of this society were to establish all the arts under the primacy of design, and to educate professionals and art lovers in the *maniera* championed by Vasari. Because of its distinguished membership, this academy became the leading arbiter in artistic matters throughout Europe. The power of the Accademia del Disegno and its conscious goal of arresting historical decline remained important features of later academies. Well-articulated theories of style, to which artists were expected to conform, survived in the academic tradition of the baroque period, and well after that. It is significant that the two most prominent theorists of late Mannerism both founded academies: Lomazzo the Accademia della Valle di Blenio of Milan, and Zuccaro the Accademia di San Luca of Rome. Like the Florentine academy, these associations combined educational aims with propaganda.

Whatever their negative impact, mannerist academies demonstrate that optimism also activated thinkers in the sixteenth century. Thus they help us to formulate an overall view of this period that counterbalances the notion of Mannerism as an era of pessimism, anxiety, and decadence. The rise of capitalism is often cited as a cause of economic crises; but we must remember that it also injected finance and society at large with a new sense of exciting adventure. Capitalism is connected with the geographical exploration that introduced new sources of wealth. This facet of the sixteenth century has yielded yet another caption, The Age of Discovery.[24] We may also note that exoticism produced a further impetus for the marvelous novelty so beloved by mannerists. Furthermore, the recognition given to scientific advancement and the utilitarian value inherent in mechanical inventions heralded the seventeenth-century preoccupation with technology. Today, historians hail the seventeenth century as the turning point between ancient and modern science. It is my view that the role of the sixteenth century—and in particular its mannerist aspects—has been somewhat misunderstood.

As did philosophy in the sixteenth century, science enjoyed a spirit of rejuvenation. But scientists believed that their work embodied the only tangible and incontrovertible advance beyond ancient knowledge, an advance that rendered classical science obsolete. While these men may not have been as original as they imagined, the important thing is that they valued novelty. Their optimism contributed to a general idea that a decisive and glorious intellectual revolution was taking place. And yet this group includes men whose work ranges from rational science to mystical occultism. Some are saluted as important inventors whereas others are dismissed as charlatans; some seem to elude classification. The widely divergent opinions evident in modern history merely indicate that scientific and philosophical progress traveled through devious paths. The salient achievements of many scientist-philosophers are obscured by their penchant for arrogant sensationalism and convoluted secrecy. Both fields, and they cannot be separated easily, combine convincing dynamism with fashionable novelty, and regressive with progressive ideas—paradoxical features that stamp them as examples of Mannerism. As in the arts, many features of intellectual Mannerism were inherited from the Renaissance; some lived only in mannerist soil, and some survived into the seventeenth century. To understand the intricacies of science and philosophy, we must abandon modern concepts of the two fields, for in the mannerist period the lines of demarcation are obscure between medicine, mechanics and magic, chemistry and alchemy, astronomy and astrology, rational philosophy and mystical hermeticism. And these were precisely the ambiguities that resulted in clashes with civil and religious authorities.

Our present topic relates to one facet of the complex neoplatonic tradition that dominated philosophy and science. This facet was based on ancient sources, but ones of a significantly different thrust from the classical texts cited as sources for this movement. Neoplatonists were intrigued by hellenistic writers of the hermetic school in Alexandria.[25] Although it may be difficult to believe today, this aspect of neoplatonism was a radical force in mannerist thought. The neoplatonists stressed the importance of material phenomena as opposed to ideal forms. They believed that by understanding the living spirit behind the variegated world of appearances, which mysteriously bound them into one cosmos, one could reach ultimate truth. This conviction underlay two related mannerist concerns: experimental science and hermetic para-scientific philosophy.

Mannerist thinkers embraced hermetic philosophy because it presented a novel and entrancing method. Its emphasis on *nous*, the faculty of intuitive comprehension, transformed dialectic reasoning into mystical experience. The result was not *logos* but *gnosis* or the divine revelation of truth. Gnosticism prided itself on its ability to see the secret meaning of the cosmos and to enjoy dominion over it.[26] The relationship of this general philosophical approach to aesthetics specific to mannerist art and literature is self-evident. With regard to the present topic, I note that this double-edged ability—passive contemplation and active mastery— was both exciting and problematic. At first, the Church tolerated this belief because its meditative side was cultivated by a small number of intellectuals. It became dangerous, however, when it developed into a school of pantheism based on individual inspiration. The idea that one mystic could attain knowledge of divine truth through his inspired *nous* challenged the supremacy of the Church at a time when it was touchy on this subject. Furthermore, gnosticism extended into practical matters where experimental magic claimed the subjugation of the secrets of the universe. Because of this presupposition, many branches of science were suspect in the watchful eyes of ecclesiastical authorities.

In effect, the neoplatonists used the tools of modern humanism to revive the ancient concept of the *magus*, the man of supernatural powers who controlled the cosmos through *magia*. Of course, the early Florentines were interested mainly in contemplative exercises fusing hermetic lore with religious faith.[27] And in its liberal phase, the Church could afford to permit the mannerist eclecticism that this philosophy represented. Trouble arose as humanism and theology diverged into increasingly disparate directions, one toward more daring beliefs in philosophy and science, and the other toward more rigid orthodoxy in religion. In fact, the syncretic aspect of neoplatonism itself was persecuted later in the century precisely because of its magical implications. In spite of this situation, many religious humanists still worked in this vein by shedding magical overtones and concentrating on religious mysticism. This approach dominated French theology. But even in Italy, where the repressive measures of the Counter Reformation exerted a strong influence, Patrizi defended hermetic mysticism as a means of restoring Catholic faith.[28]

Other iconoclasts were less fortunate. Tommaso Campanella, whom Yates calls the last philosopher-*magus* in the hermetic tradition,[29] was tortured several times but confounded the Inquisition by his subtle logic. The radical views and fiery personality of his fellow Dominican, Giordano Bruno, caused his execution in 1600. The verdict against Bruno was based less on his defense of the copernican system (although this played a part) than on his pantheism and blasphemous interest in magic. Bruno's writings flaunt extravagant style, replete with witty conceits and obscure symbolism, as well as mannerist content. They are imbued with a mystical ecstasy that stems directly from the hermetic tradition. The studies made by Yates have shown that *magia* colored his view of mathematics, astronomy, the occult sciences, the arts, and mnemonics. It was also integral to his belief in the infinite universe and the transcendence of the material world. I cite Bruno as a mannerist on two counts. His salient philosophical position entails an exaggeration of a previously restrained norm of thought, and his works straddle the areas of speculative and practical inquiry. For these reasons, the Church feared his doctrines.

The connection between *magia* and the arts surfaces in a treatise in which Bruno explores the phenomenon of "bonds," intangible forces that seem to bind all living beings. These forces operate on three interrelated levels: spiritual (rational reason and irrational *gnosis*), natural (physical love and fecundation), and material (the forming of matter through a creative act that imprints animation on it).[30] The treatise is wide ranging in the hypotheses it examines, but a significant portion of it addresses the arts and this portion warrants the caption of "aesthetics." Bruno's aesthetics in effect bypasses the traditional explanations of the arts—that is, manual crafts, sciences, imitations of nature, or liberal disciplines. Like the other phenomena in Bruno's purview, the arts constitute a kind of magic because they convey the influence of one soul upon another.[31] They are but one manifestation of magic and love.[32] Bruno talks of the arts as a group, of individual arts (i.e., painting, music, rhetoric, poetry, etc.), and of the various materials and senses through which these bonds receive concrete form and enter the consciousness of the recipient.[33] Although his pronouncements are scattered throughout the treatise and do not form any clearly logical argument, because of his hermetic and often obscure style, one can nevertheless extrapolate several important implications from his remarks. Bruno's theory of bonds can explain why the arts require eclectic amalgamations of natural beauty,[34] why they embody complex and artificial forms together with a tone of almost unattainable nobility,[35] why they divide into different styles,[36] why they exert pathos and attract the recipient through the operation of sympathetic magic,[37] why creative agents can be called geniuses,[38] and finally why the creative personality seems to be mysteriously embodied in the artwork.[39] From the above description, it is clear that Bruno's radical originality allowed him to formulate the first comprehensive philosophy of art particularly suited to Mannerism.

Pietro Pomponazzi is considered to be the founder of natural empiricism.[40] He postulated that universal principles were immutable and thus justified sciences that proved the existence of such laws. However, Pomponazzi also admitted that miracles operated outside these laws and inferred that other para-sciences, such as astrology and alchemy, were viable examples of natural magic. This ambivalent position was characteristic of many thinkers of the time. I cite as an example the case of Girolamo Cardano, an important contributor to mathematics, medicine, and mechanics, who confused his work in these eminently rational subjects with superstition and wild fantasies. The most obvious mannerist aspects of Cardano's thought emerge from his interest in palmistry, portents, dreams, astrology, and magic in general. He was a prolific writer. Of his two most popular and accessible books, Sarton says: "Their success was natural, for they provided the kind of pabulum of which learned men of that time were fond, science but not too much of it, and tempered with a sufficient amount of nonsense and magic."[41]

I have referred to two out of a rather substantial group of scientists to show the interdependence of hermetic philosophy and natural empiricism. And I take this interdependence as a signal trait of mannerist science. Much of the impression made by novelties in the so-called rational sciences was due to their supernatural implications. Neoplatonism had succeeded in synthesizing Christian mystery, humanist scholarship, and hermeticism into a metaphysical system based on the secret correspondence between macrocosm and microcosm. God was transcendent in nature and for this reason, *magi*, through ecstatic furor, shared intellectual divinity as they plumbed the depths of dynamic natural laws. As I have stated previously, the hermetic *magus* acted in two areas, one speculative and one practical. Of course, speculative thought had a long tradition of respectability, and in its new guise, it extended this aura to scientific empiricism. As a result, the sixteenth-century *magus* achieved the status of a learned and refined humanist. His activities were defended not as examples of evil black magic but rather as adjuncts to philosophy and the white magic of studies on nature. This constitutes the avant-garde contribution of mannerist thought.

The basis of astrology, a branch of the occult sciences, rested on sympathetic magic by which one could harness the powers of zodiacal constellations. Authorities permitted general horoscopes and forbade personal ones, but this official stance did not stop eminent scientists, such as Cardano, Galilei, Tycho Brahe, and Johannes Kepler, from dabbling in astrology. The power of magic over otherwise rational minds is clearly seen from the fact that astrology still flourished even after advances in astronomy had destroyed its foundations. Because astrology was natural magic, it lay outside the purview of the laws of nature.

Giovanni Pico della Mirandola posited the existence of evil and good magic. The *magus* of good magic controlled the hidden links subsisting among natural things. On to this hermetic viewpoint Pico grafted cabala, an abstruse para-science that he divided into practical and speculative kinds. The latter, in which he was particularly interested, yielded a mystical experience that formed a vital part of Catholic philosophy. The former involved mastery of supernatural powers. Pico's admission of the existence of practical magic was extremely important.[42] It encourages the later, specifically mannerist, fusion of religious mysticism and practical occultism. Perhaps the most important example of such combination is found in the writings of Cornelius Agrippa von Nettesheim. His work presented a compendium of natural magic and at the same time investigated the genuine applied sciences of chemistry and mechanics. It is significant to our theme that Campanella referred to mechanics as "real artificial magic."[43] Again we observe a typically mannerist bifocus on irrational and rational science, couched, moreover, in a startling aphorism. To us this may seem a strange symbiosis; but it was taken for granted in the sixteenth century. Like so many other theories of potential gravity, magic did not lack its trivial moments. An example of the latter can be found in della Porta's famous work that concentrates on magical curiosities, *effetti meravigliosi*, such as optical illusions, and tricks of all kinds.

This scientist also touched on alchemy, the most flagrant instance of mannerist paradox. To us, alchemy appears to be a bewildering mixture of sober experimentation and wild obfuscation. Treatises on this subject were intentionally abstruse for two reasons: *magi* insisted on the idea of esoteric lore for initiates only, and also reacted against more intelligible books on chemistry. The most famous, or infamous, practitioner of alchemy was the physician Philippus Aureolus Theophrastus Bombastus Paracelsus von

Hohenheim. His prose style is both obscure and grandiloquent; as is well known, the adjective "bombastic" derives from descriptions of his *maniera*. Obsessed with the magical transmutation of metals, Paracelsus believed that all natural substances could be reduced to aboriginal matter, the *mysterium magnum*, from which God, the divine *Magus*, created the world. If the alchemist could find this secret, he then possessed the power of transforming material at will. Although this aspect of paracelsian thought is the most controversial issue in his doctrine, one that branded him a quack, it nonetheless provided the basis for his empirical investigations. In promulgating the medicinal efficacy of sulphur, mercury, opium, iron, and arsenic, Paracelsus opened up a new field of iatrochemistry. One can easily understand why these novel ideas were considered both dangerous and fraudulent by conservative physicians. The magical side of paracelsian chemistry was also tainted by his other interests, namely chiromancy and astrology. Perhaps more than any other scientist, Paracelsus typifies the mannerist combination of irrational hermeticism and rational empiricism.

As we all know, astronomy during the sixteenth and early seventeenth centuries embodied truly radical progress over past knowledge. This progress begins with the epoch-making work of Nicolas Copernicus.[44] Copernicus did not see himself as a radical and his essentially conservative approach stressed the careful study of classical authorities. His theory was at first viewed by the Church as a harmless essay in mathematical hypothesis, a view that Copernicus himself apparently upheld.[45] But when other influential thinkers, such as Bruno and Galilei, supported him publicly and claimed greater authority for his doctrine, copernicanism came to be persecuted. Adverse reaction against the heliocentric view arose specifically because it had invaded theology. Copernicus was not a mannerist, but his theory became entangled in the complexities of mannerist philosophy and science.

Nor is the great astronomer, Galileo Galilei, son of the musical theorist Vincenzo Galilei, a mannerist by any stretch of the imagination. And yet the saga of his career symbolizes the struggle between scientific and religious interests, a struggle that is incomprehensible unless we take into account the suspicion harbored by conservative authorities for any scientific ideas that smacked of

heretical philosophy. Galilei was the unwitting victim of a milieu
that fostered unwarranted fears of his sober and objective research.
This milieu was a mannerist one. What the Church failed to realize, of course, was that Galilei had moved beyond Mannerism into
a new sphere of science. Thus the Inquisition enacted a futile
gesture when it put his treatise on the Index.[46] Kepler will close
these remarks on astronomy because in some respects he belongs
in the mannerist canon and in others he points to the new scientific
ideals of the Baroque. Kepler has been called the last in a line of
"mystical rationalists,"[47] a caption of some import. In effect, he
combined daring scientific theories with hermetic philosophy, and
his espousal of Copernicus was founded on astrological belief in
the centrality of the sun. Kepler's main work well illustrates his
paradoxical thought.[48] In it he managed to reconcile his discoveries, such as elliptical orbits, with the pythagorean theory of the
harmony of the spheres. Thus mathematical theory, astronomical
observation, and magical mechanics were united in an impressive
system imbued with hermetical conviction. Kepler stands, like a
Janus-faced symbol, looking back to the past and forward to the
future.

The origins of his outlook come from neoplatonism, a movement that activated a revolt against aristotelian science. Mannerist
magi worked according to two methods. The first, natural magic,
entailed a passionate theory of knowledge that enabled one to
learn the secrets of nature by revelation and initiation in esoteric
lore. The second, pure empiricism, entailed innovative experiments
that enabled one to investigate the facts of nature that had utilitarian value. The aim of these methods was power, and mannerist
scientists were militant practitioners of both. As the century progressed, scientific empiricism gradually overshadowed hermetic
magic. Neoplatonic hermeticism had fulfilled its purpose; it had
fostered the genuine and experimental sciences. Once their techniques were established, they produced a natural philosophy of
their own. The pantheistic universe gave way to an idea of nature
as a machine, an arrangement of parts in perpetual motion.[49]
Ancient metaphysical notions about the cosmos had literally lost
their magic. The circle was indeed broken, and the mannerist *magus* had become the baroque scientist. But the foundation of what

historians consider to be modern science was laid by the perverse experiments and intellectual convolutions of mannerist thinkers. The character, style, and some of the content found in their works are explicable only in terms of a mannerist ambience, and as such died with the waning of the Age of Mannerism. But hidden in their radical games were the seeds of modern technological science.

CHAPTER VII

§●,§●,§●,

Mannerism as
a Historical Concept

In this concluding chapter on the sister arts, I will explore the problems of positing Mannerism as a period. It is taken for granted that the methodology inherent in such historical-stylistic abstractions, in spite of its controversial nature, can nevertheless offer insights into patterns of the past.

I shall be much occupied with the Counter Reformation at the end of this discussion, and my assessment of it differs substantially from the one customarily put forward in other historical points of view. The question of whether this movement belongs to mannerist or baroque aspects of the sixteenth century is closely interrelated with the concept of Mannerism itself, and this concept revolves around the historical sequence of Renaissance, Mannerism, and Baroque. Friedländer's characterization of Mannerism as an essentially anticlassical revolt rests on a definition of classicism that stresses its normative and objective attitude toward nature.[1] He formed his conception at a time when the debate over the historical import of the Counter Reformation first began. Hauser disagrees with Friedländer because the latter scholar isolates Mannerism's concern with mystery and spiritualism, and then parallels it to the Counter Reformation's return to absolute faith and inspired vision. We have already seen that from the viewpoint of philosophy and theology this view is, in certain respects, quite accurate. But Friedländer and Hauser both discuss these abstractions in terms of art. And like Friedländer, Hauser defines Mannerism as a radical departure from classical norms in the sense that it consciously deviates from naturalism. The thrust of Hauser's argument becomes clarified if we take into account his assessment of Mannerism as a movement imbued with an antihumanist or antirenaissance spirit.[2] If we consider the Counter Reformation to be an antihumanist movement, as does Hauser, it then appears to share a common bias with Mannerism. Hauser thus links these two phenomena, but on slightly different grounds than those espoused by Friedländer. Before examining the validity of this link, we should investigate the premises behind it. Any notion of Mannerism that predicates an anticlassical style contains implications relevant both to universal history and to the more precise problem of the connection between the fifteenth and sixteenth centuries.

Historians who wish to avoid including the sixteenth century in the Late Renaissance or the Early Baroque propose to define this era as a completely independent period. In so doing, they have perhaps overemphasized the contradictory characteristics of the Renaissance and Mannerism. Generally speaking, the classical style of the former is described by words such as "congruence," "rationalism," "clarity," "harmony," "articulation," "dignity," and "idealism." In contrast, the anticlassical style of the latter invites words such as "diffusion," "irrationalism," "incoherence," "dissonance," "obscurity," "playfulness," and "distortion." The problem with these descriptions is that not all the opposing elements necessarily apply to individual artists of either period, nor are they mutually exclusive. Furthermore, all the traits ascribed to Mannerism constitute negative ones that stem from a classical viewpoint. A champion of Mannerism might take exception to the idea that this style is disordered, abnormal, and confused. In short, as abstractions taken out of context, these value criteria are not helpful to cultural history.[3]

Although such interpretations have done much to isolate Mannerism as the dominant style in the sixteenth century, they seem somewhat dubious weapons with which to combat conventional dislike of the term. It could be more advantageous to begin with positive descriptions of Mannerism; for example, a style of spontaneity, virtuosity, and refinement that contrasts sharply with a classical ideal dominated by academic rules, impersonality, and commonplaces. While certainly as biased as the other approach, this one would surely raise even more controversy. Adherents of negative descriptions can reply that they use such adjectives in defiance of the pejorative connotations usually ascribed to them. In fact, I suspect that this is their tacit point, although their usual justification draws on evaluations of a mannerist world view full of tension, alienation, and psychological unrest. At any rate, both avowed and unavowed premises represent the basis on which they flout those historians who admit the existence of Mannerism but consider it a degeneration of worthwhile values. Thus Bousquet dares to turn the tables by stating that the Renaissance is but a brief episode between two great Ages of Mannerism.[4]

Shearman points out that emphasis on anticlassicism is as mistaken as emphasis on Expressionism.[5] Indeed, these two ideas are linked inasmuch as the concept of anticlassicism lends itself to a theory of recurring styles by virtue of which both the sixteenth and twentieth centuries emerge as antipodes to classicism. Baumgart criticizes this view on the grounds that it embraces a totally one-sided interpretation based on an equally narrow view of the Renaissance as a solely classical phenomenon; and Gombrich suggests that this view obscures the continuity of certain ideals between the two centuries.[6] These points are especially important when we recall that Mannerism lives in the shadow of the past. Intellectuals of *maniera* see their task as one of perfecting the already perfect, and herein lie the reasons for their various styles. While some of their refinements amount to nothing more than trivial stylizations, others reach a level of brilliant originality. But in view of their recognition of the need to surpass the classical heights of antiquity and of the Renaissance, one can hardly call them anticlassicists.

In raising art to a liberal discipline, renaissance artists initiated a trend that mannerists carry to its ultimate limit. In their hands, art is independent even of science and learning; it represents proof of divine genius. For genuine scholars of the time, the arts support the formulation of that branch of philosophy that today is known as aesthetics. These men establish the notion of the artists as hero and of art as the civilizer of humanity. "They were the first to make art an ingredient of intellectual and moral culture."[7] Behind this mannerist viewpoint lies the fundamental assumption of progress. Gombrich believes that this idea imbues artists with a "new sense of mission,"[8] and this sense influences not only their psychological attitudes but also the institutional framework of art. By reviving ancient science, renaissance artists thought that they were recovering classical excellence. Mannerist artists naturally consider themselves to be even more progressive insofar as they refine and elaborate the scientific achievements of the Renaissance to a startling degree of sophistication. For this reason, problem solving, which in the Renaissance was tempered by a desire to emulate the naturalism of classical art, becomes in Mannerism an end in itself; *effetti meravigliosi* leave naturalism far behind because artists strive to impress connoisseurs with the ingenuity of their invention of problems and of their solutions to them. We can therefore say that Mannerism reaches its maturity when the ambiguities inherent in the renaissance ideal of progress become apparent—when Raphael and Michelangelo achieve perfection.[9] The crisis is solved by the eventual codification of Florentine-Roman *disegno* and *maniera*. This is accomplished by academic theorists when their role as learned humanists is accepted by artistic circles and society in general.

Kristeller cautions modern scholars against imposing too vague a definition on renaissance humanism, which is, in his opinion, not a philosophical movement but rather an educational program based on a limited area of studies. Of course, humanists too believed that they contributed to progress by recovering and reinterpreting ancient texts and models.[10] Even in this restricted sense, renaissance humanism had an influence on the sixteenth century. Its success added to the growing ranks of independent thinkers who worked outside the universities and who founded the first academies. Scholarly studies by humanists encouraged the development of literary criticism and debates in the mannerist period. And the great respect accorded to the *studia humanitatis* prompted artists to militate for the inclusion of the visual arts within the liberal canon. A lateral sideline of this situation, one that entails the conviction that learned men can write critically on any subject, is the rise of the amateur *poligrafo*.

Two respected authorities, Cicero and Quintilian, promote rhetoric, style, and eclecticism in their writings, both authentic and spurious. All three elements, particularly in their more exaggerated form, are hallmarks of mannerist style. In poetry, ideals of elegance, grace, and ornamental eloquence contribute to the evolution of petrarchism and concettism. The reason behind the extravagant stylization by mannerist poets of an aesthetic that aimed originally at restrained refinement is the same one that inspired artists—a search for novel perfection. The *effetti meravigliosi* of poetry and art become symbols of the ability of the moderns to surpass the ancients. Neoplatonic interest in hermetic lore also influenced the rise of experimental and occult sciences in a profound way. And so there develop in the sixteenth century two schools of philosophy. On the one hand, the aristotelians continue the medieval tradition in the universities. Outside their confines a new group of antiaristotelians, the mannerist *magi*, champion a novel concept of cosmology and natural philosophy. Although the metaphysical aspect of this movement disappears in the seventeenth century, the scientific aspect grows into the modern system. Furthermore, since humanism affirms the dignity of man and his special place in the universe, it also upholds the validity of personal judgment and experience. This conviction, magnified by mannerist thinkers, is fundamental in laying the ground for radical experiments in all fields of intellectual endeavor.

Renaissance humanism characterized a circle of academic areas restricted to a scholarly elite. This situation fits the technology of manuscript culture and the oral dissemination of knowledge. Because the Church at that time tolerated liberal thought, humanists were able to reconcile their new ideas with traditional theology. Mannerist humanism also stresses the exclusiveness of intellectual disciplines. But the audience capable of grasping esoteric knowledge through the medium of the printed vernacular has now grown to alarming proportions, alarming, that is, in the view of a reformed Church that advocates rigid orthodoxy. However, ecclesiastical reform is deliberately flouted by progressive thinkers for whom progress means rebellious iconoclasm. Their mannerist writings exhibit either bold intellectualism or a deepening of spiritual significance, and both qualities are tinged with bizarre affectation.[11]

The unique contribution of mannerist art and thought is

found in their common goal to be eloquent. And eloquence means the power to convince. This aim, one inherited from the Renaissance, can be achieved in two ways. The first toys with fantastic ornaments and surface appearances. The second embodies personal vision and creative sensibility. Mannerists exploit both methods to please and stupefy their audience with *meraviglie*, whether artistic, philosophical, or scientific. Whichever method he chooses, the *magus* hopes to prove the originality of his inspiration as well as his participation in a collective front of avant-garde progress. Progress and individualism are thus fused into a dynamic cultural configuration.

Sixteenth-century notions about progress and modern evaluation of both these notions and their historical evidence raise the problem of the connection between Mannerism and the Baroque. Just as historians try to establish Mannerism by contrasting the fifteenth and sixteenth centuries, they use the same approach with the sixteenth and seventeenth centuries. Friedländer, and many scholars after him, states that the Baroque represents a consciously antimannerist trend. To speak in general terms, Mannerism is described as facile, affected, aloof, complex, concettist, contorted, recondite, and unnatural. The Baroque, on the contrary, is deep, communicative, simple, normative, popular, vigorous, and natural. And yet these same historians admit that many features of Mannerism can be found in baroque style.[12] Such common features bespeak a continuity between the two periods, and a quality of virile productiveness in Mannerism that can be cited against derogatory connotations of this term. In the case of poetry, we can refer to concettism and dramatic monumentalism. In the visual arts, aspects of *maniera* such as figural *contrapposto*, serpentine shapes, and the illusion of dynamic depth all act as influences on baroque style. In addition, mannerists initiate academies, art history, criticism, and biography—all of which remain vital sociological forces in the seventeenth century. The grand manner in art and poetry aims at the expression of the passions and affections —in short, at dramatic pathos. Regardless of the relative success or failure in achieving this aim, Mannerism embodies the main aesthetic premise explored and extended by the Baroque. The premium put on communication and propaganda by mannerist *magi* is also espoused by baroque intellectuals, perhaps for more legitimate and socially acceptable purposes. My point is that the basic goals are the same; only society has changed.

The latter phrase pinpoints the crux of the matter. Those historians who see elements of continuity generally stress that the Baroque adapts mannerist elements into a new conception, one based on order, unity, and normality. Baroque style presupposes that a creative work must be a carefully organized totality. This attitude parallels the seventeenth-century view of the universe as a uniform mechanism. Nevertheless, we must remember that this concept was adumbrated by astronomers and mechanicians of the sixteenth century. The grandiose theatricality of the baroque intellect relies on the primacy of rhetoric, which Mirollo takes to be one common denominator behind the diverse individual and national styles in the seventeenth century.[13] Perhaps the Baroque does attain a more popular and communicative tone than the affected and aristocratic style of Mannerism. And yet, the ideal of rhetorical eloquence first appears in the sixteenth century. Although baroque specialists may recognize this fact, they also believe that this erstwhile esoteric aim is transformed by the Baroque into one of convincing appeal. And this fundamental change is attributed to the reemergence of classical norms in the seventeenth century.[14]

It should now be clear how most historians place Mannerism as a style period between the Renaissance and the Baroque. Although Shearman avoids abstractions, he does suggest that Mannerism constitutes a style that depends on the cumulative aggregation of jewellike ornaments and effects. This decorative unity is neither structural nor energetic. The Baroque revives the energy and organic unity characteristic of the Renaissance.[15] Another way of stating the sequence of these three periods is as follows: both the Renaissance and the Baroque are in essence classical styles because they grow out of balance, clarity, and harmonious organization; Mannerism is different in that its anticlassical style exhibits imbalance, obscurity, and disorganization.[16]

This general line of argument forms the basis for Sypher's four-phase cycle—Renaissance: provisional order; Mannerism:

disintegration; Baroque: reintegration; Late Baroque: academic codification.[17] In Sypher's system, Mannerism becomes a negative phase between two periods of affirmative classicism. Haydn uses a similar cyclical view as a generalization of culture. Here the sixteenth century is seen as a time of unrest and anxiety that surfaces between two highly confident and secure world views. Renaissance optimism germinates from Christian humanism and baroque optimism from faith in reason.[18] Mahood agrees with this interpretation, but she also points out that the confidence of the baroque ethos is very different from that of the renaissance.[19] Hauser explains the difference in these terms: baroque unity requires the concentration and subordination of details under a dominant organic order; renaissance unity arises from an additive multitude of details.[20] And the divergence between these two kinds of unity, then, is ascribed to the intervention of Mannerism. From it, the Baroque inherits dynamism, dramatic rhetoric, and asymmetrical composition. But the Baroque presses these elements into the service of reviving classical ideals of naturalism and rationality. Hence, its salient principle or basic aesthetic returns to that of the Renaissance. According to this historical view, the value of Mannerism lies in its transitional position between the classical thrust of the Renaissance and the Baroque. Santillana says that "all periods are of transition, but some are more transitional than most."[21] The implication should be obvious. Mannerism interests cultural historians only insofar as it represents an anticlassical aberration of classical norms, some of whose qualities manage to outlive their negative phase to become part of a new classical and commendable order.

What we have here is a nice compromise between a pejorative and a laudatory definition of Mannerism. Even though this cyclic theory posits the existence of Mannerism as a historical fact, its tacit assumptions still deny it any worthwhile characteristics of its own. The main problem is that apparently objective criteria are projected from value judgments implied by the notions of classicism and anticlassicism. I do not deny that historical and conceptual continuity binds the Renaissance, Mannerism, and the Baroque. But those elements that Mannerism inherits and transforms from the Renaissance, as well as those it invents and provides for baroque adaptation, should be used as a means of defining the unique character of this period.

Rather than indulge at this point in similar abstractions, I refer the reader to my previous treatment of the sister arts and their theoretical literature, the intellectual climate, and sociological framework of Mannerism. After investigating music during these years, I shall attempt to draw the strands together. For the moment, let us turn to the problem of the Counter Reformation, the evaluation of which partly depends on the classical-anticlassical antithesis already outlined. But this is only one side of the confusion evident in analyses of this phenomenon vis-à-vis Mannerism and the Baroque. The other side arises from a lack of clarity in distinguishing two distinct trends, one represented by the Council of Trent and one by the Jesuits.

The final meetings of the Council of Trent in 1563 dealt specifically with the role of art in religious observance. Although the actual decrees of the Council are terse and negative, they prompted a number of more detailed treatises on the visual arts and poetry.[22] The implication of these tridentine views, published concurrently with the heyday of Mannerism, are extremely important. In effect, they represent a new ideal in religious art, one that ignores artistic values in favor of moral didacticism. Because this ideal militates against a search for novelty and progress, individual expression, personal style, and technical virtuosity, it inspires an antimannerist movement. I have already indicated that the tridentine concept of religious decorum underlies critiques of *maniera* in general as well as of specific artworks. In addition to introducing a self-conscious element of prudery, tridentine theory tries to arrest that aspect of stylistic transformation that individual freedom in Mannerism precisely condones. In its place it proposes to institute an abstract, timeless stability that stands above the vicissitudes of artistic progress or decline.

It is thus only natural that an antipathy should develop between tridentine and mannerist aesthetics, except in the case of academic art. This animosity is most evident in philosophy and science. Even though free exploration suffers an initial setback, the Church is ultimately unable to deter the momentum set in motion by mannerist *magi*. But the same situation holds true for the arts; the somewhat insipid aesthetic offered by the Council of Trent is doomed to fail. When historians cite the Counter Reformation as an effective cause of the demise of Mannerism, we must realize that only the tridentine aspect of this movement pertains to such explanations. The authoritarianism embodied by this side of the Counter Reformation finds a convenient ally in the authoritarianism of the academies. Both institutions emasculate mannerist style into socially and ecclesiastically acceptable art. And a direct outgrowth of this general attitude appears in the repressive measures instituted by the Jesuits, the Inquisition, and the Index. The notorious proceedings of these two arms of the Church militant have one common goal—to keep unruly geniuses in line with official dogma. Their purview extends from the astronomical findings of Galilei to the dogs and dwarfs of Veronese. Transforming tridentine theory into practice, the Jesuits pursue its antimannerist bias with much more efficient success.

And yet, the fanaticism and practical sense of the Jesuits have their positive side. As is well known, this movement is activated by a missionary zeal to glorify the Church and to overwhelm the faithful with its majesty. Proceeding from the didactic views of tridentine morality, the Jesuits patronize art and poetry that appeals sensually and emotionally through grandiose rhetoric. To this end, they encourage those elements of mannerist style that they correctly assess as a means toward this lofty aim. Although aspects of content are still closely supervised, elements of heroic and virtuoso *maniera* (*horribile dictu*) manage, gradually, to infiltrate the canon of respectable religious art. Rather than censure and totally ignore a contemporary style, the Jesuits instead adapt it to their own purposes. Thus, what historians call "the Italian Baroque" emerges with the blessings of a Church triumphant, a Church that finds it eminently suitable to embrace this historically derived style. At the same time, we must point out that Jesuit interest in popular and communicative art produces two types of baroque style in the early seventeenth century. One is the humble naturalism of Michelangelo da Caravaggio—the antimannerist style identified by Friedländer. But the other is the dramatic and apocalyptic style of Guido Reni and Gianlorenzo Bernini, and this style develops directly from the *maniera grande* of the sixteenth century. Startling virtuosity, magnificent rhetoric, and personal vision are now found to coincide with Catholic theology. Sypher characterizes the phenomenon as follows: "This art speaks with the voluminous tones of a new orthodoxy, for the Council of Trent announced its decrees with a majestic voice; it overwhelmed heresy with splendor; it did not argue, but proclaimed; it brought conviction to the doubter by the very scale of its grandeurs; it guaranteed truth by magniloquence. . . . It is an art given to superlatives."[23]

Although it is now possible to see the soundness of his metaphorical description, it should be noted that it contains two slight inaccuracies. First of all, the style to which he refers, and which he calls baroque, represents the second of two artistic trends evident in the early seventeenth century. It is the one I define as derivative from the grand manner of the sixteenth century. It therefore seems misleading for Sypher to make the following comparison just before the last sentence quoted above—to wit, "After the bloodless and shrunken mannerist forms, the baroque is a style of plenitude, capable of absorbing, and robustly transforming to grandeur, every sort of realism." Even more misleading is his equation of voluminous tones and majestic voices with the Council of Trent; they belong rather to the Jesuit movement. Because of the encouragement given by this group, the Counter Reformation inspires baroque artists to transform certain elements of Mannerism. Although purists advocating a return to a lifeless abstraction of *arte sacre* continue to exist, even to this day, the liberal and astute attitude of the Jesuits enables the Church to patronize new styles and to retain its position as a catalyst for religious art. Had the Counter Reformation not taken this happy turn, the historical configuration formed by the Renaissance, Mannerism, and the Baroque would have been entirely different.

PART TWO

Mannerist Theory—Music

CHAPTER VIII

ઝ૰ઝ૰ઝ૰

Introduction

Writings on music thrive in an atmosphere similar to that surrounding other intellectual inquiries—an atmosphere made up of
courtly and academic institutions, humanist scholarship, criticism,
experimental science, and public controversy. Because musicians
inherit a vital tradition of theory from antiquity and the Middle
Ages, they are much more self-concious than their colleagues and
produce a voluminous literature "exceeding by far in quantity—
and diversity of approach—anything comparable in the field of
the visual arts, and also in that of literary criticism."[1] And because
music has always enjoyed a privileged position in the liberal arts as
part of the quadrivium, theorists do not have to convince anyone
of the dignity of their discipline. As we have seen, the humanist
rediscovery of classical texts on music theory gives a second lease
on life to this mathematical tradition in art.

During the sixteenth century, however, music shifts from the
scientific quadrivium to the expressive trivium. The thrust of mannerist theory is toward a novel idea of music as an art independent
of numerical systems. In effect, the older cosmology that endowed
music with its eternal significance cedes to a linear notion of progress. And this notion opens up limitless vistas for all kinds of
experiments. Mannerist theory posits music as an aesthetic experience and stresses the human factor of creativity and enjoyment.
If mathematical schemes are used, they find their justification in
relation to compositional or performance methods. And for this
reason, the medieval system of pythagorean proportions comes
under attack. As an abstract branch of speculation, it is as viable
as any other; but as a concrete part of musical practice, it no
longer furnishes an adequate foundation.

In view of the expertise required to discuss music, it is not surprising to find that most writers are musicians. They produce learned works for professionals as well as simpler handbooks for beginners. Like other humanists, musical theorists thirst for posthumous fame and use the medium of printing for purposes of self-aggrandizement. Whether advanced or rudimentary, their works are written with a view to instructing a large audience. Even when exegesis occurs on a high level, most treatises include critical passages on style. These passages are addressed not only to other musicians but also to cultivated amateurs who wish to acquire an appreciation of music. At this point we should note that the role of the music lover changes during the sixteenth century, and that this change brings about some new developments in writing about music. Whereas in the earlier part of the century secular music is still simple enough for amateurs to sing, the cumulative striving for novel effects in the late mannerist phase results in the complication of compositional and performance problems. The music lover is now cast in the role of the elite listener whom a new class of virtuoso singers seeks to bedazzle with *effetti meravigliosi*. As a result, treatises on performance practice appear to instruct the stars and more popular books on the art of music appear to edify the consumer. Some of the latter are written by professionals, and some of course by amateurs.[2] Although these essays have a decidedly popular tone, they afford intriguing glimpses into performance practices of the time as well as into a new mystique of adulation occasioned by musical talent.

Humanism plays a pervasive role in the development of musical thought in the sixteenth century. Again the influence of the neoplatonic academy at the turn of the fifteenth century must be noted. Both Pico and Ficino were interested in classical and hellenistic theories of music and incorporated them into their philosophical systems. They initiated a specifically academic tradition —to include music in discussions of the ethical effects of the arts, *paragone*, and literature. Except for some performers who focus solely on their special field, all writers who treat speculative or practical aspects of music are humanistically oriented. They quote Greek sources, either from firsthand or secondhand readings, in support of their ideas. And many of them participate in the editing of previously unknown classical works. It is important to realize that humanism fosters scholarly research into original sources as well as modern experiments in acoustics and tuning. Mathematical systems are sustained by empirical tests, thus making theory and mechanics the basis for a new science of music whose quasi-magical validity is uselessly condemned by conservative thinkers. The mannerist *magus* is equally an ideal for progressive musicians.

The self-consciousness of mannerist musicians arises from their concepts of the past and future. The case of music poses special problems that make analysis of this milieu different from an analysis of the sister arts. The latter have access to a repository of classical models. In addition, literary criticism benefits from extant theory. Artists, on the other hand, can find no treatises from classical antiquity devoted to the visual arts, except for Vitruvius, and therefore piece together a composite picture of ancient ideas from a smattering of commentaries. The situation for knowledge of musical antiquity is just the reverse. Virtually nothing is known about Greek music itself. Whether conservative or radical, theorists derive their notions as to its nature from a body of writings that are predominantly speculative. And because their interpretations can neither be proved nor disproved by live musical example, they often use identical sources for widely divergent ideas.

As for the more immediate past, the development of printing makes handwritten notation obsolete and thus renders music before 1501 increasingly inaccessible. Theorists who delve into the arcane puzzles of manuscript idiosyncracies in the late sixteenth century are motivated by an antiquarian interest. At the same time, music that survives in printed form enjoys longer life—witness the enduring reputation of Josquin des Prez as the prince of the perfect art. Generally speaking, theorists have a tendency to refer to composers of their own time, plus those of the immediately preceding generation. But their humanist education inculcates a sense of the importance of history, and they therefore pay homage to the past even if their grasp of facts and chronology is somewhat meager. The best of them seem to be aware of the issue of modern progress, and their views on this issue illuminate the change from renaissance, to mannerist, and to baroque styles.

The historical notions of Henricus Glareanus reveal the problems of style history at the juncture between the Renaissance and Mannerism.[3] His stylistic layers correspond to four ages of music: infancy, starting about 1450 (in spite of its limitations, this grave and majestic music is preferable to modern excesses); adolescence, starting about 1480 (its moderation is pleasing); maturity, starting around 1495 (the *ars perfecta* to which nothing can be added); old age, starting about 1520 (the decline of the perfect art).[4] As a conservative purist, Glareanus laments the fact that music of his day is wild and unrestrained. Young composers abandon the precepts of the perfect art, an art that observes the modes, and instead write distorted songs that please only because of their novelty. With this statement, Glareanus sheds light on the direction of new music, a direction toward free harmonic vocabulary. From his critique there emerges a negative evaluation of what we call mannerist style in music—novel exploration of new sonorities based on the distortion of classical ideals embodied in the perfect art of the Renaissance. His attitude is clarified in the famous encomium of Josquin.[5] Glareanus hails this composer as a great genius whose music balances abstract principles of construction with expression of moods suitable to the text. But at the same time, Glareanus notes with displeasure that in some motets his idol used unusual harmonies to depict highly dramatic words. This immoderate love of novelty and originality can only signify the onset of decline.

It is significant for our topic that Glareanus associates novelty in music with texts that call for vivid representation. In fact, apologists of modern music justify their mannerist experiments on the grounds of both literal and emotional expression of the words. And Glareanus is quite correct in attributing the beginnings of this modern aesthetic to Josquin, a composer who wrote many beautiful works that fit well with the notion of an *ars perfecta*, as well as a smaller number of daring essays in the new manner. At any rate, Glareanus's treatise does much to place Josquin in the position of the consummate master of perfection whom all subsequent composers can either emulate or try to surpass. Cosimo Bartoli likens him, more aptly than he realized, to Michelangelo.[6]

Hermann Finck divides Franco-Flemish composers into two groups: *veteres* and *recentiores*. Josquin, the main exponent of the older school, laid the foundation of the scientific art of counterpoint. Finck singles out Nicolas Gombert as the outstanding musician of the younger generation because his complex and subtle counterpoint represents a superior perfection over the past.[7] Finck thus is the first in a line of conservative theorists to remark on the gradual and natural transformation of a musical norm. Giovanni Maria Lanfranco betrays a nationalist bias in his twofold division. He speaks of the ancients and lists a number of Franco-Flemish composers, including Josquin. The second group, which by inference comprises the moderns, is made up mainly of Italians, with the exception of Adrian Willaert.[8] Lanfranco's perceptive comments indicate his awareness that a school of Italian composition is developing. Italian composers contribute not only to refining traditional style but also to the new genre of the madrigal. The latter, allied with petrarchist and concettist verse, is destined to become the vehicle for audacious musical techniques. Now, the techniques used in both sacred and secular music take as their point of departure the *ars perfecta* of the Renaissance. But refinements or distortions of this ideal move in many different directions, and each theorist concentrates on those aspects that seem to him to be the most significant. The general direction of radical style, however, remains clear to all up-to-date writers regardless of whether they approve of new music. The very phrase, "new music," and the popularity of this slogan, emerge from the many treatises and editions of music that appear after 1530. As early as 1537, Johannes Stomius complains that new music is too complicated; it has neither mathematical reason nor sweet sound.[9]

One fascinating view of musical progress is supplied by the fantastic and mendacious Adrianus Petit Coclico, a theorist who displays the mannerist love of calculated self-advertising. Coclico claims to have been a pupil of the great Josquin and devotes a detailed passage to describing his master's teaching method. He maintains that this method has disappeared, and that his purpose is to revive a lost style that he calls *musica reservata*.[10] Coclico divides musicians into four groups: *theorici* (the inventors of music who achieved a certain minimal harmony of the voices); *mathematici* (the developers of complicated counterpoint that lacks suavity because of its notational and technical difficulties); *praestantissimi* (the kings of music—among whom Josquin is the master

—whose sweet and affective music is much admired as the most elegant style yet achieved); *poetici* (the masters of written and extemporary counterpoint as well as of the proper art of singing whose sweetness delights everyone).[11]

Coclico's grouping begins in chronological fashion, although his knowledge of early history is rather fuzzy. He nevertheless exhibits the same viewpoint as Glareanus in relegating fifteenth-century composers to the birth and youth of musical progress. His third group includes both living and dead composers; their superior style represents the apex of a development toward elegant perfection. Unlike Glareanus, Coclico does not admit the possibility of decline after the achievements of the *praestantissimi*. Instead, he insists that a fourth group, presumably including himself, has further refined this admirable style with the art of singing. In other words, Coclico differentiates between conservative and progressive trends, both of which are alive in his own time. His criteria for praising the moderns, whom he graces with the title of "poets," are suavity, ornamentation, and artifice in singing. Hidden in his rather abstruse categories is the ideal of rhetorical eloquence.

Nicola Vicentino deliberately invites polemics over his avant-garde musical practices. He composes in a novel manner, instructs singers as to the way to perform his daring music, constructs an instrument capable of producing microtones, debates publicly on the subject of the genera, and finally writes a treatise vindicating his radical ideas.[12] By reviving ancient practice based on the three genera (diatonic, chromatic, and enharmonic), Vicentino proposes to revolutionize contemporary music and to rejuvenate the miraculous effects of ancient music. For this reason, he provides a naïve but pertinent survey of inventions that he correctly sees as influencing the development of compositional procedures.[13] In short, Vicentino employs a history of past novelties in order to justify his own startling contributions to progress. It is irrelevant to the present discussion to note that Vicentino derived his erroneous ideas about the genera from secondary sources; more to the point is his conviction that a revitalization of musical practice is possible. Vicentino's theories have two aims: first, a theoretical explanation of the chromatic music already being composed at the time; second, a further expansion of musical vocabulary through the use of microtonal intervals. Whereas for vocal music the second aim constitutes a dead end, the first mirrors an established fact.

Vicentino is quite aware that his radical views militate for the free use of peculiar intervals that cannot be explained by traditional rules. He even advocates mixing genera in one composition on the grounds that the more surprising the music, the more attracted and moved will be the listener.[14] Even the tritone is allowed because it produces *un effetto maraviglioso*.[15] Vicentino clearly emphasizes the value of startling effects; his aesthetic embraces rhetorical eloquence. Novel style is mandatory "because music is composed to a text, and is made solely to express the conceits, passions, and affections of the words with harmony."[16] Vicentino insinuates that the expressive deployment of technical elements, especially unusual intervals, produces *una bella maniera di comporre*. He admits, even relishes, the fact that this new music cannot be appreciated by everyone. The *mirabil dolcezza* of chromatic and enharmonic styles is reserved for the elite.[17] Thus, in his work we have the first formulation of a mannerist aesthetic based on three concepts: *musica nova, bella maniera, musica "riserbata."*

Ghiselin Danckerts, one of the judges who brought down a negative verdict against Vicentino in the debate, is also an outspoken critic of the new style.[18] He inveighs against those self-styled moderns who vitiate the perfect art "by imitating the *maniera* of Willaert, a style which they call 'new.'" Danckerts refers to Willaert's *Musica nova* and to the fact that "new music" is the manifesto of Willaert's radical pupils. In retrospect, we can see that he erroneously confused the two. But his opinion of radical style is not unimportant. He cites the bad use of modes and consonances, emphasis on homophony, and the exploitation of uncomfortable intervals. Danckerts concludes that this new music is lugubrious and lacks beauty as well as artful counterpoint. The notorious escapades of radicals such as Vicentino must not obscure our realization that Willaert's style is esteemed as the natural culmination of tradition.

This view appears in the writings of another of his pupils, Gioseffo Zarlino. For him, the music of antiquity represented a consummate and unique doctrine. As time passed, music degenerated from *somma altezza* to *infima bassezza* and consequently lost the respect of men with taste. But now, Willaert's *elegante maniera* has restored music to its former honor.[19] Zarlino's treatise codifies the stylistic presuppositions of Willaert's generation, a perfect art that is at once a restrained depiction of the text and an embodiment of autonomous harmony (*numero sonoro*).[20] This theorist divides good music into two historical periods, the *antichi* (classical antiquity) whose musical practice must be adduced from theoretical writings, and the *moderni* (his contemporaries) who compose polyphony according to perfect rules.[21] Zarlino also points out that radical music, which supposedly revives the ancient genera, is nothing more than an eccentric aberration.[22]

Like the Venetian visual arts, Venetian music remains largely untouched by mannerist tendencies. In view of the special place occupied by Venice, it is logical that another relatively conservative theorist should emerge from that city. Lodovico Zacconi writes at the turn of the century, and his treatise presents a traditionalist view of history along with one sidelight on modern practice. Zacconi too speaks of ancients and moderns. The *antichi* are divided into two groups: philosophers of the science of music who established proportional intervals, and composers who created music based on sounding numbers.[23] This ancient music is regulated by consonance and harmonious mathematics, and its construction features canons and imitation. Zacconi notes that this music arises from invention, and we can therefore surmise that he refers to abstract counterpoint that obeys inherently musical laws. The *moderni* search for difficult and beautiful effects, and ornamentation is very important in their music.[24] Modern style contains fewer errors and impurities than ancient style—in other words, it is more refined. Zacconi believes that good music can be reinforced by good singers, especially those who are "masters of charming *accenti* and gracious *maniere*." Because modern music is better composed and performed, it possesses more power than the old music.[25] It is clear that Zacconi judges the merit of styles from two points of view. The first focuses on the inner workings of compositional method. According to this reasoning, ancient style appears self-sufficient; its entire effect resides in the independent procedure of mathematically conceived harmony. The notes thus arranged by pure invention need no further assistance from singers trained in the art of ornamentation. This assessment of old music is a six-teenth-century fabrication, and Zacconi is only one of a number of theorists to allude to it.

The most striking formulation of this view occurs in the treatise of Nicolas Listenius. He divides the study of music into three branches: *theorica* (science), *practica* (performance didactics), and *poetica* (composition). The *poetici* are not content with theory and execution. Their aim is to produce the consummate and complete artwork (*opus consumatum & effectum*); thus, after their death, they leave behind the *opus perfectum & absolutum*.[26] It goes without saying that such emphasis on the perfect and absolute work of art in music would be impossible before the invention of printing, inasmuch as this technology fosters the notion of the accurate reproduction of music made available to posterity as well as the notion that once old music has been thus recorded, it must not be tampered with. Zacconi echoes this idea when he says that the music of the *antichi* must be sung exactly as written because of its *obblighi* and other *osservatione*. In his opinion, the refinements achieved by the moderns concern both the inner and outer aspects of music. As in the case of the *antichi*, the *moderni* fall into two groups, an older and a younger generation. The *vecchi* of new music (Willaert, Cipriano de Rore, and Giovanni Pierluigi da Palestrina) introduced new beauties, and the younger composers of new music base their art on the compositions of this group.[27] At first glance, it may seem odd to couple Rore, famous for his innovative madrigals, with Palestrina, the paragon of traditional church polyphony. But both these men changed the style of old music, the first in the direction of word-oriented melodies and rich chordal sonority, and the second in the direction of linear counterpoint based on simplified modal schemes. The point implied by Zacconi is that both new styles are amenable to improvised embellishment. And now it becomes clear why singers assume such importance for the good effect of modern compositions. Their art has caused the development of a polyphonic style suited to it. Furthermore, the new sweet beauties found in chromaticism and in the dramatization of individual lines demand sensuous and striking performances from each singer.

It is evident that conservatives and moderates see musical

progress as a natural, organic evolution toward perfection. They grapple with the problems of dissecting the elements of perfect style, but they wish to arrest this cycle at the peak of its achievement and to freeze this moment into an eternity of greatness. Writers more attuned to the new key of mannerist progress give us an entirely different picture. For example, Agostino Michele comments on the musical scene in the late sixteenth century as follows: "Take music, in which many years ago Josquin and Willaert flourished; in the past age, Rore and Lasso were famous; and in these days Marenzio and Vecchi become singular and illustrious; and nevertheless *their manners* of composing are so different that it seems they are not practitioners of the same art."[28] Of course, Michele speaks with the benefit of hindsight. But earlier writers also demonstrate sensitivity to rapidly changing fashion. The views of Stomius and Danckerts have been mentioned. One of the interlocutors in Anton Francesco Doni's popular book of 1544 remarks facetiously that Jacob Arcadelt's madrigals, published five or six years earlier, are now outmoded.[29]

Vicenzo Giustiniani, a noble amateur, provides us with a perspicacious survey of mannerist progress. He begins with the composers active during his youth (Arcadelt, Rore, and Lasso) and then cites the delightful new inventions of younger innovators (Marenzio, Ruggiero Giovanelli, and Carlo Gesualdo). Their contemporaries of the Roman school (Palestrina and Giovanni Maria Nanino) have developed good solid counterpoint and Giustiniani notes that their works are still used as models in the early seventeenth century.[30] His remarks indicate an awareness of two modern styles, one based on radical novelties and one on gentle refinement. Giustiniani also discusses at length a new style of solo singing that leapt into prominence around 1575. He lists many singers famous for their gorgeous voices and their art of improvised ornamentation. He then makes a very astute observation; this singing style inspired many composers of polyphony to texture their works as if they were written for solo voice and accompaniment.[31] He notes that the cult of the solo virtuoso quickly spread all over Italy, bringing with it a new body of literature that includes florid (ornamented) and sentimental (popular) songs.[32]

Finally, Giustiniani turns his attention to the most modern

composers, such as Monteverdi, who have added more new beauties to new music. He also notes the rise of national and regional styles of singing.[33] At the end of his informative outline, Giustiniani states that amateur singing has declined in his day. Professionals (such as Giulio Caccini) have taken over, and they have abandoned the unpolished music of old as well as the excessive ornamentation of newer solo literature. As a result, current recitative is the finest style ever developed in the history of music.[34] Giustiniani in effect traces here the radical changes in style from the earliest polyphonic manner based on renaissance precepts to the latest mannerist novelties such as concerted music and solo song, novelties that are taken up by baroque composers.

Vincenzo Galilei's two treatises present somewhat different opinions on salient elements of modern progress. Palisca evaluates his work on modern counterpoint as one of prophetic vision and originality.[35] Galilei envisages the traditional topic of the deployment of consonances and dissonances from a totally new vantage point of vertical harmony, and he therefore recognizes the logic behind modern music. His aesthetic premise about the use of intervals in a new way to express the text means that they are not to be limited by the rules of *contrapunto osservato*, a term that refers to Zarlino's idea of the perfect art. Here Galilei adumbrates a distinction between strict counterpoint of a traditional cast as opposed to free counterpoint of a radical kind. And Mannerism lies directly along the route of this stylistic change. Galilei does more than excuse the unbridled use of prohibited intervals. He insists that even though such intervals submit to no mathematical systems, they are just as natural as those intervals that do so. Scientific rules must yield to the judgment of the ear. Significantly, he singles out Rore as the founder of the new style.

Galilei's public manifesto shows the influence of Girolamo Mei insofar as Galilei supports Florentine monody and attacks his former teacher, Zarlino.[36] To begin with, Galilei states baldly that contemporary polyphony can never resurrect, let alone surpass, the affective power of ancient music. Polyphony is only 150 years old and certainly not a perfect art. In fact, it has declined since the great masterpieces of Rore. Theorists who claim that polyphony possesses the marvelous qualities of ancient music are little short of impertinent in Galilei's estimation. Their theories arise from a complete misunderstanding of ancient systems, and hence their practical tenets are also mistaken. Traditional polyphony mixes different words, rhythms, modes, registers, and intervals in a contrapuntal hodgepodge so that the affective impression of one element is simultaneously canceled by another. This procedure goes against the fundamental nature of ancient vocal music. Galilei even dismisses instrumental music as mere sensual pleasure. But he does concede that modern polyphony has some commendable points. He praises the ingenious, rare, and delicate mixture of consonance with harsh and bitter discords. This analysis refers to mannerist style in the madrigal. But at the same time, Galilei takes a dim view of the metaphorical word painting to which modern style is put, and categorizes it as *una ridicola maniera*. His point, of course, is that the solo song best deploys the free mixture of affective elements. Only this style can hope to match the fabled rhetorical eloquence of ancient music.

In many ways, Adriano Banchieri adheres to Galilei's division of counterpoint into old and new styles.[37] He sketches a rudimentary picture of musical progress ending with Marenzio's *moderna novità*. And he concludes that modern music has achieved a new kind of *gratiosa maniera*. Banchieri obviously prizes the mannerist qualities of novel sweetness and spicy refinement. He also notes that the latest innovation is the solo song, a genre based on the sense of the words. In describing modern counterpoint, he distinguishes between two styles: *osservato*, strict counterpoint using purely musical laws, and *commune*, mixed counterpoint with figuration and free dissonances. Banchieri considers *osservato* style to be the proper training for fledgling composers. It is perfect polyphony but neglects the affective power of the text. Of *commune* style, Banchieri says that although it is perfect oratory, "it is not susceptible of being written about since it has . . . no rational principles except to please the sense of hearing."[38] Banchieri's statement epitomizes the bewilderment of theorists trained in traditional theory whose analytical tools are no longer useful in analyzing the new style. More militant conservatives therefore dismiss modern music as irrational stuff perpetrated by composers unskilled in the fundamentals of the craft. This problem lies behind the controversy between Giovanni Maria Artusi and Claudio Monteverdi, as well as the unknown author from Ferrara who calls himself *l'Ottuso Academico.*

The first part of Artusi's treatise takes the form of a dialogue between Luca, who offers a feeble defense of the moderns, and Vario, who demolishes their pretensions. After Vario pulls apart some extracts from Monteverdi's madrigals (printed anonymously), Luca sums up the position of the moderns who believe "that theirs is the true way to compose, maintaining that this novelty and new order of composing can produce many effects that are not, nor ever will be made by ordinary music full of so many and such suave harmonies; and they fancy that, feeling such piquant sounds, the sense is moved and does marvelous things."[39] Vario counters that discords have been used by many eminent composers for affective purposes without transgressing established and respected rules.[40] Artusi's vocabulary clearly indicates that he sees modern practice as nothing more than an unruly and extravagant deformation that results in absurd music. The second part of his treatise records his arguments with the "stubborn academic." It rehearses the same points over again and profiles even more strongly than the first part his feeling that the novel style is simply the haven of unskilled charlatans.[41]

Monteverdi's celebrated division of contemporary music into *prima* and *seconda prattica* is, of course, a direct rebuttal of Artusi's attack. From the *Dichiaratione* we glean Monteverdi's theory.[42] The first practice, abstract counterpoint, enjoys an august tradition perfected by Willaert in composition and Zarlino in theory. Here Monteverdi alludes to the *ars perfecta* or *contrapunto osservato*. Like Galilei, Monteverdi sees the new style, the second practice, as stemming from Rore and attributes to this composer a renewal of ancient ideals. Unlike Galilei, Monteverdi posits a continuous line of refinement and progress ensuing from Rore's inspiration. He groups together composers of polyphonic madrigals, concerted madrigals, accompanied monody, and opera. His reasons are simple. In the first practice, the perfection of harmony is mistress of the words, whereas in the second practice, the perfection of melody takes precedence. Most important to the present discussion is the fact that Monteverdi tries to dignify modern music by intimating that it too has a venerable tradition based on the rejuvenation of the marvelous effects of ancient style. And the tradition of which he speaks is the one that I propose to call Mannerism between 1530 and 1630.

Monteverdi's remarks indicate that certain aspects of his mannerist tradition serve as models for baroque practice.[43] One may argue that his sharp division between two practices is "exaggerated and artificial";[44] it presents a simplistic notion exacerbated by the polemic nature of his conflict with Artusi. And Artusi's opinions are equally one-sided. Both men partake of the self-conscious spirit that imbues musical theory in the mannerist period. Their forceful statements on behalf of old and new styles are shaped by their respective concepts of progress and by their awareness that a critical change in style is at stake at the time they are writing.

The notion of the musical genius mirrors the different facets of various views about historical development. This notion is not invented by the mannerists, but it takes on a new significance for radical thinkers. The magical, quasi-divine quality of music has been a traditional topic since antiquity. In the Middle Ages, this pagan idea, one that equates the operative elements of music with a cosmos created from number, is united with Christian ethics. Conservative theorists in the fifteenth and sixteenth centuries naturally stress the scientific side of music and therefore contribute to the continuation of this notion. Music pleases God with its mathematical harmony.

Glareanus is the first writer in our purview to use the term "genius" (*ingenium*), and his concept relates to the problem of art versus nature in music. He poses the question as to whether the composer of a chant melody or the composer of a Mass on this melody is the greater of the two. Genius for Glareanus is equivalent to natural talent. He is puzzled by the fact that musically untrained people can both invent and respond to good tunes. Counterpoint, on the other hand, is a studied art with a myriad of rules to guide the composer, and its intricacies are fully understood by very few persons. Having stated the problem, Glareanus jumps to the conclusion that one musician can have the genius for the invention of melody as well as for the art of counterpoint.[45] His reconciliation of natural talent and learned artifice enables him to hail Josquin as the greatest genius of the *ars perfecta*.

Zarlino presents a more sophisticated and logical discussion of genius. True to his conviction that all usable intervals conform to the *senario*, he stresses the scientific foundation of musical study that produces the *musico perfetto*. The composer who relies on practical habit is merely a *prattico*. This does not mean that Zarlino neglects the need for practical talents, such as a good ear and a knowledge of singing. But he is wary of the radical trends in his day that promote the judgment of the ear over scientific reason, for he insists that musicians must use sense and science. Sense alone is purely subjective whereas reason adds objectivity that transcends the vagaries of personal taste.[46] Thus we see that Zarlino's concept of *ingegno* amounts to natural craft. This notion is less paradoxical than it may seem at first glance. If one takes Zarlino's precepts as a whole, his explanation of polyphony presents a remarkable crystallization of contemporary practice. He believes that the perfect musician has a natural ability for composing counterpoint on a subject.[47] Whether his chosen theme is his own or a preexistent melody, it imposes certain limitations: mode, rhythm, intervals, etc. The composer must do more than work within these restrictions; he must have the innate talent for finding, exploiting, and developing the latent possibilities of his subject as the basis for imitative counterpoint. In effect, Zarlino is the first writer to present us with what amounts to an aesthetic for the *ars perfecta*. A composer can learn the abstract rules governing the proper construction of counterpoint, but if he possesses only this knowledge, he is at best a mediocre composer. The genius is one who can manipulate the rules to create polyphony that grows in a natural and inspired fashion from the working-out of the subject. This tacit assumption underlies Zarlino's detailed discussion and comparison of different kinds of counterpoint.

The above point brings us to Coclico's description of the qualities needed by the student composer. He must be able to improvise counterpoint and more important, he must show a great desire and inner compulsion for composition. Coclico cites these requirements as those stressed by Josquin.[48] Although Lowinsky points out that Coclico's idea is not equivalent to the platonic *furor poeticus*, an idea that came to the fore in literary criticism of the late sixteenth century,[49] it is important to note Coclico's appreciation of spiritual enthusiasm. His notion is just another version of Zarlino's natural craft. Finck's discussion of the same subject shows a similar viewpoint. He speaks of *artifices* (composers) "who are drawn to composition by natural inclination and who, from childhood, regularly cultivate their natural gift by art, practice, and varied and frequent exercises." A little later in the same passage he advises the careful choice of a good master for the student "who burns by nature with love of music."[50] It is not insignificant that this discussion occurs at the start of a book dealing with singing and improvisation. Evidently, Finck wishes to distinguish between the higher qualifications required of the composer (whom he calls *musicus*) in contradistinction to the singer. And this distinction arises from his earlier definition of music and its divisions.[51] Finck's three classifications (*theorica, practica, poetica*) reflect those posited by Listenius nineteen years earlier. In fact, Listenius's words seem to reverberate in the brief explanation of *poetica* given by Finck: "*Poetica*, that invents songs and compositions, and leaves behind some constructed works after labor, and it is exclusively [the realm] of composers."

Inevitably, the definition of genius presenting the closest parallel with the mannerist concept in the sister arts comes from radical theorists of music whose approbation of the *grazia* and *dolcezza* imputed to novel techniques rests on a belief in the composer's individual gifts. Subjective inclination now becomes the excuse for musical license. Giovanni Spataro elaborates on this novel approach with an extremely pertinent comment when he suggests that learned composers—through natural instinct, a certain grace, and manner—introduce harmonies and expressions that cannot be explained by any rule or precept.[52] The implication of such a statement for later mannerist extravagances needs no elaboration.

Spataro's correspondence greatly influenced Pietro Aaron who espoused many of his radical ideas. In one of his late works, Aaron takes a very critical view of the scientific definition of music. Only the ignorant talk of this divine art as a craft. They think that the more one practices, the more grace and mastery one acquires. And yet this is simply not true, he argues, for some musicians compose well who have studied little, and some compose badly who have studied much. Good composers are born, as are poets. To be sure, composers must know the rules; but they must also possess individual skill and natural grace, as well as the instinct to know when to depart from the rules whenever they wish to create novel effects. These gifts, received from heaven, are granted only to a special few.[53] With these words Aaron pronounces the mannerist doctrine of the divinely inspired genius whose rare talent sets him apart from ordinary craftsmen. Although Vicentino does not discuss genius, his activities indicate his belief in it. And in his treatise he mentions that theories and practices vary from country to country, and generation to generation.[54] One man's poison is another's delicacy, in other words. Of course, these remarks offer an oblique vindication of his own audacious experiments.

Vicentino's avant-gardism, as well as that of others, is undertaken for the sake of surprising and startling expressivity. As the concept of music moves from the mathematical quadrivium to the rhetorical trivium, rational craft cedes its former prominence to a new aesthetic of irrational genius. This dichotomy is implicit in the Artusi-Monteverdi debate. Artusi judges modern style by the precepts of contrapuntal craft and naturally finds it lacking in logic. Monteverdi replies that modern style takes liberties with established rules in order to depict the text. It may lack logic, but it revives ancient ideals, and the latter aim is superior to that of constructing abstract counterpoint. One may even suggest, as does Lowinsky, that Monteverdi implies "it took less genius to write in the old style."[55]

This implication is made explicit in a treatise on opera by Giovanni Battista Doni. Doni makes a sharp distinction between strict counterpoint (a closed, dead language—the craft and exercise of rules) and dramatic music (an evolving, living language —the instinctive exploration of affective communication). He admits tacitly that dramatic music does not entail the rigorous application of preset rules and therefore anyone with talent can compose it.[56] And this is precisely the criterion invoked by conservatives who condemn modern style. In their opinion, the very absence of objective standards provides an open invitation to mediocrities and quacks. But Doni's position exemplifies a totally new approach. The rhetorical, dramatic, and emotional effect of the new style is the gauge by which modern music should be judged. Only those composers with the genius for creating novel and striking works are deemed superior musicians. One need not be a learned theorist to assess modern music, but one must be a sensitive connoisseur. Doni's answer is not a rebuttal of criticism of new music. Like his colleagues, he fails to see that new music has its own kind of logic. The two camps are in effect arguing at cross purposes, and their respective shortsightedness arises out of the mannerist milieu in which these debates take place. At any rate, the idea of creative genius versus pedantic craftsmanship grows concurrently with the development of expressive ideals in music, and it is used and abused by generations of radicals seeking to justify novel inventions. This situation is central to mannerist style in the sixteenth century.

There can be no doubt that the extravagances of mannerist musicians, both in their music and behavior, form yet another facet of the cult of fame and genius. Although the cultivation of biographies is not as strong in music as in the sister arts, writings exhibit a liberal dose of anecdotes about composers and their relations with patrons. Sociological realities also abet the exploitation of arrogance, and this aspect of musical culture receives an added impetus from the rise of virtuoso singers and their adoring public. But these phenomena are exterior manifestations of deeper conceptual changes. Many historians evaluate the Baroque as the beginning of modern music. Even more than in the case of the sister arts, the rise of baroque music represents a continuum of events, for the *seconda prattica* flows from the *bella maniera*, a style that thrives on aesthetic and technical novelties throughout the sixteenth century.

CHAPTER IX

§•,§•,§•

Tuning and Temperament

Theoretical sources on this subject reveal an astonishing number of methods as well as objectives, all of them subject to considerable controversy. The corollary confusion about the fundamental nature and definition of music, both as a speculative and practical phenomenon, contributes greatly to a mannerist spirit in the field of musical inquiry. We can, however, discern three general approaches to the problem of tuning and temperament. Conservative systems remain totally divorced from practice. Progressive ones reconcile contemporary style and scientific method. Radical ones attempt to reflect the most modern music. The two latter groups mirror a situation in which all kinds of musical experimentation necessitate explanations of new ways of tuning, and many of these novel theories arouse vociferous debate. In sorting out divergent opinions, I am primarily concerned with the relationship between theoretical systems and a rapidly expanding musical vocabulary in mannerist style. To understand this relationship, we must try to see it through the eyes of theorists and musicians of the time.

First of all, theories of tuning presuppose logical systems that, in both their speculative and practical aspects, rest on scientific proof. Practical methods effected solely by visual, aural, or mechanical means, on the other hand, cannot be considered logical systems for the simple reason that, by definition, logical systems entail proportional or fractional mathematics by which one produces rational numbers. It is, of course, possible to combine the two methods. But if one must choose, the very nature of science forces one to reject the practical in favor of the systematic. This specific situation pertains in the sciences in general, except that in music, mannerist *magi* have more difficulty in promoting empirical methods that lack mathematical validity.

Conservative theorists persist in harking back to the boethian formulation of the pythagorean system, even though it has lost its relevance for renaissance music, let alone the audacities of mannerist music. The crux of the matter is the definition of the semitone. The pythagorean tone, with a ratio of 9:8, consists of a minor and a major semitone; the difference between them is the comma. But only the minor semitone, whether written or extemporary, can be used in actual music. For this reason, progressions between B♭-B♮ or F-F♯, or any other equivalent intervals, are forbidden. When the chromatic madrigal begins to abound in such progressions, it raises a flurry of controversy. A teaching handbook by Biagio Rossetti explains the problem in simple terms. Although Rossetti is a staunch pythagorean with a poor knowledge of Greek theory, his discussion of certain contemporary issues seems clear enough. He says that the minor semitone appears in plainchant whereas the major semitone appears in polyphony. The latter creates dissonance in the permutation between B♭-B♮. To reconcile practice and theory at least in part, Rossetti qualifies this interval by calling it a sweet dissonance or beautiful color.[1] These terms indicate that the major semitone is heard as a peculiar sonal quality. Indeed, words such as *suavità* and *dolcezza* appear frequently in descriptions of the delicate coloring of mannerist harmony. And whenever found in a poem, these same words prompt chromatic progressions using this interval.

In his suggestion of a new tuning system, as well as other novel topics, Bartoloméo Ramos de Pareja emerges as a radical unique for his time. Furthermore, the polemical tone of his treatise also reveals him to be a militant avant-gardist, and his merciless diatribes against conservative ideas succeeded in arousing the enmity of many theorists. Ramos is not a mannerist nor does he address mannerist practice; however, he has a direct and indirect influence on later theorists whose writings relate to sixteenth-century Mannerism. The most controversial aspect of Ramos's intervallic ratios occurs in his second division of the monochord.[2] By bisecting and trisecting a string, he constructs a compromise system somewhere between pythagorean and ptolemaic tunings.

Although his approach is empirical, for the sake of practical simplicity, a mathematical translation is possible. Thus, his system includes four pure major thirds and three pure minor thirds (386 and 316 cents). It produces pure triads on C major, D minor, E minor, F major, A minor, and B♭ major. All other fifths and thirds are smaller than pure sizes by one comma (22 cents). Because Ramos advocates this system for vocal music, its assumptions come under attack from conservative writers.

The ensuing quarrel between Ramos's critics, Nicolaus Burtius and Franchinus Gafurius, and his pupil and advocate, Giovanni Spataro, carries into the sixteenth century. Spataro defends Ramos by satirizing any conservative stance that dismisses theoretical difficulties as irrational,[3] for Spataro sees this attitude as a convenient escape from problems posed by musical practice. In his letters, Spataro supports Ptolemy's syntonic diatonic tuning and Ramos's system, because they both codify intervals used in the music of his day.

Lodovico Fogliano proposes another system closer to just intonation than that of Ramos. Fogliano's keyboard requires double keys for D and B♭; the difference between these keys is the syntonic comma (81:80). He tabulates a chromatic scale based on ramian consonances in such a way as to arrive at five pure minor semitones (25:24), six pure major semitones (16:15), and one anomalous one, F♯-G (27:25).[4] This arrangement allows only six pure triads on G major, G minor, A major, A minor, B♭ major, and B minor. Barbour concludes that Fogliano's system is much inferior to the one proposed by Ramos.[5] Be that as it may, his system has been cited for two reasons. First, it heralds the coming preoccupation with tuning systems for keyboard instruments, a preoccupation that will yield a host of highly refined mathematical solutions. Second, although again Fogliano cannot be counted as a mannerist, his system will be cited by *l'Ottuso Accademico* in defense of modern, iconoclastic vocal music.[6] And the stubborn academic's defense against the criticism of Giovanni Maria Artusi, in spite of its weaknesses, falls squarely into the mannerist framework of controversial issues in the late sixteenth century.

Gioseffo Zarlino presents an astute theory that fuses contemporary practice with traditional scientific speculation. He rejects the pythagorean *tetraktys* because its thirds are not simple ratios,[7] and proposes in its place the *senario* (1:2:3:4:5:6) as the mathematical basis of the perfect art.[8] The philosophical beauty of the *senario* resides in the fact that consonances can be derived from superparticular ratios, and this fact is buttressed by symbolic analogues to celestial and worldly numbers.[9] Therefore, it is not surprising that Zarlino should favor Ptolemy's syntonic diatonic tuning.[10] He declares that this ancient system produces all the perfect and imperfect consonances in their purest form, in spite of some small problems in the calculation of the sixths.[11] Zarlino glosses over what he considers to be a minor discrepancy in his otherwise perfect system, a system that, according to him, is used for all vocal music. Fretted and keyboard instruments can only approximate the perfection of vocal tuning (which we today call just intonation).[12]

Before coming under the influence of Girolamo Mei, Vincenzo Galilei supports Zarlino's views. But in the *Dialogo* he observes ironically that on Zarlino's authority, many musicians believe that modern tuning revives the syntonic diatonic of Ptolemy.[13] Galilei goes on to prove that the divergent interval sizes in this system make it impractical, and concludes that singers must add or subtract the comma whenever necessary to avoid dissonance or loss of pitch. In other words, singers instinctively temper appropriate intervals.[14] Seen from this angle, singers imitate instrumental practice and not vice versa. As we will see, these observations are hardly new in 1581, and they do not lead Galilei toward serious consideration of equal temperament.

Whereas just intonation is associated with vocal music, keyboard instruments are tuned generally by meantone temperament. There are many ways of tempering, and these range from written versions of practical methods to learned discussions based on classical authority. The most widely accepted system is that proposed by Pietro Aaron. He calls it *participatio*; it involves tuning by successive fifths, each one tempered by one-quarter of the syntonic comma, in such a way that the comma is distributed among the intervals of the octave.[15] As is well known, two chromatic pairs of pitches in Aaron's system, D♯ and E♭ as well as G♯ and A♭, have a difference of 41 cents (almost one-half of an equal-tempered semitone), a discrepancy called the "wolf-tone." Apart from this problem, a significant number of triads combine tempered fifths with one pure third.

Although Zarlino upholds just intonation for vocal music, he suggests another way of tuning keyboard instruments—that is, tempering by two-sevenths of a comma. Because this fraction is irrational, Zarlino works from a geometric basis. His meantone method produces two sizes of semitone: seven semitones of 121 or 122 cents and five of 70 cents. All fifths are smaller than the pure size by 5 or 6 cents, except for C♯-G♯, which is 45 cents larger.[16] By extending Zarlino's calculations to enharmonic pitches, we note that his G♯ and A♭ produce a difference of 51 cents (slightly more than one-half of an equal-tempered semitone). For this reason, Zarlino describes a keyboard with nineteen keys in each octave.

Francisco de Salinas advocates yet another meantone temperament for keyboard instruments, one based on one-third of the syntonic comma. After a complicated series of geometric computations, Salinas arrives at a tone divided into three almost equal parts: C-C♯ (63 cents), C♯-D♭ (64 cents), and D♭-D (63 cents).[17] Because all tones and semitones are equal, more or less, Salinas's system resembles equal temperament. However, the difference between enharmonic pitches is the same as that between actual semitones. Therefore, double keys become necessary, again producing a nineteen-note octave. In his meantone temperament, progressions involving chromatic notes in close proximity sound extremely peculiar, although diatonic triads are pleasing.[18]

If we take these samples, as well as other meantone temperaments, as a whole, we can isolate one predominant problem—how to distribute the comma throughout the octave. Theorists approach this problem from the only mathematical point of view they know, a fractional spread of the comma defined as a simple ratio. None of these methods succeeds in achieving an unnoticeable distribution. Each system offers some elements of logic; but these elements, although viable from one vantage point, only introduce other apparently inescapable problems. The rationale behind meantone temperament is now clear. The syntonic comma has "disappeared" between enharmonic pitches. Thus, these systems work well only for music that does not mix sharp and flat chromaticism.

Of course, the only system that allows limitless chromaticism is equal temperament. Although sixteenth-century theorists dislike it, they admit that it in fact exists in fretted instruments. A few writers suggest it for keyboard instruments, and some truly radical theorists even dare to say that vocal music is best tuned this way. Because written theory for instrumental practice is a relatively new phenomenon, it remains unhampered by traditional heritage. Theory for vocal practice is another matter. Here tradition plays a weighty role, and this role dictates the necessity of scientifically valid tuning systems. The conceptual problem with equal temperament resides in its irrational ratios. Hence no mathematical calculation is possible so long as theorists adhere to fractional mathematics and euclidian geometry. The mechanician, Niccolò Tartaglia, explains the situation in the revised preface to his translation of Euclid's *Elementa*.[19] He considers proportions as common properties of musical consonance and geometric figures. Euclid's eighth proposition proves that one cannot divide superparticular ratios into two equal parts. Therefore, no matter which ratio one proposes, it will never yield equal semitones. Neither a mathematical nor a geometric method can resolve this problem.

Henricus Grammateus constructs a temperament for the organ that comes close to systematizing equal tuning. The most striking feature of his system is that the octave now has two equal halves, C-F♯ and F♯-C, each of them equivalent to 600 cents. Grammateus keeps the pythagorean semitone between diatonic half-steps (90 cents), but calculates all chromatic semitones as half of the just major tone (102 cents). Thus, all fifths and fourths not involving E and B are pure intervals.[20] Giovanni Maria Lanfranco, one of the correspondents in the Spataro circle, also suggests tempering keyboard and string instruments. His method, however, is purely practical—that is, flattening the fifths and sharpening the fourths by minute amounts.[21] Historians today surmise that the result would be equal temperament; but an equally good case can be made for meantone temperament. Lanfranco's ideas merely echo practical guides for the latter that go well back into the early fifteenth century.

As stated previously, the main hurdle faced by theorists is the lack of rational explanations for equal temperament that would support the hallowed rules of vocal music. Artusi wrestles with the problem in the course of his debate with Ercole Bottrigari without coming to any firm conclusions.[22] Galilei remarks that fretted instruments use the high diatonic tuning system of Aristoxenos—six equal tones in the octave divided into twelve equal semitones.[23] Seven years later, Zarlino tries to work out a rational system for equal tuning on the lute based on a semitone ratio of 18:17.[24] Parenthetically, we note that the validity of this hypothesis resides in the fact that 17 mediates between 18:16, a compound version of the 9:8 tone. However, twelve 18:17 semitones produce an octave that is 12 cents short of a pure interval. To us it seems but a small step from tuning on the basis of a 99 cent semitone to tuning on the basis of a 100 cent semitone. But both Artusi and Zarlino indulge in the number games prevalent at the time. The abstract approach inherent in such methods surfaces in Zarlino's emphasis on the octave discrepancy, a discrepancy that renders this particular system imperfect in his view. In practical terms of playing the lute, it is negligible.

The only thinkers in the sixteenth century to accept the irrational ratios of equal temperament as normal seem to be mathematicians and mechanicians.[25] Simon Stevin states categorically that musical pitches have nothing to do with the mathematical ratios revered by old-fashioned theorists of music. He considers it ridiculous that such sweet intervals as thirds and sixths should be classed as imperfect consonances. Stevin concludes, furthermore, that good singers equalize all intervals. Therefore, the proper division of the octave should produce twelve equal semitones by using the twelfth root of two.[26] Giovanni Battista Benedetti demolishes Zarlino's just intonation in two interesting letters written to Cipriano de Rore around 1563. His method is as practical as it is revealing. Using several measures from one of Rore's mildly chromatic madrigals, he effectively demonstrates that singers cannot retain the so-called pure intervals without losing pitch. According to Benedetti, the only solution is equal temperament.[27]

We must recognize that this debate entails several issues. One is the matter of aural discrimination. In addition to its irrationality, equal temperament ruins the sonorous quality of intervals; the only pure interval within the octave is the octave itself. A second issue involves vocal practice. Momentary tempering to avoid loss of pitch does not necessarily mean consistent equal temperament. The final issue concerns the antagonism between systematic theory and extemporary practice. We cannot expect theorists to approach problems from viewpoints foreign to their way of thinking. Even when they admit that proportional ratios are not causes of consonance and dissonance, they still must find rational systems to explain tuning. For this reason, some theorists suggest that equal temperament might be sought through mechanical aids, such as the mesolabium.[28] The practical feasibility of this device is still a moot issue today. It remains clear, however, that to the sixteenth-century mind, neither mathematics nor geometry was able to solve the puzzle of equal temperament. To counter criticisms against irrational and "rule-of-thumb" procedures, some writers have recourse to mechanics, a new branch of science that lends equal temperament an air of scientific validity. The inventions of scientific *magi* validate empiricism.

Ever since the Middle Ages, it has been generally accepted on the authority of Boethius that the Greek modes were sung according to three kinds of tetrachords: diatonic, chromatic, and enharmonic. Theorists of *musica theorica* or *speculativa* dutifully repeat this information, even though only the first genus supposedly survives in contemporary music. Theorists in the mannerist period are fascinated by the genera not only because of their humanist studies but also because of their interest in questions of tuning. Conservatives describe the genera to show the mathematical basis of intervals; this topic does not disturb their traditional definition of the diatonic tetrachord as the basis for real music of their day. Progressive theorists cite classical authority to support new systems such as just intonation or meantone temperament. Radicals refer specifically to Aristoxenos's high diatonic genus as their prototype for equal temperament. It thus becomes clear that each theorist announces the concept of the Greek genera that best suits his own theoretical position. Classical sources are interpreted, correctly or incorrectly, in order to support modern notions of the proper tuning for the best music of the time.

In view of this situation pertaining to classical scholarship, Nicola Vicentino feels no compunction about contributing his own interpretation of ancient theories. Although he derives his notions on this subject from humanist contacts in Ferrara and Rome, Vicentino consistently cites Boethius as the sole authority in his treatise. His questionable research is compounded by inconsistencies and errors in the text. Once the latter are resolved, wherever possible, Vicentino's conception emerges as a striking instance of mannerist thinking. As the title of his treatise indicates (*Ancient Music Adapted to Modern Practice*), he tries to revive the ancient genera in relation to modern practice, and modern practice, in his mind, consists of traditional everyday style and progressive ultrarefined style. Although Vicentino obviously counts his work in the latter category, his theory aims at renewing the exquisite perfection and rhetorical power of ancient music for both styles.

To understand Vicentino's convoluted arguments, we must begin with his intervallic structures. The comma, the smallest discrete pitch, does not occur in vocal music; it does, however, figure in his archicembalo. All other intervals play a part in counterpoint using the three genera.[29] The minor diesis (C-Ċ) comprises two commas, and the major diesis (Ċ-Db) comprises two minor dieses. The minor semitone is the same size as the major diesis, whereas the major semitone contains three minor dieses. There are five tone varieties: minor, two natural (10:9 and 9:8), accidental (with sharps or flats), and major.[30] Thirds constitute the most variable class: minimal accidental (D-Fb), natural minor (D-Ḟ), accidental minor (F-Ab), enharmonic minor (D-Ḟ), natural major (C-E), accidental major (D-F#), and enharmonic major (C-Ė).[31] The fourth has three sizes: natural, accidental, and enharmonic.[32] We have already mentioned that Vicentino accepts the tritone for vivid word painting. He subdivides this interval into natural and accidental types; the enharmonic tritone is omitted even though it occurs in his music.[33] Six kinds of fifths are listed: imperfect natural (B-F), imperfect accidental (F#-C), enharmonic imperfect (B-Ḟ), natural (C-G), accidental (C#-G#), and enharmonic (C-Ġ).[34]

The consistent division of intervals into natural, accidental, and enharmonic sizes relates directly to Vicentino's exposition of the three genera and their use in vocal polyphony. He describes in some detail the construction of the genera on different species of tetrachords, pentachords, and octaves.[35] To simplify matters, I will use the pentachord between C and G to illustrate his system. The diatonic pentachord consists of: C-D (natural tone), D-E (natural tone), E-F (major semitone), and F-G (natural tone). The chromatic pentachord is as follows: C-D♭ (major semitone), D♭-D (minor semitone), D-F (minor third), F-G♭ (major semitone), and G♭-G (minor semitone). And finally, the enharmonic pentachord has these intervals: C-Ċ (minor diesis), Ċ-D♭ (major diesis or minor semitone), D♭-F (major third), F-Ḟ (minor diesis), Ḟ-F♯ (minor diesis), F♯-Ġ♭ (major diesis or minor semitone), and Ġ♭-G (minor diesis). We should note that since the major diesis is twice the size of the minor diesis and equals the minor semitone, the chromatic step between D♭-D does not differ from the enharmonic steps between Ċ-D♭, and F♯-Ġ. Thus, the minor diesis is one-third and the major diesis two-thirds of the major semitone. Vicentino calls this genus enharmonic, but it rather approximates the soft chromatic genus of Aristoxenos. And it is, moreover, inaccurate to refer to it as quarter-tone tuning.

In theory, singers are supposed to differentiate among six individual pitches from the major tone down, each of them one diesis smaller than the previous one. In practice, they probably attempt to pitch the dieses somewhere in between equal semitones. By combining the comments from ancient Greek theorists as to how microtonal intervals are placed within the octave species with our present knowledge of Middle Eastern singing styles, it is reasonable to assume that these minute intonations are introduced as ornamental notes between standard stationary pitches of the modes. Vicentino, however, advocates all his notes as discrete pitches in melodic and harmonic arrangements. And his musical examples bear out this interpretation of his intentions. From his incorrect impression of the nature of classical practice, Vicentino has invented a new and extravagant style of composition, and Zarlino is correct in negating the notion that such music recreates ancient style.[36]

Vicentino maintains that each melodic genus, in order to remain pure, must not be adulterated with intervals from the other two genera, and to explicate this theory he provides musical examples illustrating each pure genus. Although the pure diatonic is very limited, the other two genera afford a rich and varied vocabulary. And because the highest aim of music is to arouse astonishment and admiration, Vicentino recommends composing in a mixture of the three genera. The converse of his theory is that a few salient intervals suffice to identify a genus. Thus, the tone and major semitone are proper to the diatonic; the major and minor semitones, and minor third to the chromatic; the major and minor dieses, and major third to the enharmonic. This construct represents the crux of Vicentino's public debate with Vicente Lusitano.[37] In simple terms, Vicentino's proof that the pure diatonic no longer exists in contemporary practice rests on its use of minor semitones as well as major and minor thirds as structural intervals.[38] Lusitano counters that only music featuring frequent progressions of successive semitones or dieses can be called chromatic and enharmonic respectively. The judges awarded the purse to Lusitano.

Extrapolating a tuning system for the genera in vocal music is a complicated matter and in the final analysis rests on conjecture. Because the chromatic and enharmonic genera are defined by intervals derived from a division of the natural tone, the ratio of this interval becomes crucial. In his preliminary discussion, Vicentino describes the ordinary pythagorean tone as 9:8 or 18:16; he also mentions the 18:17:16 division but rejects it as irrelevant to his theory.[39] Instead, he posits the *diatonico partecipato* as the tuning for vocal polyphony.[40] By gathering together his unconnected references, we can infer that Vicentino espouses just intonation, or Ptolemy's syntonic diatonic tuning. Herein lies the difficulty in calculating the semitone and diesis ratios; Vicentino repeatedly cites both 9:8 and 10:9 ratios for the natural tone.

Various methods can be tried to find the hypothetical values for the comma, dieses, and semitones in the genera. If we take the just major tone (204 cents), we arrive at the following: comma (20.4 cents), minor diesis (40.8), major diesis or minor semitone (81.6), major semitone (122.4). If we take the just minor tone (182 cents), we come up with a different set of figures: comma (18.2 cents), minor diesis (36.4), major diesis or minor semitone

(72.8), major semitone (109.2). If we begin with the traditional syntonic or didymic comma (22 cents), the computations give us: minor diesis (44 cents), major diesis or minor semitone (88), major semitone (132). It should be self-evident that if Vicentino's generic divisions are actually based on just intonation, then the sizes of enharmonic and chromatic intervals will vary depending on which of the tones, major or minor, they subdivide.

From the previously outlined pentachord, we see that Vicentino is careful to subdivide only the 9:8 natural tone (204 cents) into the chromatic genus—that is, C-D and F-G yield C-Db-D and F-Gb-G respectively. Thus, C-Db is the major semitone (122.4 cents) and Db-D the minor semitone or major diesis (81.6), and they come to 204 cents; F-Gb and Gb-G also equal the same amount. These two sets of chromatic divisions leave a minor third, D-F, of 294 cents. The latter size does occur in just intonation, and it constitutes a badly tuned minor third (equal to the pythagorean one) that causes loss of pitch. At any rate, Vicentino's chromatic pentachord is consistent with just intonation. Nevertheless, we can detect some problems. For one thing, both semitone sizes bear no relationship to the actual ones in just intonation (92 and 112 cents). These discrepancies are troublesome because C-Db should be the same size as E-F. And of course, the problems become compounded in the enharmonic pentachord. The chromatic semitone, C-Db, yields C-Ċ, a minor diesis (40.8 cents), and Ċ-Db, a major diesis (81.6); the F-G tone is also broken down into major and minor dieses of the same values. But as a result, the major third, Db-F, is 375.6 cents—9.6 cents short of the just major third. Now, if we were to predicate other figures for diesis and semitone divisions in keeping with Vicentino's proportional sizes, we would simply observe another set of discrepancies. The problem is insoluble given Vicentino's terms of reference. Even more than Rore's chromatic madrigals, Vicentino's genera vindicate Benedetti's espousal of equal temperament.

Another partial solution would be meantone temperament, and this idea brings us to Vicentino's archicembalo. This instrument, constructed before 1561, was one of the stellar items in the Ferrarese court's collection of curiosities. We need not wonder that this formidable instrument, with its 6 orders and 132 keys, frightened ordinary players.[41] In both tuning systems, the first keyboard produces Aaron's one-quarter comma meantone temperament. The systems differ in the tuning of the second keyboard. The first system contains the diesis needed for enharmonic music as well as a further comma division for some keys, whereas the second system features the pure fifths and pure thirds found in just intonation. The detailed problems of establishing precise measurements for both systems have been assessed elsewhere.[42]

Regardless of which set of figures is used, and there are several distinct possibilities, the first tuning system effects a nearly equal diesis and comma division between chromatic keys as well as between diatonic and enharmonic keys. The rationality of this tuning cannot be denied. Vicentino's first system regularizes meantone discrepancy by transforming it into a rational norm governing the second keyboard. Kaufmann hails this system, and others based on it, as a kind of equal temperament. However, its equality becomes audible only when the player consistently mingles the two keyboards—that is, when he plays in the enharmonic genus (refined with comma inflections) intermingled with the diatonic and chromatic genera. Vicentino's propaganda about music based on a mixture of the three genera now takes on added significance.

Vicentino recommends using the archicembalo to train singers in accurate pitch intonation for his brand of avant-garde music. But one cannot deny the fact that the instrument produces a preponderance of tempered intervals. Even diesis and comma inflections fail to come close to pure sizes. Of course, singers can easily adjust, but in so doing they abandon the principles of just intonation upon which Vicentino insists for vocal performance. Because the archicembalo produces a closed set of generic tunings, it is a complete system. And one is therefore tempted to view his earlier stabs at generic tunings within just intonation as a major error. Whatever the case may be, Vicentino's premise emphasizes the highly original effects of both vocal and instrumental tunings of the genera. And although he suggests that the archicembalo be used for rehearsal purposes, the first tuning system really prepares the instrument for solo renditions of modern music. Luzzaschi's lost works bear witness to this practice.

Furthermore, the second tuning system supports the thesis

that the first concerns avant-garde instrumental style. In the second system, the player can strike just triads on nearly all the degrees of the octave by a judicious combination of keys selected from both keyboards; and Vicentino carefully describes how this is to be done. The rest of his phraseology, vague as it is, must be interpreted in the context of the entire treatise. He says about this second tuning that its thirds are more perfectly tuned than the ones he uses (in the first tuning), and that the perfection of its intervals revives a marvelous ancient order (Ptolemy's syntonic diatonic, or the *diatonico partecipato*, as Vicentino calls it). He also notes that this tuning is apt for the arciorgano, a statement implying that he associates the latter system with the use of keyboard instruments to accompany vocal complements. And, rightly or wrongly, Vicentino adheres to just intonation as the tuning relevant to vocal practice. Therefore, his earlier attempts to combine just intonation and generic music for voices again emerge as incorrect. Just intonation is one thing; generic music is another. In a later chapter, we will discover that generic music is reserved for a special category of private, noble entertainment for refined ears, whereas ordinary music in just intonation belongs in the public realm.

   Vicentino's second tuning system attempts to bring keyboard instruments in line with vocal intonation. References made to concerted music by different theorists indicate their awareness of tuning problems. Bottrigari divides instruments into three categories similar to those posited by Zarlino: stable, changeable, and flexible. He insists that combining instruments with similar tunings is the best practice; but inasmuch as it is now customary to include at least one keyboard instrument with any ensemble, Bottrigari goes so far as to allow the combination of any two of his three groups.[43] Artusi makes a similar recommendation.[44]

   Vicentino's *Descrizione dell'arciorgano* (1561) is a short advertisement for a portable organ.[45] The text describes in glowing terms the various virtues of this new instrument. It first expounds on the perfection of intervals hitherto unknown on ordinary organs (i.e. just intonation). The tacit reference to the second tuning system of the archicembalo is unmistakable because Vicentino states that the arciorgano can accompany music in the pure and mixed diatonic genus—that is, *musica communa*.[46] The second virtue is the arciorgano's ability to produce the three genera (i.e. the first tuning system). The instrument therefore instructs its owner on eloquent music that follows every minute affection of the words, as well as on the nondiatonic styles of non-Western peoples. The third virtue reported in the text is more of a sales pitch than a factual account of the instrument's capabilities. With the arciorgano, one can play in tune with any group of instruments, including equal-tempered ones. It is a "compleat" instrument for all music lovers.

Performance practice evidently pays scant attention to the problems troubling theorists. Practical adjustments are made when possible, and other insoluble discrepancies are exploited as normal aspects of an extremely colorful spectrum of sound. One interesting comment appears in Thomas Morley's treatise. In it, he states that the organ is tuned half in the diatonic and half in the chromatic genera, whereas the virginal is tuned half in the chromatic and half in the enharmonic genera.[47] This comment sheds light on the spicy intonation of works written by the English virginalists. Michael Praetorius mentions a complex harpsichord suited to playing madrigals by Marenzio,[48] a comment that indicates the close connection between innovations in tuning and compositional practice in the mannerist madrigal. It also suggests that one pathway to harmonic refinements in keyboard music starts at the doorstep of radical experiments in vocal music. The ensuing chapters in Part Two of this study trace the theoretical controversies that mirror vocal practice. And such controversies over intervals, accidentals, hexachords, transposition, and the like always refer back, tacitly or openly, to tuning systems.

CHAPTER X

❧❧❧

Intervals and Modes

We can take it as symptomatic of the general situation at this time that intervallic systems arise in conjunction with historical concepts of musical style. This side of the science of counterpoint becomes increasingly allied with practice. For example, Henricus Glareanus concentrates on those intervals with a useful function in counterpoint illustrative of the *ars perfecta*: unison, fifth, and octave (perfect consonances), third and sixth (imperfect consonances), semitone, tone, fourth, and major seventh (dissonances). All dissonances except the fourth must appear in syncopation; the fourth, on the other hand, can be employed without syncopation when it participates in fauxbourdon or cadences. Glareanus distinguishes between the effect of perfect and imperfect consonances and gives rules explaining the limited deployment of dissonances, which, he feels, disturb the ear.[1] His definition of dissonances betrays the traditional bias against this category.

In the sixteenth century, it becomes customary to discuss intervals in the manner outlined by Glareanus. Thomas Morley repeats this classification as late as 1597 in his rules for improvised descant on a cantus firmus. Like other theorists, Morley makes an extensive investigation of the subject of the fourth. This special attention is necessary because according to *musica practica* the fourth is a dissonance whereas according to *musica theorica* it is a consonance. The sole practical exception that uses the fourth as a consonance noted by Morley is fauxbourdon.[2] By mid-century, however, fauxbourdon no longer functions as a normal mode of composition. It has become a special effect, usually prompted by a textual passage calling for harmonic underscoring.

Gioseffo Zarlino's contribution to traditional theory resides in his unique reconciliation between stylistic perfection in music and mathematical science. He gives practice a firm speculative basis, and this aspect of his work alone suffices to earn him the rank of a major theorist in the late sixteenth century. As indicated in the discussion of Zarlino's tuning for vocal music, this theorist classifies all intervals except the semitone, tone, and seventh as consonances. He settles the question of the fourth by uniting science and practice, both of which present this interval as an unqualified consonance.[3] In Zarlino's opinion, imperfect consonances are not as satisfying as perfect ones; the reason is that the former involve ratios from four to six, whereas the latter result from ratios between one and four.[4] But in spite of their lower theoretical status, imperfect consonances possess characteristics that fascinate Zarlino. The major species has a lively, cheerful quality, and a bright sonority. The minor species is sweet, smooth, sad, and languid. Furthermore, minor imperfect consonances tend to contract to the nearest perfect interval whereas major imperfect consonances expand in the opposite direction. Implicit in these observations is the notion that these natural patterns enhance the emotive aspects of the two categories. Zarlino also notes that these movements require linear motion by semitone, an interval he calls the salt and seasoning of good melody and harmony.[5]

This point brings Zarlino to the exposition of dissonances. Unlike his colleagues, he takes a positive stand on the subject. He postulates that dissonances are necessary for motion from one consonance to another. They constitute a condiment that lends piquancy to the blandness of consonant sounds. The only useful dissonances are those found in the diatonic order. To bolster his scientific system, Zarlino notes that in a sense these intervals also arise from the *senario*; their ratios use numbers outside the *senario* but the calculations producing them involve numbers within the sacred system.[6] It is now possible for Zarlino to construct all intervals within the octave with ratios corresponding to just intonation. One of Zarlino's original achievements is his aesthetic conception of intervallic categories, and this conception arises from his tuning system. Zarlino also describes certain extremely harsh intervals that he does not allow in good composition. The fact that these intervals produce awkward false relations is linked to their irrational ratios—one more proof of the solidity of his tuning system. However, Zarlino wishes to avoid rigidity in matters pertaining to fine points of style, and he therefore notes that the diminished fifth and the tritone may appear occasionally to good effect.[7]

The basic thrust of Zarlino's theory is now clear. He has found a respectable mathematical, ergo scientific, justification for just intonation with his *senario*. At long last, all intervals come to rest securely in an integrated system that fuses *musica theorica* and *musica practica*. In this way, Zarlino can present convincing evidence for the notion of music as sounding number, *numero sonoro*. The ancient Greek ideal is no longer a speculative fabrication; it has attained physical embodiment in the style of Adrian Willaert and his contemporaries, whose music represents a new perfection in the history of this art. The weight of Zarlino's system is felt by all conservative theorists who come after him. His treatise, reprinted a number of times, also reappears in adapted form in simpler handbooks by other writers.[8] By the end of the century, zarlinian precepts become the symbol of traditional theory, and for this very reason, his ideas are subjected to often unreasonable attacks by the younger upstarts of modern practice.

Seventy-six years before Zarlino's treatise appeared, Bartoloméo Ramos de Pareja startled his contemporaries by advocating a tuning much like just intonation. His system has repercussions on his definition of intervals. Ramos adheres to a backward viewpoint by classifying the fourth as a dissonance, but he shocks everyone by suggesting that the unison, third, fifth, sixth, and octave are pure and simple consonances without any further qualification.[9] Needless to say, this arrogant deviation from accepted theory earns him the reputation of a radical thinker. From his views there arises the Burtius-Gafurius-Spataro controversy. When we realize that it takes 100 years of musical practice to inspire someone to formulate a scientific rationale for modern style, the tenacity of traditional pythagorean theory comes sharply into focus. Only after Zarlino's treatise does just intonation become an acceptable system. The odd aspect of this development is that Ramos's notions represent an explanation of a new style, the *ars nova*, as Johannes Tinctoris calls it.[10] By the middle of the six-teenth century, this style is already the repository of conservative practice, at least in the estimation of avant-garde musicians. Thus, Zarlino's system justifies traditional counterpoint at a time when secular music is moving toward an even more daring and icono-clastic language. The diatonic boundaries of just intonation are simply incapable of accommodating this newer style, Mannerism, in the Italian madrigal.

The only theorist to work out a system codifying some ele-ments of late sixteenth-century practice is Vincenzo Galilei.[11] His conception of intervals parallels the final phase of Mannerism, a phase that in some respects carries over into the Baroque. Galilei begins by contradicting Zarlino. He believes that intervals outside the *senario* must be judged to be as natural and as viable as those within it. Galilei's justification for this viewpoint is the judgment of the ear. For Galilei, only the semitone, tone, and seventh are dissonant. The fourth and tritone form a special category of inter-mediate dissonances; they are less harsh than real dissonances and therefore may be used with fewer restrictions. He further intimates that dissonances have an autonomous existence and integral value. In effect, Galilei's novel concept liberates this intervallic category, and it therefore mirrors the free use of dissonance by composers of modern counterpoint. And this modern method is called *seconda prattica* by Monteverdi in contradistinction to the old manner, the *prima prattica* prized by Zarlino and Artusi.

Vicentino writes in the mainstream of mannerist style. His division between consonances and dissonances, as part of the ex-position of musical rudiments, presents nothing extraordinary.[12] He does, however, advocate the tritone, the most denigrated of intervals, for marvelous effect.[13] The radical side of Vicentino's intervallic theory emerges from the hyperrefined characteristics that he ascribes to individual interval sizes. His prime objective is affective and rhetorical painting of the text through musical means, and his musical vocabulary includes extravagant chromatic and enharmonic inflections. Vicentino's description of intervallic qualities reads like a precursor of baroque *Affektenlehre*.[14] Al-though his construct exhibits self-evident limitations as a manual for composition, it nevertheless represents a preoccupation with the expressive function of vocal music. Like all detailed theories of musical affections, Vicentino's system appears somewhat childish and simplistic in its attempt to categorize every conceivable interval. And yet it corresponds in a striking way to the instinctive use of intervals by mannerist composers. Madrigalian style has also been accused of infantilism by antimannerists, both of the past and of the present.

In contrast to intervallic theory, the subject of the modes exposes the conservative side of contrapuntal theory. Any ideal of modal purity militates against chromaticism and the indiscriminate mixture of modes or their wide-ranging transposition. Traditionalist attitudes, therefore, are alien to mannerist style. Even within the confines of the sixteenth-century *ars perfecta*, theorists encounter difficulties in relating linear modes to polyphony that is vertically conceived. These problems are aggravated by the fact that systematic exegesis of the modes tends to be more analytical and speculative than practical.

In the *Dodecachordon*, Glareanus explicates his new system for the modes. As a preamble, he presents the customary analysis of the accepted eight modes during which he notes that the combination of authentic and plagal varieties is called *permixtio*.[15] In laying the foundation for his own system, Glareanus criticizes the received approaches as confusing and dull. For one thing, he rejects the traditional focus on finals and constitutive species in favor of the arrangement of semitones, which, in his view, gives each mode its particular structure and character.[16] Glareanus's method of partitioning the gamut into arithmetic and harmonic divisions yields a total of sixteen modes, four of which are rejected. The remainder constitute the twelve modes pertinent to modern music, the *ars perfecta*: Dorian, Phrygian, Lydian, Mixolydian, Aeolian, and Iastian or Ionian, and of course, their plagals.[17] Glareanus has extended the modes in order to explain more fully the diatonic basis of perfect style, and because he includes four more modes, he feels that his system is more than adequate for this purpose. Hence Glareanus roundly condemns composers who venture outside the confines of this scheme. His modal theory thus contains both revolutionary and conservative elements. An interesting feature of his transposition system is that the mode on F with a B♭ is now the

Ionian once transposed. For the first time, the problem of this mode is settled in an orderly fashion.

Glareanus next presents a detailed description of the ethos of each mode with numerous examples from plainchant. He is here concerned with the art of the *phonascus*. Although he does not outline an analysis of melodic *phrasis*, the reader can arrive at his own conclusions from an examination of the illustrations. Glareanus combines the older view of modal character with a progressive approach stressing affective qualities and also gives some pertinent comments on old versus new melodies. For example, he composes chants on the rejected "tritone" modes for the sake of exegesis, but at the same time cautions that composers who use these modes are those who thirst after fame.[18] The old form of the Lydian (with B♮) is today completely altered by the use of B♭; it becomes the transposed Ionian. The alluring sweetness of the Ionian gives it an air of frivolity, and it is therefore a good mode for dances. Old church music did not use it and its present popularity dates back 400 years.[19] The Hypoaeolian occurs only in a few Graduals, while the Aeolian, with its pleasant seriousness, is primarily suitable for lyrical songs.[20] The Hypomixolydian, much used in old church music, is today changed into the Ionian by means of *connexio*; the charm of the Hypoionian, little used in old church music, enhances love songs and is particularly good for brass instruments.[21]

When Glareanus gives examples of the modes in polyphonic works, he selects them according to the ages of music. The reader can thus find illustrations of both the old and new Lydian.[22] To show the use of the Ionian, he provides excerpts from Josquin's *Ave verum*, as well as other works. Glareanus makes an important observation when he notes that the Ionian is frequently transposed to F in order to make room for the lowest voice in counterpoint, as for example, in Josquin's *Stabat mater*.[23] It is thus very important to realize that the F mode with a B♭ is not the Lydian but the Ionian mode. Glareanus closes his discussion with the Hypoionian, a mode extremely popular in his day, and prints Josquin's *Ave Maria*, a work that in his opinion embodies an especially beautiful treatment of the mode.[24] Included among the examples of the Ionian mode are several secular compositions. To sum up, Glareanus makes a clear distinction between old and new forms of certain modes, and more important, furnishes convincing evidence for his new modes.

Having established his modal system, Glareanus can embark on an analysis of the subtle combinations possible among individual modes. He describes two different techniques. The first is *permixtio*, the combination of authentic and plagal versions of the same mode. In addition to examples of *permixtio* in chant, a detailed investigation is devoted to Josquin's works because they demonstrate superior technique.[25] Glareanus's comments on the second kind of combination, *commixtio*, are scattered throughout his treatise. This kind of combination involves unrelated modes, and Glareanus takes pains to note that all kinds of *commixtio* are possible and indeed frequently seen in practice. However, not every *commixtio* is equally felicitous. Bad *commixtio* results from putting together modes whose *phrases* are very different.[26] Good *commixtio*, marking the natural genius of the *symphoneta*, arises from the smooth mixture of divergent *phrases*. The latter can be effected between Lydian and Ionian, Dorian and Aeolian, and Mixolydian and Ionian. At this point, it should be clear that *permixtio* is a necessary outcome of counterpoint with voices in different ranges. *Commixtio*, by way of contrast, is an optional procedure involving aesthetic judgment.

Glareanus spends considerable time on the subject of bad *commixtio*. He states that the combination of the Phrygian and Hypomixolydian modes is not permitted but that some composers do use this combination for the sake of *voluptas* (e.g., Josquin's *Factum est autem*).[27] In the second Agnus Dei of the *Missa Mater patris*, Josquin uses both the Aeolian and Ionian modes. This bad *commixtio* prompts Glareanus to comment that Josquin often favored the unusual rather than the customary ordering of the modes.[28] The most execrated example of bad *commixtio* is the combination of Dorian and Phrygian. It offends very strongly because it introduces frequent tritones. Glareanus describes two cases where this fault appears in Josquin's works—*Memor esto verbi tui* and *De profundis*. He is forced to admit, however, that in the *De profundis* Josquin effected the mixture with novel skill. Furthermore, the roughness seems suited to the text. Glareanus therefore concludes that the reproach "from Dorian to Phrygian" does

not apply in this instance.[29] These remarks help to clarify Glareanus's criticism of his otherwise perfect paragon. Josquin seems too
radical and liberal in his *commixtio modorum*. This is the reason
why Glareanus states that Josquin lacked full knowledge of the
modal system. And his uneasiness about the fate of the perfect art
arises from his dislike of the distorted music of the moderns.

Glareanus's twelve-mode system is by no means accepted by
all other theorists. In fact, many of them, even radicals, continue
to analyze modes in the old way. The only major theorist to take
up his system is Zarlino.[30] In the 1558 edition of the *Istitutioni*,
he keeps the order given by Glareanus; but in view of the growing
popularity of the Ionian mode, Zarlino changes the order in the
1573 edition, placing it at the head of the list.[31] From Zarlino's
work, the twelve-mode system reappears in theorists who emulate
him. Galilei takes issue with this system in the *Dialogo* because
Mei has taught him that Glareanus and Zarlino misunderstand the
basis of the Greek *tonoi*. Galilei concurs with Ptolemy in insisting
that only seven modes are possible because a mode or *tonos* is an
arrangement of the intervals within the octave. For Galilei, theoretical ignorance of the Greek system amounts to further proof of
the limitations of traditional polyphony.[32]

Glareanus's conception of modal character is fairly sophisticated insofar as it presupposes that melodic *phrasis* contributes to
the affective quality of each mode. Zarlino also stresses the importance of *phrasis*, a feature that he calls *forma*—a more humanistic
term with artistic overtones. Zarlino observes that major imperfect
consonances occur at strategic points in the cheerful modes (F, G,
and C), whereas minor imperfect consonances do the same in the
sad modes (D, E, and A).[33] Although this observation hardly
constitutes an admission of major-minor modality in the modern
sense, it does indicate that the older notion of individual ethos
is dissolving under the impact of new procedures based on vertical sonorities. The growing emphasis on rhetorical eloquence, so
obvious in the madrigal, also influences this conception.

Of course, ethos has been a commonplace topic since its ap-
pearance in medieval theory. As the authority on this subject,
Boethius's views were accepted as true to ancient Greek doctrine.
In spite of his many radical ideas, Ramos gives us a version of

boethian ethos. He describes the four modal pairs in terms of galenic psychology and astrology.[34] The triumvirate of *musica mundana, humana,* and *instrumentalis* properly belongs to *musica speculativa.* Thus, scientific treatises repeat this august doctrine. Practical works usually omit it or else pay cursory obeisance to it in short definitions of music.[35] Of course, musical cosmology survives in other scientific fields such as astrology, medicine, and astronomy. Even though the philosophical validity of modal ethos disappears, the concept of individual modal qualities hangs on with remarkable tenacity. The problem with such exegeses is that they bear little relationship to musical practice, even though we may accept them as instances of the influence of renaissance and mannerist humanism.

Conceptions of ethos in the sixteenth century move in two different directions. The first reflects humanist scholarship; ethos is approached from an antiquarian viewpoint in which writers describe specific classical or hellenistic concepts. At the same time, these interpretations foster the notion that ancient music possessed great affective power. Zarlino believes that this power lives on to some extent in modern polyphony, whereas Galilei does not. The latter argues that ethos is a linear concept related to solo singing where the ranges of the human voice influence the character of each mode. The second trend arises from a refined notion of melodic *phrasis* or *forma* based on practical considerations. Because they predicate modal structure and character on this notion, both Glareanus and Zarlino present convincing arguments supported by music of their day. Vicentino also lists affective traits for the eight modes. By themselves, these traits seem rather general and unremarkable. But when they are combined with his list created from the three genera, giving a total of twenty-four modes, there surfaces a complex and detailed system of musical expressivity.

Because modal characteristics, both technical and aesthetic, are defined from a linear point of view, theorists encounter special problems when analyzing modes in polyphony. When they begin to understand counterpoint as the simultaneous aggregation of intervals, one notices an increasing divergence between contrapuntal and modal theory. For example, Pietro Aaron, the first writer to insist on the simultaneous approach to polyphony, still maintains that the tenor governs the mode of a composition.[36] Vicentino modernizes the old eight modes by advocating cadential formulas on the fourth or fifth degree.[37] And Zarlino ignores the problem of *commixtio* because he considers it outside the pale of acceptable methods. Here is not the place to discuss in detail all theoretical attempts to systematize precepts for handling the modes in sixteenth-century polyphony.[38] However, we should note that no writer of this period confronts the realities of avant-garde audacities, even though some are aware of novelties in other technical areas. Thus, modal theory does not change apace with musical practice between the Renaissance and Mannerism, and between Mannerism and the Baroque.

CHAPTER XI

᠄᠄᠄

Counterpoint and Composition

The two words in the title of this chapter are used in apposition, for I believe that during the sixteenth century, the theoretical approach to polyphony changes from an abstraction of linear counterpoint to a concrete notion of compositional style. Within the latter idea we find concepts of vertical sonorities, expressivity, and genre. Such concepts are possible only after the development of Mannerism, a movement that informs the intense controversy between old and new, or conservative and progressive, musical practices. From a didactic point of view, earlier theorists can explain contrapuntal precepts on the assumption that basic procedures for all polyphony are the same. They have only to choose the historical generation that best exemplifies perfection. But when markedly different styles become symptomatic of their chosen group or even of their individual model, theorists must make an aesthetic as well as a historical choice. Such choices entail value judgments of a subtly different kind, for ideas of old and new music now imply something more than mere historical sequence. Conservatives support tradition as the proven principle of timeless perfection, whereas radicals militate for new music as proof of progress toward superiority. And radicals point to various aspects of mannerist style. Thus the mannerist approach to composition represents the bridge between renaissance and baroque theory.

The overall concept of style that can be gleaned from fifteenth-century treatises is a curiously inadequate one. This situation results partly from methodology—disjunct rules appear in an unconnected series. Structural elements are not discussed in any detail, and whenever present, any such concepts must be extrapolated from an unsystematic exposition. For example, Bartoloméo Ramos de Pareja makes a tantalizingly incomplete reference to styles. He distinguishes between two kinds of *tropus*—a tranquil quality achieved by stepwise motion and a babbling quality produced by disjunct and winding motion. The first elevates the listener by its serious gravity while the second amuses him with its gentle humor. Ramos also hints at future expressive techniques when he states that a change of *tropus* produces a corresponding change of affection.[1] We can surmise that such treatises are professional works written for serious students of counterpoint who would presumably augment their readings with concrete studies under a master. Because such students are already adept at singing, they have acquired practical experience as performers. With the advent of humanist education and the technology of printing, a fundamental alteration in musical treatises becomes apparent. The new type of treatise is not only a self-sufficient instruction book, but also of interest to both professionals and amateurs.

A passing reference to integrated counterpoint made by Franchinus Gafurius[2] emerges as a conscious precept in Aaron's works. As early as 1516, this progressive writer distinguishes two methods of writing polyphony: the successive and the simultaneous.[3] This notion appears even more prominently in the *Thoscanello*. Here Aaron attributes the layered approach to older composers and credits the moderns with the development of an integrated conception.[4] The implication of superiority and stylistic progress between the old and the new needs no further comment. But because Aaron believes that the older method is good for beginners, his ten rules of counterpoint espouse this viewpoint.[5] And yet, his exegesis is novel in that his rules demonstrate various four-voiced progressions, including unusual spacings and alternative intervallic arrangements. More old-fashioned are the customary rules on dissonance treatment. But on a more general level, Aaron stresses the aesthetic function of dissonances, and the fact that beautiful counterpoint embodies an artful variety of intervals.

In spite of the conservative attitudes that Aaron has in common with earlier writers, his treatise is a surprisingly progressive document. Its modernity can be attributed not so much to its espousal of a few novel theories, such as integrated counterpoint and meantone temperament, as to its approach to the science of counterpoint. Although Aaron's examples are purely didactic material, they include all voices of the contrapuntal texture in question and demonstrate progressions extending beyond two steps. In other words, Aaron's concept moves away from ideal, abstract science toward concrete, practical art. His examples are detailed enough to exemplify not only rules of correct procedure but also guidelines for artistic value. Thus, even the teaching of rudiments becomes infused with stylistic criteria. Aaron's sensitivity to musical practice of his time can be adduced from his consistent use of four voices as the norm for composition. When Glareanus next extols this style in 1547, it is already one generation old and in the process of being eclipsed by counterpoint for five or more voices, the *ingenii ostentatio* of rebellious youngsters, to use Glareanus's own words.[6]

The ostensible aim of the *Dodecachordon* is the defense of a new modal system presented by Glareanus as pertinent to music of his day. However, the full impact of this remarkable work extends far beyond a mere exposition of the twelve modes. It represents the first critical essay on music, an attempt to subject this art to historical and stylistic analysis along the same lines as writings on literature and the visual arts. The *Dodecachordon* can hardly be considered a handbook on the art of writing counterpoint. Its approach appeals to all persons interested in music, and different readers gain different insights from the many penetrating comments found in it. As far as the composer is concerned, Glareanus assumes that he has learned the rules of his craft elsewhere. From his treatise, the composer gleans delicate points about good and bad, mediocre and inspired styles. As far as the layman is concerned, he may absorb stylistic values solely from the point of view of the listener, or he may avail himself of the preliminary exposition of musical rudiments in order to better understand the subsequent discussion of aesthetic matters.

In view of the critical emphasis in this treatise, Glareanus naturally takes most of his examples from real compositions; the exceptions are notational illustrations culled from other books. In addition to eighty monophonic pieces (mostly chant), he prints ninety-five polyphonic compositions, twenty-nine of which are by

Josquin des Prez. Glareanus's historical spectrum covers the three ages of music (omitting old age). His closely interrelated ideas about the structure of the modes, their ethos, and their judicious combination in counterpoint combine to form a subtle but imposing system for evaluating musical procedure and expressivity —in short, style. At the end of his work, Glareanus adds to his analysis of Josquin's music some capsule comments on the styles of five other prominent composers.[7] His remarks can be quoted today without losing any of their authority. Above all, they demonstrate a lively awareness of individual *maniere*, an awareness that we take for granted but was quite new in the sixteenth century.

Adrianus Petit Coclico also proclaims a novel approach. Despite his bizarre personality, unverifiable statements, and mediocre talent as a composer, this theorist presents many interesting ideas that warrant serious attention. He chastises previous theorists for their frigid and obscure treatment of useless subjects, such as mathematics, cosmology, tuning, and proportional notation.[8] Coclico's disdain stems from a humanist conviction about music. In his view, music belongs to the trivium rather than to the quadrivium because it is a liberal art like rhetoric. He therefore proposes to expound on the rules governing music as an expressive discipline: the science of correct and graceful singing and composing. The art of song and composition are more than just two facets of practice; they are related to Josquin's teaching method, for he accepted as pupils of composition only those who had mastered extemporary singing of counterpoint.[9]

Coclico submits that his treatise presents three important subjects that have always been ignored by other theorists: first, elegant and graceful delivery in singing; second, the rules of counterpoint; third, a method for composing. Coclico is partially justified in making such a sweeping statement. Treatises on singing are rare but not altogether unknown during the first half of the century; Coclico evidently feels that this art needs reviving in Germany. But it is difficult to understand why he touts the originality of the other two subjects. In themselves they are not new; however, Coclico's conception of them is somewhat novel. In his scheme, "counterpoint" refers to the art of spontaneous counterpointing, whereas "composition" designates written counterpoint—the science of composed polyphony (*res facta* or *opus absolutum*).[10] Although earlier theorists mention improvised counterpoint, they treat it as an inferior branch of polyphonic science. Its importance in Coclico's treatise therefore forms part of an original system as far as theoretical works are concerned.[11]

In Coclico's case, systematic inspiration unfortunately is not matched by detailed expertise. His section on improvised counterpoint presents the customary rules supported by some dubious examples of acceptable procedures as well as some instructive examples of erroneous ones. In the section on composition, Coclico lists seven requirements. The first two are the prerequisites for the student composer: knowledge of improvised counterpoint and a natural impulse for composition. The third requirement concerns the deployment of intervals. Here the rules are essentially the same as those for improvised counterpoint, except for certain liberties allowed in written polyphony that are forbidden in the extemporary variety. Coclico provides one example of permissible licenses and numerous charts of interval combinations showing good, harsh, and absurd arrangements. He is quite adamant on the subject of the modes, the fourth requirement, and echoes Glareanus's dislike of modern novelties. In this context, he warns the student to seek sweet harmony rather than lavish, strange, and outlandish music. Careful observance of the tactus and mensuration signs constitutes the fifth requirement. The sixth concerns the text. Modes and harmonies must be appropriate to the text (no details given), and ornaments must not obscure the words. Above all, the student must take care that syllables and note lengths correspond, for music is very much like poetry. The last requirement suggests that a composition should begin with imitative voice entries *per fugam*. Coclico's concept of *fuga* is rather confused, as his closing examples demonstrate; they include canon, imitative points, and homophony. This situation seems a little surprising inasmuch as Coclico claims to be using Josquin as a model.

Zarlino's exegesis, of course, is an admirable combination of three interrelated elements: explanation of the rudiments of counterpoint, how these rudiments produce different procedures, and finally, the link between technical procedures and refined style.[12] Clearly, Zarlino views abstract science and concrete style as inseparable phenomena. Although his organization is lax at times, his writing nevertheless reveals the keen mind of a fine practitioner and teacher. Of Zarlino's six general rules for composition, only the first four concern our present inquiry: first, one must have a subject (*soggetto*) on which to base movements and harmonies; second, good composition consists mainly of consonances with some carefully deployed dissonances; third, proper voice leading, which obeys sonorous number, helps to ensure good harmony; fourth, one must strive for variety and diversity in motion and harmony.[13]

Beginning with the first general rule, it must be understood that we are dealing with a very sophisticated topic, the *soggetto* in music—a topic related to the then current notion that all the arts imitate nature. Zarlino's *soggetto* embraces a number of ideas, but only the musical one concerns us at the moment. He defines the subject as the initial voice that serves as the basis for the invention of other parts in a polyphonic composition. This subject, or theme, can be a cantus firmus invented by the composer or one borrowed from another work. If a composition has no subject in this sense, then the first voice to be composed becomes the subject. One can also devise a series of subjects as one goes along; composing in this way is known as *comporre di fantasia*. Here Zarlino refers to freely composed counterpoint utilizing canon or imitative points, a style of composition to which he will devote considerable attention. The clarity of his initial exposition is refreshing, and it also entails a very progressive attitude. From an aesthetic viewpoint, Zarlino intimates that a musical composition grows out of and extends a musical subject whose elements determine the character of the complete product.

In relation to the second rule, Zarlino offers many helpful suggestions for the deployment of intervals. For example, he points out that in a homophonic opening, perfect consonances are mandatory; however, if one opts instead for a canonic or imitative opening, then both perfect and imperfect consonances are permitted. At this point, Zarlino injects a value judgment by saying that the latter type of counterpoint possesses greater beauty and artifice than the former. But the composer must not interpret such freedom as an excuse to leave the confines of the given mode.[14]

Clear musical examples illustrate the verbal exegesis of this point as well as all subsequent comments on refined procedures. Dissonances fulfill two functions, according to Zarlino: they facilitate motion between consonances, and they cause the second consonance to sound even more pleasant. On an aesthetic level, Zarlino notes that a composition made up solely of consonances may be agreeable enough, but somehow it sounds incomplete.[15] In short, the proper use of dissonances adds grace to contrapuntal movement. Zarlino's extensive comments on the false relations created by the tritone indicate the growing popularity of this interval in practice. He does, however, recognize that this progression can enhance cadential formulas under certain circumstances.[16]

Zarlino's precepts for intervallic deployment grow out of his theory of harmonic relations, the latter here understood as sounding number in music (the third rule). He has made it quite clear that in simple counterpoint for two voices, progressions are restricted to mathematical relations between consonances.[17] Multivoiced polyphony affords greater variety. Thus, intervals forbidden in simple counterpoint may be very pleasing in the florid kind. Zarlino's specific illustrations concern triadic sonorities. Inasmuch as perfect counterpoint contains simultaneous thirds and fifths, proportional relationships provide the basis for the diversity and perfection of harmonies. The fifth contains two thirds, major and minor. When the lower third is major, the harmony sounds gay; and when it is minor, the harmony sounds sad. From these two qualities harmonic variety arises. Zarlino cautions the student against using too many minor sonorities in succession because they produce a distinctly melancholy effect that could be at variance with the text. Successive major sonorities are more pleasing because they adhere more closely to the rules of *numero sonoro*. However, Zarlino concludes that the best procedure is to vary major and minor sonorities consistently.[18] The fusion here of mathematics, abstract musical technique, and an aesthetic notion of expressive effects should be noted. It represents one aspect of Zarlino's philosophy of music and it vindicates, at least in his view, the absolute perfection of contemporaneous polyphonic practice. The import of this philosophy is well understood by the adherents of avant-garde practice who criticize it.

The concept of *numero sonoro* also relates directly to the topic of proper voice leading, a topic that encompasses rather strict and traditional rules of interval manipulation.[19] The fourth general rule is calculated to allow diversity within reasonable norms. Conjunct or moderately disjunct motion lends variety to the interrelationship of voices. Zarlino admires delayed entries, or imitative counterpoint, because this technique embodies an artful source of musical variety. He also notes that a reasonable variety of ranges is needed to avoid boredom; extreme ranges may be introduced very rarely and then only in connection with vivid expression of a text. According to *numero sonoro*, imperfect consonances sound harsh when placed in the lower voices, and such harsh harmonies may be used only if required by a specific text.[20] From the above exposition, we can see that Zarlino links the ideals of propriety and variety. The thrust of the fourth rule is to allow enough variety without disturbing fundamental precepts such as sounding number and the *senario*. Propriety and variety act as a system of mutual checks and balances; the former prevents variety from becoming excessively extravagant whereas the latter prevents propriety from becoming academically pedantic. These two ideals also surface in a number of other observations made by Zarlino. Although he begins with a blanket statement about the desirability of contrary motion, he later qualifies this rule. Parallel motion does produce variety. Indeed, the skillful composer uses parallel motion for grace, elegance, and full harmony; it is absolutely essential in canonic and imitative counterpoint.[21] In effect, Zarlino's passion for progressive styles has prompted him to revise one of the traditional rules of counterpoint. He also makes a special point of stating that the location of cadences must vary.[22] The only negative comment concerns literal repetition of a passage in one voice; this monotonous device, which shows a lack of imagination, must be avoided at all times.[23]

At this point, Zarlino makes a very interesting observation. All the rules he has elucidated thus far enable the student to write correct counterpoint. But gifted professionals also display *un non so che di bella, di leggiadro & di elegante*, "a certain undefinable quality of beauty, spiritedness, and elegance."[24] These aesthetic criteria, although based on scientific rules, somehow go beyond them into that realm where compositional technique and style are one. They arise from a particular technique in which one voice duplicates all or part of another voice after a time lag. This procedure, practiced by all talented composers, is called *fuga*, *consequenza*, or *reditta*. Zarlino has now come to the core of his doctrine—the explanation of modern forms of counterpoint.

Both the meaning and implications of Zarlino's distinction between *fuga* and *imitatione* have been misunderstood until more recent research has shown both the subtlety and clarity of his methodology.[25] In *fuga*, which can be *legata* (strict canon) or *sciolta* (free imitative points), the consequent voice must follow the guiding voice at the unison, fourth, fifth, or octave. It is restricted to these intervals for the simple reason that by definition it must duplicate exactly the interval species of the first voice. *Fuga* is most comprehensible when a short time lapse separates the different voices. However, Zarlino notes that this device is rather common and thus implies that a longer time lapse would create a more unusual composition.[26] As far as *imitatione* is concerned, Zarlino's statements clearly indicate that he considers it to be a particularly ingenious and praiseworthy ornament. Like *fuga*, it can be strict or free. But the divergent premise behind its construction is very important. The consequent voice of an *imitatione*, whether strict or free, need only imitate the steps and movement of the guide without duplicating the interval species. For this reason, *imitatione* may be written at any interval the composer chooses.[27] Zarlino's distinction between *fuga* and *imitatione* cannot be dismissed as trivial, for it impinges on the matter of *musica ficta*. The crucial flexibility characteristic of *imitatione* concerns semitone inflections, and it indicates that accidentals are not always necessary to make canon or imitation literal and exact.[28] We must add that Zarlino's *imitatione* gives us the first detailed and systematic explanation of canon and points of imitation at intervals other than the perfect consonances. Moreover, its subtle freedom makes it more elegant and ingenious than *fuga*.

Zarlino's preoccupation with elegant composition also emerges in his praise of various contrapuntal procedures, such as canon in contrary motion, double fugue, and the combination of *fuga* and *imitatione*.[29] He provides, in addition, many remarks on more minute points of good style. In this respect, I cite his discussion of the structural function of cadences as well as the technique of avoiding the cadence at intermediate points within a composition.[30] Zarlino also qualifies his earlier ban on figurative repetition by suggesting that it can be effective if the accompanying counterpoint is varied in intervals and rhythm. This kind of repetitive counterpoint tests one's skill, but if successfully managed, it shows a lively spirit and an abundance of invention. In short, *contrapunto con obligo* marks the superior composer.[31] Again in relation to grace and elegance, Zarlino admits certain licenses, provided that excessive nonharmonic intervals and chromaticism are avoided.[32] And finally, after describing counterpoint for four or more voices,[33] Zarlino closes his compendious exposition of contrapuntal composition with an exegesis of the ancient genera. His scathing critique of those moderns who believe that they can revive ancient practice in contemporary music is leveled undoubtedly against mannerist composers, composers who favor chromatic and enharmonic styles—in particular, that controversial figure, Vicentino.[34]

Taken in its entirety, Zarlino's exposition presents an astute guide on matters of science and art. He not only provides concrete and detailed rules for correct counterpoint, but also gives helpful hints on elegant style. His work represents an outstanding example of the humanistic treatise on music, a self-sufficient book covering basic rudiments as well as fine points of aesthetic value. Zarlino's refined concepts exemplify a perceptive theory aimed at preserving scientific truths as well as progressive ideals of moderately expressive, artful polyphony. The impact of his theory of counterpoint and composition can be gauged by the numerous adaptations of Book III made by other theorists. In this vein, we can count Giovanni Maria Artusi's and Orazio Tigrini's works as symptomatic of late sixteenth-century popularization of learned treatises.[35] The same holds true of Pietro Ponzio's first treatise.[36] In a later tract, Ponzio adds two more modern ideas: *imitatione* designating imitative counterpoint in contradistinction to canon, and a more systematic treatment of parody technique in the Mass.[37] Domenico Pietro Cerone also presents a *summa* of traditional polyphony that is influenced by Zarlino. But Cerone's interest in complex contra-

puntal devices such as puzzles and enigmatic canons indicates a
new antiquarian bias characteristic of early seventeenth-century
theory.[38] A similar approach can be seen in Lodovico Zacconi's
study of canons.[39] Rarely practiced in sixteenth-century polyphony, these devices have now become part and parcel of academic
expertise, a kind of schoolbook counterpoint associated with the
prima prattica. This atmosphere is also responsible for the trend
toward explaining the craft of counterpoint by means of "species"
exercises.[40]

Although Morley's treatise is not a continental source, the
composers and theorists studied by this English composer indicate
an impressive knowledge of both traditional and modern styles
prevalent in sixteenth-century Italy. Morley's work presents a
summation of the art of composition graced by readable prose and
many instructive examples. After a succinct survey of the art of
descant—that is, improvised counterpoint on a given melody—the
student proceeds to written composition wherein rudiments and
advanced techniques are carefully described. The most interesting
and relevant portions of the latter are those that elucidate Morley's
concepts of style. Again, the significance of this theorist's fusion
of composition and stylistic considerations must be stressed. For
example, after explaining interval combinations in four-voice sonorities, Morley observes that sudden changes of harmony occur
in madrigals, canzonets, pavanes, and galliards. Slower harmonic
rhythm, long notes, and bindings or suspensions characterize
church music.[41] The last portion of the treatise contains a concise
outline of different genres, according to stylistic traits. In the ditty
(secular vocal music), people admire variety. In this case, rhythm,
harmony, melody, and texture should change in reflection of the
mood of the words. In particular, poetic details often call forth
fine bindings and strange cadences. Morley concludes that this
light music evinces too much vanity. The motet, in contrast, must
always be grave, majestic, and slow.[42] Morley then lists secular
genres in the order of their lightness, starting with the madrigal
and ending with the passamezzo with text.[43] The novice composer
could not ask for a more helpful list. Nor could we ask for a more
precise expression of the sixteenth-century composer's understanding of genre and style.

It would appear that foreigners seeking to adapt Italian practice to their own needs often approach matters of style and genre
with a more analytical frame of mind than do musicians within a
tradition. Such an approach appears in Michael Praetorius's treatise, a work written for the education of German choirmasters.
Under serious composition, he classifies sacred concertos, motets,
and falsobordone. Gay style is subdivided into two categories:
first, genres that observe the text, such as the madrigal and sestina;
second, genres that treat the text freely, such as the dialogue, canzonetta, aria, and quodlibet.[44] Praetorius's rules of counterpoint
present a fascinating blend of traditional and modern principles.
The former stem from the zarlinian school; however, Praetorius
adapts them to local use by substituting the German chorale as a
source for cantus firmi. The latter appear in his explanation of
contrasting choruses supported by string and wind instruments,
concerted style with figured bass and solo ornamentation, and
most important of all, the cardinal rule of vivid representation of
the text.

Praetorius's distinction corresponds to Adriano Banchieri's
division of late sixteenth- and early seventeenth-century practice
into *contrapunto osservato* (old, traditional polyphony) and *contrapunto commune* (new, concerted counterpoint).[45] The problems faced by theorists in coming to terms with old and new styles
have already been discussed. In general, growing historical awareness on the one hand, and continued interest in progress on the
other, constitute problems aggravated by the radical techniques of
mannerist composers. Few theorists can make their peace with the
innovations of modern practice at the turn of the century. The
most famous case in point is Artusi's celebrated critique of Claudio
Monteverdi. Artusi singles out nine excerpts, seven from *Cruda
Amarilli* and two from *Anima mia perdona*.[46] The objections
raised by him amply demonstrate the fundamental divergence between the first and second practices. All of Artusi's points revolve
around the improper use of dissonance, and they can be reduced
to four basic principles. The first condemns the introduction of dissonant notes by leap or after rests. The second isolates dissonances
caused by careless voice leading. The third focuses on the diminished triad, a sonority outlawed by the rules of *numero sonoro*.

And the fourth criticizes a vertical sonority that we today call the dominant seventh.[47] In view of these aberrations, so closely compacted in short passages, it is not surprising that Artusi should be aghast at the radical style they exemplify. Such progressions make no sense whatsoever in terms of traditional counterpoint; they cannot even be excused as occasional licenses. Monteverdi's equally famous rebuttal relies on aesthetic rather than practical or scientific reasoning. It is indeed unfortunate that Monteverdi never wrote his treatise on the *seconda prattica* that he practiced so well.

However, some insight into the rationale behind the second practice can be found in Vincenzo Galilei's tract on modern counterpoint, inasmuch as his most innovative ideas relate to the treatment of dissonances.[48] Galilei states that syncopation is not mandatory for introducing dissonances on the strong beat. Furthermore, dissonant intervals may be resolved by leap as well as by step, and they do not have to move to a consonance. He divides dissonance treatment in two types—primary and secondary. In the latter, loose dissonances are permitted, and these include passing notes (*cattive*) and auxiliary notes (*note di moto locale*). Galilei's belief in great freedom for this category is evident in his comment that any two of four successive notes can be dissonant; and in addition, three *cattive* in a row are allowed. Galilei's rules for primary dissonances are liberal in the extreme. Such notes may be resolved by ascending motion, by leap, by parallel motion, by ornamented figuration, and they may ultimately "resolve" to another dissonance.[49] Among the primary dissonances, the fourth, diminished fifth, and the tritone enjoy the greatest flexibility; even chromatic resolutions now enter the canon of acceptable possibilities. Galilei also notes that the seventh, in what we call a dominant seventh chord, is not a dissonance at all, but rather an integral interval of that sonority. Both the second and seventh may be approached by leap on a strong beat, and it is possible to combine the second, fourth, and seventh in one vertical massing.

We should make note of two interrelated aspects in Galilei's theory. First of all, his radical rules for dissonance treatment arise from a new consciousness of vertical sonorities dominated by a soprano-bass polarity.[50] Galilei's conception no longer has anything to do with the traditional idea of independent linear factors operating according to abstract musical laws. In fact, Galilei states that abstract rules of interval manipulation and voice leading are valid only for two-voice counterpoint, especially when played by instruments. Vocal music, by virtue of its expressive goal, needs more flexible rules. The second aspect constitutes a tacit, but still salient, idea. In my view, Galilei's exposition of modern counterpoint rests on the assumption that there now exist two musical practices, an old and a new one. And if we accept this interpretation, Galilei's exposition of dissonance treatment fills in the gaps for Monteverdi's distinction between the *prima* and *seconda prattica*. Palisca makes a convincing case for interpreting Galilei's treatise as a study of harmony. And yet Galilei himself says he is writing about the "art of modern counterpoint," and this statement is essentially a true one. Had Artusi seen this tract, he could not have faulted it as lacking rules; but he certainly would have condemned the rules as irreverent distortions of the fundamental nature of counterpoint.

The musician most self-conscious about the impact of the new style is Nicola Vicentino. He presents a detailed, if personal, account of scientific and aesthetic premises behind mid sixteenth-century progress. The basic level of contrapuntal science appears in his rules for interval progressions in two steps, the rudimentary stage of learning the craft.[51] But even here, he makes a few pertinent remarks on stylistic niceties. Intervals must be regulated according to the words of the text.[52] As a rule, instrumental music requires sweeter and cleaner dissonances than does vocal music. Some composers claim that their music is equally amenable to vocal and instrumental renditions. But the student must bear in mind that some vocal music is not appropriate for instruments because of the diversity of its sequences.[53] Here Vicentino intimates that vocal music, given its aim of expressing the text, lacks that element of abstract logic needed to make self-sufficient formal sense. Apart from this one observation, his discussion of basic interval progressions departs very little from the customary approach to this subject. By way of contrast, Vicentino's preoccupation with larger structural considerations represents a decidedly progressive outlook.

Vicentino's unique contribution to matters of structure and

style, one that is often reprinted and plagiarized, emerges in his advice about how to organize the beginning, middle, and ending of a composition.[54] At the outset, the composer must consider his subject. If he is writing a Mass, it may be based on a cantus firmus,[55] a motet, or a fantasy. The beginning of such a composition must be grave in character, as are all things Latin. If the composer is writing a madrigal, sonnet, or canzona, the beginning should be in moderate speed. The villanella opens with a sprightly tempo. Vicentino strongly recommends an opening point of imitation written in such a way that it helps the singers maintain good intonation. This requirement is very important for church music. As far as the middle section is concerned, Vicentino comments that the character of church music does not change—that is, all three sections are the same. The implication, of course, is that contrasting characters prevail in secular music. The same implication pertains to other remarks, such as the necessity for staying in the mode in church music. The closing section is naturally very important. In church music, the mode must be carefully accentuated in order to facilitate further musical responses. But in the madrigal, the final section may end off the mode entirely, *per imitatione delle parole.*

Once again, we see that matters of structure are closely connected to problems of style. Vicentino's awareness of style appears, for instance, in his chapter devoted to the elusive subject of good melody. To extricate himself from the task of verbalizing on creative invention, Vicentino provides examples of good and bad, as well as modern and old-fashioned melodic styles.[56] Having already outlined the affective qualities of modes, harmonies, and rhythms, he can now indicate their proper deployment in various genres. Thus he notes that stability works well in motets with devout subjects; however, if a motet sets a joyous text, more mobility is permitted. A great deal of variety and simultaneous syncopation (previously disallowed) is recommended for madrigals, villanellas, and *canzoni franzese*.[57] Vicentino goes on to say that in secular vocal music, a happy text requires fast tempo, excited intervals, high registers, and liberal dissonances; a sad text requires the exact opposite. Harshness can be achieved by using descending minor thirds, minor sixths, and major sixths.[58] Church music, on the other hand, must be serious and unhurried; secular tunes are not permitted.[59] A few general precepts on compositions in two, three, four, and five voices, as well as on psalms and dialogues for double chorus, round out Vicentino's remarks on structure and style.[60]

We must not forget that Vicentino wrote the treatise to vindicate his opinion of the genera and their relation to contemporary practice. This topic is bound to influence matters of structure and style as well. His main contention at the public debate was that polyphony combines the features of the three genera as defined by ancient theorists. Indeed, even the perfect harmony and restrained expressivity desired by reactionary musicians cannot be attained without this mixture. In his treatise, Vicentino gives a systematic definition of each genus with musical examples from his own compositions. Although the diatonic genus does not exist in reality, Vicentino writes a textless composition, but he admits that it sounds extremely harsh.[61] This fact, however, only serves to prove his point that intervals from the other two genera are needed for sweet harmony. An analysis of this dull piece reveals that all the voices use only the tone and natural semitone; thirds occur only when separated by rests and are excusable for this reason.[62]

Vicentino provides two examples of the pure chromatic genus.[63] Of the *Mottetino allegro tutto Cromatico, Alleluia haec dies a4*, Vicentino remarks that he composed it to show that such music can be sung in church with full choir as well as in the chamber with solo ensemble. The work contains one tone and five major thirds. Vicentino justifies their presence on the grounds that this excited species depicts the word, *letemur*. Even more remarkable is the chamber motet, *Hierusalem convertere a5*, whose text comes appropriately from the Lamentations of Jeremiah. Only one extraneous interval slips in—a minor sixth. At the beginning of the piece, a repeated motive outlines the chromatic tetrachord in both ascending and descending motion in all the voices. This opening presents a vivid musical emblem of humanist interest in ancient theory; any knowledgeable musician would recognize the symbolism. And this melodic formula crops up in disguised form in the chromatic music of other composers as well.[64]

The pure enharmonic genus is exemplified by a partial madrigal, *Soav'e dolc'ardore a4*.[65] An examination of each voice reveals the acoustical refinement and virtuoso technique involved in performing this kind of chamber music. All intervals except for the major third are larger or smaller than their diatonic counterparts by one diesis. Nonenharmonic steps include two natural tones, five minor thirds, and one major sixth. Of course, Vicentino insists that mixture of the genera produces a *buono concento d'armonia*.[66] There are two ways of achieving this effect. The first can be seen in two partial madrigals, *Dolce mio ben a4* and *Madonna il poco dolce a4*,[67] works composed in such a way that they may be performed in five different manners: diatonic, chromatic, enharmonic, diatonic and chromatic, or in all three genera together. The second method consists in writing successive portions of one piece in each of the three genera, taking as one's point of departure the *concetto* of the text.[68] A Latin occasional motet in honor of his patron, Cardinal Ippolito d'Este, forms a fitting conclusion to this subject—*Musica prisca caput a4*.[69]

The text can be divided into three sections, each composed in a different genus: "Ancient music has only held up her head through great darkness" (diatonic) "that she, by making sweet and old numbers, your famous deeds" (chromatic), "O Hippolitus, might send high above the heavens" (enharmonic). Symbolic correlations between the text and each genus chosen are obvious —darkness with the diatonic, sweet and old numbers with the chromatic, and supercelestial heights with the enharmonic. Parenthetically, we may note that this schema, however witty and learned, is by no means new. Rather than compose another dry exercise in the first section, Vicentino alleviates the crudity of the strict diatonic with a liberal sprinkling of chromatic semitones. The predominantly diatonic character of the first part, a kind of *musica participata & mista*, emerges in retrospect from the ensuing chromatic section. This part achieves a startling flavor through its prominent semitones and minor thirds. Enharmonic character in the last part arises not only from sinewy microtonal undulation but also from enharmonic leaps, including octaves. It must be heard to be believed. This work, as well as the other examples, presents an embodiment of the theoretical, philosophical, and practical sides of self-conscious *maniera*. Even though we may count enharmonic style as a personal eccentricity, the chromatic style is shared by many other musicians of the time. And Vicentino must be recognized as the first mannerist to stress chromatic practice and to try a systematic formulation of it.

The basic premise behind Vicentino's style and that of a host of other madrigalists comes under virulent attack in Galilei's manifesto championing monody. The third part of this rambling dialogue consists mainly of a diatribe against polyphony.[70] Galilei begins by citing Plutarch's comments on the expressive use of the modes.[71] This introductory statement at first appears to be but an echo of earlier mannerist notions—to wit, modes regulated judiciously according to the words can express the passions with marvelous art. But Galilei's malicious intent soon becomes apparent, for he announces that this important aesthetic precept is not embodied in music of his day. In his view, counterpoint involves abstract rules that operate independently of textual considerations; and more often than not, these rules go against the affections of the words.[72] As we have already mentioned, this devastating critique is aimed at the *ars perfecta*, the traditional style of counterpoint now called *contrapunto osservato*. The impact of Galilei's attack goes deep, for he destroys the very foundation of conservative philosophy—that suave and sweet harmonies in the perfect art can rejuvenate and surpass ancient ideals. According to Galilei, the prime goal of vocal music should be to express the text. But the abstract means of *contrapunto osservato*, refinements and licenses notwithstanding, are incapable of attaining this noble aim. Although self-sufficient counterpoint may be suitable for instrumental music, it is certainly a poor medium for vocal music.

Galilei's attitude sheds light on the one positive comment he makes about polyphony—the treatment of dissonances whose slightly harsh and bitter quality mixes with the continuous delicacy of diverse consonances.[73] The point is that this rare and ingenious method occurs in modern counterpoint—that is, in the style that he himself describes in his other treatise. And this style is none other than Banchieri's *contrapunto commune*. Modern counterpoint evolves directly from the audacities of earlier madrigalian style, an evolution recognized by Galilei when he cites Cipriano de Rore as the last master of polyphony.[74] Although he appreciates the radical aspect of this new *maniera* insofar as it encourages the liberation of dissonance, Galilei deplores the manner in which this freedom is put to use to express the text. He concentrates on minute word painting, a technique that has become the hallmark of the mannerist madrigal. His list of examples provides an excellent sampling of both visual and aural effects. Words such as *fuggire* and *volare* prompt fast tempo, whereas words such as *morire* are set slowly or lead to a sudden stop that makes everyone laugh. Numerical diction, like *solo* and *due*, is imitated by solo and duet texture. Words evocative of color, for example *brune* or *bianche*, have the inevitable black or white notes. Words suggesting motion inspire imitative devices, such as extended syncopation for *onde* or descending lines for *dolore*, and of course, every poetic sigh finds its musical counterpart. Crude and unusual harmonies depict the ubiquitous mannerist conceits: *piangere, ridere, gridare, stridere, duri lacci, cruda donna.*[75] These metaphorical extravagances parade under the banner of affective expression, but in Galilei's estimation, they miss the point entirely.

In short, practitioners of both traditional and modern counterpoint are completely ignorant of the true nature of ancient classical music. Effective expression of the *concetti dell'animo* can be achieved only by expressing the sense of the whole. Polyphony, no matter how vivid its word painting, cannot embody organic simplicity. Monody is the proper vehicle for vocal music, and this is the reason ancient authors continually praise the *effetti meravigliosi* of music. Solo song portrays the general character of the poem by means of mode, accents and gestures, rhythm and quantity. And, of course, the words are not obscured by complicated contrapuntal treatment. Harmony to the ancients did not mean the vertical arrangement of intervals; rather, it was defined as beautiful solo singing in a mode with the proper high and low tones.[76]

With Galilei's treatise we have run the full gamut of theoretical ideas related to counterpoint and composition. The abstract rules of contrapuntal science are sufficient guides for musicians familiar with one predominant style. But even the earliest renaissance treatises evince a historical awareness that grows from the influence of humanistic nostalgia for the golden age of antiquity. This consciousness raises the problem of radical progress versus

timeless perfection. As printing makes humanist ideas widely available, notions of historical progress become commonplaces in the
musical world, and these notions inspire several generations of
ambitious composers in the sixteenth-century to seek novel refinements. For these reasons, music presents not only different genres
but also widely divergent personal styles. Theorists accordingly
temper abstract counterpoint with comments on the aesthetics of
maniera. Needless to say, evaluations of various styles depend on
the conservative, progressive, or revolutionary bias of each writer.
But it is clear that the novelties associated with avant-garde music
eventually force an artificial distinction between reactionary theorists who defend traditional polyphony against the threats of radical inroads, and radical theorists who defend modern polyphony
against the dry academicism of reactionary tradition.

By the early seventeenth century, most theorists recognize
that two basic styles of composition exist in uneasy apposition.
Contrapunto osservato represents the summation of perfect art,
proper contrapuntal procedures according to mathematical rules—
the *prima prattica. Contrapunto commune* or *moderno* represents
the new free counterpoint that aims at affective depiction of the
text—the *seconda prattica.* Both kinds of counterpoint are criticized by apologists of monody, for different reasons. My thesis is
that the fundamental motivation behind all innovations, whether
theoretical or practical, whether mildly progressive or wildly iconoclastic, is an acute consciousness of style. The use of the term
maniera is irrelevant (although we will examine this aspect as
well). Its tacit assumptions underlie all musical developments in
the sixteenth and early seventeenth centuries. To its manifold ramifications we can attribute the important changes evident during
this dynamic period. This situation constitutes one reason why it
seems viable to me to call the years between 1530 and 1630 a mannerist period, one that eventually transforms renaissance concepts
of music into baroque doctrine.

CHAPTER XII

§∾§∾§∾

Chromaticism

Many kinds of innovation are subsumed under the general term "chromaticism," and this situation explains the difficulties experienced by sixteenth-century theorists wishing to come to terms with avant-garde trends. For the most part, theorists try their best to modernize traditional concepts, and they use as tools the renaissance systems of hexachord solmization, mutation, and musica ficta.

The continuing presence of the hexachord system in numerous treatises of the time indicates that it is still deemed to be a relevant educational device. Of course, as the perfect art becomes more and more outdated when compared to radical style, the efficacy of this system wanes. A case in point is the treatise by Adrianus Petit Coclico. After explaining the gamut with its three hexachords, Coclico outlines those mutations needed for singing polyphony. Apart from a few slips, his list includes one untraditional element: *Efa* (Eb), a mutation *extra manum*, required when E does not ascend to F. This is just another way of stating the "fa-la" rule.[1] Coclico's examples, on the other hand, present nothing out of the ordinary.[2]

Nicolaus Listenius presents the same general system, but in a more successful didactic manner. He makes a significant observation about three types of vocal music, one based on *Cut* corresponding to the natural hexachord, one based on *Gut* corresponding to the hard hexachord, and one based on *Fut* corresponding to the soft hexachord.[3] Listenius also notes that mutation between soft and hard hexachords is forbidden. Now, this perspicacious analysis suggests that the hexachord system is fast becoming an integral part of sonorous and harmonic character. If a composition in the Lydian mode can be defined as belonging to the soft hexachord, then by converse logic, a composition that mixes the soft and natural hexachords can be defined as belonging to the Lydian and Ionian modes. The approach exemplified by Listenius will have a great impact on later modulatory practices in chromatic music.

A similar idea is intimated by Franchinus Gafurius. Because *proprietas* is the particular pattern of each hexachord, there are then three such proprieties: *durum, molle,* and *naturale.*[4] This definition differs substantially from the traditional one that explains propriety as the unchanging interval sequence in all hexachords. My point is that Gafurius makes a qualitative distinction among the characters of three hexachordal structures. He does not, however, elucidate his reasons. In view of his conservative bias, it may very well be that he refers simply to notational differences. But later musicians who are interested in harmonic audacities will use this concept of hexachordal character as one of the foundations of *nuova maniera.*

Gafurius offers one hint of future developments in his list of causes pertaining to mutation. These causes combine those of necessity and those of beauty. The former, of course, concern the orderly progression of intervals by which they avoid all harsh and irrational sequences. The latter are not so clear-cut inasmuch as they entail aesthetic judgments. Even in traditional practice, *causa pulchritudinis* is summoned to defend departures from the norm that cannot be otherwise justified. When such departures become norms of composition, we have arrived at mannerist style in music. Returning to Gafurius specifically, we note his references to sweeter modulation (voice leading) and mixture of modes under *causae pulchritudinis.* Both of these are relevant to incipient chromaticism because the use of flat accidentals in practice both depicts and symbolizes sweet harmony and melody. In the mannerist madrigal, flats appear consistently on words such as *dolce.* Of course, Gafurius does not admit flat accidentals beyond *Bb fa.* But in the hands of mannerist composers, mutation on the flat side gradually widens to include hexachords beyond the normal three. And when this innovation becomes commonplace, a corresponding set of mutations on the sharp side appears to add piquancy to musical vocabulary.

Gafurius's conservative ideals can be adduced from his emphasis on careful, conjunct mutation. He evidently frowns on sudden and unusual changes, precisely those that will emerge as favorites in avant-garde practice. But Gafurius also mentions that disjunct mutation occurs frequently in polyphony. Although he does not define it, we can surmise that disjunct mutation happens between soft and hard hexachords necessitating the harsh *permutatio* from *B♭fa* to *B♮mi*. Gafurius further notes that the use of unequal semitones characterizes the chromatic genus; it is therefore forbidden in diatonic counterpoint. Henricus Glareanus also adheres to pythagorean tuning, and he therefore limits his definition of mutation to the traditional one excluding *permutatio*.[5] But because he uses mutation to explicate modal structure, he inadvertently extends the boundaries normally created by this system.[6] Furthermore, his discussion of musica ficta allows fictive hexachords outside the guidonian gamut.[7] Thus Glareanus, like all traditionalists who face the task of accommodating contemporary style, must contradict his initial premise. And the broadening of the hexachord system causes logical complexities and verbal circumlocutions.

One of the earliest inroads into the neutral hegemony of this system comes from the combination of modes and hexachords. Martin Agricola uses solmization on *B♭fa* and *B♮mi* to explain the modes: *B♮mi* in the Dorian, Phrygian, and Mixolydian modes; *B♭fa* in the Lydian mode.[8] Even though he fails to mention hexachord species in this context, the pertinent syllables cannot be conceived without them. Listenius goes more directly to the point. After surveying the *voces musicales*, he states that the Dorian belongs to the natural, the Lydian to the soft, and the Phrygian and Mixolydian to the hard hexachords.[9] Glareanus also explains his two new modes according to hexachord mutation. Even Johannes Tinctoris's convoluted discursus on the Lydian mode with B♭ rests on the premise that mutation to the soft hexachord avoids the tritone.[10] When discussing counterpoint, the problem of vocal range forces Tinctoris to consider matters of modal transposition. After clarifying that transposed modes end on irregular finals, Tinctoris presents a complex exegesis that permits transposition up to two flats. This scheme requires a hexachord on B♭, which he calls a *coniuncta* on *Elami* (E♭), a term that saves him from having to admit a bona fide hexachord outside the gamut.[11]

Although Nicola Vicentino's transpositions are not very adventuresome, the context of his remarks presents a novel approach. He takes it for granted that an explanation of the modes and their treatment in polyphony cannot be conducted without *musica finta*. Furthermore, he explores the interrelationship between accidentals and modes without recourse to hexachord mutation.[12] This may at first seem a small point; however, it demonstrates that accidentals in Vicentino's theory have assumed an existence independent of the system that for generations had given them their justification. Modes for Vicentino embody expressive qualities. Therefore, the composer of secular music must vary them in order to paint a fleeting series of passions, *quando aspre, & quando dolce, & quando allegre, & quando meste*. Vicentino likens this technique to the mixture of *maniere* in architecture, a mixture undertaken for the sake of variety and ornamentation. Now he comes to his cardinal argument. The modes contain intervals from the three genera, and this is why contemporary music must be called *musica participata & mista*.[13] Generic mixture is particularly evident in the transposition of modes due to the use of accidentals, both sharp and flat. It follows that transposition retains the musical structure of the modes while changing their character. Thus Vicentino states that music in the Lydian mode (with B♭) is *Cromatica Musica*.[14] Generally speaking, he admits the possibility of transposition up to four flats in his charts. The thrust of Vicentino's point of view is now clear. Musica ficta, introduced without mutation, affect the expressive quality of the modes and produce *musica mista*. This characteristic appears most prominently in modern secular music, and it explains the superiority of the *bella maniera*.

Although Gioseffo Zarlino attacks Vicentino's radical theories, his own discussion of modal transposition shows an awareness of milder refinement. In analyzing feasible transpositions, he indicates that modes can be transposed twice on the flat and twice on the sharp side; this scheme legitimizes B♭, E♭, F♯, and C♯.[15] Once again, Zarlino indicates his willingness to accommodate practice while maintaining the precepts of the *ars perfecta*. I refer specifically to sharp accidentals, which were previously admitted only in cases of *commixtio modorum*; for example, an F♯ *subsemitonium modi* in effect mixes the Mixolydian and Ionian modes. And it could very well be that Gafurius's disjunct mutation means transposition on the sharp side.

Of course, musica ficta appear in polyphony for reasons other than transposing modes. Those connected to *causa pulchritudinis* furnish the basis for radical experiments in the mannerist period, and this concrete relationship shows us that the roots of modern style are embedded in the hidden refinements of traditional music. We can understand this situation from the discussion of *fictae* or *coloratae* given by Gafurius, a discussion that diverges from the predominantly conservative outlook characteristic of his work. He notes that coloration may be introduced in three ways: chromatic, mixed, and enharmonic. All three are ornaments of the basic diatonic genus. Gafurius limits his explanation to the mixed genus (diatonic-chromatic). Beginning with the aspect that develops from authority, he first shows how one arrives at *fa permutatum* (the ordinary B♭ *fa*). At the same time, he indicates that it is customary to sing the pitches, G F G, as G F♯ G. This kind of *subsemitonium modi* has no authoritative hexachord. Gafurius then concludes that many theorists assign mutations to every degree in the gamut. As examples, he gives *mi-fa* on E, *fa-mi* on C, and *mi-fa* on B. In effect, Gafurius is describing E♭ *fa* based on the B♭ hexachord, C♯ *mi* based on an A hexachord, and B♭ *fa* based on the traditional soft hexachord. All these notes and hexachords he calls *musica acquistata*. Gafurius does not condemn this practice, but he is careful to ascribe its acceptance to other theorists.[16] Nevertheless, his examples suggest that he is willing to concede mutation as far as two flats and two sharps.

Glareanus takes a similar view of musica ficta, which he defines as notes not found in the ordinary gamut, thereby excluding B♭ *fa*. His illustrations of unusual mutation include *mi* on F, *sol* on E, and *fa* on A.[17] Unfortunately, Glareanus does not state precisely which hexachords are involved in these mutations. If we take him at his strict word, these ficta must be pitches actually outside the gamut. It therefore appears that he means F♯ *mi*, E♭ *sol*, and A♭ *fa*.

In that case, Glareanus envisages the extension of flat mutation to a surprising degree of chromaticism—that is, to four flats. And because mutation by sharps is unusual in itself, he contents himself with the moderate admission of one sharp.

Listenius's statements indicate that extensive flat mutation is not entirely unknown in the early sixteenth century. He too defines ficta as notes outside the gamut. The progression he gives can be interpreted as either *Eb ut, Fre, Gmi, Ab fa, Bb sol,* and *Cla,* or as *Eut, F#re, G#mi, Afa, Bsol,* and *C#la.*[18] A subsequent musical illustration makes it clear that Listenius refers to the hexachord beginning on *Eb ut.* Its written accidentals (Bb, Eb, and Ab) necessitate musica ficta ranging from Bb to Db.[19] An attempt to solmizate this melody reveals why Listenius mentions that mutation of this kind cannot be effected without considerable disagreement. It also serves to stress that such a chromatic *maniera* is deliberately limited to virtuoso singers and to a select audience. However, in spite of its manifest difficulties, Listenius insists that such mutation is possible on any note of the gamut.

It should be apparent at this point that we have bridged the gap between conservative and revolutionary theory. Even conservatives feel it incumbent upon them to take cognizance of certain radical trends. In this vein we must understand the one unusual element in Coclico's mutation system. His solmization of *Elami* (E♮) and *Elafa* (Eb) disabuses the repeated statements found in secondary literature to the effect that *Elafa* was never recognized in fifteenth- and sixteenth-century theory. What is more, Listenius's example, mentioned previously, provides proof that extensive flat mutation is warily accepted as a harmonic refinement. His melody contains implicit within its vertical requirements a series of transitory modulations: C, F, Bb, Eb, Ab, Eb, and Db. The "key areas" thus suggested are, of course, a result of the natural behavior of hexachord mutation. However, any student of baroque harmony immediately recognizes the scheme as equivalent to circle-of-fifths modulation. It matters not that sixteenth-century theorists do not speak of modulation in the modern sense. It exists in practice, and writers approach this reality from the only theoretical tool they have available to them—hexachord mutation.

Circle-of-fifths modulation cannot operate in the strictly

diatonic framework of modality. Its unusual harmonic drive is clearly understood by sixteenth-century musicians to be a novelty in sonority. And this novelty, characteristic of a great deal of chromaticism, spells the breakdown of the modes. Therefore, its implications are twofold: it permits a wide-ranging use of unusual accidentals, and it introduces an entirely new way of organizing vertical triads. We here witness one of the most important aspects of hexachord mutation. Originally a neutral didactic device for singers, it has now drastically altered the harmonic and tonal spectrum of musical vocabulary at the disposal of composers.[20]

Glareanus and Listenius are by no means the only theorists to intimate the possibility of extensive flat mutation. Agricola puts the case in a straightforward manner when he notes that in polyphony, the notes A, D, and G can be sung as *fa*.[21] These ficta produce hexachords up to D♭. Twelve years earlier, Pietro Aaron advocates that all notes in the octave can be solmizated on all six *voces musicales*. His system combines the traditional three hexachords with additional flat ones up to A♭.[22] This combination, however, produces some inconsistencies in *proprietas*, the most noticeable of which is the lack of semitonal permutations on C and F. In order to produce them, Aaron would have to complete his procedure by using *C♭ fa* and *F♭ fa* based on hexachords starting on G♭ and C♭. Because of tuning problems affecting enharmonic equivalence, Aaron states that these two hexachords are not good. From the standpoint of traditional theory, Aaron's scheme appears quite daring inasmuch as its disjunct mutations result in forbidden permutations on every note except C and F. From this fact we can conclude that the hexachord system itself is undergoing a fundamental change in the hands of those theorists who seek to justify chromatic style. And for this reason, Aaron's scheme raises considerable interest in avant-garde circles. In one of his letters, Giovanni Spataro argues that it is incomplete on account of its restriction to flat mutation, and he cites John Hothby and Bartoloméo Ramos de Pareja as authorities for mutation on the sharp side.[23] Probably because of this and other letters, Aaron later revised his system to include sharp mutation as far as the hexachord on F♯.[24] For the same reasons as those given concerning the flat system, he omits the hexachords on C♯ and G♯, which need E♯ and

B♯ accidentals. Now, musical compositions that wander widely through mutations and transitory modulations raise severe problems for tuning and intonation, especially in view of the scientific premises of the latter. However, mannerist practitioners are not content with orderly exploration of either flat or sharp mutation; they frequently combine both types in close proximity. As a result, G♯ and A♭ may follow each other, and in some eccentric cases be sounded simultaneously.

We have already indicated that equal temperament provides the only solution to the problems posed by radical style. The musical theorists who support this system are few. It is implicit in Spataro's notion that all notes of the gamut without exception can be raised or lowered by applying sharps or flats.[25] In addition to very unusual accidentals, such as double sharps and double flats, Spataro's system entails a complete double cycle of circle-of-fifths modulation that ends where it began, provided equal tempering has been applied along the way. A few decades earlier, Andreas Ornitoparcnus states that musica ficta are a fact of life, and that one of their effects is *subita et improvisa mutatio*.[26] Both isolated mutation and systematic modulation undoubtedly strike sixteenth-century listeners as sudden and unexpected harmonic excitement.

Gregor Faber's discussion of ficta in terms of *causa necessitatis* and *causa suavitatis* must be considered as a document of mannerist theory. In his opinion, sweet chromaticism has two functions—to relieve monotony and to mirror the words of the text.[27] Such ideas about musical expressivity have been encountered before. But the use of the word *suavitas*, and the suggestion that purely diatonic music is a little dull, can be construed as signal mannerist concepts. Even more striking is the musical example picked by Faber to illustrate *causa suavitatis*—Matthaeus Greiter's *Passibus ambiguis*. Its cantus firmus, *Fortuna desperata*, unfolds in an ostinato scheme whereby each statement mutates one step in the flat hexachord system: F, B♭, E♭, A♭, D♭, G♭, C♭, and F♭.[28] Greiter himself wrote a brief didactic handbook that includes unusual hexachord mutation. His technical thesis maintains that any note of the gamut can be sung to any syllable. His aesthetic thesis predicates that ficta should appear in surprising places.[29] This notion demonstrates another aspect of mannerist theory and practice. Once formerly unusual accidentals have become stereotypes, musicians in search of novel effects are forced to envisage still more daring chromaticism.

We have mentioned that Ramos is one of the earliest authorities for radical mutation cited by Spataro. Even though Ramos suspects the much touted efficacy of the hexachord system, he nevertheless takes it as a point of departure. Ramos first explains *mi-fa coniunctae* on B, E, and A as well as *fa-mi coniunctae* on C and F.[30] He then constructs his own gamut with hexachords starting on F, G, A, Bb, C, D, and Eb—hexachords requiring the following accidentals: Bb, F#, C#, Eb, and Ab.[31] His progressive attitude can be adduced from the adoption of unusual ficta into a regularized system of mutation. Because Ramos is most keenly interested in devising a flexible scheme for harmonic variety and beauty, he maintains that one can arrange the natural gamut on a higher pitch on the one side and on a lower pitch on the other side. In this way, the original diatonic order engenders two chromatic ones. Ramos's tripartite system produces the five ficta previously listed. And Ramos insists his scheme proves that singing the accidental systems is exactly the same as singing the natural one; that is to say, that hexachordal *proprietas* operates on both the flat and sharp sides.[32] But like Aaron's system, it is incomplete and therefore inconsistent; not all permutations are the same size. Yet Ramos cannot be faulted for stating that contemporary composers use all the accidentals he has systematized, and that his system, furthermore, teaches singers to recognize Bb-C# as a minor third and Eb-C# as a tone. Considering the date of this treatise, we must admit the radical nature of Ramos's concept, one that presages later mannerist ideas.

The matter of harmonic audacities is approached from an entirely different angle by Vicentino. Like other radicals, he begins with the guidonian gamut but then plays his own variations on it. Altogether, he describes seven orders: two diatonic, two chromatic, and three enharmonic. The first diatonic presents the normal gamut without any accidentals, whereas the second diatonic introduces *Bb fa* in the low octave. The first chromatic gamut uses flat accidentals, so that it ascends by major and descends by minor semitones. Sharp accidentals in the second chromatic gamut produce the opposite arrangement. The first enharmonic gamut merely duplicates the first diatonic one, but with its pitches raised by one diesis. In the second enharmonic gamut, the minor semitone found in the chromatic one is divided by the minor diesis throughout. The division of the major semitone into one minor and one major diesis results in the third enharmonic gamut.[33] The complexities of this exegesis have less to do with complete generic gamuts than with Vicentino's desire to show their construction by logical steps. In their totality, the gamuts demonstrate the three genera.

In scholarly appraisals of the sixteenth century, the role assigned to Vicentino in the drama played by influential radicals has been negligible. Here is not the place to attempt a complete evaluation of his importance. However, we must stress that his theoretical views are relevant to the history of mannerist thought. Earlier, we mentioned a number of theorists in the late sixteenth century who combine excerpts from Zarlino and Vicentino. Only mildly progressive topics from his treatise are employed in these cases, and it is clear that his radical notions about chromatic and enharmonic styles hold no interest for such writers. But it is incorrect to assume that Vicentino's ideas regarding vocal styles pass unnoticed. That they are discussed in different musical circles can be adduced from the fact that several theorists, such as Zarlino, Gandolfo Sigonio, and Jean Taisnier, see fit to publicly refute them.[34] Taisnier is a known plagiarist who unashamedly lifts concepts from other theorists, and we can therefore assume that his condemnation of modern novelties comes from somewhere else. Nevertheless, his remarks are revealing. Taisnier reviews four customary divisions of music. The first is the tripartite schema of *theorica*, *practica*, and *poetica*, a division reminiscent of Listenius, Coclico, and Hermann Finck. The fourth distinguishes between chant and figured, or polyphonic music. It is at this point that Taisnier indulges in his disparaging digression. Polyphonic music itself exhibits two styles—ancient and modern. Of [*musica*] *moderna*, he says that it "is called *nova* or *reservata* by some who have decided that the imposition of one or the other diesis or diaschisma in a secular song or motet turns the diatonic genus of music into the chromatic, being completely ignorant of the divergence of the diatonic from the chromatic and enharmonic."[35]

As we mentioned earlier, Zarlino concludes his remarkable exposition of the art of counterpoint with a survey of the ancient genera. His treatment is more than mere obeisance to the antiquarian interests of humanist readers. This audience has been satisfied by the material presented in Book II. In Book III, Zarlino concentrates on practical elements appearing in modern music. After outlining the generic ingredients of the tetrachord,[36] he exposes the erroneous premise behind current theories of the genera. Zarlino dismisses abstract theories about generic integrity as well as their validity for sustaining the thesis that modern counterpoint mixes the three genera. And his refutation is more complete and convincing than either that of Vicente Lusitano or Ghiselin Danckerts. In simple terms, Zarlino insists that one must examine musical practice where these three styles are defined by the nature of melodic movement. Thus, the diatonic style presupposes tonal movement, chromatic style needs semitonal movement, and enharmonic style requires microtonal movement.[37] To demonstrate the ridiculousness of the nondiatonic genera, he deliberately picks the case of a composition built on a chant, so that the cantus firmus is subjected to some devastatingly bizarre changes.[38] Zarlino concludes that pieces in the pure chromatic and enharmonic genera are poor efforts. But it is possible to choose those intervals from the chromatic genus that blend well with the diatonic one, and to use them in order to sweeten and vary the harmony without disturbing the innate laws of music.[39]

Zarlino believes that musicians must distinguish clearly between two *maniere* of composition, one ancient and one modern. Modern style is polyphonic in contradistinction to the monophonic practice of classical times. Because polyphony demands perfection of intervals both in linear and vertical arrangements, it is impossible to introduce the pure chromatic and enharmonic genera. Modern radicals err in thinking that they have revived ancient style. Their compositions rely on a completely new genus of their own invention, and one that is imperfect inasmuch as it ignores the rules of sonorous number.[40] Zarlino also refutes the idea that all intervals, regardless of their mathematical proportions, are viable in a style that seeks rhetorical eloquence. For him, musical oratory is no substitute for musical beauty. Although Vicentino is never once named throughout this discussion, the terms of Zarlino's argument leave no doubt as to the butt of his attack.[41]

Vicentino's *Hierusalem convertere* provides us with an instructive example of chromatic experimentation in practical terms (Example XII-1). No forbidden intervals, such as the tritone, appear. However, the consistency of semitonal melodies qualifies it as a work in chromatic style according to Zarlino's definition. This characteristic is also responsible for the peculiar harmonic sequences that abound in the composition, sequences that would surely offend Zarlino. They are particularly evident in the opening and closing sections of the piece, thereby demonstrating Vicentino's precepts about the importance of these structural segments. The first one entails a constant vacillation between major and minor thirds, rendered even more strange by false relations between consecutive sharps and flats. The most fascinating feature of this motet is the sparse use of dissonances. In fact, every single constellation of vertical sounds, taken in isolation, forms a perfectly consonant triadic sonority. But the semitonal melodic motion— the linear aspect of the texture—brings these triads, some of which require unusual accidentals, into startling apposition. The ensuing description relies on modern vocabulary because sixteenth-century analytical tools provide an unwieldy method for handling vertical harmony.

The long opening point of imitation, whose *inganno* creates the unstable major and minor alternations noted above, is completed by two very unusual progressions: two triads related by semitone root-movement (D major and E♭ major) and two triads related by third root-movement (E♭ major and C major). Both semitonal relations and third-relations are foreign to diatonic style; they are, however, inherent in chromatic style and give this *maniera* its highly distinctive sonal character. The next small section produces a transitory modulation by means of a circle-of-fifths in four steps, moving from C major to E♭ major. The last two triads are repeated in reverse order, and lead into another third-related pair (B♭ major and G minor). This last triad switches immediately to G major and sets off another small circle-of-fifths containing three steps from G major to F major. The momentum of this progression is abruptly cut off by two third-relations in a row (F

EXAMPLE XII-1.   N. Vicentino, *Hierusalem convertere* (1555).
From *L'antica musica ridotta alla moderna prattica,*
Book III, Chapter 55, fols. 70v–71r.

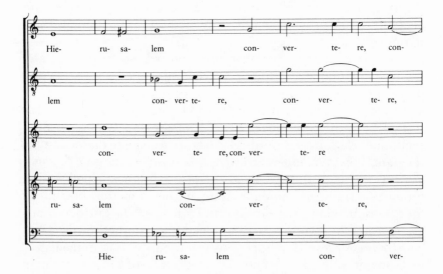

major, D major, and B major). And the piece ends with a totally unexpected plagal cadence on B major. In the short span of this eccentric miniature, Vicentino has ranged over modal areas as far as two flats and four sharps. Zarlino would point out triumphantly that it is impossible to ascertain the mode of this unruly composition. From the modern standpoint, it is equally impossible to find a predominant tonality. The work begins on G (major or minor?) and concludes on B major. We should note that this large-scale plan also encompasses a third-relation, between which a meandering series of flat and sharp sonorities wends its way. To sixteenth-century ears, semitonal melodic configurations, major-minor triads on the same degree, semitone- and third-related triads, and circle-of-fifths modulations all sound very adventurous and odd. In this composition, the nine diatonic steps (excepting the circle-of-fifths) are completely swamped by the chromatic ones. The style represented by this composition has been aptly called "floating triadic atonality."[42] And we will see that it is by no means exclusive with Vicentino.

By way of conclusion, we note that theoretical conceptions of chromaticism reflect practice in different ways. Truly conservative writers either ignore styles that go beyond normal rules or explain them away as abuses of freakish musicians. Progressive theorists modernize traditional systems in order to take into account certain inescapable facts of practical reality. Their more radical admissions, grudgingly given, can be avowed or tacit, but in all cases, they try to find a reasonable balance between old and new techniques. Radical polemicists attack the inadequacies of traditional systems and either abandon them or substitute new methods in their place. The opinions of all three groups attest to the vitality of chromaticism. When we discuss this phenomenon in the madrigal, we shall be able to judge the relationship between theory and practice more fully. It suffices here to point out that because chromaticism so obviously departs from classical precepts, both from a theoretical and a practical point of view, writers seem always to stress its aberrations. Chromaticism is an important factor of mannerist style, but it is not the only one that contributes to the shift from renaissance to baroque styles in music.

CHAPTER XIII

Imitation and Expression

Related to concepts of musical expressivity that can be traced back to the earliest treatises on music of the Middle Ages are frequent references to modal ethos that formed part of a strong tradition of citing classical authors. And to the same tradition of *auctoritas* we must ascribe the ubiquitous comments about expressive power in definitions and encomiums of music. Both tales of music's magical ability to profoundly move the listener and ethical theories of modes continued to appear in writings of the Renaissance. However, from the aesthetic viewpoint, the new ideas of history embraced by renaissance theorists changed the profile of these traditional topics in a significant way. Most important was the relegation of medieval music to crude barbarism and the concomitant belief that the *ars nova* of the fifteenth century symbolized a revival of classical ideals pertaining to harmony and expressivity. From the practical viewpoint, modal ethos enjoyed as ambiguous a relationship to contemporaneous polyphony as it did to medieval music. For this reason, theorists merely repeated commonplace characteristics for the modes as well as general injunctions about choosing a mode appropriate to the text. These perfunctory obeisances to a minor topic did not obviate music's firm place in the quadrivium.

The development of mannerist theory begins when expressivity, seen as a concrete musical matter, influences the older abstract concepts of counterpoint. Two striking examples of this phenomenon are the modal systems of Henricus Glareanus and Gioseffo Zarlino. Their subtle tools for analyzing melodic structure and modal mixture offer a flexible harmonic language for expressive style. Glareanus praises Josquin des Prez, the prince of the perfect art, for his handling of the modes to create sonorous beauty, lyrical charm, and profound pathos. But Glareanus's system is still somewhat old-fashioned in that he clings to ideas of individual modal integrity and character. Zarlino, on the other hand, adds a new analytical insight that arises from his observation of the style of Adrian Willaert, the new Pythagoras of music. On the basis of the prevalence of major or minor sonorities, Zarlino divides the modes into two groups, happy and mournful. While it is premature to attribute to Zarlino even incipient major-minor tonality,[1] the modernity of his system cannot be denied. Individual modes are losing their formerly distinct character and now coalesce into two expressive categories, each of which is defined by salient common qualities. A composer seeking sad effects can thus combine intervals proper to the Aeolian, Dorian, and Phrygian *formae*. The old taunt against inept bunglers who move from Dorian to Phrygian has lost its barb.

Both Glareanus and Zarlino are humanist scholars who read classical sources, and their new ideas concerning the modes are surely inspired by the knowledge thus gained. In these cases, humanist study allows the adaptation of carefully selected ancient theories for the purpose of making contrapuntal science relevant to modern style. Such adaptations are introduced with the understanding that they shall not disturb the primacy of self-sufficient musical laws, laws that have a mathematical base. However, another set of new ideas on expressivity does succeed in unbalancing and ultimately destroying the latter ideal. This phenomenon arises out of another happy misunderstanding of classical sources. But this tale must be told a little later. Humanist scholarship is also responsible for one of the most fecund notions in the sixteenth and early seventeenth centuries. Renewed acquaintance with Aristotle and the peripatetic school of ancient philosophy supports many novel ideas, the most important of which is the theory of *mimesis*. Its impact on the liberal arts is immediate and lasting. And the evolution of poetic and literary *mimesis* has particular relevance for musical theories of imitation.

Among the multifaceted concepts relating music and the imitation of nature,[2] we can isolate two dominant ideas, one quite radical and one moderately progressive. We begin with the latter. This facet encourages subtle transformation of neoplatonic ideas and concerns the concept of nature as a system of natural laws to be imitated by the arts. In this kind of imitation, art finds models not in the external appearance of nature but rather in its inner principles. This is the basis for the renaissance belief in ideal mathematical proportions. Musicians take for granted their place in the liberal arts and bask comfortably in the reflected glory of their perfect art, an art born from the wedlock of mathematics and abstract counterpoint. But various sociomusical pressures during the sixteenth century encourage musicians to turn their attention to practical criticism and the art of compositional style at the expense of speculative philosophy and abstract science. The neoplatonic notion of cosmological harmony falls into disrepute, and the hiatus thus created lies behind the crisis in musical theory felt by all sensitive musicians of the time. In losing its philosophical anchor, music is set adrift. Many conservatives stick tenaciously to the precept that music imitates the natural laws of the cosmos, even though they suspect that many of the mathematical formulations connected with this precept no longer seem to have any bearing on musical practice.

This predicament demonstrates why Zarlino's work makes such a resounding impact within the conservative arena. Zarlino revives the honor and relevance of speculative reasoning without neglecting empirical sense. His crystallization of the perfect art relies on two ideas that support his construct: *maniera* and *imitazione*. It is the latter idea that concerns us here. Implicit in Zarlino's system is the primacy of nature—the model for musical style. Nature gives music its *soggetto*, and music fulfills the inherent qualities of this subject.[3] But it should not, indeed cannot, improve on nature by departing from the model.[4] For this reason, Zarlino does not approve of mannerist excesses, even though they may be justified as ornaments of nature. The first and most important *soggetto* given to music by nature constitutes the mathematical laws of sound. Music is sounding number. On a superficial level, this idea seems to be nothing more than a repetition of outmoded quadrivial theory.[5] However, Zarlino expands the pythagorean *tetraktys* to the *senario*, a number set that allows him to dignify imperfect consonances with mathematical exegesis. Their incorporation into just intonation vindicates the musical style of his day. The *senario* also supports Zarlino's new arrangement of the modes. In short, music imitates the refinements of nature by embodying *numero sonoro*.[6] This remarkable scheme permits Zarlino to unite the speculative, philosophical, aesthetic, and technical aspects of music into an organic whole.

Zarlino also discusses the *soggetto* in such a way as to intimate analogies with art and literature, analogies based on technical-aesthetic ideals. Counterpoint grows out of a *soggetto della compositione*—a musical theme. Zarlino's concept of the musical imitation of nature becomes a little complex at this point. A musical theme itself cannot be natural inasmuch as it is an artificial product of the fantasy. But it possesses musical qualities that are natural to it. Its nature affects every detail of musical style, because a good composer will create his piece of music with a view to revealing the latent attributes of the subject. Furthermore, the more superior the style, the more convincing and powerful will be the embodiment of the subject.

This idea of the *soggetto* sets the stage for the entrance of an elaborate conceit. Zarlino's detailed explanation of *fuga* and *imitatione* presents these two contrapuntal styles in terms of rhetorical figures or tropes. They emerge as ornaments or refinements wrought on sound and correct (i.e. mathematical) procedure. Although *imitatione* occurs in earlier theory, Zarlino is the first writer to stress the term, probably because of the influence of the artistic notion of *imitazione della natura*. Haar suggests that Zarlino seems dissatisfied with *fuga* as a term because it lacks the humanistic and rhetorical overtones of *imitatione*.[7] Zarlino, of course, envisages both *fuga* and *imitatione* as means of attaining a graceful and beautiful style that goes beyond mere correctness. But his most lavish adjectives are reserved for *imitatione*. By definition, *fuga* represents a rigorous kind of counterpoint because of its rigid restrictions, and of course, the composer demonstrates his skill and ingenuity in handling these restrictions with good taste. But *imitatione*, by virtue of its flexibility, offers the composer more freedom of choice. He must therefore possess a greater measure of stylistic flair so that his search for variety pleases by its ingenuity and yet lacks eccentricity. Original and tasteful *imitatione* exercises the composer's innate feeling for *elegante maniera*.[8] Its fusion of rules and of their subtle working out demonstrates the composer's craft and genius.

Imitatione, then, is elastic enough to accommodate musical procedures understood as self-sufficient entities to the notion of imitating the text, this last being the third meaning of *soggetto* in Zarlino's theory. The rather fine nuances of Zarlino's views regarding the third *soggetto* have been insufficiently stressed in modern scholarship. First of all, we note that words are objective natural models for musical composition. Therefore, the structure of a work must imitate their natural qualities (prosody and grammatical sense) without sacrificing purely musical laws. Now, it is true that Zarlino also talks about the expression of the affections; but in terms of his own argument, this aspect is not connected with *imitazione del soggetto della parole*. And in this chapter, his notions about affective character will be discussed under another category, one which I call expressivity permitted within the laws of good procedure. In Zarlino's system, imitation of words involves correct declamation, and he makes this very clear in his famous ten rules, rules adapted from Giovanni Maria Lanfranco and in turn adapted by Gaspar Stoquerus.[9] These three writers share a humanist concern for verbal intelligibility. But I must stress at this point that their precepts are not equivalent to radical interest in vivid, pictorial, and affective representation of conceits and passions.

Because I consider theories propounding adherence to prosody and grammatical sense in traditional polyphony as corresponding to *imitazione delle parole*, I have created another category to comprise theories championing the deployment of musical elements for affective purposes—that is, expressivity permitted within the laws of good procedure—a category that represents a compromise concession made by conservative and progressive thinkers. Adrianus Petit Coclico suggests such a division in his definition of music: the art of singing and composing in a correct and graceful way.[10] The adjectives *recte* and *ornate* can be interpreted as recognition of the scientific basis of music on the one hand, and of rhetorical ornamentation on the other. Coclico emphatically rejects the old abstract or mathematical methods and instead treats music as a sister of rhetoric, an attitude that clearly points the way to mannerist concepts. Of course, in mature and late Mannerism, rhetorical eloquence overshadows scientific and abstract structural ideals.[11]

Even those theorists who insist on the mathematical approach cannot avoid admitting that musical materials also serve general expressive purposes. So, Franchinus Gafurius suggests that each composition must suit the text, but he does not demonstrate how to achieve such expressivity except by enumerating the customary list of vague modal characters.[12] As we have seen, Glareanus posits the expressive possibilities of modal combinations. And his disapproval of the penchant for voluptuous sound evident in these mixtures is very relevant to incipient musical Mannerism. Zarlino also discusses similar expressive devices. In true humanist fashion, he begins by referring to Plato's emphasis on the expression of the words. And he goes on to say that the composer must choose his mode carefully, and then accompany the words with appropriate harmony and rhythm. Joyful sentiments call for the tone and major semitone; sad feelings require the minor semitone, minor third, and minor sixth; harsh affections are best served by the major sixth, as well as by the syncopated fourth and seventh. Swift and vigorous rhythm expresses happiness, whereas slow rhythm expresses affliction and bitterness. Zarlino also notes that music without accidentals is sonorous and virile, whereas musica ficta produce soft and languid effects. Lest the composer take these remarks as permission to indulge in excessive novelties, Zarlino warns him that these devices must never offend the senses and reason. His comments are accompanied by musical examples taken from the works of Willaert, the composer to whom Zarlino attributes the rejuvenation of elegant style.[13]

Mannerists disregard Zarlino's plea for temperance. Because they seek startling eloquence, they have no patience with views that codify the ideals of timeless style. In their opinion, progress cannot be denied, and their refinements pave the way for the future. Once restraint has lost its meaningfulness, expressive devices can be used freely and in any exaggerated form required by the vivid conceits of poetry. But even this extreme form of iconoclasm has hidden roots in traditional practice. Radical musicians simply transform exceptions to the rule into norms of style. But before describing their approach, it might be helpful to survey those reactionary theorists (reactionary, that is, in the eyes of radicals) who admit the existence of licenses and exceptions.

Tinctoris permits the repetition of imperfect consonances for the sake of the text.[14] Glareanus allows unusual modal mixtures in connection with startling depiction of the affections. In spite of his repeated admonitions regarding the immutable primacy of sounding number, Zarlino states that some texts inspire nonharmonic progressions and extensive chromaticism. Even his praise of *contrapunto con obligo* can be construed as recognition of modern rhetorical ornamentation. When the musical repetitions characteristic of such counterpoint express a particular text, their dramatic quality becomes quite prominent. In the hands of mannerist composers of secular music, these exceptions become commonplace. At the end of the sixteenth century, this situation is admitted by Giovanni Maria Artusi when he cites the use of sweet and even harsh dissonances in the madrigals of Cipriano de Rore, Orlando de Lasso, Giaches de Wert, and others.[15]

Conservative theorists, then, permit musical licenses to a greater or lesser extent, provided that the mathematical foundation of correct rules is not too shaken up. Textual exigencies are to be followed; however, they form but one consideration for the compositional act. As mannerists turn their attention more and more to petrarchist and concettist verse, the text assumes primary importance. The underlying aesthetic of radical style can be thus summed up—*imitazione del concetto delle parole*. In this phrase we witness the deep influence of poetic theory and practice on composers who come into contact with literary notions through courts, academies, and humanist books. Minute and graphic representation of poetic conceits becomes a matter of pride, and composers often advertise their talent for this kind of composition. For instance, in his prefatory remarks to an edition of funereal madrigals, Giulio Bonagionta states that the music therein presents *concenti molti proprii alli concetti delle parole*.[16] Monteverdi's celebrated apology for the second practice is anticipated as early as 1569 in another preface by Marc Antonio Mazzone. This com-

poser considers critics of modern music stupid and ignorant because they do not realize that while the notes are the body of a
composition, the text is its soul. Just as the body follows the soul,
the notes must follow the sentiments of the words. Furthermore,
the composer may even neglect the rules for affective purposes.[17]
In the words of Giulio Cesare Monteverdi, *l'oratione sia padrona
dell'armonia e non serva.*[18]

The idea that music should imitate the conceits of poetry
inspires composers to match the wit, elegance, and grotesqueness
of poetic invention with a barrage of pictorial devices. These can
be purely visual eye music or aural figures, and they quickly develop into a stereotyped set of madrigalisms. And this duality has
caused some misunderstanding. It is clear that in the minds of
mannerist musicians, concrete word painting relates to the imitation of the affections. Poetic *enargeia* is transformed into an aesthetic for eloquence in music. As I have stated previously, this
aesthetic is widely promulgated by humanist writers. By imitating
the conceits of poetry with pictorial devices, mannerist composers
therefore believe that they also express the passions of these conceits in a particularly vivid and moving way.

The intellectual objectivity inherent in affective representation
arises from its link with the imitation of conceits. Just as literary
theorists conceive *concetti* to be rhetorical ornaments of poetic
style, so musicians consider visual and aural figures, figures depicting poetic conceits, to be ornaments of madrigalian style. It should
be further noted that modern historians err when they classify
pictorial devices as realistic.[19] Realism today connotes naturalism,
and the highly eccentric representation of words and affections in
the sixteenth-century madrigal is anything but natural. In fact, the
zarlinian school of theory, which bases its aesthetic on the imitation of nature, criticizes madrigalisms precisely on the grounds
that they are unnatural; they distort the perfect art that imitates
the inner laws of nature and are therefore very artificial and mannered. Champions of musical rhetoric would admit the artificiality
of their aesthetic but at the same time would consider this aesthetic
to be wonderful and marvelous—in short, mannerist rather than
mannered. Of course, the conservative view forgets that even the

imitation of natural laws idealizes and ornaments nature. The same problems and the same divergent values can be found in theories of the visual arts and literature.

The theoretical conception and practical use of musical conceits is a complex phenomenon. Purely pictorial word painting consists of eye music whose visual effect depends on esoteric puns grasped only by performers. This tradition is a very old one going back to the Middle Ages; but even then it was viewed as a witty rhetorical trope. Aural figures are more ambiguous inasmuch as they depict conceits and affect the listener. They have a double purpose: to imitate *concetti* by their graphic shape and to dramatize the affective meaning of the conceits by drawing the listener's attention to them. The effectiveness of aural figures remains a matter of debate to the present day, and this debate not only plumbs the depths of musical aesthetics but also influences assessments of Mannerism.

Aural figures, then, entail musical shapes based on rhythm and motion: running melismas, sighing contours, unexpected stops, jagged intervals, rising and falling melodies. Such devices concretize aspects of motion contained in the words and dramatize innate gestures implied by the affective meaning of the conceits. Some of them appear in renaissance polyphony as well, but here they are employed as abstract symbols. And they never reach exaggerated proportions that disturb the proper mathematical basis of counterpoint. Mannerists, on the other hand, manipulate such devices until they become stylized components of rhetorical *enargeia*. To them, they add other startling figures that not only disrupt organic structure but also augment an undeniably dramatic dimension. We must understand that we are here dealing with an illusion —an illusion of affective drama created by the use of these devices. But this illusion appears very real because of the mannerist conviction that music can match the tangible rhetoric of speech. To this conviction we must also attribute the infiltration of soloistic voice treatment within polyphonic procedure, together with its concomitant features of recitativelike declamation and virtuoso embellishment. Mannerist delight in affective dramatization thus leads to the breakdown of the *ars perfecta* and ultimately to the development of the concerted madrigal and monody. In this context, the degree of self-conscious affectation separates mannerist from baroque music.

Another means of aural eloquence surfaces in the deployment of unusual harmonic progressions. Although precedents exist in the perfect art, the invention and elaboration of a new musical language must be ascribed to mannerist style. Liberal musica ficta, startling hexachord mutation, circle-of-fifths modulation, free dissonance treatment, false relations, nonharmonic intervals, and semitonal melodies all contribute to the astonishing growth of chromaticism. Insofar as harmonic rhythm and shape are concerned, these devices share the characteristics of the aural figures previously described. In other words, harmonic novelties can be graphic and affective at the same time, and are so conceived by most mannerist composers. In isolated usage, audacious harmony merely impresses by its intrusion into traditional sounds. But this aspect of compositional technique also develops into a stereotyped battery of rhetorical ornaments.

If we take madrigalisms as a group, we then notice a situation analogous to that of music's sister arts. If the affective power of music resides in its ability to surprise, former novelties that have become commonplaces of style must be replaced by newer novelties. Insofar as even the most expressive and convincing compositions retain an element of artificiality, this element arising from the intellectual objectification of imitative-affective principles, such compositions easily stand as models. Thus, the best and worst examples of Mannerism contribute to a self-conscious attitude toward musical achievement. Attenuated stylization is an inescapable feature of *maniera*. And this quality of contrived rhetoric is cherished by an elite circle of professionals and amateurs who equate connoisseurship with appreciation of the refined and bizarre. Considering this climate, it seems paradoxical that everyone in the sixteenth century insists so much on the expressive power of *maniera*. Spontaneous reaction to artificial conceits would appear to be a contradiction in terms, but the delicate balance struck between deliberate intellectualism and involuntary emotionalism can be taken as the hallmark of musical Mannerism. Profiled against the musical heritage of the Renaissance, artificial conceits emerge as the weapons with which mannerists convince their sophisticated audience of the emotional power of music. Both creators and consumers play the game of willing disbelief. The salient point is that music's expressive capability rests entirely on the objective imitation of conceits and the objective representation of the affections. I have stressed this point because the premise of the mannerist aesthetic remains foreign to twentieth-century philosophy of music, and it requires a considerable effort to understand the issues in their proper historical framework.

Our search for sixteenth-century formulations of concepts related to imitative-affective style brings us to theories that lie clearly outside the rubrics of music understood as the imitation of natural laws and expressive devices allowed within these laws. Compared to the theorists of ordinary counterpoint who can depend on a weighty tradition, champions of novelty represent a small but vocal minority. Avant-garde theory does not adequately mirror the popularity or extent of mannerist elements as they exist in practice. In the framework of the history of musical thought, however, radical views attest to a growing conviction that new music is far superior to old music. Unlike writers on the visual arts and literature, radical thinkers in music must combat a firmly entrenched establishment that upholds the revered precepts of a perfect art. The latter, as we have seen, furnishes two hints elucidating the impact made by novelty: first, the frequent attacks on modern practice, and second, the exceptions to accepted rules. The first hint casts a violently negative light on *maniera* whereas the second provides wary recognition of some of its technical refinements.

Nicola Vicentino presents a detailed and very militant statement on behalf of Mannerism in music. Those aspects of his theory already discussed show that for Vicentino, imitative-affective aesthetics are inseparable from technical features. Considering the date of his work, this amalgam is highly original. Notions about musical expressivity are no longer appended as afterthoughts to the science of counterpoint. On the contrary, they arise naturally from considerations of compositional principles predicated on style.

Vicentino stresses throughout his treatise that intervals, harmonies, modes, rhythms, and the genera have expressive character. This premise vindicates both his title and his opening remarks— the *effetti musicale* and *dolci concenti*[20] of ancient music can be rivaled and surpassed by modern music. In his instructions for composing sweet and harmonious compositions, Vicentino singles out three important aspects of musical eloquence. First of all, the composer must arrange the intervals (in linear succession) *al suggietto delle parole*. Then, these melodic intervals must be accompanied by appropriate harmonies and by pertinent movements.[21] Vicentino stresses the role of tempo, and distinguishes among four general speeds: slow, medium, fast, and very fast. He also warns the student that the rate of motion can alter the affective qualities of intervallic structures.[22] Most relevant to our present topic is Vicentino's description of the components that make up good, bad, and indifferent effects. The good type arises from excited intervals accompanied by excited harmonies and fast movement, or from sad intervals accompanied by sad harmonies and slow movements. Any combination of opposites will produce a bad effect because the expressive elements contradict each other. His final illustration is a striking commentary on mannerist opinions of ordinary style. Vicentino states categorically that if the composer mixes sad and excited elements throughout a composition, the effect is neither good nor bad; it is at best confused.[23] If we compare this evaluation with Zarlino's advice to mix interval species and rhythms in order to achieve variety and harmonious composition, the widely divergent views of conservatives and radicals about *bella maniera* emerge with particularly strong force.

Vicentino also repeats Ramos's division between devout stability and mobile joyousness. But this general declaration, which refers to basic mood evocation, relates to the motet.[24] Secular music, by way of contrast, features minute word painting and rapidly changing expressive effects. It is in this context that we must read Vicentino's famous summation of the aesthetic premise behind mannerist style:

For music is written to a text and is made solely to express the conceits, passions, and affections of the words with harmony. And if the words speak of modesty, the composition should proceed modestly, and not in an infuriated way; and if they speak of joy, the music must not be sad; and if of sadness, it should not be composed gaily; and when they are bitter, it should not be sweet; and when sweet, it should not accompany them differently because they will seem distorted from their conceit; and when they speak of swiftness, it should not be slack or slow; and when of standing, it should not run; and when they demonstrate going together, the music should be arranged so that the parts are joined with a breve because the latter is more obvious than a semibreve or minim. . . .[25]

After continuing with still more concrete advice, Vicentino concludes that careful observance of all his recommendations enables the composer to produce *una bella maniera*. It is in relation to the above comments that Palisca makes the following observation: "Vicentino's greatest contribution to musical aesthetics was that he replaced the renaissance ideal of harmoniousness and proportion with the baroque ideal of expressiveness."[26] Although many of Vicentino's notions survive in later *Affektenlehre* and *Figurenlehre*, his aesthetic better exemplifies Mannerism between 1530 and 1630. His conception profiles the development of a distinct style that takes as its premise the norms of the perfect art of the renaissance, transforms them and distorts them into a convention of affected refinement, and contributes to the ideal of rhetorical power in music, an ideal to be fully exploited by the Baroque.

References to imitative-affective style in other writings illustrate that Mannerism is a fully mature phenomenon, and that, at the close of the century, it has caused a seemingly irreparable breach between traditional and modern music. This bifurcation lies at the heart of Claudio Monteverdi's celebrated remarks, annotated by his brother, Giulio Cesare.[27] The source is too well known to require detailed comment; I therefore concentrate on its mannerist import.

Monteverdi takes issue with Artusi's accusation that he composes haphazardly. Had Artusi provided the words for the excerpts he criticized, then everyone could discern the error of his judgment. Monteverdi's style takes the text as its point of departure, and therefore, its dissonance treatment differs fundamentally from that found in the music Artusi values. The attitude exemplified by this rebuttal is typical of mannerist aesthetics, and my interpretation receives support from other comments, such as the list of composers supplied to give the second practice a historical tradition. Of special importance is Giulio Cesare's reference to Cipriano de Rore, the first composer to renew the second practice. This fascinating remark suggests that modern music rejuvenates ancient classical ideals (hence the reference to Plato), and that it is the unruly heir of the first practice. To achieve its superior goal, modern music distorts and abandons traditional precepts. Monteverdi states deliberately that modern music is a second practice and not a second theory. He therefore proposes to call his forthcoming treatise, *The Perfection of Modern Music,* a title that stresses two things: first, modern music embodies the perfection of melody, or the expressive union of word and tone; and second, its premises embrace practical rather than theoretical considerations.[28]

Lest Artusi or any of his conservative colleagues continue to attack modern music on the grounds that imitative-affective devices create a totally absurd style with no musical merit whatsoever, Monteverdi closes his argument with the proposition that the second practice satisfies both reason and sense. When dealing with reason, Giulio Cesare's logic becomes a little fuzzy. His second proof is self-evident only to those who accept the ideal of modern music—to wit, that textual supremacy produces melodic perfection. To those who do not accept it, perfection of melody cannot condone imperfection of harmony. His first proof is manifestly untrue. He claims that modern music uses the consonances and dissonances approved by mathematics. Artusi's and Zarlino's disapproval of novel *maniera* involves the incontestable fact that nonharmonic progressions, lying outside sonorous number, abound in modern music. Monteverdi's text goes on to say that modern music pleases the senses because textual command over rhythm and harmony results in a total effect that can influence the disposition of the mind. Here he clearly refers to the affective and rhetorical power of the second practice. Self-sufficient harmony alone is incapable of producing extrinsic effects. It can prepare the mind for general moods, but it cannot express extramusical things. Zarlino agrees with these ideas, but of course, he evaluates them from a different point of view.

The preceding notion is clarified by one concrete excursus. Giulio Cesare points out that in the first practice, harmony remains the same regardless of the variety of compositions and genres. Its abstract and immutable laws do not allow it to follow the text. This idea will recur in our discussion of *maniera*. Monteverdi concludes that the second practice, a term which he claims to have invented, builds on the foundation of truth. In other words, it is not a false practice favored by inept musicians. Even if Monteverdi's defense seems insufficient, his brother emphasizes that in his day, discerning people admire only a style of music that admits the command of the words. Thus is Artusi summarily dismissed as a carping pedant.

While on the subject of Monteverdi, we should remember that in one other instance this composer talks about a new style of music based on reviving a forgotten ancient practice—the *stile concitato*. Monteverdi indicates that in his reading of classical philosophy, he encountered the concept of the three main passions: anger, moderation, and humility or supplication. These mental states were paralleled by the three ranges of the human voice, and by three styles in music (*concitato*, *temperato*, and *molle*). Turning to music of the past, he found only examples of the soft and moderate styles. Monteverdi then set out to rediscover the agitated style, on the theory that opposites move the mind with greater force. It is significant that the same aesthetic idea underlies excessive mannerist devices in literature and the visual arts. Monteverdi cites the *Combattimento di Tancredi e Clorinda* as his first attempt in *stile concitato*, and explains that he chose this section of Tasso's epic for specific reasons, principally its representation of antipodal passions in startling proximity. Now that the *stile concitato* has become a norm for contemporary music, Monteverdi writes this preface so that the world might know that he invented a new style.[29] Monteverdi's explanation of *stile concitato* falls squarely in the mannerist framework, and his music, replete with vividly pictorial, even grotesque, *moti di cavallo* and *moti di guerra*, represents a striking exemplar of both the strengths and weaknesses of this aesthetic. One scholar warns us against overplaying the significance of this preface because its appearance is ex post facto to the musical event.[30] Since documents concerning the writing of the preface do not exist, we can only speculate about the reasons that prompted Monteverdi. It may very well be that he arrived at this style through an intuitive response to the problems of setting a particular text, and that someone else later pointed out to him the classical authority by which he could name and justify it. Whatever the case may be, Monteverdi's obvious pride in his personal invention can be taken as another manifesto of the mannerist outlook. His preface also illustrates another typically mannerist ploy—vindicating novel stylistic extravagance by claims of rejuvenating ancient practice. Both his words and his music attest to the vitality of *maniera* in the early seventeenth century. They represent the last great flowering of Mannerism in music.

Furthermore, Monteverdi's *Combattimento* spans the realms of vocal chamber music and theatrical presentation, and thus it serves as an indicator of a general trend. The imitative-affective devices of modern music, bolstered by notions of rhetorical eloquence, force increasingly dramatic qualities on to the lyrical premises of polyphony. What begins as a refinement of the perfect art of counterpoint soon evolves into a drastic distortion of this style. The final result of this trend is the emergence of the solo voice accompanied by instruments. At this point, the musical conceits of the polyphonic madrigal come under fire from two camps: the reactionary adherents of traditional counterpoint who feel that affective *maniera* has gone too far, and the radical champions of monody who feel that affective *maniera* has not gone far enough. Strangulated in this vise, rhetorical polyphony dies in the most elegant and graceful tradition of mannerist demises, but not without leaving behind a legacy for the future.

For some eighty years, the dramatic novelties grafted onto the polyphonic madrigal are nevertheless hailed as stellar achievements of stylistic progress. Adriano Banchieri's statement sums up the mannerist position. Older composers wrote perfect *contrapunto osservato*, but their music contains no verbal expressivity. Modern composers of *contrapunto commune* breathe life into polyphony by emulating the perfect orator. Their eloquent music imitates the affections of the words with harmony. For this reason, modern music delights not only the composer, but also the singers and audience.[31] Here we have two salient requirements characteristic of Mannerism. Music is now a vehicle for virtuoso display by singers, and this virtuosity produces audience-oriented music.

Both requirements derive from the inherently dramatic aspect of imitative-affective ornaments.

Because the depiction of the text justifies musical experiments that transcend and break traditional rules, it also explains the greater genius of composers who explore *effetti meravigliosi*. Rhetorical ornamentation contributes to an aesthetic of creative excellence based not on the observance of the rules, but rather on individual talent, innate genius, personal *idea*, and inspired poetic furor. Music has moved out of the sphere of quadrivial science into that of the rhetorical trivium. Of course, mannerists hail expressive devices as testimony of their iconoclastic originality. But a trend toward systematization evident in the early seventeenth century manages to gather these willful eccentricities into a docile scheme of musical rhetoric. These schemes first appear under the rubric of *musica poetica*, in itself a suggestive term, and develop subsequently into the *Figurenlehre* and *Affektenlehre* of baroque theory.

Coclico calls the composers of traditional counterpoint the *mathematici*. Their opposites, the *poetici*, are the most modern exponents of expressive style. The humanist bias of this statement is obvious, and Coclico's encomium of musical poets could be a covert attack on the authority of Boethius who held the *genus poetarum*, the makers of songs, in such low esteem.[32] Giovanni Spataro's and Pietro Aaron's belief that composers are born with talent as are poets also reflects humanistic emphasis on expressivity in music. But humanism in musical theory, supported by the printing technology, also fosters the aristotelian notion of the composer as a fabricator of the perfect and absolute work of art. The phrase is first coined by Nicolaus Listenius, who is also the first in a line of German theorists to use the term *musica poetica* as an aesthetic-technical category.[33]

Simply put, *musica poetica* means a theory of musical composition.[34] But the matter is not so simple as it appears on the surface. Listenius's three branches of music seem to be nothing more than an attempt to clarify meaningful terminology and to introduce *musica poetica* as a more fashionable alternative to *arte sive scientia contrapuncti*. However, *musica poetica* subsumes more than the ordinary concept of contrapuntal craft; it refers really to the art of composition. As we have seen, this humanist idea of composition develops from stylistic considerations, and style, or *maniera*, is inseparable from expressive content. Thus, it is not inappropriate to call Vicentino's fourth book on musical practice, *musica poetica*.[35] Most important of all, theories of *musica poetica* are frequently couched in descriptive and prescriptive terms borrowed from literary rhetoric. The significance of this vocabulary has yet to be investigated in any systematic way. From what we know of this subject, it seems clear that rhetorical figures function as convenient means of describing features of style in an admittedly artificial, hence, self-conscious, manner.

Treatment of some musical figures or devices, garnished with authentic or transmogrified classical names, appears intermittently in a number of sixteenth-century treatises. But I shall limit the discussion to Joachim Burmeister's work, which presents a complete and systematic exposition of the art of counterpoint in terms of rhetoric and style. Its sixteen chapters begin with the rudiments of music and culminate in a detailed exegesis of expressive and structural techniques. He defines *musica poetica* as "that part of music that teaches one to write vocal music, joining the sounds of melodies in harmony adorned by various periodic affections to turn the spirits and hearts of man to different emotions."[36] Burmeister divides musical style into four categories. The *stylus humilex* uses smooth intervals and consonances. Its opposite, the *stylus grande*, is based on large leaps and numerous dissonances. Between these two extremes there lies the *stylus mediocre*. A fourth category, the *stylus mixtus*, freely combines elements of the previous styles according to the affections of the text.[37] Given the discussion of sixteenth-century ideals presented in this chapter, it should not be necessary to stress that the fourth category represents the best style. Indeed, Burmeister selects Lasso as the ideal stylist for students to emulate, precisely because he adheres to the *stylus mixtus*.[38] And although most of Burmeister's examples are culled from church music, their characteristics can be found in secular genres as well.

Burmeister's figures, labeled with rhetorical names wherever possible, fall into three groups: *figurae harmoniae* (sixteen), *figurae melodiae* (six), and *utriusque figurae* (four). Twelve are clearly formal or structural, and fourteen have expressive connotations.[39] The formal figures describe matters of artistic structure; they therefore function as ornaments that transform correct counterpoint into stylish style. Out of the twelve, seven are harmonic, two are melodic, and three belong to the category combining both aspects. Among the traditional ornaments of correct counterpoint we may include imitation (*fuga realis*), canon (*fuga imaginaria*), double fugue (*hypallage*), fugue with two themes (*metalepsis*), syncopation (*syncope* or *synaeresis*), and *Faux Bourdon*. Of newer vintage are musical embellishments such as incomplete fugue (*apocope*), dissonance at cadence points (*pleonasmus*) or permitted by voice leading (*parrhesia*), double-choir repetition of homophonic passages (*anaploce*), full consonant sonorities (*parembole*), and sequential harmonic repetitions (*congeries*).

Needless to say, the expressive figures provide a catalog of the devices associated with *nuova maniera*. They include a set of figures describing various kinds of homophonic textures: a single homophonic passage in the midst of counterpoint (*noema*), a double *noema* (*analepsis*), two repeated homophonic phrases on different pitch levels (*mimesis*), a double *mimesis* (*anadiplosis*), and varied repetition of a homophonic passage in ascending motion (*auxesis*). Two figures pertain to dissonances—the first (*symblema* or *commissura*) to the affective use of passing notes, and the second (*pathopoeia*) to the affective use of chromatic semitones. Burmeister also explains the rhetorical function of the general pause (*aposiopesis*), the overstepping of modal limits (*hyperbole* and *hypobole*), as well as three kinds of repetition: melodic (*pallilogia*), ascending sequences (*climax*), and partial repetition of some voices in a complex (*anaphora*).

The above excursus covers all but one of the figures, *hypotyposis*. This one deserves special attention inasmuch as Burmeister's definition is somewhat problematic: "*Hypotyposis* is that ornament by which the meaning of the text is revealed in such a way that whatever [elements] are hidden in the text and lack soul and life, seem to be endowed with life."[40] Ruhnke suggests that *hypotyposis* involves the musical representation of abstract ideas (a kind of emblematic symbolism) rather than word painting.[41] In the Lasso example quoted by Burmeister, however, we find the following features: a melisma under *Laetatur cor*, triple meter under *gaudebit*, busy counterpoint under *laborem*, and long notes under *dolorem*. Considering this excerpt and Burmeister's definition, it is more likely that *hypotyposis* is the means whereby composers achieve vivid musical *enargeia*. Thus *hypotyposis* corresponds to *imitazione del concetto delle parole*, and in this sense, it is a broad aesthetic trope covering other individual figures or concrete effects.

Nine harmonic, four melodic, and one harmonic-melodic figure comprise a total of fourteen expressive devices. They can be found in polyphonic works ranging from progressive examples in traditional style to radical experiments in avant-garde style. Burmeister appears particularly taken with homophonic passages in various dramatic sequences. *Noema* and *analepsis* appear often in the works of Josquin's generation where they serve both structural and mildly expressive purposes. It is indicative of mannerist procedures that these techniques should be exploited for their rhetorical power and developed into *mimesis*, *anadiplosis*, and *auxesis*. Repetition also contributes to eloquent effects, one of which is called *climax*. Although Zarlino discusses *pertinacie*, he ignores their extramusical potential, a potential that will be realized in mannerist style. Exceeding the modes for affective considerations is recognized by Glareanus, and the new mannerist emphasis on these devices can be seen from Burmeister's terms. He is also the first to stress the dramatic quality of pauses, devices often used and abused in mannerist music. Finally, Burmeister's explanation of word painting and chromaticism (*hypotyposis* and *pathopoeia* —literally, the making of patterns and pathos) clearly demonstrates how mannerist aesthetics survive in baroque doctrine. The actual influence of this theorist on subsequent writers must await more detailed study of early baroque sources.[42] The same holds true for his concepts in relation to rhetoric in contemporary and earlier writings on literature and music. Most scholars agree, nevertheless, that Burmeister contributes to the heritage binding the Renaissance and the Baroque,[43] a heritage, it seems to me, that is best understood as a period of Mannerism.

CHAPTER XIV

§✿§✿§✿

Singing and Ornamentation

Documents reveal that in the Renaissance, musicians received their education first as singers and then as masters of the science of counterpoint. Before the advent of printing and the full impact of humanism, theorists assumed the existence of a master-pupil apprenticeship and therefore felt free to omit certain topics. Because sixteenth-century writers are preoccupied with producing complete and systematic books, they incorporate previously unwritten practices and knowledge gained in the studio or on the job, as it were. Thus they rationalize in print the didactic relationship between the training of singers and composers.

The topic of improvised ornamentation becomes an issue of cardinal importance in the work of Adrianus Petit Coclico. We have already noted that he relates music to rhetoric, and from this position comes his focus on "correct and beautiful singing as well as artificial, sweet and colored delivery."[1] In Coclico's view, the salient aspect of a singer's art is his mastery of alluring cadences (*clausulorum lenociniis*), that is, ornamenting simple cadential patterns with elegant diminutions.[2] To aid the student, he includes several examples of embellished cadences supposedly taught by Josquin des Prez as well as others presumably of his own invention. The chapter concludes with two French chansons by Claudin de Sermisy and his own motet, all replete with ornamentation. Disregarding the dubious attribution to Josquin, the examples demonstrate Coclico's interpretation of typically renaissance procedures. In the ornamented passages, either the first or last note corresponds to the original version. The ornaments themselves do not seem very inspired and comprise a limited repertory of stereotyped patterns, labeled variously as "elegant," "colored," "spicy meat," or "meat seasoned with salt and mustard."

Now, the art of diminution represents one of Coclico's justifiable claims to novelty. Along with the art of improvising counterpoint on a given tune, an art that is closely connected to ornamented cadences, this practice raises the musician to the rank of poet. Such an artist not only creates music by extemporary procedure, but also delights the audience with the beauty of his voice and with the artistry of his voluptuous ornamentation. He becomes an orator. This implicit idea prefigures the mature phase of Mannerism when the virtuoso singer reigns supreme. Because of the breath control and sheer physical vigor required by excessive embellishment, boy sopranos and falsettists are quickly supplanted by female singers and a new phenomenon, the male castrato. It is significant that the castrato first appears in the Papal Chapel in 1562. The subsequent craze for this voice type, a fad that invades baroque opera, can be attributed to the mannerist love of artificiality and stylization.[3]

Apart from furnishing evidence for the new social prominence of solo singers, Vicenzo Giustiniani makes other interesting observations in his book. He notes the growing emphasis on solo singing and the development of a musical style tailor-made for professional display; these phenomena produce a milieu in which connoisseurs have been transformed into appreciative listeners for a new class of wonderful singers. Giustiniani concludes that music has reached an unusual and almost new perfection.[4] This short statement reveals yet another facet of mannerist aesthetics: refinement whose zenith of perfection is both novel and startling. Manneristic stress on elegant stylization in singing also emerges from Giustiniani's comments on singers. After describing the styles of specific virtuosos, such as the men from Naples, the famous *concerto delle donne* in Ferrara,[5] Roman and Florentine singers (especially Vittoria Archilei),[6] Giustiniani offers a very pertinent comment: it is possible for a singer to have a poor voice and a graceful style.[7] In typical mannerist fashion, he attributes *maniera* to natural talent rather than to art.

Giustiniani ascribes the invention of a reformed solo style to Giulio Caccini who, in his words, has abandoned the unpolished and exaggerated embellishments of earlier practice with the result that in Caccini's compositions, the words are clear, and graceful ornaments enhance the poetic thought. Giustiniani concludes this encomium with a general pronouncement—solo style has been so perfected that nothing remains to be added.[8] It is well known that Caccini himself, when writing about solo singing, favored a subtler kind of ornamentation; nonetheless, modern scholars find that his songs frequently embody the mechanical roulades of textbook notoriety.[9]

The appearance of a specialized class of virtuoso singers has important repercussions on the musical scene. Their popularity inspires composers to create a style for their exclusive use. Herein lie the roots of the fabled tyranny of singers. Their demand for dazzling *passaggi* and *gorgie* brings about two changes in the music then being written. On the one hand, composers begin to incorporate ornamental figures into their written style, thereby distorting a balanced polyphonic idiom. This point is made explicit by Giustiniani. And in this regard, we note an assessment made of Luzzasco Luzzaschi's concerted madrigals for the Ferrarese ladies—"among the most extreme examples of the rather tiresome sixteenth-century art of diminution."[10] On the other hand, these singers strongly influence composers of unaccompanied polyphonic madrigals. Florid diminutions penetrate the texture of the works of Giaches de Wert's eighth book (1586) as well as Benedetto Pallavicino's fourth book (1588). For the same reason, Claudio Monteverdi explores free dissonances in the florid sections of his madrigals from the fourth book on. Both the sociological and the musical prominence of virtuoso singers are such that every pupil aspires to fame, and the ensuing educational crisis is solved by the rationalization of "spontaneous" ornaments in instruction manuals. This rash of books reduces an inspired and improvised art into a pedantic and often ludicrous system of technical excesses.[11] The parallels to art and literature are striking.

Ornamentation provides two salient influences on the development of mannerist style; first, the rise of virtuoso singers, whose startling acrobatics satisfy the current love of *effetti meravigliosi*; and second, the use of an array of iconoclastic dissonances that drastically alter the traditional rules of counterpoint. It is true that diminution and dissonances in instrumental music also help the incipient definition of a new musical language. But the most audacious features in instrumental harmony are linked sociologically as well as musically to vocal style. Furthermore, the development of instrumental music is by and large not impeded by the opposition of conservative theory, whereas the conflict between old and new styles takes place in the realm of vocal music, and especially, the mannerist madrigal. At first, the improvised art of ornamentation does not figure prominently in the controversy over unorthodox music. Most theorists, like Zarlino, are content to caution against overly florid embellishments.[12] But when the techniques of *gorgia* are absorbed into the vocabulary of written *concertato* style, the battle lines are clearly drawn. Critics such as Giovanni Maria Artusi in effect fight a rearguard action against modern practice. And my thesis posits that this *maniera*, and all it entails, helps transform the *ars perfecta* of the Renaissance into the various styles and genres associated with the Baroque.

The literature dealing with ornamentation presents a confusing picture of vaguely defined terms, ambiguous usage, and even indiscriminate mixture of performance media. Most treatises of the late sixteenth century explain extremely elaborate and difficult figures that dissolve notes of the original melody into brilliant runs and turns of all kinds. Although these ornaments adhere to principles similar to those described by Coclico, they make his illustrations seem like child's play. This situation is evident in one of the earliest manuals written by Girolamo della Casa, a singing teacher, a manual describing improvised trills (*groppi*), tremolos (*trilli*), and the more extravagant art of coloratura *passaggi*.[13] Giovanni Bassano's precepts and examples further demonstrate the growing virtuosity of ornamentation that now includes dotted rhythms and wide leaps.[14] Lodovico Zacconi stresses the importance of sweet and effective rendering by singers whose artistry makes good composition all the more enjoyable. In his view, the most modern and perfect composers write in a style that allows singers to display their enticing wares. And these wares consist of vocal embellishments. His examples of *gorgia* technique range from simple intervallic fillers (*accenti*) to elaborate twisting runs (*vaghi*). Zacconi also makes a significant statement to the effect that in his day, singers win public favor and professional esteem only if they are masters of this art.[15]

After 1592, writings in this field concentrate almost exclusively on solo virtuosity. Singers may change one voice from a polyphonic complex to a highly ornate version sung with instruments, or they may compose their own melodies for this purpose. This dual method is made clear in the title of Giovanni Luca Conforto's treatise.[16] A falsetto singer himself, Conforto naturally propagates his personal technique, and his excessive *gorgia* style, which even entails harmonic alterations, is attacked as an abuse by Giustiniani.[17] Rampant complexities in the new dazzling style of ornamentation are also amply illustrated in Giovanni Battista Bovicelli's work. Even though this writer talks about tasteful application of ornaments, his extreme examples fall into the category of showpieces. It is also interesting to note that Bovicelli is the first theorist to attempt a description of accelerated tempo in *trilli, groppetti,* and *passaggi.*[18] Because of the intricacy involved in these types of ornaments, Adriano Banchieri stipulates that *gorgie* must be used only in solo singing with instrumental accompaniment. He introduces an element of systematization by dividing the techniques of *gorgia* into two kinds: *accenti* and *fioretti,* corresponding to simple and complicated ornaments.[19]

My purpose in describing briefly the preceding handbooks is not to give a history of ornamentation, but rather to provide a context for evaluating the innovations featured in Caccini's system.[20] The very fact that his publication comprises newly composed monodies for solo voice and instrumental accompaniment is sufficient reason for calling it *New Music.* But the mannerist ideal of novelty goes deeper. Caccini states that his purpose is to reveal the secrets of the noble manner, or style, of singing, a manner forgotten by singers and composers alike in their inordinate love of running divisions that only maim the music.[21] He also wishes to rectify the confusion surrounding the proper way to perform *trilli, gruppi, esclamazioni,* and *il crescere o scemare della voce.* Caccini further indicates that from discussions he heard in Giovanni de'Bardi's Camerata, he came to realize that polyphony puts the text in a subordinate position, lacerating the poetry and ruining the *concetto* of the verse. Even solo songs of his time are deficient

because they submerge the text beneath a proliferation of divisions. The vulgar love this style. By inference, refined connoisseurs
find it boring and inexpressive. His precepts are aimed at remedy-
ing both ills, ills that reflect a state of decadence.

First of all, Caccini tackles the aesthetic premise of his new
style, the *nobile sprezzatura del canto*. From a compositional viewpoint, it relies on novel treatment of dissonances in the melody.
From the viewpoint of performance practice, it posits new criteria
for the use of ornaments. Florid ornaments, such as *gorgie* and
the like, which belie the passions and only tickle the ear, must be
carefully restricted to the lighter sentiments, and even in such
cases, they are acceptable only on long syllables and at cadences.
On the other hand, short ornaments, such as *accenti*, contribute to
a passionate manner of singing that is appropriate for serious and
affective verse. Caccini also mentions in passing that his songs
are considered superior to solo versions of polyphonic madrigals.
From his comments, we can conclude that *sprezzatura* arises from
his personal style (*maniera*) of using written and spontaneous dissonances. The term indicates, moreover, that Caccini realizes his
dissonance treatment does not adhere to the rules of counterpoint.
Nobile sprezzatura imbues this novel technical feature with a noble
aesthetic idea—expressing the conceits and the passions of the
text without undue excesses.

Of course, Caccini's new style of monodic composition should
be matched by a noble manner of singing, a *maniera* that also entails *sprezzatura*. According to this ideal, the singer must alter
note values and rhythmic patterns in infinitesimal ways to suit the
conceits of the words. With this subtle practice, he achieves an
excellence that arises from graceful negligence. He must also cultivate clear intonation as well as a natural rather than a feigned
voice; these two skills allow the singer to vary dynamics and
tempo, both of which are important elements of Caccini's ornamentation practice. Caccini concludes with the comment that
feigned voices can never attain the noble manner of singing. Until
recently, this passage has drawn insufficient attention. One aspect
of *sprezzatura* is identified correctly as the difficult art of rhythmic
and dynamic flexibility, an art that frees the singer from the written notes. But the other aspect of the noble manner of singing

refers to a new way of producing the voice.[22] This fundamental innovation abandons the falsetto in favor of the natural full voice, known today as the "mid-voice." The mid-voice possesses a ring and brilliance ordinarily lacking in the falsetto, or feigned voice as Caccini calls it, as well as a natural vibrato that facilitates uniform control over the singer's entire register. The point is that in Caccini's day, the noble manner of singing required a very striking and contrived voice type. In the context of his time, the *nobile maniera di cantare* represents a delightful mannerist novelty.

Caccini's exposition of desirable ornaments, then, depends on this new element of the poised mid-voice. Apart from this element of mannerist novelty, his description of some embellishments also reveals mannerist values. For instance, Caccini lists two accepted manners of stylized intonation. The first entails beginning a third below the note and rising up to it, a technique corresponding to improvised *accenti*.[23] Caccini rejects it on two counts: it produces indiscriminate dissonances and, more important, it has become a tedious commonplace. The second manner entails beginning on the note itself and then increasing its dynamic level. Caccini recommends this method because it is still relatively unusual. At this point, Caccini admits that he always searches for novelty that delights and moves the affections. He therefore suggests yet a third way of intoning. In this manner, one sings the note and then immediately decreases its dynamic level. The element of surprise should be obvious. And Caccini makes this clear in stressing that if one sings softer on the initial intonation, a subsequent increase in dynamics then appears extremely passionate. In Caccini's system, *l'esclamazione* is one of the principal devices for moving the affections, and its efficacy is greatly augmented when it follows his third manner of intonation. Clearly, these effects require a voice of considerable flexibility, and Caccini comments that crescendos are particularly insufferable in falsetto voices. It is equally evident that his new ornaments are based on mannerist values.

Caccini's noble style of solo songs brings up the subject of theories of monody and the circles from which they emanate. Conceptions of monody and their relationship to early opera form a perplexing network of notions that bespeaks a highly experimental and fluid milieu. Technical, aesthetic, and sociological problems are further exacerbated by the petty rivalry of not one, but three, identifiable groups in Florence.[24] The earliest of these is the Camerata proper, a typically mannerist academy that congregates at Bardi's home between roughly 1575 and 1582. This informal salon, composed of Giovanni de' Bardi himself, Vincenzo Galilei, Piero Strozzi, and Ottavio Rinuccini, indulges in casual discussions on science, poetry, astrology, and of course, music. In the latter field, these men concentrate on solo monody as the means whereby it is possible to revive the marvelous effects of ancient music.

The gist of the Camerata's views can be gleaned from Bardi's letter to Caccini. Like all champions of new music, Bardi starts with a rejection of established style. After citing Plato's definition of music and the innumerable marvelous effects described by ancient authors, Bardi dismisses sixteenth-century polyphony in terms which are remarkably similar to those employed by Galilei. The art of good singing, by implication far superior to counterpoint, comprises ensemble or solo performance. For ensembles, Bardi recommends blending the voices, ornamentation in strict time, and a reserved style of production. He does not describe the music, but one can suppose that he refers to *contrapunto commune*. The soloist, of course, may take liberties with tempo and rhythm. These liberties should serve the noblest aim of the singer —to express exactly the affections of the song with all the suavity and sweetness he can muster. *Dolcezza* in voice and melody represents the most important aesthetic foundation of good singing, and in Bardi's estimation, Caccini is unsurpassed in this regard.[25] The remarks of this patron suggest two things about the Camerata's ideal. First, its members wish to vindicate solo melody for its own sake, and second, they wish to vindicate the sweet voluptuousness of the solo voice. Admonitions for correct prosody and declamation take on secondary importance, because the very medium of solo singing without elaborate *gorgie* ensures textual clarity. We can conclude, therefore, that pure recitative style and striking dramatic quality do not figure prominently in the kind of monody prized by Bardi and his colleagues.

Bardi's letter also reveals another fundamental theme in the talks of the Camerata—namely, the dispute between the relative merits of ancient and modern style. Whereas earlier mannerists abide by the belief that their stylistic refinements raise polyphony to that level of affective power characteristic of ancient music, the Camerata stands for outright rejection of counterpoint on the grounds that it cannot even approximate this fabled excellence. The main source for this viewpoint, the last in a line of progressive ideologies, is the great humanist, Girolamo Mei. Mei had many academic affiliations, among them the Accademia degli Alterati.[26] His approach to music departs from the premises of aristotelian *mimesis*. What is most interesting is that Mei adopts this notion in conscious opposition to Zarlino and his followers, whose theories stress numerical proportions as the common link between nature and music. In effect, Mei rejects this concept by defining musical imitation in terms of rhetoric. The very fact that polyphony must obey the laws of sonorous number renders it incapable of imitating the passions. And this superior goal can be attained only by the solo song. Palisca characterizes Mei's influence with the following statement: "In a time of experiment, uncertain esthetics and academicism, Mei ignited the imagination of the influential men of Bardi's Camerata and inspired them to refashion the languishing and casual salon art of monody in the image of a noble and cultivated art of the past."[27] The above quotation, admirable in its summation of the monodist approach, alerts us to the mannerist premise behind it—self-conscious stylization.

Galilei was first apprised of Mei's research into ancient music in 1572, and the two men corresponded between that date and 1599.[28] Mei's patient letters eventually turned Galilei into an acrid critic of Zarlino and an ardent exponent of monody. The fruits of his labors finally appeared in a somewhat garbled version in Galilei's *Dialogo della musica antica e della moderna* (1581). In the course of his letters, Mei describes the techniques whereby ancient solo song expressed and aroused the passions; in addition to fidelity to the metric structure of Greek verse, this music utilized the three ranges of the human voice and the three degrees of rhythmic motion. In fact, the effective deployment of these elements constituted the ethos of the ancient modes, so greatly misunderstood by contemporary musicians. Furthermore, the Greeks recognized three modes of melodic composition, modes which were allied to three styles: the grand manner proper for elevated effects; the restrained manner appropriate for love and lamentation; and the serene manner for tranquil, hymnlike effects.[29]

Galilei transforms Mei's quiet scholarship into a petulant polemic against polyphony. His negative attack is telling, but his description of monody lacks both originality and systematic organization. Reflecting the general views of the Camerata, Galilei neglects the problem of tragedy recited to music and stresses monody as a vehicle for natural declamation and beautiful melody. He first cites Plutarch's comment that the modes must relate to the affections of the words, and then remarks that music was invented in ancient times for one sole reason—to express the conceits of the soul with great efficacy.[30] By itself, this statement is hardly remarkable and merely echoes earlier mannerist mottoes concerning imitative-affective music. But Galilei continues to the effect that in ancient music this aim was attained by the exploitation of the solo voice accompanied by the lyre or cithara.[31] It is at this point that Galilei's argument diverges from the mannerist aesthetic of the polyphonic madrigal. He notes that ancient poets and musicians were usually one and the same, and that performers recited their verse to an improvised melody. Galilei readily admits that this custom still exists in his day in the solo recitation of poetry with the support of a lute or keyboard instrument.[32] However, one receives the distinct impression that this type of improvised performance is not very highly rated by Galilei. This theorist really wishes to restore the place within *res facta* improperly usurped by counterpoint to the composition of melody. Modern counterpoint operates on the worthless principle of pleasing the ear and thus has lost the marvelous effects of ancient vocal practice. Galilei does not deny that some elements of ancient harmony survive in contemporary counterpoint; however, they have been debased by a false and pernicious aesthetic. The attempts of more radical style (i.e. the imitative-affective madrigal) to express the text are at best puerile. For these reasons, learned men of superior judgment prefer the simplicity, virility, and gravity of the solo song.[33] So much for Galilei's aesthetic view.

As for practical advise to contemporary songwriters, Galilei recommends that they imitate classical orators whose art can be discerned, to some extent, in modern performances of spoken drama. If the composer ignores the immoderate laughter of actors, and instead observes their graceful manner of using voice ranges, accents, gestures, and rhythms to portray character, he then penetrates the secrets of ancient style.[34] Here it seems that Galilei is arguing for increased dramatization in the vocal medium. But the full implications of his notion are not realized until the first essays in the *dramma per musica*, a genre in which Galilei shows no interest whatsoever. In the chamber monodies cultivated by the Camerata, we can discern two incipiently divergent styles; but the distinction between them becomes clear in the seventeenth century. One style, called the solo madrigal, stays close to the imitative-affective devices of through-composed, affective music, and it uses many of the devices associated with the much-denigrated madrigal. The other style, the aria, is a strophic song in which beauty of melody takes precedence over recitative principles. From the context of his entire treatise, we conclude that Galilei militates for rejuvenating the second style. This is the implication of his statement to the effect that in ancient times, harmony meant the beautiful and graceful procedure of the aria of the song.[35]

Partly from mannerist arrogance and partly for polemic reasons, champions of monody claim they are the first musicians to have discovered the true nature of ancient music. Exponents of traditional counterpoint are cast in the ungrateful role of pedantic reactionaries who base their rules on ignorance and poor scholarship. Of course, monodists fail to see that their own interpretation of how one revives ancient practice is just as fanciful. And because Zarlino seems to be the most respected figure among conservatives in the last half of the century, he automatically becomes a target for ridicule by the radicals. His critics conveniently overlook those portions of his treatise that demonstrate the depth of Zarlino's humanist learning and musical sensitivity.

Zarlino presents quite a perceptive comparison between ancient and modern styles. At the outset, he repeats the traditional notion of progress leading to the music of his day. Ancient music was predicated on simple and somewhat crude principles; its theoretical literature shows that it suffered from an impoverishment of consonances. Because modern counterpoint contains more consonances, it naturally embodies great heights of refinement in the development of musical vocabulary. It is the perfect art to which nothing can be added. From this historical fact alone, Zarlino believes that one can deduce the imperfection of ancient harmony.[36] After a digression on Pythagoras,[37] Zarlino brings up the paradox that prompts so many mannerist experiments. If ancient music was so imperfect, his readers may find it impossible to believe that it could imitate vivid affections as recounted in classical sources. And he freely admits that modern polyphony, in spite of its musical perfection, does not produce such marvelous effects as those credited to ancient music. How does one, then, resolve these incompatible facts? Zarlino proposes to proceed from the thesis that ancient music did indeed express the passions in a manner unknown to modern style. And this despite the imperfection of the former and the perfection of the latter.[38]

Zarlino builds up his argument by first describing ancient practice. Greek musicians used solo melody. They recited their tragedies and comedies to musical song; dance and mime took place at the same time as this recitation, and instruments were chosen to suit the mood of the scenes.[39] At this point Zarlino cannot refrain from throwing a dart in the direction of mannerist pride: modern upstarts who base their cult of fame on their imitation of ancient style are guilty of gross temerity. The stupidity of their notions is shown by the incontrovertible fact that modern counterpoint cannot paint warlike weapons, nor move the listener to violent or peaceful feelings and actions. However, this mistaken view does not mean that both ancient and modern praise of Greek music as an eloquent art is unjustified. Lest his readers conclude that ancient marvelous effects are purely fictitious, Zarlino examines the grounds for their existence. He isolates four elements and stresses that all four must be present in musical composition in order for it to imitate and arouse the passions. The first is melodic harmony, the mathematically sonorous deployment of intervals. The second, number, is determined by the verse and is therefore called meter. Narration of a story, which depicts customs and characters, comprises the third element; it can be referred to as speech or oration. And the fourth requirement is a well-disposed subject whose nature responds to musical recitation and submits to the arousal of passions.[40]

Having listed the four cardinal elements of ancient art, Zarlino can now make his point. Because modern polyphony depends solely on harmony, it is incapable of producing extrinsic effects. Harmony may dispose the mind to experiencing certain intrinsic, general affects, such as gaiety or sadness. However, beautiful counterpoint, which imitates the numerical harmony of nature, only arouses a feeling of pleasure in its proportions.[41] These statements represent the crux of Zarlino's aesthetic concerning the perfect art. It imitates the inner laws of nature and thus affords noble pleasure. The affective qualities of modes and harmonies that he describes elsewhere only contribute to a vague emotional appeal. Therefore, attempts within this style to depict and arouse concrete images and objective affections are misplaced; they only distort the perfection of polyphony.[42]

Zarlino goes on to say that when a polyphonic composition combines harmony and meter, it acquires a more obvious ability to move the soul. This situation pertains to the dance which adds extrinsic bodily movements to the intrinsic motion of harmony and meter. The next step, of course, is to unite harmony, meter, and oration. In this instance, the composition expresses character by recounting a story or historical theme. Zarlino avers that it is impossible to estimate the expressive force of this tripartite fusion (in effect, the *dramma per musica*) because it is nonexistent in modern practice. Finally, he notes that the composition must strike a sympathetic chord in the listener's emotional makeup. Harmony alone can incline the soul to happy or sad moods. Metrical rhythm doubles music's affective power. One assumes that Zarlino would grant more concrete passions to stylized dances on the grounds that their metrical structure suggests unseen movements.[43] However, he insists that these two elements by themselves cannot generate extrinsic passions. This power belongs to oration. Thus, the marvelous effects of ancient musical style depend on melody, the principal medium of oration.[44]

The views presented above should not be interpreted to mean that Zarlino rejects the affective power of all contemporary music. On the contrary, he admits that one kind of modern music can move the affections as did ancient music. To be precise, *effetti meravigliosi* occur when beautiful, learned, and elegant verse is recited by a soloist to the sound of an instrument. The listeners are then moved deeply and inspired to tears, laughter, and so on. As a concrete example, Zarlino cites the recitation of Ariosto's poetry. Ancient music operated in the same way—that is, spontaneous monodic recitation based on formulas. Zarlino also notes that careless composers produce polyphony without any effects at all. They forget that meticulous declamation can give this style a measure of ancient dignity and power.[45] This is the reason he stresses the rules for correct text underlay. But he does not equate this requirement with the dramatic representation of concrete passions. If the latter objective means the destruction of sound contrapuntal procedures, then Zarlino rejects it out of hand. His thesis rests on the eminently reasonable assumption that *effetti meravigliosi*, admirable in their own right, belong properly to the province of the solo recitation of a narrative. Their presence in ancient music or modern song has nothing to do with the perfection of polyphony.

This view is made explicit in the work Zarlino wrote answering Galilei's blistering critique. In it he points out that monodists attack counterpoint on two counts: its mixture of musical elements and its self-sufficient rules governing these mixtures. In Zarlino's opinion, however, these procedures are necessary for good contrapuntal writing; they are inherent in the craft. He further points out that in his first treatise, he emphasized that the composer must never neglect the text. He meant to say that within the limits of reason, harmony and number are servants of the words. Therefore, Galilei's criticism is both one-sided and unfair. Zarlino repeats his contention that the marvelous effects of ancient style were related to the solo song, and thus do not in any way vitiate the perfections of modern polyphony. Furthermore, Galilei's advice to composers to imitate orators and actors has nothing to do with counterpoint or even with beautiful melody in song. His recommendation is viable only for the recitation of a dramatic subject.[46] In a way, Zarlino's comments underscore the confusion evident in Galilei's discussion of monody. They certainly establish Zarlino as a perspicacious theorist of musical styles.

Moderation and sanity in public debates of this period constitute poor weapons for contending with impassioned and flamboyant tactics. As the mannerist belief in progress gains momentum, theorists of radical persuasions can afford to be more and more daring. Thus, a truly avant-garde movement at the turn of the century promulgates a new *maniera* without suffering the fate that hounded Bartoloméo Ramos de Pareja 100 years earlier. Galilei and his cohorts support monody, a new style no longer conceived as a mild or even an extreme distortion of the old, but rather as a complete departure from it that relegates old style to oblivion. Though many musicians acknowledge the existence of two practices, their value judgments imply that traditional counterpoint has degenerated into academic craft, the study of which is restricted to students. After thorough mastery of a closed language with finite rules, the student then tries his hand at modern style, a style that presents a different kind of challenge to his genius and inspiration.

The quarrel between ancient and modern music is a complicated affair informed by variegated notions of history and progress. The dichotomy outlined above involves two ideas: first, that ancient music comprises a reputedly perfect art whose scientific premises are no longer alive; and second, that modern music embodies the potential for unlimited progress to true perfection. If we shift the terms of reference back a few decades, we observe a different set of opposites. Generally speaking, modern music can mean the perfect art, radical chromaticism, or solo monody; conversely, ancient music can refer to old-fashioned counterpoint, medieval music, or the music of classical Greece and Rome. However, below this patchwork of ideas there runs one persistent thread. All concepts of historic-stylistic progress culminating in some form of new and perfect art are based on notions about revising, equaling, and surpassing the glories of antiquity. This attitude, together with the opposition it occasionally engenders, survives in the baroque period, and well beyond it.

Although the works of Giovanni Battista Doni lie for the most part outside the chronological limits of the mannerist period, many of his views reflect, either directly or indirectly, the theoretical and practical controversies of that time. I cite first of all his dissident view of modern superiority over classical music, a view explicated in detail in his *De praestantia musicae veteris* (1647). The attributes given by Doni to ancient singers (e.g., good voices, marvelous ornamentation, elegance, and suavity)[47] are precisely those claimed for modern music by proponents of mannerist nov-elties in both polyphonic and monodic styles. Doni's negative opinion aims at destroying the reputation of modern progress, and his list of composers who believe in such progress as well as his description of specific details of a musical nature amount to a catalog of mannerist musicians and mannerist tendencies in com-position and performance.[48]

Doni's analytical rigor yields fruitful results when he turns his attention to the newest styles and genres. As a humanist scholar with considerable knowledge of ancient culture, Doni is fascinated particularly by the phenomenon of opera, a genre that tries to fuse poetry, drama, and music in a manner similar to ancient repre-sentation. Of special interest is his tripartite division of monodic styles.[49] Narrative monody, with its small intervals and rapid rhythmic configurations imitating speech patterns, represents the most straightforward style of the three. Recitational monody re-sembles the style given to heroic poems. Doni notes that its fre-quent cadences create a monotonous effect; Giustiniani makes a similar comment.[50] The affective elements in melody and harmony characteristic of the third kind, expressive monody, are reserved for moments of great pathos. All three can be taken as musical stylizations of oratorical or histrionic mannerisms. They therefore adhere to one point in Galilei's advice to monodists. And they demonstrate yet another aspect of mannerist aesthetics in that they omit arias, or strophic songs. The reason for this omission, one that strengthens the monodists' cause, resides in the fact that arias embody the same self-sufficient musical logic that supports tradi-tional counterpoint.

Systematic aesthetics of opera in independent writings do not surface until the Baroque. The early cameratas of Jacopo Corsi and Emilio de'Cavalieri concentrate on practical experiments and not on abstract theorizing. In view of this situation, literary hu-manists provide the first major sources. Notions linking music to poetry and drama with references to aristotelian catharsis and *mimesis* begin in the mid-sixteenth century. Later, theorists of the new mannerist epic and pastoral acknowledge the utility of music in these genres. Furthermore, readings of pastoral poems, such as *Il pastor fido*, always feature incidental music in the form of polyphonic choruses, dances, instrumental interludes, and even solo songs. Of course, we are not dealing with a completely musical presentation of a dramatic poem. But both the pastoral and epic genres constitute one stream that leads eventually to the *opera in musica*. In addition to setting a precedent for the use of music, their structures are fused in early operatic librettos.

The other important influence on early operatic experiments comes from humanist research into the nature of ancient drama. Although Francesco Patrizi belongs to an antiaristotelian minority, his criticism of the confusion present in Aristotle's definition of *mimesis* illustrates the commonplace sixteenth-century interpretations of this topic. Patrizi finds no less than six different meanings of imitation, four of which are relevant to our discussion. The second one refers to depicting concrete and vivid images (*enargeia*); he does not mention that this ideal animates the mannerist madrigal. When an imitated action is put on the stage, the fourth kind of imitation results—the dramatic presentation of real action. Such imitation, of course, also relates to opera. As an extension of the fourth one, Patrizi lists a fifth kind of imitation, that found in narrative poetry. And this kind of imitation has a profound influence on various musical genres that set such texts. Finally, musical imitation itself comprises a sixth kind; Patrizi here refers to singing narrative poetry or actual drama.[51] Through the media of academic discussion and humanist books, these notions circulate widely in learned and dilettante circles. And we must recognize the significance of this situation insofar as early opera is encouraged by this segment of society. Patrons and amateurs of music are the persons who prompt professional poets and musicians to experiment with a novel musico-poetic form. And by its very nature, the *dramma per musica* appeals to the same sophisticated lovers of mannerist refinements who previously enjoyed the eccentricities of the polyphonic madrigal.

We should also note that private academies play an important role in fostering revivals of the ancient manner of presenting drama. For example, the members of the Accademia degli Alterati had a scholarly interest in music as well as the four other liberal arts: grammar, rhetoric, dialectic, and poetry. The idea of including music in an expanded trivium is not entirely new. But the conviction of this group that music and rhetoric imitate and express the affections has a tangible influence on certain members of the academy who will champion monody and opera—Bardi, Corsi, and Rinuccini.[52] There can be no doubt that these men transfer ideas from the academy into their own groups where they are put into practice by professional musicians.

With respect to Bardi's Camerata, we can glean its high reputation from a document left to us by his son, Pietro de'Bardi.[53] The elder Bardi's list of accomplishments is impressive: he encouraged Galilei's studies of ancient theory as well as his first solo performances, Caccini's monodies, as well as Rinuccini's and Peri's *Dafne*.[54] Pietro also gives Corsi credit for supporting novel operatic style, and cites Monteverdi as the greatest living composer of opera. Research into the elder Bardi's life has shown that he ceased to be active in Florentine circles after 1592. Nevertheless, Caccini pays him a supreme tribute by dedicating to him the publication of his *Euridice*. Animated by jealousy because Peri was commissioned to compose Rinuccini's text through Corsi's influence, Caccini wrote his own score and rushed it into print in order to claim the distinction of being the composer of the first published opera on record. Copies rolled off the press one day after the premiere of Peri's version. In the dedication, Caccini indicates that the style of his opera derives from his earlier work on the solo madrigal. Like these monodies, the voice parts of his opera are to be performed with *sprezzatura*, the noble manner of singing. Caccini cannot refrain from pointing out that his style embodies the improvised practice of Vittoria Archilei, who sang the title role in his rival's opera.[55]

Peri subsequently published his score in 1601, and his dedication is more informative for students of early operatic theory.[56] Peri attributes his inspiration to the knowledge that classical tragedies were recited throughout, in a style that was more melodic than plain speech and less melodic than song. To arrive at his own *stile recitativo*, Peri quickened the melodic movement so that it lay in between the leisurely pace of song and the swift motion of speech. A study of speech patterns also revealed to him an important and useful feature. Some words are so intoned that in setting them to music the composer can base a harmony on them. Others are amenable to quick passage on the same harmony (complete with dissonances) until the composer reaches another word that can support a new consonant harmony. Using this characteristic as a basis for the *basso continuo* part, the composer thus arrives at a flexible system paralleling the nature of the words. This alternation between intoned and nonintoned words effectively reproduces the passionate accents of speech. It follows, therefore, that if musical style reflects verbal style, it too will express affective qualities. The procedure outlined by Peri also avoids the feature of having the melody dance to the movement of the bass, a defect that Peri notices in Caccini's recitative. At cheerful or gay moments in the libretto, the composer may use pure song style; but grave and sad passages must be set in *stile recitativo*. Peri concludes that his recitative may not be equivalent to ancient recitation, but it is the only one possible in modern music that sets dramatic poetry.

Peri is proud to indicate that his style has pleased learned gentlemen as well as professional composers and eminent singers, such as Vittoria Archilei. This comment perhaps represents an oblique apology for those listeners who disliked the opera. Peri also has the generosity to admit that in the performance itself, Euridice's solo airs as well as a few choruses were provided by Caccini.[57] However, he does wish to point out that his opera was composed and performed before Caccini's appeared in print.

Both Peri's and Caccini's dedications demonstrate the continuing vitality of mannerist aesthetics and attitudes. Their works are the productions of musical genius inspired by humanist notions. Both make claims to ingenious novelty based on the idea of reviving and surpassing ancient *effetti meravigliosi*. Performed in the rarefied atmosphere of one of the most sophisticated courts of Europe, their settings of Rinuccini's dramatic pastoral represent the culmination of the *cinquecento*'s craving for startling rhetorical devices in music. As works of art, their operas stand on their own intrinsic merits. As cultural documents, they cannot be isolated from the mainstream of musical Mannerism. And the acrid personal rivalry between the two men attests to their acute self-consciousness and their desire to garner priority in posterity's historical hindsights.

Maniera

The term *maniera* in musical theory entails a fusion of technical and aesthetic ideas which influence the evolution of concepts of style. One scholar correctly points out that the history of *maniera* as a technical term in music has yet to be investigated.[1] The same may be said of its history as an ideal of style. This chapter bypasses specific problems of interpretation and concentrates instead on cases where the stylistic implications of *maniera* are clear.[2] In view of the interrelationship between style concepts and topics such as history, artistic values, genius, and composition, the reader will notice some duplication of material found in previous chapters. At the same time, these topics can serve to illuminate and reinforce a more narrow focus on *maniera*.

The absolute meaning of *maniera*—that is, poise, elegant deportment, or style—prevails throughout the fifteenth and sixteenth centuries. Implicit in the initially social concept is the idea of refined preciosity and artificial etiquette. And exaggeration of this aspect occurs naturally in the sophisticated atmosphere of mannerist life-styles. It is significant that in music the term *maniera* first appears in fifteenth-century dance manuals, and its import derives directly from social conventions. Domenico da Piacenza lists five abilities that mark the good dancer: *mesura* (a sense of musical rhythm), *memoria* (memorized steps), *maniera* (fluid and moderate bodily motion), *mesura di terreno* (patterned arrangement on a floor space), and *aiere* (alternation between movement and repose).[3] Piacenza's ideal is one of gentility, cultivation, and elegant artistry. His pupil, Antonio Cornazano, includes the same requirements plus a sixth one, *diversità di cose* (great variety of steps), and thereby hints at the future mannerist emphasis on prolific ornamentation. But it is Cornazano's interpretation of *maniera* that points to facets of this concept destined to become associated with mannerist style. He defines *maniera* as the intensive swaying of the body, both from side to side as well as up and down. In Cornazano's view, *maniera* adds grace to the dance.[4] The most famous dancing master of the time, Guglielmo Ebreo, presents a list of six abilities similar to that of Cornazano. Under *aiere*, Ebreo discusses light and graceful motion of the body in rising and falling cadences. *Maniera*, on the other hand, refers to the turning of the body from side to side.[5] In spite of minor differences, the general unanimity of the three treatises is pronounced, and demonstrates that from the very beginning, *maniera* denotes gracefully improvised decoration for a form of courtly entertainment. Although these writers talk of *maniera* in terms of a refined adornment, an artificial stylization of gesture, the ties between *maniera* in the dance and a social code of high-class civility remain strong. When the term is resurrected in musical writings of the sixteenth century, after a hiatus of some sixty or seventy years, it appears in a different framework, one informed by notions of historical progress and artistic value.

Whereas *maniera* in the dance represents a natural extension of an ideal of civilized behavior, *maniera* in the visual arts arises from an intellectual adaptation of its original import. In this context, it takes on other meanings, and its absolute sense becomes adulterated by the typically renaissance view of cultural history. *Bella maniera* now functions as an ideal for good art, based on the model of antiquity. By inference, its opposite lacks the primary trait of this ideal, *grazia*, and for this reason, it is called *cattiva maniera*. The technical elements that produce *bella maniera* are the mathematical proportions of music translated into geometry, anatomy, and perspective. We have noted that classical harmony has both philosophical and practical repercussions for renaissance art. On the practical side, it fosters the art of design, and this art admits both realistic imitation and eclectic idealization of nature. The latter, of course, is seen as a type of decorative trope, one that will be increasingly stressed in the mannerist period. Surpassing nature in search of elegant and graceful *maniera* will change to distorting nature in search of novel and bizarre *maniera*.

Musical theorists in the Renaissance take for granted the secure place of music in the liberal arts and the tradition of master-pupil education. Harking back to classical models seems unnecessary inasmuch as both theoretical and practical sides of music remain vital inheritances from the Middle Ages. And it also seems unnecessary to investigate stylistic premises in any detail because such matters are relatively simple and are learned from practical experience. Furthermore, theorists overlook the fact that speculative systems do not coincide with practice. As we have seen, the most revolutionary theories of this period are put forward by Bartoloméo Ramos de Pareja. His awareness of contemporary style prompts his exposition of radical ideas, ideas condemned by his conservative colleagues. Most pertinent to the present topic is Ramos's formulation of a general concept of musical expressivity in terms of happy or sad styles. Because this concept takes as its point of departure the text being set to music, it signals the eventual emergence of mannerist aesthetics.

In summing up this transitional phase of musical thought, I stress one point. A few writers adumbrate stylistic concepts when attempting to view their contemporary practice in some sort of historical continuum. But these attempts are sporadic at best, and the relationship between such notions and methodologies of prescriptive rules for composition is vague and unsystematic. In none of these writings does a clear and dominating concept of style emerge as a central focus.

Between 1520 and 1540, artistic theory experiences a lull. In the field of literary theory, on the other hand, three important ideas come to the fore, ideas that will be favorite themes later in the century. Poetry and music are linked as arts with the power to influence the passions, and this ideal of eloquence accentuates rhetoric as a common element in both arts. Writers also evince an interest in the lyric genre, whose aim is to please. To this end, it should embody graceful and suave style characterized by sweet and elegant figures of speech. These ideas as yet lack the emphasis on novelty and extravagance found in mannerist aesthetics of literature.

In comparison with the sister arts, musical theory at this time presents many progressive and even radical ideas. Pietro Aaron offers a well-defined distinction between linear counterpoint and integrated polyphony, a distinction that implicitly posits modern musical style as a superior refinement over older style. Furthermore, his examples furnish concrete and practical guidelines for elegant techniques. Thus, contrapuntal theory is transformed into stylistic criticism. And many of Aaron's other progressive concepts can be ascribed to his desire to bring theory more in line with contemporary practice.

By and large, handbooks on musical rudiments tend to explicate conservative doctrine. And yet, we can discern small hints of radical practice even in this area. For example, Biagio Rossetti admits the major semitone as a sweet dissonance; and his authority is modern style. A similar situation obtains in the work of Nicolaus Listenius. Among the progressive ideas in this otherwise ordinary little book, we must count his praise of the *opus perfectum & absolutum*—the first theoretical admission of the benefits of printing. This technology, in effect, allows compositional styles to be disseminated as models for emulation by other musicians. And this is an important sociological impetus behind the stereotyping of mannerist novelties. It also underlies the growing cultivation of fame, because musical works remain accurately recorded for posterity. Listenius exhibits progressive views in connecting hexachordal propriety to harmonic character; in particular, his admission of a mixed category of composition anticipates the new elasticity of mannerist style. And the harmonic audacities of the latter are prefigured in his mutation example, especially its circle-of-fifths organization.

The most radical writer of this period is Giovanni Spataro whose writings do much to enliven the musical scene. Symptomatic of his attitude is his spirited defense of Ramos. Spataro's militant views arise from an understanding not only of contemporary style, but also of coming developments. Seated on the barely marked crossroads from which mannerist style will move in a divergent path away from traditional practice, Spataro sees into the future with sibylline talent. I refer to his ideas about tuning as well as to his aesthetic notions. Spataro insists that art and grace cannot be taught because good composers are born as are poets; inspiration moves the composer to use musical elements that defy the rules. The implications of this statement for mannerist aesthetics cannot be overestimated. Spataro makes a clear distinction between the accepted and commonplace rules of science as opposed to the novel and unusual innovations inspired by individual genius. The first support craft whereas the second permit the unruly and instinctive shaping of personal style.

Vindication of Spataro's position will not come until the full range of musical audacities is explored and exhausted by the mannerist madrigal. The converse situation holds true for theory in the visual arts between 1540 and 1560. In the wake of early mannerist works, theorists begin to formulate aesthetic and technical precepts applicable to the new *maniera*. Even the traditional *paragone* between painting and sculpture reveals some new arguments that betray the influence of incipient mannerist virtuosity. For example, violent foreshortening is exalted because forced and strained poses, corresponding less with nature and more with the intellectual *idea*, exude a mysterious quality of vanquished difficulty. Both sides of this debate tout mental or manual brilliance, the *effetto meraviglioso* worthy of awed admiration.

Artistic theory in this period is dominated by Giorgio Vasari's seminal work, in which he analyzes the worth of individual styles in the light of each artist's historical position. Thus, chronology and artistic value are fused into a concept of cultural history seen as causal progression toward perfection. Vasari constructs stylistic abstractions separated into four epochal *maniere*. In the third of these, artists have developed consummate mastery of technique and medium. Their natural and graceful depiction of nature is so perfect that nothing can be added to the arsenal of scientific knowledge and manual capability. Vasari is faced with the possibility of a decline following this acme. In order to prolong perfection into a timeless ideal, artists can imitate the sweet and grand manners, as Vasari himself suggests; or else they may try to surpass the giants of the perfect art by refining, exaggerating, and distorting their aesthetic principles. Vasari's sensitivity to the mannerist dilemma is substantiated both by artistic practice and by subsequent evaluation of this practice, for historians criticize Mannerism as empty epigonalism or an hyperrefined preciosity and bizarre monumentalism.

Vasari's description of the components of the *bella maniera* shows his realization that this style represents a *summa* of its classical heritage and that, at the same time, its subtle new refinements form the basis for future mannerist trends. These two aspects are seen in a number of dual characteristics that he highlights: mastery of natural proportions as opposed to *sprezzatura*, a quality of graceful negligence and novel spontaneity; clear distinctions among various orders as opposed to abundance and variety of decoration; skill in harmonious measurement as opposed to a tone of polish and elegance that exceeds the rule of proportion. Above all, perfect art possesses *maniera*. This fundamental requisite of stylishness has reached an unprecedented peak of perfection. And from this viewpoint, modern style has equaled and surpassed the glories of ancient art. Vasari's emphasis on *maniera* bespeaks his awareness of the thrust of modern practice. He explains the basis of *bella maniera* as a kind of perfection arising from eclectic procedures. Eclecticism produces a repertory of idealized models that in turn produce a homogeneous base for the artist's personal *maniera*. I take this tenet as a cardinal one for Mannerism. Each artist must find his own inner vision, and then execute it with originality and virtuosity so that people are astounded by his novel style. The emphasis now lies on individualism and inspiration, and according to Vasari, artists may even take as their model the style of another artist.

Now, Vasari sees all this as a natural outcome of progress. His view is not shared by Lodovico Dolce who, under the influence of Pietro Aretino, criticizes Florentine Mannerism. Among the four necessary attributes of good style, argues Dolce, Michelangelo and his vapid imitators excel only in invention and design. Their intellectual virtuosity, lacking in rich naturalistic color and emotional depth, has indeed produced a *maniera*. But this *maniera*, a kind of empty and shallow manneredness, has distorted the revered laws of classical style. It is therefore not a virtue of the perfect art, but rather a vice of *cattiva prattica*. In Dolce's opinion, Venetian style has successfully surpassed ancient ideals by adding refinements that do not disturb traditional principles. The battle lines in the visual arts are now clearly drawn.

Because of a strong antiquarian and scholarly strain, poetic criticism of this period does not demonstrate so lively an interest in contemporary issues. Rampant petrarchism, which has already reached its full stride, finds only faint echoes in theory. Critics are engrossed with explicating ancient ideas and demonstrating their humanistic prowess, as for example, in the controversy over allopathic and homeopathic catharsis. Not quite as learned but more to the point is the discussion of poetry in terms of imitating and moving the affections. This concept reflects an increasing tendency to link poetry and rhetoric, and to claim powerful eloquence for epic and narrative verse. In this regard, poetic rhetoric is seen as directed to pleasing the fantasy or imagination, and it therefore utilizes elevated diction. Although this idea is not as yet related to lyric poetry, its emphasis on style points to a distinctly mannerist propensity. Rhetorical figures of speech are supposed to ensure vivid and realistic imitation, or *enargeia*. But the appearance of criticism against extravagant imagery also suggests that theorists are aware of certain radical trends. Some state that both *maniera* (affected stylization) and *mimesis* (straightforward expression) are necessary elements of imagery. The former produces marvelous effects and novel style. At this point, poetic theory starts down the mannerist pathway.

Writings on music between 1540 and 1560 present us with a striking adjunct to practical matters—the marked bifurcation between radical and conservative styles. The crossroads have been passed. From this time forward, conservative tracts form a secondary body of books that expound traditional topics in blissful ignorance of the musical ferment present in contemporary practice. Progressive writers formulate the precepts of the perfect art in such a way as to make this style relevant to modern music and, more important, to elevate musical perfection into a timeless ideal. Theirs are the theories that clash with a growing number of militant avant-gardists who espouse the cause of new styles that either refine and distort the perfect art, or else depart entirely from its sacrosanct rules.

Because of his critical orientation (in itself an original approach to music), Henricus Glareanus combines analysis of compositional practice with a historical viewpoint. Like Vasari, he charts the rise of modern art and divides its development into four ages. Glareanus's historical outline precedes that of the eminent art critic by some eleven years.[6] When one realizes that no precedent for this approach exists in musical theory, the originality of his departure from established ideas seems even more outstanding. Equally progressive is this theorist's preoccupation with musical style. Glareanus's subtle tools of *phrasis*, *mixtio*, and *commixtio*, related to his new system of twelve modes, become the foundation for evaluating elegant and expressive composition. The latter ideal furnishes, in certain exceptional cases, an excuse for inventive license. But Glareanus's essentially conservative bias emerges from his criticism of contemporary predilection for violent and distorted music. This tendency heralds the decline of the perfect art, in Glareanus's view, and the beginning of mannerist style, in my view. It is true that Glareanus does not use any Latin term that can be construed as equivalent to *maniera*. Nevertheless, his interest in stylistic problems represents the core of his aesthetic, and because his aesthetic addresses expressivity in particular, we must assess Glareanus as a progressive thinker.

A similar goal motivates the work of Adrianus Petit Coclico, who speaks of reviving a lost perfection. This theorist, however, devises his own version of historical progress, one that presents the music of his own generation not as a decline but rather as a further refinement of perfection. In order to teach the precepts of modern music, Coclico proposes a novel system of three related areas: elegant singing, improvised counterpoint, and written composition. The technique of polyphonic diminution forms the main topic in the second area. Along with a good voice and a natural grace in delivery, improvised embellishments contribute to the oratorical power of the singer. This concept parallels Coclico's progressive notion that music belongs in the liberal arts as a sister of rhetoric. Yet, his pedestrian rules of counterpoint and composition reveal little that can be interpreted as integral to expressive polyphony. The only hint of adventurous vocabulary appears in his admission of E♭ in the hexachord system. This minor point at least suggests the widening scope of harmonic language that will furnish mannerist composers with one affective weapon. A somewhat similar approach can be seen in Hermann Finck's treatise. This theorist too is aware of a fundamental distinction between the styles of an older and a younger group of composers. Finck does not attribute this change to the art of singing, but rather to *stylus* and *musica poetica*—in other words, to compositional style. Finck's comments indicate that he feels modern musicians have achieved a greater measure of refinement compared to the more restrained principles of the older perfect art.

In spite of their progressive side, the theories of these two men do not confront the most important feature of avant-garde style of their time: experimentation with radical harmonies. However, we can find some explanations of mannerist chromaticism in two ordinary handbooks. Matthaeus Greiter extends mutation far beyond traditional limits. His colleague, Gregor Faber, pronounces the mannerist credo of refined novelty and startling effects by suggesting that chromatic elements alleviate monotony. From this idea, we can conclude that even mild expressivity within the canon of accepted contrapuntal theory is now too commonplace for the jaded taste of connoisseurs. Progress in musical art must take the route of expanding and distorting any potentially flexible system, in this case, hexachord mutation.

Spataro and Aaron also contribute radical theories in this area, theories that reflect current style. Even though Aaron does not use *maniera*, the following ideas in the *Lucidario* indicate his mannerist leanings. Superior composers rely on native talent and, for this reason, their works result from divine inspiration rather than from laborious study; they have mastered the secret of satisfying the ear with supernatural modulations. It should be noted at this point that Aaron's daring notion precedes similar ideas in the sister arts by some forty years, and it further implies that whereas natural modulations embody rational principles, supernatural ones embody ornaments and refinements insofar as they deviate from mathematics. Relying on their genius, modern composers have transformed the perfect art into ingenious, artificial, and wonderful stylization.

This pertinent definition of radical style occurs but once in Aaron's work. In Nicola Vicentino's militant treatise, this definition becomes an artistic program.[7] We have seen that his rules of counterpoint belong to the progressive school; but his systematic explanation of structural elements in composition, borrowed from rhetoric, adds a new dimension to this tradition. For this reason, later theorists are able to combine Vicentino's and Zarlino's progressive ideas into retrospective compendia of perfect counterpoint.

From the many revolutionary theories put forward by Vicentino, we cite his justification of accidentals without the hexachord system, and his idea that transposition changes the expressive character of the modes. The latter concept is linked with the most innovative item in the treatise—the threefold system of the ancient genera adapted to modern practice. Vicentino constructs no less than seven gamuts on the basis of generic inflections. The inherent characteristics of each one produce the expressive qualities of melodic and harmonic intervals as well as the individual and mixed modes. If the expressive use of rhythm and erstwhile forbidden intervals are added, we arrive at an astonishing array of imitative-affective devices.

Vicentino's awareness of stylistic differentiations among current genres is fundamental to his aesthetic. I have referred to his admonition that church music should be grave and restrained in contrast to the greater freedom and startling effects reserved for secular music, in which minute pictorialism reflects changing poetical conceits. Vicentino is also aware, and delighted, one suspects, that his system of chromatic and enharmonic music deviates so profoundly from traditional precepts. Caught on the horns of the mannerist dilemma, he prides himself on the esoteric and exclusive nature of his style, and at the same time, betrays a desire to instigate a new and popular fashion. For the latter purpose, he writes his treatise on vocal music and also reveals the secrets of his archicembalo whose six orders permit virtuoso solo performance in all three genera combined.

Because I have repeatedly cited Vicentino's treatise as the first mature presentation of mannerist aesthetics, an examination of his understanding of the term *maniera* seems to be in order. His frequent use of both *maniera* and *modo* certainly attests to a preoccupation with style. Although Vicentino is not always consistent in his distinction between the contexts and meanings of the two words, a careful reading of his treatise reveals that most often, *modo* refers to technical matters, and *maniera* to aesthetic concepts. To put it another way, *modo* means method whereas *maniera* means style.[8] But because method is inseparable from stylistic considerations in Vicentino's thought, the terms tend to overlap in some instances. In view of the inconsistency evident in his treatment of other subjects, such as vocal and instrumental tunings, the relative clarity of *modo* and *maniera* warrants some comment.

The technical significance of *modo* can be adduced from its repeated occurrence in chapter headings (e.g., *Modo di far*, *Modo d'accordare*, and *Modo di comporre*).[9] In the text, its singular or plural form appears prefaced by words such as "first," "second," "many," or "various" to designate specific points about counterpoint.[10] While such cases clearly demonstrate the use of *modo* as method, another group shows the infusion of aesthetic notions. In these instances, method is prefaced by "beautiful" or "good" (*bel modo*). Such phrases occur in explanations of modal freedom, canonic artifices, improvised counterpoint, homogeneous texture in church music, and the skill required for switching orders on the archicembalo.[11] These contexts indicate that *bel modo* still refers to technical methods, but in this case, ones that embody a certain amount of aesthetic refinement or *grazia*. In short, Vicentino seeks to distinguish between correct and stylish methods of manipulating specific technical ingredients of performance or composition.

On the other side of the coin, we find several instances where *maniera* appears in contexts parallel to the usage of *modo*. Two of these are clear-cut cases of equivalent meaning; they appear in discussions of methods for instrumental tunings, and specifically for the archicembalo.[12] Another set occurs in Vicentino's explanation of the problems inherent in canon. He here insists that the demanding nature of this kind of artificial counterpoint does not obviate the need for proper and stylish method.[13] In these cases, *maniera* is the same as *bel modo*, and like it, implies aesthetic preferences.

These few cases of ambivalent connotations attached to *maniera* are balanced by a number of passages that present a well-defined distinction between technical method and musical style, underscored by consistent usage of *modo* and *maniera* respectively. As examples, I cite the chapters devoted to performance problems on the archicembalo and in singing. In the former, Vicentino extols the novelty and marvel of his invention, which for the first time in history allows a player to produce a new style of sweet music.[14] In the latter, he emphasizes that singers must be educated to recognize divergent compositional styles so they can accordingly vary their methods of singing, including tempo, dynamics, voice quality, and improvised ornaments.[15] These particular passages, both in their contexts and their terminology, clearly illustrate a systematic differentiation between *modo* and *maniera*.

As far as compositional ideals are concerned, I have already shown Vicentino's sensitivity to matters of style. And it is significant that *maniera* figures prominently in these key passages. For example, he compares the composer to the architect; both rely on good technique (*bel modo*) to ensure that their structures rest on sound support, in other words, on good design. Musical design, in Vicentino's terms, depends on the structural intervals of the chosen mode. However, he goes on to suggest that correctness is not enough when he notes that painters often delight the viewer with optical illusions,[16] and that architects accompany their basic design with *diverse maniere*. In spite of their diversity, these styles may be combined in an orderly variety of ornaments, just as an orderly variety of sounds ornaments the basic mode of a musical composition. But musical variety must conform to the requirements of different genres. In secular music, great variety is permitted for the sake of depicting the text in contradistinction to sacred music, where gravity should be observed.[17] These observations indicate that Vicentino knows, either from firsthand or secondhand sources, about certain typically mannerist ideas in the sister arts, the most important of which is the connection of eclecticism with refined *maniera*.

Elsewhere in the treatise, Vicentino returns to the topic of coloring music's basic design. This component of *maniera* can only attain its full potential in secular music. First of all, Vicentino advises the composer to take great care with the *modo della pronuntia*, the technical element of prosody. At the same time, the composer must not forget that the accents of impassioned speech correspond to the expressive qualities of musical elements other than rhythm. He points to generically inflected intervals in particular. Vicentino concludes that all expressive material must imitate the sequence of affections and concrete conceits embodied in the words. The resultant musical style will not only ensure a variety of harmonies and rhythms but also an illusion of rhetorical eloquence. Hence his earlier parallel with optical illusions in painting. What is more important, by emulating the accents and inflections of the moods of specific languages, the composer creates a musically vivid analogue, or embodiment, as Vicentino would perhaps prefer, of a style of speaking. This twofold power of music relies on what we have called the mannerist combination of intellectual and emotional imitation, the *effetto meraviglioso*. Composition that takes as its premise this kind of rhetorical eloquence is considered by Vicentino to be *una bella maniera di comporre*.[18] This kind of *bella maniera*, by its very nature, appeals to a select group of connoisseurs. It is therefore different from and superior to *musica communa*, or ordinary and rather dull academic craft.

To sum up, Vicentino distinguishes, for the most part, between *modo*, understood as technical method, and *maniera*, understood as stylistic aesthetics. It is even significant for his general outlook that the vast majority of appearances of both terms occurs in Book IV, the book that concentrates on a complete theory of composition (*musica poetica*). At least half of the other occurrences of *maniera* in other books also relate directly to matters of style. For these reasons, I consider it an accurate proposition to state that Vicentino's thought is dominated by stylistic considerations, and in particular, those that contribute to the marvelous effects of novel and stunning rhetorical power.

In previous chapters, note was made of various polemics and antagonistic views engendered by Vicentino's treatise. At this point, the reader need only be reminded of Ghiselin Danckert's statement to the effect that the moderns debase good counterpoint by emulating the *maniera* of Adrian Willaert, a style that they consider to be new. This gibe more than adequately demonstrates current recognition of a *nuova maniera*, a new stylization in musical composition championed by a group of iconoclasts. Danckerts also pronounces his disapproval of those who "pretend to compose *alla musica maniera*."[19] Although Kaufmann's interpretation of the latter words as "without knowledge" is not incorrect, I suggest that, in the light of Vicentino's theory of *bella maniera* and of Danckert's complete phrase, a more pertinent reading would be "affected or stylized musical manner."

A similar conservative appraisal, put in more learned terms, appears in Zarlino's important treatise. It will be remembered that this theorist speaks quite openly about two *maniere*, the ancient and the modern, and in Zarlino's opinion, the two are entirely incompatible. Because the chromatic and enharmonic genera are alien to modern counterpoint based on sound technical procedures, radical composers have not revived ancient practice. Instead, they have invented a new style—to be more precise, a bad style. Their aesthetic manifesto, which promulgates the notion that they compose polyphony with marvelous effects like those of ancient music, ignores other important facts as well. Solo singing in antiquity could paint concrete affections and extrinsic conceits because it was dramatic recitation based on four indispensable ingredients: harmony, meter, narration, and subject. Modern polyphony, on the other hand, relies solely on the first two of these and therefore cannot match the rhetorical eloquence of ancient song. Of course, Zarlino maintains that his limitation is more than compensated for by the greater perfection of harmony characteristic of sixteenth-century polyphony.

The relationship between *maniera* and Zarlino's ideal of polyphony is a complex one, as is the more mundane matter of terminology.[20] Apart from the reference to ancient and modern styles,[21] a reference that forms incontrovertible evidence for his awareness of style concepts, *maniera* figures prominently in two other sections of Zarlino's writing. In the first of these, he traces the development of melodic styles in primitive and ancient cultures. In his words, men soon discovered *una maniera di compo-*

sitione called the hymn, among many other *maniere* including the heroic, tragic, comic, and dithyrambic. After the debasement of these antique musical styles, according to Zarlino, Willaert has shown a reasonable method of composing *con elegante maniera.*[22] There can be no doubt that here Zarlino refers to elegant style, but one displaying rational order as well. The other section where *maniera* appears in the unequivocal sense of style comprises the introductory material to Zarlino's study of the modes. Altogether, I have found twenty-nine instances of *maniera* or *maniere* connected to the exegesis of ancient and modern poetic styles as well as the melodic formulas associated with them.[23] Even in this context, Zarlino cannot refrain from criticizing modern radicals yet again. He says that the reader should marvel at those who think they can use the chromatic and enharmonic genera, whose principles have long been forgotten and of whose *maniera* (musical style) there remains not a single tangible trace.[24]

It seems reasonable enough to assume that Zarlino's use of *maniera* is motivated partly by the term's current popularity in theories of the visual arts.[25] But from passages referring obliquely to Vicentino, as well as those presenting more direct paraphrases,[26] it may also be assumed that Zarlino uses *maniera* in conscious opposition to Vicentino's definition. At any rate, both these interpretations indicate that Zarlino's understanding of *maniera* involves something more than a general meaning of type or kind.[27] Like Vicentino, Zarlino is not a philosopher and we should not be surprised, therefore, to find a substantial number of cases where both *modo* and *maniera* do have such a neutral import, not to mention instances where both words refer to technical methods. But this observation does not weaken the case made for interpreting the meaning of *maniera* as one of style in the passages discussed in this chapter.

Because Zarlino's main aim is not to explicate an aesthetic or philosophical doctrine, his stylistic ideals must be extrapolated from the various technical points he makes in the treatise. To this end, we now review the aesthetic implications of the *soggetto.* Because music imitates nature, as do art and literature, it derives from nature three basic subjects or models: sounding number, words, and theme. The aim of the composer is to discover the innate qualities of these models and to fulfill them in a natural manner. The laws of sounding number relate to the portrayal of the inner principles of nature. This ideal dictates all aspects of the act of composing. Vocal music must also obey the laws of *imitazione delle parole*, in Zarlino's case understood as correct declamation and not as the imitation of conceits and passions. The third *soggetto*, the musical theme, suggests the influence of nonmusical aesthetics on a topic that was, traditionally, a simple matter of craft. Closely related to Zarlino's idea of theme as the carrier of musical character is his concept of modal *forma*. In this case, modal decorum involves more than observing the correct finals. The intervals peculiar to specific modes, their *forma*, influence the style of counterpoint. Thus, the composer, like the artist and poet, works out the possibilities of his themes by creating the finished artwork.

In the light of the subtle premises of the *soggetto*, Zarlino's discussion of the aesthetic value of different contrapuntal styles now assumes a deeper significance. As we have seen, complete mastery of composition demands beauty, elegance, and polish. These qualities are to be found in *fuga* and *imitatione*, the structural categories that impart to music a stylishness transcending mere rules of correctness. And Zarlino favors *imitatione* because it affords the most flexible scope for fine style. Furthermore, he chooses a popular name for this kind of superior counterpoint to emphasize the fact that, in his opinion, *imitatione* embodies the most felicitous imitation of nature possible in a musical idiom.

Although Zarlino condemns radical style, he does recognize that harmony and number possess affective qualities of a general kind. All his examples are taken from the works of Willaert, the paragon of *elegante maniera*. Emotional characters must be arranged according to the overall tone of the text and not with a view to picturing minute details. At the same time, this kind of mood evocation must not interfere with the proper imitation of nature. Zarlino wishes to be as broad-minded as possible. He therefore acknowledges that modern solo recitation reflects the marvelous effects of ancient style. And he even goes so far as to permit some breaking of the rules in the case of very unusual affective demands made by certain texts.

My thesis is that Zarlino's theory, comprehended in its entirety, reveals a concern with both craftsmanlike expertise and elegant stylization. *Maniera*, for Zarlino, does not designate organic constructivism,[28] although self-sufficient musical logic remains a fundamental requisite of good counterpoint. *Maniera* rather fuses mathematics, abstract precepts, and concrete stylistic niceties into a perfectly balanced ideal of vocal music. And Zarlino's use of *maniera* in some key passages indicates that he is talking about style. I do not believe that it is correct to attribute his concept of *maniera* to any one source, but if one were to choose a main source, that source would surely have to be Vicentino. The context of Zarlino's arguments suggests very strongly that he adopted the term in order to profile the difference between Vicentino's and his own views. But this is admittedly a hypothesis, based on amalgamating various remarks made in the course of a lengthy, complicated, and rather subdued treatise.

I conclude the discussion of Zarlino's treatise with two general but important points. First of all, the idea that music imitates nature has never been so stressed by a theorist concerned with traditional polyphony. *Imitazione della natura* and *imitazione delle parole* are mottoes of mannerist theory and practice. Zarlino's espousal of this aesthetic shows his awareness of radical ideas as well as of humanist notions about the liberal arts. Ancient arts, especially music, were based on the imitation of nature. Zarlino wishes to demonstrate that polyphony has evolved naturally to a culmination—a perfect style imitating nature in a different and superior manner to ancient style.[29] One might say that the revered, but rather abstract, rules of conservative counterpoint have been imbued with refined stylishness. Glareanus's *ars perfecta* has become the *elegante maniera*, which Zarlino seeks to codify into an immutable ideal.

The second point to be made concerns historical context, inasmuch as the split in musical practice exemplified by Vicentino's and Zarlino's concepts of *maniera* is unique for its time. One must not be misled because *elegante maniera* in this study is called conservative or traditional. For Zarlino, *elegante maniera* is modern, but in a special way. It embodies the ultimate stage in the perfection of unchanging ideals—music as a mirror of the harmonious cosmos. Of course, Zarlino does not broach the problem of the future's relation to the present state of perfection. My thesis maintains that his *elegante maniera* appears conservative from the viewpoint of Vicentino's *bella maniera*. The mannerist quest for striking rhetorical power relegates zarlinian ideals to the realm of academic craft. Thus, his modern art becomes the first practice when the fruits of the second practice ripen. The causes of this uncomplimentary development are both the radical thrust of mannerist progress and the conservative thrust of stationary perfection. Both trends are mannerist insofar as they entail self-conscious ideals. But in contrast to the visual arts, musical Mannerism of a revolutionary cast has yet to attain its full conquests. As art becomes increasingly academic, music becomes increasingly adventuresome, and its innovations continue into baroque practice.

Musical controversy between 1560 and 1580 abates to a lull before the storm. Debates over different styles exist in the sister arts, but they present a somewhat different picture of intellectual ferment. In the visual arts, the battle continues between Venetian and Florentine styles. Literary criticism exposes two new themes. One of these concerns the mannerist distortion of a classical concept. Realistic imitation of believable character and reasonable passion (*enargeia*) has ceded to fantastic imitation of supernatural persons and grotesquely violent passion (*meraviglia*). And the great popularity of lyric verse initiates controversy over its relative merits compared to the epic.

The years between 1580 and 1630 witness the ripening of mannerist theory in poetry and art. Artificial and virtuoso proportions change the illusionistic potential of renaissance design into a vehicle for secret and bizarre *effetti meravigliosi*. And the violent elements of mannerist design reputedly create vivid affectiveness. A small group of antimannerists criticize this *maniera* as extravagant and vapid artificiality. But unreality, and its power to astonish, win the day. *Dipingere di natura* and *dipingere di maniera* become commonplace distinctions of style. By implication, realistic naturalism adheres to an older tradition whereas artificial stylization belongs to modern radicalism. This distinction has already been made in musical theory.

In poetic theory, conservative denial of imitative power for lyric poetry is engulfed by overwhelming support for the idea that the lyric imitates particularly well the elements of character, thought, and, of course, the passions and affections. The poet is the maker of the "marvelous." This mannerist view is echoed in the numerous treatises dwelling on *furor poeticus*, the irrational source of mystical inspiration. All these notions indicate that grace and elegance are no longer sufficient values for *maniera*; preciosity, extreme artificiality, and monumental grandeur now enter the canon of novel modern style. It is therefore fitting that the first works praising concettism should make their appearance at this time. Novel *concetti* are taken as proof of the poet's sublimity, and the more hyperbolic the conceit, the more sublime the poet. When passionate lyric moments are strung together in a sequence, the poet creates a *favola pastorale*, the mannerist genre that attempts to monumentalize the amorous conceits of lyric poetry.

From these observations, we can conclude that as far as music's sister arts are concerned, the balance has swung finally toward recognition of radical *maniera*, in both its technical and aesthetic aspects. That this situation is even more pronounced in the musical climate of these decades can be attributed to two factors: first, the earlier appearance of revolutionary thought and polemics, and second, the apparent success of practical innovations. At this particular juncture we witness the sharp division between traditional and modern practices, a division sharpened by evaluations of radical polyphony and, especially, of monody. Taking the case of polyphony first, we now notice an exaggerated sense of radical progress in style; this sense pushes Zarlino's formerly progressive ideal further back into the world of recalcitrant conservatism. I have noted Agostino Michele's remarks on the vastly different *maniere* characteristic of three successive generations of madrigalists in the sixteenth century, as well as Vincenzo Galilei's views of modern counterpoint. Although the latter commends the technical side of this style—its novel and ingenious use of dissonances—he also finds that the new musical language serves a childish aesthetic aim—word painting. Galilei therefore calls this madrigalian approach *una ridicola maniera*. Nor is he the only writer of this period to question the prevalent style of modern counterpoint.[30]

A contextual understanding of the values discussed by Galilei, Tasso, and others can help us clarify contemporary issues. These writers do not dismiss entirely the novelties and radical innovations of modern music, but they do indicate some uneasiness about modern music's extravagance and frivolity—in other words, its somewhat superficial stylization. Their criticism does much to explain the full import of several apologies made by prominent composers of the time. The first one we will discuss is of special interest for several reasons. To scholars of the sixteenth-century madrigal, Luca Marenzio is famous, if not notorious, for his predilection for word painting of all kinds. The apology in question here appears in a publication dedicated to Count Mario Bevilacqua, the patron of an illustrious private *ridotto* in Verona. Marenzio states that the works in this collection are composed "in a style quite different from that of his earlier one" (*con maniera assai differente dalla passata*). Their new manner embodies a quality of "serious gravity" (*mesta gravità*) arising both from considerations of imitating the words and observing stylistic propriety.[31]

The second apology also comes from the pen of a noted composer, Luzzasco Luzzaschi, a well-known practitioner of many avant-garde techniques. Luzzaschi's dedication presents a more general justification of the basic aesthetic premise behind madrigalian Mannerism. His words remind us of many accusations leveled against radical novelty by his contemporaries as well as by writers before his time, and we must consider it significant that the word "style" (*maniera* and *stile*) occurs several times in the course of his brief remarks. First, Luzzaschi repeats the rhetorical ideal of modern music by pointing out that the styles of poetry and music are interrelated. He states, furthermore, that a new, very novel, and perfect style in the madrigal has developed alongside a new style in modern poetry, featuring *brevità, acutezza, leggiadria, nobiltà*, and of course, *dolcezza*. Luzzaschi concludes with these militant and pertinent remarks: "[And] this commendable style (*stile*), our musicians, too, have attempted to discover, imitating new techniques (*nuovi modi*) and new inventions sweeter than usual ones. Out of these, they have fashioned *una nuova maniera*, which can please and win the world's applause not only because of its novelty, but also because of its exquisiteness of artifice."[32]

The third document embraces similar ideas and ideals, but in the context of monody and virtuoso performance by famed soloists. Sigismondo d'India here produces, as evidence for his superior personal achievements, a testimony from Vittoria Archilei, "most excellent above all other women singers, who, as the most intelligent in this profession, urged me to pursue this my own style (*questa mia maniera*), saying she has not heard a style (*stile*) that has so much force and at the same time displays the *concetto* with such a diversity of chords, variety of harmony, and with such a new style (or manner) of ornamentation (*con sì nova maniera di passeggiare*)." Earlier in this preface, d'India stresses the novelty of what he considers to be the *vera maniera* of composing in contradistinction to commonplace, ordinary music, which always adheres to the same style (*medesimo stile*). The detailed points he mentions in connection with his achievement are unusual intervals, novel progressions between consonances according to the variety of the sense of the words, as well as new modulations and ornaments. All these techniques, in his opinion, contribute to a musical style with greater affective power and greater force in moving the affections than the more customary practice.[33] In this instance, d'India's denigrating comments about ordinary, unremarkable style refer not to polyphony (old or new) but rather to solo songs characterized by bland lyricism and trite tunes.

Before continuing with our discussion, I digress briefly to inform the reader that in addition to treatises, a large body of evidence for the significance of style concepts in music exists in the form of prefaces, dedications, or letters attached to publications of madrigals, monodies, and music for the theater. These musical sources are not only more numerous, but also more provocative, than similar sources in art and literature. Preliminary investigation brings together some thirty-five documents of this kind written between 1580 and 1630, and in these we find anywhere from one to seventeen appearances each of *maniera* or *stile* in the sense of musical style.[34] Although an exhaustive comparative study of these sources cannot be undertaken in this chapter, a representative sampling is offered.

To the two sources related to polyphonic madrigals, the prefaces by Marenzio and Luzzaschi, we now add a few others. The dedication to a collection composed by Ruggiero Giovanelli refers, as does Luzzaschi's preface, to the parallel between poetry and music. In this instance, the writer remarks on the charming conceits of Sannazaro's *stile* appropriately set to music by Giovanelli *con dolce & dilettevol maniera*.[35] This sweet and delightful style is so much in vogue in Italy, and evidently represents novelty of some kind, that Filippo di Monte, in his dedication to his patron, Rudolph II, admits that he has attempted to change his *stile* in order to please those who do not approve of his other compositions.[36] The inference here is that Monte's customary style appears old-fashioned. Three other prefaces from the early seventeenth century refer, in a more concrete way, to the features that make this style so fascinating. Mariano Tantucci, himself a composer, praises the madrigals of Tomaso Pecci and cites specifically the new sentiments evident in the *artificiosa maniera del compor moderno*.[37] A similar reference to modern style occurs in the dedication to a publication by Alessandro Scialla. The writer recommends these madrigals, which are immune from criticism because of *la novità, & vaghezze dello stil moderno*.[38] In the last source pertinent to polyphonic madrigals, the composer, Marsilio Casentini, expounds on the delights of modern style in a suggestive and humorous way. After a reference to the popularity of Guarini's *Il pastor fido*, Casentini notes that many people applaud *le licenze del moderno comporre* because of the delight they derive *da questa maniera*. He then goes on to personify Methodical Rules as venerable matrons in dignified clothing and with maternal feelings. Modern Licenses, on the other hand, appear in the guise of gracious young damsels, lasciviously dressed and with a thousand charms. Rather than displease either group of ladies, Casentini gallantly tries to steer a middle road and concludes his preface with a typically mannerist pun to the effect that he therefore set out blindly to compose this book of madrigals.[39]

Whereas the above documents address matters of compositional style, our sources pertaining to solo and theatrical music cover a broader range of topics. Although the relationship between early opera and the humanistic conception of ancient drama is universally recognized today, the influence of mannerist aesthetics on these corollaries has been overlooked. The opening statement in the dedication written for Emilio de'Cavalieri's *Rappresenta-tione di anima et di corpo* announces the presentation of this composer's new and singular work, composed in that style (*quello stile*) with which the ancient Greeks and Romans used to move the affections of the spectators in their theaters.[40] The point that needs to be stressed here is that these remarks can be taken as illustrative of the aesthetic premises behind the first essays in the *opera in musica*. And these premises, based as they are on humanist ideas, have two elements in common with the mannerist viewpoint evident in other writings, regardless of the different musical practices that they explain. The common elements are first, a fascination with style as such, and second, an emphasis on the rhetorical power of a style. Even though the reader surely realizes that the practical outcome of this aesthetic in a polyphonic madrigal, a solo song, or an opera can be quite different—because of the diverse technical ingredients required by each genre—I suggest that the philosophy embodied in these ideas is one and the same, and furthermore, that it is symptomatic of mannerist values.[41]

These values are tacitly presumed in one remark found in Marco da Gagliano's preface to his *La Dafne*—to wit, his reference to the discussions about the *maniera* used by the ancients in their tragedies, discussions leading up to the composition of the "libretto" by Ottavio Rinuccini. Later in the preface, Gagliano surveys the elements of *rappresentazioni in musica*, and his list gives us an excellent idea of the interrelationship between early opera and the mannerist intermedio: invention, disposition of the *favola*, symbolism (*sentenza*), sweetness of rhyme, musical art, *concerti* of voices and instruments, exquisiteness of singing, the charm of ballet and gestures, and the visual aspect of scenery and costumes.[42] Because monodic composition requires extraordinarily fine voices and virtuoso technique, references to the high quality of singing abound in documents pertinent to monodies and theatrical music of all kinds. In addition to Gagliano's comments, I cite here those made by Cristofano Malvezzi about the intermedios for *La Pellegrina*, presented at the wedding of Ferdinando de'Medici and Christine of Lorraine (1589): the sounds of various instruments, the sweetness of the voices, and the charming style (*vaga maniera*) of the singing.[43]

In addition to general comments on the excellence of singing, we also find remarks on specific styles of monody, styles that have both a compositional and a performance basis. For example, Gagliano, having set the same text as Jacopo Peri, praises the latter as the inventor of *quella artifiziosa maniera di recitar cantando*, a style admired throughout Italy.[44] And in the preface to a collection of monodies, Severo Bonini singles out Giulio Caccini as the *Inventore di questa nobilissima maniera*.[45] These comments clearly show that the writers have a pronounced concept of individual styles, and in the case of Peri and Caccini, the concept is borne out by their music. By way of a conclusion, I note that the preponderant bias of these sources points to a preference for new or modern style with connotations of refinement, artificiality, personal ingenuity, and of course, marvelous effects.

Even though Vincenzo Galilei champions the cause of monody, he nevertheless takes pains to construct a theory for the novel use of dissonance in polyphony. His precepts represent a tacit recognition of two distinct practices, traditional and modern counterpoint. In this context, adherents of zarlinian principles become regressive rather than progressive. Thomas Morley's and Lodovico Zacconi's comments on various styles would have ensured them a place in the progressive group twenty years ago. But their attempts to retain a common foundation for older and newer styles now relegate them to the placid backwaters of antiquarian theory. The one radical element in Zacconi's treatise is his emphasis on singers who are masters of *gratiose maniere*, or improvised ornaments. The decorative gesture of the dance has now become the rhetorical gesture of song.

Any view of music that maintains abstract and self-sufficient rules, however flexible, succumbs to the onslaught of the solo song and the cult of the new virtuoso singer. The attitude of the Florentine Camerata reflects this situation. In their view, only monody is capable of reviving the *effetti meravigliosi* of ancient style. Any claims to expressivity made on behalf of traditional, and even modern, counterpoint are summarily dismissed. Although *maniera* as such does not appear in the writings emanating from this circle, concepts of style, often couched in related vocabulary, are fundamental to their ideals.

The spokesmen of the Camerata, apart from Caccini, have little to say about the current craze for florid diminution. This practice enjoys scant authority from classical sources. But there is no doubt that mannerist practitioners and their audience find many marvelous effects and affective qualities in *accenti, fioretti,* and *gorgie.* Both the exuberance and conventionality of such ornaments attest to the rapid infiltration of mannerist ideals into this area of performance. The singer is seen as a musical orator who embellishes discourse with a dazzling array of affective ornaments. And with these means, he manipulates the feelings of his listeners much in the same way as the skilled orator. And just as an orator can improve an apparently unpromising text, so a singer can heighten the effect of an ordinary piece of music. Their art therefore arouses wonder and admiration. Mannerist excesses in the field of ornamentation eventually dwindle to a staple diet of reasonable flourishes; but the abuses of the coloratura singer remain legendary. It is also worth noting that many mannerist ornaments are taken over and systematized in baroque practice. One scholar points out that the frequent use by sixteenth-century theorists of terms such as *maniera di far passaggi* leads to the seventeenth-century technical term, *Manieren.*[46] In this case, of course, *maniera* and its derivative are not centrally connected to concepts of style.

Many aspects of *maniera* during this period signal the transformation of Mannerism into the Baroque. In the visual arts, *maniera* is codified as an acceptable academic practice. The success of academies of design promulgates mannerist style at the expense of natural imitation. Had Vasari been alive, he probably would have recognized two separate *maniere*: an older naturalist one based on scientific rules and a newer mannerist one based on personal and original invention. Poetic theory at this time vindicates the *favola pastorale* as well as a lyric style that is completely dominated by startling *concetti.* And literary critics of the Baroque ascribe concettism to sixteenth-century mannerist style in Italian poetry.

The same interpretation can be drawn from some ideas espoused by progressive and radical theorists of music. The Monteverdi brothers reply to Giovanni Maria Artusi's attack on modern music with the celebrated division of contemporary practice into two styles: an older polyphonic one that depends on the perfection of harmony and on the subordination of the text as opposed to a newer polyphonic one that depends on the perfection of melody and on the subordination of musical laws. They do not use the term *maniera*, but they nevertheless stress stylistic premises. And their distinction between conservative and radical practices must be understood as the culmination of many decades of preoccupation with *maniera*. Their view is also found in Adriano Banchieri, a mild progressive, when he differentiates between *contrapunto osservato* and *contrapunto commune*, the latter being modern counterpoint *con gratiosa maniera*.[47] And the notion of these two *maniere* survives into baroque theories of style.

Chromaticism and eloquence continue to function as basic elements within modern practice. Thus, Ercole Bottrigari reviews the Vicentino-Lusitano debate, and sides with Vicentino. He also comments on the greater freedom and complexity of modern counterpoint, commendable characteristics arising from the adventurous potential of *musica mista*. As proof of this evaluation, Bottrigari prints his own setting of Petrarch's *Così mi sveglio*, composed according to the practice and style of the moderns (*secondo l'uso & lo stile de'Moderni*); Bottrigari further remarks that this madrigal demonstrates both *il vero modo, & la vera maniera* of the chromatic genus.[48] And like Monteverdi, he cites Cipriano de Rore as the initiator and prime exponent of the madrigalian style.[49] Theory of new music at this time contributes one more important notion to the arsenal of baroque concepts, the *musica poetica* of Burmeister. On the basis of the now commonplace idea that music is an expressive art, Burmeister divides musical procedure into four styles and illustrates them with some twenty-six rhetorical figures. His model is Orlando di Lasso. A more significant bridge beteen sixteenth- and seventeenth-century ideas cannot be found. And regardless of the actual term employed by any of these writers, whether *maniera*, *prattica*, *stile*, *modo*, or *stylus*, the context of their usage implies consistent preoccupation with "stylization."

The mannerist delight in profuse ornamentation can be adduced from instruction books on diminution. We have seen that Vicenzo Giustiniani provides music lovers with an astute survey of the development of modern composition and performance practice. He states that in his day a composition wins favor if it is composed according to the rules and at the same time embodies rare and unusual difficulties.[50] He also charts the rise of the virtuoso singer, whose exquisite voice production and magnificent technique inspire a new style of music. The popularity of improvised embellishment is such that composers now incorporate florid *passaggi* and affective *accenti* in written counterpoint, thereby introducing the unruly dissonances that so anger conservative theorists. Giustiniani attributes the latest refinement in solo singing to Caccini, "the inventor of a new manner in singing."[51]

The importance of stylishness and stylization in Caccini's outlook can be gauged by the frequency of the word *maniera* in the preface to his *Le nuove musiche*.[52] It should be noted that seventeen of the twenty-eight substantive cases of *maniera* imply stylistic criteria; the remainder appear in contexts suggesting "method" or "way," and thus are equivalent to the words *arte* and *modo*, which Caccini also uses in the latter sense. Most of the stylistic uses refer to singing, although *buona maniera* appears once in connection with composition. The word *stile* appears three times in relation to ideas of style. It seems clear, then, that because Caccini's precepts of performance and composition have nothing to do with the traditional science of counterpoint, they are explained by him in terms of style (*nobile maniera, nobilissima maniera, buona maniera, affetuosa maniera,* and *nuovo stile*). Caccini's estimation of his new, noble, and good style implies that previous monodic conventions are inferior because the latter are too closely predicated on certain features of the polyphonic madrigal. But other musicians assess novel style in the solo song from the opposite point of view inasmuch as they believe that iconoclastic devices transferred from madrigalian conventions impart dignity, affectivity, and eloquence to monody. Such is the case with d'India's avowed search for *vera maniera*. Just as Zarlino and Vicentino use *maniera* to refer to their different ideals of good counterpoint, so Caccini and d'India do the same concerning their ideals of good song.

Novelty is also claimed by both Caccini and Peri in their rivalry over precedence in the composition of opera. Peri stresses this new genre's unprecedented rhetorical power. In other words, operatic monody has fulfilled Galilei's recommendation to imitate histrionic style. This concept is clearly set forth by Giovanni Battista Doni when he describes the differences among narrative, recitational, and expressive recitative. And he also distinguishes not only the various styles of monody, but also separates them from melodic writing in the *maniera madrigalesca*.[53]

On a general level directed to all the arts, it is important to realize that the concept of a classical Renaissance is itself a mannerist construct, and that at the very moment of its formulation, a self-consciousness about style sets in. Perhaps because such historically oriented ideas become prominent in the sixteenth century, Mannerism develops with such a dominant impact on all the arts. This is certainly the situation with musical ideas. Avant-garde composers are aware not only of the novelty of their procedures, but also of the highly artificial, personal, and extravagant aspects of their experiments. They are creators of the "marvelous," distorting traditional and classical principles. They have mastered the art of the illusion of musical drama. As Doni states, counterpoint is a craft to be studied by the rules, but dramatic music is born of natural talent and irrational genius. Modern music, whether it be madrigalian audacity or monodic boldness, cannot be evaluated by mathematical precepts, no matter how close to nature they may be. On the contrary, the excellence of modern music must be judged by subjective standards of sensibility that respond to originality, rhetorical force, and dramatic power. These form the fundamental aesthetic premises of effective and affective *maniera*, whose successful embodiment in music represents for mannerist musicians the vindication of ancient ideals.

❧❧❧

CHAPTER XVI

Musica Reservata

The enigmatic term, *musica reservata*, has long fascinated modern historians, and the controversial interpretations found in their writings reflect the diversity and ambiguity of the primary sources on which their ideas are based. In this discussion, I intend to explore the possible connections between *musica reservata* and elements isolated by sixteenth- and early seventeenth-century theorists as pertinent to current issues about musical style, and specifically, those elements that I see as pertinent to a definition of musical Mannerism. Like so many mottoes of the time, *musica reservata* constitutes a fashionable slogan. It is so widely used that scholars conclude *musica reservata* denotes no single meaning but rather a number of divergent connotations, all of them equally valid and at times mutually exclusive.[1] The term emanates mostly from northern European centers and seems to designate imitations of Italian *maniera*—hence the primary reason for investigating it. Although its lack of clarity can be exasperating, its richness of meaning touches all areas of cultural history between 1530 and 1630.

The earliest appearance of the term links it to a revival of a neglected style of music. Adrianus Petit Coclico's intention is to elucidate Josquin's style, which, according to him, is generally called *reservata*.[2] A similar aim, this time connected to a revival of ancient Greek style, underlies Nicola Vicentino's theories. In his view, chromatic and enharmonic music are properly reserved for a different use than the diatonic.[3] Although it is true that in Vicentino's text, *riserbata* is not an adjective modifying *musica*, we cannot deny that he intends to prove the possibility of adapting ancient practice in modern music.[4] Furthermore, this adaptation produces an extremely novel style; *musica "riserbata,"* if we may be permitted to adapt Vicentino's terminology somewhat, is thus equivalent to *bella maniera.*

Two letters written by Dr. Seld, chancellor to the Bavarian court, support the above explanation. In the first, he recounts that Egidius Fux and some other singers performed *reservata* and other unknown music in his house in Brussels. Dr. Seld also notes that the new choirmaster favors *reservata* more than did his predecessor.[5] It appears, then, that the term relates to a newly emerging fashion.[6] In the second letter, Dr. Seld recommends Filippo di Monte as a master of *new art* and *musica reservata.*[7] One scholar suggests that these two sets of terms represent opposites; however, most others maintain that they are synonymous, in view of Dr. Seld's other letter.[8] This interpretation is borne out by Vicentino's treatise, and by the title of his first book of madrigals, which advertises works written *al nuovo modo* rediscovered by his celebrated master, Adrian Willaert.[9] And we have mentioned several times that Ghiselin Danckerts makes fun of self-styled moderns who imitate the *nuova maniera* of Willaert. This writer does not use the term *musica reservata*; he does, however, dwell on the abuses of radical composers who, in his words, espouse affected stylization. The source of Vicentino's affected stylization is precisely the ancient genera reserved for special purposes. This eccentric style, to be sure, does not appear in the 1546 book of madrigals. But it is my contention that Vicentino, rightly or wrongly, develops his earlier somewhat vague notions about a *nuovo modo* into a systematic aesthetic of radical *maniera.*

Other indisputable equations of *musica reservata* with the excesses of avant-gardism appear in two works by Jean Taisnier.[10] In the first of these, Taisnier scoffs at *musica moderna*, called by others *nova* or *reservata*. In the second, he promises to write a treatise about the differences between old and new music or *musica reservata*. From the general tenor of such comments we can deduce one thing. The controversy surrounding novel *maniera* seems to spark markedly militant opinions in writings concerned with *musica reservata*. Our task is to ascertain exactly what elements of *musica reservata* arouse such violent reactions.

One set of sources implies a connection between *reservata* and improvised ornamentation. In the case of Coclico, several scholars deny that any relationship exists between diminution and his concept of *musica reservata*; but on the other hand, I remind the reader that Coclico's novel educational plan relies on the interplay between mastery of improvised embellishment and mastery of written counterpoint.[11] In yet another letter, Dr. Seld records his admiration for Netherlandish excellence in extemporary ornamentation.[12] Because he mentions Fux, some scholars link this statement to Dr. Seld's private performances of *musica reservata*. The opposing view maintains that inasmuch as Dr. Seld does not actually use this term in the same letter that describes *die Art des Colorierens*, *reservata* and ornamentation cannot be construed as equivalent.[13] However, among the abuses of the new *musica reservata* listed by Taisnier is the propensity of singers to revive old practices by improvising counterpoint. It is not clear whether he refers to improvised embellishment or to extemporary polyphony, especially because the art of diminution, improvised counterpoint, and written figural polyphony are so closely interwoven in the sixteenth century. Taisnier's wording, nevertheless, is most provocative: "Likewise, they recall to mind extemporary counterpoint in three, four, five, six, and seven parts, modulated by diverse singers, from the testimony of their predecessors. In short, they make of singers Poets, [who], aroused by the example of their predecessors, leave behind in their own memory and for the use of posterity, the absolute (finished) work (*opus absolutum*)."[14] Those historians who seek as broad a definition of *musica reservata* as possible include improvised ornamentation as one component of this style.[15] The implications of this viewpoint are important. If *reservata* does relate to embellishment, then the entire corpus of treatises on ornamentation is by inference connected to the topic of new music.

Another interpretation connects *musica reservata* with the cult of the solo performer, a connection that adds another dimension to the one discussed above. Coclico's emphasis on refined singing and his praise of modern musicians provide the first source for this view. Perhaps his poets are practitioners of *musica reservata*. Dr. Seld's references to intimate chamber music also suggest performances by a select group of soloists. Moreover, Vicentino's radical works are meant to be executed in a delicate manner by a solo ensemble, and the novel style of such works arises from their use of the ancient genera. In this regard, it seems significant that the Besançon writer should consider the mutation of genera as particularly pleasing in *monodia*—that is, in part-music for soloists.[16] And I have noted Taisnier's disapproval of the fact that in *musica reservata* singers fancy themselves to be poets and usurp the role of the composer. In a petition to his patron, Archduke Ferdinand, Raimundo Ballestra asks permission to publish a collection of music including *etlicher reservata*.[17] One scholar connects Ballestra's *reservata* to a style contrasting solo monody with choral sections, whereas another denies emphatically any relationship between this term and the cultivation of monody in Graz.[18] It may be that Ballestra merely wished to publish music hitherto restricted to private court circles. Our last source is a document from the court at Neuberg that lists Biagio Marini as *musico riservato*.[19] Even if *reservato* has nothing to do with monody, it may in this case refer to Marini's status as a soloist. This interpretation forms one more bit of proof, albeit a small one, that certain concepts originally associated with mannerist novelty become integral elements of baroque practice.

In contrast to the preceding sources, all of which suggest some kind of new music (in spite of their differences), there exist documents implying a connection between traditional values and *reservata*. The latter seem on the surface to contradict the premises imputed to the former, and this problem is exacerbated by potentially opposite readings of one and the same source in certain instances. One of these is Coclico's treatise. We must admit the possibility that Coclico's *musica reservata* may designate the compositional refinements that Josquin developed into classic perfection. In other words, Glareanus's *ars perfecta* has the same implications as Coclico's *musica reservata*. The desire of both theorists to eternalize an ideal can be considered progressive for their time inasmuch as they seek to explicate the norms of a recent style. That Glareanus has a more sensitive understanding of Josquin's style is due less to his temporal proximity to this composer than to Coclico's inferior musicianship, evident in the motets published under the title *Mu-*

sica reservata consolationes piae ex psalmis Davidiciis (1552). Modern scholars have combed these compositions for concrete traces of *musica reservata*. Several gave up in disgust, declaring that this inept music shows Coclico to be a complete ignoramus.[20] But to be fair, we must concur with the view put forward by another musicologist—namely, that with the exception of three works, the motets adhere to the principle of successive points of imitation.[21]

Musical events in mid-century force slightly antiquarian overtones on to theories idealizing established *maniera*. Because radicals degrade abstract rules and traditional craft, their opponents upgrade them to hallmarks of refined ingenuity. Among these hallmarks are elegant imitative points, canonic artifices, double and invertible counterpoint, and other *osservati* or *oblighi*. These elements are still seen as components of a living style; they refine mildly progressive *maniera*. This is the thrust of Gioseffo Zarlino's epoch-making treatise. A similar attitude informs the dedication to a publication by Orlando di Lasso. The composer addresses a patron who enjoys music that is called *osservata* and wishes everyone to understand it.[22] Because Lasso seems to refer to a style that is somewhat unappreciated, a number of scholars equate *osservata* and *reservata*. Others disagree on the grounds that *reservata* does not include the connotation of learned counterpoint associated with *osservata*.[23] But evidence to the contrary exists, even if we discount the problematic case of Coclico. On the authority of writers such as Pietro Aaron[24] and Andreas Ornitoparchus,[25] who use the adjective *reconditus* in reference to artful and hidden complexities, historians related contrapuntal artifices to *musica osservata*.[26] They then connect recondite *osservata* with a tradition of refined counterpoint subsumed as one aspect of *musica reservata*. Additional evidence is found in the title of Vincenzo Ruffo's fourth book of madrigals, which contains the phrase *con dotte arte et reservato ordine*.[27] Ruffo, or his publisher, offers no explanation. Now, *reservato ordine* is linked to *musica reservata* by one contingent of scholars simply because of their similarity as terms, whereas another group equates them on the grounds that *reservata* means learned, refined, and delicate counterpoint.[28] On the other hand, those historians who define *musica reservata* as novel rhetorical style deny the connection between *reservato ordine* and *musica reservata*. According to them, the former term indicates a reserved manner and an orderly technique; in fact, they suggest that Ruffo is boasting of a dual achievement insofar as he has succeeded in uniting the older, traditional ideal with a newer one based on sweet and suave harmony.[29] Even in this context, Ruffo's *reservato ordine* still belongs to mid-century progressive outlook, especially in its combination of rational order and reasonable expressivity—ideals also espoused by Zarlino.

Later appearances of *reservata* embody an undeniably retrospective and academic attitude. For instance, Antonio Brunelli indicates that the success of a previous tract on singing practice has prompted him to publish a work dealing with *altre regole più riservate e recondite*—in this case, the strict and learned rules of double counterpoint.[30] And it may very well be that Ballestra's *etlicher reservata* refers to works built on contrapuntal artifices. This meaning is especially relevant to one grandiose motet that features crab canon, a repeated hexachordal cantus firmus, and polytextual symbolism.[31] Pieces such as this one attest to the antiquarian stylization of older polyphonic norms, a form of emulation of the perfect art characteristic of early seventeenth-century counterpoint. Conservative ideals also underlie a statement made by Giovanni Maria Trabaci to the effect that his ricercars are composed *con tutte quella osservata diligenza*.[32] Although this last source concerns instrumental music, the idea of "observed or strict diligence" casts some light on the ricercar as a genre and its relationship to abstract vocal polyphony. All these documents, then, intimate close connections between *musica reservata* (abstract contrapuntal refinements and complexities) and *contrapunto osservato* (traditional, strict counterpoint). As we have seen in another context, *contrapunto osservato* is the opposite of *contrapunto commune*, the modern style of expressive polyphony.[33]

To sum up, the above interpretation of *musica reservata* links it to a historical development that culminates in the concept of two distinct polyphonic *maniere*—the *prima* and *seconda prattica*. The *ars nova* of Tinctoris becomes the *ars perfecta* of Glareanus, then the *musica reservata* of Coclico, and finally, the *musica reservata-osservata* of late sixteenth- and early seventeenth-century theorists. In a sense, this evolution merely sketches the normal life span of any style seen through the eyes of its practitioners. However, I wish to suggest as well that this particular evolution is but another symptom of values inherent in the stylization characteristic of musical Mannerism. Its pattern, accompanied by praise or condemnation, indicates the self-consciousness of the age. On the surface, the concept as I have explained it seems to contradict any definition of *musica reservata* as radical style. But I further maintain that a comprehensive understanding of Mannerism shows that *osservata-reservata* is the siamese twin of *communa-reservata*; in other words, just as Zarlino and Vicentino use *maniera* to designate opposing ideals, so do theorists who discuss *reservata*.

We now return to our survey of the evidence for interpreting *reservata* as a description of radical techniques. Glareanus willingly praises Josquin's restrained expressivity, and somewhat unwillingly his more exuberant rhetoric. Coclico's joining together of expressivity, *musica reservata*, and Josquin's music reminds us of Glareanus's assessment. And Coclico pointedly contrasts the ability of the kings of music to depict every affection with the mathematical predilections of earlier composers. Furthermore, the poets invent new refinements for their regal heritage insofar as Josquin's legendary mastery of affective power has been augmented by a cultivation of singing. Both kings and poets practice music not as a science but as a rhetorical art. On this basis, several scholars insist that Coclico's works, their crudities notwithstanding, do attempt to portray the text.[34]

Vicentino's viewpoint is dominated by rhetorical eloquence and dramatic expression. These form the ideals of the *bella maniera di comporre*. Nearly all his radical devices develop from the use of the chromatic and enharmonic genera. Moreover, Vicentino's sole reference to "reserved music" occurs in relation to ancient ideas about generic styles; it therefore coincides nicely with his polemic for affective music. Elsewhere in the treatise, Vicentino uses *musica communa* to designate straightforward diatonic counterpoint in an academic vein. Although *musica "riserbata"* and *musica communa* do not appear in the same passage, Lowinsky's suggestion that Vicentino employs these terms to differentiate two musical styles[35] is supported by the general temper of Vicentino's writing as well as by subsequent theoretical emphasis on the bifurcation between old-fashioned and fashionable counterpoint.

Coclico's *musica reservata*, of course, still rests comfortably within the progressive aspect of the perfect art. Vicentino's *musica "riserbata,"* on the other hand, relegates *musica communa* to a secondary plateau. Furthermore, his concept must be taken as a distinctly mannerist one that champions refined distortion of hidden radical tendencies in the perfect art. Both deviation and departure from classical norms are justified on the grounds of expressive goals. It is significant that among the characteristics of *musica moderna, nova,* or *reservata,* Taisnier omits vivid depiction of the words. In this regard, Palisca surmises that Taisnier realized the benefit for his polemic to be derived from neglecting the one positive element of *musica reservata.*[36] All of Taisnier's antiradical criticisms stem from his tacit belief in the supremacy of self-sufficient musical rules. Thus, he presages Giovanni Maria Artusi's later attack on the *seconda prattica.*

Two famous references to *musica reservata* link the term to specific compositions by Lasso. One is a document in the Munich court archives, dated 1559, concerning *Tityre tu patulae.* Dr. Seld cites this setting of a bucolic eclogue by Virgil as an example of *musica reservata* but gives no explanation for this appellation.[37] The style of the work in question embodies no striking features except for predominantly homophonic declamation. Kaufmann suggests that this piece belongs to a tradition of experimental works with classical or humanistic Latin texts, such as Josquin's *Dulces exuviae,* Willaert's *Quid non ebrietas,* and Vicentino's *Musica prisca caput.*[38] It should be noted, however, that most of these compositions involve extravagant harmonic novelties. In fact, Lasso's *Prophetiae Sibyllarum,* a very chromatic cycle on a humanist text, is a better candidate in this regard.

Our second source comes from the pen of a humanist physician, Dr. Samuel Quickelberg. His famous commentary accompanies the lavish miniatures that decorate an elegant manuscript version of Lasso's *Penitential Psalms.*[39] Quickelberg provides a succinct formulation of the aesthetic premise behind *musica reservata*—depicting the affections of the text in a vivid, lively, poignant, graphic, and realistic manner. To paraphrase his words, musical elements seem to be so intimately fused with verbal emotions as to form one indissoluble entity. Lowinsky rightly singles out one striking phrase in his statement: *ad res et verba accommodando, singulorum affectuum vim exprimendo rem quasi ante oculos ponendo.*[40] Lasso accommodates his music to the content of his text, and so vividly expresses the affections that the listener thinks he sees things represented before his very eyes. All students of rhetoric immediately recognize this last attribute as the one given to rhetorical figures of speech by Marcus Fabius Quintilian and the author of the *Ad Herennium.* Hence we might forgive its mixture of metaphors. The comment echoes Vicentino's plea for pictorial and rhetorical effects, and it also anticipates Burmeister's *hypotyposis.* In short, mannerist theorists of music, like their counterparts in poetic theory, put their own interpretation on Horace's dictum: *Ut pictura poesis.* The number and nature of sources relating *musica reservata* to a rhetorical ideal are so overwhelming that no modern historian disputes this specific explanation.

Harmonic audacity represents one of the most controversial devices characteristic of rhetorical music. Coclico's adventuresomeness is very limited in his treatise, but his musical publication, *Musica reservata,* reveals two elements of experimentation: daring *commixtio* between Dorian and Phrygian modes, and some chromatic passages.[41] Vicentino's use of the genera for extremely bizarre *effetti meravigliosi* has been described in some detail, and it is clear that harmonic novelty lies at the heart of his notorious *bella maniera-musica "riserbata."* And, as we have seen, Vicentino's avant-gardism arouses considerable controversy. From his many detractors, I cite Taisnier's remarks. The reference given earlier in this chapter, which equates *musica moderna, nova,* and *reservata,* continues to the effect that *reservata* style is composed by misguided musicians who believe that they can change the diatonic genus into the chromatic by applying the *diesis* or *diaschisma.* Taisnier's equation of radical *musica reservata* with the new chromatic style is unequivocal.[42] That Taisnier means Vicentino specifically is shown by his complaint that the moderns fail to see the real difference between the traditional diatonic genus of current polyphony and the chromatic and enharmonic genera of ancient practice. Like Danckerts, Zarlino, and other critics of innovative harmony, Taisnier condemns modern style as iconoclastic irreverence.

The sources linking chromaticism to mannerist *imitazione delle parole* are many. Two others that associate this feature specifically with *musica reservata* deserve some comment. In the Besançon essay, the praise of generic mutation in *monodia* can be construed as a feature of *musica reservata* inasmuch as this device prevents monotony and excites the listeners.[43] Eucharius Hoffmann states that in ancient times, the chromatic genus was limited to instruments; in his day, some composers have revived it in vocal music that they call *musica reservata*.[44] It is also worth noting that subtle chromatic nuances form one element of Vicentino's *nuovo modo*; and chromatic and enharmonic intervals characterize the recondite motets of Giovanni Spataro and Ballestra. From all this evidence, there can be no doubt that chromaticism, one of the chief features of radical *maniera*, constitutes an important aspect of *reservata* style.

Vicentino's *nuovo modo* also exploits rhythmic breathlessness and continuous texture. Similar trends are evident in the madrigals found in his treatise. This is why Danckerts isolates fast tempo and short notes as faults of the *nuova maniera*.[45] Taisnier too describes the incessantly flowing quality and rhythmic eccentricity of *contrapuncta fluentia* as an aspect of *musica reservata*.[46] And the author of the Besançon tract indicates that in continuous rhythm, one should avoid the cadence so that what is called *musica reservata* results. Now, continuous rhythm and deceptive cadences are ubiquitous features neither in mannerist practice nor in theoretical conceptions of *reservata*. Vicentino, however, describes the techniques of *fuggir la cadenza* at some length. These closely related treatises seem to reflect the influence of Vicentino's work, and at the very least, they attest to the custom of associating *musica reservata* with his *bella maniera*.

The rhetorical figures of *musica poetica* have received insufficient attention, both in their own right and as adjuncts to mannerist ideals. We have noted that the use of *musica poetica* to describe the art of composition appears in theory before Burmeister's figural system. From its inception, this term grows out of the humanist desire to associate music with the expressive arts. Although Coclico does not mention *musica poetica*, his pairing of music and rhetoric is prophetic. And he calls modern musicians "poets." The inference that musical rhetoric is related to *musica reservata* receives support from his musical publication. Modern scholars have found figures corresponding to Burmeister's *noema*, *climax*, *analepsis*, and *mimesis*,[47] not to mention *fuga realis* and *fuga imaginaria*. Vicentino's incredible list of affective intervals can also be taken as a forerunner of later more systematic treatment of musical figures. And his music abounds in techniques that could be analyzed in Burmeister's terms. It is significant that Taisnier's writing, which contains so much criticism of Vicentino's style, lists many abuses found in *musica reservata* that accord with Burmeister's terms. Taisnier mentions *hypotyposis*, metrical changes, repetition, and homophony as aberrations of the new style. The Besançon work also mentions four rhetorical figures that anticipate Burmeister's categories: imitative texture (*fuga*, *ploke*, or *copulatio*), repetition of homophonic passages on ascending degrees (*tone*), conjunct motion (*agoge*), and disjunct motion (*petteia*).[48] Palisca notes that rhetorical terms are rare in musical theory before Burmeister. For this reason, both Taisnier and the Besançon writer provide extremely important sources for linking early seventeenth-century *musica poetica* with sixteenth-century *musica reservata*, the latter, of course, denoting radical *maniera*.

Inasmuch as Burmeister's *figurae* are illustrated by excerpts taken from motets by Lasso, we should not be surprised to discover that his *Penitential Psalms* are replete with rhetorical figures. This cycle does not contain the chromaticism that relates some of Lasso's other works to *musica reservata*. The most convincing assumption, therefore, is that Quickelberg's adulation of the vivid and affective style of this composition refers to the presence of rhetorical figures. Both the musical style of the *Penitential Psalms* and the appearance of a number of passages from it in Burmeister's treatise point to a strong connection between *musica poetica* and *reservata*. Burmeister's system gathers together nearly all the expressive devices of sixteenth-century *maniera*, including elements ranging from the ornaments of canon and imitation, and the fast-running figures of *contrapuncta fluentia* and florid diminutions, to minute word painting, affective chromaticism, and dramatic intensification. In this way, mannerist stylization is transformed into a stylistic basis for baroque music. *Musica reservata* becomes *musica poetica*, and iconoclastic elements of *maniera* become the rational and academic *Figurenlehre* and *Affektenlehre*.[49]

My final point has to do with social function. Many documents reveal that new music is reserved for some kind of elite audience. In this respect, *musica reservata* affords a striking parallel with the general mannerist pride in superior refinement and extraordinary exquisiteness beyond the reach of the masses. The motets in Coclico's *Musica reservata* are intended for private performance in the home. Dr. Seld's description of the private renditions of *reservata* indicates a similar function. Ruffo's *dotta arte et reservato ordine* is also aimed at the private delectation of musical connoisseurs.[50] Vicentino's treatise contains the most extensive statement about the social function of *musica "riserbata."* Four sets of parallel opposites comprise the characteristics of ordinary as opposed to reserved music: diatonic versus chromatic and enharmonic styles, communal places versus aristocratic courts, public festivals versus the praise of noble persons or heroes, and common versus refined ears. The elitist element of cultivated audiences also extends to highly trained singers. Vicentino himself taught a select group of performers in Rome with the greatest of secrecy until they were ready to dazzle Cardinal Niccolò Ridolfo's entourage (ca. 1549). Throughout his treatise, Vicentino repeats the requirement that chromatic and enharmonic pieces must be sung in the hyperrefined style appropriate to private chamber music. This is the reason he prefaces his chromatic motet with the statement that this work can be sung by a church choir—it is an exception to the rule. And his *Musica prisca caput*, a virtuoso combination of all three genera, sets a Latin humanistic text in honor of his patron, Cardinal Ippolito d'Este. Vicentino's views not only set forth the sociological milieu for *musica "riserbata"* but also link it to the exclusive appreciation of novel and bizarre *effetti meravigliosi*. His *bella maniera* belongs to private collections of courtly curiosities, as does his notorious archicembalo, in a more tangible and physical way.

Among the many examples of this cultural ambience, I refer

to a few works that have been cited in other contexts. Spataro's recondite motet is dedicated to Pope Leo X, and Ballestra's *musica reservata* praises Archduke Ferdinand. Willaert's "chromatic duo," *Quid non ebrietas*, is a private puzzle piece designed to test, and foil, the abilities of the papal choir. It is also possible that Dr. Seld calls *Tityre tu patulae* an example of *reservata* because Lasso meant it for a restricted court audience. This hypothesis is substantiated by the fact that his *Penitential Psalms*, together with Quickelberg's comments, appear in a sumptuous manuscript that is the exclusive property of his patron. Another magnificent set of handwritten part-books with miniatures by Hans Muelich preserves his *Lamentations of Jeremiah* and the *Sibylline Prophecies* (1560). Its contents are thus immortalized as an art book gracing the Duke's private library. We thus conclude that chromaticism of the most outrageous kind is limited to those *cognoscenti* who love esoteric art of all kinds. Mannerist love of secrecy also shows itself in the practice of hidden chromaticism, the secret chromatic art of the Netherlands and its Italian imitations. Such *musica reservata* is reserved for select performers. In another context, that of improvised ornamentation, Ercole Bottrigari records that the performance of chamber music at the court of Ferrara was effected with the greatest of secrecy[51] and the jealous guarding of the *concerto delle donne* is well known. Francesco Corteccia, court composer to the Grand Duke of Tuscany, applied self-imposed secrecy, an attitude evidently intended to enhance his infinitely more mediocre music. Perhaps Marini was called a *musico riservato* because he performed his virtuoso solos only for a small and select gathering at the court.[52] These are just a few of the facts surrounding the aesthetic and sociological implications of *musica reservata*.

Although not all interpretations are sure, the connection between *reservata* and exclusive social circumstances cannot be denied. This milieu encourages experimentation with esoteric effects whose *meraviglia* raises the reputation of musicians and their patrons alike. Even early operas, which by their very nature address a fairly large audience, are produced in this rarefied atmosphere. They represent the last mannerist striving for startling rhetorical power in music, but rhetorical power that pleases only refined and learned persons. When opera becomes a public commodity, it loses its most precious mannerist traits, traits that are directly attributable to the sociological and stylistic premises of *musica reservata*.

Hucke finds it astonishing that studies on *musica reservata* do not relate this topic to Mannerism in sixteenth-century music.[53] Although this statement is not entirely accurate,[54] it nevertheless reflects the status of both *musica reservata* and *maniera* in modern scholarship. The more current spate of books on Mannerism in the sister arts is finding increasing echoes in musical historiography, and several scholars make stimulating but as yet incomplete associations among these matters.[55] In the preceding chapters, I have traced in some detail the changing profile created by conservative, progressive, and radical theory from the viewpoint of historical ideas, aesthetic values, tuning, rudiments, counterpoint, composition, imitation, *musica poetica*, singing, and *maniera*. *Musica reservata* touches on all these topics in subtle and often obscure ways. The total picture is quite complicated in its small-scale topography. But this topography in turn delineates one dominant trend in the sixteenth and early seventeenth centuries: the eventual technico-aesthetic formulation of two norms of style. And in my opinion, the formulation of a norm for traditional polyphony develops under the pressure exerted by radical stylization in the form of *nuova maniera* and *musica reservata*.

Recalcitrant reactionaries, moderate progressives, and militant avant-gardists exhibit an acute awareness of the serious upheaval taking place in this period. That they sometimes foment unrest by undue exaggeration of polarities can be ascribed to several mannerist characteristics: love of debate, desire for personal aggrandizement, and polemical self-importance. This upheaval, whether real or imaginary, leaves its indelible mark on all theoretical subject areas, and it represents, "in short, Mannerism, a term adopted from art history to designate what only recently has been recognized as a move separate from the traditional sixteenth-century idiom."[56] Stylistic abstractions seem most difficult to promote in music, a field in which scholars hesitate to make analogies and comparisons. This situation is particularly unfortunate with regard to Mannerism, because, in my view, theoretical and aesthetic writings about music between 1530 and 1630 provide a more fecund and convincing body of evidence than similar sources in the sister arts. There remains the task of examining mannerist style in musical practice, an examination that takes into account both the elements described by theorists and those neglected by them. The combined force of theoretical conceptions and musical activity will, it is hoped, justify my hypothesis that these years embrace a distinctive historic-stylistic entity—an Age of Mannerism whose style mediates between that of the Renaissance and that of the Baroque.

PART THREE

Mannerism in Music

CHAPTER XVII

ઙ૰ઙ૰ઙ૰

Introduction

Any attempt to crystallize the essence of a style poses particular problems in music, and the case with Mannerism is no different. The first studies of this phenomenon, initiated under the influence of awakening interest in art history, reflect opinions characteristic of the first stage of the historiography of Mannerism, opinions that have been revised by subsequent scholarship. These early musical writings provide us with many valuable and provocative ideas, but they also present certain difficulties. For one thing, they often indulge in vague and occasionally irrelevant comparisons with intellectual and social factors informing the background of the sister arts. Even more disconcerting is their formulation of musical analysis in analogical terms borrowed indiscriminately from the methodology of art criticism.[1] These limitations have been criticized in more recent musical scholarship. Benefitting from the rigorous modern investigation of Mannerism in the sister arts, musicologists have refined their notions about Mannerism in accepting or rejecting its validity. Most important of all, musicologists now pointedly stress the need for purely musical tools—technical, aesthetic, and historical—for examining Mannerism in music.[2]

Inasmuch as a cultural approach to music presupposes that this art is not created in a vacuum, it follows that period concepts, be they propositions on behalf of a Renaissance or of Mannerism, rest on the hypothesis that music shares certain elements with other areas of artistic and intellectual endeavor. Now, cross-currents between music and such areas seem most viable when advanced from sociological and theoretical evidence. But even here, musical configurations must be framed in the context of musical behavior and thought. Using this approach, one may appreciate mannerist attitudes in musical terms, and also ascertain any parallels with or distinctions from other facets of culture. As far as musical works are concerned, attention must focus primarily on musical elements contributing to mannerist style in this medium. Technical analysis, couched in terminology proper to music itself, serves this purpose. On the other hand, critical analysis of aesthetic aims inherent in these works depends on the findings of technical analysis, but it uses a vocabulary that adapts to similar questions in the other arts. Style cannot be grasped adequately without the combination of technical and critical apparatus. And it is precisely in style criticism that the observant researcher discovers striking evidence of both similarities and divergences between musical Mannerism and Mannerism in the sister arts.

At the outset of the sixteenth century, musical practice evinces unanimity with theory. The contrapuntal procedures of Josquin des Prez and his generation form a musical norm, a classical model for subsequent mannerist stylization.[3] Mannerism in this sense has a twofold influence. The first relates to the style that, in general, becomes the *prima prattica*. To musicians of the sixteenth century, the music of what we call the Renaissance seems to embody remarkable equipoise between abstract laws, textual exigencies, and stylistic flexibility. These elements comprise the base for notions of an *ars perfecta*, of *musica reservata-osservata*, and finally of the *prima prattica*. I believe that this idea of a stylistic base is an apt one, because in their striving for ideal perfection, musicians emphasize the style of their model—its *maniera*. In short, they seek to understand the stylistic components of a norm that can be isolated, explained, and put into practice. This norm, of course, does not remain unchanged throughout its history. Quite the contrary, each successive generation adds its own refinements, and theorists, depending on their sensitivity and astuteness, recognize this fact. But, as each group reaches that level it believes to be consummate perfection, writers cling tenaciously to the chimera of a timeless ideal whose prolongation supposedly guards against degeneration. At the same time, the medium of print, which encourages the preservation of the composer's *opus absolutum*, in effect establishes an ever-widening corpus of precedent models. As the sixteenth century progresses, the line of authority becomes longer and longer, and theorists accordingly begin to distinguish among older and younger practitioners of the perfect art. This situation inculcates a strong sense of tradition that leads ultimately to the marked antiquarianism associated with *prima prattica* in the early seventeenth century. Refined details are certainly different, but the stylistic base of such polyphony remains the same. At the same time, the drastic changes evident in secular music, together with the militant opinions of radical musicians, force the proponents of conservative style to stress the revered continuity of the perfect art, a continuity that bespeaks its essential immutability.

The second mannerist influence relates to the multifarious styles and genres of secular music, elements that quickly transform the frottola and the lyrical diatonic madrigal into the later chromatic and dramatic madrigal, the concerted and soloistic madrigal, monody, cantata, and opera. The breeding ground for the startling novelties that effected this amazing change is the polyphonic madrigal.[4] In the early sixteenth century, this genre embodies a mild stylization of the norms of renaissance polyphony. It begins as hedonistic court entertainment,[5] setting Italian verse in a contrapuntal idiom that takes as its point of departure the imitative style of the perfect art. The madrigal is meant to amuse cultivated amateur singers and perhaps a small group of listeners. Occasional expressive touches, inspired by the conceits of petrarchist verse, are also stylizations of the more adventurous details present in the classical norm. These seemingly innocuous excursions, considered by their creators as refined ornaments of the *dolce maniera*, are the seeds of an unforeseen explosion that will distort the classical norm beyond recognition.[6] Style consciousness, infused with a new ingredient of arrogance and pride, is clearly evident in the attention given from mid-century on to *nuovo modo, nuova maniera, musica reservata, bella maniera, nobile maniera, contrapunto moderno,* and *seconda prattica*. The basis for "modern" stylization takes various forms. Its earliest manifestation depends on the exaggerated refinement of the sweet ornaments of early Mannerism, but what ensues can be characterized as refinement of these refinements as well as completely iconoclastic innovations. Inherent in this cumulative approach is a belief in the necessity for deliberate departure from the norms of any previously established style. It grows stronger with each generation of inventive mannerists until the division between the staid refinements of the first practice and the excessive refinements of the second practice becomes an accomplished fact.

Radical musicians emphasize the importance of rhetorical devices, devices they conceive as types of imitative-affective ornaments. Surrounded by humanist chattering about passionate expression, mannerist composers at first invent musical effects that represent and arouse the affections within the polyphonic idiom. Minute word paintings, from individual words to more complex *concetti*, are created by eye music and aural figures. But these expressive excursions as yet do not totally disrupt the musical logic of contrapuntal procedures. Later in the century, we observe that the violent *contrapposti verbali* of concettist poetry go hand in hand with increasingly exaggerated effects in musical settings. Each generation of madrigalists sets out to outdo the previous one with more sweet, more striking, more unusual, more daring, and of course, more numerous novelties. The *maniera dolce* of the early madrigal is now challenged by the *maniera grande*. The literary inspiration of *imitazione delle parole* stretches the norm of imitative counterpoint in the madrigal to such a degree that it eventually disintegrates.[7] Out of its ashes arises the phoenix of the concerted solo madrigal and monody, genres performed by a new class of virtuoso performers. This last development, adapted to the narrative presentation of a dramatized story, represents the final outcome of the mannerist tradition of literalizing and rhetoricalizing music.

We have noted that imitative-affective devices in the polyphonic madrigal embody a strange combination of intellectual wit and intensely charged emotion. Because eye music is associated solely with a penchant for witty punning, this device has been decried by detractors of madrigalian excesses as childish and absurd.[8] But we must remember that even visual eye music, whose imitation appeals only to singers, is considered by its practitioners as a contribution to the imitation of the passions.[9] It forms part of the magical tricks of music. From this viewpoint, eye music is no different than aural figures whose wit and *enargeia* appeal to both singers and listeners—in effect, the aesthetic premise behind the two is identical. We should also recognize that the minute and fleeting manifestations of aural figures are more obvious to the connoisseur or even to the analyst. At any rate, musical devices such as melodic shape, rhythmic patterns, and harmonic coloring share the paradoxical fusion of calculated rationality and spontaneous expressivity that characterizes ambivalent Mannerism. Furthermore, these aural imitative-affective figures embody the disruptive forces that change the classical norm into a distinctly manneristic style.[10]

Because of their dual nature, rhetorical devices in music are notoriously amenable to vapid imitation. The more novel and unusual a device, the greater its immediate impact. It soon becomes a stock-in-trade within a growing body of stereotypes. Thus, the musical genius who invents a cliché must move on to another in order to maintain his status as a trend setter. At the same time, clichés enjoy popularity, and composers using them contribute to the propagation of current madrigalisms and thus transform inspiration into banal fashion, a superficial stylish mode. The very fact that novel inventions pass rapidly into common use helps to stabilize a repertory of musical devices, and, more important, a musical attitude. Both the technical and aesthetic aspects of mannerist stylization build up a tradition, one clearly recognized as such by early seventeenth-century apologists of new music. But this tradition, in contradistinction to the one associated with the perfect art, serves as the authority for radical experiments.

Since mannerists stress their ability to rival the fabled *effetti meravigliosi* characteristic of ancient rhetorical style, modern scholars tend to attribute every innovation in musical language to this aim. The touting of classical authority by avant-gardists represents an aesthetic justification for their stylized novelties. Sometimes these aesthetic pronouncements come after the artistic fact, and evidently show an awareness of current ideas, ideas that musicians capitalize on to sell their product. Musicians are also very much aware of the fact that their procedures depart from the sacrosanct rules of the science of counterpoint. Indicative of this attitude is that these innovations, when they can be explained at all, are explained as distortions, extensions, and deviations from normal precepts. If their music no longer embodies scientific rules, as every conservative critic says, radical writers counter with the polemical notion that such music embodies refined *maniera* to an extent unknown in dry academic science. Moreover, new style, the result of innate talent and divine genius, must be judged by the canons of dramatic expressivity. In short, the rhetorical ideal functions as a convenient criterion for any avant-garde stylization that transcends the rules of science. Mannerists cannot talk about *scientia* but they certainly can talk about *bella* and *nuova maniera*. This characteristic defense against attacks made by traditionalists must not make us forget that some mannerist inventions are purely technical and musical ones without any connection to the rhetorical manifesto.[11] Nor must this characteristic defense mislead us into thinking that *nuova maniera* always lacks its own musical rules.

Both technical and expressive novelties, which contribute to the many individual styles of the mannerist period, arise from an overwhelming desire to experiment. Once the magic circle of renaissance cosmology has been broken, nothing seems to stand in the way of the enthusiastic propagation of stylistic progress. As experimentation moves along its inexorable spiral toward iconoclasm, it relegates formerly progressive style to the uncomplimentary rank of conservative academicism. If traditional musicians seem at times to be uncharitable to new music, the same can be said of the reverse assessment made by radical musicians concerning traditional values in music. And in spite of the many warnings voiced by reactionaries, some patrons of the *ars perfecta* eventually accept certain elements of the *nuova maniera*. For example, the Church militant of the Counter Reformation cannot afford to ignore the great appeal of secular style. In the end, the uninspired reforms advocated by the Council of Trent fall by the wayside as religious leaders utilize the novelties of rhetorical music for their own catholic purposes.

These interacting trends, and the complex picture they form, possess one common element—a search for novel techniques in music calculated to astonish, to create *effetti meravigliosi*. The polyphonic madrigal, with its minute word painting and rampant chromaticism, the concerted madrigal, with its soloistic voices and expressive dissonances, the solo song, with its florid diminutions, and monodic recitation, with its dramatic impact, all belong in the same arena of radical *maniera*, of musical Mannerism—"the most extremely experimental period in the history of art save for the present."[12]

CHAPTER XVIII

ꙮ ꙮ ꙮ

Incipient Mannerism, 1530–1550

Before examining the early madrigal, a review of some radical tendencies in certain works of the Renaissance will elucidate the framework of mannerist developments. Although Henricus Glareanus does discuss expressive elements in the music of Josquin des Prez, elements that transgress against his concept of modal purity, he wisely omits the most adventurous compositions by this composer. I mention first two Latin pieces, the secular motets *Fama malum a4* and *Dulces exuviae a4*, setting passages from Virgil's *Aeneid*, because they contain expressive traits that anticipate mannerist style. Isabella d'Este greatly admired this epic, and Josquin may have composed the works when he visited Ferrara around 1503.[1] Both their court performance and their style suggest connections with *musica reservata*. In the first piece, Josquin's depiction of Fama, the malignant deity responsible for the rupture between Dido and Aeneas, abounds in subtle pictorial details and small-scale rhetorical figures. Even more prophetic is the setting of Dido's famous lament, *Dulces exuviae*. As in the case of *Fama malum*, a shift from Dorian to Phrygian modes gives this work an affective quality striking for its time. I must stress that such compositions are hardly exemplary of mature Mannerism; however, like their counterparts in art and literature, they contain hints of traits destined to be exaggerated by radical composers of the later sixteenth century.

Two other works of Josquin, one secular and one on a Biblical text, demonstrate harmonic experimentation by means of hexachord mutation. *Fortuna d'un gran tempo a3* (1501), as is well known, features three conflicting signatures (two, one, and no flats) as well as mutation to six degrees in the circle-of-fifths scheme, requiring ficta from B♭ to D♭. These devices do not paint specific words of the text; they amount rather to a musical emblem that symbolizes the vicissitudes personified by Fortuna.[2] In this respect Josquin's work belongs to the same "iconographical" tradition as Matthaeus Greiter's *Passibus ambiguis a4*, which was mentioned in connection with Gregor Faber's radical hexachord system. Perhaps the most famous of Josquin's expressive compositions is *Absalon fili mi a4*, a work that sets the lament of David for his dead son.[3] Scholars agree on the authority of the earliest manuscript source (1516–22) that preserves the work for four low voices with conflicting signatures (two, three, and four flats). The tessitura and rich harmonies bespeak Josquin's goal of affective eloquence. And because the text is nonliturgical, it also belongs to *musica reservata*. The most striking part of this unusual piece occurs in the final, repeated passage where an extended circle-of-fifths progresses from B♭ major to G♭ major. This passage is noteworthy because it presents an affective rendering of David's anguish as well as a graphic depiction of his desired descent to infernal regions. Both these features become characteristics of mannerist style.

Dulces exuviae and *Absalon fili mi* also feature an aspect of mannerist ambiguity found in the later madrigal. They set very strong personalized sentiments of grief and sorrow, couched in verbal terms of the first person singular, in the somewhat depersonalized medium of polyphony, embodying the first person plural. And inasmuch as the personal passion of concettist verse is clearly more extravagant, the continued use of polyphonic texture appears even more odd. As we will see, different techniques employed by sixteenth-century composers in their effort to overcome the limitations of counterpoint become disruptive elements within the premises of polyphonic precepts. Be that as it may, the polyphonic tradition seems to bear an ambivalent relationship to the mannerist creed of rhetorical power, and some modern historians call the madrigal a mannerist genre for this very reason.

Another work in the early avant-garde stream that warrants some discussion is Adrian Willaert's *Quid non ebrietas* (ca. 1519), an astonishing composition that circulated for years as a "chromatic duo," and was printed as such in Giovanni Maria Artusi's treatise in 1600. Its earlier history relates directly to the debate over equal temperament and extensive hexachord mutation.[4] Giovanni Spataro sent this *opera subtillissima et docta* to Pietro Aaron with an accompanying letter (1524) in which he recounts that Willaert avenged a slight perpetrated against him by the papal choir by submitting to them this puzzle piece; and their unsuccessful performance of it proved to his satisfaction their limited musical expertise. In notated form, the duo ends on a seventh after an enigmatic series of dissonant intervals. The key to the solution lies in the tenor part. After a guileless beginning in the Dorian mode once transposed, this voice starts down the familiar path of flat mutation, and so that there can be no mistake, Willaert writes in the cumulative accidentals from E♭ to C♭. Needless to say, this last audacious fictum is unheard of even in the most progressive hexachord systems of the time (except for that of Spataro). Written accidentals suddenly disappear at this point. But the singers are supposed to take C♭ as a signal to continue the circle-of-fifths by applying even more abnormal ficta to the last half of the tenor: F♭, B♭♭, and so on up to C♭♭. With this radical procedure, Willaert has gone through the full circle back to the B♭ in the key signature, now read as the enharmonic equivalent of C♭♭.

Willaert's arrangement of the humorous text, taken from the fifth epistle of Horace, wittily underscores the main sections of his harmonic scheme. The first line, "What can drunkenness not manage? It reveals secrets," is set to the opening section, whose character is quite ordinary. The word "secrets," however, signals the appearance of hexachord mutation, which occurs through notated accidentals (E♭ to G♭) under the second line, "It orders hope to be confirmed [presumably that of the papal singers], it leads the coward into battle." And the battle cry comes with the subsequent C♭, the last written accidental, which is followed directly by an unwritten F♭. These two ficta appropriately mark the start of the third line, "From the anxious soul." By the end of this line, "From the anxious soul it removes the burden, it teaches skills," all the other outrageous ficta should have been introduced. If the singers have indeed attained the skills necessary to interpret the piece thus far, they should have no trouble with the rest: "Full cups, whom have they not made eloquent?" The full cups of inebriation are the profuse accidentals that certainly befuddle sober musicians accustomed to less potent fare. But a drastic amount of daring is required to achieve eloquence.

From one viewpoint, this fascinating work can be constructed as yet another general symbol of its text, a learned emblem. However, the close connection between individual passages of both text and music, which has hitherto gone unnoticed, adds a distinctly graphic dimension, a kind of humorous *enargeia*, to the composition. It is tempting, but erroneous, to relate Vicentino's early *nuovo modo* to Willaert's chromatic experiment.[5] Moreover, Vicentino's later chromatic and enharmonic compositions depart from an entirely different premise than that of hexachord mutation. And yet, it should be noted that the sectional arrangement of his *Musica prisca caput a4* follows the scheme of *Quid non ebrietas*. We do not know whether Vicentino was acquainted with Willaert's duo, although both works may be considered examples of mannerist striving for bizarre rhetoric in music. It is true that the full impact of such early harmonic experiments will not be felt until the mid-sixteenth century, and to understand this side of Mannerism in secular music, we must first consider the early phase of the madrigal.

Although works in madrigalian style antedate the use of the name itself, scholars concur in starting the history of the genre in 1530, the date of the first appearance of the word in a musical publication (*Madrigali de diversi musici libro primo de la serena*). After this date, "madrigal" remains a generic term for polyphonic, concerted, and solo music throughout the sixteenth and early seventeenth centuries, a phenomenon that in itself suggests a continuity between styles normally associated with the Renaissance and the Baroque, not to mention Mannerism. Now, even in its initial stage, the madrigal reveals a conscious stylistic eclecticism that is typical of Mannerism, for it represents an amalgamation of national characteristics (especially those of the Parisian chanson and the Italian frottola), welded together by the international language of imitative counterpoint. The reason behind the intrusion of northern polyphony into the indigenous frottola has puzzled historians of music. To attribute it to the fact that northern composers become interested in setting Italian verse is not an adequate explanation, for these musicians can and do write perfectly good frottolas. Harrán suggests that the sluggish frottola, with its reliance on homophonic declamation, does not permit much musical development; it is somewhat of a dead end. And because musicians lack ancient models like those that inspire Mannerism in art and literature, they turn to the more flexible and adaptable medium of motet style, a kind of "classical" model for them. In short, imitative polyphony imparts to the setting of Italian poetry a more respectable artistic flair.[6] This hypothesis has much to recommend it, for it points out the perverse development of the madrigal. In its early phase, the madrigal abandons Italian heritage to become a version of northern style. And yet, in later stages it returns to the ideals of the frottola through the use of declamatory solos accompanied by homophonic texture. Those scholars who consider the frottola to be an Italian renaissance phenomenon and later declamatory monody or pseudo-monody to be an Italian baroque phenomenon place the polyphonic madrigal in a mannerist tradition that represents a degeneration of rhetorical and dramatic ideals.

I mentioned previously that the frottola belongs to the last and most artistic phase of *poesia per musica*. As interest shifts to the more mannerist style of poetic petrarchism, imitative polyphony begins to appear in musical settings, even those still called frottolas. The precepts of this *maniera*, adapted to the Italian language, answer the requirements of refined musical artistry. Hints of northern influence on early Mannerism in art have been isolated by modern historians. In the case of music, this kind of influence is more profound and far-reaching. And yet—and I consider this to be an important point—contrapuntal madrigals that closely mirror the premises of northern style, the *ars perfecta*, have a very short vogue. Even though the frottola disappears as a form after the establishment of the polyphonic madrigal, its melodic style and its vertical procedure by root progressions soon invade madrigal settings. These elements, plus the nature of Italian verse, alter the madrigal in a subtle way so that it quickly becomes differentiated from traditional style. Northern composers pay petrarchist verse the supreme compliment of setting it to an idiom based on the fundamental principles of the perfect art. But at the same time, they unconsciously bring in features not found in this stylistic model. I therefore submit that, despite its imitative counterpoint, the polyphonic madrigal even in its initial stage embodies a stylization of the *ars perfecta*.

Among the many technical features found in such stylization, two can be cited by way of a general introduction. Others will be discussed in the course of examining specific composers and their works. Madrigal publications at this time often refer in their titles to *nuovo modo* and *musica nova*. These terms signify something more than first printings or hitherto unpublished music. Novelty is connected to *madrigali cromatici* or *madrigali a note nere*, and chromaticism here means the use of small rhythmic values resulting in a plethora of black notes. *Note nere* herald a new spirit of rhythmic animation entirely foreign to traditional polyphony. Such stylization of a classical model, destined to have important repercussions on the future of the madrigal, is inspired by expressive needs and by purely musical interest in novel *maniera*.[7] This dual import allows, on the one hand, a more lively declamation, and on the other, a more subtle use of dissonances. Again, it is important to remember that *madrigali cromatici* retain the basis of imitative points borrowed from the *ars perfecta* but adapt it to a new *maniera*, a fact recognized by musicians of the time.

A second and equally important feature relevant to stylization of northern polyphony concerns the deployment of chromatic harmonies to paint the sweetly languid *concetti* of petrarchist poetry. When the madrigal comes into prominence, theorists of the perfect art already admit the legitimacy of B♭, E♭, F♯, C♯, and G♯. The next steps, according to the dual mutation system, are A♭ and D♯. It is interesting to note that early madrigalists go as far as A♭ but not D♯. Compared to the daring experiments of Josquin and Willaert, these chromaticisms seem pale and dull. However, their significance lies in the reasons for their use. They are written accidentals, and appear at odd moments within a predominantly diatonic framework solely *per causam suavitatis* and are always associated with key words in the text. This technico-aesthetic evidence points to later mannerist ideals.

Having sketched a general picture of the salient features of the early madrigal, we can turn now to some specific works to assess how these features are deployed in concrete instances. We find, in the works of Filippo Verdelot, an eclectic combination of frottola, chanson, and northern counterpoint.[8] To be specific, they exemplify the mannerist union of four-voice imitative texture with homophonic style stressing the highest voice.[9] Verdelot's *Madonna qual certezza* (ca. 1525–26; Bonifazio Dragonetto) serves as a good example of his technique because, in spite of some archaisms, it exhibits a number of novelties connected with text setting. For example, chords utilizing E♭ appear on *fuoco, poco a poco*, and *Haimè*. The latter anguished interjection is emphasized by its long notes, which are set off from the preceding and following phrases, as well as by the surprising third-relations formed between it and the previous cadence (Example XVIII-1). In this case, the harmony underscores a kind of rhythmic contrast whose only justification is the words. A similar but less obvious technique, can be seen in the opening of the madrigal. Here, the rhetorical address to the poet's *madonna* becomes more poignant by the subsequent dancelike meter of the next few phrases. These lead to the word *consumarmi*, which prompts a sudden animated movement that in turn dwindles to the slower pace of *poco a poco*, leading to a sectional cadence.

EXAMPLE XVIII-1.   F. Verdelot, *Madonna qual certezza* (ca. 1525–26). From H. Colin Slim, *A Gift of Madrigals and Motets*, 2:379. Chicago, 1972. Used by permission of The University of Chicago Press.

We should note that the varying textures and tempos—from slow, to moderate, to fast, and finally to slow again—characterize the entire opening section of the piece, and that from the abstract viewpoint interest in heightening the successive conceits of this poem does not disrupt the independent flow of the music up to this point. But immediately after the cadence marking this point, we hear the E♭ major sonority on *Haimè*. Later in this section we find an unexpected rest after *diviso* that does indeed interrupt the musical flow.

These few remarks suffice to show that this work shares the madrigalisms characteristic of a number of Verdelot's other pieces, such as *I vostri acuti dardi* (ca. 1525–26). Harmonic coloring, rhythmic contrasts, pauses, and sighing figures all contribute to a growing arsenal of imitative-affective devices. Prompted by the conceits of the poetry, such devices often occur as nonstructural elements. In view of the dating of these compositions, Slim presents convincing evidence for placing Verdelot before Jacob Arcadelt as one of the early masters of the polyphonic madrigal.[10] In this regard, I mention the testimony of his friend and contemporary, Cosimo Bartoli, who states that Verdelot's works are admired because they contain *del facile, del grave, del gentile, del compassionevole, del presto, dal tardo, del benigno, dello adirato, del fugato, seconda la proprietà delle parole.*[11] Had these comments, stressing as they do the rather divergent musical qualities mustered to depict the text, been applied to a later composer—such as Luca Marenzio or Giaches de Wert—we would easily consider them indicative of mature and fully developed rhetorical *maniera*. However, it is apparent that such value judgments are relative. And at the very least, in my view, Bartoli's description does indicate the presence of incipient Mannerism, or mannerisms if you will, in the works of this composer.

Adrian Willaert dominates the musical scene in northern Italy, and pupils flock to Venice to study with him: Andrea Gabrieli, Costanza Porta, Nicola Vicentino, Gioseffo Zarlino, Francesco della Viola, Antonio Barre, and Cipriano de Rore. This roster has just about all the leading figures of the next generation. Willaert's most important publication is the *Musica nova* (1559), a collection of thirty-three motets and twenty-five madrigals. But his early style reflects the secular works in this publication, the *nuovo modo* that inspires future trends. *Amor mi fa morire a4* (1536; Dragonetto) indicates the direction that Willaert's mature *maniera* will take. In general, we can isolate two characteristics. The first is an imitative procedure imbued with subtle and flexible rhythmic liveliness. The second concerns Willaert's treatment of the text, which eschews word painting but includes occasional excursions into chromaticism, showing his sensitivity to sensuous musical language[12] (Example XVIII-2). In *Qual dolcezza giammai a5* (1538; Anton Francesco Doni), a work composed for the private *musicales* of Polissena Pecorina's *ridotto* and dedicated to this cultivated lady, Willaert deploys five voices in a changing kaleidoscope of four higher and four lower groupings. The *ars perfecta* is represented by imitative texture, and the *nuovo modo* by refined declamation. Most striking is the new rich sonority achieved by the five voices.

The adventurous aspects of Costanzo Festa's output, one of the few Italians to challenge northern domination in these decades, pertain to an ideal of expressivity. Although his contrapuntal style stays closer to classical norms than that of Willaert, Festa uses unusual techniques, such as chromatic melodies built on semitonal configurations. One such instance occurs on the words *dolor* and

EXAMPLE XVIII-2.   A. Willaert, *Amor mi fa morire* (1536).
From *Opera Omnia*, 14:4. Edited by H. Zenck,
W. Gerstenberg, and B. and H. Meier. American Institute
of Musicology, 1977. Used by permission of
Dr. A. Carapetyan.

morte in *Quanto più m'arde* (1539),[13] and the entire phrase—
from both the linear and vertical viewpoints—forms a striking
contrast with the diatonic character of the rest of the madrigal
(Example XVIII-3). Festa's antidiatonic learnings are also reflected
in the fact that one of the first cases of a written A♭ occurs in a
composition published in 1537.

EXAMPLE XVIII-3.   C. Festa, *Quanto più m'arde* (1539).
From H. Osthoff, *Theatergesang und darstellende Musik
in der italienischen Renaissance*, 2:219. Tutzing, 1969.
Used by permission of Hans Schneider Verlag.

Mannerist stylization and eclecticism also dominate the madrigals of Jacob Arcadelt, written during his Italian period (1539–
55). The opening of *Crudel acerba inesorabil morte a5* (1538;
Petrarch) features dissonant suspensions obviously designed to
paint cruel, bitter, and inexorable death with a vivid stylization of
classical points of imitation. *Ecco pur che doppo sì lunghi affanni
a4* (1539), on the other hand, illustrates some interesting dramatic
tendencies. *Ecco* is twice stated, the second time in shortened note
values, and its treatment suggests an oratorical gesture. In fact, the
overall homophonic texture of the work gives it a rhetorical flair
that suggests a dramatic premise.[14] Such dramatic moments, however, are rare in Arcadelt's music. He favors lyrical style but
infuses it with his personal exploitation of languid and sensuous

sentimentality, a quality that raises Arcadelt to the rank of the most celebrated representative of the *dolce stile nuovo*.

The single most famous madrigal embodying the sweet new style is his *Il bianco e dolce cigno a4* (1539; Alfonso d'Avalos). From northern style, Arcadelt takes the technique of setting each verbal phrase to a new musical section. But other traits—such as syllabic text treatment, repeated homophonic chords, and polyphonically animated homophony—belong to the new *maniera* of the madrigal. The ironic similes and hidden erotic conceits of d'Avalos's poem are matched by Arcadelt's subtle interplay among various techniques. A picture of the white, sweet swan who dies singing is evoked immediately by the range of the three higher voices. And the contrasting image of the poet who dies weeping prompts a musical contrast in the form of lower voice ranges for all four parts and a striking E♭ major chord on *piangendo* (Example XVIII-4). By itself, this sonority is not particularly daring, but in context it is a subtle stroke of genius. Arcadelt repeats the line to emphasize the bittersweet chromatic chord. The straightforward syllabic setting of the swan's disconsolate death serves as a foil for the beautifully soaring melisma picturing the happy death of the poet. And the ensuing recitativelike, homophonic passage

EXAMPLE XVIII-4.   J. Arcadelt, *Il bianco e dolce cigno* (1539). From *Opera Omnia*, 2:38–39. Edited by A. Seay. American Institute of Musicology, 1970. Used by permission of Dr. A. Carapetyan.

underscores the morbidity of the poet's joy and desire in death. Then comes the final witty point. Here Arcadelt mirrors the ingenuity of the words with a light, sentimental play on musical imitation that repeats over and over, *Di mille mort'il di, di mille mort'il dì.* Although the composition derives unity from the predominant Lydian modality and the homogeneity of its texture, we are already moving toward a madrigal style that contrasts elements purely for the sake of the text.

Arcadelt's chromatic excursions usually stay within the bounds of mildly progressive techniques. But he does use A♭ in an unorthodox fashion on *inusitata* in *Dov'ito son a4* (1540), and his witty pun, more witty than the affective import of a similar occurrence on *i tutte la mia doglia* in Claudio Veggio's *Per quei begli occhi a4* (1540),[15] can be taken as a harbinger of the highly intellectual and abstruse aspects to be found in madrigalian devices later in the century. Another harbinger of eccentric *maniera* can be seen in the opening of Alfonso della Viola's *In me cresce la voglia* (1539) (Example XVIII-5). First, we should note the semitonal line in the soprano, outlining a kind of chromatic tetrachord that paints in a graphic way the first words of the poem. Extremely unusual triadic relations support the plaintive wail of this voice. The major-minor versions of the same triad, as well as most of the third-related triads, are connected by none, one, or two linear semitone(s); the single case of two triads related by semitone root progression, A major and B♭ major, requires three linear semitones, although one of these is omitted.[16] Viola adds more fuel to his chromatic fire by introducing an anticipatory suspended seventh dissonance between the outer voices.[17] Practically all the ingredients of avant-garde madrigal style are here present. Later mannerists will refine and magnify their potential.

Among the works of Francesco Corteccia, one madrigal in particular stands out from his otherwise unremarkable style. *Quest'io tesseva a4* (1544) exploits the rhythmic animation inherent in *note nere* to create a striking representation of the impassioned lament. The poetic meter is completely distorted in an effort to achieve dramatic pathos. And in assessing this work, Einstein is certainly correct when he states that Corteccia is one of the first madrigalists guilty of *laceramento della poesia.*[18] In this respect,

Example XVIII-5.   A. della Viola, *In me cresce la voglia* (1539).
From *Primo libro di madrigali.*

Corteccia points to the coming freedom with which composers will treat their texts. Perhaps Corteccia was influenced by his participation in the sumptuous Florentine intermedios where music enhanced a dramatic context. But in all fairness, we should note that Haar finds rhythmic agitation in other madrigals, there used solely as a technical novelty.[19] The early madrigals of Vicentino do not hint at his later eccentricities. In his first book (1546), which contains his *nuovo modo*, we find mild rhetorical figures and restrained chromaticism. However, a rather novel element of harmonic agitation enters in the form of circle-of-fifths modulation, sudden diminished chords, and deceptive cadences.

The composers of the 1540s were eclipsed by the rising star of Cipriano de Rore, the initiator of the *seconda prattica* and *moderno contrapunto*. Rore went to Ferrara in 1547 where he lived with Vicentino and took part in the musical events of this brilliant court. Vicentino had already begun work on the ancient genera in 1534, and there is reason to suspect that Rore's later chromatic experiments are due in part to the influence of his friend and colleague. At this point the schoolbook truism that Rore changed the course of the development of the madrigal in a decisive way bears repetition. He also taught Luzzasco Luzzaschi, who will become the leading composer in Ferrara during the reign of the *concerto delle donne.*

Rore's first three books (1542, 1544, and 1548) establish the norm of five-voiced polyphony for subsequent madrigalian tradition. This *ingenii ostentatio* (to use Glareanus's words)[20] provides greater flexibility in textural groupings that can be used for affective and dramatic effects, as well as for structural purposes. It is universally recognized that Rore chooses his texts for their high literary quality and their vivid *concetti*, and that from the outset, he concentrates on painting in music their passions and affections. To this end, Rore treats the verse very freely, compressing and expanding it at will. And all the musical techniques he deploys serve but one idea—*imitazione delle parole*. We must remind the reader again that aesthetic judgments are relative. Compared to the eccentricities of the late sixteenth-century madrigal, Rore's style seems almost classical; but when compared to the *ars perfecta*, his style seems quite mannerist. Furthermore, he is the first composer to embody in his style a forceful individual inspiration. He cultivates his own inner vision, twisting the natural elements of both poetry and music into a design that is purely of his own making.[21] For all these reasons, Rore emerges as the first madrigalist with a strikingly personal *maniera*, one copied by a host of lesser talents. He is the first great mannerist master.

The tone painting evident in two Petrarch sonnets, *Hor che'l ciel e la terra a5* and *Per mezz'i boschi a5* (1542), illustrates tendencies that will become more pronounced as Rore matures. His third book contains the famous setting of Petrarch's *Vergine canzone*. These *madrigali spirituali*, unsurpassed in their flexible counterpoint and sensitive declamation, appear subdued in comparison with Rore's secular madrigals. But they nevertheless depart from the madrigal norm rather than from traditional sacred polyphony. His cycle inspires similar settings as well as other spiritual madrigals, and this tradition, with all the aesthetic tenets it entails, provides an analogous facet to the sensuality seen in religious art of the Counter Reformation.[22]

Rore's most celebrated madrigal, *Anchor che col partire a4* (1547; Avalos),[23] merits detailed discussion, not only because of its fame but also because of its intrinsic merit. I have already analyzed its epigrammatic verse, whose *maniera* consists of the ultimate in refined preciosity and subtle wit. Rore matches, indeed surpasses, the poem with his elegant and incredibly supple manipulation of serious charm and charming seriousness. It is a difficult task to put into words the elusive and delicate quality of this music; however, some characteristics of Rore's treatment of the text can be isolated. The two thoughts of the opening line are mirrored by contrasting textures: "Again in parting" has paired imitation, and "I feel myself dying" has a sonorous uplifting and then sensuous falling off of all four voices. Playfully animated movement underscores the idea, "I would like to part from you every hour, every moment"; in the music, the moments are shorter than the hours. After repeating "So great is the pleasure I feel" by means of three climactic statements, the singers then savor, in gloriously full, melismatic ecstasy, the thought of "the life that I acquire in returning" (Example XVIII-6). At this point, Rore creates contrasting texture and a quickening pace leading to the final line by means of intricate yet transparent points of imitation. But this section also functions as a felicitious rendering of the words, "And so, a thousand and a thousand times each day I should like to part from you"—a passage that inspires emulation by later composers, as we will see. A sensuous passage concludes the composition on the words, "So sweet are my returns," and the final cadence ends tantalizingly on the dominant of the Aeolian mode, leaving the perfumed sentiments hovering in the air after the last notes have sounded.

The great esteem enjoyed by this exquisite mannerist flower is attested by the fact that no composer after Rore dared to set this text except in emulation of his marvelous madrigal.[24] We have here a well-known and thoroughly investigated case of "parody" technique—in the widest sense of the term—associated with a single composition. Whereas parody technique in Masses of the sixteenth century has drawn considerable attention in modern scholarship, the extent of this approach in secular music, and especially in the madrigal, has only recently been recognized. The research of two scholars concerning specific pieces and composers clearly indicates that there exists "a whole sixteenth century tradition of the transformation, disguise and purloining of madrigals."[25] This tradition awaits systematic investigation, but nonetheless, the surprising discoveries made by Haar and Bianconi certainly add a

EXAMPLE XVIII-6. C. de Rore, *Anchor che col partire* (1547).
From *Opera Omnia*, 4:31–32. Edited by B. Meier.
American Institute of Musicology, 1969. Used by
permission of Dr. A. Carapetyan.

EXAMPLE XVIII-6, *continued*

new dimension to our understanding of a sixteenth-century practice arising from self-conscious and deliberate stylization. The
music they discuss demonstrates that *maniera* is a tangible musical
ideal, one that can be described in musical terms. Furthermore, the
repertory in question here suggests to us that "iconographical"
traditions in music, if we may be permitted to adapt a visual term,
represent striking analogues to mannerist trends in literature and
art.

CHAPTER XIX

§●§●§●

Mannerism Established,

1550–1580

In the previous chapter, I alluded to *note nere* as an agent of stylization in the madrigal, one that was responsible for a basic change in the genre and recognized as such at the time. The vogue of advertising the novelty of *note nere* is still alive in the early decades of the mid-century, and evidence for the importance attributed to this technical feature can be found even at the end of the period under consideration—Orazio Vecchi's charming and humorous travesty of Arcadelt's *Il bianco e dolce cigno* (1580). The text of the first stanza of *Fa una canzone a4* deserves to be quoted here: "Make a canzona without *note nere*; / If ever you have coveted my favor, / Make it in a tone (E♭ major triads) that invites sleep, / Sweetly, sweetly making it come to an end." The basis of Vecchi's musical parody (apart from subtle reminiscences of Arcadelt's harmonic idiosyncrasies) is the same as the one behind Anton Francesco Doni's evaluation of Arcadelt's *maniera* in 1544: *madrigali cromatici* have rendered earlier style obsolete. However, at mid-century, *madrigali cromatici* also designate another meaning—that of chromatic style. The examples are many; I cite Cesare Tudino's *Madrigali a note bianche et negre chromatiche* (1554), Giulio Fiesco's contrast between two madrigals, one *diatonico* and one *cromatico* (1554), Francesco Orso's *due madrigali cromatici* (1567), and two similarly labeled works by Ludovico Agostino (1570). And of course, Nicola Vicentino's treatise (1555) contains compositions so designated.

This sampling signals the most important development in

novel *maniera*, chromatic experimentation, whose greatest flurry of activity takes place between 1550 and 1560. Spurred on by academic and humanist interest in ancient theory and by courtly cultivation of *meraviglie*, composers explore some extravagant parameters of chromatic procedures. After 1560, rampant chromaticism dies down to become one component in the repertory of imitative-affective devices, but not before it has succeeded in revolutionizing musical language in a fundamental way. Nonetheless, theoretical and practical ferment at this time suggests a spirit of revolt against classical normality inasmuch as chromaticism furnishes an all too obvious element of intense preciosity, bizarre capriciousness, and dazzling virtuosity. The absolute meaning of *maniera* now embraces a truly mannerist ideal, and this change constitutes a musical crisis keenly felt by all sensitive musicians of the time.[1]

One chromatic method takes as its point of departure the addition of musica ficta. As such, it represents the final flowering of renaissance experiments, but after 1560, it also amounts to eccentric antiquarianism. Because most of the examples of this technique appear in northern Europe, they fall outside our purview. I refer to the dozen or so motets emanating from the Netherlands and works such as Matthaeus Greiter's *Passibus ambiguis a4* and Adrianus Petit Coclico's *Non derelinquat Dominus a4*.[2] All these works can be interpreted as examples of *musica reservata* on sociological, aesthetic, and technical grounds. To date, research has uncovered very few Italian madrigals that use this technique, although there may be more yet to be discovered. One that we do know of is Stefano Rossetti's *Mentre ch'el cor a4* (1560; Petrarch). The ending of the work poses problems similar to those encountered in the northern repertory. A diatonic reading entails three prohibited progressions, and for this reason, Lowinsky favors a chromatic interpretation.[3] As in the case of Willaert's duo, a C♭ fictum indicates further mutation to F♭ and B♭♭, producing a cadence on G♭ major. The piece thus ends one semitone below its notated form and concretely paints the mannerist conceit, *Et pianger di dolcezza*. Orso's two chromatic madrigals referred to earlier, in fact, two parts of the same Petrarch poem—*Il cantar novo* (a significant *capoverso*)—deliberately exploit bizarre

harmonies and equally bizarre notation.[4] In one spot, each successive sharp in the music indicates another semitonal rise in the
melody (Example XIX-1). Thus, the bass G♯ G♯ G♯ should be sung
as G♯ A A♯ (B♭) and the tenor C♯ C♯ C♯ should be sung as C♯ D
D♯ (E♭), and so on. Singers who can ferret out the secret of this
puzzle will perform a series of third-related triads.

EXAMPLE XIX-1.   F. Orso, *Il cantar novo* (1567).
From T. Kroyer, *Die Anfänge der Chromatik im
italienischen Madrigal des XVI. Jahrhunderts*, p. 90.
Leipzig, 1902.

The second, and by far more widespread, chromatic method
entails unorthodox progressions effected by means of written accidentals. Two of the earliest madrigals in the new avant-garde
wave represented by chromaticism at this time appear in Tudino's
book, whose title was cited at the start of this chapter. Both are
also labeled *cromatico* in the collection itself. *Altro che lagrimar*
features one flat and four sharps, and we can therefore count Tudino as one of the first composers to consistently notate D♯ and to
exploit chromaticism in the sharp direction. In addition to circles-
of-fifths on the sharp side, Tudino's chromaticism relies on third-
related triads and some minor-major shifts on the same root. These
radical triadic relationships usually occur between isolated pairs

of triads, except for one instance of an interlocking double progression (i.e., where the middle triad forms semitonal relations
with the preceding and following chord) and four instances of
triple progressions comprising one pair separated by a diatonic
step from an interlocking double set. The latter chromatic progressions are held together by ordinary diatonic steps and by circles-
of-fifths (Example XIX-2a).

The above excerpt, setting the second and third lines ("Nor
does my soul feed on anything but grief, / For he knows that he is
the master of my injury"), illustrates the techniques we have described. It opens with a triple progression, goes through a small
circle-of-fifths (B minor to D minor) that leads directly to another
triple progression (separated by a rest), through a longer circle-of-
fifths, and then ends with one pair of third-related triads. Aside
from the A minor-A major shift, two of the first three third-relations (C major A minor, and G major B minor) need no linear
semitone; these are the least audacious chromatic pairs and involve
major to minor progressions by descending-third root movement.
There are five other instances of such mild chromaticisms in the
madrigal. The remaining four cases in the given example all require
one linear semitone (G major B minor, B♭ major G major, G major
E major, and C major A major); the first of these progresses from
major to minor by ascending-third root movement whereas the
other three progress from major to major by descending-third root
movement. Only one other instance of the latter kind appears
elsewhere in the madrigal. All the root movements described thus
far form minor thirds, and all cases of triads connected by one linear semitone have been accounted for save two (Example XIX-2b).
One of these appears in the second excerpt under the words, "To
close one's eyes in eternal slumber": the triadic pair, F♯ minor and
D major, whose roots descend by a major third. In another spot in
the piece we find the opposite arrangement—that is, ascending
major thirds between the roots of F major and A minor. This
minority group represents slightly more audacious techniques. But
the most daring of all occurs in the second example (*sempiterno*),
for here two major triads involving ascending major thirds between their roots produce two linear semitones. This is the sole
case of this type of chromaticism in the entire piece. Finally, it

EXAMPLE XIX-2a.   C. Tudino, *Altro che lagrimar* (1554).
From T. Kroyer, *Die Anfänge der Chromatik im italienischen Madrigal des XVI. Jahrhunderts,* pp. 151–52. Leipzig, 1902.

EXAMPLE XIX-2b.   C. Tudino, *Altro che lagrimar* (1554).
From T. Kroyer, *Die Anfänge der Chromatik im
italienischen Madrigal des XVI. Jahrhunderts*,
pp. 152–53. Leipzig, 1902.

is worth noting that both restrained and audacious chromaticisms
as well as circles-of-fifths are based on a predominance of sharp
accidentals, and taken together, these traits give Tudino's madrigal
a piquant and volatile flavor.

Fiesco's diatonic madrigal of 1554 need not detain us here.[5]
The chromatic one begins with the significant words, *Bacio soave*,
and it employs the same accidentals as Tudino's *Altro che lagrimar*.
After an ordinary opening, Fiesco presents a rapid modulation
through six steps in the sharp circle-of-fifths (B major to C major)
and then jumps suddenly from C major to A minor (third-relations
with no linear semitone). Although his chromatic language does
not go beyond that of Tudino, Fiesco's setting of the text is much
more rhetorical in orientation. The high point comes on the words,
Che l'un'e l'altro sente, where melodic contours, rhythmic motives,
and harmonic colors combine to provide a vivid painting of the
two lovers' fluctuating passion.

We come now to Vicentino and his *"antikisierende Manier."*[6]
Because the madrigals found in his treatise are only fragmentary,
they do not show the full extent of Vicentino's chromaticism, a
feature that can be better evaluated in the two motets, one religious

and one secular. *Hierusalem convertere a5* (see Example XII-1) represents a textbook exemplar. In the light of our assessment with respect to Tudino's techniques, a brief recapitulation of Vicentino's is a useful point of comparison. The major-minor-major shifts in the first ten measures, of course, require a single linear semitone. Their unrelenting sequence is followed, in measures 10–11, by the triadic pair with semitonal root movement, noted before on account of its three melodic semitones. This eccentric and bizarre progression has not been encountered before. In the last half of the motet, circles-of-fifths separate various chromatic progressions, four of which involve two major triads connected by root movement in descending minor thirds (one linear semitone), and only one of which is the more ordinary major-minor pair with descending roots forming a minor third (no linear semitone). Compared to the chromaticism of Tudino and Fiesco, we observe a heightening of *effetti meravigliosi*. And if we then compare the chromatic section of Vicentino's *Musica prisca caput a4* to the motet just analyzed, we discover even more astonishing features. In the first part of this section, Vicentino sticks mainly to third-relations and root shifts that involve one linear semitone between two triads. Of course, their close proximity is peculiar in itself, for double and triple series of chromatic relations are separated by single diatonic steps. What happens in the last part of this section is that diatonic connections disappear entirely, until we arrive at the closing cadential passage, and even here, they are decorated with diminished triads. Before this cadential passage, Vicentino presents chromatic chords almost totally made up of semitone-related triads that require two or three simultaneous linear semitones (Example XIX-3). These relations permit triads with sharps and flats to appear adjacent to each other. I have mentioned several times that the three sections of this piece (diatonic, chromatic, and enharmonic) reflect the basic *concetti* of the Latin text. The middle, chromatic one sets the conceit of the "sweet and old numbers" of ancient music, and they become sweeter and older, or harsher and newer (depending on one's bias) as this section unfolds.

The year 1555 seems to be a stellar one for chromaticism. Pietro Taglia's first madrigal book is intended for the delectation

EXAMPLE XIX-3.   N. Vicentino, *Musica prisca caput* (1555).
From *L'antica musica ridotta alla moderna prattica*,
Book III, Chapter 54, fols. 69v–71v.

of a Milanese academy, and we can deduce their taste from *Il mal mi preme a4* (Petrarch). The madrigal abounds in extremely strange harmonies as well as perverse syncopations violating the principles of traditional contrapuntal balance and verbal accentuation. The vertical progressions follow neither circle-of-fifths modulation nor typical chromatic relations linked by linear semitones. One can only describe them as capricious.[7] On the words, "And the worst frightens me," Taglia introduces some wild voice leading that is truly frightening: the soprano leaps up a tritone, the tenor down an augmented octave, and the bass down one octave and immediately up another a semitone higher than the first. The effect is grotesque. In this same year, Orlando di Lasso, whose career reads like a mannerist odyssey, enters the musical scene with one of his first publications, in which he proudly announces some works *à la nouvelle composition d'aucuns d'Italie*. This phrase undoubtedly refers to two chromatic secular motets on Latin humanist texts, one by Lasso himself and the other by Cipriano de Rore. Lasso's *Alma nemes a5*, written in emulation of Rore's work, contains two flats and five sharps (note the appearance of A#). Between short diatonic passages setting the straightforward portions of the text, Lasso uses extended circles-of-fifths on the

sharp side and third-related triads connected by semitonal movement. The latter, in particular, paint minute details of evocative
words (Example XIX-4). In the case of Rore's work, *Calami sonum
ferentes a4*, unusual harmonies are enhanced by the tessitura of
four bass voices. Chromatic exploration utilizes the same accidentals as in Lasso's piece but contributes more to the general mood
than to pictorial details.

One of the most notorious examples of extensive chromaticism and *musica reservata* is furnished by Lasso's cycle, *Prophetiae
Sibyllarum a4*. The date of this group of secular motets has been
the subject of some debate. Earlier scholars placed it among the
composer's later works on the basis of its posthumous publication
in 1600 and its radical style. We know now that it must have been
written before 1560, the date of the private manuscript belonging
to Lasso's patron, Duke Albrecht V of Bavaria. When Charles IX
of France wrote to Albrecht praising Lasso's *grande et rare science*
(1571), Albrecht permitted a copy of the cycle to be sent to the
French court where it was performed to the great astonishment of
gallic connoisseurs.[8] The text comprises twelve sibylline prophecies whose mysterious statements were interpreted as foretelling
the coming of Christ. Needless to say, their enigmatic prognostica-
tions receive appropriately enigmatic musical treatment.

Any attempt to find organic logic within the cycle is thwarted
by the unruly aberrations of each member. Neither the arrangement of key signatures, accidentals, nor final cadences reveals
an architectonic plan. The accidentals include three flats and five
sharps, but their number in any one piece is not always an indication of the most daring harmonies. It seems clear that Lasso's aim
is to put the listener off balance.[9] Except for the odd tritone and
passing "dominant-seventh" massing, nothing out of the ordinary
occurs. Of course, this statement omits the liberal, even profligate,
usage of semitonal motion. Herein lies the secret of this cycle's
unorthodox quality. Each composition wanders about at will in an
entirely unpredictable manner among natural, flat, and sharp triadic sonorities. That Lasso leans heavily toward sharp chromaticism shows yet another side of his innovative approach. Chromatic
triads feature third-related and semitone-related root movements.
Particularly effective for the luscious sonority of the work are the

EXAMPLE XIX-4.   O. di Lasso, *Alma nemes* (1555).
From *Trésor musicale: Musique profane*, 3:4. Edited
by R. van Maldeghem. Brussels, 1867; 1965.

numerous major triads related by third movement; no composer up to this time employs so many and especially so many in downward motion. Although triadic relationships requiring two or three linear semitones are relatively few (roughly 9 out of 215), they herald the coming eccentricities of later mannerists. Lasso builds up chromatic meandering by separating these highly charged sequences with one or at most two ordinary diatonic steps. It is significant that the most widely spaced chromatic progressions are those separated by circles-of-fifths. This technique adds a great deal to the enervating quality of the harmonic vocabulary. A circle-of-fifths will set up a dynamic, goal-oriented motion toward a projected modal area, only to be interrupted by a chromatic turn. This happens in the vast majority of cases; for the rest, a relaxing cadence is followed immediately by another chromatic surge before the cadence has a chance to settle down. These cumulative and extremely capricious chromatic moments are strategically placed to destroy any incipient diatonic stability.

Although the cycle belongs to *musica reservata* by virtue of its exclusive social circumstances and its chromatic language, the matter of expressive intent has been argued. Very little by way of pictorialisms appear: in *Sibylla Samia*, black notes portray *dies nigras . . . tenebris*; in *Sibylla Europea*, *altos* occasions a leap of a seventh; in the Prologue, *arcana salutis* stands out because of its closely packed unorthodox harmonies. In assessing its expressive import, some scholars see the cycle as adhering to an older tradition of abstract symbolism or emblematic allegory, a tradition having nothing to do with dramatic and affective devices in the madrigal.[10] One cannot deny, however, that chromaticism, no matter how it is used in a particular composition, embodies an exciting and affective character within the historical context of traditional modal purity. This is why one cannot justly say that the *Prophetiae Sibyllarum* relies on inexpressive chromaticism exploited purely for the sake of abstract *maniera*.[11] Haar correctly points out the highly artificial and mannerist tone of this cycle; but in my view, its *maniera* depends on the affective resonance of extreme chromaticism. That there are no diatonic passages that contrast with the chromatic ones only augments the utter strangeness of the work. In effect, Lasso stretches his chromaticism, which in technical terms is not as extravagant as that of Vicentino, over grandiose proportions. His style here becomes *la grande maniera.*

Chromaticism in Lasso's madrigals is a less prominent component among his pictorial and affective techniques. Occasional chromatic flurries function as deliberate word painting, and from the musical viewpoint, these flurries represent digressions from the principal mode. Such is the case with *Cantai hor piango a5* (Petrarch) and *Crudel acerba inesorabil morte a5* (Petrarch), both printed in 1555. In his later madrigals, this feature is extremely rare. Lasso at this time shows a marked proclivity for petrarchan and petrarchist poetry, and the absence of more recent concettist verse suggests that he has lost touch with the newer *maniera* popular in Italian intellectual circles.[12] In general, great rhythmic energy and masterly deployment of concise motives characterize his counterpoint. The heritage of classical style is still discernible, but the plasticity of Lasso's personal *maniera* creates a style that is far removed from the placid lyricism of the Renaissance. His madrigals furnish examples of all the techniques of *musica poetica* enunciated by Joachim Burmeister. But with Lasso, even graphic word painting (*hypotyposis*) acts as an integral element of organic structure. In this sense, Lasso is less a mannerist and more a precursor of baroque ideals.

If Lasso is already drifting to the periphery of madrigal activity, the opposite holds true for the companion in arms of his youth, Rore. After establishing five-voiced texture as the norm for the madrigal, this composer goes on to imbue both four- and five-voiced complements with a new transparency and madrigalian expressivity destined to remain legendary for generations to come. The books published in this period secure for Rore the position of the most influential innovator in the *maniera madrigalesca.* His two books for four voices (1550 and 1557) are published in an epoch-making edition, the first printed score on record; the title of the 1577 edition ends with the words *spartiti et accommodati per sonar d'ogni sorte d'istrumento perfetto & per qualunque studioso di contrapunti.* They stress two important things. First, the score permits students to plumb the depths of Rore's *maniera*, thus facilitating Burmeister's precepts of analysis and emulation. Second, it allows performance by perfect instruments—that is, instruments whose tuning accommodates his novel harmonic style.

Although chromaticism remains a striking element of Rore's late style, it has been overemphasized by modern scholars.[13] The most important aspect of his seminal influence, one clearly understood by later mannerists, is his attitude toward poetry. Rore achieves what seems to be a new and miraculous symbiosis of word and tone. Every single device departs from a basic aesthetic of imitating and representing every minute image and emotional connotation of the text. Counterpoint versus homophony, serene diatonicism versus dynamic chromaticism, traditional versus radical dissonance treatment, quiet versus agitated rhythms and tempos, consistent texture versus soloistic disintegration, homogeneous sonority versus extreme ranges, and so on—all are called into play to depict the words. In spite of the artificiality inherent in his *effetti meravigliosi*, Rore manages to saturate them with dignity and emotional conviction. In retrospect, Vincenzo Galilei and Claudio Monteverdi are correct in tracing the roots of *moderno contrapunto* and *seconda prattica* to the individual genius and inspiration of Cipriano de Rore, for in his hands, early mannerist eccentricities have coalesced into full-fledged and successful stylization.

The varied texts of Book II *a5* (1557) prompt Rore to create vastly different moods. *Un'altra volta la Germania strida* demonstrates his serious and heroic style. In the case of *Schiet'arbuscel*, a somewhat feeble imitation of petrarchan imagery, we find a different approach to handling amorous conceits. Hand in hand with homophonic texture goes his use of flats and sharps to produce appropriately bittersweet harmonies (Example XIX-5). The gentle languor of the sentiments is enough to bring out Rore's chromatic touches, touches that enhance the verse. This madrigal abounds in third-related and semitone-related triads, as does *Beato mi direi*. One of the highlights in the collection, *O Sonno* (Giovanni della Casa), features prominent homophonic declamation, a texture strengthened by Rore's masterful use of four self-sufficient and beautiful lines. Rhythmic contrasts, chromatic surges, and alternate excursions to flat and sharp areas all serve to paint the striking similes and metaphors of the poem. Even fauxbourdon has a role

EXAMPLE XIX-5. C. de Rore, *Schiet'arbuscel* (1557).
From *Opera Omnia*, 4:62–63. Edited by B. Meier.
American Institute of Musicology, 1969. Used by
permission of Dr. A. Carapetyan.

in affective harmony. The musical style of Johannes Tinctoris's *ars nova* has now become a stylized device of the *dolce stile nuovo*, Palisca, who provides an excellent analysis of this madrigal, sums up Rore's *maniera* with the following words, "Sacrificing the homogeneity of style admired by the Renaissance, he creates a melange that has fittingly been called *mannerism*."[14]

Rore's noble tone and magnificent mood painting is also exemplified by his setting of Petrarch's double sestina, *Mia benigna fortuna/Crudel acerba inesorabil morte*. A conflicting key signature (one and two flats) and additional accidentals (A♭, F♯, C♯, B♮, and E♮) provide the basis for a wide harmonic spectrum. Petrarch's opening contraposition of cheer and gloom is underscored in the music by a contrast between major and minor sonorities: *Mia benigna fortuna* has sustained harmonies based on large-scale third-relations, whereas *e'l viver lieto* has more active diatonic harmonies. In this case, harmonic character as such is enhanced by harmonic rhythm. The overall plan of the two halves of this line highlights two areas (F major and B♭ major) whose diatonic connection relates to the notion of benign fortune and joyful living. However, the inner instability of third-related triads hints at unspoken anguish (Example XIX-6a). *I chiari giorni* begins after a general pause and ends with melismatic runs; *le tranquille notti* forms a vivid contrast achieved through quiet homophony, a very low bass range, and luscious harmonies moving from flat to sharp areas. Prominent third-related triads accompany *E i soavi sospiri*, the last word of which phrase receives rhetorically deployed rests; the remainder of this line, *e'l dolce stile*, which ends with semitone-related triads, runs into the next line without a break, and Rore keeps up the momentum thus created by compressing the line into a short time span. *Volti subitamente* is depicted subtly by an imitative point and *in doglia e'n pianto* causes the voices to dwindle to a lone C♯ (Example XIX-6b). The final line, *Odiar vita mi fanno et bramar morte*, represents the climax of the stanza, and Rore sets it twice to virtually the same music. *Odiar vita* appears on a surprising progression whose chords introduce B♮ and E♮ for the first time. The harshness and bitterness of the poet's feelings come sharply to the fore by means of a prominent upward leap of a major sixth in the bass and tenor; this

EXAMPLE XIX-6a.   C. de Rore, *Mia benigna fortuna/Crudel acerba inesorabil morte* (1557).

From *Opera Omnia*, 4:79. Edited by B. Meier. American Institute of Musicology, 1969. Used by permission of Dr. A. Carapetyan.

EXAMPLE XIX-6b.   C. de Rore, *Mia benigna fortuna/Crudel acerba inesorabil morte* (1557).
From *Opera Omnia*, 4:79–80. Edited by B. Meier. American Institute of Musicology, 1969. Used by permission of Dr. A. Carapetyan.

unorthodox interval, of course, profiles the two accidentals. The rest of the line features many third-related triads as well as a magnificent upward leap of an octave (A♭-A♭) in the bass on *morte*, a leap that joins two third-related sonorities. The second part of the madrigal opens with another major sixth on *Crudel*, and in this instance, the iconoclastic thrust of the interval is even more prominent, coming as it does on an opening point of imitation. This startling beginning will inspire other composers who set the same text. Rore's setting of the second half of Petrarch's double sestina furnishes evidence similar to that described with respect to the first half. In its totality, the work admirably demonstrates Rore's interest in portraying internal affections and external conceits through all the musical means at his disposal.

Rore's *Da le belle contrade* a5 (1566) shares certain traits with the double sestina, most notably the attention paid to details of the text as well as the colorful harmonies marshaled at affective points. The last portion of this work demonstrates a rather different kind of word painting. While depicting as literally as possible the entwining embraces of the unhappy girl with animated imitative points, Rore uses the simile of the acanthus plant as an excuse for a twisting figure whose visual and aural character suggests the object itself; here *hypotyposis* and *enargeia* are combined. The anonymous poem can be best described as an amorous dialogue in a pastoral setting. Rore parallels the narrative and dialogue portions of this text with a setting that approaches the miniature cantata as closely as a single madrigal for five voices will permit.[15] The most interesting passages occur when the beloved speaks (Example XIX-7). Her tortured cries, *T'en vai, haimè! Sola mi lasci! Adio!* receive graphic treatment by means of a rising chromatic line punctuated by extremely arresting rests. Each exclamation follows the natural accents of impassioned speech. As she resorts to plaintive wailing after this outburst, *Che sarà qui di me scur'e dolente?* Rore uses smoother lines culminating in an inconclusive, unresolved cadence. After a dramatic pause, she exclaims, *Ahi, crud'amor!* Love's fleeting sweetness is marvelously profiled by an unexpected turn to D♭ major.

Before leaving the topic of harmonic audacities, we should look at two other outstanding examples. Gioseppe Caimo, a Mi-

EXAMPLE XIX-7.   C. de Rore, *Da le belle contrade* (1566).
From *Opera Omnia*, 5:97–98. Edited by B. Meier.
American Institute of Musicology, 1971. Used by
permission of Dr. A. Carapetyan.

lanese composer and pupil of Taglia, employs extreme chromaticism learned both from his teacher and from an association with Vicentino. A typical illustration of his approach can be seen in *Piangete valli a4* (1564). This anonymous poem indicates the direction that mannerist verse will take toward tortured images ("dark lilies and black violets"), images appropriate to a tone of lugubrious lamentation. It is difficult to select the most striking passage from this strange composition. However, the opening point of imitation, with its descending chromatic motive, serves to show just how much the classical model of polyphony has become stylized and self-consciously mannered.

Luzzasco Luzzaschi, pupil of Rore and friend of Vicentino, spent his career at the glittering court of Ferrara where he had occasion to perform much experimental music. His playing of Vicentino's archicembalo was greatly admired at the time, but today he is mostly remembered for his concerted madrigals written for the Ferrarese ladies. However, Luzzaschi wrote many fine five-voiced madrigals. And because of his court affiliations, he set many poems by Tasso and Guarini and was evidently encouraged to explore novel techniques in his music. Luzzaschi's most radical madrigal, *Quivi sospiri* (1576; Dante, *Divine Comedy*) features expressive chromaticism allied with detailed pictorial touches, and the result is a deeply moving representation of the torments of the damned. The accidentals are not at all unusual for the time, but the sonorities produced by their deployment are certainly so. Among the many third-related triads, a significant number have descending motion. Luzzaschi augments the gloomy atmosphere evoked by these sequences with other ambivalent series of chords, such as erratic switches between major and minor sonorities and triads related by roots a tritone apart. The latter chromatic progression, not encountered before, appears in measures 4–5, a point where the words *sospiri* and *pianti* overlap. The chords in question are A minor and Eb major. But the most dramatic moments are left for last (Example XIX-8). *Accenti d'ira* features appropriately ascending figures; *voci alti* rises even higher in a strident chromatic motive; and [*voci*] *fioche* falls suddenly into the nether regions of voice range accompanied by third-related triads that provide the illusion of constricting strangulation. Indeed, musical illusionism

EXAMPLE XIX-8.   L. Luzzaschi, *Quivi sospiri* (1576).
From *The Golden Age of the Madrigal*, pp. 57–58. Edited
by A. Einstein. New York, 1942. Copyright, 1942, by
G. Schirmer, Inc. Used by permission.

of the most violent and tortured kind is the keynote of this madrigal. The refined music lovers of the Ferrarese court surely found much enjoyment in Luzzaschi's monumental *effetti meravigliosi*.

The better part of this chapter has been devoted to chromaticism because this trait stands out among the devices of avant-garde experimentation. For one thing, chromaticism reaches its mature phase by mid-century, and it therefore emerges as the first clear signal of avowed radical intentions and self-conscious Mannerism. Its unsettling capacity for destroying the rules of the perfect art are so obvious that theorists tend to equate novelty with chromatic aberrations, regardless of whether they approve of *nuova maniera*. Furthermore, a substantial number of instances of chromaticism in compositions can be related to general humanist ideas, and specifically to musical ideas concerning ancient authority. Admittedly, the latter range from self-evident connections between a theoretical position and its practical outcome, as in the case of Vicentino, to more camouflaged connections between humanist texts and their musical settings, as in the case of Lasso, and even to decidedly cryptic ones between single poetic conceits not originally conceived as references to ancient theoretical matters but so interpreted by musicians, as in the case of Rore (i.e. *e'l dolce stile* in *Mia benigna fortuna/Crudel acerba inesorabil morte*). The latter type of arcane connection between ideas connoting antique resonances and musical representations of such resonances will become more common after 1580. At any rate, taken as a whole, this body of evidence proves that notions of reviving ancient aesthetic ideals and ancient technical devices antedate by many years the monodic and operatic experiments in Florence, experiments that are usually cited as the first incontrovertible documents supporting the hypothesis that music too partakes in the cultural rejuvenation of ancient glories.

The history of musical chromaticism up to this point involves a steady accumulation of written accidentals that follows a widening of the hexachord system as well as a steady tendency toward increasingly daring and iconoclastic progression between vertical sonorities, and the latter entail connections by root movement as well as connections by semitonal inflections. Moreover, the compositions themselves elucidate two aspects of mannerist stylization.

In the first, chromaticism acts as an imitative-affective device, and in this framework it expands harmonic language without destroying modal dominance. Such stylization can be called the *dolce maniera*. In the second, chromaticism is used throughout a composition to the exclusion of modal centricity whenever a composer seeks monumental rhetorical eloquence. This kind of stylization can be construed as the *grande maniera*.

The phase of Mannerism under consideration here provides several other important tendencies in madrigalian stylization, tendencies that although relatively new at this time, will figure more prominently in later phases. I close the chapter with a discussion of these aspects. Antonio Barre's *Il primo libro delle muse a4* (1555) bears the subtitle, *madrigali ariosi*, a phrase referring to homophonic settings of Ariosto's *Orlando furioso*. In another context, I mentioned the tradition of reciting passages from this beloved poem to popular formulas (*arie*), formulas that appear in disguised versions in the madrigals of this collection.[16] Barre's publication has two implications for mannerist style. First, consistently homophonic texture throws the soprano into high relief, and for this reason, these works can be performed as solo songs with instrumental accompaniment. Their pseudo-monodic character is augmented by a decidedly declamatory penchant featuring pairs of repeated notes. The second element concerns the large number of settings of dramatic monologues. This phenomenon relates directly to a growing emphasis on concrete dramatization rather than on illusionistic effects.

The second tendency that merits discussion concerns the somewhat elusive character (elusive from the viewpoint of classification within a concept of Mannerism) of a musical style that is neither blatantly radical nor blatantly reactionary. The main figure who exemplifies this style is Adrian Willaert. The significance of the title of his *Musica nova* (1559) is a disputed one in modern scholarship. The most plausible explanation postulates that "new music" means progressive style, characterized by sensitive yet controlled text expression, as indicated in Francesco della Viola's dedication when he states that the great Venetian composer *fa sentir nell'animo tutti gli affetti*. On the basis of this statement, one might expect to find all kinds of extravagant devices in this collection. But such is not the case. However, Willaert's careful declamation laced with note repetition, his melodic elasticity born of consideration of verbal values, his use of frequent pauses and varied cadences, and his subtle deployment of third-related triads of a moderate variety all contribute to the ideal of expressing the text. In short, Willaert strikes a perfect balance between reactionary and radical facets of musical practice of his time. Hence, Gioseffo Zarlino's praise of his *elegante maniera*. Willaert's *musica nova* establishes an important model for those composers who wish to absorb novel devices into sound musical procedures. In view of the condemnation of extreme Mannerism as an aberration perpetrated by willful upstarts, this trend has added importance in keeping alive a sane approach to mannerist stylization. Through Willaert and his spiritual followers, innovations uniting dramatic impetus and architectonic structure become accepted elements of Mannerism. Shearman is quite correct in stressing Willaert's connection with baroque dramatic style.[17] But he is not entirely correct in stating that this composer bypasses Mannerism.

A third trend, one related to the aesthetic premises of the second, comes to the fore in another *Musica nova* (1569), this time by Giulio Fiesco. The dedication states that the madrigals were composed *ad instanza del S. Batt. Guarini*. Novelty in this case resides in the choice of these highly concettist verses, and Fiesco's publication is indeed the first one devoted to poems by Guarini. The elegantly pointed *maniera* of the poet's epigrammatic forms is reflected in the composer's refined musical *maniera*. Fiesco's overly polished delicacy derives from the "height of artificiality and mannerism"[18] embodied in the *concetti* of the poetry. In the context of their time, these madrigals may not seem very remarkable. But they must be considered as the first musical settings whose aesthetic premise embraces ideals of lyrical preciosity. Ideals destined to become more exaggerated later in the century, particularly in music setting the hyperrefined verse of Guarini and his imitators. This trend in madrigalian stylization is balanced by another that attempts to infuse the madrigal with dramatic monumentalism. The latter development brings us to Giaches de Wert.

Wert, court composer to the Gonzaga family in Mantua, fuses the traditions established by Rore, Barre, and Willaert in the works of his early period. This fusion is saved from descending into superficial eclecticism by a quality of originality discernible from the start. From Barre and Willaert, Wert adopts declamatory style; from the latter he also learns the refined techniques of melodic and contrapuntal plasticity. From Rore, Wert takes harmonic coloring as well as the typically mannerist combination of wittily imitative and deeply affective figures. Wert's personal characteristics arise from his penchant for dramatic monumentalism, a predilection that is perhaps inspired by the mannerist arts in the Mantuan court. In general terms, Wert seems to favor rough and uncomfortable intervals, odd harmonic progressions, sharp dissonances, and at times, artificially graphic imagery.[19] In his later madrigals, this composer explores a very individual kind of novelty, a manneristic *maniera* that appeals only to a select circle of connoisseurs. For this reason, these works are seldom reprinted; his late style has become a kind of *musica reservata*. At any rate, the young Claudio Monteverdi and Luca Marenzio knew Wert's earlier work well, and each of them took from this master those elements of madrigalian technique that most suited his personality.[20]

Wert's second book of madrigals (1561) indicates that he is already making a distinction between polyphonic and homophonic *maniere*. *Amor io fallo a5* (Petrarch) illustrates polyphonic style, a style in which dramatic touches form a secondary albeit piquant aspect. For example, the opening leap of a seventh acts both as a concrete musical rendition of the conceit, "Love, I fall short," and an affective image of anguish. It thus admirably shows the mannerist combination of wit and pathos. The leap dramatizes the sentiment; but for musical initiates, the seventh (one short of the perfect octave) suggests "falling short."[21] In *Dolce spoglie a5*, the lament of Dido, Wert achieves surprising contrast by uniting homophonic declamation and intense contrapuntal imitation. The first part, especially, explores a declamatory style that hints at choral recitative, whereas the second part proceeds by means of imitative counterpoint in the Phrygian mode, giving the words an emotional lyricism whose premises go back, consciously or not, to Josquin's *Dulces exuviae*. Both works also contain a few free dissonances and forbidden intervals, elements that will become more prominent in Wert's mature works.

Wert's indebtedness to Rore appears most clearly in Book III (1563). But I must stress that Wert's chromaticism is even more sharply pictorial than that of his model. *Nova amor nova fiamma* *a5* exemplifies this characteristic. A rising chromatic line depicts the visual metaphor of the flames of new love as well as the affective connotations of burning sentiments. A highly unusual dissonant clash of a minor second and seventh paints *cruda guerra* in the same way; the notes are at war with one another and their duel produces harsh sounds. Internalization and externalization operate in mutual cooperation. Thus Wert translates older *maniera* into his own kind of *effetto meraviglioso*. The fourth book (1567) swings in the direction of extreme *enargeia*. It is full of "musical realism that goes beyond the merely symbolic."[22] Indicative of the style of this collection is *Qual nemico fortuna a5* (Federigo Affanni), a work abounding in witty madrigalisms and affective harmonies (including triads related by roots a tritone apart). Whereas the fifth book (1571) reverts to conspicuous eclecticism (perhaps reflecting the taste of Count Mario Bevilacqua's Veronese academy, to which it is dedicated), the sixth one (1572) shows the fruition of Wert's mature style, a style dominated by declamation and dramatic impetus. Wert now transforms the homophonic *maniera* of his earlier madrigals into a vehicle for violent pathos. He abandons the dancelike formulas of popular *arie* and adds affective chromatic and dissonant touches to the predominantly diatonic language of *madrigali ariosi*. Concomitant with this change is the appearance of more modern concettist verse (i.e., two cycles by Luigi Tansillo, *Era dunque ne'fatti* and *Se quel dolor*). Masterful as these works are, I shall reserve detailed investigation of Wert's mature *maniera* for later.

The ideal of musical *enargeia* that inspires serious musical imitation in courtly and academic madrigals also prompts composers to explore the humorous possibilities of graphic pictorialism. I refer to Alessandro Striggio's *Il cicalamento delle donne al bucato* (1567), a comically descriptive madrigal, and his *Il gioco di primiera* (1569) in which Striggio depicts with astonishing realism a game of cards among five players. Part of the effect of such pieces depends on onomatopoetic devices of virtuoso proportions, devices that also figure in more serious works such as Striggio's

Non rumor di tamburi a6 (1571; Ariosto, *Orlando furioso*). When Vincenzo Galilei criticizes madrigalisms, one of the first examples he gives of the *ridicola maniera* is the imitation of drums and trumpets.[23] The delight taken in these musical games must be understood in the framework of madrigalian aesthetics. Quite apart from their inherent virtuosity, comic madrigals exploit current conventions for *imitazione delle parole*. They are oblique travesties of their serious counterparts, and their emphasis on humor and parody shows a self-conscious relationship to learned style. They form yet another body of evidence for the importance of stylization or *maniera*.[24] Jokes, parodies, and witty puzzles also appear in the works of Ludovico Agostini, a strange personality on the peripheries of Ferrarese and Mantuan circles. His settings of bizarre poems by Andrea Calmo (1567) and his book of musical riddles (1571) bespeak a close connection between madrigalian wit and the mannerist grotesque.

The transformation of the madrigal from mild stylization to more exuberant stylization parallels three rough stages of musical Mannerism: early (1530–50), middle (1550–80), and late (1580–1630). This transformation can be gauged by assessing the career of Filippo di Monte who spent the early part of his life in Italy (1540–68), and then moved to the court of Maximilian II in Vienna. When that archmannerist monarch, Rudolph II, ascended the throne in 1576, Monte became court composer in Prague. In the period under discussion, Monte shows himself to be a progressive mannerist in the Willaert-Rore-Barre tradition. Lively and artful counterpoint with occasional affective harmony forms the basis of his style, although eclecticism is also quite a noticeable component. At the midpoint of his career, Monte is content to work within the stylistic clichés he had mastered as a young composer.

His prolific output attests to the longevity of fashionable stylishness. Monte's *maniera* has been described in terms of accomplishment, stereotyped pleasantness, and well-mannered charm.[25] Monte's turn from youthful modernism to middle-aged conformity suggests interesting parallels with Lasso. And both men take on a distinctly conservative tone in madrigals written in northern European centers when compared to the innovative spirit of their

Italian contemporaries. One suspects that the change in Monte is only partially attributable to the fact that he now moves in circles tangential to musical Mannerism. His staid style seems out of joint with the flamboyant Mannerism of the Rudolphine court. It may be that his patron's taste in music is less advanced than his taste for extravagant experiments in other areas. But I believe that the real reason lies in Monte's creative intellect. Even in his youthful phase, he does not indulge in any of the more outrageous icono-clasms prevalent in the early decades of the mid-century. More than Lasso, Monte is a musician who adheres to self-sufficient musical considerations. He never allows expressive needs to overrule ab-stract logic, and this tendency simply becomes more pronounced in his maturity. And it is at this point precisely that lyrical and dramatic ideals in the Italian madrigal justify the extreme manifes-tations of novel *maniere*. The most telling evidence for Monte's situation is his self-appraisal, found in the dedications to his eighth and tenth books of five-voiced madrigals. In the former (1580), Monte as much as admits that he has not as yet fully mastered the *nuovo stile* of the madrigal. I have cited in a previous chapter comments in the latter (1581) that allude to *maniera* and *stile* in terms of a current and sophisticated taste responsible for the adverse assessments of his earlier works.

In Part I, I indicated that after 1560, art was losing the in-spired momentum of earlier Mannerism. But music, like poetry and science, is only catching its second wind, as it were. It will go on to more marvelous and more new *maniere*. Artists may be pessimistic, but musicians of radical persuasion have just cause for the most blatant optimism.

CHAPTER XX

ॐॐॐ

Mature Mannerism, 1580–1600

When considering this stage of Mannerism, we are confronted with a complex network of different features and styles not only in the output of individual composers but also in single compositions. And yet, it is possible to discern one common trait, or better, approach—sophisticated eclecticism. In this context, masters of modern *maniere* stand out by virtue of their brilliance and ingenuity in manipulating mannerist clichés. In addition, this context is enriched by the appearance of some new musical techniques as well as a decided emphasis on concettist poetry.

Generally speaking, the eclecticism rampant in this period makes a survey of madrigalisms very difficult. The technique most easily isolated is eye music. Its innate reliance on intellectual wit also characterizes the technique of painting individual words and conceits by means of aural figures. Of course, the mannerist concept exemplified by this approach is not new; however, between 1580 and 1600, it dominates to such an extent that it results in mosaiclike texture. Quite often, but not necessarily always, graphic figures are used intentionally to externalize the text. Such dramatization operates within the limits of a polyphonic style animated by a series of vivid illusionist devices. In short, fragmentary *imitazione delle parole* can be either lyrical or dramatic in intent. Concomitant with these techniques is the deployment of audacious harmony to paint internalized affects. This feature now exhibits two aspects: chromaticism and the unorthodox treatment of dissonances. The former, of course, enjoys a previous mannerist tradition, whereas the latter is quite new. Both expressive realism and dramatic trends can appear in works predicated on homophonic declamation. Because of its musical premise, homophony often endows musical figures, chromatic harmony, and bold dissonances with their most modern and unusual manifestations. And finally, the introduction of soloistic virtuosity also permits the use of radical intervals in written counterpoint. In opposition to the aforementioned devices, devices which cause the disintegration of balanced polyphony, is the continuation of refined imitative counterpoint based on purely musical logic and characterized by grace, elegance, charm, and the rich diatonic sonorities of the Venetian style.

The punning tricks of eye music count among the most notorious madrigalisms, and they enjoy their greatest vogue between 1580 and 1600. Most common, of course, is the use of black notes to "color" pertinent words. Einstein remarks with some justification that "in Marenzio's work, no passage involving *notte, color,* or *discolora* is allowed to go by without an abrupt shift to black notation; conversely, all passages involving 'light' or 'day' are written in 'white.'"[1] But Marenzio's ingenious fancy invents other more unusual, ergo more witty, visual puns. In *O bella man a4* (1585; Petrarch), the phrase, *di cinque perle* inspires the appearance of five breves strung on a single line of the staff. In another case, *Occhi lucenti e belli a5* (1582; Veronica Gambara), eye music allies with *enargeia*. The slow motion of the soprano, pitted against livelier rhythm in the lower voices, dramatizes the poet's repeated address to the eyes of the beloved; the singer receives added amusement because on the page the repeated breves look like a pair of eyes. Marenzio is not the sole composer to utilize these witty devices. We find one such instance, admittedly a rare case, in Monteverdi's *Non si levava ancor a5* (1590; Tasso). The poet likens the embracing of the lovers to the convoluted shape of the acanthus plant. As did Rore,[2] Monteverdi invents interweaving melodic figures whose visual outline reproduces the acanthus leaf and whose aural sound depicts the ardor of their embrace.

Historians agree that among practitioners of eye music, Marenzio is the most adroit and prolific. And in this respect it may be correct to suggest that Galilei's satire of the *ridicola maniera* refers to the notoriety of Marenzio's eye music. However, Galilei's comments also refer to the wanton concatenation of tiny realistic figures. And Marenzio is an accomplished master of this technique as well. Thus, our survey of musical pictorialism begins with an outstanding mannerist who dominates musical stylization at this time.

The somewhat shallow virtuosity[3] of Book III *a5* (1582), dedicated to Count Mario Bevilacqua's Veronese academy, results from the aesthetic attitude evident in its contents. Drastic musical imagery prevails. Every poetic conceit and every evocative word is thrown into high relief to the detriment of affective expressivity and organic structure. It is not insignificant that this style relates to the concettist verse of Guarini, although Marenzio applies it to older poetry as well. Exemplary of this mannerist approach to madrigalian *maniera* is the setting of Guarini's O *dolce anima mia*, in which Marenzio capitalizes on the poet's finely turned conceits. In this work we see Marenzio's brilliance in handling a series of jewellike imitative devices. But Marenzio's setting of Luigi Alammani's *Scaldava il sol (Favola di Narcisso)* represents a superior masterpiece inasmuch as imitative devices are here united with overall mood painting effected by means of harmonic color. The charming description of midday lethargy is underscored by a firm harmonic plan that creates a marvelous illusion and at the same time holds the work together. This dual function is achieved by harmonic pace that supports melodic, rhythmic, and textural devices deployed for the sake of pictorialism. Marenzio sets the mood with two striking conceptions at the very start. "The sun burned" has a leisurely imitative point over sustained minor chords. The effect of this passage is strengthened by the ensuing spectrum that veers away toward more animated major chords, and these in turn contrast with the sustained dronelike minor harmonies picturing "The shepherd slept" (Example xx-1). To suggest silence, Marenzio uses repeated stationary chords that eventually dwindle to a single D. The final line contains the most unusual and witty device of all: "Only the cicada did not feel peaceful." *Sol* appears twice, first on a single G (*sol* in the natural hexachord) and then on a C major triad, thus reaffirming the pun. *Cicala* inspires an onomatopoetic rendering of the cicada's buzzing whose vivid humor is matched by a novel technique—parallel-third figuration creating double dissonances against static harmony. Marenzio is the first

EXAMPLE XX-1.   L. Marenzio, *Scaldava il sol* (1582).

From *Publikationen älterer Musik*, 4¹:127. Edited by
A. Einstein. Leipzig, 1929; Hildesheim, 1967. Used by
permission of Breitkopf & Härtel, Wiesbaden.

madrigalist whose attempt at this kind of descriptive exaggeration is successful, and his work will not be challenged until Giaches de Wert's *Vezzosi augelli* (1586) and Claudio Monteverdi's *Ecco mormorar l'onde* (1590).

Similar effects can be found in many of Marenzio's works for four and five voices published between 1580 and 1590. They are rare in his late madrigals, although there exists one exception, *La bella man a5* (1599), where a pair of canonic voices symbolizes the elaborate *concetto* of Guarini's poem. In connection with *Disdegno e gelosia a5* (1585; Tasso), Einstein remarks that Marenzio's emphasis on pictorial detail makes him a mannerist.[4] This statement holds true for all the works embracing this aesthetic, for Marenzio's aim is to match the eccentric virtuosity of the poetry with an appropriate musical *maniera*. In these cases, his madrigals cannot be appreciated without their texts, even more so than is true for the works of Cipriano de Rore.

Few composers go to the realistic extremes of Marenzio.

Monteverdi, for example, never allows minute word painting to weaken logical structure. Yet modern scholars cite one work, *Dolcissimi legami a5* (1590; Tasso) as an example of detailed pictorialism.[5] Monteverdi certainly alternates textures and voice groupings in a kaleidoscopic manner that graphically represents the successive conceits of the poem. He also treats the text very freely, but less for the sake of realistic expression than for architectonic form. A comparison between this madrigal and those of Marenzio reveals that Monteverdi's pictorial techniques are not nearly so drastic as those of Marenzio, and that harmonic sectionalization, albeit in modal terms, holds the piece together.

I mentioned in a previous chapter, in connection with Rore's *Da le belle contrade a5* (1566), a new tendency toward dramatization in music. Under dramatization I include any musical techniques based on external rhetorical effects that create the illusion of spoken dialogue. When viewed from the vantage point of later monody and opera, polyphonic drama seems a curiously pale and mannered phenomenon. But the point is that for contemporaries, this style embodies evidence of *enargeia* and *effetti meravigliosi* in music. Mastery of descriptive realism gives composers the expertise necessary to explore dramatic realism. In other words, dramatization is but an extension of the established canon of *imitazione delle parole*. Within this larger framework, Marenzio's setting of Guarini's obscene dialogue, *Tirsi morir volea a5* (1580), initiates a particular tradition.[6] Minute word painting relies on very short phrases and frequent changes of tempos, note values, rhythms, and textures. These fluctuating musical devices, appearing as they do throughout the work's three parts, indeed produce the illusion of a miniature cycle,[7] if not a miniature cantata. Particularly noteworthy are the seemingly endless points of imitation with overlapping cadences that cleverly pictorialize the lovers' delay in sexual consummation. As in *Scaldava il sol*, the exterior wit of the musical depiction of poetic conceits is tempered by the sensuous sheen of Marenzio's harmonic vocabulary.

A similar fusion of descriptive and dramatic realism characterizes Wert's *Solo e pensoso a5* (1581; Petrarch) in which *enargeia* emerges from a very original use of unconventional ranges and linear contours. The young Monteverdi demonstrates mastery of this approach quite early in his career, especially in the second book of five-voiced madrigals, a book that marks his personal discovery of Tasso's lyrics. The poet's pointed and elegant concettism is in part responsible for the maturation of Monteverdi's technique. In *Non si levava ancor*, for example, Monteverdi lavishes Tasso's evocative imagery with a myriad of pictorial devices. He matches the poem's descriptive portions with music that is both agitated and sweet, and enhances the words of the dialogue with dramatic treatment.

In his six-voiced madrigals, Marenzio composes in a nondescriptive style. These "hedonistic"[8] works are pure musical entertainment enhanced by rich texture and the diatonic palette of the Venetian school. And yet, Marenzio cannot give up his propensity for dramatization even in this style, as is evident in *Piangea Filli a6* (1585). Luscious homophonic harmony, including third-related triads, underlies the description of Filli as she laments as well as the direct quotation of her pathetic words. And her cry, *O Tirsi*, is given a rhetorical treatment that features, among other elements, a plaintive suspension. Filli's exclamation recurs throughout the poem, and each time Marenzio sets it to identical music, creating at once a dramatic and architectonic effect anticipating baroque tendencies. Filli's second cry precedes a most unusual mood painting of the murmuring waves.[9] We have already seen a similar instance in Marenzio's depiction of the cicada. He goes even further with the waves. Another prophetic element appears in Marenzio's *O tu che fra le selve a8* (1580; Tasso). The poet indulges in a delightful game of echo. Each pair of lines poses a question that is answered by a punning reverberation. "Who is my life and love (*amore*)? Death (*more*). Am I not the lover's exemplar (*essempio*)? Impious (*Empio*)! Did I not have pity on her laments (*lamenti*)? You lie (*menti*)." And so on. As we might expect, Marenzio reflects the poetic scheme with musical echoes between two complementary choirs. He even continues this device at the end of the poem where the textual echo has been dropped. Quite possibly, such virtuosity may be responsible for the subsequent popularity of echo effects in dramatic music of the baroque period.

Up to this point, I have discussed dramatic elements in relation to dialogue techniques in the amorous pastoral. Inasmuch as this genre continues the tradition of witty *concetti*, its musical settings correspondingly exploit descriptive and dramatic realism. Imitative-affective devices in both poetry and music contribute to the artificiality and preciosity that characterize this phase of Mannerism. A different kind of dramatic polyphony originates from settings of the marvelous episodes of Tasso's *Gerusalemme liberata*. The monumental pathos of these sections inspires composers to new heights of *imitazione delle parole*. Because Wert knew the poet personally and had access to manuscript versions of the epic, he is the first in a long line of distinguished musicians to set portions of it to music. Wert found material worthy of his *furor poeticus*, and he enhanced the poem with a number of musical settings whose daring and novelty rivals the *meraviglia* so much touted by the poet.[10]

Our present topic, graphic dramatization, is reflected in two works by Wert in Book VIII *a5* (1586). The first, *Qual nemico gentil*, comprises a cycle of five stanzas describing Armida's reaction to Rinaldo's decision to leave her. The first, depicting her low voice and soft sighs, suggests a pastoral lament, and Wert creates an apt mood for this part. In addition to mannerist touches, such as the treatment of *sospir*, his music reveals two novel techniques: interlocking dotted figures with at least one voice in syncopation, and florid melismas. These virtuoso features undoubtedly owe their inspiration to the improvised art of the famed Ferrarese *concerto*. While relatively subdued in this instance, they soon become extreme and standard mannerisms. Wert's increasingly eccentric use of such devices functions as a hallmark of his personal *maniera*. The last four sections present Armida's outburst, and they therefore mirror the cadences of her impassioned speech with flexible textures and rhythms. In the last two parts, the musical style is very agitated; some passages even hint at Monteverdi's later *stile concitato*.

Wert exploits virtuoso techniques to an entirely different end in *Vezzosi augelli*, the description of Armida's magic garden. The first notable feature of this madrigal is its strong diatonic character. Static harmonies are often retained over long periods of time while the voices move about in an animated fashion. Three high voices pronounce the first two lines in quick succession. On *lasci-*

vette, Wert indulges in playful figuration reminiscent of Marenzio. Then the two lower voices enter with the first phrase of the third line, *Mormorar l'aure*; this tiny figure paints the murmuring of the breeze. Wert then combines all the lines and their motives in free counterpoint that can only be considered as mood painting. Later, *Garrir* receives a graphic motive that actually "chatters" in close imitation. *Quando taccion gl'augelli* has homophony for low voices, and *Alto risponde* has imitation for higher voices. *Cantan* prompts dazzling melismas derived from improvised diminutions (Example xx-2). *Alterna i versi lor* is vividly characterized by alternating pairs of voices. Finally, florid written diminutions on *Musica* bring this gem to a brilliant close. It has been noted already that Tasso's stanza impels the reader to experience the beauties of the subject through active images and sonorous word values. If Armida's garden is magical in Tasso's verbal terms, it is even more so in Wert's musical terms. The content of both poem and music is descriptive, but the intent and result are highly dramatic.

Tasso's *Ecco mormorar l'onde*, an independent lyric in a style similar to the above stanza from his epic, inspired Monteverdi to write an impressionistic madrigal (1590) whose style rivals that of both Marenzio and Wert. Static harmony and diatonic modality characterize its language. And its vocabulary is clearly related to both *Scaldava il sol* and *Vezzosi augelli*. Every passage, from the first to the last, presents an inventive pictorial and affective reflection of the words (Example xx-3). Furthermore, the vocal trios spun out over fundamental parts demonstrate that Monteverdi is already thinking and composing in *moderno contrapunto*—the *maniera* that will become a basis of baroque style. Although a tradition of mood painting binds these three composers, a comparison of their pieces clarifies the thrust of evolving Mannerism. Marenzio's basic approach is still geared to linear counterpoint; moments of *moderno contrapunto* are isolated, and for this very reason produce striking effects. Wert maintains a balance between linear and vertical considerations. In his style, a stable harmonic plan permits the efflorescence of ornate soloistic writing, and, in addition, syllabic declamation produces a semblance of vertically conceived sonorities stressing the highest voices. However, all parts are equal partners in textural deployment. In Monteverdi's

EXAMPLE XX-2.   G. de Wert, *Vezzosi augelli* (1586).
From *Opera Omnia*, 8:14. Edited by C. MacClintock and
M. Bernstein. American Institute of Musicology, 1968. Used
by permission of Dr. A. Carapetyan.

EXAMPLE XX-3.   C. Monteverdi, *Ecco mormorar l'onde* (1590).
From *Tutte le opere*, 2:74. Edited by G. F. Malipiero.
Vienna, 1927.

EXAMPLE xx-3, *continued*

masterpiece, we witness the first overt division of labor insofar as the lower parts act as harmonic foundations and the upper ones as soloistic free agents. All that is needed to transform Monteverdi's polyphonic madrigal into a concerted solo ensemble is the addition of a *basso continuo.*

In introducing the topic of audacious harmony, it is important to note that composers who search for novelty introduce detailed refinements grafted onto the chromatic innovations of previous generations of avant-gardists. For instance, customary accidentals appear in strange combinations, and triadic relations stress double and triple linear semitones. More remarkable is the use of the tritone in four-note chords that seem like dominant sevenths. Finally, novel suspended dissonances and free chord inversions render chromatic passages more piquant. In short, stylization has become more stylized.

Marenzio presents us with harmonic experiments verging on the excessive in two madrigals. One of these, the celebrated *O voi che sospirate* (1581; Petrarch), features five flats and five sharps. The lover's plaintive entreaty to end his misery marks the first highly chromatic passage in the work. Third-related triads, major-minor shifts, and occasional diminished chords are intensified by consistently semitonal motives (Example xx-4). What follows constitutes the most famous passage in the entire piece. A dazzling circle-of-fifths to the area of remote flat harmonies vividly paints the words *Muti una volta quel suo antico stile.* This striking device both symbolizes and graphically represents the poetic conceit of "changing ancient style." Its use proves that circles-of-fifths still retain their affective and radical impact even in the 1580s.[11] And the spelling of the accidentals adds another element of radicalism. Just at the point where Marenzio reaches the most chromatic mutation, he introduces the following pairs of notes simultaneously in two voices: A♭ and G♯, D♭ and C♯, and G♭ and F♯. These accidentals result from individual voice leading. Their significance, however, is more than technical. Marenzio's daring concept highlights the current vogue of eccentric *maniera* based on classical theory. His music demonstrates literally how musicians can change their ancient (traditional) style into modern (mannerist) *maniera* by refining antique procedures.

EXAMPLE XX-4.   L. Marenzio, *O voi che sospirate* (1581).
From *Publikationen älterer Musik*, 4¹:70. Edited by
A. Einstein. Leipzig, 1929; Hildesheim, 1967. Used by
permission of Breitkopf & Härtel, Wiesbaden.

The second work, *O fere stelle a6* (1588; Sannazaro), appears in the collection, dedicated to Count Mario Bevilacqua, whose dedication announces Marenzio's new, serious *maniera*—a typically mannerist advertisement. The work in question admirably shows the constitutive elements of his novel style. Minute word painting recedes in favor of evocative mood illustration.[12] The madrigal is full of chromatic progressions, including less bold varieties and more daring kinds. The sestina contains the line, *E tu fortuna muta il crudo stile* (Example xx-5). Marenzio harks back to the now well-known circle-of-fifths technique to depict Fortune's revolving wheel. However, he enriches the scheme by introducing extra chords between some of the traditional steps; minor triads, "dominant sevenths," and third-related chords add harmonic piquancy to the diatonic modulation characteristic of this device. As in the previous work, this dynamic excursion to flat tonal areas represents the one striking departure from sharp harmonic vocabulary.

In these works, chromaticism and circles-of-fifths lend graphic and affective depiction to vivid *concetti*. This means that avant-garde techniques now constitute elements recognized as madrigalian devices, devices which are further refined by forbidden intervals and progressions. One might say that composers have taken up Vicentino's challenge concerning the *effetto meraviglioso* of the tritone. In technical terms, this interval creates diminished triads and dominant-seventh sonorities, all of which are not accepted as legitimate entities in the perfect art. Only Vincenzo Galilei's *moderno contrapunto* admits them into the hierarchy of respectable chords. In the face of these latest radical experiments, the chromatic tradition that still adheres to earlier triadic atonality fades in importance. It no longer contributes anything new to style, but rather exploits an established technique. Giuseppe Caimo's spiritual madrigal *E ben raggion a5* (1585) is a case in point. For all its strange beauty and affective eccentricity, the *maniera* of this piece now represents mannered epigonalism.

As is well known, Carlo Gesualdo's fame rests on the chromatic madrigals composed after his stay in Ferrara. Perhaps he picked up hints about chromaticism from some of Luzzasco Luzzaschi's music or from his performances on Vicentino's archicem-

EXAMPLE XX-5.   L. Marenzio, *O fere stelle* (1588).

From A. Einstein, *The Italian Madrigal*, 3:253. Translated
by A. H. Krappe, R. H. Sessions, and O. Strunk. Rev. ed.
Princeton, 1971. Copyright, 1971, by Princeton University
Press. Used by permission of Princeton University Press.

balo.[13] Gesualdo also learned the secrets of florid counterpoint from the concerted madrigals written for the Ferrarese *concerto delle donne*. All these influences will come together in his late works. However, the madrigals published during this period, particularly those in the third and fourth books, contain some hints pointing to Gesualdo's mature and very eccentric *maniera*. In addition to commonplace chromaticism, *Moro e mentre sospiro a5* (1596) includes a few radical passages. Both aspects of this piece relate to the decidedly violent tone of the poetry and music. In the opening section, Gesualdo contrasts homophonic texture with third-related triads against polyphonic texture with sharp passing dissonances. The first two pairs of third-related triads (E♭ major G major and C major A major), found in the homophonic opening, illustrate Gesualdo's imaginative stylization of double counterpoint.[14] Throughout the madrigal, we notice peculiar voice leading and small motives in obverse syncopation, elements that create a mannered disintegration of balanced polyphony. Gesualdo's rhetorical treatment of *d'un mio sospiro* demonstrates this point (Example xx-6). Noteworthy is the double dissonance E♭/C (soprano and tenor) approached by leap, and the insertion of a rest in

EXAMPLE XX-6.   C. Gesualdo, *Moro e mentre sospiro* (1596).
From *Sämtliche Werke*, 4:46. Edited by W. Weismann.
Hamburg, 1958. Used by permission of VEB Deutscher
Verlag für Musik.

the bass after the note A that interrupts its resolution and stresses
the precarious diminished fifth, E♭-A, between the outer voices.
Such eccentricities will become "normalities" in his later works.[15]

In spite of these audacious moments, Gesualdo's chromaticism appears conservative when compared to that of other composers of the time. Luzzaschi's *Dolorosi martir a5* (1594; Tansillo)
occurs in a book dedicated to Gesualdo and is obviously written
with a view toward surpassing Marenzio's chromatic setting of the
same text (1580). The Dorian mode in Luzzaschi's composition is
hidden completely by a marked tendency toward sharp harmonic
areas, extended chromatic progressions, and semitonal melodic
configurations. Marenzio also exhibits bold style in his late works.
In many ways, Book IX *a5* (1599) represents the summation of
Marenzio's personal *maniera*. Radical harmony, including floating
atonality as well as bold and pungent dissonances, unusual voice
leading, and a wealth of imitative devices fuse to produce the
remarkable style of these late madrigals.[16] In addition, Marenzio
exhibits the mannerist trait of self-conscious stylization and exag-

geration of previous audacities. For example, in *Crudel acerba inesorabil morte* (Petrarch), he sets about to outdo Rore's expressive setting, written over forty years earlier. This aim seems clear from the opening passage that begins with Rore's affective and unusual ascending major sixth. After comparing the two pieces, we must conclude that Marenzio's personal approach does indeed surpass that of the initiator of the *maniera madrigalesca* from the point of view of its extreme chromaticism, weird cadences, and overall virtuoso effects.

The penchant for grotesque exaggeration evident in all the arts penetrates secular music in a profound way. The refinements grafted onto earlier innovations provide only one proof of this situation. Even more salient is the fact that conservative elements, such as diatonic and contrapuntal ideals, fade into the background as composers seek to pile up one musical shock after another. These are the means they use to surprise and move the jaded tastes of connoisseurs who are all too familiar with novel stereotypes. Madrigalisms now reach a level of unprecedented extravagance. This situation is evident in another setting of Petrarch's sestina (1588) that furnishes us with yet another self-conscious attempt to surpass Rore's madrigal. I refer here to Wert's unusual composition, a work replete with startling effects of all kinds. In the words of MacClintock, this "deeply emotional composition . . . reaches a new peak of 'expressiveness' in its mannered, baroque contrasts of color and emotion."[17]

In his sixth book of five-voiced madrigals (1594), Marenzio applies the panoply of radical novelties to the precious agonies of Guarini's *Il pastor fido*. Thus does Guarini's poetic grotesqueness find its musical counterpart. A particularly instructive example is *Udite lagrimosi spirti*. After a diatonic imitative point with one chromatic inflection, Marenzio unfolds the incredible sophistication of his harmonic techniques. His main affective weapons are unorthodox dissonances and other forbidden intervals. Rather than restrict these to diatonic passages, Marenzio uses them most prominently in chromatic ones, and this odd technique produces a heretofore unknown *meraviglia* (Example xx-7). After a pair of triads whose roots move by semitone (A major Bb major; three linear semitones), Marenzio interlocks a third-related pair (Bb major

EXAMPLE XX-7.   L. Marenzio, *Udite lagrimosi spirti* (1594).
From *Publikationen älterer Musik*, 6:110. Leipzig,
1931; Hildesheim, 1967. Used by permission of Breitkopf
& Härtel, Wiesbaden.

G minor) whose lack of linear semitone is compensated by a piquant suspended dissonance in the bass voice. At measure 15, we find a "dominant-seventh" massing, produced by a suspended dissonance, on the strong pulse of the tactus. There then occurs a most peculiar confluence of intervals at measure 16: the bass and tenor sing G, the seeming root of a triad; the alto has a suspended D, while the two sopranos sing a tritone, B♮-E♭. This "chord" can be interpreted in one of two ways—either as a G major triad with an E♭ dissonance anticipating the ensuing C minor triad (in second inversion), or as an E♭ major triad in first inversion with a dissonance (D) resolving by step to the root note of C minor. Whichever interpretation one chooses (and the ambiguity is deliberate), one cannot deny the eccentricity of this sonority. Immediately after it (measure 17), Marenzio writes another ambiguous chord whose components parallel exactly those just described. The final observation to be made about this excerpt concerns the last three third-related triads (measures 19–20). These are interlaced with harsh dissonances, some of which appear in unrelenting and surprising series. Now, on one level, the entire passage functions as a highly charged affective depiction. But on another level, Marenzio is playing an intellectual game. Mirtillo calls on the audience to observe new sorts of spiritual torments and to marvel at cruel affection. Marenzio calls on his audience to observe new sorts of musical pain and to marvel at crude progessions. I note, once again, the mannerist combination of wit and passion.

We should not leave the topic of Marenzio's harmonic innovations without treating one final example of his extreme affectation—the celebrated showpiece of Book IX, *Solo e pensoso a 5* (1599; Petrarch), a work full of expressive passages. Its opening alone, however, is enough to ensure the composer lasting fame and a prominent place in the ranks of mannerist masters. In Petrarch's sonnet, the vivid imagery of desolate nature fuses with the lover's despondent state of mind. And Marenzio captures this symbiosis in his astonishing setting of the first two lines. The first notable feature is the deliberate contrast between the slow, measured rise of the soprano and the more agitated descent of the lower voices, a feature heightened by the apposition of conjunct and disjunct motion. Marenzio further reflects the text by starting with two voices in the same range and slowly increasing their number to five. They progress in contrary motion until they reach an ambitus of four octaves; they then reverse this motion until they come to rest where they began. Marenzio carefully lays out the harmonic plan with a view to creating points of maximum tension, each of which is surpassed by movement to another such point. A series of dynamic passages, consisting of diatonic and chromatic chords, come to rest with a diatonic pattern that raises the expectation of a cadence. But Marenzio foils this ingrained response by using third-related triads that act as deceptive cadences. Moreover, when the sonal climax of four octaves arrives, Marenzio again foils any expectation of repose on this plateau, for he immediately reverses the direction with a most audacious third-related deceptive cadence. The descent continues with a dizzying series of chromatic chords. Just when the outer voices seem to be getting together in anticipation of final musical serenity, Marenzio introduces an unstable diminished triad that precedes the bass leap of ninth. The passage then ends quickly with a cadence in the modal area from which we embarked on this incredible journey. It is no wonder that this section remains to this day a "constant source of amazement and admiration."[18] It represents one of the most felicitous *effetti meravigliosi* ever invented by this mannerist composer, *il più dolce cigno d'Italia*.

Instances of unorthodox dissonance treatment have cropped up during the discussion of chromatic harmony. But chromatic excursions can be effected without recourse to unruly dissonances. Both trends evident in mature Mannerism relate to the governing aesthetic of *imitazione delle parole*, but when the two are merged, composers have attained the limits of their expressive language. As early as 1582, Marenzio is already experimenting in this vein. *Ohimè se tanto amate a5*, an excellent example of the mosaic madrigal, contains many harmonic devices used to paint Guarini's images. Among them, I cite here Marenzio's audacious dissonances on the words, *Languide et doloroso ohimè* (Example xx-8). First, a passing dissonant C appears against G♯. Then another such dissonance (D) forms a seventh against E and a tritone against G♯; the result is a "dominant seventh" in third inversion. After a consonant A major triad, Marenzio introduces a dissonant G shared

EXAMPLE XX-8.   L. Marenzio, *Ohimè se tanto amate* (1582).
From *Publikationen älterer Musik*, 4¹:110. Leipzig,
1929; Hildesheim, 1967. Used by permission of Breitkopf
& Härtel, Wiesbaden.

by two voices against F and A, followed by a double passing dissonance (C/E) against D, followed by another double passing dissonance (C/E), this time against D and B♭. These adventurous and
affective clashes result from suspensions and are used with third-
related triads. Marenzio here relies on traditional means, but bends
them to suit his own *maniera*.

A host of similar techniques occurs in his highly mannered
setting of *Giunto alla tomba a5* (1584; Tasso). Marenzio chose
this section from the *Gerusalemme liberata*—a description of Tancredi's lament at the tomb of Clorinda—in order to compete with
Wert's earlier setting (1581), of which we shall have more to say a
little later. Two more divergent conceptions can hardly be imagined. Wert's is an ingenious study in choral declamation verging
on total dramatization. Marenzio's adheres to the earlier tradition
of detailed word painting to such a degree that his composition
disintegrates into a long mosaic. Pictorialism survives in miniature
dimensions but not in gigantic four-part cycles such as this. Although each effect is expressive by itself, the variegated structure

of the whole possesses no sustaining power. In this case, the experiment simply does not work.

Dissonance treatment in the madrigals written by Wert about this time seems pale in comparison with Marenzio's audacity. However, Wert does introduce innovative touches on particularly evocative words. *Misera non credea a5* (1586; Tasso) sets the episode from the epic where Erminia laments over the inert body of Tancredi. Although the texture is mainly contrapuntal, Wert dramatizes her anguish by using syllabic declamation. Agitated rhythms, wide leaps, and chromatic harmonies abound in this masterpiece. Its affective tone will be much admired in the Baroque, and Berardi cites it in 1689 as an exemplar of the new style. One striking instance of forbidden intervals occurs when Erminia finds the courage to kiss Tancredi's bloody lips. At this point, Wert employs third-related triads (Bb major D major) and stresses the horrible fascination of Tancredi's *labbra esangui* by making the bass jump directly from Bb to F#.

The composer who will carry these unorthodox techniques to their height of modernity is, of course, Monteverdi. His dissonance treatment represents a bridge between mannerist and baroque practices, and for this reason arouses the ire of Artusi. Hints of Monteverdi's mature style in this respect already appear in his first book of madrigals (1587). Several prominent examples can be found in his setting of Guarini's *Baci soavi* (Example xx-9). On *C'hor m'involate*, Monteverdi uses his favorite device of double dissonances three times in a row. In the space of two measures, no less than seven dissonances appear, and five of them are combined in simultaneous fashion. Although these clashes are momentary passing notes, their congregation in condensed alignment intensifies their effect. From the vantage point of traditional voice leading, they are incorrect; but from the vantage point of modern harmony, they make perfect sense. Scholars generally agree that certain of Marenzio's chromatic and dissonant audacities are undertaken under the influence of Mantuan composers, principally Wert and Monteverdi.[19] However, a number of works suggest that the reverse is also true. One such case is Marenzio's *Ohimè se tanto amate a5* (1582; Guarini), which in many ways stands as a model for Monteverdi's later setting of the same text (1603). I cite here

EXAMPLE XX-9.   C. Monteverdi, *Baci soavi* (1587).
From *Tutte le opere*, 1:14. Edited by G. F. Malipiero.
Vienna, 1926.

one small but prophetic detail from Marenzio's *Così nel mio parlar a 5* (1599; Dante), a work embodying dissonant virtuosity (Example XX-10). Over a sustained D in the middle voice, Marenzio causes the two upper parts to rise in parallel thirds from consonances to dissonances,[20] and the latter he resolves in an irregular fashion by leap. The total effect admirably depicts the image of *ancide*. And of course, we will encounter this figure frequently in Monteverdi's later madrigals.

EXAMPLE XX-10.   L. Marenzio, *Così nel mio parlar* (1599).
From A. Einstein, "Dante im Madrigal." *Archiv für Musikwissenschaft* 3 (1921): 418.

A survey of some general trends in the use of dissonances is now possible. At first, dissonant sounds are introduced by means of the accepted technique of suspension. When suspensions move slowly, forbidden intervals occupy one complete metric pulse. Composers also deploy novel ways to intensify dissonant effects— that is, doubled or simultaneous dissonances. After 1590, we discern a new trend toward using dissonant constellations without the benefit of suspension. This more daring technique signals the emancipation of dissonance treatment from the strictures of traditional rules. Suspension lives on, however, as a means of introducing consecutive dissonances, and multiple dissonances in chains of suspensions soon become a conscious stylization in radical *maniera*. Greater novelty results from using dissonances with unruly approaches and resolutions. When all these eminently mannerist innovations are gathered together, balanced polyphonic style receives the final *coup de grace*. Upper voices become soloistic vehicles for unusual dissonances, strange and affective intervals, and virtuoso coloratura. Lower voices are given a supportive role against which these freewheeling dissonances can operate. When this function is taken over by a continuo instrument, the concerted ensemble makes its appearance. But this new genre also receives an important impetus from another aspect of stylization evident in this period—that found in declamatory madrigals.

The latter *maniera* entails many distinct but interrelated elements. The earlier mannerist propensity for *note nere*, a novelty that by now has become a norm in the madrigal, means that syllables are set to small note values. From the start, the technique of *note nere* is allied with syllabic declamation. Together, these two characteristics infuse the madrigal with lively representation of verbal rhythm. Even before the advent of *note nere*, mannerists tended toward paired repetition of homophonic sonorities. After *note nere*, these pairs become not only more rapid but also more frequent. For this reason, other polyphonic devices, such as melismas and imitative points, function as expressive figures. Now, syllabic text setting may be homophonic and include changing or repeated vertical chords as well as slow or rapid motion. The small-scale rhythmic configurations within large metrical units may or may not mirror closely the natural inflections of speech.

The same holds true for melodic configurations; they may or may not reflect the accentuation of speech patterns. The degree of declamatory and dramatic effect of musical settings depends on the number of factors marshaled at any point. These characteristics also operate in polyphonic texture. When the motives are small and concise, the declamation rapid and natural, and the rhythm fast and animated, imitative texture verges on *concertato* style. This element becomes even more prominent if balanced points of imitation are distorted for the sake of contrasting tempos or sonorities.

Marenzio's *Partirò dunque a5* (1580; Guarini) demonstrates this aspect of his artistry. With the exception of expressive melismas on *sguardo* and *ardo*, the text receives syllabic treatment. Word painting through melodic figures is thus at a minimum, although harmony and texture contribute to the evocation of appropriate moods. Marenzio achieves a very subtle balance between the outer and middle parts of the piece. Whereas the middle one is based on imitative counterpoint, the outer ones feature homophonic textures, textures characterized by stationary chords at the start and mobile harmonies at the close; and the latter lead into small sections of imitative counterpoint whose effect is one of mounting tension. In general, declamatory style seems to predominate, but Marenzio actually manipulates various tempos and textures to achieve a fluid representation of the poetic conceits. This approach appears in many other madrigals discussed in other contexts. Rhythmic agitation, syllabic treatment of the text, and declamatory motives in flexible imitative points also give Wert's setting of passages from Tasso's epic (Book VIII, 1586) their very individual *maniera*. But Wert surpasses Marenzio in giving syllables to rapid dotted figures and to sequences of sixteenth notes.

Wert's original approach to the dramatic quality of Tasso's epic and of Guarini's pastoral has already been mentioned. His unusual setting of *Giunto alla tomba* (1581) has been rightly called a "semi-dramatic narrative" and a "real dramatic scene."[21] The first section describes Tancredi's anguish, and here Wert adopts an almost totally homophonic style. The very first words, set to repeated A minor and E major chords in extremely low registers, establish the tone of Wert's personal *effetto meraviglioso*. In the rest of the opening section, up to *il viso affisse*, Wert keeps up a chordal style that contains several subtle changes of texture. Initially, static harmonies cause repeated notes in every voice, but a little later, the bass and tenor leap up and down octaves to contrast *prigion'il ciel*. Immediately following this animated passage, Wert repeats an A major chord no less than eleven times to dramatize the words, *Di color, di calor di moto privo*. The next section describes Tancredi's sudden eruption of weeping and sighing. Wert responds with a sudden eruption of astonishing virtuosity. Long, florid diminutions appear on *sgorgando*, and Wert intensifies their electrifying effect by repeating the phrase four times. *Rivo* also receives graphic representation by means of rising and falling eighth-note figures spun over several triads. *In un languido* begins with repeated notes and then jumps down with a sudden leap on *oimè*. The second part of the madrigal sustains the style established in the first part: declamatory homophony with occasional touches of imitative texture to provide musical momentum. Both parts feature frequent third-related triads and constant vacillation between major and minor shifts. These harmonies add immensely to the pathetic tone of the setting. Wert does not go to any harmonic extremes; his vocabulary is limited mainly to vertical sonorities proper to the Aeolian mode. Within this limitation, he deploys diatonic and chromatic progressions to create a somber tonal palette, and for some especially poignant phrases, he compacts a series of unusual chromaticisms. Wert has achieved a "first" in the history of sixteenth-century radicalism because his madrigal is the earliest polyphonic setting of Tasso's epic and because it embodies a very daring musical conception. After several decades of mannerist stylization based on polyphonic models, Wert turns to a self-conscious stylization of recitation associated with epic poetry. But his musical vision, intensely personal and striking, is far removed from the bland *madrigali ariosi* of Barre. Gone are the symmetrical lines and formulaic dance patterns. In their stead, Wert deploys flexible phrases and rhythmic configurations that mirror verbal declamation. Gone also are the predictable diatonic patterns of earlier declamatory works. All in all, Wert's mannerist masterpiece admirably exemplifies the precarious balance between convincing inspiration and artificial preciosity.

When he sets Guarini's *Tirsi morir volea a7* (1581), Wert goes a step further with regard to declamatory style. This madrigal appears six years before Gabrieli's setting, and it surpasses the latter in dramatic realism. Although Wert's composition is not the first to distinguish between narrative and discursive sections of the text, it is certainly the first in which this distinction acts as a basic aesthetic premise. The entire work relies on homophonic declamation similar to that found in *Giunto alla tomba,* except for the last line. The narrative portions and Tirsi's words are given to four low voices, whereas a female trio presents the nymph's words. The madrigal begins with Wert's subtle alternation of static and dynamic chords, but after this leisurely start, it then gains momentum. A slight hint of imitative polyphony appears at an appropriate spot (describing Tirsi's ardor). Dramatic moments, such as the homophonic cadential pattern on *Li disse,* add an almost operatic flavor (Example xx-11a). When the nymph is finally ready for love, she literally flutters with languid and trembling eyes (Example xx-11b). The subsequent dialogue between the two lovers as they consummate the sexual act is a masterpiece of realism. Even before Gabrieli, Wert has explored the possibilities of the cantata. By comparison, Vincenzo Galilei's *Poi che'l mio largo pianto a4,* published in the same year, appears an insipid attempt at choral declamation. Regular phrases, dancelike rhythms, and predictable harmonic patterns are alleviated by the occasional chromatic element. Einstein suggests that this work conforms with Galilei's thesis that polyphonic music should imitate histrionic style.[22] And in a sense, it does. However, Wert is really the composer who embodies this precept to an extent unsurpassed by any other contemporary mannerist before Monteverdi.

Monteverdi puts declamatory *maniera* to his own personal use. Even in his earliest works it is possible to detect his incipient interest in *concertato* texture. Symptomatic of this tendency is the rapid, almost parlando declamation in *Mentre io miravo fiso a5* (1590; Tasso). Whereas this madrigal reflects the superficial concettism of mannerist poetry, Monteverdi employs declamation for serious dramatic aims when he turns to Tasso's epic. Here parlando style becomes impassioned drama, as is clearly evident in a striking setting of Tancredi's lament, *Vivrò fra i miei tormenti*

EXAMPLE XX-11a.   G. de Wert, *Tirsi morir volea* (1581).
From *Opera Omnia*, 7:57. Edited by C. MacClintock
and M. Bernstein. American Institute of Musicology,
1967. Used by permission of Dr. A. Carapetyan.

EXAMPLE XX-11b.   G. de Wert, *Tirsi morir volea* (1581).
From *Opera Omnia*, 7:60. Edited by C. MacClintock
and M. Bernstein. American Institute of Musicology,
1967. Used by permission of Dr. A. Carapetyan.

(1592). This magnificent madrigal certainly equals any of Wert's works, and Monteverdi's quasi-operatic recitative has been noted by many modern analysts. In Einstein's words, the setting gives the impression of "frustrated monody."[23] Frustrated monody is just as prevalent in the homophonic settings given to Guarini's lyrics, as for example, in *Perfidissimo volto* (Example XX-12). In this madrigal, imitative texture and linear counterpoint with suspended dissonances appear solely to intensify expressive aspects of the text. The same general traits can be seen in Marenzio's settings from *Il pastor fido* (Book VI a5, 1594).[24] Monteverdi's madrigals seem to have a more modern flair because of their livelier rhythms, tonal leanings, and distinct dramatization. Marenzio, by comparison, stays closer to more placid rhythms, modal bases, and languid lyricism.

EXAMPLE XX-12.   C. Monteverdi, *Perfidissimo volto* (1592).
From *Tutte le opere*, 3:69. Edited by G. F. Malipiero. Vienna, 1927.

In his last book of madrigals (1595), one that forms the culmination of a long career, Wert devotes half of the contents to Guarini's pastoral drama. And the style he had developed in dealing with Tasso's epic is now applied to Guarini's languid sentimentality. In this way does Wert monumentalize the precious and exquisite affections of amorous pastoralism. Declamatory recitation is most prominent in *Udite lagrimosi spirti*, a work that MacClintock calls a *recitativo ed aria*.[25] Wert even approximates cantata structure in his cyclic treatment of *O Primavera*; after Mirtillo's celebrated monologue, Amarilli and her girl friends gather to play their adult version of blindman's bluff. In Wert's version, the choral parts are given homophonic recitation. One scholar notices a certain lack of variety in texture and rhythm, an unusual feature in Wert's music. But perhaps Wert intended this setting for dramatic presentation on the stage with instrumental doubling of the choral portions.[26] At any rate, whether performed on stage or not, madrigals such as this one reveal a fascination with stylization of the polyphonic idiom.

Even Marenzio, the master of the contrapuntal mosaic, succumbs to this mannerist trend in his later works. The culmination of this phase of Marenzio's evolution as a composer comes in a tripartite "dramatic scene" setting the dialogue between Dorinda and Silvio from Guarini's pastoral (1598). To prove his point that the so-called invention of monody by the Camerata is just around the corner, Einstein reproduces a portion of this work as an accompanied monody.[27] And indeed, from the vantage point of melodic recitation, it could be mistaken for a product of the Florentine circle. One point must be clarified here. Although the change in Marenzio's style is significant, especially when we consider his earlier penchant for mosaic effects, homophonic declamation of a mild sort does exist in his early works. The more dramatic, or "premonodic," or "pseudo-monodic" elements characteristic of his later works arise from the startling rhetorical novelty of passionate declamation within the limits of polyphonic pastoralism made famous by Monteverdi and Wert—and not from the influence of Florentine notions about recitative.[28] My thesis is that declamatory dramatization appears first in the polyphonic madrigal, and it constitutes a kind of *effetto meraviglioso*. At the same time, it stretches the genre to its utmost limits. The madrigal has certainly come a long way from its beginnings. Through a series of deliberate stylizations, it has taken on a number of features normally associated with baroque style. When is a madrigal not a madrigal? And when does Mannerism become the Baroque?

Before addressing these problems, mention must be made of several other important innovations evident in late sixteenth-century practice. The first of these concerns the influence of improvised ornamentation on polyphonic composition, a characteristic that further blurs the distinction between late mannerist and early baroque styles. Emphasis on high female voices and florid diminutions have been described in connection with some works by Wert and Monteverdi. Because of Wert's close association with Ferrara, he naturally emphasizes this more novel tessitura. Thus, when Wert decides to set *Giunto alla tomba* for soprano, alto, two tenors, and bass, he does so in order to produce an unusually deep sound. An earlier norm is now a startling mannerism. Of course, Wert is also known for his mastery of florid embellishment, a trait inspired by the improvised art of the Ferrarese singers. One of his most evocative works, *Non è sì denso velo a5* (1586), exploits their coloratura style in a magnificent manner (Example xx-13). The work opens with a lengthy female trio featuring *concertato* effects. And the first octave leap is most unusual and striking. Wert subsequently contrasts the deeper five-voiced sonority to paint the words, *Nè sì remoto cielo*. And because the fame of the ladies tends to obscure the presence of virtuoso male singers, we note the melismatic treatment of the bass on *fiumi*. Similar vocal efflorescences characterize Wert's *Vezzosi augelli*.

Monteverdi's *Ecco mormorar l'onde* is also replete with written-in ornamentation. Equally virtuoso is the opening of *Lumi miei cari lumi a5* (1592; Guarini). Here, rapid parlando and florid diminution are welded together in dazzling *concertato* style. And it is but a small step from such works to the concerted duos and trios in Monteverdi's later output. This mannerist device, one that transforms the balanced contrapuntal madrigal into a genre stressing soloistic display, has connections with specific Italian courts. Its glamorous appeal, related to the adulation of singers, represents the ultimate stylization of the unaccompanied madrigal. It not only causes the disintegration of traditional voice leading, but also introduces a plethora of forbidden intervals. Many composers

EXAMPLE XX-13.   G. de Wert, *Non è sì denso velo* (1586).

From *Opera Omnia*, 8:33–34. Edited by C. MacClintock and M. Bernstein. American Institute of Musicology, 1968. Used by permission of Dr. A. Carapetyan.

EXAMPLE XX-13, *continued*

consciously imitate this clearly recognized *maniera*. A case in point is Marenzio, who generally favors doubling one of the inner parts, but who, in his later career, writes a number of works featuring the brilliant sonority of three high female voices.[29]

The discussion of mannerist elements in the courtly madrigal, though central to my thesis, must not overshadow the popularity of the Venetian style. Andrea Gabrieli develops refined madrigalian procedures based on the approach of his teacher, Adrian Willaert. Apart from rare instances of pictorialism and chromaticism, Gabrieli explores musically self-sufficient settings of light pastoral verse. Clear structural diatonicism, animated rhythm, fine motivic imitation, and sumptuous multi-voiced sonority characterize a *maniera* geared for high-class yet simple entertainment music. In the hands of Ippolito Baccusi, Giuseppe Caimo, Giovanni Croce, and Giovanni Gabrieli, pastoral playfulness attains its most sophisticated charm and sensuality. Most of Marenzio's six-voiced madrigals, with some exceptions noted earlier, belong to this tradition. In many ways, Venetian style represents the epitome of the original meaning of *maniera*—studied and stylized *grazia*. And in a limited way, Venetian music presents interesting analogues to Venetian art.

Lighthearted entertainment, first evident in single comic madrigals, now develops into cyclic arrangements based on a theme of some sort. With regard to Adriano Banchieri's *La pazzia senile a3* (1598), the singers may enjoy the musical humor by performing the madrigals and silently reading the connective material, or they may include an audience by reading aloud the narrative portions found between the madrigals. The latter procedure is recommended by Banchieri in his preface. Undoubtedly, the most accomplished and famous madrigal-comedy in this period is Orazio Vecchi's *L'Amfiparnasso a5* (1597), and in this case, the comic drama is to be perceived solely through the music, as Vecchi himself states. The work includes an astonishing range of madrigalian *maniere*: sentimental pastoralism, grotesque parodies on famous works, and subtle takeoffs on passionate *imitazione delle parole*. Quite apart from its musical bravura, the madrigal-comedy as a genre demonstrates a highly developed sense of style consciousness in this period.

Similar consciousness informs the growing body of *madrigali spirituali*, a genre encouraged by Counter Reformation circles. When such works come from composers well-versed in the latest mannerist devices, as for example, Marenzio, we observe a transference of pictorial tricks characteristic of secular style to quasi-religious music. Even Lasso, the erstwhile paragon of light and lascivious music, turns to the more salubrious spiritual madrigal which he invests with all the mastery of expressive techniques evident in his secular music. Lasso's very last work is a setting of Luigi Tansillo's lugubrious cycle, *Lagrime di San Pietro* (1595). And these activities seem to accord with Lasso's gloomy state of mind and his morbid preoccupation with death.

They may also reflect fatigued resignation from a modern world whose novel virtuosities eluded him. Such is certainly the case with his northern colleague, Filippo di Monte, who, together with Lasso, complains about the irrational eccentricities of younger composers.[30] Monte attempts to modernize his style by writing settings of the concettist verse of Guarini, Tasso, and even of Marino. But he cannot match the daring *effetti meravigliosi* of Marenzio, Wert, and Monteverdi. Monte's rather staid temperament relegates him to the rank of an unimportant imitator of Italian *maniera*. He possesses neither the fiery eloquence of rhetorical dramatization, the witty ingenuity of pictorial realism, the luxuriant color of Venetian pastoralism, nor the virtuoso brilliance of *concertato* techniques. And these are the characteristics destined to bring the *maniera madrigalesca* to its final and most glorious phase, a phase that will finally bridge Mannerism and the Baroque.

CHAPTER XXI

§◦§◦§◦

Mannerism in Transition,

1600–1620

The years between 1600 and 1620 are dominated by two composers, Carlo Gesualdo and Claudio Monteverdi, and their respective approaches to the polyphonic madrigal provide insights into the dual nature of late Mannerism. An almost pathological *morbidezza*[1] permeates Gesualdo's works, works that thrive on grotesque and strangely powerful effects. In bringing chromaticism to its final efflorescence, Gesualdo attains the most exaggerated manifestation of mannerist stylization. Monteverdi too follows a personal inspiration in his quest for radical refinements. But his mannerist stylization yields more fruitful avenues for baroque style. In Monteverdi's music we observe a transition from polyphony to concerted music. And every aspect of this transformation, whether subtle or blatant, is handled with the sure hand of a master craftsman.

Because of the impact of these two *maniere*, the eclectic mixture of word painting and descriptive-dramatic realism becomes outdated. Although it continues to be popular after 1600 from a historical point of view, it must be considered to be a fashionable stereotype. The composers who cultivate this convention are many. I cite here the example of Marco da Gagliano, a Florentine known for his monodies and dramatic music. In his polyphonic madrigals, Gagliano favors pastoral poetry of a lightly sentimental cast, and his musical settings are characterized, appropriately enough, by elegance and gentility. Generally, Gagliano's style consists of counterpoint based on declamatory motives with occasional instances of chromaticism and minute word painting. Exceptions can be found in a few passionate works, such as *O Sonno a5* (1602; della Casa), a madrigal featuring suspended dissonances and third-related triads. Atlhough effective, Gagliano's technique is neither new nor particularly radical for the time. And yet, it comes under fire in a treatise by Muzio Effrem, who censures the liberties evident in Gagliano's counterpoint. His tract, of course, represents another piece of evidence for the musical turmoil engendered by the second practice.[2]

The degree to which the *maniera madrigalesca* now constitutes a self-conscious tradition is further demonstrated by a student publication of Heinrich Schütz, who studied in Venice between 1609 and 1612. This talented young man learned his stylistic lessons well; and the book of madrigals in question (1611) reveals Schütz's understanding both of Venetian and of courtly madrigalian styles. From the Venetians and Monteverdi, Schütz acquired the modern art of firm tonal organization on which pictorial effects can be mounted without disturbing organic unity. From Monteverdi, he also developed his mastery of declamatory motives as well as affective harmonies and melodic contours, as is shown in *Dunque addio care selve a5* (Guarini, *Il pastor fido*). But Schütz's distinct predilection for figural word painting, often involving virtuoso elements, comes from the older tradition of mosaic madrigalism. This tradition reaches manneristic, we might even say mannered, extravagance in *Fuggi o mio core a5* (Guarini), a study in musical "flying." *Selve beate a5* (Guarini, *Il pastor fido*) contains many such remarkable passages. The eighth-note runs on *frondi*, with their complex permutations, entail scalar motion between tritones as well as tritone leaps, thus representing written versions of the most exaggerated *passaggi* recommended in treatises on vocal ornamentation. The ending presents a noteworthy *fioritura* (Example XXI-1). Here, *ridente* is depicted by a figure that every voice student recognizes as a stereotyped vocalise. Mannerist playfulness, if not superficiality, is admirably demonstrated by this *effetto meraviglioso*.

The overlapping of older and newer radicalism can be seen clearly if we turn now to Monteverdi's famous fifth book of madrigals (1605), a book that represents both the end of the unaccom-

EXAMPLE XXI-1.   H. Schütz, *Selve beate* (1611).
From *Neue Ausgabe*, 22:23. Edited by H. J. Moser.
Kassel, 1962. Used by permission of Bärenreiter-Verlag.

panied madrigal and the beginning of the concerted madrigal. It
is a remarkable publication on many counts. The preface, later
glossed by his brother, sounds the trumpet of attack on behalf of
champions of the second practice. And Monteverdi deliberately
includes four works criticized by Giovanni Maria Artusi.[3] Of the
nineteen pieces (the last six with obligatory continuo), sixteen are
set poems by Guarini,[4] and eleven of these are from *Il pastor fido*.
Inasmuch as many of the Guarini texts also appear in Luca Marenzio's Book VII *a5* (1595), Einstein suggests that Monteverdi
wishes to compete with his illustrious predecessor.[5] At the same
time, there exists the possibility that Monteverdi's choice is motivated by an aesthetic ideal, for he focuses on elegant concettism
whose sweet lamenting accents hide the potential for lyric and
dramatic passion. Guarini's *maniera* is eminently well suited to
Monteverdi's novel concept of polyphony as the perfection of
melody. With this poetry, he explores the novelty of *recitar cantando*[6] in modern counterpoint. As is well known, five of the pieces
form a cycle, *Ecco Silvio a5*, setting the dialogue between Silvio
and Dorinda from the fourth act of *Il pastor fido*. This set of
madrigals retains Monteverdi's earlier declamatory style characterized, on the one hand, by moderate or even rapid parlando
melodies, and on the other hand, by polyphonic moments with

expressive dissonances. In other words, its harmonic language and stylistic principles derive from approaches that Monteverdi had previously established. Modern scholars cite it as a forerunner of his future essays in the concerted madrigal and the chamber cantata.[7] And yet, for all its inherent modernism, it lacks dramatic shape and articulation. And it does not commeasure with the radical elements of *concertato* style evident in other works in this book, or for that matter, equally innovative ones in previous books.

Monteverdi's setting of Guarini's *Non più guerra!* (1603) illustrates this point. He gives the text, a dramatic lyric much like the monologues of *Il pastor fido*, his typical treatment consisting of declamatory motives in imitative textures. Homophony and linear suspension each appear once for the sake of sharp pictorialism. The style of this madrigal, agitated and humorously vivid, tends to be much closer to the *stile concitato* than *Ecco Silvio* (Example XXI-2). The opening exclamations have two distinct, rhythmically concise motives that are combined with the second and third lines of the poem. During this section, each voice stands out as a soloistic combatant, and thus, the opening reproduces the unusual and artfully mannered *contrapposto* of Guarini's conceit. The repetition of the first line contributes to the evocation of an agitated mood; it also hints at the musical and expressive significance of the two motives that comprise it, for the entire madrigal is based on configurations of them. Their rhythmic contours yield various permutations for subsequent motives that appear in brilliant imitation and kaleidoscopic combination. Thus does Monteverdi exploit elements of similarity and contrast to link and profile the two basic *concetti* of the poem—war and peace.

The subtlety of his rhythmic technique is incredible. The patterns of *Non più guerra!* and *trionfanti* share the same warlike rhythms. The more placid rhythm of *Pietate!* is echoed by *Occhi miei belli*. The bellicose rhythm reappears on *A che v'armate? Ancidete i rubelli* and on *Ancidete chi*, a truncated line. *Contr'un cor che già* appropriately reflects the beloved's animosity by varying the warlike pattern. The remainder of this line, *pres'e vi si rende*, features the first occurrence of syncopated suspensions, "bindings" that again mirror the words. *S'arm'e si difende* is related rhythmically and conceptually to *Contr'un cor*, and therefore, the phrase

EXAMPLE XXI-2.   C. Monteverdi, *Non più guerra!* (1603).
From *Il quarto libro de madrigali a cinque voci.*

EXAMPLE XXI-2, *continued*

EXAMPLE XXI-2, *continued*

EXAMPLE XXI-2, *continued*

EXAMPLE XXI-2, *continued*

contains an implicit reference to *Ancidete chi*—which is actually the first part of the line. Up to this point, these motives are freely combined, dovetailed, and varied to create a sonal illusion of inimical agitation. The "point" of the lover's protest comes with the words, *Non chi vinto v'adora*. Here, Monteverdi introduces his first new figure in a sensuous and sweet trio for high voices. The effect in context is very striking, and includes the only gentle melisma in the entire piece. There follows immediately a passage of declamatory homophony for low voices on *Volete voi ch'io mora?* And the lover's happy acquiescence to this wish is brought out by rhythms recalling the fact that he is already conquered and adoring. The melancholy repetitions of *e del morir* present quieter versions of *Non più guerra!* and harsh suspended dissonances paint the anguish of death. Monteverdi achieves rounded unity and witty expressivity by setting the "point," *ma sarà vostr'il danno*, in a rhythmic pattern modeled after the warlike figure of the opening. Now, this abstract analysis cannot do justice to the instinctive compositional process by which Monteverdi arrived at this magnificent setting; as Giovanni Battista Doni would insist, the madrigal is a result of natural talent. This kind of dramatic genius cannot be conveyed by prosaic descriptions, for it arises from inspired *furor poeticus*.

Monteverdi generally avoids extreme chromaticism in his mature works. One exception can be found in *Piagne e sospira a 5* (1603; Tasso, *Gerusalemme conquistata*),[8] a madrigal built on semitonal melodies and third-related harmonies obviously inspired by the pathetic tone of the verse. In comparison with that of Monteverdi, Gesualdo's style, in his fifth and sixth books (1611), exemplifies the ultimate in chromaticism. In the seclusion of his Neapolitan palace, Gesualdo now concentrates on short poems characterized by violent and highly mannered melancholy. The torments of love and death described in this doggerel verse certainly fit the extreme contortions of his musical *maniera*.

Tu m'uccidi o crudele (Book v, 1611) serves as a fine illustration of Gesualdo's techniques and their resultant *effetti meravigliosi*. Unusual harmonies appear in syllabic sections whose relatively slow pace contrasts sharply with two distinct sections of animated counterpoint underscored by clear-cut diatonic vocabulary; the polyphonic sections set one word, *amando*. In spite of this surface dichotomy, Gesualdo's chromaticism and dissonance treatment are still linear in orientation. The opening of the madrigal constitutes a model of harmonic ambiguity. Its surprising effect arises from consecutive and multiple dissonances (with and without suspensions), triads whose roots are related by thirds and semitones, frequent tritones, unorthodox seventh-chords, and juxtaposition of flat and sharp accidentals. The setting of the words, *Ch'io moro*, stated twice, is very strange and warrants further comment (Example XXI-3). At the end of the first statement, we find an A minor seventh-chord (the seventh being a suspension) and an F♯ major chord; this third-relation involves three linear semitones. The second time, an F major seventh-chord moves to an E major one via four linear semitones, all clearly shown in Gesualdo's voice leading.[9] To sum up, the main characteristics of the chromatic episodes reside in a very flexible manipulation of chords in various positions, peculiar root movements, unusual syncopations and suspensions, and bizarre false relations. The fol-

EXAMPLE XXI-3.   C. Gesualdo, *Tu m'uccidi o crudele* (1611).
From *Sämtliche Werke*, 5:62. Edited by W. Weismann. Hamburg, 1958. Used by permission of VEB Deutscher Verlag für Musik.

lowing remarks made by Einstein apply to this work, even though they are made with reference to another equally eccentric madrigal in the fifth book: "The 'expression' in this sort of piece is astonishing, but it would be difficult to determine exactly where sincerity of feeling ends and mannerism begins."[10]

The elongated descending motives at the start of *Languisco al fin a5* (Book v, 1611) have drawn the attention of several scholars, one of whom identifies this figure with the *inganno*, a motive that appears later in keyboard music (e.g., in the works of Giovanni Maria Trabaci and Girolamo Frescobaldi).[11] In Gesualdo's madrigal, the *inganno* bears a striking resemblance to Nicola Vicentino's reconstruction of ancient tetrachords, and this fact intimates the influence of Ferrarese experiments. Although the pattern does not occur so prominently in other madrigals by Gesualdo, it does crop up from time to time.[12] I mention it here because this phenomenon suggests one tantalizing link between chromaticism in works of the middle and late mannerist periods and those of the early baroque period.[13]

Book VI (1611) contains many outstanding and expressive works. Among them, *Moro lasso* is deservedly famous because it manages to fuse extreme stylization and affective conviction. A cursory glance at the music shows that Gesualdo organizes its structure by alternating sections of fairly slow chromaticism with sections of faster counterpoint. The two types correspond nicely with the verbal images that Gesualdo repeats at will in order to create harmonic contrasts. Within these larger sections, there exist unit correspondences that also reflect verse repetitions.

The two polyphonic sections, on the words *E chi mi può dar vita*, are built on the brisk imitative interplay of a single motive that presents a characteristic aural figure on *vita*. In the first of these sections, a carefully planned harmonic climax receives support from the contrapuntal arrangement of the voices. Although the second section parallels the first with regard to its two sets of imitative points, its harmonic and motivic plan is rearranged to create maximum tension. It is important to realize that occasional semitonal inflections do appear, in spite of the predominantly diatonic character of these polyphonic sections. Indeed, the latter create a diatonic feeling by virtue of the extreme chromaticism of the other alternating segments of the madrigal. The diatonic sections are also closely related inasmuch as the first one gravitates to C major and the second to F major. By way of contrast, the chromatic sections range far afield from this stable relationship.

Gesualdo establishes an eccentric tone in the very first short chromatic section, a compendium of radical Mannerism (Example XXI-4a). Low voices, slow motion, and slithering semitonal melodies create a lugubrious atmosphere; and triadic floating atonality begins in the outré region of C♯ major and slides through third-relations to G major. When this ordinary harmony is reached, acerbity appears by means of peculiar dissonances and leaps. The first and last chords of this section form third-relations (C♯ major and E major), as does the ending of the chromatic part with the ending of the ensuing polyphonic section (E major and C major). Whereas the first chromatic portion gives the illusion of homophony, the second is built on the strangest possible points of imitation (Example XXI-4b). The voice entries are best described as unruly and eccentric in the extreme. Surely Zarlino never envisioned such

EXAMPLE XXI-4a.   C. Gesualdo, *Moro lasso* (1611).

From *Sämtliche Werke*, 6:74. Edited by W. Weismann. Hamburg, 1959. Used by permission of VEB Deutscher Verlag für Musik.

EXAMPLE XXI-4b.   C. Gesualdo, *Moro lasso* (1611).

From *Sämtliche Werke*, 6:74–75. Edited by W. Weismann. Hamburg, 1959. Used by permission of VEB Deutscher Verlag für Musik.

unorthodox relationships even in his most casual *imitatione*. This imitative point not only dramatizes in a vivid way the word *Ahi!* but also symbolizes Gesualdo's penchant for grotesque stylization of traditional procedures. Furthermore, this weird kind of counterpoint produces five third-related chords in succession, ranging from C minor to C# major. After concluding this chromatic section with a homophonic passage, Gesualdo then repeats the first three lines of the poem together with their alternation of chromatic, diatonic, and chromatic sections. The first two now appear on a sonorous plane a fourth above the original statements. But because of the modulatory scheme of the diatonic section, the outrageous setting of *Ahi! che m'ancide* is pitched a tone below its counterpart. Its homophonic closing portion begins as it did the first time, but Gesualdo suddenly jumps up an octave so that the rest sounds a ninth above the original. The effect is electrifying.

But the most extraordinary effects come at the end of the piece (Example xxi-4c). *O dolorosa sorte* begins with a slow, wailing imitation that increases the number of multiple dissonances with each voice entry. Beneath them lies a diatonic support. On the last B♭ major chord, Gesualdo perversely repeats the note, A, in the alto (from the preceding F major seventh-chord), creating a harsh B♭DFA massing that leads directly to an E major chord. The harmonic components of these two vertical sonorities, including root notes, are a tritone apart; furthermore, they rely on three linear semitones. What can one say about this totally grotesque progression? Nothing approaching its audacity has been seen in the annals of mannerist radicalism. Gesualdo repeats this passage, complete with the "tritone-related" chords, on a harmonic plane a fifth above the original. Then, a short, fairly diatonic section introduces the final staggering setting of *ahi! mi da morte*. Two overlapping imitative sections, based on a most peculiar chromatic motive,[14] produce a network of intricate dissonances, diminished triads, and "dominant seventh" chords. Scarcely one vertical sonority goes by without piquant dissonances. A cataloging of the latter cannot reproduce the bitter flavor created by their unrelenting appearance. Gesualdo manipulates seconds, sevenths, and tritones in a most eccentric manner. Six such cases of passing single dissonances on strong and weak subdivisions of the pulse are over-

EXAMPLE XXI-4c.   C. Gesualdo, *Moro lasso* (1611).

From *Sämtliche Werke*, 6:76–77. Edited by W. Weismann.
Hamburg, 1959. Used by permission of VEB Deutscher
Verlag für Musik.

EXAMPLE XXI-4c, *continued*

shadowed by nine cases where these disturbing intervals occupy entire metric units of the tactus.

I have already indicated that Gesualdo's chromaticism and dissonance treatment arise from linear considerations. At the same time, certain third-relations seem to arise from vertical considerations. Gesualdo's carefully planned repetitions, featuring different harmonic planes, also attest to an awareness of sonorous values and blocks of color. The commonplace idea that Gesualdo reserves chromaticism for homophonic sections and counterpoint for diatonic ones is somewhat misleading. His chromatic sections seem homophonic simply on the basis of a comparison with the polyphonic ones. By the same token, the diatonicism of the contrapuntal sections seems bland only in comparison with the chromatic excesses of the so-called homophonic sections. In reality, Gesualdo's style departs from linear voice leading, with the exceptions noted above. Gesualdo indeed unites traditional polyphonic procedures with avant-garde trends,[15] but in a very special way.

Apart from a general consensus on the matter of Gesualdo's harmonic extravagances—characterized as "musical seasickness," "extreme but stillborn fantasies," or products of a "psychopath" and a "pathological case"[16]—there exists considerable disagreement as to the exact technicalities that constitute his *maniera*. Several scholars stress the novelty of Gesualdo's sharp contrasts between slow homophony and rapid counterpoint.[17] But I have suggested that his basic viewpoint is always contrapuntal. However, rhythmic novelty is evident in his characteristic freedom in dealing with imitative points; entries are spaced at irregular intervals, and the configurations varied to obtain agitated effects. Another prominent element of avant-gardism hitherto unnoticed is Gesualdo's tendency to use very irregular vertical intervals as points of entry for imitative voices. His radical approach often features extreme registers and startling dissonances. The total effect is one of complete distortion of homogeneous polyphony. There are moments in Gesualdo's texture when the listener experiences the peculiar sensation that one more step, either higher or lower, will cause the tenuous structure to collapse—a relative illusion, of course, but still a very telling one.

With regard to dissonance treatment, Gesualdo's use of diminished triads and seventh-chords is hardly novel, considering the appearance of such sonorities in the works of Marenzio, Wert, and Monteverdi. Insofar as these constellations result from linear elements, however eccentric, Gesualdo's usage is much closer to that of Marenzio than to that of Monteverdi. This comparison, of course, omits factors such as the number and congregation of chromatic elements. Monteverdi's novel treatment of such chords, chords that furnish one important basis for the new *maniera*, makes him the first archmodernist. But with Monteverdi, unorthodox chordal entities become the norm of a new style; they are positive factors in the *seconda prattica*. In Gesualdo's *maniera*, unorthodox treatment of nonharmonic components remains a deliberate deviation from the *ars perfecta*; in this sense, it functions as a negative factor in an extreme stylization of past tradition. And from this point of view, Gesualdo emerges as an archmannerist whose audacities presume an ingrained response to normal procedures. Gesualdo uses his tricks to shock and surprise. Monteverdi too seeks *effetti meravigliosi*, but in his hands the regressive aspects of mannerist stylization are transformed into progressive ingredients of baroque style.

As far as chromaticism is concerned, scholars agree that Gesualdo's personal audacities stem from the isolation and new function of semitonal relationships between vertical progressions.[18] For example, G-G♯ can produce E♭ major and E major triads. This specific instance is important inasmuch as the roots are a semitone apart, and motion from one to the other entails three linear semitones. There is no doubt that such cases abound in Gesualdo's harmony, and they constitute one of the most outrageous vertical-linear relationships possible in chromatic style, barring the introduction of dissonances. One way of exaggerating the shock value of chromatic sonorities is to compound the semitonal connections from three to four. Another method is to connect a four-note chord and a triad whose roots are a tritone apart. The latter type of progression produces three linear semitones and three linear tritones at the same time. And Gesualdo uses both methods whenever he strives for particularly striking effects. Close examination of his audacious vocabulary reveals certain interesting features.

Gesualdo's small-scale chromaticism—that is, from chord to chord —tends to rely on progressions that involve two or three linear semitones. Thus, it is correct to conclude that semitonal motion, the theoretical basis of Vicentino's chromatic genus, finds its apotheosis in Gesualdo's *maniera*. When Gesualdo desires especially surprising effects, he then moves on to extreme forms of chromaticism heretofore unknown: triple and quadruple semitone connections, bizarre accidentals such as B♯ and E♯, and/or semitone and tritone root movements. The eccentricity of these progressions can be exacerbated by sharp dissonances and angular voice leading. Simpler chromatic relations (those characteristic of earlier mannerist experiments) now occur in contrapuntal sections, or between the beginnings and endings of larger phrases and sections. The point to be stressed here is that chromatic elements that were previously considered highly volatile become, for Gesualdo, relatively stable.

All these techniques produce a style whose violent contortions have been noted frequently by historians. Gesualdo's *maniera* has occasioned comparisons with El Greco, Pontormo, Parmigianino, Tasso, Marino, and Gracián. Without subscribing to concrete analogies between different media or between creative artists from different generations, we can agree that Gesualdo represents the mannerist love of excessive distortion and stylization in an unmistakable way. With reference to musical Mannerism, his personal *maniera* is a dead end, not only because of its highly individual avant-gardism, but also because this composer develops one aspect of mannerist stylization to its ultimate limits. After Gesualdo, there is virtually nothing new to be done with chromaticism understood as a self-conscious, deliberate deviation from tradition. One may emulate but one cannot develop this approach any further. But from the viewpoint of chromaticism seen as a vehicle for strong affective expression, Gesualdo joins the ranks of mannerists who build up an aesthetic taken over by baroque composers. His style is known and appreciated by several exponents of the second practice. Thus, on the one side, Gesualdo's style represents a "minor current"[19] inasmuch as its technique is the end and not the beginning of a musical trend. On the other side, however, his style

belongs to a major current inasmuch as its aesthetic premise is the
start and not the end of future developments.[20] In Gesualdo's case,
it is clear that *maniera* has a special and provocative meaning.

In my view, the novel use of dissonances, allied with the
mannerist creed of *imitazione delle parole*, provides the real link
between Mannerism and the Baroque. The reader will recall that a
number of madrigals published between 1580 and 1600 feature
successive and simultaneous dissonances that occur in linear suspension. Benedetto Pallavicino's *Cruda Amarilli* (1600; Guarini,
Il pastor fido) adheres to this principle (Example xxi-5). The opening, the only section where linear counterpoint prevails, contains
a series of suspended single dissonances, two cases of double dissonances, and two cases of irregularly resolved tritones. Such progressions are certainly "pungent,"[21] and they paint a vivid picture
of cruel Amarilli. However, they are not in themselves novel, for
we have seen similar instances in earlier works by Marenzio and
Monteverdi. Nonetheless, this particular composition is important
in that it furnished a model for settings by a number of eminent
composers, including Sigismondo d'India (1607) and Monteverdi
(1605). And Monteverdi's work is singled out by Artusi as an
exemplar of unruly modernism.

The first few measures of Monteverdi's madrigal suffice to
indicate the connections between the two Mantuan composers
(Example xxi-6). Although Monteverdi's version is less dissonant
than Pallavicino's, it has a distinctly modern tone lacking in the latter work. Monteverdi repeats the first phrase on two closely related
tonalities, and the dissonances, repeated verbatim, act as harmonic
propellents within vertically conceived cadential patterns. There
follows a passage of animated homophony (including a diminished
triad) that dissolves into written ornamentation on *ahi*. The last
part of this passage is torn apart by Artusi. Monteverdi commits
the cardinal sin of introducing a dissonance after a rest in the
soprano, and then of resolving it by a leap to another dissonance.
Of course, according to the precepts of modern counterpoint, this
second "dissonance" is an integral consonance belonging to a
dominant seventh chord. At the same time, the dissonances just
described also serve as affective depictions of the words. The same
holds true for the other excerpts selected by Artusi, who neglects

EXAMPLE XXI-5.   B. Pallavicino, *Cruda Amarilli* (1600).
From *Das Chorwerk*, 80:17. Edited by D. Arnold.
Wolfenbüttel, 1961. Used by permission of Möseler Verlag.

EXAMPLE XXI-5, *continued*

the primacy of the text as well as the tonal logic that regulates dissonance treatment. Compared with Monteverdi's work, the dissonances in Pallavicino's madrigal still retain obvious ties with older sixteenth-century counterpoint.

   This difference is even more evident in Monteverdi's *Ohimè se tanto amate* (1603; Guarini), a witty reflection of the tongue-in-cheek *concetti* of the amorous poem. Several significant passages can show Monteverdi's consummate handling of modern dissonances. The opening begins with a very rhetorical and dramatic rendition of the exclamation. Both entries of the soprano duet high above the bass involve irregular dissonances.[22] Besides being a startling *effetto meraviglioso*, the passage forms evidence that Monteverdi is thinking in terms of trio texture. These drawn-out wails are followed by rapid homophonic parlando spiced up by occasional dissonances. Only one of the latter would pass muster as a passing nonharmonic note; the rest represent willful ornaments of the type disallowed by traditional theorists. Monteverdi depicts *dolorosa* with some of the most unorthodox voice leadings in the composition: a number of single and double dissonances culminate in a descending leap of a seventh from a consonance to

EXAMPLE XXI-6.   C. Monteverdi, *Cruda Amarilli* (1605).
From *Tutte le opere*, 5:1. Edited by G. F. Malipiero.
Vienna, 1927.

Example XXI-6, *continued*

mar,		ahi las-	so,
mar,	ahi	las-	so,
mar,	ahi	las-	so,
mar, ahi		las-	so,
mar, ahi-		las-	so,

a dissonance. Had Artusi seen this madrigal, he certainly would have accorded it a place of honor in his diatribe. The concluding section presents another aspect of Monteverdi's inventiveness in devising yet another original idea for the commonplace conceit, *Havrete mille mille dolc'ohimè*. He underscores the words with a sequence of interlocking fauxbourdon chords, a series that produces a bittersweet set of false relations. The passage gravitates from B♭ major to G major (third-relations). And the penultimate triad in this sequence exemplifies Monteverdi's modern musical wit. Its components make it out to be a B minor triad in first inversion; as such it belongs to the fauxbourdon sequence. But Monteverdi seems to realize that the ear hears it differently, especially after it "resolves" to G. It sounds rather like a D major triad whose consonant A has been replaced by a dissonant B, inasmuch as the V-I movement of the bass voice is very strong. This ambiguity becomes explicit at the end of the piece (Example XXI-7). All in all, this charming work embodies the earlier tradition of mosaic fragmentation in which every detail of the poetry finds its appropriate musical image. From this viewpoint, the madrigal "remains manneristic and experimental."[23]

Another work from the fourth book, *Ah dolente partita* (1603; Guarini, *Il pastor fido*), exhibits more modern polyphonic techniques similar to those explored by Wert. We can discern his influence in the declamatory motives that furnish the basis for textural procedure.[24] But we can also isolate several features that must be ascribed to Monteverdi's personal ideas. One of these is a very vivid musical *contrapposto*: agitated parlando declamation for *Un vivace morire* combined with a slow melody for *Per far che moia*. The other instance concerns his use of dissonance in the beginning and closing sections of the piece (Example XXI-8). The opening duet presents a rather novel deployment of harsh and affective intervals in a two-voice idiom. Unisons, seconds, and thirds outline a tortuous contour that unites musical and emotional tension. This dual technique will become an integral element in Monteverdi's concerted duets. The ending brings out Monteverdi's vertical conception in terms of fundamental bass versus *concertato* upper parts in an even more palpable way than examples previously given for this approach.

EXAMPLE XXI-7.   C. Monteverdi, *Ohimè se tanto amate* (1603).
From *Il quarto libro de madrigali.*

EXAMPLE XXI-8.   C. Monteverdi, *Ah dolente partita* (1603).
From *Il quarto libro de madrigali.*

It is not accidental that Monteverdi's essays in polyphonic declamation center on speeches from *Il pastor fido*.[25] The inherent impetus toward musical dramatization is intimately connected with Guarini's attempt to dramatize lyric passion. Aristocratic audiences know well this beloved pastoral, and even single madrigalesque settings can rely on the tacit narrative background. Furthermore, the quasi-dramatic style given to Guarini's poem is so well understood by everyone that it can be easily transferred to independent lyric poems. All passionately amorous outbursts thus become potential excerpts from imagined pastoral romances. After all, the themes are commonplace, and many single lyrics by Tasso, Guarini, and other poets could just as well be inserted into *Il pastor fido*. By inference, a highly self-conscious and stylized inference, anonymous lyric sentiments become intensely personalized as unnamed Mirtillos, Silvios, Amarillis, and Dorindas speak within the confines of polyphonic dramatization. Such is the case with Monteverdi's celebrated setting of Ottavio Rinuccini's *Sfogava con le stelle a5* (1603). Here Monteverdi devises real choral recitative. It seems reasonable to assume that learned connoisseurs would immediately get the point of Monteverdi's allusion to the fact that in ancient drama the choral responses were chanted in recitative style. Through a genial stylization, Monteverdi has dramatized the drama.

Two other madrigals in Book IV alternate homophonic or polyphonic declamation with virtuoso soloistic passages reminiscent of Wert's florid style. In *Quel augellin che canta a5* (1603; Guarini, *Il pastor fido*),[26] words such as *canta, vola, l'albetta, faggio, mirto, ardo,* and *vago* prompt extended roulades. Most of these figures, which feature a great deal of quasi-instrumental sequences, appear in the two soprano voices which are deployed either in parallel thirds or in imitation. To this extent, they share the characteristics of Luzzasco Luzzaschi's concerted madrigals. But Monteverdi also varies the florid texture by using similar diminutions for other combinations as well. By far the most virtuoso madrigal is *A un giro sol* (1603; Guarini) (Example XXI-9). Its first part is built out of four coloratura figures that correspond to the poet's lively metaphors: *A un giro sol, Ride l'aria d'intorno, E'l mar s'acquesta,* and *e i venti.* A more charming and vivid depiction

EXAMPLE XXI-9.   C. Monteverdi, *A un giro sol* (1603).
From *Il quarto libro de madrigali.*

EXAMPLE XXI-9, *continued*

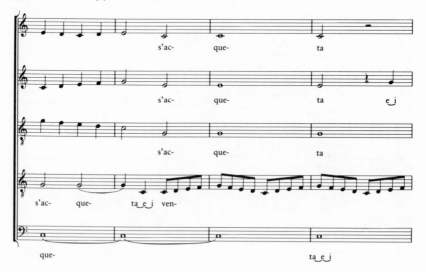

of Guarini's conceits can hardly be imagined.[27] It is also true that the preciosity of the verse finds equally precious echoes in the music. Gay and animated homophony describes the effects of the beloved's eyes. And a sudden turn to strange harmonies and suspended dissonances gives the last four lines their proper contrasting expression: the lover's eyes are sad and full of tears. One scholar suggests that Monteverdi uses surprise as a weapon in this madrigal in order to startle the listener into sharp awareness of the concettistic opposition embodied in the poem.[28] At any rate, Guarini's stylized *maniera* seems to inspire some of Monteverdi's most brilliant, yet most contrived, musical effects.

As everyone knows, Monteverdi takes the step to accompanied ensembles in the last six madrigals of Book v (1605). He is not the first composer to think of adding a keyboard support to secular polyphonic works.[29] However, his notion as to the role of this support differs fundamentally from that of his predecessors. In Rossi's and Signorucci's publications, the keyboard is a *basso seguente*, whereas in Luzzaschi's music for the Ferrarese ladies, it is completely written out and embodies a reduction of five-voiced counterpoint. Monteverdi's continuo comprises an unfigured bass; in polyphonic sections it acts as a *seguente* part, but in soloistic sections it becomes a real fundamental part. The six works in question do not belong to the category of monodic recitative or aria as practiced by Florentine composers. Passages for solo voice exist and some of them are in recitative style. But for the most part, Monteverdi concentrates on ensembles and through them explores *concertato* style.

E così a poco a poco a6 (Guarini) exhibits the loosest structure of the six concerted pieces. The reason resides in the nondramatic nature of the poem. In this case, Monteverdi's alternative textures merely provide an element of variety. But in *Troppo ben può a5*, Guarini's division between narrative portions and direct speech forms the basis for Monteverdi's more dramatic sectionalization. Yet, Monteverdi does not forget to highlight individual words and conceits by means of various textures, rhythms, and florid diminutions. The last three lines of the poem parallel the fourth through sixth lines in their structural arrangement, and they contain the witty "point" of the basic conceit. For this reason,

Monteverdi repeats the general characteristics of his setting of the earlier lines at the end. This "rather manneristic"[30] madrigal, in spite of its artificial moments, has a clear structure, a structure with both absolute and dramatic import. Whereas Monteverdi sticks closely to the poetic structure in *Troppo ben può*, in *T'amo mia vita a5* (Guarini), he takes more liberties with the text. These liberties reflect Monteverdi's desire to construct a small-scale lyrical drama,[31] a chamber cantata. During the lover's soliloquy, the words, *T'amo mia vita*, occur twice—at the start of the first line and at the start of the last line. Monteverdi extrapolates these words from their context to transform them into a musical presentation of the beloved speaking to her lover. Each time they appear, the words are sung by a solo soprano, often to the same music. Thus, they form a "ritornello" framework within which the words of the lover appear for three low voices in homophonic declamation.[32]

The highlight of the concerted madrigals, *Ahi come a un vago sol a5* (Guarini), is a masterpiece in dramatic and musical structure. In this case, clear sectional organization and rondolike form point toward Monteverdi's later chamber cantatas.[33] The madrigal is comprised of sections for two solo tenors alternating with a choral refrain for a varying number of voices. The refrain, *Ah che piaga d'amor non sana mai*, corresponds to the tenth line of the poem. Again, it is the composer who transforms this line into a refrain. The duet sections reveal some noteworthy features in their arrangement. Each time, the number of lines decreases by two; this means that the duet sections get progressively shorter. At the same time, Monteverdi augments the temporal reduction by changing the musical style. The first and longest duet is also the most elaborate one, featuring ornate ornamental figuration both in parallel motion and in animated *concertato* imitation. The second one alternates segments in passionate declamation with segments of ariosolike embellishment. In the third duet, only one brief melismatic portion disrupts the declamatory style. And the final one consists solely of declamation. This organization, of course, brings the refrain sections closer and closer together. And in this way, Monteverdi achieves a hitherto unrivaled intensity as the music approaches its final climax. At the same time, the vocal ritornellos follow a carefully planned scheme of their own. The longer, more florid duets alternate with relatively short refrains. When the duets reach their declamatory stage and become quite cursory in length but intense in style, the refrains get progressively longer. This opposing but complementary arrangement in section lengths is balanced by the overall tonal organization. The first duet and refrain establish the key of D major. The ensuing pairs of duets and refrains revolve around the dominant, a key they affirm with cadences in related areas. And the final duet and refrain return once more to the stable area of D major. Not only the expressive but also the musical structure of this magnificent work presages baroque practice, and the structure carries with it the mannerist devices of ornamentation, contrapuntal declamation, and affective harmony. Without such genial transformation, these sixteenth-century techniques might not have survived.

Monteverdi closes the fifth book with the most grandiose of the concerted madrigals, *Questi vaghi concenti a9* (Guarini). The vocal music requires two separate choirs, one of five and one of four voices, arranged in antiphonal fashion after the model of dialogue madrigals. Occasionally, soloistic phrases with *basso continuo* interrupt the choruses, and these sections correspond to the more impassioned moments of the poetry. The work is introduced by a five-voiced instrumental sinfonia that reappears in an abbreviated form about midway through the madrigal. More than any other piece in this book, *Questi vaghi concenti* points toward the cantata. But still, its basic inspiration belongs to the mannerist tradition insofar as the combination of double-chorus technique, solo passages, and instruments creates a vivid emblem for Guarini's *concetto, Questi vaghi concenti.*

In many ways, the madrigals contained in Book v demonstrate Monteverdi's instinctive move away from mannerist artificiality and stylized affectivity to the overtly theatrical and rhetorical style usually associated with the Baroque.[34] However, elements of the *maniera madrigalesca* are still present—individual word painting, very precious and virtuoso ornamentation, and extravagant dramatization of lyric poetry.[35] His art remains one that appeals to the aristocratic tastes of his day. Both restrained and exaggerated *effetti meravigliosi* still animate the fundamental aesthetic premise behind his style. As Arnold suggests, Monteverdi is the greatest of the mannerist composers who practice their art in northern Italian courts.[36] Historians who separate Monteverdi—along with Adrian Willaert, Cipriano de Rore, and Carlo Gesualdo—from the mannerist stream and insist that they are prebaroque composers,[37] base their view on the idea that mannerist and baroque styles are mutually contradictory. I propose, on the other hand, that baroque vocal practice is inconceivable without the mediation of mannerist elements. And Monteverdi's works admirably illustrate this stylistic phenomenon, for in the madrigals discussed in this chapter, we can discern the coexistence of the two *maniere*, with different degrees of emphasis on one or the other.

Before leaving this period, mention must be made of Adriano Banchieri's masterful madrigal-comedies. *Il zabaione musicale a5* (1603) is exactly what the title suggests—a frothy concoction made up of conventionalized pastoral scenes.[38] Banchieri usually mixes serious madrigals with fanciful *capricci*. Typical of the latter type, at which Banchieri excels, is a piece in the *Barca di Venetia per Padova a5* (1605) in which he depicts a singing master by means of extravagant solfeggio exercises. But the crowning glory of this genre is without a doubt his *Festino a5* (1608), a work consisting of twenty musical numbers preceded and completed by narrative material.

Banchieri's forward is a speech by Modern Delight who recounts how he was accosted by a moth-eaten figure, Ancient Rigor, on the stairs as he came up to the evening's entertainment. This pedantic professor of traditional counterpoint warns Modern Delight against listening to works by composers who flagrantly disobey the sacred rules of true music. Modern Delight replies that he has no patience with academic sophistry, a failing that causes one to overlook the "great taste in their modern inventions." Ancient Rigor wished to pursue the argument, but Modern Delight left him with the helpful suggestion that he peddle his manuscripts among the fishmongers for use as wrapping paper. Then Modern Delight warns his audience that they will not hear any learned disquisitions this evening. The serious theorists of the group are busy settling an argument in the kitchen. The cook and the maid are discussing the matter of how one should categorize the sound of a braying ass. "The cook, arguing platonically, maintains that it is a bastard sound, whereas the maid, using a polycratesque demonstration, says that it is a mixed consonance." After this broadside aimed at academic controversy, Modern Delight bids the guests to simply enjoy singing his music before dinner.

The whole point of the madrigal-comedy is that the various characters and situations are represented within the confines of five-voiced secular style. This genre lacks acting, costumes, or scenery, and everything is depicted by means of the music. It is evident that the artfully contrived compositions of the *Festino*, in their own humorous way, reflect the mannerist concept of *imitazione delle parole*. Banchieri's madrigal-comedy, full of lighthearted spirit, draws us a graphic picture of aristocratic and academic entertainment. It is a healthy sign that mannerists are able to laugh at themselves and to poke good-natured fun at the basic pretensions of *maniera*.

CHAPTER XXII

ॐॐॐ

The Concerted Madrigal
and Monody

In previous chapters, I had occasion to mention different kinds of solo singing in the sixteenth century. The oldest of these are, on the one hand, improvised *poesia per musica,* and on the other, the related but more artistic convention of solo performance of homophonic frottolas. The latter tradition coexists as late as the 1530s with a newer, contrapuntal orientation in the frottola. But at this stage, the frottola yields to the madrigal, disappearing as a genre and leaving its legacy of musical style to this mannerist invention. At the same time, improvised solo singing receives another vehicle in the form of Ariosto's *Orlando furioso* (1516), a poem sung to a new repertory of stock formulas, many of which survive as ground basses in the baroque period. Recitation of Ariosto's poem stays in vogue throughout the century, and, as we have seen, inspires declamatory madrigals in the 1550s. And these works furnish one basis for the development of dramatic tendencies in the later mannerist madrigal.

It is clear that in spite of the stylization of northern polyphony, a stylization that provides the foundation for incipient Mannerism in the madrigal, solo singing remains a popular way of making music. So much so, that any polyphonic madrigal amenable to soloistic adaptation is so rearranged. As in the case of the frottola, much of this activity remains improvised in nature. Occasionally, we find published versions of such arrangements; for example, Adrian Willaert's edition of a group of madrigals by Filippo Verdelot (1536). Such transcriptions appear rarely in print because

[410]

they do not require professional skill. Indeed, solo performances of an improvised nature occur not only in chamber music, but also in the numerous theatrical presentations associated with courts. When *concertato* techniques and mosaic fragmentation dominate the later madrigal, solo adaptation is no longer practicable. But these works can be, and often are, transformed into concerted ensembles, such as duets and trios with instrumental accompaniment.

The fact that in 1601 Caccini vaunts the superiority of his songs over solo arrangements of polyphonic madrigals attests to the long history of this practice. Caccini, of course, refers to versions featuring excessive ornamentation. Our main sources for this phenomenon come from singing manuals published between 1580 and 1600, and these sources seem to codify an existing tradition. But such highly mannered solos are far removed from the simplicity of solo arrangements, even though one may infer the use of ornamentation in the early sixteenth century. The point is that improvised embellishment undergoes the same process of refinement and exaggeration that characterizes written madrigals, except that little documentation survives to help us chart the change from restrained to complicated ornamental figuration. But it remains clear, nonetheless, that earlier ornamentation could be mastered by accomplished amateurs, whereas later solo arrangements require highly trained singers. Improvised florid embellishment, which has its roots in a long-standing practice of solo singing, also leaves behind it a legacy for composed monodies and arias. Once again, we witness the transformation of a musical conception from simple classical ideals, through mannerist artificiality, to dramatic vocal style.

One consistent feature found in written sources should be noted here. The music of frottolas and madrigals often appears in two versions, one for ensemble and one for solo plus accompaniment. It is only in the late sixteenth century that composers begin writing music expressly for solo performance. The popularity of this novel idea can be gauged from the hundreds of solo songs emanating from printing presses in the early seventeenth century. This does not mean that the older practice of dual versions disappears entirely. For example, Paolo Quagliati's concerted madrigals (1608) can be performed, according to the composer, with all four voices or with soprano and *basso continuo*. And Giovanni Priuli advertises his third book of five-voiced madrigals (1612) as madrigals *di due maniere, l'una per voci sole, l'altra per voci & istromenti*. These examples still predicate a polyphonic texture as the original conception, but one written in such a way as to make solo performance possible. Of course, the reverse can also happen, as is the case with Claudio Monteverdi's celebrated *Lamento d'Arianna* (Rinuccini), the affective solo from his opera, *Arianna* (1608). Apparently at the request of a Venetian nobleman, Monteverdi reworked the solo into a five-voiced madrigal, *Lasciatemi morire* (1614). Needless to say, champions of monody do not approve of this seemingly retrogressive adaptation.[1]

The accompanied madrigal is still a madrigal as long as its aesthetic focuses attention on the detailed imagery of concettist poetry. Word painting by means of aural figures and affective harmony characterizes such through-composed works, works that represent the culmination of a trend toward rhetorical dramatization. In its early phase, the concerted madrigal belongs to the last stage of mannerist stylization. Luzzasco Luzzaschi's compositions written for the *concerto delle donne* of Ferrara illustrate this stylization particularly well. I have already mentioned that the keyboard part is a written-out reduction of the five-voiced texture typical of polyphonic madrigals. Over this part, Luzzaschi writes either solo songs, duets or trios for female voices. Although written between ca. 1570 and 1597, these pieces did not appear in print until 1601, with the encouragement of Emilio de'Cavalieri. This gentleman, a rival of the Florentine monodists, wishes to prove that solo madrigals antedate the polemical statements of Bardi's Camerata. And Caccini's *Le nuove musiche* (1601), with its attack on "pseudo-monodic" compositions, is essentially a rebuttal of Cavalieri's position.[2]

O Primavera (Guarini, *Il pastor fido*) can be taken as a representative example of Luzzaschi's solo style as well as of his approach to ornamentation. The soprano part, considering its octave range and its melodic and rhythmic elements, suggests simple, popular songs; it even has a dancelike triple section in the middle. Luzzaschi treats Mirtillo's monologue quite freely, repeating lines in order to achieve balanced, rounded forms. The harmony for the most part is straightforward. *Ma non son io già quel*, the first intimation of the speaker's sadness, prompts a subtle turn to the only minor harmonic area in the entire composition. In spite of this basic simplicity, a quality of harmonic and structural design, the song radiates a contradictory air of preciosity and artificial complexity (Example XXII-1). The latter quality can be ascribed to the ornamentation. A close look at the ornaments reveals that they answer a purely musical function insofar as they embellish cadential patterns, even when they happen to fall on significant words. It is evident that Luzzaschi works with conventional melodic and rhythmic patterns, patterns divisible into two stereotyped categories: *passaggio* and *gruppo*. Although the ornate figuration becomes predictable in its combination of the two types of ornaments, Luzzaschi manages to manipulate them in asymmetrical

EXAMPLE XXII-1. L. Luzzaschi, *O Primavera* (1601).
From *Madrigali per cantare et sonare a uno e doi a tre soprani*. Monumenti di Musica Italiana; Serie 2: Polifonia, 2:34. Edited by A. Cavicchi. Brescia, 1965. Used by permission of Paideia Editrice.

arrangements with a view to variety and degrees of intensity. These embellishments are just similar enough and just different enough to demand the utmost attention and virtuosity from the singer.

Declamatory style, pathetic lyricism, and restrained ornamentation characterize the duet, *Cor mio deh non languire* (Guarini). The only elements of avant-garde *maniera* missing in this piece are the telling deployment of dissonances and parlando recitation. Luzzaschi's balanced interplay between passages of homophonic declamation and passages of imitative *concertato* is obviously adapted from the *maniera madrigalesca*. They simply gain more prominence because of the duo-instrumental idiom. And yet, in spite of the fact that the textures suit the words to which they are appended, their arrangement verges on the mechanical. Apart from a few isolated instances of pictorialism, the ornaments obey the same conventions noted in the works for solo voice. Of course, the presence of two voices complicates matters somewhat, but once again, we can discern a stereotyped method for the use of ornaments in duo texture. If each voice is taken alone, the ornate figures exemplify *passagio-gruppo* combinations, as in the solo works. If the two voices are taken together, we again deduce two categories: those which overlap, and those which follow one another in close proximity, giving an echo effect. One final observation concerns Luzzaschi's attempt to inject word painting on three occasions—*potessi*, *aita*, and *viva*. In these cases, the effect is less than striking because of the predictable nature of the ornaments.

The somewhat contrived *effetti meravigliosi* found in this duet form a sharp contrast with the warmth and beauty of *O dolcezze amarissime d'amore*, a trio in which Luzzaschi grafts an independent lyric by Guarini (*Quest'è pur il mio cor*) onto the famous line from Mirtillo's lament, *O Primavera*, from *Il pastor fido*. Every device—ranging from ornamentation, harmony, rhythm, and dissonance to texture and structure—is carefully deployed to enhance the poetical conceits. The music requires sensitive performance with alternations of soothing legato and excited staccato singing as well as dramatic changes in dynamics. Considering the descriptions of the singing style of the Ferrarese ladies,[3] one can well imagine the affective and sweetly lyrical affectation with which they would project this little gem. Such fine singers could also improve the less inspired quality of Luzzaschi's other pieces. However, this composition is outstanding because its style suggests points of departure for interpretive ingenuity.

Although the concerted madrigals written by Monteverdi and other composers depart from polyphonic norms more emphatically than those by Luzzaschi, this genre still shows traces of its origin.[4] The reason is that two, three, or more concerted voices tend to retain certain technical, and hence aesthetic, features of modern counterpoint. The degree to which such madrigals diverge from the unaccompanied model depends on the degree of assimilation of elements associated with monody. Concerted works for four or five voices stay closest to the premises of earlier mannerist polyphony; for the most part, they seem to be contrapuntal madrigals with continuo. Duets and trios, on the other hand, embody the most modern traits. The favored idiom for ensemble *concertato* is the duet, and with good reason. Two solo voices, usually in the same range, afford the closest approximation of monodic presentation while still providing the composer with means for textural and sonal structure. I believe this is the reason why Monteverdi concentrates on the duet.

Generally speaking, the duet comprises two styles. The first, a carry-over from sixteenth-century madrigals and canzonettas, features a *basso seguente* as the lowest part. The second, much more progressive, features two independent voices proceeding in *concertato* over a real *basso continuo*. These duets range from simple strophic songs to through-composed madrigals and use declamatory recitative, affective arioso, florid ornamentation, and lyrical melody as well as strophic variations and different forms of sectionalization. Duet sections may be combined with solo and choral passages, or may include obbligato instruments. Many amount to lyrical interpretations of amorous poetry. But the medium of two voices lends itself so well to discourse that duets become a prime vehicle for dialogues, and the resultant genre, the dialogue duet, is considered at the time to be the most dramatic kind of chamber music.[5] This idea emerges from the title of Francesco Rasi's *Dialoghi rappresentativi* (1620). *Rappresentativo*, of course, is a term coined by monodists to refer to solo melody that narrates a story with staged action of some kind. By using it in connection with chamber music, Rasi calls attention to the narrative and dramatic potential of his pieces. In short, if any one genre in mannerist solo music can be singled out as the most influential forerunner of the baroque cantata, this honor must be accorded to the *concertato* dialogue duet.

The greatest master of duet composition is Monteverdi. This genre makes its debut in his sixth book (1614) whose eighteen works present a combination of traditional *maniera* (unaccompanied five-voiced madrigals) and modern *maniera* (concerted works with continuo). The first group includes settings of two Petrarch sonnets, the four-part cycle *Lasciatemi morire*, and a magnificent setting of Scipione Agnelli's sestina on the death of Caterina Martinelli, the *Lagrime dell'amante al sepolcro dell'amata*. The latter, whose *capoverso* is *Incenerite spoglie*, shows in particular Monteverdi's ability to imbue the superficial imitative-affective devices of the mannerist madrigal with persuasive emotional depth. In spite of its traditional cast, the sensibility of this madrigal cycle rivals that of any of the more modern works in the collection.

The remaining six works set poems from Giambattista Marino's *Rime boscherecce*. In my view, the meeting of Marino and Monteverdi in these progressive pieces is hardly a coincidence. Just as Marino's poems represent in many ways the bridge between Mannerism and the Baroque in poetry, so Monteverdi's settings do the same in music. The madrigal here becomes the cantata. Marino's *A Dio Florida bella* transforms the lyrical sonnet into a dramatic dialogue between two lovers interrupted by narrative and descriptive passages. Monteverdi accordingly uses a five-voiced chorus for the nonspeaking portions, and differentiates Floro's and Florida's words with tenor and soprano solos. In this madrigal-cantata, Monteverdi draws the two solo parts from the complement of five that make up the chorus. He goes a step further in *Presso un fiume a7*, which he calls a *dialogo concertato*, by separating the five-voiced chorus from two solo parts. Marino's free-form poem has four stanzas. At the beginning of each, the chorus provides connective material for the loving conversation between Eurillo and Filena. Each time, Monteverdi employs a homophonic chorus with continuo. For the speeches of the lovers, he uses soprano and tenor solos characterized by a very declamatory style, a style that definitely shows the influence of Monteverdi's operatic recitative. The final stanza forms a musical and expressive climax. Its first two lines are set for the chorus, which describes the lovers murmuring together; charming rhetorical figures adorn the evocative words, *Sì, sì.* The next two lines are presented as a declamatory duet, and the last two are again given to the chorus. Monteverdi pointedly contrasts *guerre* (with aggressive motives prefiguring the *stile concitato*) and *pace* (with serene and static figures). He even paints *mille i baci* with short imitative, *concertato* motives. Thus does Monteverdi weld together various elements from older and newer *maniere* to create a mannerist masterpiece.

The impetus toward dramatic interpretation is so strong that Monteverdi injects it when setting to poetry that does not in itself project dialogue character, as in his treatment of the sonnet *Qui rise O Tirsi a5.* As in the case with *T'amo mia vita* and *Ahi come a un vago sol* (1605), Monteverdi transforms the first line of the sestet into a choral refrain that appears three times during the course of the composition. The rest of the music features different pairs of duets, one solo, and one quartet. Most of the *concertato* sections display redolent ornaments in overlapping, echo, and parallel textures whose deployment depicts especially vivid words. Their suave and undulating lines create a musical atmosphere that admirably captures the erotic tone of the poem.

The title of Book VII (1619), *Concerto*, emphasizes the novel primacy of the concerted ensemble. Most surveys of the traditional madrigal stop at this point because the works in this collection seem closer to baroque practice than to that of the late renaissance madrigal. But in truth, most of them are still madrigals disguised as cantatas, and their ties with certain aspects of sixteenth-century ideals emerge more clearly when we view them and the preceding tradition in terms of Mannerism. Apart from four solo monodies and a *ballo concertato, Tirsi e Clori* (produced in Mantua in 1616), the works in question comprise fourteen duets, one quartet, and one sextet. Their texts range from poems representing the established mannerist style (Guarini, Tasso, and Marino) as well as the latest fashion (Gabriello Chiabrera and Claudio Achillini).[6] In general, Monteverdi's style exhibits a new and masterful fusion of popular canzonetta tunes, declamatory recitative, florid embellishment, strophic variation, and through-composed madrigalesque settings with word painting. Such eclecticism is itself a mannerist trait, regardless of the success with which the composer handles all the elements. These concerted ensembles rely on a continuo, and in two works Monteverdi expands the instrumental role by using an orchestra.[7]

Interrotte speranze (Guarini) is a miniature masterpiece of intense duo recitative. The first section has two almost identical parts, each describing a harmonic arc between D minor and A minor. The two tenor voices present similar melodic contours in both parts but with different declamatory rhythms embodying the accents of the words with sensitive fidelity (Example XXII-2). They begin on a unison, expand to a third with a telling dissonance, expand again in similar fashion to another higher third, then to a sixth, and finally to a high third, after which they cadence with the first semblance of linearly independent motion. The slowly rising melody, carefully designed with acrid dissonances and euphonious consonances, mirrors the tormented sentiments of the unhappy lover. His anguish is augmented in the next three short lines. Here the two voices proceed in parallel thirds with each motive ascending one degree higher. They then separate to share in alternation and echo the repeated words, *Questi* and *Donna crudel*, the first words of the twelfth and thirteenth lines of the sonnet. Monteverdi's truncation of the poem is a deliberate one, and the careful listener realizes the emotional climax of this section after he has heard the completion of the respective lines later in the piece. Indeed, the entire composition is permeated by subtle and exquisitely mannerist affectation. Now, the passionate quality of this duet is at the opposite end of the scale of vocal style when compared to the more decorative works, such as *Ecco vicine o bella Tigre* (Achillini) and *Dice la mia bellissima Licori* (Guarini). Monteverdi seems to be exploring every possibility, and also to be vaunting his mastery of extremely diverse *maniere*. Among the decorative pieces, *O come sei gentile* (Guarini) exhibits the most profuse ornamentation and exuberant virtuosity, elements that suggest that vocal coloratura has become an end in itself. Long imitative runs and extended dotted-note figures appear on every conceivable word. They form a dazzling array of *effetti meravigliosi*. More

EXAMPLE XXII-2.   C. Monteverdi, *Interrotte speranze* (1619).
From *Tutte le opere*, 7:95–96. Edited by G. F. Malipiero.
Vienna, 1928.

EXAMPLE XXII-2, *continued*

than any other work in the collection, this madrigal celebrates the sonorous beauty and breathtaking flexibility of the human voice.

Perhaps the most remarkable duet in this remarkable publication is the setting of Bernardo Tasso's *Ohimè dov'è il mio ben*. The continuo presents the romanesca bass, a pattern used for improvised recitation of *ottave rime*. Monteverdi treats this stock formula quite freely, shortening and lengthening it at will, and over its repetitions he causes the two concerted sopranos to weave an impassioned web of declamatory recitative and affective arioso. The entries and exits of these voices, now parallel, now staggered, never coincide with the regular cadencing of the bass. Their tensile melodies create alternating points of tension and repose against the predictable phrases of the continuo. Furthermore, their melodies comprise a set of continuous variations, but variations constructed in such a way as to reflect the *concetti* of the words. Monteverdi has created a form that fuses strophic principles with madrigalesque through-composition. In this way, the unruly side of word painting is disciplined by the cohesion of strophic variations.[8]

Monteverdi's concerted madrigals for three and four voices derive their stylistic character not from polyphonic models but rather from concerted duets. Instead of representing reductions of five-voiced counterpoint, they expand *concertato* duo technique. For this reason, they seem much more modern than similar works by his contemporaries. We can see this novel approach most clearly in the active and florid bass part of *Parlo miser o taccio a3* (Guarini) and *Al lume delle stelle a4* (Tasso) (Example XXII-3). Monteverdi exploits tremendously varied textures ranging from solos to entire vocal complements. Inasmuch as every tiny detail of the poetry is painted through figures, we can say that these works wed madrigalian Mannerism to *concertato* style of more recent mannerist invention. The highly experimental nature of this volume is further evident in the sextet, *A quest'olmo* (Marino), in which Monteverdi accompanies the voices with continuo plus a small orchestra of two flutes and violins. In this case, he explores the potential of new sonorities and timbres.

Monteverdi's *Scherzi musicali* (1632) contains mostly monodic compositions. The two exceptions are justly famous duets for two tenors and continuo. *Zefiro torna* (Rinuccini), a brilliant

EXAMPLE XXII-3.   C. Monteverdi, *Al lume delle stelle* (1619).
From *Tutte le opere*, 7:130. Edited by G. F. Malipiero.
Vienna, 1928.

work based on an ostinato chaconne, is really an extended aria in concerted style; as such, it must be set aside for the moment. The other duet, *Armato il cor*, a study in *stile concitato*, reappears in the eighth book of madrigals. The preface to this publication, *Madrigali guerrieri et amorosi* (1638), contains the celebrated statement concerning the three styles of musical expression. Because no musician has tried to rejuvenate the warlike, agitated style mentioned by ancient Greek authors, Monteverdi claims to be the originator of the *stile concitato*. The two parts of this collection, divided between works on war and on love, embody a deliberate and very self-conscious study in opposing techniques, moods, and genres. In short, this book serves as the ultimate testament to mannerist conceptions of *maniera*, and its contents remind us of countless mannerist paintings treating the amorous dalliance between Venus and Mars. Both parts deal with the theme of love couched in witty and stylized *concetti*. Only the *Combattimento di Tancredi e Clorinda* (Tasso, *Gerusalemme liberata*), a stage piece among the warlike compositions, achieves a measure of serious passion. It has been suggested that the arrangement of the two parts shows a careful symmetry.[9] Although such a schematic reading is not convincing in every detail, it is nonetheless evident that Monteverdi selected appropriate works from his earlier output and added to this selection some new compositions. His choices obey one aesthetic aim—the demonstration of amorous and warlike affections. This fact stresses Monteverdi's acute awareness of questions of style, or more properly, of stylization. In the *madrigali amorosi*, he relies on his already fully developed mastery of moderate style. But in the *madrigali guerrieri*, he exploits to the full a startling and new approach to musical imitation and expression.

The compositions vary from multivoiced grandiose conceptions to small-scale chamber ensembles, and the instruments range from simple keyboard continuo to string orchestras with two to six members. On the surface, the most old-fashioned pieces seem to be the five-voiced settings of Guarini's *Dolcissimo usignolo* and *Chi vol haver felice*, but even here, Monteverdi is experimenting with choral renditions of French style.[10] A direct contrast to these works appears in the tenor duet, *Mentre vaga Angioletta* (Guarini). The poem takes the form of a lover's description of his beloved's singing, and naturally, its concrete imagery provides the perfect foil for minute and graphic word painting. In Monteverdi's setting, every poetic conceit is graced with different and astonishing devices (Example XXII-4a and 4b). Two examples suffice to indicate both the extreme virtuosity and the extreme preciosity of Monteverdi's conception. However, this concerted madrigal is more than a paradigm of ornamentation.[11] Guarini merely presents through words the *effetti meravigliosi* of dramatic, passionate, and decorative solo song. Monteverdi actually embodies these marvelous effects in music. The style demands singers who have command of flexible recitative, affective arioso, and incredibly virtuoso techniques. Most important of all, Monteverdi's duet requires the utmost precision in *concertato* singing, more so than in other works examined up to this point. And, of course, it is a vibrant testament to a kind of *enargeia* possible only in music.

EXAMPLE XXII-4a.   C. Monteverdi, *Mentre vaga Angioletta* (1638).
From *Tutte le opere*, 8:252. Edited by G. F. Malipiero. Vienna, 1929.

EXAMPLE XXII-4b. C. Monteverdi, *Mentre vaga Angioletta* (1638).
From *Tutte le opere*, 8:258. Edited by G. F. Malipiero.
Vienna, 1929.

Other compositions steer away from dazzling lyric style and point to miniature dramatic proportions. Such is the case with the masterpiece in this vein, *Non havea Febo ancora* (Rinuccini). This composition can be classified as a cantata in three sections. The outer ones, setting narrative and descriptive material, feature homophonic declamation for two tenors and bass. The middle part, the *Lamento della Ninfa*, is a soprano solo whose style exploits affective recitation reminiscent of the great moments in *Orfeo*. The nymph's flexible lines are composed over an ostinato bass of four descending notes;[12] and her lamenting is interrupted by the male singers, who now take on the role of a dramatic chorus, drawing the audience into the lyrical core of the presentation. To enhance this effect, Monteverdi indicates that these interjections must follow the *affetti* of the solo voice. He calls this madrigal a *canto rappresentativo*, not because it is a work to be staged as are other *genere rappresentativi* in the book, but rather because he wishes to stress its highly dramatic tone. The lament of the nymph is "represented" realistically by the music, not just suggested by veiled musical allusions. Monteverdi's conception is the solution to the mannerist desire of putting things before one's very eyes.

Among the *madrigali guerrieri*, featuring all sorts of *stile concitato*, *Ardo avvampo a2* and *Ogni amante è guerriero a3* (Rinuccini) stand out as brilliant examples of this *maniera*. But the most exuberant in this group is *Altri canti d'Amor*. Here, Monteverdi combines a vocal sextet with a large string orchestra to create a series of vivid depictions for the strained, mannerist conceits. The work is introduced by a sinfonia, and the body of the work alternates solos, duets, and small ensembles with magnificent *tutti* sections. Whereas this madrigal seems to have a somewhat shallow affective quality, *Hor che'l ciel e la terra a6* (Petrarch) attains intense and noble dramatic impact. In the case of these two works, the divergent musical qualities reflect similar ones in the poems. *Altri canti d'Amor* is a superficial occasional piece of unknown authorship whose antithesis of Love and War, modeled on Marino's *Altri canti di Marte*, presents only the outer shell of a mannerist *concetto*. Petrarch, on the other hand, treats the contrast between peaceful nature and the lover's torment with convincing lyrical passion. And Monteverdi is inspired to write a setting appropriate to the poet's sensitive style.

Regardless of the issue of evaluating various levels of inspiration within the Monteverdi canon, we can conclude that all of his concerted works represent a superior level of achievement in contrast with the efforts of some other composers. A case in point can be found in the concerted duets by Quagliati, published in *La sfera armoniosa* (1623), a collection dedicated to Cardinal Odoardo Farnese and his circle of Roman connoisseurs. Quagliati's pieces furnish a useful point of comparison not only with reference to Monteverdi's artistic merit, but also with reference to the problem of stylized *maniera* in general. Because the tradition of conservative counterpoint remains strong in the papal city, its resident composers try to balance basic principles of the *ars perfecta* with the new aesthetic of the *stile moderno*. This approach embodies various degrees of success, but in general, their solo music tends to be somewhat dull and unadventurous. Thus, in his through-composed solo madrigals, Quagliati takes on the trappings of declamatory recitative and ornamental virtuosity. But his duets suffer from overtly symmetrical phrases, regularized *concertato* imitation, monotonous eighth-note recitation, stereotyped ornaments, and predictable cadence patterns. *Come cantar poss'io* (Guarini), for soprano and bass, contains many mannerist elements, elements that, however, contribute neither to musical nor to expressive shape. All in all, the work's aura of blandness without charm compares poorly with other settings of this poem.

Although the word "monody" is accepted today as a generic term for solo song, scholars differ in their understanding of its precise meaning, and their views reflect the confusion existing in primary sources. Does monody include solo arrangements of polyphonic models (which some writers call pseudo-monody), floridly embellished melody, improvised recitation, choral recitation, narrative recitative in early operas, expressive arioso, and closed forms or arias proper? In the late sixteenth and early seventeenth centuries, musicians employ terms such as *madrigali a voce sola, arie a voce sola, stile recitativo, stile rappresentativo, canzonetta, cantada,* and *aria.* Their quandary as to appropriate names for their works is evident in the frequent use of neutral words, such as *Le nuove musiche* or *Musiche da cantar solo.* Although Bardi's Camerata seems to be the first group of musicians to deliberately militate for solo song as the only medium capable of reviving the marvelous effects of ancient music, none of the participants uses the term *monodia.* It first appears in the writings of Giovanni Battista Doni (1630s–1640s).[13] As we have seen, Doni's antiquarian leanings lead him to a conception of *monodia* that is inextricably linked with the dramatic narration of a story on the stage. His definition thus omits a vast repertory of solo music. Now, this background situation, limited as it is to terminological matters, again illustrates that from the theoretical viewpoint the solo song at this time is neither clearly renaissance nor clearly baroque in essence. It does, however, indicate a fluid and somewhat confusing mixture of self-conscious ideals and, therefore, can be fittingly called mannerist in essence.

For our purposes, monody can serve as a general term covering all aspects of early solo music. For one thing, it avoids the tacit connotations of "song," and its ambiguity invites further clarification. Moreover, the pseudo-classical origin of the term draws attention to the mannerist premise behind its divergent manifestations. From the historiographic point of view, monody eventually leads to completely modern forms associated with baroque vocal music; however, it begins its career as the final embodiment of Mannerism. Monody also connotes opposition to polyphony, and this opposition is paramount in both the technical and aesthetic principles of the Florentine musicians who stress this new *maniera*. Stylization based on antique models, progress beyond previous limitations, imitation of natural speech accents, expression of the passions and affections, striving for novel *effetti meravigliosi*—all these elements are present in the attitudes of early monodists. Einstein correctly interprets the rise of monody in relation to a rivalry between Florence and Mantua.[14] Caccini himself intimates the existence of a rivalry between Florence and Ferrara. It is in these self-conscious social circumstances that monodic experimentation takes roots.

The pronouncements of the Florentine circle isolate solo melody as the vehicle of natural declamation. Most highly prized are the imitation of rhetorical speech and the lack of purely musical procedures. Of course, these elements appear in a clear way in the first operas produced by Florentine musicians. Their less consistent appearance in lyrical and dramatic chamber music blurs the picture somewhat. In these genres, the use of madrigalisms brings monody closer to the polyphonic madrigal, the *maniera madrigalesca*, against which monodists protest so much. But in addition to free recitative style, monody from its inception also embodies another antithetical ideal—the cultivation of rounded and sonorous tunes. As Galilei says, composers seek the beauty of the air. And such arialike works affirm the primacy of musical considerations. Both *maniere*, later distinguished as solo madrigals and solo arias, can be found in Caccini's *Le nuove musiche* (1601).

As for technical elements, solo monody has recourse to two different methods. *Stile recitativo* requires melodies of small range, whose contour and rhythmic articulation follow as exactly as possible the natural accents and inflections of speech. In order to give this style a rhetorical quality, symmetrical phrases must be avoided even when setting poetry with lines of equal length and similar metrical organization; furthermore, melodic repetitions are disallowed except when the composer encounters repeated elements in the text. Finally, singers must master the subtle art of *sprezzatura* so that they may infuse this *maniera* with eloquent spontaneity. At the other end of the scale we have the beauty of the air. In this case, simple and self-sufficient melodies, marked by a pleasing abstract design, accord both with the speech values and the mood of the text, but at the same time are general enough to permit the setting of several stanzas to the same tune. In between aria and recitative there exists a blending of the two which, for want of a better word, I call arioso style. This hybrid procedure does not totally abandon the precepts of natural declamation, but it combines them with just enough elements of the aria to allow the creation of soaring melody, descriptive devices, and passionate imitations of lyrical affects.

As for types, monody can be divided into two categories. The solo madrigal, as its name suggests, retains certain traits from established *maniera*. It is through-composed, following the conceits of the poem with fidelity. Its artistic pretensions can be seen in the choice of aristocratic mannerist verse very much like, and often identical with, the poems set by composers of polyphonic madrigals. Composers sometimes add abstract structural elements, such as variations over ostinato patterns, instrumental ritornellos, or choral refrains. They may even insert passages in aria style. When all these characteristics fuse into dramatic-structural schemes, we arrive at the cantata. The solo aria, of course, is a strophic song with folklike melodies derived in part from the canzonetta. Melody, rhythm, and harmony combine to create clearly sectionalized forms. The texts chosen for such songs tend to be rather light in tone, often verging on amorous doggerel.[15] Arias too can be organized as strophic variations, but the effect in this case is quite different from that of solo madrigals. In its most insignificant manifestation, the solo song embodies salon music of dubious artistic merit. At its best, however, this genre contributes to the development of expansive melody that culminates in the sonorous radiance of the baroque aria. While many monodies in this period adhere to the division outlined above, a fair number coalesce these ingredients into a masterful synthesis. In his later years, Monteverdi in particular composes some solos and duets in which this fusion attains an unprecedented and unrivaled brilliance.

Although mediocre music can be found in the annals of the polyphonic madrigal, the act of writing part-music presupposes a modicum of technical expertise. Of course, second-rate composers work in the mannerist period as they do in any other, and many succeed in getting their music published. And we cannot discount the fact that there also exists a market for unimaginative but pleasant entertainment music. With the advent of monody, this sociological profile undergoes a change. The high number of publications of monodies indicates, on the one hand, the popularity of this latest mannerist invention and, on the other hand, the realization that monodies are not costly to print. Furthermore, the surface simplicity of solo songs attracts many amateur composers. As a result, these publications contain much good and much bad music. In its initial phase, at a time when the solo madrigal predominates, monody still remains a sophisticated court art. After 1620, the courts decline in importance and broader commercial networks emerge in Rome and Venice. This switch also signals a growing emphasis on the solo aria. From a very limited point of view, it signals the start of the Baroque. Most of the composers of early monody are amateurs—singers, such as Caccini, Peri, and Rasi; lawyers, such as Domenico Maria Megli; and aristocrats, such as Lodovico Bellanda and Claudio Saracini. After proving its staying power and artistic potential, monody attracts professionals as well—Monteverdi, Sigismondo d'India, Antonio Cifra, and Giovanni Ghizzolo. By far the most progressive and experimental music emanates from the enthusiastic circles of Florence.[16] A noteworthy exception is presented by the case of Monteverdi, a master who manages to combine youthful daring and mannerist iconoclasm with the maturity born of developed craft and seasoned experience.

Caccini appears as a virtuoso singer in the Florentine court in 1564. His association with the Medici ambience coincides with the most extravagantly mannerist phase of this cultural center; luxurious decorativeness and extreme elegance characterize every aspect of court life. This *maniera* is particularly evident in the sumptuous theatrical productions presented on festive occasions. Music, and Caccini himself, play a prominent role in these lavish entertainments. In addition, the philosophical discussions of the Camerata concerning the *meraviglia* of ancient Greek music make a deep impression on this singer. Indeed, the notion of emulating and surpassing the past glories of classical style reveals that the essence of Mannerism lies behind monody.[17]

Of the two collections published by Caccini,[18] the most important and relevant to our topic is *Le nuove musiche*, a publication containing monodies composed between roughly 1580 and 1600. Caccini's book has two parts, the first containing solo madrigals on texts by Guarini and other concettist poets, and the second containing solo arias on poems by Chiabrera. As far as the madrigals are concerned, we can observe that Caccini's method is very flexible, and that each work presents an individual solution to its particular poem. Even the degree of ornamentation varies from piece to piece. *Cor mio deh non languire* (Guarini), for example, illustrates his ornate *maniera*. As a technical demonstration included in the preface, its every ornament appears on the score. The pieces in the body of the publication include only the elaborate diminutions, the shorter ones being left to the discretion of the singer. Similar in style to the above-mentioned madrigal is *Amor io parto* (Guarini). Long *gorgie* appear on words such as *rire, cor, morto, amore*, and *pungente*; they always elongate long syllables (Example XXII-5a and 5b). However, shorter decorative ornaments are used for insignificant words such as *può, non, mai, il, più*, and *mi*. In these cases, the embellishments answer the musical need of emphasizing the cadence. Somewhat less complex, but still exhibiting considerable coloratura, is *Vedro'l mio sol* (Guarini), a work particularly favored by Bardi's circle.[19]

Other madrigals embody a much more subtle and restrained use of ornamentation. A comparison between two such pieces demonstrates the different aspects of Caccini's technique. *Amarilli* (Guarini) belongs to that category of sweet lyrical style so much prized by theorists of monody. Caccini not only observes the rhythmic values of the words, but also arranges phrase lengths and cadences in such a way as to reflect the general scheme of the

EXAMPLE XXII-5a.   G. Caccini, *Amor io parto* (1601).
From *Le nuove musiche*.

EXAMPLE XXII-5b.   G. Caccini, *Amor io parto* (1601).
From *Le nuove musiche*.

poem. The entire melody has an octave ambitus, and individual
phrases are restricted to smaller ranges, except for the sixth line.
Its swooping contour forms a climax just before the last line of the
poem, a line that receives the longest musical phrase in the composition. Its passionate style, complete with written *accenti*, contrasts sharply with the more sedate style of the first six lines. All in
all, this madrigal is an excellent example of Caccini's mastery of
delicate sweetness, an attribute of *maniera* in the sister arts as well.
The piece is not without charm, and it is perhaps unfair to characterize such works as "spineless diatonic lyrics."[20] *Perfidissimo
volto* (Guarini), on the other hand, comes much closer to recitative

and arioso, and it provides an insight into Caccini's *stile rappre-sentativo* as it is found in his opera, *Euridice*. The recitational style of the melody is accompanied by affective harmonies at points of emotional intensity. And the arioso portions permit short or-naments of the type that Caccini recommends because of their affective quality.

There are, of course, a number of other important monody collections in this period, and I mention only a few of them. Peri's monodies must be counted among the finest specimens of the genre. His *Tu dormi* exemplifies an imaginative approach to the strophic variation principle that is welded together with the prem-ises of the through-composed madrigal. Because Rasi is an espe-cially accomplished singer, his monodies show a keen sense of vocal felicity, particularly in the arched structure of his arias and the affective contours of his madrigals.[21] On the other side of the coin are the solo madrigals of Quagliati, works that evince the same characteristics as those already noted in his duets. In a few instances, Quagliati adds obbligato violin and optional theorboe; the latter belongs to the continuo whereas the former adds a new timbre but stays close to the style of the vocal part. Works such as *Felice chi vi mira* (Guarini) alternate madrigalian recitative and arioso sections with short segments in slow triple meter derived from aria style. Occasionally, these arialike sections feature only the violin and fundamental instruments. But the placement of the instrumental segments seems quite haphazard, and no musical links are made between them. Nevertheless, these elements do point to the future division between recitative and aria found in the mature Roman cantata.

It is significant that Monteverdi shows a marked preference for concerted ensembles. Monodies, on the other hand, form a minority genre in his lyric chamber music, and quite often, they contain some elements of polyphony whether they be choral re-frains, ensemble sections, or orchestral interludes. Monteverdi is above all a musical architect, and seeks to form large organic structures with abstract and expressive power. He does not, of course, neglect the solo voice entirely. In previous discussions of ensemble works, note was made of the use of solo texture in both short and long passages. And it is interesting and pertinent to point out that on a conceptual level, it is difficult to decide whether such works are solos with polyphonic moments, or polyphonic works with solo moments. Be that as it may, monody makes its first prominent appearance in the sixth book of madrigals (1614). The one work in this publication that is usually designated as a solo piece is *Misero Alceo* (Marino). Marino's sonnet belongs to that group in which dramatic elements invade lyric sentimentality. The first two lines and the final stanza comprise descriptive narration. The rest of the sonnet presents Alceo's lament to Lidia in direct speech. Naturally, Monteverdi sets the outer portions for five-voiced chorus with continuo, whereas Alceo's pathetic words are pronounced in declamatory recitative, real *stile recitativo*, with very affective harmonies at the most passionate moments.

Book VII (1619) contains four vastly different and equally original solo works. The *Lettera amorosa* (Achillini) and *Partenza amorosa* are each labeled *stile rappresentativo*, a nomenclature that emphasizes their operatic style. Both compositions are, in effect, rather lengthy studies in free declamation to be performed *senza battuta*. Schrade surmises that Marino's *Tempro la cetra* was chosen deliberately by Monteverdi as the first number in the book.[22] The poet's self-image as a singer who tunes his instrument to sing the praises of Mars but finds that he is obsessed by Love becomes in Monteverdi's hands a musical reality. The four stanzas of the sonnet are separated by short ritornellos for strings whose music corresponds to the first line of the sinfonia that opens and closes the composition. At the same time, the harmonic underpinning given to the continuo for each sung stanza remains basically the same; over it, the tenor sings in affective arioso style. Thus, the work can be considered a kind of double strophic variation.

By far the most revolutionary monody is *Con che soavità* (Guarini), subtitled *Concertato a una voce e 9 istrumenti*. The instruments are arranged in three orchestras or "choirs"—the first consisting of fundamental instruments, the second of high strings, and the third of low strings. Monteverdi deploys these groups by themselves and in various combinations to color the successive conceits of the amorous lyric. The vocal part also shifts among different style in accordance with the affections of the text. The three main styles—passionate declamation, arialike melody, and animated *concitato* figuration—can be seen in the opening section of the composition (Example XXII-6). At the start, syllabic declamation and ascending sequential motives reach their climax on *labbre odorate*, a climax that leads into a more arialike setting for *E vi baccio e v'ascolto; Ma so godo un piacer, l'altro m'è tolto.* The second instrumental choir makes its appearance in the second half of this portion, a portion that contains the rhythmic cell from which the ensuing *concitato* is constructed: *Come i vostri diletti S'ancidono fra lor.* It is worth noting, by way of an aside, that the word *ancidono* prompts agitated figuration in both vocal and instrumental parts, and that Monteverdi pointedly contrasts this *concitato* effect with the interpolated recitation of *se dolcemente Vive.* The second appearance of this phrase goes on to include the entire line, complete with a coloratura figure on *l'anima mia* calculated to represent the sensuously sweet life of the lover's soul. At this point, the third instrumental choir enters to accompany the recitative on the words *Che soave armonia Fareste.* Considering these characteristics, the vocal part cannot simply be called an aria.[23] Rather, it represents an amalgam of *maniere* and one accomplished, moreover, in a consciously eclectic way. Fortune justifiably connects this unique work to operatic style and suggests

EXAMPLE XXII-6.   C. Monteverdi, *Con che soavità* (1619).
From *Tutte le opere*, 7:137–44. Edited by G. F. Malipiero. Vienna, 1928.

EXAMPLE XXII-6, *continued*

EXAMPLE XXII-6, *continued*

ni-ma mi- a? Che so- a- v'ar-mo- ni-

Terzo choro

EXAMPLE XXII-6, *continued*

that it may have been written for the Accademia degli Invaghiti, a group associated with the production of *Orfeo*.[24] Except for the *concitato* passages, the vocal part presents nothing particularly extraordinary. Indeed, the affective force and evocative mood painting is supplied by the orchestra. Although this piece bears comparison to certain passages in *Orfeo*, it is even more closely connected with the intermedio tradition and gives us a concrete idea of the suave and luxurious sounds required by such entertainments. In fact, the characteristics held in common by certain passages in *Orfeo* and by *Tempro la cetra* are inspired by the intermedio tradition.[25]

The radical left wing of the monodists,[26] whose most gifted exponents are d'India and Saracini, transfers all the imitative-affective devices of the mannerist madrigal to monody. Chromaticism, strange modulations, prolific dissonances, and false relations abound in these pieces. Because the voice is now liberated from its prior task of blending with other parts, it now embodies wide and unusual intervals as well as unexpected rhythmic changes. And because such works are through-composed, they can paint every conceit with appropriate fidelity and *enargeia*. Above all, composers strive for violent contrasts in mood. In their hands, the solo madrigal reaches its most self-consciously mannered stage. Precisely because this music looks backward at the mannerist aesthetic, it does not engender any tradition after 1620. Its extremely intense stylization explores the limits of artificial expression. Nonetheless, it does furnish a repertory of devices that baroque composers can use for rhetorical effects.

Saracini's passionate madrigals on poems by Guarini, Tasso, and Marino represent his best works, works in which the dramatic potential of arioso style is carried to mannerist heights of intensity and pathos. *Lasso perchè mi fuggi* (Guarini; 1620) embodies the most extravagantly affected and pathetic *maniera* (Example XXII-7). *Lasso*, set to a sobbing figure, reappears constantly to interrupt the discursive logic of the text. And the urgent intensity of the declamatory style given to the other lines contrasts sharply with this interjection, one invented by the composer and not by the poet. Saracini also repeats other lines of the poem less for abstract structure and more for the sake of evoking a mood of

EXAMPLE XXII-7.   C. Saracini, *Lasso perchè mi fuggi* (1620).
From R. Haas, *Die Musik des Barocks*, pp. 55–56.
Potsdam, 1929.

Cru- del, far- mi mo- ri- re? Ah non si può

mo- rir, ah non si può mo- rir, Las-

so, sen- za do- lo- re, Las- so,

E do- lor non si può chi non h'a

co- re, chi non h'a co- re.

violent emotion. The conclusion of the work, starting with *Ah non si può morir*, affords a particularly striking illustration of Saracini's technique. Its first four words have a precipitously rushing motive, echoed by the continuo, that ends abruptly with a surprising rest, after which appears the word *morir*, set to a descending fourth. This word leads directly into a sequential repetition of the line a tone higher. This time, *morir* descends by tritone and immediately ascends by a diminished fifth, leading to yet another *Lasso*, which interrupts the completion of the line: *senza dolore*. One final *Lasso* introduces the witty point: *E dolor non si può chi non ha core*. The grammatical sense of the words matters less here than does the forceful expression of tortured feelings. Performed with the proper verve, this madrigal recreates the ranting of an impassioned lover.[27]

D'India's radical madrigals rise above these unruly eccentricities because this composer balances dramatic instinct with professional discipline. His craft permits him to endow the violent contrasts inherent in imitative-affective devices with musical unity.[28] Of d'India's four books of monodies, the first one (1609) represents his most original work. In the preface, d'India criticizes monodists for their monotonous harmony and dull declamation, and announces his quest for a *vera maniera* based on unusual and novel intervals. This style, he believes, will endow his songs with greater affectivity and force in order to move the affections of the mind. Both d'India's goal and its realization can be assessed by examining any of the solo madrigals whose texts entail passion or pathos; for example, the opening of *O dolcezze amarissime d'amore* (Guarini, *Il pastor fido*) with its third-related chords, chromatic contours, tritones, dissonances, and expressive *passaggi*, or the opening and closing portions of *Là tra'l sangue* (Tasso, *Gerusalemme liberata*), which present similar elements (Example XXII-8). Of particular interest is d'India's setting of the words, *labbra esangui*, in *Ma che squallido*, a setting that bears comparison to Wert's treatment in *Misera non credea a5* (1586). Of course, d'India is not the only master of the mannerist solo madrigal. Marco da Gagliano's *Valli profondi* (1615; Tansillo) is an impressive study in melancholy equal to the best works of d'India. Like the latter, Gagliano has a sense of balance between detailed variety

EXAMPLE XXII-8.   S. d'India, *Ma che squallido* (1609).

From *Le musiche da cantar solo*. Instituta et Monumenti;
Serie I: Monumenti, 4:95. Edited by F. Mompellio.
Cremona, 1970. Used by permission of the Fondazione
Claudio Monteverdi.

and expressive unity. For this reason, the work in question has
been justly called "one of the greatest Italian songs of the time."[29]

Inasmuch as the aria stresses organic melody and formally
abstract structure, some scholars consider it to be a retrospective
genre, one harking back to the frottola, the villanella, and other
popular forms.[30] Actually, the principles of well-formed melody
are not forgotten during the heyday of mannerist rhetoric, for they
exist not only in dance music and folk and urban songs, but also in
polyphonic madrigals setting light, anacreontic verse. A relatively
late genre belonging to this kind of entertainment music is the
canzonetta. Although basically simple in all its elements, the canzonetta attempts to combine popular elements with a sophisticated
veneer of urbanity and polish, and for this reason it exudes preciosity and stylization. These qualities are preeminent even in Monteverdi's canzonettas, as for example in *I bei legami a3* (1607).
The polyphonic canzonetta is important for another reason. It
provides the single most influential model for the new solo, strophic air. This type of song, which can be called an aria, a canzo-

netta, or a scherzo, is quite popular in Florence. Both Peri and
Caccini include such pieces in their monodic collections; outstanding among the strophic arias in the latter's 1614 publication are *Al
fonte al prato* and *Amor ch'attendi?* (Chiabrera). Among the most
gifted Florentine composers in this vein is Vincenzio Calestani,
who develops intricate melodic organization over clear tonal patterns.[31] Rather than being retrospective, these characteristics are
quite progressive and point to the baroque aria. This historical
evaluation is possible only when elements of Mannerism are put in
proper perspective, and the vindication of abstract melody emerges
as a kind of reaction against established mannerist ideals.

Although Monteverdi is not particularly enamored of the solo
strophic air, he does write a number of these trifles in his *Scherzi
musicali* (1632). The simplest and most charming is *Maledetto sia
l'aspetto.* However, Monteverdi's dramatic instinct drives him
toward the fusion of isolated genres. Such is the case with *Eri già
tutta mia* in which he combines symmetry, tonality, refrains, and a
dancing bass with a vocal line blending aria and arioso styles. For
all their musical guile, Monteverdi's strophic songs do not compare with the easy elegance and effortless polish of such works as
Gagliano's *Mie speranze lusinghiere* (1615) or Calestani's *Damigella tutta bella* (1617). Perhaps Monteverdi's most felicitous essay
in this genre is the duet, *Chiome d'oro* (1619). And it is significant
that Monteverdi feels most at home in the idiom of the concerted
ensemble. The duet is introduced by an instrumental ritornello for
three voices that recurs in abbreviated form between each strophe
and concludes the work in its full form. The vocal style adheres
to the bouncing rhythms of the canzonetta, and a few sparkling
coloraturas paint individual words without disrupting organic coherence. If Monteverdi is eclipsed by the less rigorous superficiality
of other composers of the solo air, he surpasses them handily in
the field of the strophic duet.

The variation principle provides greater artistic scope for
composers of strophic songs. When the composer wants simplicity,
the variations are slight and consist of nothing but conventional
patterns. Caccini includes three such strophic variations in *Le
nuove musiche,* among which *Ard'il mio petto* is the best known.
Other Florentine composers, including Peri, and Roman compos-

ers introduce features from either declamatory or arioso styles, thus making the variations more complex. This kind of strophic variation becomes very popular with Roman composers such as Quagliati, Antonio Cifra, and Stefano Landi. The reason for this situation is obvious; not only does an ostinato bass give musical unity to a composition, but it also affords a challenge to compositional ability. Cifra, for example, demonstrates his prowess by writing thirty different strophic variations on the romanesca bass.

Considering Monteverdi's interests, it is not surprising to find that some of his best strophic songs belong to the variation type. Two solos from the *Scherzi musicali* (1632) stand out in particular. *Quel sguardo sdegnosetto*, a charming work fusing canzonetta and arioso elements, enhances the tongue-in-cheek *concetti* with gracefully florid word painting. *Ed è pur dunque vero*, on the other hand, is a more ambitious work. Here Monteverdi manipulates the variation principle in such a way as to allow him scope for expressing specific sentiments and images. But as always, Monteverdi's masterpiece in the field of the strophic aria with variations comes in the form of a duet. In this instance, I refer to his justly famous *Zefiro torna* (Rinuccini), called *ciacona* in the title of the *Scherzi musicali*.

The duet presents an unbelievably dazzling and carefully organized series of melodic variations over a short ostinato bass that appears no less than sixty-one times. Monteverdi's artistry is amply illustrated by the subtle interplay between the *concertato* voices and the chaconne. Seldom do the entries and exits of the vocal lines coincide with the steady symmetry of the bass pattern; when they do, they emphasize important textual segments by providing a sense of closure. Most often, the voices weave overlapping imitative motives that form a continuous web of echoing musical ideas. The opening of the work, for example, paints the turning of the wind in just this manner. But all kinds of figurations and textures appear in order to depict the words. No vivid poetic image is left without its musical counterpart (Example XXII-9). At the same time, Monteverdi maintains a gay mood appropriate to the tone of the poem. When Rinuccini suddenly changes, by way of mannerist contrast, to the lover's first-person enunciation of melancholy, Monteverdi suddenly drops the dancing motion of

EXAMPLE XXII-9.   C. Monteverdi, *Zefiro torna* (1632).
From *Tutte le opere*, 9:14–15. Edited by G. F. Malipiero.
Vienna, 1929–30.

the chaconne and writes totally free and impassioned recitative. The effect is very telling and hides beneath its passion an artificial reference to the *dramma per musica* for the delectation of connoisseurs. The juncture between this free section and the reappearance of the chaconne is most subtly managed. All in all, the alternation of simple aria style, florid embellishment, and parlando recitative allows Monteverdi to display the utmost harmonic and melodic variety within the limits imposed by the ostinato pattern. Every texture and every musical phrase depicts graphic images and moods inherent in the text. And yet, the composition is dominated by a strict muscial logic.

It should be obvious to the reader that up to this point all the individual elements discussed in relation to divergent genres contribute to the emergence of the secular cantata. Indeed, many of the works called by other names are cantatas; furthermore, many compositions called cantatas bear striking resemblances to works called by other names. For example, Alessandro Grandi's well-known collection, *Cantade et arie* (1620), which is customarily given as one of the first examples of the baroque cantata, contains three *cantade*, two *sonetti*, two *madrigali*,and some *arie*. The *arie* are ordinary strophic songs, and the *madrigali* adhere to the through-composed arioso style characteristic of this genre, whereas both the *cantade* and *sonetti* are strophic variations. In some of the latter instances, their texts comprise dramatic dialogues, and these are the works cited as forerunners of the baroque secular cantata.[32] But in spite of the presence of dialogue poetry, the basic orientation of these early cantatas remains a lyrical one. In short, these compositions stay within the confines of mannerist settings of dialogue poetry that has been described in this and previous chapters. After 1620, however, the cantata becomes the genre in which new approaches are explored.[33] More clear-cut distinctions between recitative and aria sections allow a broader dramatic framework, so that *stile recitativo* is given to narrative portions and *arie* to lyrical moments. When instrumental sinfonias and ritornellos as well as choral sections are added, then the dramatic cantata expands into the baroque oratorio. Thus, the initial dramatic impulse, hidden in the polyphonic context of the mannerist madrigal, blossoms into the largest and greatest form of baroque dramatic music outside the realm of staged opera.

The overpowering fascination that dramatic possibilities in music hold for the mannerist mentality can be gauged from the invasion made by monodic and concerted styles into sacred music. Up to the end of the sixteenth century, sacred music represents a bastion of conservative ideals, a situation supported by the tridentine reformed style. Very few composers permit affective and rhetorical elements from the mannerist madrigal to intrude on the inviolable rules of scientific counterpoint. As one example, we can cite the radical approach evident in Emilio de'Cavalieri's *Lamentations of Jeremiah* (ca. 1599). The solo soprano part abounds in affective intervals and chromatic relations. Some of the sections, for which Cavalieri had built a special organ, even presume the enharmonic genus. The *Lamentations* created quite a stir when they were performed in Florence, perhaps because of the singing of Vittoria Archilei.[34] An important point about this composition is that religious content has become a vehicle for *effetti meravigliosi*, and therefore I would like to suggest that Cavalieri's work qualifies as one exemplifying mannerist values. Equally mannerist, but for a slightly different reason, is Quagliati's collection of spiritual monodies, *Affetti amorosi spirituali* (1617). The title of this publication, like so many other similar ones of this period, stresses the peculiarly hybrid nature of the genre. Religious sentiments are expressed in the limpid melodies and redolent *passaggi* associated with secular amorous music. The happy and unhappy loves of pastoral persons become religious adoration and anguish. Mannerism has forced its way into the church in spite of the injunctions of the Council of Trent. Generally speaking, just as Gianlorenzo Bernini's sensuous statuary cannot be fully understood without its mannerist precedents, the same evaluation holds true for certain early baroque styles in religious music.

In searching for the roots of monody and lyrico-dramatic influences on church music in the early seventeenth century, we are inevitably drawn to Monteverdi's work. Compositions such as the beloved *Lamento d'Arianna* form a stylistic model for countless Biblical laments, both monodic and polyphonic,[35] voiced by Rachel, Mary Magdalene, and the Blessed Virgin Mary. Undoubtedly the most iconoclastic religious work by Monteverdi is the celebrated Vespers of 1610. His choice of texts for this liturgical service has occasioned considerable scholarly controversy.[36] Most thought-provoking for our theme is the observation that the radical elements of Monterverdi's musical conception occur in the substitute antiphons, precisely those sections of the Vespers whose liturgical function seems unclear. These sections range from virtuoso monodies, such as *Nigra sum*, to virtuoso ensembles, such as *Duo seraphim*; and in either case, their religious texts could be replaced by secular ones without violating stylistic decorum —provided, of course, that one is not offended by their secular overtones in the first place. It is true that vesper services since the Middle Ages have been traditionally subjected to personal inspiration. However, few composers can match Monteverdi's individual vision and *maniera*, elements that transfigure the aloof church service into a rapturous expression of religious feeling. Even more important is the fact that Monteverdi theatricalizes this service in a successful effort to move the passions and affections of the congregation.

Monteverdi's startling initiative receives a sympathetic response from his followers and disciples. Saracini, in particular, concentrates on affective recitative in his sacred monodies. The most interesting of these are *Christo smarrito*, the *Lamento della Madonna* and *Stabat mater dolorosa*, and the *Pianto della B.V.M.* (1620). Deep religious emotion and the theatrical potential of such texts provide ample opportunity for drama. The problem as to whether these works, sacred and secular, are mannerist or baroque in spirit is a difficult one. Their eclecticism, their surprising effects, and their ambivalent combination of sincerity and affectation suggest strong links with past mannerist techniques and aesthetics. Other elements, of course, point to the Baroque. But considering their historical position, this is as it should be.

CHAPTER XXIII

Music in the Theater

When thought of in relation to the early seventeenth century, the title of this chapter immediately brings to mind the rise of opera. Even though opera may be viewed as a unique invention of a group of Florentine enthusiasts, it nonetheless retains many elements from previous traditions. These may comprise anything from components of style and form, instruments and texts to staging, scenery and costumes, pantomime and ballet, social circumstances, personnel, and the like. There exists no one specific kind of theatrical event incorporating music that can be called the forerunner of opera, for the simple reason that many different facets of staged entertainment contribute to this phenomenon. Historians cite the advent of opera around 1600 to support the thesis that this year marks the beginning of the baroque era. And in view of subsequent events, their thesis is justified. In my opinion, however, early operatic essays up to 1630 or so evince characteristics suggesting a strong mannerist bias as well. Like so much other music, opera adapts many older elements of musical Mannerism and fuses them with entirely new aesthetic and technical concepts. Because the latter have been assessed in some detail in scholarly literature devoted to opera, and because of the theme of this study, the ensuing discussion focuses on the mannerist side of opera. To evaluate the historical position of this genre in the early seventeenth century, we need an assessment of the precedents for utilizing music in the theater. A myriad number of sumptuous entertainments take place during festivities financed by the courts and academies throughout the sixteenth century. Despite the great variety of such fare, it is possible to discern three general types: incidental music in spoken plays, the intermedio and related genres, and finally opera itself.

The practice of using musical numbers in the course of spoken drama is, of course, a very old one. Although copies of such plays include information about the musical requirements, these sources, as a rule, supply neither the works nor the names of the composers. However, many of the compositions are preserved elsewhere. Thus, we have left to us today musical works that appear to be independent pieces, but in reality have as texts portions of the plays to which they originally belonged. Until thorough research in correlating dramatic and musical sources is made, many compositions will remain detached from the social circumstances that gave them birth. The proportion of sixteenth-century secular works originally written for presentations of plays has not been recognized until the appearance of a recent study.[1] Italian productions before 1530 illustrate several trends destined to gain prominence later. For example, the use of frottolas is indicated for the comedy, *Trinumo* (Mantua, 1499), and for Jacopo del Legname's *Tragedia* (Treviso, 1517); the latter play concludes with a danced *moresca*, a type that will figure prominently in the sixteenth-century intermedio.[2] Most interesting are the cases where works by known composers turn out to be occasional music for the theater. We know that Bartolomeo Tromboncino wrote several frottolas for Galeotto dal Carretto's comedy, *Beatrice* (Casale, 1499), as well as for his pastoral romance, *Nozze di Psiche e Cupidino* (Casale, 1502). Furthermore, it has been noted that the melancholy tone of this composer's *Queste lacrime a4* derives from the dramatic situation of the pastoral, *Tirsi* (Urbino, 1506) by Baldassare Castiglione and Cesare Gonzaga.[3] In my view, the theatrical ambience of a surprising number of frottolas certainly encouraged, if it did not directly inspire, their performance as solo songs.

Another kind of solo singing, the improvised *poesia per musica*, is also associated with theatrical productions. Apparently, Serafino dell'Aquila, one of its foremost exponents, wrote an allegorical drama (Mantua, 1495) in which he played the role of Voluptà; from documents, we learn that he sang and accompanied himself on the lute.[4] Literary historians hail Angelo Poliziano's *Favola d'Orfeo* as one of the first Italian pastoral poems. It is less well known that staged productions, including music, are connected with this genre from its inception. Considering the subject matter, this situation is eminently natural. In a Mantuan presentation of 1480, the famous improviser, Baccio Ugolino, played the leading role and used his talents to sing certain portions of the verse.[5] Apart from setting a precedent for the use of solo singers in a dramatic context, improvised recitation formulas themselves have a definite technical connection with early opera.[6] In addition to solo singing, both of preexistent polyphonic music and of an improvised nature, the polyphonic madrigal too is enlisted into dramatic service. Several of Filippo Verdelot's madrigals are associated with plays by Niccolò Machiavelli;[7] for example, *Quanto sia liet'il giorno a4* written for *La Clizia* (Florence, 1525). In one spot in this madrigal, the phrase, *Io nimpha e noi pastori*, features the soprano voice pitted against three lower parts. One scholar calls this a preoperatic touch; it certainly indicates a desire for graphic dramatization which can be appreciated by an audience.[8] This distinctive trend in the polyphonic madrigal, one discussed at length, represents a transference of idiom and style. The profiling of *dramatis personnae* in a polyphonic context can be considered a mannerist stylization inspired in part by theatrical works.

After 1530, music in the theater assumes definite characteristics according to the kind of drama in which it is used. Under the antiquarian and pseudo-classical influence of mannerist culture, interest in comedy wanes, although certain centers still cultivate this genre. Two documented performances in the private theater of the Prince of Salerno bring together the traditions of Siena and Naples. Although no music for *Gl'ingannati* (Naples, 1545) or for Antonio Mariconda's *La Filemia* (Naples, 1546) survives, the roster of actors includes all the leading musicians of the city: Luigi Dentice, Scipione del Palla (Giulio Caccini's teacher), Giovanni dell'Arpa, Fabrizio Dentice, and Giulio Cesare Brancaccio. Judging from the players, we can assume that both comedies featured a great deal of singing; and indeed, documents indicate that a musician named Lo Zoppino was in charge of the first play and that Vincenzo da Venafro composed music for the second one.[9]

Italian tragedy, a mannerist genre insofar as its stylized imitation of classical models is concerned, seems a natural vehicle for music. In practical terms of dramaturgy, writers accommodate music primarily in the canzona structure given to the chorus, a form obviously designed with a view to musical setting. Composers are then commissioned to furnish polyphonic music for these sections. In many cases, the compositions have been lost, as for example, in the case of Alfonso della Viola's choruses for Giambiattista Giraldi Cintio's *Orbecche* (1541), Alberto Lollio's *L'Aretusa* (1563), and Agostino degli Argenti's *Lo sfortunato* (1567), all produced at the court of Ferrara. In other cases, scholars have rediscovered certain madrigals composed for specific tragedies. Such is the case with two surviving choruses by Cipriano de Rore written for Cintio's *Selene* (Ferrara, 1548).[10] These works retain the descriptive realism and affective harmony that characterize Rore's chamber madrigals. Andrea Gabrieli too keeps his style intact in four impressive choruses written for a very elaborate production of Sophocles's *Edipo tiranno* (1585).[11] The production was undertaken by the Accademia Olimpica to inaugurate Palladio's Teatro Olimpico in Vicenza. Palladio's magnificent design, a paragon of mannerist stylization of classical elements, could not have received a more fitting christening.

Apart from tragedy, the most favored form of theater in courtly circles is the *favola pastorale*. This eminently mannerist genre, embodying the dramatization of lyrical passion, represents more than a mere stylization of theatrical conventions. From the very start of its history, the pastoral receives live dramatic performance. A case in point is Agostino Beccari's *Sacrificio* (Ferrara, 1554) with music by Alfonso della Viola. Of the two surviving numbers, one takes the form of a final chorus or canzona, *O Dei silvestri a4*, and the other is a strophic solo with improvised lira accompaniment and choral interludes, *Tu ch'ai le corna*. The style of the solo portion resembles the arias used to improvise recitation for *ottave rime*. Even though this piece is hardly a recitative in the sense that operatic composers comprehend this style, it nevertheless indicates the importance of solo singing in dramas well before the appearance of opera proper. One can imagine the electrifying effect of this solo in its dramatic context. Surely such instances gave later innovators the courage to believe that they could imitate and surpass the recited dramas of ancient times. Little documentation exists concerning the premiere of Torquato Tasso's *Aminta* (Ferrara, 1573), except for a verbal description of four choral numbers (texts by Tasso) interspersed between the acts.[12] But the structure of the pastoral as well as the theatrical tradition in Ferrara suggest that music played an important role. At least the choruses at the ends of the acts must have been sung. This hypothesis is supported by information concerning a later production done in Florence (1590) for which Emilio de'Cavalieri provided the music.[13] It is worth noting that for this luxurious presentation, the celebrated Bernardo Buontalenti devised machinery to create illusionistic stage effects.

The above parenthetical observation concerning the Florentine production of *Aminta* draws our attention to but one instance of a general situation. In the sixteenth century, realistic natural scenery and astonishing transformations of all kinds become a *sine qua non* of theatrical entertainment. The importance of musical and scenic *effetti meravigliosi* emerges when we realize that writers deliberately arrange matters to furnish the maximum number of possibilities for ostentatious display. Mannerist productions are meant to be feasts for the eyes and ears, and upon occasion, even the sense of smell. No opportunity for striking effects is allowed to go unexploited. As we will see, this approach to staging and structure holds true not only for the pastoral, but also for the intermedio and for opera as well.

In view of the dominant aesthetic in staging pastorals, and especially in view of the close connection between Guarini's *Il pastor fido* and musical settings, one can imagine the stunning productions that were lavished on this beloved *favola pastorale*. It is indeed unfortunate that so little documentation about these presentations has survived. However, we do know Guarini always intended that music should have an important role in his pastoral. For example, sometime between its first draft (1583) and its printed form (1601), the final scheme of *Il gioco della cieca* (Act III) was designed. According to Guarini, he collaborated with Leone, a ballet dancer, and Luzzasco Luzzaschi, the composer, to create an original scenic ballet. First, Leone invented the choreography, and then Luzzaschi composed the music. Guarini's contribution came last when he wrote the verse according to the music.[14]

Luzzaschi's music has disappeared, and when other productions were contemplated, this scene was set to music by Giaches de Wert and Francesco Rovigo, as well as by Giovanni Giacomo Gastoldi and Cavalieri in turn.[15] Court documents connected with the latter production (Florence, 1599) list Jacopo Peri as a singer;[16] we may thus assume that some solo songs were also used. After scenic ballets became a consistent feature in the dramatic pastoral, thanks to the fame of *Il pastor fido*, they also entered the sphere of operatic productions. The mutual influence between music and the pastoral is very important from different viewpoints. Not only does the pastoral encourage dramatic tendencies in individual settings of excerpted speeches, but it also draws music into central focus in the theater.

If we lack documentation about productions of pastorals, the opposite holds true for the intermedio. This magnificent form of courtly entertainment, a specifically mannerist invention, represents the social pride of princely families and city states. A great deal of music exists in published form, and minute descriptions of the productions themselves survive, because patrons wished to arouse admiration and envy in rival political enclaves. The intermedio began its career as a small *tableau vivant* or scenic pageant inserted between the acts of a spoken play by way of offering visual and aural variety; hence the emphasis on music and dance. As later intermedios grew in length and complexity, their allegories became very arcane and their staging very elaborate. A single intermedio could be made up of many musical numbers, and take up as much time, if not more, than the acts surrounding it. This phase also brought with it a semblance of dramatic action within each intermedio; but the action remains an excuse for displaying marvelous effects.

Of such charming stuff are made the truly lavish Florentine intermedios that dominate the sixteenth century. By the 1550s, the intermedio has become an independent art form complete with its own traditions. The spoken drama is now a drab foil for the dazzling spectacle of several intermedios presenting one continuous theme. It is not even necessary to have a play in order to produce such "total theater" events. Scenic ballets and mascheratas can be presented as independent entities, or a banquet may be graced with a series of *tableaux* whose ingredients do not differ in the least from those of the intermedio. Humanist scholars, writers, artists, and musicians collaborate to produce these fantastic shows. No effort and no expense are spared to achieve something new, wonderful, brilliant, and surprising. As Shearman suggests, the intermedio represents the most comprehensive manifestation of Mannerism.[17] The intermedio declines after 1600 largely because many of its spectacular aspects are taken over by opera, which supplants it as formal court entertainment. Whereas incidental music always serves in a relatively humble capacity in spoken drama, in the intermedio it comes into its own, inasmuch as elaborate musical numbers are principally responsible for the intermedio's increasing length. The spoken drama now functions as an interlude between the "acts" of the intermedio. Pirrotta records an especially apt satire on this state of affairs; in Antonfrancesco Grazzini's *La comedia*, the personification of Comedy bewails that audiences treasure only *la meraviglia, ohimè, degli intermedi.*[18]

The first real extravaganza was an academic performance of Antonio Landi's *Il Commodo* featuring elaborate intermedios written by Giovanni Battista Strozzi and composed by Francesco Corteccia (Florence, 1539).[19] The latter comprise a series of scenes unified by the theme of time, and they more than adequately illustrate the mannerist love of variety and fantasy. Different exotic settings—nocturnal, pastoral, bacchic, and maritime—are enhanced by instrumental groupings whose timbres are associated with specific moods. The nasal and coarse sounds of crumhorns and cornetts go well with pastoral peasantry; lutes and transverse flutes depict the sea, trombones the mystery of night, whereas trumpets, flutes, drums, and strings accompany the orgiastic carousing of mythical creatures. Corteccia's music is rather ordinary, the pieces being straightforward, homophonic, and simple in every respect. Of course, the colorful orchestra added a great deal of variety not evident in the music itself.

Some aspects of the intermedios for Francesco d'Ambra's *La Cofanaria* (Florence, 1565), presented for the delectation of the pleasure-loving Francesco de'Medici, deserve mention here. First of all, it is worth noting that many important artistic figures cooperated in this undertaking—namely, Giovanni Battista Cini,

Giorgio Vasari, Federico Zuccaro, Bernardo Buontalenti, Alessandro Striggio, and Francesco Corteccia.[20] In general, the lavishness of these intermedios can be adduced from the fact that no less than fifty-four instrumentalists were needed. In particular, the use of monody in some of the scenes is worth noting. For example, in the second intermedio (Striggio), Cupid appears holding a swan; when he plays on the swan with a bow, while singing, the audience realizes that it is a disguised violin. The fourth one (Corteccia) features a group of Furies carrying drums and arms that conceal instruments. They fight in a stylized ballet accompanied by a *moresca*. In the fifth intermedio (Striggio), Psyche goes to the underworld followed by Envy, Jealousy, Care, and Scorn who carry serpents hiding four violins. Psyche sings a solo supported by their instruments as well as by four offstage trombones and a lirone.[21]

The mascherata presented in Florence in 1579, *Carro della Notte*, to celebrate the wedding of Francesco de'Medici and Bianca Capello, is famous because of the appearance of Giulio Caccini. This celebrated virtuoso, who took the role of Night, sang two monodies accompanied by his own viol and other offstage instruments. Only Piero Strozzi's *Fuor dell'humido nido* (Palla Rucellai) survives, and this work clearly approaches the style of music championed by the monodists in Giovanni de' Bardi's Camerata, of which Strozzi was a member. When Caccini sang, the audience apparently fell into a "hush of amazement,"[22] so great was their surprise. Now, the entertainment in question here demonstrates that monody is by no means restricted to opera. Indeed, its success in intermedio performances probably acted as a catalyst for the invention of the *dramma per musica*. Furthermore, we have records that Vittoria Archilei sang during a ballet presented in Florence in 1584.[23] We can safely conclude, therefore, that monody with elaborate diminutions occurred in all kinds of pageants during the sixteenth century.

The close connection between intermedio, monody, and opera is also evident in the fact that Giovanni de'Bardi invented the intermedios that went with his own pastoral, *L'amico fido* (Florence, 1586), produced during the wedding festivities of Virginia de'Medici and Cesare d'Este. In this case, the luxurious instrumental forces, the rich scenery, and the amazing transformations effected by machinery devised by Buontalenti all illustrate the mannerist heights which Florentine spectacles had reached. The chronicle calls the intermedios "stupendous, new, and magnificent."[24] Twelve different categories of instruments make up a large orchestra. And in addition to choral and ensemble works (composed by Bardi, Striggio, and Cristofano Malvezzi), there are a number of solo pieces. In the first intermedio, Mercury sings a monody accompanied by viols, lutes, organ, and cembalo. In the next one, Flegias appears in a boat and sings a solo with trombone and bass viol support. He then transports a group of sinners to Hades where they are chased into a cave by screaming Furies. A charming pastoral in the third intermedio alleviates the feigned terror of the previous scene. Flora and Zefiro, appearing on the frozen countryside, each sing with lute and harp accompaniment; Primavera answers them in song supported by lutes, harps, muted cornetts, dulcians, and trombones, while the scene is transformed into one of springlike paradise. During the maritime setting of the fourth intermedio, Thetis rises from the sea to sing a solo with lute; she and a group of tritons then disappear into a stormy sea whose violent waves are calmed by Neptune singing a solo accompanied by lutes, harps, trombones, and recorders. In the fifth one, the audience was treated to a real storm, complete with black sky, thunder, lightning, and torrents of rain. Juno causes the sky to clear and a rainbow to appear with her song, performed with lutes, harps, and cembalo. Finally, the famous sorceress, Fiesolana, renews the seasons with a monody accompanied by lute and cembalo.[25]

This extravagant spectacle was surpassed by the even more excessive pageantry of the festivities surrounding the marriage of Ferdinand I and Christine of Lorraine (Florence, 1589). Three different and equally luxurious entertainments were given in succession. The first, a *sacra rappresentatione*, *L'esaltazione della croce*, had intermedios composed by Luca Bati which rivaled the splendor of the secular productions. Nonetheless, the highlight of the events was without a doubt the three performances of Girolamo Bargagli's *La pellegrina* presented by the Sienese Accademia degli Intronati, with intermedios invented by Bardi. Bitter rivalry between Bardi and Cavalieri almost spoiled the show. In the end,

Cavalieri insinuated himself into the production, contributing some music; in one instance, the final *ballo* of Intermedio VI, he collaborated with his friend, Laura Guidiccioni, who provided the text. It is worth noting, parenthetically, that both Guidiccioni and Ottavio Rinuccini—who wrote the texts for Intermedio I (except for the first number by Bardi himself), Intermedios II and III, Intermedio V (except for the second number by Bardi), and Intermedio VI (except for the *ballo*)—later wrote operatic "librettos." While on the subject of texts, I also mention that those of Intermedio IV were written by Giovanni Battista Strozzi. The scenery, costumes, and machines—designed by Buontalenti—were the most lavish ever devised. Most of the music survives in Malvezzi's 1591 publication, except for Caccini's monody from Intermedio IV, omitted because of personal intrigue but extant in another manuscript, and Luca Marenzio's instrumental sinfonia from Intermedio III.[26] The main burden of composing the music was divided between Malvezzi (Intermedios I, IV, V, and VI) and Marenzio (Intermedios II and III); however, a substantial number of individual pieces were supplied by Antonio Archilei, Giulio Caccini, Jacopo Peri, and Cavalieri. Most of these pieces, interestingly enough, involve solo performance. Altogether, there are six solo numbers. Three of them adhere to the older convention of solo performance for a polyphonically conceived composition (designated below by the number of voice parts) and three seem to have been composed as monodies with either simple or orchestral accompaniment.

In the first intermedio, which comprises six numbers and dramatizes the neoplatonic notion of the harmony of the spheres, Vittoria Archilei sang a floridly diminuted version of her husband's composition, *Dalle più alte sfere a 5* (Bardi), accompanying herself on a grand-lute with offstage cembalo and two chitarrones. The third intermedio (four numbers by Marenzio) presents the battle between Apollo and the python; the actual duel occurred in what must have been a stylized ballet-pantomime danced to a five-voiced sinfonia called *Moresca per combattimento*, the music of which has not survived. In the fourth one, which also comprises four numbers and depicts the good and evil demons—a notion culled from philosophical views on *magia*—a sorceress sang an elaborate monody supported by her own lute as well as by hidden instruments: archlyres, bass viols, lutes, violin, double harp, trombones, and organ. This solo, *Io che dal ciel cader*, composed by Caccini and sung by his wife Lucia, has been located in a manuscript version that provides the melody and *basso continuo* line. The fifth intermedio shifts to a maritime scene and features three solos among its nine numbers. The first two of these (numbers one and three respectively) are by Malvezzi. *Io che l'onde raffreno a5* features Anfitrite, who sings the soprano line while playing a lute; her solo is supported by a group of nymphs playing viols and bowed lyres. The second piece by Malvezzi, *Godi coppia reale a5*, calls for similar presentation. The highlight of this intermedio comes with Peri's monody, *Dunque fra torbid'onde*, sung by Peri himself in the character of Arion. This virtuoso solo includes two echo voices and four parts for instruments. The dazzling ornamentation of the song was so marvelous that it attracted the dolphin that rescued Arion from the sea. In the final intermedio, the theme returns once more to neoplatonic symbolism, this time dealing with the gifts of the gods to mortals. Among its five numbers is a solo rendition of Cavalieri's *Godi turba mortal a5*. In this case, all the verses of Rinuccini's text, save the last one, were sung by a chorus of muses and cupids seated on clouds; the exception featured the renowned castrato, Onofrio Gualfreducci, who sang alone to the accompaniment of four instruments. The last chorus, *O che nuovo miracolo*, takes the form of a lesson on the *ballo*, taught by the divinities and learned by twenty mortal couples who appear on the scene after the celestial clouds are lifted into the sky.[27] Alternating with a five-voiced chorus are a number of trio sections for three female voices (obviously modelled on Ferrarese style), which were sung by Vittoria Archilei, and Lucia and Francesca Caccini. This grandiose finale required thirty voices and the full complement of all instruments featured in the previous intermedios.

Needless to say, these intermedios represent the climax of mannerist style in entertainment. Dazzling virtuosity in execution, learned symbolism, and an array of amazing *effetti meravigliosi* penetrate every aspect of the genre—theme, text, decor, and music. Even more spectacular, especially from the visual point of view, was the entertainment given for the same occasion in the Palazzo Pitti, an entertainment that centered on a realistic *naumachia* in the flooded courtyard.[28] It is perhaps unnecessary to point out that this production, along with the *Pellegrina* intermedios, demonstrates the fine dividing line between exaggerated Mannerism and grotesque extravagance. All the presentations of 1589 mark the high point of lavish spectacle. Their importance subsequently declines, and they cease to exist after 1630 when the courts themselves lose their primacy as patrons of the theatrical arts. But they leave a legacy to opera, in more ways than one.

For a time, however, intermedios and mascheratas continue to rival the new mannerist invention—the *dramma per musica*. Illustrative of this state of affairs is the production of Guarini's play, *Dialogo fra Giunone e Minerva*, with intermedios by Cavalieri, which was given at the same wedding festivities as Peri's celebrated opera, *Euridice*, and Caccini's less well-known opera, *Il rapimento di Cefalo* (Florence, 1600).[29] The Mantuan wedding entertainments of 1608 centered on Claudio Monteverdi's second opera, *Arianna*, the stellar event after his great success with *Orfeo* (1607). Nonetheless, this did not prevent the directors from also producing Guarini's *L'Idropica* with intermedios written by Gabriello Chiabrera. The music is lost, but we know that Monteverdi composed the Prologue and his brother the fourth intermedio.[30] For the same occasion, Rinuccini and Monteverdi collaborated on *Il ballo delle ingrate*, a mascherata *in genere rappresentativo*. The ballet sections, some of them accompanied by choruses, alternate with solo recitatives in operatic style. In this way, older traditions of intermediolike pageantry are wedded to the newer phenomenon of declamatory narrative. According to contemporary accounts, the pathetic subject matter and the highly affective music moved the audience deeply.[31] Similar techniques occur in Monteverdi's ballet, *Tirsi e Clori* (Mantua, 1616). The use of solo singers and of *stile recitativo*, as in the case of two Florentine mascheratas of 1590 and 1611, again shows the rapprochement between static *tableaux* and dynamic musical drama.[32] This fusion is so deceiving that a number of intermedios have been mistaken for operas by modern scholars. I cite two instances of this problem. Paolo Quagliati's *Il carro di fedeltà d'amore* (Rome, 1606), is a through-composed work with solo and choral sections, and yet, in spite of its "operatic" appearance, it was merely a mythological *tableau* on a wheeled float. Domenico Belli's *Orfeo dolente* (Florence, 1616), because of its subject and style, was long thought to be an opera; in reality, it comprises five intermedios for Tasso's *Aminta*.[33]

It should be evident that courtly traditions take a long time to die. In spite of all the hullabaloo raised about the superiority of the *favola in musica*, its chief exponents do not shy away from providing music for old-fashioned pageantry. Thus, Monteverdi, at the height of his career in Venice, accepted a commission for a choreographed tournament, *Mercurio e Marte* (Claudio Achillini), to be given at a Farnese wedding (Parma, 1627). The music is lost, but we can surmise that Monteverdi found the idea attractive because of its adaptability to the *stile concitato*, which he was currently exploring.[34] Somewhat more ludicrous is Peri's contribution to a tournament and of all things, an equestrian dance (Florence, 1616).[35] Horse ballets, the last word in mannerist extravagance, were a popular form of court entertainment, and they represent another kind of total theater involving elements of the intermedio, ballet, joust, and tournament.[36]

Although opera abandons the more grotesque aspects of intermedio conventions, it nonetheless embodies a striking continuity with such traditions, a continuity that permeates not only general questions of aesthetics but also details of a technical nature. This assessment does not vitiate the truly novel aspects of opera. Its uniqueness must be measured precisely against those elements it has in common with earlier theatrical ideals and practices. Operas are still court entertainment, and many of them appear at celebrations along with intermedios, jousts, ballets, and pageants. Even when operas are produced independently of such festivities, they remain essentially exclusive affairs. Some productions take place in rooms, perhaps with set-off stage areas. Others are given in actual court theaters. But it is interesting to note that these theaters were constructed by noble patrons not for opera *per se*, but for presentations of plays with intermedios.[37] The fact that such theaters are amenable to operatic production only points to the common external characteristics between the two genres. When the

Barberini family opened its Teatro delle Quattro Fontane (Rome, 1632), we encounter yet another mannerist extravaganza. This private theater, located inside the palace, seated no less than 3,000 persons. Opera was the main focus of the Barberini stage, and private or not, the very size of the building dictated a certain trend toward the monumental in the operatic scale. Peri's *Euridice* would be lost in such a setting. The final transformation of mannerist courtly opera into baroque opera comes, of course, with the public theaters of Venice.

As all devotees of opera well know, this genre has never shed its aura of social glitter. But after 1637, pure court opera—"the spectacle of princes" as Marco da Gagliano calls it[38]—is eclipsed by public opera that caters to another spectrum of musical taste and faces totally different problems, both artistic and practical. Gagliano's phrase is an apt one in many ways. In relation to external elements such as staging, early opera still adheres to the aesthetic of scenic pageantry. Marvelous backdrops featuring optical illusions of all kinds are obviously geared to the current craving for hidden and astonishing surprises. And the fabulous machinery of the intermedio also serves similar functions in opera. Scenic transformations, real water, flying gods, and mysterious entries and exits are all integral elements of operatic staging, and as such remain prominent throughout baroque opera. Indeed, even the more pseudo-classical decor of baroque opera—receding columns and triumphal arches—owes its inspiration to mannerist intermedios. And we must not forget the lavish costuming that is even today considered appropriate to the mounting of opera. All in all, this aesthetic of extravagant decor, which, incidentally, differentiates baroque opera from baroque spoken theater,[39] stems from the incontrovertible fact that early operas still manifest an interest in *la meraviglia, ohimè, degli intermedi*.

Operatic texts provide the first instance in which a story is written with the express intent that it be set to continuous music. Hence one can speak of librettos. The earliest of these, in particular those by Rinuccini, are modeled not on spoken plays but on the *favola pastorale*. In this respect, then, opera is an evolution of the staged pastoral poem. In effect, librettos adapt both the spoken pastoral with incidental music and the pastoral-intermedio to a new conception of musicalized drama. Even the intermingled themes taken from mythology, allegory, and historical sources bespeak ties with mannerist forms of theater. One scholar points out that all the subjects listed by Bousquet in relation to mannerist poetry and art can be found in opera: melancholy, dreams, magic, night scenes, madness, death, suicide, demons, fire, hell, cruelty, eroticism, captive women, sex changes, etc.[40] Of course, many of these are proper to ancient drama and its renaissance imitations as well. What is more important than the presence of such motifs is the way in which they are treated. Whenever such themes appear as central or secondary aspects of opera with a view to creating marvelous, surprising, and technically brilliant effects, then we can speak of mannerist tendencies in seventeenth-century opera. The stories chosen for librettos demonstrate that early operas continue the eclectic tradition of mannerist literary conventions. As examples, we cite *Dafne* (aborted abduction and transformation), *La Galatea* (magical transformation), *Il rapimento di Cefalo* (abduction), *Euridice* and *Orfeo* (the mysterious power of music, return from the dead, infernal and celestial scenes), *La liberazione di Tirreno ad Arnea* (rescue of captives), *Andromeda* (captive women, potential torture, dragons and rescue), *Istoria di Iudit* (lust and murder), *Armida* and *Erminia sul Giordano* (unfaithful lovers and abandoned women), and *La flora* (pastoral allegory).

The matter of musical styles and forces is a complex one that can be elucidated best by investigating specific operas. Generally speaking, those operas that can be called chamber works—that is, those presented in ordinary rooms—use small orchestras of strings and fundamental instruments. More ambitious operatic productions naturally utilize larger orchestras much like the ones found in the grandiose intermedios previously described. In fact, the instruments are grouped in such a way as to present timbres associated with scenic moods. This usage stems directly from experience with the courtly intermedio. The central focus of early opera is on narrative and lyrical recitative. This in itself represents the novelty and *meraviglia* of the *favola in musica* as well as its pseudo-classical pretensions—both qualities being essentially manneristic.[41] The question as to how long and how successfully one can maintain a musico-dramatic entity on recitative alone need not detain us here.

The point to be made is that this basic premise, emphasizing the dynamic and dramatic potential of a musical style or *maniera*, becomes the criterion for differentiating between opera and the more static structure of the intermedio. However, the division is not so clear-cut as modern historians would have it. Many intermedios possess incipient dramatic impetus in that they contain a brief narrative, a dramatic action, conveyed through solos, choruses, and ballet.[42] And when composers of opera come to the realization that recitative cannot sufficiently articulate the external and internal shape of their librettos, they inevitably return to sectionalized forms such as arias, ariettas, choruses, concerted ensembles, instrumental interludes, and dances. Of course, these elements are organized on a much larger scale than in intermedio scenes. And in the hands of gifted musicians, such as Monteverdi, their musical arrangement answers the need of formal and affective articulation to a degree unknown in the more haphazard intermedio.

Scholars also stress that opera, from its inception, seeks to involve the listener in the passionate lyric core of the story in a manner foreign to polyphonic madrigals and theatrical intermedios. Their thesis seems to be supported by numerous contemporary accounts of how deeply moved were the audiences, even to the point of weeping openly. In effect, scholars who hold this opinion wish to distinguish between wondrous amazement arising from detached intellectual appreciation of mannerist games, and wondrous amazement arising from emotional reaction to baroque communication. But we must remember that spontaneous emotional involvement occurs only in isolated, climactic moments in opera, moments when the composer falls back on old mannerist tricks, successfully deployed for decades to depict affections and passions. It is the realistic and novel dramatic context of such mannerist moments—imitative-affective moments—that gives them their impact. Musical connoisseurs dispassionately admired the virtuosity of polyphonic or monodic madrigals by Marenzio, Wert, Monteverdi, or Caccini; when Caccini sang a solo evocative of night in the midst of an intermedio, they fell silent with amazement; and when Virginia Ramponi sang Arianna's lament in an opera, they were moved to tears. Arianna's lament is a good case in point. Its polyphonic version does not differ in quality or effect from any other highly affective madrigal by Monteverdi. But in its operatic context, it takes an unsuspected emotional power. At the same time, we must not discount the power of suggestion surrounding the earliest essays in opera. Their audiences, comprising refined patrons of humanist persuasion, are conditioned by the operatic aim of surpassing the legendary impact of ancient theater. Such recipients are all too ready to enter the game of willing disbelief and to raise themselves to the ranks of ancient *cognoscenti* who appreciate the noble accents of impassioned musical drama. Their proclivity to lachrymal activity is but another testament to the *meraviglia* of music. And *meraviglia*, whether arrived at by gigantic scenic effects or by deliberate play on emotions, remains a basic mannerist aesthetic.

The operas in question, with their very artificial and stylized *modus operandi*, are a curious hybrid of mannerist and baroque traits when viewed from a historical vantage point. They combine static scenic effects from the courtly intermedio, affective imitation from the madrigal, and the dynamic recitation or declamation of a narrative. This fusion, eclectic at its core, results in an entirely novel genre. At the same time, these works hide within their overtly refined *maniera* the seeds of real music drama—the baroque conception of more popular and communicative opera. Einstein warns us against misapplying our notion of music drama (a notion that developed historically from the Baroque) to early seventeenth-century operas.[43] Even though many of their ingredients were subsequently adapted to the needs of modern opera, early *favole in musica* are not equivalent to baroque opera. Neither are they related to the ideals of the *ars perfecta*. They represent the final outgrowth of nearly a century of mannerist trends in secular music, trends moving toward intensification of lyricism and dramatization of pastoral sentimentality. Without the cumulative background of the *maniera madrigalesca* in all its forms and with its attendant aesthetic theories, early opera would never have been "invented."

The place of honor as the first opera on record is accorded to *Dafne* (Florence, 1597).[44] The circumstances behind the writing of this work warrant some discussion, for they well illustrate the close connection between early opera and the intermedio. With

Jacopo Corsi's encouragement, Rinuccini wrote a short pastoral poem that was, in effect, nothing more than an amplification of his earlier text for the intermedio about Apollo and the python (1589). Then the two men convinced Peri to set the *favola pastorale* to music, in collaboration with Corsi. Most of Peri's music has disappeared except for the Prologue (*stile recitativo*), the second scene (canzonetta style), and the fifth scene where a messenger recounts Dafne's transformation into a laurel tree (*stile recitativo*). Porter notes that only the messenger's nonstrophic music hints at the style of Peri's *Euridice*; the other music uses typical sixteenth-century formulas.[45] I must reiterate at this point that the inspiration for using these formulas comes directly from the mannerist intermedio. According to Gagliano, who also set this "libretto" in 1607, the performance of Peri's work aroused great pleasure and amazement.[46] But so did the intermedios for *La pellegrina*.

The artistic merit of Peri's *Euridice* (Florence, 1600; Rinuccini) has been open to debate from the very beginning. Roman music lovers present at the premiere found the opera monotonous and somewhat annoying.[47] This reaction and similar ones voiced by critics of opera up to modern times can be attributed to the fact that the work is being judged by inapplicable standards. The Romans probably expected a grand spectacle with many marvelous effects, including large choruses, virtuoso ornamentation, varied orchestration, and scenic ballets. They were disappointed to hear a narration of gentle pastoral sentiments conducted mainly through the medium of restrained *stile recitativo*. Peri did insert ballets, some strophic songs, and some choruses, but these assume a decidedly secondary role compared to that given to the recitative, the carrier of dramatic action and lyrical passion. Peri's recitative style is subtly flexible and controlled; it mirrors exactly the inflections of speech. It is worth noting that although Monteverdi surpasses Peri in his impassioned recitative, many of the patterns discernible in his early operas were invented by Peri.[48] It is true that Peri's recitative and its supporting bass tend to fall into predictable contours in the more mundane passages. However, at intense moments, such as the justly famous lament of Orfeo, *Funeste piaggi*, Peri succeeds in creating an affective style characterized by chromatic harmony and a freewheeling melody with pungent dissonances.

All in all, given its historical context, Peri's conception must be assessed as innovative and experimental. His *maniera* fulfills Galilei's idea of histrionic style in song.[49]

Peri's opera qualifies as a mannerist composition not only because its recitative is a stylized essay in *imitazione delle parole*, but also because every page of the score, every moment in the music, exudes a quality of self-conscious refinement and overtly noble *maniera*. Those critics who judge the work by the criteria of later opera necessarily find it lacking in dramatic shape, in-depth characterization, and so on. The music does not in any way convey the inner life of emotional conflict that we have come to expect of opera as a matter of course. But as Einstein says, Peri's opera and other works like it are not synonymous with modern music dramas. For one thing, Rinuccini's text is modeled on Guarini's *favola pastorale*,[50] and its pasteboard characters do not go beyond the conventional lyricism of this mannerist genre. The main onus of the musical setting falls on the narrative elements of the text, and emotional intensity is both subtle and fleeting. Indeed, subtlety and artificiality stand out as the main traits of the music. Only those noble and refined connoisseurs who are fascinated by the sole problem of reciting a pastoral poem on a mythological theme will appreciate the pastel shades so finely wrought by the composer. Those listeners expecting the external *meraviglia* of grandiose spectacle or the internal *meraviglia* of musically dramatized emotion will be inevitably disappointed. Peri's opera, then, is an archmannerist composition addressed to a select circle of initiates who can understand his solution to the problem of the *dramma per musica*. In view of the rather unpromising libretto and the main focus of the operatic problem as he conceives it, Peri achieves a remarkable degree of dramatic and lyrical dynamism.

Peri's achievement appears in a different light if his opera is compared to the setting made by Caccini. The latter composer's score has a *maniera* that stems from the more placid lyricism of his solo songs. In Giovanni Battista Doni's opinion, Caccini's opera presents more variety of musical styles whereas Peri's possesses a more noble and tragic character.[51] Doni's critical remarks are quite perspicacious. Compared to Caccini, Peri attains a new level of dignity and pathos through the restriction of virtuosity and more important, through the sensitive use of bold dissonances and chromatic harmony for affective passages. Although its noble accents were drowned out by the more extravagant sound effects of other entertainments presented on this occasion, Peri's *Euridice*, far more than Caccini's inferior product,[52] represents the starting point for operatic development. Before going on to discuss the mannerist side of this development, I remind the reader of the bitter rivalry between the two composers, a rivalry fomented by the mannerist ambience of the court at which they worked.

We come now to Monteverdi's first opera, and the greatest work he wrote in the courtly tradition, *Orfeo* (Mantua, 1607). The fame of this opera in its own time and in subsequent history rests not so much on its historical significance, which is considerable, but rather on its artistic merit. The premiere took place before the members of the Accademia degli Invaghiti, after which the opera was produced several times for the court. Everyone was apparently stupefied by its unprecedented dramatic power and affective pathos. One member of the audience records that both the writer and composer "have presented the affections in such an extraordinary manner that nothing remains to be criticized."[53]

Alessandro Striggio's *favola pastorale*, as he himself calls it, fuses Florentine conventions with a new element of dramatic tension and incipient character delineation. His verse shows an awareness that various poetic forms adapt to different musical procedures. For example, the speech of La Musica (Prologue) is written in rhymed metrical style. In the ensuing acts, Striggio alternates this poetic type with rhymed blank verse. The text of Orfeo's famous aria in Act III, *Possente spirto*, employs *terza rima*, a unique form in the libretto. Monteverdi's use of recitative and choral declamation corresponds mainly to the sections in blank verse, whereas arias, canzonettas, strophic variations, and danced choruses appear in the metrical portions.

On a more general level, the style and structure of the libretto serve as indicators of the peculiarly hybrid nature of the opera as a whole. A quality of artificial nobility marks the poetic conception, and this quality reminds us of Rinuccini's poems. Large static sections alternate with real dramatic depiction, a minority aspect, and with long sections of lyrical expression. In the latter, Striggio writes mannerist poetry featuring conceits typical of Guarini, Tasso, and Marino. Although the total narrative makes logical sense, each act is a separate entity, a scenic *tableau* animated by minor dramatic motion; narrative links between the acts are missing. The first pastoral act is devoid of any dramatic impetus, and it does not differ appreciably from an intermedio. The second presents two contrasting mood studies—pastoral gaiety and mournful lamentation—with a dramatic climax in the middle where Euridice's death motivates spontaneous emotional reaction. In the third act, which shifts abruptly to infernal regions, two relatively static sections flank a lyrical climax in the center, Orfeo's great aria. The fourth act begins after Orfeo's plea to Pluto. Again, a static opening leads to the dramatic crisis—Orfeo's decision to disobey. The consequences of this action are swift, and the remainder of the act concentrates on static presentation of his lament. From the dramaturgical viewpoint, the last act is the least satisfactory of all. It opens with typical pastoral lamenting (complete with echo effects), and then changes to celestial apotheosis through the convenient offices of an arbitrary *deus ex machina*. As Arnold observes, the libretto sacrifices the potential of dramatic action for the sake of emphasis on a series of lyric poems;[54] this organization produces the *tableaux vivants* described above.

Monteverdi's musical setting naturally reflects the structure of the book. In addition, the composer's own techniques reflect a hybrid conception that looks back to the intermedio and forward to dramatically activated conflict. His score represents the first instance where the instruments of the operatic orchestra appear in detail, and of course, they comprise a group typical of the grandiose intermedio. When Monteverdi wishes to underscore a specific scenic mood, he indicates combinations for pastoral, infernal, and celestial settings. Again, this use of instruments comes directly from the intermedio tradition, and it contributes to static sonal symbolism. Monteverdi employs four diverse instrumental forms in the opera. The introductory toccata is merely a fanfarelike overture in a style common to earlier theatrical productions. The concluding *moresca* also represents a staging convention drawn from incidental music and the intermedio alike. Within the opera itself, Monteverdi's customary procedure is to use instrumental ritornellos or sinfonias several times within an act to frame a number of vocal sections. In the case of strophic variations, ritornellos function as refrains dividing the sung strophes, and these numbers, depending on the vocal style, hark back either to his earlier strophic madrigals or strophic arias. During some of the sinfonias, stylized silent action takes place. We have observed such devices in the intermedio as well. Monteverdi, however, employs his instrumental sections with remarkable skill to articulate dramatic entities and to alleviate through-composed sections of recitative. Consequently, he achieves a new ideal of operatic formalization unknown in earlier Florentine style. At the same time, these sections add to the static quality of his opera, a quality that renders it closer to the intermedio than to modern opera.

The chorus, although dramatically integrated with the story, has two conventional roles. At times it presents moral commentary or lyrical summation of dramatic phases of the narrative. One such chorus, *Lasciate i monti* (Act I), is a *ballo* in the best intermedio tradition. All in all, these choruses, like the instrumental music, contribute to static effects. But Monteverdi's most impressive music is given to those moments when the chorus takes part in dramatic action, as in the case of *Ahi caso acerbo* (Act II). Monteverdi is perhaps the first composer to so successfully develop this rather novel approach. Thus, choral sections have a dual significance: traditional intermedio usage and progressive structural articulation. The most powerful effects occur at points where the chorus joins in the emotional expression of the main characters to integrate all the vocal forces into the dramatic action. The other closed vocal form that Monteverdi employs in a way similar to instrumental and choral pieces is the air or aria. These songs appear in the guise of both solos and concerted ensembles, and their style strongly resembles his chamber music: simple canzonettas, *scherzi musicali*, and strophic songs. Significantly, most of these pieces appear in the static sections of the opera, and they help maintain gay or mournful moods. Such numbers, particularly in the first act and at the start of the second act, add statuesque variety to the grandiose scenic pageantry reminiscent of the intermedio. Two solo songs, Orfeo's *Rosa del ciel* and Euridice *Io non dirò* (Act I), exemplify the through-composed monodic madrigal, and like similar works among his chamber music, they embody Monteverdi's union of abstract patterning and free declamation. The other form where this union appears is, of course, the strophic variation. In *Orfeo*, two stellar examples of this technique are the Prologue by La Musica and Orfeo's *Possente spirto* (Act III). The latter takes the form of a dazzling series of variations featuring vocal ornamentation and obbligato instruments interspersed with ritornellos. The use of coloratura style as a musical symbolization of the affective power of music has been encountered in the intermedio. However, Monteverdi surpasses the external virtuosity of such examples with his more psychologically oriented bravura piece.[55] Given the dramatic context and Monteverdi's ingenious symbiosis of external spectacle and internal drama, this aria must have impressed the audience very deeply.

The third act is the only one in which the main dramatic-lyrical focus falls on the aria. In the rest of the opera, all dramatically and lyrically intense moments are rendered in recitative, and in this respect, we can say that Monteverdi continues in the tradition of Florentine opera. But his superb synthesis of realistic declamation and affective arioso owes very little to previous conventions. It is rather Monteverdi's own invention, a product of that dramatic instinct of which Doni speaks. In general, Monteverdi's recitative exhibits the three styles listed by this writer. The acknowledged glory of this opera is the passionate recitative used at all points of maximum affective tension.[56] In these passages, Monteverdi reaches hitherto unprecedented levels of convincing expression. The attributes of normal recitative are here wedded to free arioso style, giving the melodic lines great sweep and intense linear arcs. Fragments of melodic and rhythmic sequence appear not so much to give musical shape to these passionate utterances as to mirror the spiritual agony behind the poetic conceits. Here Monteverdi attains his most daring and iconoclastic use of strange harmonies and affective dissonances. In my view, the most fascinating aspect of this *maniera* is that the composer imports madrigalian devices, and at the same time writes recitative that reflects every single word so closely that it is inconceivable without the text. No other composer of the time comes close to Monteverdi in this regard.

Now, the portions of the libretto set in this magnificent recitative correspond to Monteverdi's most progressive dramaturgy. They contribute to the opera's undeniably novel quality of lyric and psychological intensity. For historians and critics of the music drama, these sections constitute the most important aesthetic and technical achievements of *Orfeo*. And rightly so. But I hasten to point out that this side of Monteverdi's genius must not obscure the fact that the opera as a whole retains equally weighty and important elements from the intermedio. The latter convention entails the scenic display of *tableaux*; in addition, orchestration, closed song forms, and choruses belong to this tradition. So do the personifications of Music, Hope, and the figure of Apollo. Marvelous stage effects—Orfeo crossing the Styx, Euridice fading into a shade, Apollo's entrance and his ascent into heaven with Orfeo—adhere to the cult of miraculous machinery. And finally, we must not forget the toccata, the *moresca*, and Orfeo's echo lament. Monteverdi's opera, in short, represents one of the last extant and greatest mannerist syntheses of tradition and originality in the theater. This synthesis is described by Palisca as follows:

The agglutinative process that is at the basis of the madrigal is applied on a broader time span. There results a collection of musical manners drawn from many sources. This reflects a similar tendency in the libretto. Despite the disintegrative forces of mannerism, Monteverdi achieves a certain unity within several acts, thanks to judicious use of recurrent choruses, orchestral symphonies and *ritornelli*. That one feels an encompassing unity is also owed to the forceful personality that asserts itself throughout.[57]

Only the famous *Lamento d'Arianna* survives from Monteverdi's next opera (Mantua, 1608).[58] Rinuccini's libretto is a shorter and more compact book that observes the three aristotelian unities. For this reason, the opera probably possessed more dramatic integration than *Orfeo*. All the same, devices such as the descent of Apollo on a cloud, the appearance of Venus from the sea, a depiction of Jove seated in majesty in the heavens, and a ballet of Bacchantes again suggest that the *meraviglia* of the intermedio is still alive. Similar combinations of intermedio elements and incipient musical drama characterize many other courtly operas of this period, both in Mantua and Florence. Even after his move to Venice, Monteverdi's interest in this genre prompted him to accept numerous commissions from his former employer. And this in spite of the fact that court intrigues resulted in his operas being dropped from the list of productions at the last moment.[59] The curious overlapping of older courtly traditions and newer public opera can also be deduced from the following events. The year 1637 marks the opening of the first public opera house in Venice. That same year, the Medici family in Florence were treated to a grandiose spectacle, *Le nozze degli dei*, a production requiring elaborate decor, choreography, and 150 singers plus a huge orchestra.

Even though Venice was not a court center, individual patrician families assumed the role of patrons. Thus, Monteverdi composed two operas for the musical maecenas of this city, Girolamo Mocenigo. The music for *Proserpina rapita* (1630; Giulio Strozzi) is lost. However, the social circumstances of its performance in the palace, together with the documents concerning the need for complex choreography and machines, indicate that this work still belongs to the courtly tradition. The case of the *Combattimento di Tancredi e Clorinda* is different. So different, in fact, that scholars disagree to this day as to the proper designation of this work. I include it in the survey of operas on the grounds that the composition is sung throughout and is meant to be staged in a quasi-dramatic manner. It has been called a scenic madrigal, an opera, an operatic ballet, a cantata, an oratorio, and an intermedio. Performed in 1624, the *Combattimento* appears in Book VIII (1638) under the heading, *In genere rappresentativo*. The unique nature of the musical setting arises from the "libretto," for Monteverdi chose the stanzas from Tasso's epic that describe the duel between the Christian knight and the pagan Amazon.[60] The work calls for a tenor as narrator (*testo*) for the nonspeaking portions, by far the longest of the poem, whereas the speeches of Tancredi and Clorinda are to be sung by a costumed tenor and soprano respectively. The singers are supported by a continuo and a small string orchestra, and during their performance, two actors depict the story with choreographed steps and gestures. This element of ballet and pantomime comes from the traditions of the intermedio and the scenic ballet.

The words are set entirely in recitative style. Simple *recitativo* appears when the voice is accompanied by the orchestra, and more florid arioso appears when the continuo alone forms the foundation. Apart from a few cases of highly affective recitation, most of the imitative-affective devices are given to the orchestra. Herein lies the novelty of this work. The instruments describe Clorinda's walking gait as well as Tancredi's galloping horse with the famous *Motto del cavallo*. During the lengthy description of their battle, the narrator's recitative exhibits simple melodic lines but very animated rhythm. Again, the main burden of graphic depiction lies with the orchestra. Its *stile concitato* begins slowly, and gathers momentum through a series of dotted figures, eighth-note figuration, brilliant runs, and sequences of repeated sixteenth-note patterns until it reaches a paroxysm of rhythmic activity. This section, subtitled *Principio della guerra*, begins with the words, *Non schivar non parar*. When the *testo* describes their fatigue, Monteverdi's instructions call for pizzicato strings. Throughout this long section, leading to Tancredi's fatal blow, the harmonies project a markedly static character, vacillating between "tonic" and "subdominant" tonal areas. In the relatively short ending, Monteverdi reverts to colorful harmony and melodic arioso. Clorinda speaks, asking forgiveness and expressing her desire to be baptized, in an arioso style that is a miracle of affective simplicity. Her words are accompanied by a "halo of strings." The narrator's arioso rises to the expressive heights of *Orfeo* when he tells of Tancredi's anguish upon recognizing the woman he loves. The work ends in a studied, yet effective, mood of utter pathos as Clorinda sighs: "The heavens open, I depart in peace." Monteverdi's final touch of a delayed cadence on *pace* is a stroke of genius.

A more mannered and yet delightfully stunning work can hardly be imagined. The music hovers precariously on grotesque *enargeia*. But Monteverdi's lyrical instincts save it from degenerating into vulgar exaggeration. Appreciation of this miniature musical drama depends on a detailed knowledge of Tasso's epic, itself a mannerist masterpiece. Only literary and musical connoisseurs derive full benefit from Monteverdi's obvious exploitation of mannerist novelty. This composition is one of the happiest embodiments of *bella maniera*, or highly stylized imitative-affective music, and of *musica poetica* and *musica reservata*. It is also very daring and experimental.

In Roman operas of this period we can discern hints of what scholars identify as baroque style. The interest of Roman composers in beautiful melody, noted in connection with solo and concerted chamber music, also invades their operatic efforts. The incipient distinction between recitative and aria informs the evolution of baroque dramaturgy, in which recitative is reserved for narrative portions of the libretto whereas lyrical outbursts find their embodiment in real arias. Detailed investigation of this generality goes beyond the scope of this book. It is worth noting, nevertheless, that choruses form an important part of Roman opera. Their deployment in Stefano Landi's *Sant'Alessio* (1632; Giulio Rospigliosi) and Michelangelo Rossi's *Erminia sul Giordano* (1633; Rospigliosi, based on Tasso's *Gerusalemme liberata*) gives these operas a statuesque tone proper to their role of courtly decoration. Both works, graced by decor designed by Gianlorenzo Bernini, were performed in the private theater of the Barberini family. Roman operas also show a growing complexity in plots. We might consider this to be a retrospective feature reminiscent of the heyday of the intermedio, except for the consistent element of comic subplots. In any event, this tradition survives into the later seventeenth century, as does the castrato singer, another kind of artificial Mannerism.

For commercial reasons, the chorus disappears in Venetian opera, and for artistic reasons, virtuoso singers now reign supreme. However, I consider the roots of this phenomenon to be embedded in the mannerist delight in ostentatious display, a delight manifested both in chamber music and in theatrical productions of the sixteenth century. After the opening of the Teatro di San Cassiano (1637), the door finally closes on the mannerist phase of opera. Dramatic rigor and integrity lose the firm, if artificial grip they enjoyed in the earlier *dramma per musica*. Opera has become a public commodity, and composers must satisfy current demand for musical titillation with dazzling arrays of showpieces. Monteverdi's last operas represent an unheeded oasis in the midst of rampant exploitation of a new kind of virtuosity. Of course, this new trend will develop into a different operatic aesthetic, and a viable one in its own terms. New concepts of structure will emerge based on narrative recitative versus passionate arias featuring magnificent embodiments of *Figurenlehre* and *Affektenlehre*. All the adaptable elements of mannerist dramatization will be gathered up into this new form. And from it there arises a stylistic era known to historians of music as the Baroque.

CHAPTER XXIV

§♠§♠§♠

Mannerism as
a Cultural Phenomenon

As far as the superficial side of mannerist personalities is concerned, the reader need only be reminded that the ranks of musicians furnish numerous instances of melancholiac and eccentric artists. But on the serious side, we must recognize that philosophical concepts of divinely inspired genius and personal *furor poeticus* are integral aspects of awakening self-consciousness about original *maniera*—about style and stylization. In true humanist fashion, musicians turn back to classical sources as authorities justifying their search for a radical aesthetic of music: the imitation of nature. Inherent in their experiments is a steadfast belief in the feasibility of progress to higher levels of refinement and perfection. These notions, related as they are to expressive ideals, transform music from a mathematical science to an art dominated by ideals of rhetorical eloquence.

As mannerists gain in experience and boldness, they also succumb to the most pressing problem of radical movements. The cult of progress produces inflated virtuosity, exaggerated novelty, and extravagant *effetti meravigliosi*, all of which represent means of distorting older norms. Furthermore, because the love of recognition is part and parcel of the radical's outlook, original inventions quickly become stereotypes, and historical precedents live in the present. Thus, avant-garde musicians must deliberately seek ways to surpass not only the legendary marvels of ancient music but also the real marvels of previous innovators. The quest for external novelty and individual internal vision, framed by a careful

[481]

program of audience education, means that musical circles become extremely refined and demanding. Therefore, we can consider the *bella e nuova maniera* to be synonymous with *musica reservata*, the latter denoting exclusive music for an elite. By the same token, ordinary music that clings to traditional principles, in spite of its mild stylization, can be seen as equivalent to *musica communa*, or old-fashioned and stuffy craft. The mannerist composer is faced with a clear-cut decision.

Because of this situation, it is possible to distinguish three groups of writers on music. Radicals espouse iconoclasm to fight against the authority of an equally powerful group of traditionalists. Between these two antipodes there exist the progressive thinkers who attempt to fuse ideas of evolving perfection with the timeless rules of mathematics. In their view, it is possible to fuse *maniera* and *scientia*, and thus attain elegant and expressive music that does not destroy the primacy of reason. However reasonable and attractive their arguments, this group gets the worst of the bargain at both ends, being too modern for conservatives and too traditional for avant-gardists. All in all, the many musical controversies in the Age of Mannerism attest to an unprecedented atmosphere of intellectual ferment.

The intellectual background of musical Mannerism is also permeated by optimism, the spirit of adventure that informs all facets of contemporary endeavors. Ancient treatises not only bolster confidence in music's ability to move the passions and affections but also justify new ideas about theoretical subjects. The most fundamental of these is tuning, where interpretations range from dogged pursuits of rational systems or practical experiments to cavalier dismissals of science in favor of the judgment of the ear. The new vistas opened up by this knowledge form the basis for all other innovations attempted in this period. By subjecting acoustics, a branch of inquiry into the very nature of sound, to debate and experimentation, musical theory opens a Pandora's box of hitherto forbidden delights to every practitioner of the art. When these delights are taken up by musicians intent on garnering fame with their dazzling *meraviglie*, then timid stylization develops into blatant and exorbitant *maniera*.

The prominence of musical arguments, from arcane quibbling

over the pythagorean comma to sweeping questions of meritorious style, must be, in part, attributed to the force of the printing press. The book market is flooded by militant tracts, learned works, instruction manuals, and of course, popular discussions of famous performers and musical events. Professional musicians, trained amateurs, and outright *poligrafi* all use this exciting medium to reach as wide an audience as possible. The importance of printing in the intellectual life of musicians is clearly evident from the large number of polemical treatises, short manifestoes, public letters, and argumentative prefaces that appear in this period. Verbal debate, while exhilarating and challenging in its own way, is theatrical but ephemeral. Printed debate may be slower in effect and more impersonal, but it is arguably more permanent. And although controversial works crop up at specific moments in such a way as to bespeak their authors' uncanny sense of exploiting contemporary feelings, they also indicate that writers have a keen eye on their historical place when present events become past facts to be evaluated by posterity.

Just as printing of theoretical works ensures fame for writers, so the publication of music does the same for composers. Considering the high cost and the arduous process entailed in printing music, the indomitable persistence of publishers and composers indicates the importance given to printed music. At first, such publications merely furnish novel curiosities for musical bibliophiles. They cannot compare in beauty, and in some cases, in accuracy and legibility, with manuscripts. But even after the technology of printing music has been perfected, some patrons still prefer handwritten volumes. At this stage, the manuscript becomes a collector's item as opposed to the communal property represented by multiple printings. Nonetheless, publication is both a source of prestige and a means of ensuring wide dissemination of personal *maniere*. Indeed, the rapid distribution of printed music means that mannerist innovations quickly enter the mainstream of musical convention. This situation contributes greatly to the fast pace of stylistic change discernible in the later sixteenth century.

Although technical advances in the printing of verbal material are considerable, they pale in front of those made in music printing, especially when we consider the many technical obstacles surmounted by music publishers in their efforts to establish profitable firms.[1] To be sure, the earliest music prints are more expensive than manuscripts. But rapidly increased expertise between 1501 and 1525 means that after this date, publishing is the main means of reproducing music. And by 1550, the manuscript has become obsolete, and both the commercial market and musical attitudes are dominated by the unmistakable benefits of printed works.[2] These rough dates have a particular significance when they are compared to the evolution of Mannerism in music. In practice, innovations move at a comparably slow rate before 1550. After 1550, new styles appear in quick succession until the irrevocable division between first and second practices at the turn of the century.

For sociological and philosophical reasons, musicians associate this division with one made between sacred and secular music. We have noted that ecclesiastical music does not remain untouched by elements associated with *maniera* inasmuch as style consciousness influences the composition of church music in subtle ways. However, the striking innovations effected by avant-gardists are to be found in secular music, principally in the madrigal and the dramatic genres it engenders. There can be no doubt that the aristocratic courts of Italy, permeated by mannerist ideals in philosphy, art, science, and poetry, constitute the main sources of encouragement for the exploration of similar ideals in music. The cultivation of refined elegance, artificial preciosity, and grotesque novelty characterizes every aspect of court life, and radical musicians thus find inspiration to pursue their own ingenuity.

The musical scene encompassed by Mannerism is dominated by four major courts—Ferrara, Mantua, Florence, and to a lesser extent, Naples. Smaller courts emulate the grandiose establishments of these centers, as do the many patrician families of comfortable means. Venice presents a somewhat different picture. As in the case of art and literature, musical development follows a largely independent course sparked by a few minor touches of Mannerism. Venetian musicians are by no means unaware of the drastic iconoclasm espoused by mannerists elsewhere in Italy. In effect, they adapt selected mannerist traits in such a way as to merge them with their strong sense of a renaissance heritage; and they do this much more successfully than their Roman colleagues. The result is a distinct musical style, a Venetian practice, one that heralds the style and genres of the seventeenth century and can be justifiably called "pre" or "proto" Baroque. The greatest single infusion of mannerist style comes with the arrival of Claudio Monteverdi, a court composer. But this musician changes under the influence of his new surroundings, and his late works, especially the operas, belong to an ambience peculiar to this city.

The importance of academies (a mannerist phenomenon) in the musical life of this period has been acknowledged in modern scholarship. However, the deep force these societies exerted on various phases of Mannerism has generally escaped the notice of historians. The notions of ethos, catharsis, and affective music represent outgrowths of humanist attitudes spread by academies. Leaving aside those musicians who participated in such gatherings, even those who never joined such groups could not escape the influence of their widely propagated views. In short, academies are largely responsible for the commonplace conception of music as a member of the expanded trivium, a conception with both learned and popular guises. Even more important, the new place of music as a sister of rhetoric is thus introduced not only to musicians but also to other artists, noble dilettantes, and patrons of music. In this way, there develops an audience that is singularly attuned to the many stylized experiments invented by musicians. It is true that the connections between music and rhetoric were not neglected during the Middle Ages. But the renaissance and mannerist evaluation of this period stresses the medieval linking of music and mathematics and thus introduces yet another criterion for dismissing the barbarities of the "Dark Ages." And, inasmuch as mannerists believe that they alone have succeeded in reviving classical ideals of eloquence, they can hail their aesthetic as a new perfection.

In some academies, interest in music does not go beyond philosophical debate. But in others it functions as refined entertainment, and these academies are patrons of music, buying printed material or commissioning works, accepting dedications, and hiring professionals. From the point of view of employment, those academies that concentrate on theater are especially important insofar as their activities require the services of trained performers and composers. But the delight in amateur singing fostered by some academies also encourages the formation of countless groups whose sole purpose is to enjoy secular chamber music. Largely because these societies are very informal, an exact count of their numbers is impossible. Yet, enough names survive in scattered documents[3] to suggest that they comprise an important factor in the economic and social background of the madrigal.

Like other academies, societies for the serious study of music begin in the late fifteenth century as somewhat informal groups such as Lorenzo de'Medici's small "academy" of musicians including Antonio Squarcialupi. The first formal academy of music, one of the most famous in Italy, is the Accademia Filarmonica (Verona, 1543). This group maintained a house with a large collection of instruments and a library; from its inception, the academy retained the services of a keyboard player. In 1546 the group began the practice of hiring a professional composer as director of music; many prominent musicians, including Giovanni Nasco and Vincenzo Ruffo, held this post. The archives contain fascinating documents concerning the contracts between the academy and its directors, contracts that spell out in some detail the mutual obligations of both parties.[4]

The interests of the Accademia Filarmonica ranged far outside the confines of Veronese musical circles. Although the dedications accepted by this group are too numerous to list in detail, I note that they include many important composers of madrigals. In addition, the Filarmonica collaborated with the Ferrarese Accademia degli Rinnovati in publishing an anthology entitled *Il lauro verde* (1583) in honor of the marriage of Laura Peperara.[5] In the late sixteenth century, the activities of the Filarmonica were temporarily eclipsed by the fame and generosity of Count Mario Bevilacqua's private *ridotto*. But the latter association disintegrated after the death of its patron, whereas the Accademia Filarmonica survived into the seventeenth century.

Music lovers in Padua were among the first to emulate the precedent set by Verona. A group known as the Accademia dei Constanti engaged Francesco Portinaro as their musical director in 1556. But the association lasted only one year, and many of its members regrouped to form the Accademia degli Elevati (1557).

Portinaro became director for this academy whose main aim was to provide musical instruction for its members. At meetings, musical entertainment occurred along with formal lectures. Portinaro, who stayed with the group until it disbanded in 1560, was helped in his teaching and performance duties by seven professional assistants, called *conservatori della musica*.[6] When Cardinal Scipione Gonzaga instituted the illustrious Accademia degli Eterei in his palace (1558), Portinaro and other Paduan musicians also worked for this group. In 1573, another set of music lovers formed the short-lived Accademia degli Rinascenti and hired Portinaro as their principal. But this conservatory ceded to the competition of a better organized association, the Accademia degli Animosi (1573), which enjoyed a prosperous life under the guidance of Gabriele Martinengo. This sketchy outline highlights one socioeconomic fact in Padua, a fact symptomatic of many Italian cities: there existed groups of composers and performers who made their living by moving from one formal academy to another.

The inconstant fortunes of these musical academies can be attributed to financial problems. Occasionally, however, politics interfered, as in the case of the Venetian Accademia della Fama (1558), quickly outlawed by the Council of Ten. Early seventeenth-century academies of music, like their counterparts in art and literature, seem to have had greater success. For example, Ferrara's Accademia degli Intrepidi (1601) became a revered group of musical enthusiasts. Its membership included Claudio Saracini, and Claudio Monteverdi dedicated to it his fourth book of madrigals. The considerable influence that Monteverdi had on Saracini's style might be attributed to this academy's ideals. In any event, the popularity of such institutions prompted professional musicians to form their own groups. I here mention only two—Marco da Gagliano's Accademia degli Elevati (Florence, 1607) and Adriano Banchieri's Accademia dei Floridi (Bologna, 1615). The latter became the Accademia dei Filomusi, and finally the famous Filarmonica. One more important group deserves mention—the Virtuosi Compagnia dei Musici di Roma (1584). This association, which included Luca Marenzio, Paolo Quagliati, and Cristofano Malvezzi, very shortly changed its name to the Accademia di Santa Cecilia, and became an honorary society of famous composers pledged to support and aid its members throughout Italy.[7] The prestige of such respected academies is seen in the fact that Monteverdi's election to the Accademia di Santa Cecilia at the age of twenty-three was considered a singular honor for so young a composer. If documentation is scarce for musical academies, the situation is even more frustrating with regard to private *ridotti*. These ephemeral groups evince the same range of interest characteristic of the academies. It is known, for example, that Ercole Bottrigari had a private *ridotto* in his home in Bologna. Undoubtedly, his theoretical writings on Aristoxenos and Nicola Vicentino were prompted by the proceedings of his group. Carlo Gesualdo received his early musical training from members of an informal *ridotto* that met in his father's palace. Later, Carlo imitated the paternal model by forming his own *ridotto* in Naples comprising figures such as Giovanni Leopardo Primavera, Muzio Effrem, Rocco Rodio, Scipione Cerreto, and Giovanni Leonardo dell'Arpa.

Consistent music-making in the homes of patrician families also fostered many transitory affiliations among literary critics, poets, musicians, and gifted amateurs. Such musicales formed the sociological foundation for the performance of madrigals, madrigal-comedies, and in the case of wealthy patrons, concerted music of quite ambitious proportions. In Rome, for instance, many cardinals maintained their own private musical establishments. Thus, Vicentino was given the opportunity to train, with the greatest of secrecy, Cardinal Ridolfo's musicians in the art of chromatic and enharmonic singing. In this specific case, the merging of the *ridotto* and *musica reservata* is obvious. The prosperity of Venice's leading citizens made this city a veritable mecca for musicians. Letters and other sources attest to elaborate musical entertainments carried on in many different houses. An informative account in Anton Francesco Doni's *Dialogo della musica* (1544) affords us a glimpse into the scale of sophistication characteristic of the *ridotti* gathered around such personages as Pietro Aretino and Polissena Pecorina, to mention only two examples.[8] And Girolamo Mocenigo's patronage of Monteverdi has been noted. But the most famous and influential private *ridotto*, before the advent of the Florentine Camerata, is that of Count Bevilacqua in Verona. His group comprised no less than fifteen full-time musicians hired to compose and perform in the latest fashion. This maecenas was the recipient of countless dedications, all of them praising the high standards of his taste. Among the many illustrious dedicators are Orazio Vecchi, Giovanni Giacomo Gastoldi, Luca Marenzio, Orlando di Lasso, and Filippo di Monte.[9]

The last important *ridotti* that fall in our purview are the three interrelated groups active in Florence. The Camerata proper flourished under the aegis of Giovanni de'Bardi. Philosophical and aesthetic speculations of its members concerning the nature of classical music constitute a direct motivation for the first theoretical and practical manifestations of monody. I have mentioned that Bardi, Jacopo Corsi, and Ottavio Rinuccini were also members of the Accademia degli Alterati, a society with humanistic interests in music, and that they introduced ideas from the academy to musicians in the Camerata, the most prominent of which were Vincenzo Galilei and Giulio Caccini. The other groups, one centering on Corsi, and one on Cavalieri, were mainly responsible for the earliest essays in the *dramma per musica*. The musical styles of musicians in these *ridotti* and the sociological circumstances of their work clearly demonstrate that the invention of monody and opera represents the culmination of mannerist attitudes. This assessment is not intended to minimize the relationship between Florentine music and ensuing musical events belonging to the baroque era. At the same time, it is intended to draw our attention to the sixteenth-century roots of this phenomenon, roots that took firm hold in mannerist soil.

Because of these background factors, liturgical polyphony in the first half of the sixteenth century remains largely untouched by the more extreme forms of mannerist stylization. The situation with paraliturgical music, as always, is somewhat more fluid. Because musical innovations are associated with unruly attitudes prevalent in secular music, ultraconservative and mildly progressive thought naturally gravitates to sacred music. Thus, this field remains inextricably linked with an idealized *ars perfecta*. But even this idealization must be counted as a symptom of Mannerism. As I have endeavored to show, progressive theorists reconcile the new awareness of style or *maniera* with the sacrosanct rules of timeless counterpoint. But in spite of such efforts on both the theoretical and practical sides, the division between old and new, outdated and modern, regressive and progressive trends becomes sharper and sharper as the century draws to a close. The outcome in the early seventeenth century is that no composer who considers himself to be "modern" would write secular music in the style of the *prima prattica*. And if he composes church music in the style of the *seconda prattica*, he consciously transfers the premises behind secular *maniera* to the realm of sacred music. When this happens, as it does with increasing regularity, we notice that church music, long the bastion of conservative principles, succumbs to the attractions of Mannerism. This fact testifies to the influential position won for modern style by successive generations of radicals. And the situation in the early seventeenth century is all the more striking when we consider the basic thrust of the Counter Reformation and its relation to aesthetics of musical reform.

That thoughtful lovers of sacred music were dissatisfied with traditional approaches and that they sought ways of reforming them long before modern style became established and respected can be seen from a document dating from 1549, a letter by Bishop Bernardino Cirillo Franco to a colleague in Rome, in which Franco complains about the state of church music at the time. His distaste for secular material in the Mass is to be expected from an ecclesiastic, and will be repeated in the admonitions of the Council of Trent. But his comments on matters of sacred style are quite instructive as well as pertinent to my thesis concerning the tension between conservative and radical ideas. Franco notes that composers concentrate solely on abstract demonstrations of skill through exercises on standard contrapuntal artifices to the detriment of expressivity. In his view, the result leaves much to be desired. Sacred music, regardless of form or text, always embodies one and the same *maniera*, and consequently, it lacks the power to inspire feelings of devotion and piety. Franco goes on to say that church music must be imbued with "affective harmony that moves the listener." And he asks the recipient of his letter to find a composer in Rome who can restore to sacred music the "marvelous effects" of ancient style.[10] In view of later attitudes typical of the Council of Trent, Franco's letter has been interpreted as an attack on polyphony in the church. However, it seems much more likely that this prelate is motivated by the same humanist notions concerning rhetorical eloquence[11] that activated exponents of new *maniere*; indeed, his words are curiously evocative of Vicentino. Franco does not, unfortunately, provide us with details about his ideals, apart from the reference to affective harmony. Whether he would be satisfied with Gioseffo Zarlino's idea of harmonic character or whether he would be happier with Vicentino's chromatic genus is a moot point. Nonetheless, his evaluation of traditional polyphony as an abstract, undistinctive, and impersonal art certainly receives affirmation from avant-gardists of his own and subsequent generations.

Polyphony came under heavy fire during the meetings of the Council of Trent,[12] and its ultimate triumph must be accredited to the careful politics of a few lay and clerical connoisseurs. The edicts concerning music, accepted on 17 September 1562, are too well known to require rehearsal here. But it would be well to recall that they stress negative rules: the abolishing of instruments, the prohibition of lascivious tunes, and the statement that aesthetic aims must not focus on giving pleasure to the congregation. The one positive recommendation is very general and vague—to wit, that the words of the service must be intelligible at all times. In March 1563, two new cardinals replaced deceased members of the Council. These men, Giovanni Morone and Bernardo Navagero, proposed a motion to ban polyphony, or *musica troppo molle*, in favor of monophonic chant. After a flurry of debate and imperial intervention, the Morone-Navagero motion went down to defeat, with the understanding that the details of reform should be worked out by provincial synods (11 November 1563). To create a precedent, Pope Pius IV appointed eight cardinals to implement the reforms in Rome (1564). These churchmen, chosen for their knowledge in specific areas, were divided into four separate commissions. The task of reforming music was delegated to Cardinals Carlo Borromeo and Vitello Vitellozzo. Borromeo, Archbishop of Milan and nephew of the pope, was a man of considerable re-

finement and musical expertise. Vitellozzo also had a deep concern for salvaging polyphony inasmuch as he too was a musical
connoisseur.

The Commission of Cardinals set about its task in January of
1565, and there ensued a quiet struggle between it and the Camera
Apostolica. It is difficult for us to determine the details of these
negotiations, because the papal choir forbade its delegates from
communicating with outsiders. We do know that Borromeo re-
quested a polyphonic Mass in simple style with clear textual treatment from Ruffo, who was then in Milan (10 March 1565). In a
second letter (31 March 1565), he also suggested that Vicentino be
invited to submit a chromatic Mass. No record of Vicentino's com-
pliance exists. In any event, Borromeo's contemplation of church
music of such a radical cast certainly indicates a remarkably open
mind. Most certainly, Cardinals Morone and Navagero would
have classified Vicentino's *maniera* as *musica troppo molle*, to say
the least. The secretive document by one of the choir representatives recording the meeting at which Masses were performed and
judged (28 April 1565) provides no details as to specific compositions or their reception by those present. Dismissal of fourteen
singers from the papal choir was the last action taken by the
commission before it disbanded. Again, no reasons for this disci-
plinary act are recorded. Thus, precise facts remain a matter of
conjecture.

The main focus of the commission seems to have been on
polyphony that presented an intelligible rendition of the text. What
this aesthetic means in terms of modifications in contrapuntal procedure must be adduced from music composed expressly in reformed style. Borromeo's espousal of musical reform undoubtedly
influenced Milanese composers, especially Ruffo. His first publication in this style, a collection of Masses (1570), contains a preface
in which Ruffo states that his initial essay in the "new style" was
undertaken for Cardinal Borromeo, referring perhaps to the Commission of Cardinals.[13] Ruffo's music illustrates the reformed
manner, a *maniera* in which verbal clarity takes precedence over
all other aspects of composition. Extremely simple unaccompanied
polyphony (really contrapuntally animated homophony) forms the

basic procedure with relatively short sections of counterpoint balanced by long passages in completely homophonic texture. Linear melismas and text repetitions seldom occur. Short of writing harmonizations of chant melodies, everything possible is done to align the text in all voices. And, of course, the prosody of the Latin language is scrupulously observed. Such works represent forerunners of the later *Missa brevis*.[14]

In my view, the impact of reformed style on musical events in general is negligible. Works written in accordance with its aesthetic and technical principles comprise a minority corpus based on a specific stylization of both the *ars perfecta* and the *elegante maniera* typical of church music of the time. It should be noted, however, that both ecclesiastics and musicians would have been unable to grasp the issues at stake without the benefit of writings on musical style, regardless of their conservative or radical bias. In its own limited way, tridentine musical reform is but another manifestation of Mannerism. And it is significant that both the abstract exhortations of the Council and Synods as well as practical application of them by Ruffo and a few other composers embody, in effect, stylizations of *a cappella* polyphony. The fact that their notions perpetrated a myth about the performance practice of renaissance sacred music need not detain us here. But their combined efforts may be interpreted as an attempt to impede the development of mannerist extravagance and to transform traditional style (as they understood it) into a timeless, but this time, also pious ideal. In practical terms, reformed *maniera* tends toward impersonal music that leaves little scope for individual inventiveness and the overcoming of technical or expressive challenges. This is why it did not expand beyond a little group of devoted adherents. Considering the advanced and highly sophisticated mannerist attitudes of the late sixteenth century, this situation is not in the least puzzling.[15] Posttridentine reform has few practical implications. And yet it does foster cultivation of the *prima prattica*, that idealized conception of traditional counterpoint destined to become known as the *stile antico* in the Baroque.[16] Regardless of whether one sees this legacy as a positive one, its foundation goes back to mannerist ideas, and in this respect, it furnishes some clarification concerning the fortunes and transformations of renaissance ideals.

The Council of Trent represents but one facet of the Counter Reformation as a whole. Much more influential is the widespread patronage of the Jesuit order, the militant arm of the Church triumphant. The Jesuits saw more clearly than the befuddled committees of the Council the realities of the artistic situation of their time. To their more flexible attitudes we must attribute the growing popularity of the spiritual madrigal, a genre in which religious sentiments of serious and even lugubrious tone are clothed in the mannerist trappings associated with concettist poetry and madrigalian style. Such music, replete with pictorial devices, affective harmonies, dramatic declamation, and soaring coloratura, answers Franco's desire for *effetti meravigliosi* much more forcefully than the sober polyphony of the reformed manner. Just as the Jesuits manipulated the sensuous decorativeness of mannerist art to their religious aim of communicating feelings of ecstasy and penance, they did the same with mannerist music.

Furthermore, the Jesuits interpreted tridentine views on verbal clarity as permission to introduce monody in both liturgical and paraliturgical roles.[17] To the latter belong the many *Diletti spirituali* and *Affetti spirituali* with which religious and moral ideas could be displayed attractively in a *maniera* calculated to appeal to audiences brought up on mannerist novelties. Once the door had opened to simple solo and concerted versions of religious texts, it was but a small step to more complex forms and genres typical of the *seconda prattica*. From the accompanied lauda as used in Roman oratories, there develops the religious cantata and oratorio. These forms, on either a small or a large scale, simply transfer the literary and musical conventions of secular drama to religious themes. In those centers where elaborate concerted music has been the norm, church music now erupts into a glorious panoply of dramatic lyricism and pathos. Saints and holy figures conquer devoted congregations by means of sweet accents formerly given to characters of pastoral fame. The Church enfolds mannerist music to its bosom and joins other Italian institutions in their inevitable thrust to the grandiose and theatrical Baroque. I here repeat the acknowledgment made earlier concerning the existence of simple, natural, and even humble styles in music, styles like those in art and literature, that represent a kind of reaction against mannerist preciosity and artificiality. The reformed style of church polyphony is only one of these. But this recognition does not alter my views as to the origins of the grand manner in the baroque arts. In closing, I once again reiterate my basic hypothesis—every aspect of musical development between renaissance and baroque styles gains in precision if we posit the viability of an Age of Mannerism.

CHAPTER XXV

§⠙§⠙§⠙

Mannerism as

a Historical Concept

That the concept of Mannerism has earned belated recognition in the field of music is a fact recognized by many scholars.[1] This situation can be attributed to two factors. Among them one cannot count the idea that musical scholars are unaware of developments in other areas of cultural history. Quite the contrary, our heritage posits musicology as a humanist discipline through the adaptation of approaches and tools used in artistic and literary criticism. Indeed, this heritage can be considered as the indirect cause of the first factor. Because younger scholars have been influenced by recent trends in the philosophy of history, they hesitate to support the assumption that historical-stylistic terms are helpful or even necessary. Obviously, if one refuses to accept notions of renaissance and baroque music, then attention to Mannerism is also superfluous. The second factor concerns the use of such notions by those scholars who see some value in them. Because the profile of the period under discussion here seems extremely complicated, it encourages musicologists to examine it from the viewpoints inherent in renaissance or baroque scholarship. These avenues provide ready-made conceptual implements. Inasmuch as both are viable, they must be accepted as means of gaining insights for historians interested in tracing the life of styles in music. As I have mentioned several times during the preceding chapters, my thesis maintains that both interpretations gain if they are understood within the framework of Mannerism, an abstraction that allows us to see the years between 1530 and 1630 as an entity.

Blume makes the tentative suggestion that Mannerism might be a useful term for those aspects of music that are more usually labeled Late Renaissance or Early Baroque.[2] Scholars attempting to define a stylistic continuum of Renaissance-Mannerism-Baroque concentrate on analogical relationships between music and the other arts as well as on facets common to their social and intellectual background. In general, they take for granted the validity of importing style terms from art history together with the methods implied by them. Their delimitation of Mannerism or *maniera* in music depends on definitions of the other two contingent periods. And insofar as they depart from a preconception of both the Renaissance and the Baroque as major stable periods in music history, their notions of Mannerism entail ideas of a transitional, negative, and unsatisfactory stage. Musicologists who stress the continuation of renaissance style well into the sixteenth century confine Mannerism to a small epigonal phase bridging the sixteenth and seventeenth centuries. Other musicologists, on the other hand, trace baroque style well back into the sixteenth century, and therefore consider the early decades of the sixteenth century as a mannerist phase. A third group encompasses the hundred years between 1530 and 1630, thereby elevating Mannerism to a major era in its own right.

To the latter group belongs a recent study by Haar, a scholar who correctly insists that Mannerism must be described in purely musical terms in order to gain respect in musicology.[3] His work offers a refreshing look at technical features of music whose mannerist significance is explicable in ideas proper to the medium itself. However, it seems to me that in certain areas of musical activity, such as theory or aesthetics and productions relying heavily on social conventions, parallels between music and other cultural phenomena are more than mere analogies. And although it is possible to agree with Haar's statement that musicians think in musical terms, we must also remember that aesthetic commonplaces have a way of entering into creative attitudes and coming out through the technical apparatus of a medium.[4] This is particularly true of the self-consciousness prevalent among mannerist musicians.

Before we can consider the profile of Mannerism, the idea of a musical Renaissance must be reviewed. Basing their concepts on a somewhat simplistic view of a rejuvenation of classical style, a number of musicologists deny the existence of a Renaissance in music. They point out that actual ancient music was unknown and that if proponents of the so-called renaissance of mannerist music had been able to hear such music, they would have been greatly disappointed.[5] Moreover, the contention that a true musical Renaissance never occurred leads to the conclusion that the crisis responsible for Mannerism in art and literature also failed to materialize in music.[6] Now, it is true that generalities concerning the Renaissance have been subjected to critical scrutiny. In spite of the refurbishing of detailed data on this subject, the leading authority in the field still maintains that renaissance ideals—that is to say, rebirth or rejuvenation of classical heights—represent a driving force behind Italian thought in the fifteenth and sixteenth centuries. And he believes this to be true even though these ideals must be taken with a grain of salt insofar as they can be embodied in actual artistic creations.[7]

This is especially true for music. Tinctoris's notion of the *ars nova* may be humanistically inspired aesthetics misapplied to musical facts. Nevertheless, his concept established a precedent. And I have traced in some detail sixteenth-century ideas about perfection and progress from Glareanus's *ars perfecta* to Monteverdi's *prima prattica*. Rightly or wrongly, traditionalists throughout this period uphold an ideal *maniera* that they believe can attain unsurpassed perfection by balancing expressivity with abstract logic. Different theorists' views about natural and subtle refinements of this perfection vary according to their individual preferences. Whereas Coclico's views may be simply figments of his overdeveloped imagination, Finck's evaluation seems to be borne out by musical evidence. Musicologists, therefore, attribute to the composers cited by Finck the first mannered stylization of the perfect art, wrought in purely musical terms.[8] Regardless of the assessments of the factual import of any musical writings of the time, I maintain that theoretical as well as practical attitudes toward progress are impossible without an aesthetic premise about *maniera*. For better or worse, we take style concepts for granted; but in the sixteenth century, as I have endeavored to show, such concepts are new and difficult abstractions. But in spite of the problematic nature of style norms of a descriptive and prescriptive nature, *maniera* informs practically all aspects of musical activity. For example, Haar suggests that parody technique is based precisely on conceptions of style. This widespread compositional tool is thus another proof of the inroads made by mannerist attitudes, inroads that can be discussed in musical terms.[9] And as I have indicated, even the reformed sacred style advocated by tridentine authorities would have been impossible without a sense of style.

Because radical departures from classical-renaissance norms in secular music tend to minimize the stylization found in music of a conservative cast, Zarlino formulates his theory of the *elegante maniera*. By revamping the mathematical basis of counterpoint, the basis that gives music its philosophical validity as a revival of Greek ideals, Zarlino updates musical style and restores it to contemporary value and future timelessness—in his own opinion, at least. He picks Willaert as his exemplar because this composer's style incorporates elements of the idealized *ars perfecta* along with some newer mannerist refinements. From Willaert's initiative, there develops an indigenous tradition in Venice, a tradition based on blending a few select elements of radical Mannerism with ideals taken from traditional polyphony. Schrade differentiates Venetian style from other manifestations of *maniera* in the sixteenth century, but his comparison between music and painting (*disegno* versus *colorito*) is misleading.[10] One cannot deny that one important aspect of Venetian style arises from a strong appreciation of musical "color." Equally important, however, is the formal element of design, and this aspect arises from the *maniera* of the perfect art as understood by musicians of the time. In the hands of Venetian composers, the transformation of this *maniera* is effected in a completely natural and unconscious manner.

In other cultural enclaves of Italy, composers of traditional polyphony work in an ambience which fosters self-consciousness toward radical and conservative *maniere* alike. The touting of a long and hallowed history of antiradical counterpoint serves as a useful tool in defending *contrapunto osservato* and attacking *contrapunto moderno*. It is for this reason that supporters of radical *maniera* in turn construct historical justifications for modern music. At the same time, we must not overlook the fact that the precepts of *contrapunto osservato* represent a vital musical language for its practitioners. Even though Palestrina and other members of the so-called Roman school, being educated musicians, may be ready to acknowledge their heritage, they are also convinced that their style is a living one and still a vehicle for the artistic personality. This is the very reason they do not follow the precepts of tridentine reform.

Federhofer rejects the approach that classifies this group of composers as mannerists who perpetuate the norms of the *ars perfecta*. He believes that this attitude is much more symptomatic of the Palestrina cult evident in the seventeenth and eighteenth centuries.[11] In my view, his opinion is valid if we define Mannerism as epigonal imitation of dead languages. And in truth, both Palestrina's style and that of the more monumental counterpoint of other Roman composers at the turn of the century embody a virile stylization that allows contemporary theorists to hail them as the summit of classical refinement and perfection. In fact, the grandiose polychoral works of Roman composers have been called "baroque."[12] Although recognizing the importance of Federhofer's warning against imputing later values about the mannered imitation of renaissance counterpoint to Palestrina and his contemporaries, our study shows that the seeds of this evaluation are planted in the sixteenth century. For traditionalists, their music is alive, but for radicals, it is dead. The seeds of this controversy belong to Mannerism, the fruits to the Baroque.

In the earlier part of this period, traditional *maniera* develops apace with radical *maniera*. But when avant-garde tendencies reach their full stride, the musical novelties they accumulate force a much sharper distinction between *contrapunto osservato* and *moderno*. In spite of theoretical pigeonholes, this distinction is in practice a somewhat fluid one. Nonetheless, the inherent opposition of these two ideals, in its extreme form, does not escape the notice of Zarlino and Vicentino in mid-century. And when Monteverdi finally sums up the opposition between *prima* and *seconda prattica*, this fluidity cedes to a very self-conscious and rigid separation. The notion that the first practice represents a closed set of principles is evident in numerous writings of that time, and the further away musicians get in the ensuing decades from the actual music of the *prima prattica*, the more abstract and lifeless become their conceptions of the *stile antico*. Monteverdi might have been appalled if he could have foreseen this outcome. This conjecture, however, does not obviate the fact that baroque ideas concerning the *stile antico* go back to his division.

Because Monteverdi and other exponents of modern practice trace novel *maniera* to Rore, their collective attitude indicates that many elements we associate with baroque style go well back into the sixteenth century. In attempting to crystallize Mannerism as the period during which this transformation takes place, it is wise to recall the cautions against too facile analogies between music and other artistic, social, and intellectual currents.[13] Whatever their individual decisions about Mannerism in music, historians agree that this phenomenon entails a disintegration of the balanced, harmonious, and natural ideals of the High Renaissance. We add the point that the very notion of a High Renaissance, or a classical perfection in music, is a mannerist construct. From aesthetic, comparative, and technical points of view, everyone comes to the same conclusion—under a new emphasis on affective expression and novelty, *maniera* effects a stylization of traditional norms. Some scholars apply notions of spiritual crisis, grotesque exaggeration, and monumental grandeur to this phenomenon, whereas others restrict *maniera* to elegance, stylishness, and precious artificiality. My interpretation includes elements of both. Federhofer does not agree that expressive ideals are peculiar to Mannerism, stating that Josquin's output contains a respectable number of motets that evince such characteristics. But several historians consider these traits to be part of a tentative *maniera* understood as radicalism.[14] Their view is substantiated by the judgments of sixteenth-century theorists such as Glareanus. At the same time, the same scholars also stress that the hidden seeds of Mannerism take root and blossom in the field of Italian secular music. Out of the distortion of the *ars perfecta*, however subtle, there emerges a new style during a very experimental period.[15]

This kind of emphasis on sixteenth-century experimentation has been also attacked on the grounds that it is too one-sided an assessment of this period.[16] Certainly, one cannot discount the view that a great deal of theoretical and practical activity between

1530 and 1630 goes on quite oblivious to the avant-garde experiments that preoccupy militants of both conservative and radical persuasions. And this situation is as true of secular music as it is of sacred music. It is also true that a number of theorists fabricate controversies in order to call attention to themselves. Nonetheless, this kind of tilting at windmills cannot obscure the basic thrust of musical thought. Most treatises dealing with experiments of one kind or another are in some way connected with real changes in musical style. Furthermore, these treatises demonstrate a remarkable sense of both contemporary and coming trends in music. Even those musicologists who deny the existence of a crisis in musical composition do not gainsay the atmosphere of intellectual ferment indicated by the most seminal writings on music. Those who relate verbal debates to the innovations and stylized novelties in musical artworks focus on a profile of Mannerism as a period dominated by all kinds of experimentation.[17]

Although Haar stresses purely technical elements of stylized novelty, he also recognizes the importance of a new rhetorical ideal that animates Italian secular music after 1530.[18] The search for bold and surprising *effetti meravigliosi* produces a variety of styles whose sole aim is the vivid and astonishing depiction of poetical conceits. Concentration on decorative details and minute imitation results in a mosaiclike *maniera* in which eye music, aural figures, affective harmony, and unusual dissonances can be called into play in manifold combinations. Inspired by the idea of emulating the legendary marvels of ancient Greek music, musicians embark on a self-conscious program of surpassing at first the precepts of renaissance polyphony and then the stylized refinements of mannerist precedents. Because of the social and intellectual climate surrounding mannerist culture, audacious devices rapidly degenerate into conventional madrigalisms. On the one hand, this situation encourages an increasing grasp of imitative-affective figures as normative clichés, and on the other hand, it inspires ambitious mannerists to ever greater heights, or depths, of exaggerated and strained novelties.

As polyphony becomes more and more dramatic in intent, it eventually explodes into the soloistic concerted ensemble. At this point, the indigenous Italian love of solo singing emerges as the solution for dramatic vocal music. According to some historians, we have reached the Baroque. But the fact that musicians of the time emphasize the distortion and neglect of conservative rules demonstrates their mannerist outlook. Very few talk about new, viable musical laws operating as technical and self-sufficient guides for the second practice. And truth to say, much of this music, in spite of its logic (which we today observe from an impartial position), is still a product of the mannerist mentality. It shares with earlier Mannerism the deliberate exploitation of daring and even shocking *effetti meravigliosi*. And it also shares a curious blend of intellectual detachment—that plea for admiration and astonishment—with more direct emotional communication. This paradoxical ambivalence lies at the heart of an expressive and dramatic ideal that depends on rationalized imitative-affective devices. And insofar as traces of this ambivalence are still evident in any musical works of the Baroque, they bespeak a mannerist heritage.

At any rate, the intense experimentation, the vaunting of individual and virtuoso *maniere*, produces a plethora of styles, idioms, genres, and forms at the turn of the century. To be sure, distinctions among genres and styles existed in the Renaissance,[19] but they entailed very subtle gradations of variety within uniform musical practice. The distinctions we are talking about (which can be interpreted as another link between the three periods under review) are augmented by the force of accumulated experimentation with *imitazione delle parole*. I believe that the bewildering diversity of styles around 1600 must be seen as something more than an indication of transition. This situation is symptomatic of Mannerism itself, an artistic milieu that prizes above all the mystique of unusual and novel *maniere*.

Many historians with differing opinions as to the proper definition of Mannerism settle on the Italian madrigal because they see in it the most concrete manifestations of mannerist attitudes. This interpretation attests to the many styles and genres encompassed by the term. The first point on which there is general agreement concerns the exclusive and artificial atmosphere of courts, academies, and *ridotti*.[20] These circles encourage both high literary ideals and ultrarefined chamber music. The earliest stylizations, stylizations that present an eclectic combination of frottola, chanson, and motet principles, represent a desire to raise the act of setting Italian verse to equally refined musical *maniera*.[21] Most scholars who connect Mannerism or *maniera* to the madrigal emphasize its artificial and rational approach toward pictorializing every detail of the text. They speak of eye music and musical figures that, in the late phase of the madrigal, underlie a completely "literalized" style. In their view, the polyphonic madrigal at the end of the century constitutes a series of astonishing and marvelous rhetorical effects.[22]

Einstein sums up their assessments when he characterizes the polyphonic madrigal as an aberration or mannerist deviation from the solo song. Federhofer accepts this interpretation of the polyphonic madrigal, but rejects its connection with Mannerism because he sees it as a legitimate stylization.[23] This notion reveals his tacit definition of Mannerism, one that excludes any positive connotations. Federhofer thus contradicts the basic aesthetic premise of *maniera* as understood by all artists, poets, and musicians who practice it. The historical development of this side of madrigalian Mannerism begins with the occasional descriptive touches introduced in the lyrical works of the earliest generation of composers. The ensuing exaggeration of descriptive details may be attributed to two purely musical issues. One of these arises from the intellectual cultivation of startling effects, and it drives each generation of madrigalists to more intense and extravagant pictorialisms. The second issue is related to the first in that radical thought, the breeding ground of daring iconoclasm, continually stresses the need for progressive refinement and for surpassing the fabled eloquence of ancient music. But equally important is the rise of petrarchism and concettism in poetry itself. Mannerist composers are motivated not only by aesthetic and social circumstances connected with musical values, but also by the greater flights of fancy in poetry currently in fashion. And we must not forget that musicians, by virtue of their social affiliations, are constantly bombarded by ideas about *maniera*, genius, and the illusionistic magic of the *magus*—the maker of the "marvelous."

Most scholars stress the essentially rational aspect of madrigalisms, and do so with some justification. Their interpretation, however, is at odds with the mannerist conviction that such imitation of conceits also expresses and arouses the affections. To view this aesthetic as a crude and childish approach to fusing word and tone is tantamount to judging sixteenth- and early seventeenth-century beliefs by the canons of modern philosophy of music. And this unflattering assessment, moreover, relegates a group of gifted and sophisticated composers to the rank of infantile artists. Only eye music among the many pictorial tricks used by madrigalists may perhaps qualify as an artificial game of punning. Even in this case we may be imputing a glibness to this convention that is completely out of character. Aural devices of a graphic nature also belong to the category of imitative-affective madrigalisms. It is true that these elements of musical radicalism soon congeal into conventional idioms, a development that allows theorists to codify them as techniques of *musica poetica*. But precisely because these audacities become stereotypes, they also become the carriers of musical revolution. In the hands of gifted composers, these rational clichés take on qualities of inspired dramatic and lyrical pathos whose marvelous effect is unprecedented in the history of vocal music. Even if the reader does not agree with this historical assessment, he must remember that radical mannerists see their innovations in this light.

Scholars have tended to neglect the impulse toward overt dramatization evident in the madrigal from its inception. The countless rhetorical renderings of *sospiri*, *ahi*, and *oimè* in otherwise undramatic madrigals presage later exploitation of declamatory melody. When we arrive at soloistic treatment of individual voices, replete with elements of recitative and coloratura, musicologists talk of premonodic or preoperatic compositions. These terms reveal the customary bias of viewing certain traits as prebaroque features. And as long as the concept of Mannerism is ignored, one has no choice. Without any intention of minimizing the originality of such composers as Wert and Monteverdi, I insist that premonodic works do not spring from a void. On the contrary, they represent the final stylization of a long tradition, a tradition that reaches its climax only when poets themselves dramatize the lyrical sentimentality of earlier mannerist style in their own medium. It is my contention that this last phase of mannerist poetry receives its impetus from musical Mannerism, and that prebaroque dramatic music is really a phenomenon of Late Mannerism. This historical view does not attempt to deny that mannerist dramatization lives on, in certain adapted guises, in the baroque period. It merely draws our attention to the roots of this *maniera*, roots that are not to be found in renaissance music.

When these dramatic devices are finally fused with harmonic innovations established through long experimentation, the polyphonic madrigal attains its zenith. It can go no further as a genre in itself, and consequently yields to the accompanied ensemble and to monody. Now, harmonic audacity, especially chromaticism, seems to be such a glaring deviation from traditional style that it becomes the focus of both contemporary and modern analysts of *maniera*. Federhofer's rejection of chromaticism as a hallmark of Mannerism on the grounds that Josquin uses it in some motets arises from a misunderstanding of the historical situation.[24] Theorists and musicians alike realize that these audacious works depart drastically from the *ars perfecta*. When radical composers explore extended flat and sharp mutation, the old hexachord system in effect becomes circle-of-fifths modulation. Although such schemes are effected so that they seem to result from linear voice leading, they awaken an instinctive awareness of the dynamic properties of chordal entities. Elements of modern tonality may be present in the cadential patterns of popular and dance music. But we must attribute the gradual change from modal to tonal organization in some measure to this aspect of chromaticism, inasmuch as it throws "tonal cadences" into high relief. This very general statement is made with full cognizance of the modal-tonal ambiguities of much seventeenth-century music.

The other salient feature of chromaticism is, of course, the use of triads whose roots progress by thirds, semitones, and tritones. In my previous analyses, I have spoken in terms of vertical alignments for the sake of convenience, pointing out at the same time that these daring progressions result mainly from contrapuntal part-movement in semitonal configurations. Indeed, the number of successive and simultaneous linear semitones has been used to gauge degrees of complexity in that *maniera* Lowinsky calls floating triadic atonality. Chromatic experimentation is most popular in the middle decades of the sixteenth century. Usually, it appears in works whose texts require vivid and violent forms of expression; but it also develops into an independent musical *maniera*, a technical stylization as understood by Haar. This aspect permits chromaticism to make inroads into early seventeenth-century instrumental music, especially keyboard genres. After its initial paroxysm of activity, chromaticism subsides to become one element, but an extremely telling one, among many deployed for the sake of pictorial and dramatic purposes in the mosaic madrigal. Before being amalgamated into baroque vocabulary, it erupts once more in the personal eccentricities of Gesualdo's style.[25] Whereas the oft-repeated statement that Gesualdo's aberrations constitute a mannered decline is partially justified, the same cannot be said of chromaticism as a whole. Excessive chromaticism certainly does not dominate the *maniera* of all composers of madrigals.[26] Yet it is the acknowledged carrier of profound upheaval in the evolution of musical language. After 1570, its subtle nuances appear in every major composer, including Monteverdi. From a broad historical perspective, it is fair to say that mannerist chromaticism has a negative impact, distorting and destroying modal centricity. Even if we conclude that it contributes little to the rise of tonality, its widespread influence certainly augments the boldness of radical tendencies, boldness from which springs yet another mannerist stylization—the new freedom of dissonances.

In my view, it is not accidental that the first experiments with free dissonances as means of injecting startling effects begin after chromaticism has been transformed into a docile convention. Dissonances, no matter how they are deployed, always appear in graphic or emotionally charged contexts and thus fall into the category of imitative-affective devices. In their most extreme guise, free dissonances seen from a technical angle are farthest removed from renaissance practice and closest to baroque practice. And from this point of view, it makes sense to classify them as pre-baroque elements. Nonetheless, when we take into account contemporary discussions of such dissonances, discussions that stress their imitative-affective power on the aesthetic side and their deviation from standard rules on the technical side, the mannerist outlook of late sixteenth- and early seventeenth-century musicians becomes clear. In general terms, the degree of novelty connected with dissonance treatment depends on many factors: the number of accumulated dissonances in either horizontal or vertical alignment, the use of regular or irregular preparation and resolution, and the contexts created by stable diatonic or unstable chromatic harmonies. Although dissonance treatment in polyphony remains essentially linear in orientation, it contributes a new vertical sonority in one important instance—the dominant seventh chord. The reader is no doubt familiar with the commonplace idea that the introduction of the *basso continuo* is seminal to the development of free dissonances in baroque music. And yet, we have discovered many concrete instances where such dissonance treatment occurs in polyphonic madrigals without instrumental support. For this reason, I view the phenomenon of free dissonance treatment as one bridging the two eras.

As far as the other end of our historical continuum is concerned, we note Federhofer's rejection of free dissonance treatment as a criterion for differentiating between Mannerism and the Renaissance. This scholar believes that this assessment depends on a comparison of "modern" style with that of Palestrina rather than with that of Josquin, whose dissonances are admittedly more "free" than those of the former composer.[27] In my view, there are certain problems with this position. For one thing, one need only compare a circle-of-fifths passage in Josquin with one effected together with pungent dissonances in Marenzio, Pallavicino, or Monteverdi to grasp the fundamental change in harmonic sense between mature renaissance and mature mannerist styles. Moreover, in the period under discussion—that is, the turn of the sixteenth century—*contrapunto osservato* by and large embraces a *maniera* of its own, a decorous stylization of idealized renaissance principles. By this time, Josquin and his music have become a legend rather than a living reality. And contemporary assessments of *contrapunto moderno*, whether positive or negative, are always made in reference to traditional *maniera*. It is not a question of imposing value judgments on the styles of, let us say, Josquin and Monteverdi. Both are exceptionally gifted and imaginative composers. But Josquin's dissonance treatment presumes renaissance ideals whereas Monteverdi's cannot be understood without his mannerist heritage. For this reason, I conclude that even an historical comparison between the two presumes a false premise, a premise that can be corrected by inserting Mannerism between the Renaissance and the Baroque.

Bold dissonance usage remains a rhetorical ornament for more traditional mannerist polyphony in the case of composers such as Marenzio and Pallavicino. In the music of Wert, Luzzaschi, and Monteverdi, on the other hand, it becomes the moving force behind the intrusion of declamatory recitative and vocal coloratura. The reader will note that at this stage we can speak of conservative and radical Mannerism. The emergence of the latter represents at once the end of the mannerist career of the madrigal and the start of its baroque phase. Any comparisons made between Late Mannerism and the High Renaissance in musical terms leave no doubt that a fundamental alteration in style norms has taken place, and furthermore, an alteration that notions couched in terms of late-renaissance or early-baroque principles cannot adequately explain. However, it is equally true that a comparison between early and late Mannerism in itself reveals a startling change. The mannerist aesthetic, cherishing as it does the vaunting of novelty, forms the background for this development.

Although the manifestations of *maniere* are as many as the cases of personal inspiration, mannerist style in the madrigal can be divided into two general types. The first corresponds to the *maniera dolce*, the sweet lyrical style in which decorative variety leads to artificial preciosity and refined elegance. This *maniera* is evident in both polyphonic and monodic madrigals, as we have seen. Because Shearman restricts his definition of Mannerism to this particular aspect, he considers composers such as Verdelot, Corteccia, Striggio, Marenzio, and Monte as mannerists. By the same token, he excludes Willaert, Rore, Gesualdo, and Monteverdi, composers whom he prefers to see as belonging to the early or mature Baroque,[28] because he views their decided emphasis on affective pathos and dramatic monumentalism as foreign to Mannerism. And, of course, he does not mention the bizarre qualities evident in the music of Vicentino, Lasso, and Gesualdo. I take the opposite stand, for I believe that elements of grotesque virtuosity, grandiose illusion, and dramatic pathos (the *maniera grande*) are integral to the mannerist outlook. They are present in art, poetry, and the madrigal as well. In the case of the madrigal, whether polyphonic or monodic, the use of imitative-affective devices can create an aura of languid sentimentality or of forceful psychological drama. Both qualities, which can be fused in one composition, rely on self-conscious stylization, and they are bound up with the dominating aesthetic that inspires composers from Arcadelt to Monteverdi—*Ut musica poesis*. This aesthetic certainly comes to the fore in the numerous writings on *maniera* and its virtues produced by theorists, musicians, and music lovers during the sixteenth century.

However one may choose to evaluate the artistic merit of any mannerist phenomenon in music, the historical fact remains that the aesthetic legacy of this period becomes the touchstone of baroque style. Both the stylized *maniera* of traditional polyphony and the rhetorical stylization of madrigalian notoriety are transformed into a rational system of figures by Burmeister. His notion of *musica poetica* in turn provides the basis for the baroque *Affektenlehre* and *Figurenlehre*. Monteverdi's famous formulation of the *seconda prattica* is recognized by musicologists as the first detailed announcement of a new style of music that departs from older practice in a radical way. However, I have taken some pains to demonstrate that Monteverdi's statement is by no means the first one to defend this viewpoint. Even if we restrict the present discussion to Monteverdi's pronouncement, I here remind the reader that this composer traces the development of the second practice or style through composers who represent various stages of Mannerism. And Monteverdi's consciousness of style, which I interpret as the ultimate outcome of generations of writings on *maniera*, is transmitted to the Baroque, an era preoccupied with theories of style.

Following the initiative of baroque theorists as well as earlier exponents of new music, historians searching for the beginnings of baroque practice look to the polyphonic madrigal. The combined force of its rhetorical aesthetic and its technical innovations is hailed as a salient precedent for both general and concrete elements evident in baroque music. In opposition to this position, Shearman and Haar both believe that the second practice cannot be considered mannerist on the grounds of its dynamic, sensuous, and forceful emotional expression. Haar, however, concedes that this style can be seen as an outgrowth of certain earlier *maniere*, only those that embody ideals of rhetorical eloquence.[29] Naturally, I agree with Haar's point of view, and differ only in finding more evidence of the rhetorical ideal in the polyphonic madrigal than he does. At any rate, if one concedes that baroque criteria are potentially and sometimes actually present in earlier forms of Mannerism, then it is possible to see at once the continuation of mannerist techniques and the invention of newer baroque ones as coexisting in the works of the *seconda prattica*. This interpretation also has the advantage of facilitating a distinction between the *seconda prattica*, a transition between mannerist and baroque attitudes, and mature baroque style.

Interpretations that stress a sharp division between sixteenth-century Mannerism and the seventeenth-century Baroque receive apparent support from the attitudes of Galilei and the Camerata. However, their attack on both traditional and mannerist polyphony stems less from the real musical situation than from polemical exigencies. Harrán links their protestations to Friedländer's concept of the Baroque as an antimannerist movement.[30] This evaluation is viable inasmuch as it reflects the avowed values of militant monodists. But the musical facts also speak for themselves. Early monody owes much to the late mannerist madrigal. To see early seventeenth-century solo music as a return to simplicity and to contact with reality is to oversimplify the truth. As Fortune points out, a great deal of solo and ensemble music of this period retains the extravagant and audacious elements of mannerist style.[31] Even the bland diatonicism of Caccini's arias partakes of stylized artificiality.[32] And opera, which might be cited as a truly baroque invention, is in reality an amalgamation of mannerist intermedios, dramatic pastorals, and recitative principles. All these musical *maniere*, regardless of their leanings toward either mannerist or baroque techniques, seek to astonish and delight the refined tastes of connoisseurs. In short, I believe that the mannerist elements of early seventeenth-century genres and styles have been underestimated. At the same time, I do not deny that the baroque specialist justly stresses those elements that bespeak a technical continuity with musical language characteristic of the seventeenth century.

But even in this case, I maintain that the aesthetic premise behind the usage of such technical ingredients is a mannerist one.

It is only after 1630, when, incidentally, terms such as "solo madrigal" and *favola in musica* disappear, that transitional elements give way to those associated with the practice of the mature baroque style. To trace this evolution lies beyond the scope of the present study. Suffice it to say that most specialists in baroque studies agree in singling out the "early," "proto" or "pre" qualities in the late sixteenth and early seventeenth centuries. But when these qualities are traced further back into the sixteenth century, the need for a concept of Mannerism becomes all the more necessary. To illustrate this point, I cite the case of one writer who, being aware that Monteverdi's *Orfeo* is qualitatively different from his later operas, suggests, in terms that are difficult to fathom, that *Orfeo* is more "baroque" than Monteverdi's later baroque operas.[33] My thesis is that Monteverdi's *Orfeo*, while containing some "baroque" elements, is more mannerist than his later baroque operas.

Musical theory and composition between 1530 and 1630 demonstrate that thought and practice alike are dominated by concepts of *maniera*. And *maniera* comprises not only purely musical or technical stylization but also aesthetic stylization of rhetorical ideals. *Maniera* also embraces idealization of a conservative cast as well as various manifestations of radical experimentation. As far as the radical side of *maniera* is concerned, I believe that humanist notions about classical antiquity, historical progress, refinement, novelty, and genius form a complex of interrelated issues that animates every aspect of mannerist activity. In general and in specific terms, intellectual ideas are not just antiquarianism; they inform artistic practice. The startling and often strikingly beautiful works created by composers during this period form a continuous historical and stylistic whole that can be grasped and described in musical terms. At the same time, both theoretical and practical evidence strongly suggests that music is an integral element of a cultural framework.[34] Music does not lag one hundred years behind the other arts. On the contrary, during the mannerist period, music not only keeps pace with other developments, but also stands in the vanguard of stylistic trends. In all its aspects—technical, aesthetic, intellectual, and social—music between 1530 and 1630 represents one of the stellar achievements of the Age of Mannerism. In its own terms and in its manifold connections with intellectual history, music embodies the *effetto meraviglioso*, the *bella maniera*, with particular distinction, felicity, and significance.

Notes
Bibliography
Index of Names
Index of Titles

Notes

Chapter 1

1. See Maria R. Maniates, "Musical Mannerism: Effeteness or Virility?"
2. Eugenio Battisti, "Lo spirito del manierismo," p. 3; Craig H. Smyth, *Mannerism and Maniera*, p. 3; and Angus Fletcher, *Allegory*, p. 101.
3. As in Walter Friedländer, *Mannerism and Anti-Mannerism in Italian Painting*; Wylie Sypher, *Four Stages of Renaissance Style*, pt. III; and Gustav R. Hocke, *Der Neomanierismus*.
4. See John Shearman, *Mannerism*.
5. Various historical views can be found in the following: Battisti, "Sfortune del manierismo"; Giusta Nicco Fasola, "Storiografica del manierismo"; E. H. Gombrich, "Introduction: the Historical Background"; Friedrich Piel, "Zum Problem des Manierismus in der Kunstgeschichte"; Ezio Raimondi, "Per la nozione di manierismo letterario"; Shearman, "Maniera as an Aesthetic Ideal"; Smyth, *Mannerism and Maniera*; Marco Treves, "*Maniera*, the History of a Word"; and Georg Weise, "Storia del termine 'Manierismo.'"
6. See especially, Fritz Baumgart, *Renaissance und Kunst des Manierismus*; Arnold Hauser, *Mannerism*; and Hocke, *Die Welt als Labyrinth* and *Manierismus in der Literatur*.
7. Hauser, *Mannerism*, p. 112; and Johan Huizinga, *Homo ludens*.
8. By Rosalie Colie.
9. Renato Poggioli, *The Theory of the Avant-Garde*, p. 14.
10. Ibid., p. 74.
11. Ibid., p. 79.
12. Linda Murray, *The Late Renaissance and Mannerism*, p. 30.
13. Battisti, *L'antirinascimento*. Hiram Haydn calls his study *The Counter-Renaissance*.
14. Shearman, *Mannerism*, p. 15.
15. For example, Jacques Bousquet, *La peinture maniériste*; Alastair Smart, *The Renaissance and Mannerism in Northern Europe and Spain*; and Franzsepp Würtenberger, *Mannerism*.
16. Hauser, *Mannerism*, p. 28.
17. Friedländer, *Mannerism and Anti-Mannerism*, p. 49.
18. Hauser, *Mannerism*, p. xvii.

CHAPTER II

1. Würtenberger, *Mannerism*, p. 7.

2. André Chastel, *Art et humanisme à Florence au temps de Laurent le Magnifique*, p. 96.

3. For example, Leon Battista Alberti's *Della pittura* (ca. 1535) and Piero della Francesca's *De prospectiva pingendi* (ca. 1482). Paul O. Kristeller, "The Modern System of the Arts," p. 182; and Smart, *The Renaissance and Mannerism in Italy*, p. 35. Further information on treatises, letters, artworks, and poems can be found in the Bibliography of primary sources.

4. Since Dürer refers only to someone in Bologna, scholars presume he meant Pacioli. "Letter to W. Pirckheimer" (1506).

5. *Divina proportione* (1509).

6. *Dialogo di pittura* (1548), Venice, 1946, pp. 105–7.

7. *Paragone* is the modern title given to the first "chapter" of the *Trattato della pittura*, a set of notes compiled by Leonardo's pupil, Francesco Melzi.

8. Irma A. Richter, ed., *Paragone*, p. 61.

9. Ibid., pp. 94–109.

10. As in, for example, Pino's *Dialogo*, p. 85.

11. Jean H. Hagstrum, *The Sister Arts*, p. 66.

12. As indicative of this situation. I cite the following works: Benedetto Varchi's famous circular (1549); Pino's treatise championing painting; and Anton Francesco Doni's rebuttal defending sculpture (*Disegno*, 1549).

13. Shearman, "Maniera as an Aesthetic Ideal," p. 204.

14. *Il riposo* (1584), p. 159.

15. Weise, "La doppia origine del concetto di manierismo," pp. 184–85.

16. Erwin Panofsky, *Idea*, p. 47. For an analysis of the meanings of nature in renaissance aesthetics, see Harold S. Wilson, "Some Meanings of 'Nature' in Renaissance Literary Theory."

17. Anthony Blunt, *Artistic Theory in Italy, 1450–1600*, p. 30; and Panofsky, *Idea*, p. 48.

18. Panofsky, *Idea*, p. 49.

19. "Letter to Pope Leo X" (1519), Vatican City, 1971, p. 85.

20. *Le vite de'più eccellenti architetti pittori et scultori italiani* (1550; second enlarged edition, with a slightly different title, 1568). The ensuing discussion amalgamates material from the "Prefaces" to pts. II and III of the *Vite*.

21. Gombrich, *Art and Illusion*, p. 10 (italics mine). This confusion is in part responsible for current debate over Mannerism, but it also underlies sixteenth-century debates over the merits of mannerist art and music.

22. The reader will note the paradoxical words, "effortless intensity."

23. Blunt, *Artistic Theory*, pp. 90–91.

24. "Introduction: Of Sculpture," chap. 8, sec. 37. The original Italian reads as follows: *più di maniera che di natura*.

25. Shearman, "Maniera," p. 206.

26. *Trattato dell'arte della pittura scultura et architettura* (1584) and *L'idea del tempio della pittura* (1590). Mark W. Roskill, *Dolce's 'Aretino' and Venetian Art Theory of the Cinquecento*, p. 65.

27. *Trattato*, bk. I, chap. 1. This excerpt, taken from a sixteenth-century English translation, is also available in the following sources: Elizabeth G. Holt,

ed., *A Documentary History of Art*, pp. 77–79; and Robert E. Wolf and Ronald Millen, *Renaissance and Mannerist Art*, p. 11. A modern English version can be found in Shearman, *Mannerism*, p. 81.

28. Bk. I, chap. 2 of Lomazzo's *Trattato* is devoted to this subject.

29. Ibid., bk. VI, chap. 2.

30. Ibid., bks. III and VII.

31. Ibid., bks. V and VI.

32. Rensselaer W. Lee, "*Ut pictura poesis*," p. 207.

33. Charles Bouleau, *The Painter's Secret Geometry*, p. 147.

34. *L'idea del tempio della pittura* (1590), chap. 26.

35. Panofsky, *Idea*, pp. 25–32 and 96; Blunt, *Artistic Theory*, p. 142; and Gombrich, *Art and Illusion*, pp. 155–56.

36. *L'idea de'pittori scultori e architetti* (1607).

37. Ibid., bk. II, chaps. 4 and 6.

38. Ibid., bk. I, chap. 3.

39. Ibid., chaps. 3 and 7. Zuccaro demonstrates this notion with a mannerist pun—*di-segn-o* interpreted as *segno di dio in noi*. Ibid., bk. II, chap. 16. Panofsky, *Idea*, p. 188.

40. *L'idea*, bk. II, chaps. 3 and 4.

41. *Dialogo della pittura intitolato l'Aretino* (1557). All citations come from the modern edition, New York, 1968.

42. Ibid., pp. 23 and 118–57.

43. Ibid., p. 91.

44. Ibid., pp. 176–77.

45. Aretino published a bitter condemnation of the *Last Judgment*. Although part of his attitude stems from aesthetic convictions, a great deal of it results from purely personal enmity. See Edward Hutton, *Aretino, Scourge of Princes*; and Robert Klein and Henri Zerner, eds., *Italian Art 1500–1600*.

46. *Dialogo*, pp. 163, 167. This painting is also the prime target of the criticism directed against *maniera* by Giovanni Andrea Gilio da Fabriano in his *Due dialoghi . . . nel secondo si ragione degli errori de'pittori* (1564).

47. The reason for this defense, of course, is Aretino's involvement in the escapade. See Hutton, *Aretino*; and James Cleugh, *The Divine Aretino*.

48. Noted by Roskill, *Dolce's 'Aretino,'* p. 6.

49. Blunt, *Artistic Theory*, pp. 94–96. These characteristics will be strongly condemned by antimannerist critics of the seventeenth century. From their opinion evolves the commonplace notion of Mannerism referred to in the first chapter.

50. Würtenberger, *Mannerism*, p. 44.

CHAPTER III

1. The rhetorical view of poetry was not unknown in medieval theory; however, its renewal by humanists endows it with special potential for mannerist aesthetics.

2. For example, Baxter Hathaway, *The Age of Criticism*; and Bernard Weinberg, *A History of Literary Criticism in the Italian Renaissance*.

3. The two treatises that thrust this topic into prominence are: Francesco Robortello's *In librum Aristotelis de arte poetica explicationes* (1548); and

Vincenzo Maggi's and Bartolomeo Lombardi's *In Aristotelis librum de poetica communes explanationes* (1550). Hathaway, *Age of Criticism*, pp. 205–6.

4. *Discorsi del poema eroico* (1594), Pisa, 1823, 12:9–10, and Oxford, 1970, pp. 7–8.

5. For a detailed discussion of this controversy, consult Nicolas J. Perella, *The Critical Fortune of Battista Guarini's "Il Pastor Fido."*

6. *Della poesia rappresentativa e del modo di rappresentare le favole sceniche* (1598), p. 37.

7. *Compendio della poesia tragicomica* (1601), Venice, 1602, pp. 15 and 22. This idea also appears in Francesco Buonamici's *Discorsi poetici* (1597). See Hathaway, *Age of Criticism*, p. 278.

8. Hathaway, *Age of Criticism*, p. 3.

9. *I romanzi* (1554), pp. 15–16 and 50.

10. *Della imitatione poetica* (1560), pp. 92–94.

11. *Della difesa della Comedia di Dante* (1587), pt. I, secs. 18–19. Mazzoni's two platonic categories are also discussed by Tasso in the *Discorsi*, Pisa, 1823, 12:34, and Oxford, 1970, pp. 28–29.

12. *Discorsi poetici* (1597), pp. 24–25. In theories of art, these three classifications are defined as extravagant stylization, classical naturalism, and subtle stylization.

13. *Della poetica* (1586); *La deca disputata*, bks. III and IV. This mammoth treatise was projected as ten separate books of which only two, *La deca istoriale* and *La deca disputata*, appeared in print in 1586; five other books exist in manuscript. *La deca istoriale* contains a discussion of musical theories of antiquity that sparked a bitter argument between Ercole Bottrigari, whose *Il Patricio overo de'tetrachordi armonici* (1593) was attacked by Giovanni Maria Artusi in his *Considerationi musicali*, appended to *L'Artusi overo delle imperfettioni della moderna musica*, pt. II (1603). Even though much of this debate concentrates on interpretations of ancient sources, it nonetheless impinges on the controversy over modern trends in music, particularly in those cases where ancient authorities are cited as justification for iconoclastic devices put into practice in contemporary music (i.e., Nicola Vicentino, Claudio Monteverdi, and the anonymous L'Ottuso Accademico).

14. *Della poetica* (1590), p. 583. The same point is made in pt. III of Varchi's earlier tract, *Lezzione* (1549), Bari, 1960, 1:55.

15. *Ragionamento sopra le cose pertinenti alla poesia* (1581), p. 49. Hathaway, *Age of Criticism*, pp. 47–48.

16. *Lezione* (1599), Naples, 1733, 1:347–49. Hathaway, *Age of Criticism*, p. 59.

17. Giulio Cesare Cortese is apparently one of the first writers to analyze systematically the *concetto*, a device whose presence seems to define poetry as such. *Avvertimenti nel poetare* (1591), *Dell'imitatione e dell'inventione* (1591), and *Delle figure* (1591). Cortese warns that the *concetto* must be complex but not too difficult to comprehend. Its function is to imitate an action of the mind. Weinberg, *History of Literary Criticism*, pp. 235–36. These views, like those of Vasari, entail contradictory criteria—namely, obscurity versus comprehensibility.

18. *Del concetto poetico* (1598), Naples, 1898, p. 332.

19. These references occur in some letters quoted by James V. Mirollo in *The Poet of the Marvelous: Giambattista Marino*, p. 116.

20. *Agudeza y arte de ingenio* (1642; revised edition 1648), Madrid, 1929, p. 7.

21. Bousquet, *La peinture maniériste*, p. 231.

22. *Considerazioni sopra l'arte dello stile e del dialogo* (1646), Modena, 1819, p. 79. Mirollo, *Giambattista Marino*, p. 117.

23. *Il cannocchiale aristotelico* (1654; second enlarged edition 1663), chap. 1. The praiseworthy evaluation of artistic illusion also emerges in Tasso's use of the word "dissimulators" to characterize poets, rhetoricians, musicians, and actors. *La Cavaletta* (1587), Pisa, 1822, 7: 297–301.

24. *Agudeza*, p. 6.

25. Frank Kermode, *Romantic Image*, p. 2. They also exhibit strong similarities to art theory.

26. *I romanzi* (1554), p. 51.

27. *Discorso intorno al comporre de i romanzi delle comedie e delle tragedie* (1554), Milan, 1973, p. 75.

28. Ibid., pp. 58–60. Elsewhere, Cintio cautions the poet against labyrinthine poetry. Ibid., p. 87.

29. Ibid., pp. 76–77.

30. Ibid., p. 88.

31. *Discorsi sopra Virgilio* (ca. 1562), p. 174. In spite of Hathaway's denial that Speroni defines Mannerism (in *The Age of Criticism*, pp. 196–97), I feel that his ideas on ornamentation represent one source from which mannerist extravagance stems. Speroni himself was the foremost member of the Paduan Accademia degli Infiammati, a group which supported concettist style in literature, and Speroni's own dramas aroused some controversy because of their mannerist leanings. Hathaway, *Marvels and Commonplaces*, p. 13. Moreover, Speroni's apposition between Virgil and Homer can be construed along the lines of an apposition between "serious" and "rhetorical" literatures as enunciated by Richard S. Lanham in *The Motives of Eloquence*. Lanham's audacious reevaluation of rhetorical style addresses primarily a set of literary works and not a body of critical literature, but it seems to me that his principles, applied to sixteenth-century treatises, would yield some surprising and provocative results.

32. *Della imitatione poetica* (1560), pp. 34 and 80.

33. *Del concetto poetico* (1598), Naples, 1898, p. 336.

34. *Il Caraffa overo dell'epica poesia* (1584), Bari, 1972, 3:321 and 338.

35. *Discorsi del poema eroico* (1594), Pisa, 1823, 12:124–25, and Oxford, 1970, p. 120. Tasso uses the following words to describe the high style: *grave, grandezza, splendido, sublime*. In addition, bk. v explores the figures of rhetoric that contribute to the sublime style. For a discussion of the sublime and other style categories in the sixteenth century, see Annabel Patterson, *Hermogenes and the Renaissance*.

36. Shearman, *Mannerism*, p. 151. In Bk. I, Tasso compares Virgil with Homer, concluding that the former lacks the latter's fecund abundance of ornaments. *Discorsi*, Pisa, 1823, 12:63, and Oxford, 1970, p. 55. Earlier in the same book, Tasso notes that a narrow definition of the epic as a solely heroic genre, one based on Aristotle's description of Homer, has caused critics to deny the propriety of love themes and to castigate such amorous episodes in his own poem. Ibid., Pisa, 1823, 12:51–52, and Oxford, 1970, pp. 44–45. Tasso, of

course, stresses the importance of *meraviglia* and variety, even suggesting that these qualities can please jaded tastes. Ibid., Pisa, 1823, 12:88–89, and Oxford, 1970, p. 77. And he also insists that the epic should unite the solemnity of tragedy with the flowery ornamentation of the lyric. Ibid., Pisa, 1823, 12:160, and Oxford, 1970, p. 137.

37. *Considerazioni sopra l'arte dello stile e del dialogo* (1646), Modena, 1819, pp. 54–55. Hagstrum, *The Sister Arts*, pp. xx–xxi; and Mirollo, *Giambattista Marino*, p. 119.

38. *Il cannocchiale*, chap. 7.

39. Colie, *Paradoxia epidemica*, p. 304; and Robert J. Clements, *Picta Poesis*, p. 27.

40. Edward E. Lowinsky, "Matthaeus Greiter's *Fortuna*," p. 512.

41. *Agudeza*, p. 7.

42. *Il cannocchiale*, chap. 2.

43. Mirollo, *Giambattista Marino*, pp. 166–67.

44. Weinberg, *History of Literary Criticism*, p. 773. This phrase becomes a commonplace; but I cite one source here—the title of bk. IV of Patrizi's *La deca ammirabile*, "Come il poetà è facitore del mirabile."

45. Kermode, *Romantic Image*, pp. 2–3.

46. *Discorso della diversità de i furori poetici* (1553). The tracts on this subject are too many to list here. But I mention two: Lorenzo Giacomini's *Del furor poetico*, presented to the Accademia degli Alterati in Florence (1587); and Giordano Bruno's celebrated work, *De gl'heroici furori* (1585).

CHAPTER IV

1. For this kind of technical comparison, see Daniel P. Rowland, *Mannerism —Style and Mood*. Sypher uses a similar method to compare art and literature in his *Four Stages of Renaissance Style*.

2. Weise, "Storia del termine 'Manierismo,'" p. 33. This view goes back to Vasari.

3. Sylvie Béguin, *L'école de Fontainebleau*, p. 30.

4. Hans Hoffmann, *Hochrenaissance, Manierismus, Frühbarock*, p. 175.

5. Hauser, *Mannerism*, pp. 201–2.

6. Shearman, *Mannerism*, pp. 15–19.

7. Friedländer, *Mannerism and Anti-Mannerism*, p. 48. Mario Praz supports this notion of virile and epigonal phases in his *Bellezza e bizzarria*, p. 36.

8. Frederick Hartt, "Power and the Individual in Mannerist Art," p. 238.

9. *St. Sebastian* (1525).

10. The transfiguration of Christ, and the boy possessed by the Devil, from St. Matthew and St. Mark. Hauser, *Mannerism*, p. 160. There may also exist a covert symbolic meaning known only to learned humanists.

11. *Last Judgment* or *St. Michael* (1538).

12. *Visitation* (1514–16).

13. *Dead Christ with Angels* (ca. 1526).

14. Wolf and Millen, *Renaissance and Mannerist Art*, p. 81.

15. *Eleonora of Toledo* (ca. 1545–46) and *A Young Man* (ca. 1538).

16. Friedländer, *Mannerism and Anti-Mannerism*, p. 27.

17. Nicolaus Pevsner, "The Architecture of Mannerism," p. 121.

18. *Conversion of St. Paul* (1555).

19. Hauser, *Mannerism*, p. 210.

20. Wolf and Millen, *Renaissance and Mannerist Art*, p. 114.

21. For a discussion of this peculiar phenomenon, see Shearman, *Mannerism*, pp. 124–26.

22. Three scholars—Hauser, *Mannerism*; Bousquet, *La peinture maniériste*; and Rudolf Wittkower, *Architectural Principles in the Age of Humanism*—consider Palladio to be a mannerist; two others—Wolfgang Lotz, "Mannerism in Architecture"; and Werner Hager, "Zur Raumstruktur des Manierismus in der italienischen Architektur"—dispute this view.

23. Consult Wittkower's *Architectural Principles* in which he explores the use of zarlinian proportions by Palladio.

24. Shearman, *Mannerism*, p. 118. These steps are now located in S. Stefano.

25. Ibid., p. 122; plate 65.

26. Hoffmann, *Hochrenaissance, Manierismus, Frühbarock*, p. 175.

27. Francis Haskell, "The Moment of Mannerism," p. 69.

Chapter v

1. The estimate put forward by Hauser—to wit, that literary scholarship makes no use of Mannerism—is misleading. *Mannerism*, p. 272. Nor is it accurate to emphasize, as do Federhofer and Mirollo, the debate over literary Mannerism as if this situation were unique. Hellmut Federhofer, "Zum Manierismus-Problem in der Musik," p. 110; and Mirollo, "The Mannered and the Mannerist in Late Renaissance Literature," p. 7.

2. Mirollo, *Giambattista Marino*, p. 271. In his later article, "The Mannered and the Mannerist," Mirollo revises his negative view of Mannerism in a careful way.

3. Ferruccio Ulivi, "Il manierismo del Tasso e altri studi," p. 149.

4. Iain Fletcher, "From Tasso to Marino," p. 129.

5. Odette de Mourgues, *Metaphysical Baroque and Précieux Poetry*, p. 108.

6. This specific mannerist tendency is explored by Paolo Fabbri; however, he does not make parallels with the grand manner in the visual arts. "Tasso, Guarini e il 'divino Claudio.'"

7. Joseph Kerman, *The Elizabethan Madrigal*, p. 3. I refer here to extemporized solo recitation.

8. Leonard Forster, *The Icy Fire*, pp. 24–25.

9. Mirollo, *Giambattista Marino*, p. 196.

10. From *O bella man* (*In vita*, No. 166). The fingers or fingernails of the beloved's hand are "five pearls of oriental color."

11. (*In vita*, No. 208). "The air that the verdant laurel and her golden hair Rustles, sweetly sighing"; Tasso cites this line in his *Discorsi del poema eroico* (1594), Pisa, 1823, 12:172, and Oxford, 1970, p. 176. My translations aim at reflecting as closely as possible the diction and verse structure of the original. Although they are presented in paragraph form, capitalization parallels the line structure of the Italian given in the text.

12. (*In vita*, No. 172). "Sweet angers, sweet disdains, and sweet reconcilements, Sweet ill, sweet pang, and sweet burden, Sweet speaking and sweetly understood, Full now of a sweet air, now of sweet torches. . . ."

13. The parallel to pictorial *contrapposto* is made by two scholars. Shearman, *Mannerism*, p. 83; and Weise, "Manierismo e letteratura," p. 7. Weise also gives several pages of examples.

14. (*In morte*, No. 86). "Sweet harshnesses and placid repulses, Full of chaste love and of pity, Charming disdains, that my inflamed Desires have tempered. . . ."

15. "O you, who sigh in [long for] finer notes [nights], Who harken to Love or speak in rhyme, Entreat that for me Death be not more mute, Haven of miseries and end of lamenting; Let her change, for once, her antique style, That grieves all men and can make me so happy."

16. Shearman, *Mannerism*, p. 42.

17. Evidence for this approach can be found in Bembo's verse as well as in his writings; for example, *Prose . . . nelle quali si ragione della volgar lingua* (1525).

18. Kerman, *Elizabethan Madrigal*, p. 3; and Hans Engel, "Werden und Wesen des Madrigals," p. 46.

19. "O wild stars, henceforth give me peace, And you, Fortune, change your rough style; Give me back to the shepherds and to the woods, To primal (ancient) singing, to those customary fires; For I am not strong enough to sustain the war That Love makes on me with his ruthless string."

20. "Nothing else is my love than actual hell, And because it is nothing but hell it is deprived of meeting, Of contemplating in the sky one single living god, And there is no other grief in the eternal fire; Therefore, actual hell is my love, Because I am totally deprived of seeing that sun, my beloved, which I solely desire to see; Ah, the power of love, how strong it is, If it rather feel hell instead of death!" For a detailed discussion of this poem, see James Haar, "Altro non è il mio amor."

21. "Again in parting, I feel myself dying; I should like to part from you every hour, every moment, so great is the pleasure I feel in the life I acquire in returning; And so, a thousand and a thousand times a day I should like to part from you, So sweet are my returns."

22. Claude V. Palisca, *Baroque Music*, p. 13. It is confusing to use the epithet, antipetrarchist, to characterize poets who seem to express sincere intensity, as does Joseph Tusiani, *Italian Poets of the Renaissance*, Preface. We must simply distinguish between good and bad imitators of petrarchan style.

23. The two poems are analyzed in Mirollo, *Giambattista Marino*, pp. 185–86. This scholar does not mention a sonnet by Antonio Minturno that is clearly related to them:

O Sonno, de'mortai mirabil freno,
O caldo spron del pensier vago e scorto,
O d'afflitte virtuti almo sereno,
O de le pene altrui dolce conforto;
O di pace beato e lieto seno,
A le tempeste mie tranquillo porto,
O riposo, non mai laudato appieno,
Se non fosse il tuo ben fugace e corto;
Placido re di sogni, antico padre
Di forme erranti, che dal ciel discendi
A serenar le notti oscure e adre;

Manda, prego, il mio sole; e col bel raggio
D'amorosa dolcezza il cor raccendi,
Ch'altro diletto, che'l sognar, non aggio.

"O Sleep, of mortals the miraculous restraint, O hot spur of erratic and broken thought, O serene soul of afflicted powers, O sweet comfort of others' pains; O womb of blissful and happy peace, Tranquil haven of my tempests, O rest, nonetheless praised, Even if your benefit be fleeting and short; Placid king of dreams, ancient father Of errant forms, who from the sky descends to clear the dark and angry nights; Send, I pray, my sun; and with a beautiful ray Of amorous sweetness mend my heart, So that I need no other delight except to dream."

24. "O Sleep, O placid son of the quiet, humid, dark Night; O, of Afflicted mortals the comfort, the sweet oblivion of ills so grave, because of which life is harsh and burdensome; Relieve my heart, at last, that languishes and rest Does not have; and these tired and frail limbs Comfort; fly to me, O Sleep, and Your brown wings over me spread and rest; Where is the silence that flees both the day and the light? And the soft dreams that with vague Traces usually follow you? Alas, that in vain I call you; and these dark And frigid shadows in vain I coax; O feathers Filled with bitterness! O harsh and cruel nights!" It is interesting to note that Tasso cites the effective use of enjambement in this poem. *Discorsi* (1594), Pisa, 1823, 12:145–46, and Oxford, 1970, p. 143.

25. "So sweet is the fire and the knot With which Love inflames me, with which it binds me, That I rejoice both burned and caught; Nor would I seek ever to extinguish or untie The fire and the string; instead I continuously desire My heart to consume itself in such sweet tempers."

26. "It is not, alas, torture To die, lady, to please you, If the reason for my death is such That it makes good every ill; But what torments me Is that you may be contented with my death, And at the first glimpse of another gallant, Your heart may change; Is it not, then, torture, To die, lady, to please you?"

27. "Mercy, I shriek, wailing, But who hears me? Ah alas! I faint; I shall die, therefore, silently; Ah, for pity's sake at least, Sweet treasure of my heart, Would that I could have told you before I died: 'I die! I die!'"

28. "Painful tortures, violent torments, Hard fetters, pitiless ropes, hard chains, In which I, the night, the days, hours, and moments, Miserable, weep for my lost love; Sad voices, complaints, howls, and laments, Thick tears and continuous pains, Are the food and the dear solace As well as every wormwood of my bitter life."

29. Forster, *Icy Fire*, p. 64. Needless to say, frivolity can be stretched to giddy proportions, as in comic *capitoli*; for example, Angelo Bronzino's *To a Brush and a Radish*, and Benedetto Varchi's *To Hard Eggs*.

30. *La Cavaletta* (1587), Pisa, 1822, 7:310–11.

31. *Considerazioni sopra tre canzoni di M. Gio. Pigna* (1568), Pisa, 1823, 11:33.

32. Fletcher, "Tasso to Marino," p. 129.

33. "Behold, the waves murmur, And the leaves tremble, In the morning breeze [so do] the little bushes, And over the verdant branches the charming birds Sing sweetly, And the east smiles; Behold, already the dawn appears And is mirrored in the sea, And the sky brightens, And the sweet dew adorns the countryside with pearls, And gilds the high mountains; O beautiful and charming

Aurora, The breeze is your messenger, and you [are the messenger] of the breeze That restores every parched heart."

34. "No more war! Pity! My beautiful eyes; My triumphant eyes, for whom do you arm yourselves? Against a heart that is already captured and surrenders to you! Slay the rebellious, slay the one who arms and defends himself, Not him who, vanquished, adores you; Do you wish that I should die? Then I shall die for you, and death's sting Will I feel, yes, but yours shall be the loss [wound]."

35. Alfred Einstein, *The Italian Madrigal*, p. 542.

36. Fletcher, "Tasso to Marino," p. 135.

37. "Here I am ready for kisses; Kiss me, my Ergasto, but kiss me in such a way That from your biting teeth No mark remains engraved on my visage; So that others do not point at me and then there Read my disgrace and your kisses; Ah, you bite and do not kiss! You have marked me, ah! ah! May I die if I kiss you ever again!"

38. Mirollo, *Giambattista Marino*, p. 126.

39. "'Farewell, fair Florida, my wounded heart In my parting I leave with you, and I carry with me, The memory of you, just as with him The wounded stag bears the winged arrow'; 'My Floro, farewell, for the bitter state Of our blind life may Love console you, For if your heart stays with me, mine goes with you, Just as the little bird flies to her beloved food'; Thus by the Tiber, at the rising of the sun, Here and there was heard a confused sound Of sighs, of kisses, and of words: 'My love, live in peace'; 'And you, my love, go in peace'; 'And let it be as heaven wills, Farewell Floro!' they said, 'Florida, farewell!'"

40. Mirollo, *Giambattista Marino*, p. 53.

41. Wolfgang Osthoff, *Theatergesang und darstellende Musik in der italienischen Renaissance*, p. 317; Barbara R. Hanning, "The Influence of Humanist Thought and Italian Renaissance Poetry on the Formation of Opera," p. 3; and Fabbri, "Tasso, Guarini e il 'divino Claudio,'" pp. 239–42.

42. Some statistics on musical settings are given by Arnold Hartmann, Jr., "Battista Guarini and *Il pastor fido*." I note here the publications devoted solely to Guarini's pastoral: Filippo di Monte, *Musica sopra il pastor fido* (1600); Giovanni Piccioni, *Il pastor fido musicale* (1602); Claudio Pari, *Il pastor fido* (1611); Giovanni Nicolò Mezzogorri, *Il pastor fido armonico* (1617); and Scipione Cerreto, *L'Amarillide* (1621). By way of general statistics, the reader should note that the speeches treated in this chapter have over 100 settings, not counting the publications listed in the footnote.

43. "Ah, painful parting! Ah, end of my life! From you I part, and do not die? And yet I feel The pain of death, And I feel in parting A living death That gives life to pain, And in so doing, my heart dies immortally."

44. Approximately forty settings use the excerpts discussed in this chapter. Significantly, the proportion of solo compositions is considerably higher than in the case of *Il pastor fido*.

45. "Having come to the tomb, where for his living spirit A painful prison Heaven decreed, Pallid, chilled, mute, and as if deprived Of movement, on the marble he affixed his eyes. Finally, disgorging a tearful river, With a languid: 'Alas!' he exclaimed, and said: 'O stone so beloved and greatly honored, Which inside has my flames and outside my weeping; Not of the dead, are you, but of living Ashes a refuge, where Love reposes; And well I feel from you the usual torches, Less sweet yes, but not less hot in my heart. Ah! receive my sighs, and

these kisses Receive, which I bathe with my sorrowful humor; And give them, because I cannot, at least To the beloved remains that you have in your bosom.' "

46. " 'Go, then, cruel man, with that peace That you bequeath to me; go at last, iniquitous man. My untimely disembodied spirit, a shadowy pursuer From the first to the last at your back shall you have. A new fury, with serpents and with the torch Shall I torment you as much as I have loved you. And if it be destiny that you escape the sea, that you elude The reefs and the waves and that you arrive at the battle, There among the blood and the dead lying mortally wounded You shall pay me for my pains, pitiless warrior. The name Armida shall you often invoke In your ultimate sobs: this I hope to hear.' Now at this point she yielded her spirit to pain, Nor did she utter completely this last sound [word]; And she fell fainting and was diffused With cold perspiration, and closed her lights [eyes]. Your eyes have closed, Armida; avaricious Heaven has envied the comfort of your torments. Open your eyes, unhappy woman; the bitter weeping In the eyes of your enemy, why do you not see? O how lovingly Would the sound of his sighs relieve you! He gives as many as he can, and takes (and you do not believe it!) his final farewells, pitiable in appearance."

47. C. P. Brand, *Torquato Tasso*, pp. 129–30.

48. Ulivi, *L'imitazione nella poetica del rinascimento*, p. 131.

49. *Considerazioni al Tasso* (1589–1600), Tasso, *Opere*, Pisa, 1828, 23:8. It is also worth noting that elsewhere, Galilei makes a parallel between the nudity in Michelangelo's *Last Judgment* and certain lines in the *Gerusalemme liberata* that he considers to be obscene. Ibid., p. 173. Panofsky cites Galilei's comparison between Tasso's allegorical method—we might say, concettistic method—and anamorphotic art as one factor behind Galilei's equation of "the intent of the *Orlando furioso* (completed about 1515) with that of classic High Renaissance art, and that of the *Gerusalemme liberata* (completed about 1575) with that of Mannerism." *Galileo as a Critic of the Arts*, p. 17. The equation that Panofsky extrapolates from Galilei's comments is, of course, a tacit one, and Galilei does not use terms such as High Renaissance or Mannerism. Nevertheless, the words he does use imply qualities that I associate with the two styles. See *Considerazioni*, ibid., pp. 221–22.

CHAPTER VI

1. Giorgio de Santillana, *The Age of Adventure*, p. 26; Otto Benesch, *The Art of the Renaissance in Northern Europe*, p. 1; Bousquet, *La peinture maniériste*, p. 55; and Giuliano Briganti, *Le maniérisme italien*, p. 6.

2. Poggioli, *The Theory of the Avant-Garde*; and Lowinsky, "The Musical Avant-Garde of the Renaissance," p. 113.

3. Margery H. Nicolson, *The Breaking of the Circle*, p. 44.

4. Shearman, *Mannerism*, p. 135.

5. Rudolf and Margot Wittkower, *Born under Saturn*, p. 78. Among mannerist eccentrics in the arts I list Pontormo, Parmigianino, Rosso Fiorentino, Il Sodoma, Michelangelo, Salviati, Cellini, Tasso, Marino, Orlando di Lasso, Francesco Corteccia, Stefano Rossetti, Nicola Vicentino, Giaches de Wert, Luzzasco Luzzaschi, Orazio Vecchi, Ludovico Agostino, and Carlo Gesualdo. Some of the more colorful personalities in philosophy and science are Pico della Mirandola, Tartaglia, Cardano, Tycho Brahe, Bruno, Campanella, and Paracelsus von Hohenheim—not to mention Pietro Aretino and his vivacious pupils.

6. Shearman, *Mannerism*, p. 171.

7. Wittkower, *Born under Saturn*, pp. 91–93.

8. Colie, *Paradoxia epidemica*, p. 439.

9. *Iconologia* (1593). The entries in this book are arranged in alphabetical order. My translation is based on the edition, Rome, 1603, p. 178.

10. Bousquet, *La peinture maniériste*, p. 70.

11. Klein and Zerner, *Italian Art 1500–1600*, p. xiii; and Blunt, *Artistic Theory in Italy, 1450–1600*, p. 55.

12. Shearman, *Mannerism*, p. 44.

13. Wolf and Millen, *Renaissance and Mannerist Art*, p. 11.

14. Santillana, *Age of Adventure*, p. 19.

15. Hathaway, *The Age of Criticism*, p. v.

16. Roland H. Bainton, "Man, God and the Church in the Age of the Renaissance," p. 80.

17. Hauser, *The Social History of Art*, 2:44.

18. Works such as Giovanni della Casa's *Il galateo* (1558) afford a glimpse into the mannerist affectation of courtly circles.

19. Porta wrote the well-known work, *Magia naturalis* (1558).

20. Angelo Ingegneri's treatise, *Della poesia rappresentativa e del modo di rappresentare le favole sceniche* (1598), describes his experiences in producing the play. The academy also commissioned the theater designed by Palladio, one of its founding members.

21. Like many other literary works, Varchi's two sets of publications, cited in the chapters on artistic and poetic theory, were originally given as lectures to the Accademia Fiorentina.

22. Camillo Pellegrino started the debate with his encomium of Tasso in *Il Caraffa* (1584). He was rebutted by Lionardo Salviati, who presented the views of the Accademia della Crusca in his *Difesa dell'Orlando furioso* (1584). Francesco Patrizi also defended Ariosto against Pellegrino, *Parere in difesa dell'Ariosto* (1585), and Tasso answered Patrizi with his tract, *Discorso sopra il Parere* (1585).

23. Guarini published his *Il Verrato* in 1588, Denores his *Apologia contra l'auttore del Verrato* in 1590, and Guarini his *Il Verrato secondo* in 1593. The two Guarini tracts were later combined and printed as the *Compendio della poesia tragicomica* (1601).

24. Bousquet, *La peinture maniériste*, p. 51. I also remind the reader of Santillana's title, *The Age of Adventure*.

25. Although I am not concerned with assessing the application of Mannerism to other historical periods, I cannot resist pointing out in this context that one eminent scholar uses the term in connection with alexandrine and byzantine culture. Ernst R. Curtius, *European Literature and the Latin Middle Ages*, pp. 273–301.

26. Frances A. Yates, *Giordano Bruno and the Hermetic Tradition*, p. 4.

27. Marsilio Ficino, for example, translated the *Corpus Hermeticum*, a set of mystical tracts mistakenly attributed to Hermes Trismegistus. For a description of the contents of this arcane collection, see Yates, *Giordano Bruno*; and Wayne Shumaker, *The Occult Sciences in the Renaissance*.

28. *Nova de universis philosophia* (1593).

29. Yates, *Giordano Bruno*, p. 360.

30. *De vinculis in genere* (1591–92), "pt. I," chap. 2; "pt. II," chap. 1; and "pt. III," chap. 1.

31. Ibid., "pt. I," chaps. 3 and 12.

32. Ibid., "pt. III," "Preface."

33. Ibid., "pt. I," chaps. 3, 10, 12, 13, 17, 18, and 30; "pt. II," chap. 6; and "pt. III," chap. 8.

34. Ibid., "pt. I," chap. 12. Bruno refers to Zeuxis in this context.

35. Ibid., chaps. 3 and 8.

36. Ibid., chaps. 10 and 13.

37. Ibid., chap. 9; and "pt. II," chaps. 17 and 6.

38. Ibid., "pt. I," chaps. 3 and 7.

39. Ibid., chap. 3.

40. *De naturalium effectuum causis* (1556).

41. *De subtilitatem rerum* (1550) and *De rerum varietate* (1557). George Sarton, *Six Wings of Science in the Renaissance*, p. 33.

42. Yates, *Giordano Bruno*, p. 116.

43. *Magia e grazia* (ca. 1630), Rome, 1957, p. 180.

44. *De revolutionibus orbium coelestium* (1543).

45. The reader should note, however, that the frequently cited cautionary sentence about mathematical hypothesis was added to the preface by Copernicus's friend and colleague, Andreas Ossiander. Sarton, *Six Wings of Science*, p. 60.

46. *Dialogo sopra i due massime sistemi del mondo Tolemaico e Copernico* (1632).

47. Santillana, *Age of Adventure*, p. 206.

48. *Harmonice mundi* (1619).

49. Nicolson, *Breaking of the Circle*, pp. 1–2.

CHAPTER VII

1. Friedländer, *Mannerism and Anti-Mannerism in Italian Painting.*

2. Hauser, *Mannerism*, pp. 3–5, 11, and 12. See also, Battisti, *L'antirinascimento*, p. 378.

3. At the same time, it is worth noting that in the context of sixteenth-century writings on music these negative evaluations do have a very precise and illuminating import.

4. Bousquet, *La peinture maniériste*, p. 31. The Ages of Mannerism are the fifteenth and sixteenth centuries, whereas the classical episode (the Renaissance) lasts only a few decades between roughly 1490 and 1520. Bousquet's conception is based on a more general model of historiography whereby all classical styles amount to brief moments of perfection in a broad continuum of artistic events.

5. Shearman, *Mannerism*, pp. 31 and 38.

6. Gombrich, "The Leaven of Criticism in Renaissance Art," p. 27. See also, Baumgart, *Renaissance und Kunst des Manierismus*, p. 156.

7. Hauser, *The Social History of Art*, 2:75.

8. Gombrich, *Norm and Form*, p. 3.

9. Ibid., p. 9.

10. Kristeller, *Renaissance Thought*, pp. 10–11.

11. Hauser, *Social History of Art*, 2:90–91.

12. Friedländer, *Mannerism and Anti-Mannerism*, p. 54; Hauser, *Social History of Art*, 2:94, 161–62, and 176–77; Shearman, *Mannerism*, p. 180; Ulivi, *Il manierismo del Tasso e altri studi*, p. 172; Frederick B. Artz, *From the Renais-*

sance to Romanticism, p. 162; and Bouleau, *The Painter's Secret Geometry*, p. 172.

13. Mirollo, *Giambattista Marino*, p. 276.

14. Hocke, *Manierismus in der Literatur*, p. 145.

15. Shearman, *Mannerism*, p. 146.

16. Hoffmann, *Hochrenaissance, Manierismus, Frühbarock*, p. 179.

17. Sypher, *Four Stages of Renaissance Style*.

18. Haydn, *The Counter-Renaissance*, p. 17.

19. Molly M. Mahood, *Poetry and Humanism*, p. 137.

20. Hauser, *Social History of Art*, 2:163–64 and *Mannerism*, p. 152.

21. *The Age of Adventure*, p. 9.

22. For example, Johannes Molanus, *De historia ss. imaginum* (1594); Cardinal Gabriele Paleotti, *Discorso intorno alle imagini sacre e profane* (1582); and Cardinal Carlo Borromeo, *Instructiones fabricae et supellectis ecclesiasticae* (1577).

23. Sypher, *Four Stages of Renaissance Style*, p. 181.

CHAPTER VIII

1. Lowinsky, "Renaissance Writings on Music Theory," p. 359. See also, Shearman, *Mannerism*, pp. 96–97.

2. In the latter category, I list the following: Anton Francesco Doni, *Dialogo della musica* (1544); Luigi Dentice, *Due dialoghi della musica* (1552); Cosimo Bartoli, *Ragionamenti accademici* (1567); and Vicenzo Giustiniani, *Discorso sopra la musica* (ca. 1628). For further information concerning writings on music as well as musical compositions, consult the Bibliography of primary sources.

3. *Dodecachordon* (1547), bk. III, chap. 13.

4. The echo in Vasari is striking.

5. *Dodecachordon*, bk. III, chap. 24.

6. *Ragionamenti accademici*, bk. III, pp. 35–36.

7. *Practica musica* (1556), bk. I, "De musicae inventoribus."

8. *Scintille di musica* (1533), "Preface."

9. *Prima ad musicen instructio*. Palisca, "A Clarification of 'Musica Reservata' in Jean Taisnier's 'Astrologiae' 1559," p. 138.

10. *Compendium musices* (1552), "Praefatio"; pt. I, "De his quae futuro Musico sunt necessaria"; pt. II, "De musica figuralis" and "De compositionis regula, & notarum sincopis, & ligaturis."

11. Ibid., pt. I, "De musicorum generibus." This fourfold division is taken up by Claudius Sebastiani in his *Bellum musicale* (1563), chap. 27. For a fivefold grouping by Pietro Gaetano, *Oratio de origine et dignitate musices* (ca. 1570), see H. Colin Slim, *A Gift of Madrigals and Motets*, pp. 42–44.

12. *L'antica musica ridotta alla moderna prattica* (1555). The treatise is divided into two sections, one book on *theorica musicale*, and five books on *prattica musicale*. In subsequent citations, the first section will be designated simply by its title, whereas specific books, with their pertinent chapters, will indicate references to the second section.

13. *L'antica musica*, bk. I, chaps. 2–4.

14. Ibid., chap. 35.

15. Ibid., bk. III, chap. 48.

16. Ibid., bk. IV, chap. 29.

17. Ibid., bk. I, chap. 4.

18. *Trattado . . . sopra una differentia musicale* (ca. 1556), pt. III, chap. 2. The Italian quotation and subsequent remarks can be found in Palisca, "A Clarification of 'Musica Reservata,'" p. 138.

19. *Le istitutioni harmoniche* (1558), pt. I, "Proemio."

20. In a later work, Zarlino distinguishes among various kinds of musical imitations of nature and concludes that the composer should imitate only the rhythm and stress of the words. *Sopplimenti musicale* (1588), bk. IV, chaps. 11 and 13.

21. *Le istitutioni harmoniche*, pt. III, chap. 70.

22. Ibid., chaps. 78–80.

23. *Prattica di musica* (pt. I, 1592), bk. I, chap. 9.

24. Ibid., chap. 10.

25. Ibid., chap. 12.

26. *Musica* (1537), chap. 1.

27. *Prattica di musica* (pt. I, 1592), bk. I, chap. 10.

28. *Discorso in cui . . . si dimostra come si possono scrivere . . . le comedie e le tragedie in prosa* (1592). Cited from Hathaway, *The Age of Criticism*, p. 106 (italics mine).

29. *Dialogo della musica* (1544), Cremona, 1969, p. 109.

30. *Discorso sopra la musica* (ca. 1628), American Institute of Musicology, 1962, p. 68.

31. Ibid., p. 69.

32. Ibid., p. 71. Giustiniani's division is still useful today.

33. Ibid., pp. 71–72.

34. Ibid., pp. 76–77.

35. *L'arte et la pratica del moderno contrapunto* (1591). Because this source was not available, the ensuing discussion relies on Palisca, "Vincenzo Galilei's Counterpoint Treatise." Galilei's list of composers is revealing. Except for Josquin, all his models come from the sixteenth century, and many of them are important representatives of radical composition.

36. *Dialogo della musica antica e della moderna* (1581), pp. 76–77, 79, and 81–89. Zarlino answers Galilei with his *Sopplimenti* (1588), and Galilei counters with his *Discorso intorno all'opere di messer Gioseffo Zarlino da Chioggia* (1589).

37. *Cartella musicale* (1614); *Discorso sopra la moderna pratica musicale*, pp. 165–67.

38. This notion also crops up in Heinrich Schütz's educational ideals, and Schütz, of course, was responsible for introducing modern counterpoint to German musicians. *Geistliche Chormusik* (1648), Preface.

39. *L'Artusi overo dell' imperfettioni della moderna musica* (pt. I, 1600), "Ragionamento secondo," pp. 39r–40r.

40. Ibid., pp. 42r–42v.

41. *L'Artusi* (pt. II, 1603). Artusi inserts the Stubborn Academic's letter (pp. 6–11) and his own reply (pp. 13–21). As a sampling of Artusi's vituperative style in this part of the treatise, I give the following phrases used by him to characterize modern music: "false" (p. 13); "it leads one to laughter and ridicule; the folly capricious compositions; a new nausea and a new contempt" (p. 27); and "confusion; brutality of style" (p. 41).

42. The "declaration" consists of Claudio Monteverdi's letter, originally printed in bk. v (1605), with a glossary by his brother, Giulio Cesare. It appeared in the *Scherzi musicali* (1607). The ensuing discussion is based on the annotated version.

43. Several baroque theorists turn Monteverdi's division into systems of style and genre; for example, Marco Scacchi, *Breve discorso sopra la musica moderna* (1649); Christoph Bernhard, *Tractatus compositionis augmentatus* (ca. 1660); and Angelo Berardi, *Miscellanea musicale* (1689).

44. As does Robert M. Isgroe in "The First and Second Practices of Monteverdi," p. 309.

45. *Dodecachordon*, bk. II, chap. 38.

46. *Le istitutioni harmoniche*, pt. I, chap. 11, and pt. IV, chap. 36.

47. Ibid., bk. III, chap. 26. In this chapter, Zarlino lays out six basic requirements for good counterpoint. The rest of bk. III and a substantial part of bk. IV provide the details for each requirement. My description of Zarlino's concept of genius is an extrapolation of the context of these details. The reader will be able to judge the validity of this interpretation from subsequent chapters, especially the ones on counterpoint and composition, and on *maniera*.

48. *Compendium musices*, pt. II, "De compositionis regula, & notarum sincopis, & ligaturis."

49. Lowinsky, "Musical Genius—Evolution and Origins of a Concept," p. 42. At the same time, we should recall that this topic emerged with some importance in the mid-century.

50. *Practica musica*, bk. v, "De arte eleganter et suaviter cantandi."

51. Ibid., bk. I, "Musica quid sit."

52. "Letter to Giovanni del Lago" (1529). Spataro's correspondence will become available in a collected edition done by Lowinsky. The excerpt referred to here can be found in his "Musical Genius," pp. 481–82 and K. Jeppesen, "Eine musikhistorische Korrespondenz des frühesten Cinquecento," p. 24.

53. *Lucidario in musica* (1545), bk. II, chap. 15.

54. *L'antica musica*, bk. I, chap. 1.

55. "Musical Genius," p. 340.

56. *Trattato della musica scenica* (ca. 1635), chap. 45. The relevant excerpt is quoted in Lowinsky's "Musical Genius," p. 339.

CHAPTER IX

1. *Libellus de rudimentis musices* (1529), [p. 28]. The *Libellus* lacks any form of numbered pages. My references presume that the first page begins after the prefatory material. Rossetti's discussion of the major and minor semitone occurs near the beginning of his excursus on the intervals of the gamut [pp. 26–34].

2. *Musica practica* (1482), pt. I, bk. I, chap. 3. The first division of the monochord, which presents the traditional boethian approach, appears in pt. I, bk. I, chap. 2.

3. His *Honesta defensio* (1491) demolishes the arguments presented by Nicolaus Burtius in the *Musices opusculum* (1487), and his *Dilucide et probatissime demonstratione* (1521) attacks Franchinus Gafurius.

4. *Musica theorica* (1529), bk. III, chap. 4.

5. J. Murray Barbour, *Tuning and Temperament*, p. 11.

6. "Letter to Artusi" (1599). The Stubborn Academic's reliance on Fogliano is pointed out by Artusi in his reply along with a gleeful exposition of his opponent's misunderstanding of this source. *L'Artusi overo della imperfettioni della moderna musica* (pt. II, 1603), p. 30.

7. *Le istitutioni harmoniche* (1558), pt. II, chap. 2.

8. Ibid., pt. I, chap. 15.

9. Ibid., chap. 14.

10. Ibid., pt. II, chaps. 39 and 40.

11. Ibid., pt. I, chap. 16.

12. Ibid., pt. II, chaps. 41 and 42.

13. *Dialogo della musica antica e della moderna* (1581), p. 2.

14. Ibid., pp. 2–31.

15. *Thoscanello della musica* (1523), bk. II, chap. 41. The term *participatio* recalls to mind Gafurius's reference to organists who temper the fifths on their instruments by ear with a small, vague quantity called *participata*. *Practica musicae* (1496), bk. III, chap. 3. The latter probably approximates meantone temperament, and not equal temperament as suggested by Barbour and Lowinsky, in *Tuning and Temperament*, p. 5, and *Tonality and Atonality in Sixteenth-Century Music*, p. 46, respectively.

16. *Le istitutioni harmoniche*, pt. II, chap. 43.

17. *De musica libri septem* (1577), bk. III, chaps. 22–25.

18. Salinas seems to be aware of the drawbacks of the one-third comma system, for he also envisages tuning by five-part, seven-part, and twenty-one-part divisions of the comma. Ibid., bk. III, chaps. 15–21.

19. *Euclide* (1569). My discussion is indebted to Stillman Drake, "Renaissance Music and Experimental Science," pp. 487–88.

20. *Ayn new kunstlich Buech* (1518). The description of Grammateus's system comes from Barbour, *Tuning and Temperament*, pp. 139–41. It is interesting to note that all conservatives condemn both Ramos and Aristoxenos for supporting the equal division of the octave.

21. *Scintille di musica* (1533), bk. IV, chap. 10.

22. *Considerazioni musicali* (1603), chaps. 9 and 10.

23. *Dialogo* (1581), p. 47.

24. *Sopplimenti musicali* (1588), bk. IV, chap. 28.

25. See Drake, *Galileo Studies* and "Experimental Science"; and Palisca, "Scientific Empiricism in Musical Science."

26. Drake, *Galileo Studies*, p. 51 and "Experimental Science," p. 491.

27. Palisca, "Scientific Empiricism." See also, Drake, *Galileo Studies*, pp. 53–55 and "Experimental Science," pp. 493–95.

28. For example, Salinas, *De musica*, bk. III, chap. 27; and Zarlino, *Le istitutioni harmoniche*, pt. II, chap. 25.

29. *L'antica musica ridotta alla moderna prattica* (1555), bk. I, chap. 10.

30. Ibid., chaps. 21–24. Ordinarily, the 10:9 and 9:8 ratios designate the minor and major tones of just intonation; however, Vicentino uses these terms to refer to the first and last sizes given in our list, sizes that diverge from the natural tone by one diesis.

31. Ibid., chaps. 25–31.

32. Ibid., chaps. 32–34.

33. Ibid., chaps. 35–36.

34. Ibid., chaps. 37–41. Because the larger intervals are composites of those listed, Vicentino does not go into further analysis.

35. Ibid., bk. III, chaps. 2–4, 36–38, and 45–48. Each set of generic species culminates naturally in the exposition of generic modes—that is, the eight diatonic modes in chaps. 5–12, the eight chromatic modes in chaps. 39–42, and the eight enharmonic modes in chap. 49.

36. *Le istitutioni harmoniche*, pt. III, chap. 72.

37. The documents of this debate are reprinted by Vicentino, *L'antica musica*, bk. IV, chap. 43.

38. Vicentino calls this kind of music *"Musica participata & mista"* in *L'antica musica*, bk. III, chap. 15. The controversy did not end with Vicentino's writing. Much later, Gandolfo Sigonio's criticism of Vicentino, *Discorso intorno a madrigali et a'libri dell'Antica musica . . . da N. Vicentino* (1602), was refuted by Ercole Bottrigari, *Il Melone* and *Il Melone secondo* (1602), who decides in favor of Vicentino's position.

39. *L'antica musica*, "Libro della theorica musicale," chap. 15.

40. Ibid., bk. I, chap. 16.

41. Domenico Pietro Cerone, *El melopeo y maestro* (1613), bk. XXI, chap. 4. Cerone notes that Luzzaschi wrote compositions for this instrument on which he himself played. A similar reference occurs in Bottrigari's *Il desiderio* (1594), p. 41, and American Institute of Musicology, 1962, p. 51.

42. Henry W. Kaufmann, *The Life and Works of Nicola Vicentino*, pp. 163–74, and "More on the Tuning of the Archicembalo"; and Maniates, "Vicentino's 'Incerta et Occulta Scientia' Re-examined."

43. *Il desiderio* (1594), pp. 5–12, and American Institute of Musicology, 1962, pp. 15–23.

44. *L'Artusi* (pt. I, 1600), pp. 27v–27r. These comments could very well have been borrowed from Bottrigari's *Il desiderio*; this is very likely in view of Bottrigari's complaints about Artusi's plagiarism made in another context.

45. A reproduction of this sheet can be found in Kaufmann, *Nicola Vicentino*, facing p. 172. See also, Kaufmann, "Vicentino's *Arciorgano*."

46. The words *musica communa* occur in *L'antica musica*, bk. III, chap. 15, referring to the Dorian mode "that composers should use in common music—that is, in that [style] in which all the professionals of music compose at this time." Of course, in the context of Vicentino's propaganda on behalf of music that is reserved for elite listeners, common music takes on a distinctly disparaging ring.

47. *A Plaine and Easie Introduction to Practicall Musicke* (1597), "Annotations" to pt. I, p. 103.

48. This instrument, the Universal-Clavicymbel, featured four black keys between every tone as well as one black key between the diatonic semitones. *Syntagma musicum* (bk. II, 1619), pt. II, chap. 40.

CHAPTER X

1. *Dodecachordon* (1547), bk. I, chaps. 8 and 9.

2. *A Plaine and Easie Introduction to Practicall Musicke* (1597), pp. 141–42. The interval of the fourth is treated in the "Annotations" to pt. II, pp. 205–7.

3. *Le istitutioni harmoniche* (1558), pt. II, chaps. 4 and 5.

4. Ibid., pt. III, chap. 6.

5. Ibid., chap. 10.

6. Ibid., chap. 17.

7. Ibid., chaps. 22–24.

8. The 1558 edition reappeared in 1562; it was revised in 1573 and reprinted in that form in 1589 and 1602. Both Orazio Tigrini, in his *Il compendio della musica* (1588) and Artusi, in his *L'arte del contraponto* (1598) condense Zarlino's rules of counterpoint. Other adaptations in German and French are mentioned in Guy A. Marco and Claude V. Palisca, eds., *The Art of Counterpoint*, p. xiv.

9. *Musica practica* (1482), pt. II, bk. I, chap. I.

10. *Proportionale musices* (ca. 1474), "Proemium."

11. *L'arte et la pratica del moderno contrapunto* (1591). This description is indebted to Palisca, "Vincenzo Galilei's Counterpoint Treatise."

12. *L'antica musica ridotta alla moderna prattica* (1555), bk. II, chap. 12.

13. Ibid., bk. I, chap. 35. When Vicentino enunciates this principle, it is a startling and new idea. However, such harmonic audacities later become commonplaces in the madrigal.

14. A chart of the various intervals with their inflected sizes appears in ibid., chap. 42. Vicentino's attribution of affective qualities to each size runs through the chapters devoted to them (i.e. bk. I, chaps. 15–41). As examples, I cite his characterization of the natural fifth in upward motion as very excited, and in downward motion as very sad (chap. 39). The imperfect fifth, on the other hand, is excited in downward motion and sad in upward motion (chap. 37). The major tone—the one larger than the natural tone by one diesis—is the most exciting of all the tone sizes (chap. 24).

15. *Dodecachordon*, bk. I, chaps. 11 and 14.

16. Ibid., bk. II, chap. I. This new definition has important repercussions on Glareanus's concept of *phrasis*. Semitone configurations govern the intervals and hence the melodic contours proper to a mode.

17. Ibid., chaps. 5–7.

18. Ibid., chap. 18.

19. Ibid., chap. 20.

20. Ibid., chaps. 24 and 17.

21. Ibid., chaps. 26 and 27. *Connexio* refers to the sharpening of the *subsemitonium modi*, a practice that, in effect, introduces the *phrasis* of another mode.

22. Ibid., bk. III, chap. 21.

23. Ibid., chap. 16.

24. Ibid., chap. 23.

25. Ibid., chap. 24.

26. Ibid., chap. 11.

27. Ibid., chap. 36.

28. Ibid., chap. 13.

29. Ibid., bk. II, chap. 36 and bk. III, chap. 24. The phrase, "from Dorian to Phrygian," signifying musical ineptitude, appears in Desiderius Erasmus's *Adages* (1500).

30. *Le istitutioni harmoniche*, pt. IV, chap. 10. Gregor Faber discusses

Glareanus's system but decides in favor of the traditional number of eight. *Musices practicae* (1553), bk. I, chap. 17. Nicolaus Roggius, however, adopts the twelve-mode scheme in his *Musicae practicae* (1566), "De modis musicis," as does Eucharius Hoffmann, *Doctrina de tonis seu modis musicis* (1582), chap. 3.

31. Zarlino already effected this change in the *Dimostrationi armoniche* (1571), "Ragionamento" v, "Proposta" 14 and 15.

32. *Dialogo della musica antica e della moderna* (1581), pp. 71–78.

33. *Le istitutioni harmoniche*, pt. III, chap. 10.

34. *Musica practica*, pt. I, bk. II, chap. 3.

35. Such terse references to the boethian system are many. I cite the example of Pietro Aaron, a very practical theorist with many modern ideas, who still mentions this old concept. *Thoscanello della musica* (1523), bk. I, chap. 4.

36. *Trattato della natura et cognitione di tutti gli tuoni di canto figurato* (1525), chap. 2. This idea, repeated in the 1529 edition, is strangely outmoded in comparison with Aaron's conception of counterpoint.

37. *L'antica musica*, bk. III, chap. 32.

38. The reader is referred to Imogene Horsley, "Fugue and Mode in 16th-Century Vocal Polyphony"; and Bernhard Meier, *Die Tonarten der klassischen Vokalpolyphonie*.

CHAPTER XI

1. *Musica practica* (1482), pt. I, bk. III, chap. 2. It should be noted that these remarks are made in conjunction with an excursus on the modes, and show Ramos's classical learning.

2. *Practica musicae* (1496), bk. III, chap. 1.

3. *Libri tres de institutione harmonica* (1516), bk. III, chap. 1.

4. *Thoscanello della musica* (1523), bk. II, chap. 16.

5. Ibid., bk. III, chaps. 21–30.

6. *Dodecachordon* (1547), bk. III, chap. 13.

7. Ibid., chap. 26.

8. *Compendium musices* (1552), "Praefatio."

9. Ibid., pt. I, "De his quae futuro Musico sunt necessaria."

10. Ibid., pt. II, "De regula contrapuncti secundum doctrinam Iosquini de Pratis" and "De compositionis regula."

11. The fact that Morley's work presents two similar branches of music suggests that Josquin's method remains a flourishing tradition in education throughout the sixteenth century. *A Plaine and Easie Introduction to Practicall Musicke* (1597), pt. II "Treating of Descant" and pt. III "Treating of Composing or Setting of Songs."

12. *Le istitutioni harmoniche* (1558), bk. III.

13. Ibid., chap. 26. The fifth rule concerns modes in polyphony and the sixth addresses the relationship between text and music.

14. Ibid., chap. 28.

15. Ibid., chap. 27.

16. Ibid., chap. 30.

17. Ibid., chap. 40.

18. Ibid., chap. 31.

19. Ibid., chaps. 28, 29, 32–36, and 38.

20. Ibid., chaps. 31, 35–37, 44, 46, and 57.

21. Ibid., chaps. 35 and 36.

22. Ibid., chap. 53.

23. Ibid., chap. 55. The one exception to this rule will be discussed a little later.

24. Ibid., chap. 51.

25. Haar, "Zarlino's Definition of Fugue and Imitation." To avoid confusion, I retain the original Italian names for canonic and imitative procedures. It should also be noted that Zarlino's verbal descriptions are studded with helpful musical illustrations.

26. *Le istitutioni harmoniche*, bk. III, chap. 51.

27. Ibid., chap. 52.

28. Haar, "Zarlino's Definition," pp. 232–33. Haar points out that Aaron makes a similar distinction in his *Lucidario* (1545), bk. II, chap. 10. Aaron's first use of the term *imitatione* occurs in the *Libri tres* (1516), bk. III, chap. 52.

29. *Le istitutioni harmoniche*, bk. III, chaps. 51, 62, 56, and 52.

30. Ibid., chaps. 53 and 54.

31. Ibid., chap. 63. Zarlino calls these melodic repetitions *pertinacie*, and his treatment of them shows that stylistic and inventive refinement now grace the erstwhile forbidden *redictae* of Johannes Tinctoris. *Liber de arte contrapuncti* (1477), bk. III, chap. 6.

32. *Le istitutioni harmoniche*, bk. III, chap. 57.

33. Ibid., chaps. 65 and 66.

34. Ibid., chaps. 72–80.

35. *L'arte del contraponto* (1598) and *Il compendio della musica* (1588), respectively.

36. *Ragionamento di musica* (1588). Both Tigrini and Ponzio also include simplified versions of Vicentino's fourth book, especially the chapters on compositional structure.

37. *Dialogo ove si tratta della theorica e prattica di musica* (1595), pt. II, p. 45 and pt. III, p. 106. For the relevant excerpts and a discussion of their import, consult Lewis H. Lockwood, "On 'Parody' as a Term and Concept in 16th-Century Music."

38. *El melopeo y maestro* (1613), bks. XIV and XXIII.

39. *Canoni musicali* (n.d.). This book, which explores four kinds of canon, was probably written in the early seventeenth century.

40. For example, Zacconi's *Prattica di musica* (pt. II, 1622), bk. III, chap. 15.

41. *A Plaine and Easie Introduction*, pt. III, p. 228.

42. This apposition recalls Vicentino's ideas.

43. *A Plaine and Easie Introduction*, pt. III, pp. 290–97.

44. *Syntagma musicum* (bk. III, 1619), pt. I.

45. *Cartella musicale* (1614); *Discorso sopra la moderna pratica musicale*, pp. 165–67.

46. *L'Artusi overo delle imperfettioni della moderna musica* (pt. I, 1600), "Ragionamento secondo," pp. 39v–40r. These two madrigals appear subsequently in bk. V (1604) and bk. IV (1604).

47. Ibid., pp. 40r–44r. This portion, plus musical examples, is available in O. Strunk, *Source Readings in Music History*, pp. 393–404.

48. *L'arte et la pratica del moderno contrapunto* (1591), described in Palisca's "Vincenzo Galilei's Counterpoint Treatise."

49. For a discussion of Cerone's comments on free dissonance in modern counterpoint, consult Ruth Hannas, "Cerone, Philosopher and Teacher." In particular, Cerone's example of primary suspended dissonances includes progressions often found in Monteverdi's concerted duos.

50. It may very well be that Galilei's orientation toward vertical harmony stems from his abiding interest in the solo song, even though his rules apply to the five-voiced unaccompanied madrigals of Monteverdi. On the relationship between dissonance treatment in monody and polyphony, consult Carl Dahlhaus, "Domenico Belli und der chromatische Kontrapunkt um 1600."

51. *L'antica musica ridotta alla moderna prattica* (1555), bk. II.

52. Ibid., chaps. 1, 2, and 31.

53. Ibid., chap. 2.

54. Each section of the composition takes up one chapter in bk. IV—chaps. 14, 15, and 16.

55. Vicentino elsewhere points out that canonic treatment of the cantus firmus is old-fashioned. In modern style, composers write freely invented imitative counterpoint around their chosen melody. Ibid., bk. III, chap. 22.

56. Ibid., bk. IV, chap. 9.

57. Ibid., chap. 20.

58. Ibid., chap. 21.

59. Ibid., chap. 26.

60. Ibid., chaps. 25–28.

61. Ibid., bk. III, chap. 26. That Vicentino did not attempt to set a text in the pure diatonic genus is significant, at least in his theory.

62. The reader should note that my analysis follows Vicentino's precepts—that is, generic identity is purely a linear matter and depends on the melodic contour of each voice, not on vertical sonorities or interval combinations.

63. *L'antica musica*, bk. III, chaps. 44 and 55.

64. In instrumental practice it is known as the *inganno*. See Roland Jackson, "On Frescobaldi's Chromaticism and its Background."

65. *L'antica musica*, bk. III, chap. 51.

66. Ibid., chap. 48.

67. Ibid., chaps. 52 and 53.

68. In view of Vicentino's highly developed appreciation of word-tone relationships, one is tempted to suggest that the presence of the word *dolce* in the chromatic and enharmonic madrigals is not an accident.

69. *L'antica musica*, bk. III, chap. 54.

70. *Dialogo della musica antica e della moderna* (1581), pp. 77–90.

71. Ibid., p. 79.

72. Ibid., pp. 77, 79, and 81.

73. Ibid., p. 87.

74. Ibid., p. 80.

75. Ibid., p. 89.

76. Ibid., pp. 90 and 105. Galilei's exposition on monody will be treated in more detail in a later chapter. At this point, it should be noted that his explanation of the ancient modes and tuning is indebted to Girolamo Mei, as is the first printing of the Alypios table. Ibid., pp. 52–78 and 92–94.

CHAPTER XII

1. *Compendium musices* (1552), "Declaratio sive expositio mutationum scalae sive manus." "Fa-la" here refers to the couplet, "Una nota supra la, Semper est canendum fa." Of unknown origin, this admonition concerns ficta introduced to avoid the tritone.

2. Ibid., "De mutationibus."

3. *Musica* (1537), chap. 6. Listenius gives five monophonic and two polyphonic illustrations for these types.

4. *Practica musicae* (1496), bk. I, chap. 4.

5. *Dodecachordon* (1547), bk. I, chap. 6.

6. Ibid., bk. II, chap. 3.

7. Ibid., bk. I, chap. 3.

8. *Rudimenta musices* (1539), chap. 2.

9. *Musica*, chap. 7.

10. *De natura et proprietate tonorum* (ca. 1470), chaps. 7, 8, and 11.

11. Ibid., chaps. 45–50. The pitch E corresponds to Coclico's *Elafa*.

12. *L'antica musica ridotta alla moderna prattica* (1555), bk. III, chaps. 13 and 15–22.

13. Ibid., chap. 15.

14. Ibid., chap. 13.

15. *Le istitutioni harmoniche* (1558), pt. IV, chaps. 16 and 17.

16. *Practica musicae*, bk. III, chap. 13.

17. *Dodecachordon*, bk. I, chap. 3.

18. *Musica*, chap. 6; the final section, subtitled "De cantu ficto."

19. *Cut* (natural hexachord), to *Alami* (soft hexachord), to *Futsol* (B♭ hexachord), to *Fsolre* (E♭ hexachord), and to *B♭ solre* (A♭ hexachord), and to *A♭ fasol* (D♭ hexachord).

20. For a discussion of this development, see Lowinsky, *Secret Chromatic Art in the Netherlands Motet* and *Tonality and Atonality in Sixteenth-Century Music.*

21. *Rudimenta musices*, chap. 2.

22. *Trattato della natura et cognitione di tutti gli tuoni di canto figurato* (1525), chaps. 26–35.

23. "Letter" (1529). Cited by Lowinsky, "Matthaeus Greiter's *Fortuna*," p. 72. Agricola too includes sharp mutation and goes as far as the hexachord on B with a *D#mi*. *Rudimenta musices*, chap. 2.

24. *Lucidario* (1545), bk. IV, chap. 11.

25. "Letter" (1533). See Lowinsky, "Matthaeus Greiter's *Fortuna*," p. 73.

26. *Musicae activae micrologus* (1517), bk. I, chap. 10.

27. *Musices practicae erotematum* (1553), chap. 13.

28. The relationship between the striking harmonic and emblematic symbolism of Fortune's wheel is treated in detail in Lowinsky's "Matthaeus Greiter's *Fortuna*."

29. *Elementale musicum iuventati accommodum* (1544), chap. 2.

30. *Musica practica* (1482), pt. I, bk. II, chap. 2. *Coniuncta* is also the circumlocution employed by Tinctoris.

31. Ibid., chap. 3.

32. Ibid., chaps. 4 and 5.

33. *L'antica musica*, bk. I, chap. 5.

34. Although Taisnier does not name Vicentino specifically, his critique of the extravagances found in modern style leaves no doubt as to his reference to Vicentino's *maniera*. Palisca, "*Ut oratoria musica*," pp. 38–39.

35. *Astrologiae iudiciariae ysagoge* (1559), "Epistola dedicatoria." See Palisca, "A Clarification of 'Musica Reservata' in Jean Taisnier's 'Astrologiae' 1559," pp. 135–36.

36. *Le istitutioni harmoniche*, pt. III, chap. 72.

37. Ibid., chaps. 75 and 76.

38. Ibid., chap. 73.

39. Ibid., chaps. 77 and 78.

40. Ibid., chaps. 74 and 79.

41. Ibid., chap. 80. Several other passages in the treatise indicate that Zarlino has read Vicentino's work.

42. Lowinsky, *Tonality and Atonality*, pp. 38 and 41 and "The Musical Avant-Garde of the Renaissance," p. 133.

CHAPTER XIII

1. As does Robert W. Wienpahl, "Zarlino, the Senario and Tonality."

2. The various interpretations of aristotelian *mimesis* are covered by Armen Carapetyan, "The Concept of *Imitazione della natura* in the Sixteenth Century."

3. *Le istitutioni harmoniche* (1558), pt. III, chap. 26.

4. Leo Schrade, "Von der Maniera der Komposition in der Musik des 16. Jahrhunderts," p. 12.

5. Schrade makes this assumption. Ibid., p. 12.

6. *Le istitutioni harmoniche*, pt. III, chap. 3.

7. Haar, "Zarlino's Definition of Fugue and Imitation," pp. 239–41.

8. This phrase, referring to the music of Adrian Willaert, occurs in *Le istitutioni harmoniche*, pt. I, "Proemio."

9. Ibid., pt. IV, chap. 33. The relationship between Zarlino and Gaspar Stoquerus, *De musica verbali* (ca. 1570), is described by Lowinsky in "A Treatise on Text Underlay by a German Disciple of Francisco de Salinas," and that between Zarlino and Giovanni Maria Lanfranco, *Scintille di musica* (1533), is discussed by Don Harrán in "New Light on the Question of Text Underlay Prior to Zarlino." In my view, Harrán's grouping of Zarlino, Nicola Vicentino, and Samuel Quickelberg as theorists with similar ideas is an oversimplification.

10. *Compendium musices* (1552), pt. I, "De his quae futuro Musico sunt necessaria."

11. In a rather general and vague way, Stephano Vanneo also hints at a more modern approach when he suggests that modes influence the affections. *Recanetum de musica aurea* (1533), bk. III, chap. 39.

12. *Practica musicae* (1496), bk. IV, chap. 15.

13. *Le istitutioni harmoniche*, bk. IV, chap. 32.

14. *Liber de arte contrapuncti* (1477), bk. III, chap. 3.

15. *L'Artusi overo delle imperfettioni della moderna musica* (pt. I, 1600), "Ragionamento secondo," p. 42r.

16. *Corona della morte dell'illustre signore il Sig. Comendator Anibal Caro* (1568), "Preface."

17. *Il primo libro de madrigali a quattro voci* (1569), "Preface."

18. *Scherzi musicali* (1607), "Dichiaratione."

19. For example, see Carapetyan, "The Concept of *Imitazione della natura*," p. 52.

20. *L'antica musica ridotta alla moderna prattica* (1555), "Libro della theorica musicale," chap. 1.

21. Ibid., bk. II, chap. 1.

22. Ibid., chaps. 1 and 31.

23. Ibid., chap. 1.

24. Ibid., chap. 20.

25. Ibid., chap. 29.

26. Palisca, "The Beginnings of Baroque Music," p. 122.

27. *Scherzi musicali*, "Dichiaratione."

28. This last point reminds us of Banchieri's opinion to the effect that modern counterpoint defies rational, scientific rules.

29. *Madrigali guerrieri et amorosi* (1638), "Preface."

30. Nino Pirrotta, "Scelte poetiche di Monteverdi," p. 250.

31. *Cartella musicale* (1614); *Discorso sopra la moderna pratica musicale*, pp. 165–67.

32. Dahlhaus, "Musica poetica und musikalische Poesie," p. 112.

33. Heinrich Faber, *Musica poetica* (1548); Hermann Finck, *Practica musica* (1556); Gallus Dressler, *Praecepta musicae poeticae* (ca. 1564); Johannes Avianus, *Isagoge in libros musicae poeticae* (1581); Sethus Calvisius, *Melopoiia sive melodiae condendae ratio quam vulgo musicam poeticam vocant* (1592); Joachim Burmeister, *Musica poetica* (1606); Joachim Thelamonius, *Tractatus de compositione sive musica poetica* (1610); Johannes Nucius, *Musicae poeticae sive de compositione cantus praeceptiones* (1613); and Johann Andreas Herbst, *Musica poetica sive compendium melopoeticum* (1643). This list is by no means an exhaustive one, but it does provide an enumeration of the principal works in this tradition.

34. Dahlhaus, "Musica poetica," p. 110; Walter Wiora, "Musica poetica und musikalisches Kunstwerk," p. 579; and Palisca, "*Ut oratoria musica*," p. 56.

35. As does Kaufmann, *Nicola Vicentino*.

36. *Musica poetica* (1606), "Preface." Burmeister's concept of a period has to do with integrated structure in individual compositional members, be they phrases or sections. Ibid., chap. 5.

37. Ibid., chap. 16. These categories are borrowed from rhetoric, as are many of his technical and aesthetic terms.

38. Examples and references from this composer's motets are sprinkled throughout Burmeister's exegesis. His detailed analysis of Lasso's *In me transierunt* (ibid., chap. 15) is discussed in detail by Palisca, "*Ut oratoria musica*."

39. *Musica poetica*, chap. 12. Three scholars recognize this division: Palisca, "*Ut oratoria musica*"; Martin Ruhnke, *Joachim Burmeister*; and Hans-Heinrich Unger, *Die Beziehungen zwischen Musik und Rhetorik im 16.-18. Jahrhundert*. Ruhnke criticizes Heinz Brandes's *Studien zur musikalischen Figurenlehre im 16. Jahrhundert* for overemphasizing the expressive import of these figures. See Ruhnke, *Joachim Burmeister*, pp. 147–48. In several cases, arbitrary categorization is somewhat difficult. The reader should also be aware that rhetorical names and terms of reference appear elsewhere, in a rather consistent fashion, in Burmeister's treatise. For example, the idea of *syntaxis* in relation to contrapuntal procedures, and the list of licenses or *soloecismi* (*Musica poetica*, chap. 4), as

well as the cadential extension or *supplementum* (ibid., chap. 9), and the prescription for *imitatio*, or the emulation of a model after a stylistic analysis of it has been done (ibid., chap. 16).

40. Ibid., chap. 12, no. 14.

41. Ruhnke, *Joachim Burmeister*, p. 155. On the other hand, Palisca connects this figure to the graphic realism prized by humanist theorists who consider music from a rhetorical viewpoint. "*Ut oratoria musica*," p. 47.

42. Unger, in his *Beziehungen zwischen Musik und Rhetorik*, has made an initial but incomplete essay in this regard.

43. Brandes, *Studien zur musikalischen Figurenlehre*, p. 7; Unger, *Die Beziehungen zwischen Musik und Rhetorik*, p. 29; Federhofer, "Zum Manierismus-Problem in der Musik," p. 117; and Palisca, "*Ut oratoria musica*," p. 59.

CHAPTER XIV

1. *Compendium musices* (1552), pt. I, "De his quae futuro Musico sunt necessaria."

2. Ibid., pt. II, "De elegantia, et ornatu, aut pronuntiatione in canendo."

3. Manfred E. Bukfozer points out that castrati are called *soprani naturali* in contrast to falsettists who are *soprani artificiali*—another mannerist paradox. *Music in the Baroque Era*, p. 399.

4. *Discorso sopra la musica* (ca. 1628), American Institute of Musicology, 1962, p. 76.

5. Adriano Cavicchi, in the preface to his edition of Luzzaschi's *Madrigali per cantare et sonare* (1601), and Anthony Newcomb, in his review of this edition, both observe that the so-called three ladies of Ferrara never actually sang together as a trio. The full story about all the singers at this court is told in more detail in Newcomb's book, *The Madrigal at Ferrara*, which was published by Princeton University Press in 1978.

6. *Discorso* (ca. 1628), American Institute of Musicology, 1962, pp. 69–71.

7. Ibid., p. 74.

8. Ibid., pp. 76–77.

9. Nigel Fortune, "Solo Song and Cantata," p. 148.

10. *Madrigali per cantare et sonare a uno e doi e tre soprani* (1601); Fortune, "Solo Song and Cantata," p. 147.

11. Horsley, "The Diminutions in Composition and Theory of Composition," p. 126.

12. *Le istitutioni harmoniche* (1558), pt. III, chap. 45.

13. *Il vero modo di diminuir* (1584).

14. *Ricercate passaggi et cadentie* (1598) and *Motetti madrigali et canzone francese . . . diminuiti* (1591).

15. *Prattica di musica* (pt. I, 1592), bk. I, chap. 66.

16. *Breve et facile maniera d'essercitarsi ad ogni scholaro non solamente a far passaggi sopra tutte le note si desidera per cantare a far la dispositione leggiadra et in diversi modi loro valoro con le cadenze ma ancora per potere da se senza maestro scrivere ogni opera at arie passeggiata che voranno et come si notano* (1593).

17. *Discorso* (ca. 1628), American Institute of Musicology, 1962, p. 69.

18. *Regole passaggi di musica* (1594), "Avertimenti intorno alle note."

19. *Cartella musicale* (1614); *Brevi et primi documenti musicali,* pp. 49–50.

20. *Le nuove musiche* (1601), "Preface."

21. Caccini notes that *gorgie* and *passaggi* belong to instrumental music. He is obviously exaggerating in order to emphasize the reforms he advocates. Nonetheless, both Caccini's and Giustiniani's remarks suggest that excessive ornamentation, as indicated in standard manuals, is very much in vogue. We are therefore not misled into thinking "that singers actually sang the monstrosities they illustrate." Einstein, *Italian Madrigal,* p. 842.

22. For a discussion of the mid-voice in Caccini's system, see James Stark, "Giulio Caccini and the 'Noble Manner of Singing.'"

23. I note, as an aside, that a brief digression on this topic occurs in Artusi's treatise. Luca defends certain accented dissonances in Monteverdi's madrigals because that they are composed versions of improvised *accenti*; the resultant clashes produce remarkable effects. Vario replies that *accenti* are not excuses for barbarisms. *L'Artusi overo delle imperfettioni della moderna musica* (pt. 1, 1600), "Ragionamento secondo," pp. 41r–41v.

24. Pirrotta, "Temperaments and Tendencies in the Florentine Camerata," pp. 170–71; Fortune, "Solo Song and Cantata," pp. 151–52; and Palisca, "The Alterati of Florence," p. 10.

25. "*Discorso mandato a Caccini sopra la musica antica*" (ca. 1580). I consider it noteworthy that Bardi admits a limited amount of expressive potential in contrapuntal music that is characterized by careful treatment of the text, and that, moreover, he cites the excellence of Cipriano de Rore in this regard.

26. It is significant that both Bardi and Jacopo Corsi were members of the Accademia degli Alterati.

27. Palisca, *Girolamo Mei,* p. 70. See also, ibid., pp. 43–45, 47, and 11.

28. The correspondence between Galilei and Mei is reproduced in ibid.

29. Ibid., pp. 46–47, 54, and 71. Monteverdi's *stile concitato* corresponds to Mei's grand manner.

30. *Dialogo della musica antica e della moderna* (1581), p. 79.

31. Ibid., pp. 81, and 82–83.

32. Ibid., p. 99.

33. Ibid., pp. 83 and 86.

34. Ibid., pp. 89–90.

35. Ibid., p. 105.

36. *Le istitutioni harmoniche,* pt. II, chap. 1.

37. Ibid., chaps. 2–3.

38. Ibid., chap. 4.

39. Ibid., chaps. 4 and 5.

40. Ibid., chap. 7. The parallel between Zarlino's description and practical attempts at dramatic forms, including mannerist madrigals and early operas, is striking.

41. Ibid., chap. 7. Zarlino's comments on the nature of polyphony help us deduce the source of Giulio Cesare Monteverdi's remarks in this vein. Monteverdi's brother, of course, is aiming at a conclusion quite different from that of Zarlino.

42. Ibid. Although Zarlino is careful throughout this discussion to assume the objectivity of an antiquarian humanist, his initial exposition of musical history, tantamount to an evolutionary theory of progress, leaves no doubt as to

which style he deems superior. Modern counterpoint, which imitates the inner mathematical principles of nature, its cosmic harmony as it were, stands for Zarlino as a quintessential embodiment of neoplatonic ideals. In this regard, I am tempted to cite Lanham's characterization of the literature of the *homo seriosus*, the unified and dignified concept of the self, as creator, in harmony with the universe. Moreover, Lanham's characterization of the literature of the *homo rhetoricus*, the playful and ironic concept of the self, as creator, in the self-conscious act of role-playing and pose-assuming guises, bears a striking resemblance to the rhetorical thrust of the mannerist madrigal and even of mannerist monody, the assumed sobriety of monodists and composers of opera notwithstanding. The *homo seriosus* does not understand nor does he esteem the attitudes of the *homo rhetoricus*, and, in Lanham's view, this antipathy still generates misunderstanding of rhetorical style today. *The Motives of Eloquence*, especially pp. 1–25 and 111–15.

In the historical framework of our topic, I return to my hypothesis that Zarlino places ancient "rhetorical" music on a lower plateau than modern "harmonious" music as well as to my exposition of the more obviously denigrating remarks made by Zarlino about aberrant grafting of rhetorical tricks onto polyphony. Moreover, we shall discover in the next chapter that a number of prominent madrigalists whose works espouse rhetorical values consistently polemicize for the seriousness of their music. In Lanham's terms, they represent the *homo rhetoricus* combatting those musicians who represent the *homo seriosus*, and who consider rhetorical music to be frivolous and superficial.

43. I remind the reader that much of the affective content attributed to music in the *Figurenlehre* and *Affektenlehre* of the Baroque relies on stylized dance patterns.

44. *Le istitutioni harmoniche*, pt. II, chap. 7. Again, we witness the source for Giulio Cesare's contention that the second practice arises from the perfection of melody.

45. Ibid., chap. 9.

46. *Sopplimenti musicali* (1588), bk. VIII, chap. 8.

47. *De praesantia musicae veteris* (1647), bk. III, pp. 105–7.

48. Ibid., bk. II, pp. 54–59.

49. *Annotazioni sopra il compendio de'generi* (1640), pp. 60–62. Although written after the rise of Venetian public opera, Doni's work still focuses on early court opera. Palisca, *Baroque Music*, p. 33.

50. *Discorso sopra la musica* (ca. 1628), American Institute of Musicology, 1962, p. 77.

51. *Della poetica* (1586); *La deca disputata*, bk. III.

52. The academy presented a masque entitled *Gli Affetti* during the Florentine carnival of 1574. Palisca, "The Alterati of Florence," pp. 21–23.

53. "Letter to G. B. Doni" (1634).

54. This opera was first performed privately in 1594, and then given a second time officially during the carnival of 1597. The score is lost; however, several musical fragments have been discovered. William V. Porter, "Peri's and Corsi's *Dafne*."

55. *Euridice* (1600), "Dedication."

56. *Euridice* (1601), "Dedication."

57. This fact attests to Caccini's successful lobby against being excluded from this historic occasion.

CHAPTER XV

1. Helmut Hucke, "Das Problem des Manierismus in der Musik," p. 223.

2. A survey of these exegetical problems and methods for solving them will appear in a forthcoming study by the present author, "*Maniera* in the Writings of Vicentino and Zarlino." An earlier draft of this chapter has appeared in the *Journal of the Canadian Association of University Schools of Music* 7 (1977): 1–30.

3. *De la arte di ballare et danzare* (ca. 1450). Artur Michel, "The Earliest Dance Manuals," p. 123.

4. *Il libro dell'arte del danzare* (1455). Otto Kinkeldey, *A Jewish Dancing Master of the Renaissance: Guglielmo Ebreo*, pp. 9–11; and Michel, "The Earliest Dance Manuals," p. 124.

5. *Trattato dell'arte del ballo* (1463). Kinkeldey, *Guglielmo Ebreo*, pp. 9–10; Michel, "The Earliest Dance Manuals," p. 124; and Weise, "Maniera and pellegrino," p. 357.

6. A letter written by Glareanus in 1540 states that his treatise was finished in 1539 after twenty years of preparation. Willibald Gurlitt, "Die Kompositionslehre des deutschen 16. und 17. Jahrhundert," pp. 86–87. Because this work was apparently begun in 1519, Glareanus's association of the perfect art with Josquin seems less retrospective. Federhofer maintains that, for this very reason, any attribution of style consciousness to Mannerism cannot be substantiated—in other words, Glareanus formulated an ideal of the *ars perfecta* while this style was in full bloom. Federhofer, "Zum Manierismus-Problem in der Musik," p. 115. But in my view, given the circumstances of theoretical tradition in music at the time of Glareanus's writing, his ideal is a self-conscious one, and more important, it is later codified into a decidedly antiquarian notion of traditional style.

7. Hucke correctly supposes that Aaron and Vicentino would furnish thought-provoking material on *maniera*. "Das Problem des Manierismus," p. 224.

8. Federhofer errs in stating that *maniera* is a synonym for *modo*. "Zum Manierismus-Problem," p. 108. A detailed investigation of the grammatical, neutral, and substantive meanings of both terms will be undertaken in my forthcoming study.

9. *L'antica musica ridotta alla moderna prattica* (1555), bk. IV, chap. 16; bk. V, chaps. 5 and 6; bk. II, chaps. 9, 10, and 12; bk. III, chaps. 25 and 35; bk. IV, chaps. 18, 21–27, and 35.

10. Ibid., bk. II, chap. 1; bk. IV, chaps. 22 and 24, for instance.

11. Ibid., bk. IV, chaps. 15, 16, 33, 23, 13, and 26; bk. V, chap. 45.

12. Ibid., bk. I, chap. 6, and bk. V, chap. 3.

13. Ibid., bk. IV, chaps. 37 and 40.

14. Ibid., bk. V, chaps. 1 and 45.

15. Ibid., bk. IV, chap. 42.

16. Vicentino's detailed exploration of the use of illusionistic harmony in music takes place in another chapter. It will be discussed later.

17. *L'antica musica*, bk. III, chap. 15.

18. Ibid., bk. IV, chap. 29.

19. *Trattado . . . sopra una differentia musicale* (ca. 1556), p. 407. Quoted from Kaufmann, *Nicola Vicentino*, p. 192: "*fanno professione di comporre alla musica maniera.*"

20. The characteristics of Zarlino's text will also be examined in detail in my forthcoming study.

21. *Le istitutioni harmoniche* (1558), pt. III, chap. 74.

22. Ibid., pt. I, "Proemio."

23. Ibid., pt. IV, chaps. 1 and 2.

24. Ibid., chap. 3.

25. Schrade suggests that Zarlino borrows the term directly from Vasari. "Von der Maniera der Komposition in der Musik des 16. Jahrhundert," p. 6. This interpretation is repeated by Friedrich Blume in his *Renaissance and Baroque Music*, p. 17.

26. Zarlino's paraphrase from Vicentino's text appears in *Le istitutioni harmoniche*, pt. II, chap. 16, and his oblique references, apart from those at the end of pt. III and the start of pt. IV, already noted, occur in pt. II, chaps. 16 and 38.

27. Two scholars believe it is just a general term without technical or aesthetic connotations. Hucke, "Das Problem des Manierismus," p. 224; and Federhofer, "Zum Manierismus-Problem," p. 109.

28. This limitation is put forward by Schrade, "Von der Maniera der Komposition," pp. 7 and 101.

29. Zarlino's evaluation of modern perfection vis-à-vis the ancient imitation of nature is clearly recognized by Girolamo Mei, who, as we have seen, takes pains to refute it, for the benefit of Galilei.

30. The reader will recall Tasso's call for more gravity in musical settings of lyrical verse.

31. *Madrigali a quatro cinque et sei voci*, bk. I (1588), "Dedication."

32. *Il sesto libro de'madrigali a cinque voci* (1596), "Dedication."

33. *Le musiche da cantar solo* (1609), "Preface."

34. Most of the documents were collected from Emil Vogel's *Bibliothek der gedruckten weltlichen Vocalmusik Italiens*, as well as a number of articles that update his findings. Even so, I suspect that these sources do not yield a complete coverage. More systematic work on these sources is necessary, perhaps on the basis of the new edition of Vogel's *Bibliothek*, which is due to be published soon. However, a stimulating survey of selected documents has been made by Haar in "Self-Consciousness about Style, Form and Genre in 16th-Century Music."

35. *Il primo libro de madrigali a quatro voci* (1587), "Dedication."

36. *Il decimo libro delli madrigali a cinque voci* (1581), "Dedication."

37. T. Pecci's *Madrigali a cinque voci* (1602), "Preface."

38. *Primo libro de'madrigali a cinque voci* (1610), "Dedication."

39. The pun, *alla cieca*, refers to the title of the book and to the *Gioco della Cieca* excerpt from Guarini's *Il pastor fido* contained therein. *La Cieca madrigali a cinque voci libro quarto* (1609), "Preface."

40. *Rappresentatione di anima e di corpo* (1600), "Dedication."

41. In Part III of this book, I shall examine and evaluate the technical ingredients common to the mannerist styles of polyphonic and monodic music as well as opera.

42. *La Dafne* (1608), "Preface."

43. *Intermedii et concerti* (1591), "Dedication."

44. *La Dafne*, "Preface."

45. *Madrigali e canzonette spirituali* (1607), "Dedication."

46. Hucke, "Das problem des Manierismus," p. 223.

47. *Cartella musicale* (1614); *Discorso sopra la moderna pratica musicale,* p. 165.

48. *Il Melone* (1602), p. 38. Bottrigari's use of *modo* and *maniera* implies a distinction between the technical application of the chromatic genus and the resultant chromatic style of the finished piece. This distinction seems to be drawn from Vicentino's treatise. In a previous chapter, I mentioned my opinion that Vicentino's influence has been underrated. One theorist of the late sixteenth century who borrows from Vicentino is Pietro Ponzio. This writer discusses the stylistic differences among various genres, and substitutes for Vicentino's *maniera* the more up-to-date term, *stile*; however, he fails to grasp Vicentino's careful separation of method from style, and therefore uses *modo* and *stile* as synonyms. *Ragionamento di musica* (1588), "Ragionamento quarto," pp. 153–55.

49. *Il Melone secondo* (1602), pp. 4–5. Bottrigari's adjectives for Rore as a composer can be easily adapted as adjectives for his musical style (i.e. *il più artificioso,* and *il più leggiadro & polito*).

50. *Discorso sopra la musica* (ca. 1628), American Institute of Musicology, 1962, p. 72.

51. Ibid., p. 74.

52. Federhofer's count of thirty appearances of *maniera* is slightly inaccurate. "Zum Manierismus-Problem," p. 109. There are altogether twenty-nine occurrences of *maniera,* of which one has a clearly grammatical function.

53. Table of contents for the *Discorso sopra la perfettione delle melodie,* in the *Compendio del trattato de'generi e de'modi della musica* (1635). See Haar, "Classicism and Mannerism in 16th-Century Music," p. 59, n. 8. Haar points out that in the text of this tract, Doni uses the term *stile madrigalesca.*

CHAPTER XVI

1. Palisca, "The Beginnings of Baroque Music," p. 234, and "A Clarification of 'Musica Reservata' in Jean Taisnier's 'Astrologiae' 1559," p. 133; and Meier, "The Musica Reservata of Adrianus Petit Coclico and its Relationship to Josquin," pp. 67–68.

2. *Compendium musices* (1552), "Praefatio."

3. *L'antica musica ridotta alla moderna prattica* (1555), bk. I, chap. 4.

4. Lowinsky, *Secret Chromatic Art in the Netherlands Motet,* p. 90; and Kaufmann, *Nicola Vicentino,* pp. 189–90.

5. "Letter" (28 April 1555).

6. Kaufmann, *Nicola Vicentino,* p. 191; and Palisca, "A Clarification of 'Musica Reservata,' " pp. 148–49.

7. "Letter" (22 September 1555).

8. Gustave Reese, *Music in the Renaissance,* p. 516, as opposed to Adolf Sandberger, *Beiträge zur Geschichte der bayerische Hofkapelle unter Orlando di Lasso* 1:55–56; and Kaufmann, *Nicola Vicentino,* p. 191.

9. *Madrigali a cinque voci* (1546). In the dedication, Vicentino expands a little on the *nuovo modo* by indicating that his audience should realize that this *modo raro di comporre* is based on true musical *concenti* rediscovered by his teacher after their undeserved neglect in the past. What is particularly fascinating about this statement is its relation to Zarlino's later praise of Willaert, a composer

whose *elegante maniera* epitomizes the contemporary rediscovery of ancient harmony, in his opinion.

10. *Astrologiae iudiciariae ysagogica* (1559) and *Opus mathematicum* (1562), "Prefaces." Palisca, "A Clarification of 'Musica Reservata,' " p. 137; and Kaufmann, *Nicola Vicentino*, p. 192.

11, Reese, *Music in the Renaissance*, p. 515; Lowinsky, *Secret Chromatic Art*, p. 97; and Marius van Crevel, *Adrianus Petit Coclico*, p. 296, versus Sandberger, *Beiträge zur Geschichte*, 1:53–55; Kurt Huber, *Ivo de Vento*, p. 109; and Theodore Kroyer, "Von der Musica Reservata des 16. Jahrhunderts," p. 130.

12. "Letter" (1 July 1555).

13. Reese, *Music in the Renaissance*, p. 515; Lowinsky, *Secret Chromatic Art*, p. 97; and Van Crevel, *Adrianus Petit Coclico*, p. 296.

14. *Astrologiae*, "Preface."

15. Palisca, "A Clarification of 'Musica Reservata,' " pp. 143–47; and Robert Wangermée, *Flemish Musical Society in the Fifteenth and Sixteenth Centuries*, p. 253.

16. *De musica*, Acts of the Synod of Besançon (1571). Palisca, "A Clarification of 'Musica Reservata,' " pp. 150 and 154.

17. (Ca. 1611). This source is reprinted by Federhofer in "Eine neue Quelle der Musica Reservata."

18. Palisca, "A Clarification of 'Musica Reservata,' " p. 154, versus Federhofer, "Monodie and musica reservata," p. 33.

19. (1619). Willene Clark discusses and reproduces various versions of the document in "A Contribution to Sources of Musica Reservata." See also, Kaufmann, *Nicola Vicentino*, p. 216; and Palisca, "A Clarification of 'Musica Reservata,' " p. 154.

20. Reese, *Music in the Renaissance*, p. 515; and Einstein, *Italian Madrigal*, p. 226.

21. Meier, "The Musica Reservata of Adrianus Petit Coclico," pp. 67–68, 90, and 104.

22. *Il primo libro dove si contengono madrigali* (1555), "Dedication."

23. Sandberger, *Beiträge zur Geschichte*, 1:110; Lucie Balmer, *Orlando di Lassos Motetten*, p. 19, as opposed to Palisca, "The Beginnings of Baroque Music," p. 235; and Van Crevel, *Adrianus Petit Coclico*, pp. 301–2.

24. *Libri tres de institutione harmonica* (1516), bk. II, chap. 9. The reader should note that Aaron uses the words *inconsueta atque recondita* to describe a motet by Spataro because of its use of intervals from the chromatic and enharmonic genera.

25. *Musicae activae micrologus* (1517), bk. II, chap. 8.

26. Einstein, *Italian Madrigal*, p. 225; Federhofer, "Monodie und musica reservata," p. 34; and Hucke, "Das Problem des Manierismus in der Musik," p. 226.

27. *Opera nuova di musica intitolata armonia celeste nella qualle si contengono 25 madrigali pieni d'ogni dolcezza et soavità musicale composti con dotte arte et reservato ordine* (1556).

28. Lowinsky, *Secret Chromatic Art*, p. 94; Van Crevel, *Adrianus Petit Coclico*, p. 299; Helmut Osthoff, *Die Niederländer und das deutsche Lied*, p. 274; Edgar R. Scholund, "The *Compendium Musices* of Adrianus Petit Coclico," p. 123; and Kaufmann, *Nicola Vicentino*, p. 214.

29. Einstein, *Italian Madrigal*, pp. 227 and 464, and "Vicenzo Ruffo's *Opera nova di musica*," p. 234; and Palisca, "The Beginnings of Baroque Music," p. 230.

30. *Regole et dichiaratione di alcuni contrappunti doppii* (1610).

31. Federhofer, "Monodie und musica reservata," pp. 32 and 34.

32. *Ricercate*, bk. 1 (1603), "Preface."

33. Adriano Banchieri's description of these two styles has been mentioned several times. At this point, we add to our collection of documents the comments of Girolamo Diruta concerning free counterpoint (*contrapunto commune*) and strict counterpoint (*contrapunto osservato*); Diruta considers the latter style to be more beautiful and charming than the former. *Il transilvano* (pt. II, 1603), p. 3.

34. Reese, *Music in the Renaissance*, p. 515; Carapetyan, "The *Musica Nova* of Adriano Willaert," pp. 266–67; Meier, "The Musica Reservata of Adrianus Petit Coclico," p. 104.

35. Lowinsky, *Secret Chromatic Art*, pp. 88–89 and 109.

36. Palisca, "A Clarification of 'Musica Reservata,'" p. 155.

37. The full citation of the original source can be found in Kaufmann, *Nicola Vicentino*, p. 206.

38. Ibid., pp. 204–5.

39. Munich (1560).

40. Lowinsky, *Secret Chromatic Art*, p. 92.

41. A detailed discussion of these motets is given in Meier, "The Musica Reservata of Adrianus Petit Coclico."

42. Kaufmann, *Nicola Vicentino*, p. 192; and Palisca, "A Clarification of 'Musica Reservata,'" p. 137.

43. Palisca, "A Clarification of 'Musica Reservata,'" p. 150. Gregor Faber and Matthaeus Greiter adumbrate similar ideas without reference to *musica reservata*.

44. *Doctrina de tonis seu modis musicis* (1582), chap. 2. See Meier, "Eine weitere Quelle der Musica Reservata."

45. Kaufmann, *Nicola Vicentino*, p. 194.

46. Palisca, "A Clarification of 'Musica Reservata,'" p. 157.

47. Kaufmann, *Nicola Vicentino*, p. 187; Meier, "The Musica Reservata of Adrianus Petit Coclico," p. 92; and René B. Lenearts, "Parodia, Reservata-Kunst en muzikaal symbolisme," p. 108.

48. Palisca, "A Clarification of 'Musica Reservata,'" pp. 142 and 155–56.

49. See Palisca, "*Ut oratoria musica*."

50. Lowinsky, *Secret Chromatic Art*, p. 94.

51. *Il desiderio* (1594), p. 42, and American Institute of Musicology, 1962, p. 52.

52. Kaufmann, *Nicola Vicentino*, p. 217.

53. Hucke, "Das Problem des Manierismus in der Musik," p. 225.

54. Before 1961, three scholars connect *musica reservata* with mannerist tendencies or with the cultural spirit of Mannerism in the sixteenth century—to wit, Federhofer, "Monodie und musica reservata"; Palisca, "A Clarification of 'Musica Reservata'"; and Robert E. Wolf, "Renaissance, Mannerism, Baroque."

55. For instance, Wangermée places *musica reservata* in the mainstream development of musical style that bridges Mannerism and the Baroque. *Flemish*

Musical Society, p. 253. The fourth chapter of Kaufmann's *Nicola Vicentino* is entitled, "Reservata—A Problem of Musical Mannerism." And Palisca links Mannerism to incipient baroque figures in "*Ut oratoria musica.*"

56. Palisca, "A Clarification of 'Musica Reservata,'" p. 159.

CHAPTER XVII

1. The following essays demonstrate the inherent weaknesses of this approach, one that lessens the impact of their often penetrating insights: Schrade, "Von der Maniera der Komposition in der Musik des 16. Jahrhundert"; Wolf, "Renaissance, Mannerism, Baroque"; Rowland, *Mannerism—Style and Mood*; and in a few instances, Harrán, "'Mannerism' in the Cinquecento Madrigal?"; and Lowinsky, "The Problem of Mannerism in Music."

2. Harrán, "'Mannerism' in the Cinquecento Madrigal?"; Hucke, "Das Problem des Manierismus in der Musik"; Federhofer, "Zum Manierismus-Problem in der Musik"; Haar, "Classicism and Mannerism in 16th-Century Music"; Pirrotta, *Li due Orfei da Poliziano a Monteverdi*; and Palisca, "Towards an Intrinsically Musical Definition of Mannerism in the Sixteenth Century."

3. Haar, "Classicism and Mannerism," p. 57; Wolf, "Renaissance, Mannerism, Baroque," p. 42; and Beekman C. Cannon, Alvin H. Johnson, and William G. Waite, *The Art of Music*, p. 182.

4. Cannon, Johnson, and Waite, *The Art of Music*, p. 182; Einstein, *Italian Madrigal*, p. 29; and Lowinsky, "The Problem of Mannerism in Music," pp. 133, 140.

5. Harrán, "'Mannerism,'" p. 543.

6. Lorenzo Bianconi, "Giulio Caccini e il manierismo musicale," pp. 25–26.

7. Wolf, "Renaissance, Mannerism, Baroque," p. 42.

8. Meier, "Hieroglyphisches in der Musik des 16. Jahrhunderts," pp. 127–28; Einstein, *Italian Madrigal*, pp. 224 and 234–35; and Wangermée, *Flemish Musical Society in the Fifteenth and Sixteenth Centuries*, p. 240.

9. Haar, "Classicism and Mannerism," p. 66.

10. Ibid., p. 66; and Engel, *Luca Marenzio*, pp. 98–99, 100–101. Another scholar calls these elements of the mid-sixteenth-century madrigal "baroque." Susanne Clercx, *Le baroque et la musique*, p. 42. In my view, this is a misnomer. Many of these characteristics survive into baroque style, to be sure, but they represent an integral aspect of Mannerism, the period that intervenes between the Renaissance and the Baroque.

11. Haar, "Classicism and Mannerism," pp. 61–63.

12. Wolf, "The Aesthetic Problem of the 'Renaissance,'" p. 91.

CHAPTER XVIII

1. *Fama malum* may have been performed as a wedding entertainment in Milan in 1489. See Lowinsky, "Josquin des Prez and Ascanio Sforza," p. 19. Complete information concerning the musical works can be found in the Bibliography of primary sources.

2. Lowinsky, "Matthaeus Greiter's *Fortuna*," p. 515, and "The Musical Avant-Garde of the Renaissance," p. 116. New documentary evidence is cited by Lowinsky as support for the possibility that *Fortuna d'un gran tempo* "was

composed in 1499, under the immediate impression of the fall of the house of Sforza." Lowinsky, "Ascanio Sforza's Life," p. 71.

3. This piece could be a lament on the death of Juan Borgia, son of Pope Alexander VI, who was assassinated in 1497. Lowinsky, "Josquin des Prez and Ascanio Sforza," pp. 20–21.

4. Lowinsky, "The Musical Avant-Garde," pp. 118 and 120, and "Echoes of Adrian Willaert's Chromatic 'Duo' in Sixteenth- and Seventeenth-Century Compositions," p. 183; and Reese, *Music in the Renaissance*, pp. 369–70. Lowinsky has reconstructed the complete composition in "Adrian Willaert's Chromatic 'Duo' Re-Examined," pp. 33–36.

5. This association is suggested by Kroyer, *Die Anfänge der Chromatik im italienischen Madrigal des XVI. Jahrhunderts*, p. 34.

6. Harrán, "'Mannerism' in the Cinquecento Madrigal," pp. 538–43. Another scholar sees imitative counterpoint as a decorative device. Jerome Roche, *The Madrigal*, p. 19.

7. Haar, "Classicism and Mannerism in 16th-Century Music," p. 62.

8. Einstein, *Italian Madrigal*, p. 246.

9. Adrian Willaert rearranged many of them in 1536 for solo soprano and lute accompaniment. An example, *Con lagrime et sospir*, is available in Einstein, *Italian Madrigal*, 3:319–20.

10. Slim, *A Gift of Madrigals and Motets*, p. 189. Slim's analysis of *I vostri acuti dardi* isolates rhythmic, textural, and rhetorical figures. Ibid., pp. 176–77. His conclusion that this work is a comic satire on poetical-musical conventions, however, belies the seriousness with which these madrigalisms were explored at the time.

11. *Ragionamenti accademici* (1567), p. 36: "some facileness, some gravity, some gentility, some compassion, some quickness, some slowness, some kindliness, some anger, some fugacity, according to the propriety of the words."

12. Einstein, *Italian Madrigal*, p. 326; and Erich Hertzmann, *Adrian Willaert in der weltlichen Vokalmusik seiner Zeit*, p. 40.

13. Kroyer, *Anfänge der Chromatik*, p. 40.

14. Wolfgang Osthoff, *Theatergesang und darstellende Musik in der italienischen Renaissance*, pp. 270–71. Osthoff suggests that, originally, the madrigal must have been the epilogue to a comedy.

15. The examples are cited in Kroyer's *Anfänge der Chromatik*, pp. 40 and 42.

16. The terms "linear semitone" or "melodic semitone" designate semitonal relationships between any two notes of adjacent triads. In the case of Viola's madrigal, for instance, the triads of B♭ major and G minor entail no linear semitone; A major and F major, on the other hand, have two such semitones (E-F and C♯-C), whereas A minor and F major entail only one (E-F). The semitone-related pair of triads, A major and B♭ major, involve schematically three linear semitones (A-B♭, C♯-D, and E-F); the latter does not appear in the music. This analytical approach to chromaticism, which to my knowledge has not been systematically exploited, is useful and instructive for several reasons. First, it creates a counterbalance to a vertical consideration of triads, and thus reinstates the primacy of linear voice leading, a consideration never forgotten by sixteenth-century madrigalists. Second, by isolating both the number of such linear connec-

tions between a triadic pair as well as the nature and number of the accidentals involved, it acts as a guide for charting the development of chromatic language.

17. At the point in question, one finds parallel fourths between the soprano and alto, a not uncommon occurrence in Viola's output.

18. Einstein, *Italian Madrigal*, p. 288.

19. Haar, "Classicism and Mannerism," p. 62.

20. *Dodecachordon* (1547), bk. III, chap. 13.

21. Wolf, "The Aesthetic Problem of the 'Renaissance,'" pp. 92–94; and Haar, "Classicism and Mannerism," p. 63.

22. Alec Harman and Anthony Milner, *Late Renaissance and Baroque Music*, p. 543. Rore set six of the canzonas (found at the close of the *In morte di Madonna Laura*) in 1548; and he completed the cycle in the 1552 reprint of this book.

23. The year 1547 marks the first publication of this composition in Perissone Cambio's first book of four-voiced madrigals. It was reprinted in the *Madrigali de la fama a quattro voci* (Venice, 1548) and then reappeared in Rore's *Il primo libro de madrigali a quatro voci* (Venice, 1550). The madrigal was reprinted many times and, of course, it was included in Angelo Gardano's full-score edition, *Tutti i madrigali di Cipriano di Rore a quattro voci spartiti et accommodati per sonar d'orgi sorte d'istrumento perfetto & per qualunque studioso di contrapunti* (Venice, 1577).

24. The numerous imitations, arrangements, parodies, and the like are examined by Ernst T. Ferand, *"Anchor che col partire."*

25. Bianconi, "The Caccinian Workshop of Pietro Maria Marsolo," p. XXXVII. Bianconi's study concerns Marsolo's polyphonic elaborations of solo songs, principally those of Giulio Caccini, published in 1614. Haar, on the other hand, in *"Pace non trovo,"* presents evidence for "parody" techniques in both poetry and music relating to a Petrarch sonnet and three settings of it by Arcadelt, a certain Ivo, and Palestrina—evidence spanning the sixteenth century. The translations, paraphrases, and petrarchist parodies in French, Spanish, and English literature occasioned by *Pace non trovo* are dealt with by Emanuela Hager, *Übersetzungen und Nachdichtungen von Sonetten Petrarcas in der europäischen Lyrik des 16. Jahrhunderts*, pp. 127–76.

Parenthetically, I note that even in the case of sacred music, in the Mass to be specific, the phenomenon of parody—insofar as it addresses stylistic principles in the original and their stylization in the refashioned version—seems to point to current awareness of *maniera*, together with all the musical premises and problems it entails. This point is made by Glenn Watkins, "Carlo Gesualdo and the Delimitations of Late Mannerist Style," p. 62.

Chapter XIX

1. This evaluation of the musical scene differs substantially from that put forward by other scholars who deny that music embodies a crisis analogous to that in the sister arts; for instance, Bianconi, "Giulio Caccini e il manierismo musicale," pp. 25–26.

2. All these pieces have been intensively studied by Lowinsky in the following works: "The Goddess Fortuna in Music"; *Secret Chromatic Art in the Netherlands Motet*; "Matthaeus Greiter's *Fortuna*"; and "The Musical Avant-Garde of the Renaissance."

3. Lowinsky, "Matthaeus Greiter's *Fortuna*," pp. 500–503, and *Tonality and Atonality in Sixteenth-Century Music*, pp. 48–49.

4. Kroyer, *Die Anfänge der Chromatik im italienischen Madrigal des XVI. Jahrhunderts*, pp. 88–92.

5. An analysis can be found in Kaufmann, "A 'Diatonic' and a 'Chromatic' Madrigal by Giulio Fiesco"; and Lowinsky, "The Problem of Mannerism in Music."

6. Dahlhaus, "Zur chromatischen Technik Carlo Gesualdos," p. 90.

7. Einstein, *Italian Madrigal*, p. 427; and Edward J. Dent, "The Sixteenth-Century Madrigal," pp. 50–51.

8. Wolfgang Boetticher, *Aus Orlando di Lassos Wirkungskreis*, p. 29; and Einstein, *Italian Madrigal*, p. 480. Lowinsky also notes a letter written to Lasso by Adrian Le Roy (1574) in which the cycle is mentioned. *Secret Chromatic Art*, p. 93.

9. Lowinsky, *Tonality and Atonality*, p. 41.

10. Willem Elders, *Studien zur Symbolik in der Musik der alten Niederländer*, pp. 37 and 168–69.

11. As does Haar, "Classicism and Mannerism in 16th-Century Music," p. 63.

12. We see here the disillusionment of a master who had his avant-garde fling as a youth and now has lost patience with the latest fads.

13. Dent, "The Sixteenth-Century Madrigal," p. 48; and Louis D. Nuernberger, "The Five-Voiced Madrigals of Cipriano de Rore," p. 314.

14. Palisca, *Baroque Music*, p. 16.

15. Some of the pictorial devices are enumerated by Roche, *The Madrigal*, p. 44.

16. Einstein, *Italian Madrigal*, p. 645. An example by Barre, *Dunque fia ver dicea a4*, is available in Peter Wagner, "Das Madrigal und Palestrina." The *arioso* style is not limited to Barre's publications. We see it, for example, in an early work by Giaches de Wert, *Dunque baciar a4* (1561; Ariosto, *Orlando furioso*). Like Barre's work, Wert's madrigal is certainly amenable to solo performance. See Einstein, *Italian Madrigal*, 3:219–20.

17. Shearman, *Mannerism*, p. 100. Willaert's *Liete e pensose a7* (Petrarch) is a good example of this particular characteristic—that is, fusion of dramatic and structural elements.

18. Einstein, *Italian Madrigal*, pp. 555–57.

19. Denis Arnold, "Monteverdi and his Teachers," pp. 100, 103, and 105–6; and Carol MacClintock, *Giaches de Wert*, p. 69.

20. Arnold, "Monteverdi and his Teachers," p. 99; and MacClintock, *Giaches de Wert*, p. 100.

21. MacClintock, *Giaches de Wert*, p. 80. This scholar recognizes the expressive value of the seventh leap but not its witty meaning.

22. Ibid., p. 94.

23. *Dialogo della musica antica e della moderna* (1581), p. 89: "& facendo mentione il concetto che egli [moderni] hanno tra mano (come alle volte occorre) del romore del Tamburo, ò del suono delle Trombe, ò d'altro strumento tale, hanno cercato di rappresentare all'udito col canto loro i suoni di esso, senza fare stima alcuna, d'haver pronuntiate tali parole in qual si voglia maniera inusitata."

24. Haar, "Classicism and Mannerism," p. 62.

25. Dent, "The Sixteenth-Century Madrigal," p. 58.

CHAPTER XX

1. Einstein, *Italian Madrigal*, p. 242.

2. *Da le belle contrade a5* (1566). Although Giaches de Wert's *Aspro cor e selvaggio a4* (1561; Petrarch) is earlier than the period now under discussion, I mention it here to point out the use of black notes on *e notte oscura*.

3. Einstein, *Italian Madrigal*, p. 627.

4. Ibid., p. 638.

5. Hans F. Redlich, *Claudio Monteverdi*, p. 55; and Hugo Leichtentritt, "Claudio Monteverdi als Madrigalkomponist," p. 262.

6. There exist at least twenty-eight other settings of this poem, a great many of which represent emulations of Marenzio's madrigal. Of particular interest is Andrea Gabrieli's piece for seven voices, a work published posthumously in 1587. Gabrieli's approach differs from that of courtly madrigalists inasmuch as word painting is passed over in favor of a structural projection of the poem. The narrative and dialogue portions are set to alternate choirs of low and high voices, and the final erotic moral of the poem constitutes a musical climax with all parts in seven-voiced counterpoint. Gabrieli's declamatory melodies and sonorous planes presage baroque monumentalism, and in this respect, Einstein's description, "cantata in madrigal clothing" appears fully justified. See his "Anfänge des Vokalkonzerts," p. 10. However, we should note that the dialogue segments of Gabrieli's setting are stylistically similar to the narrative segments. Although this homogeneity contributes to organic continuity, it also minimizes the dramatic impact of the poem.

7. Einstein, *Italian Madrigal*, p. 617; Arnold, *Marenzio*, p. 8; and Roche, *The Madrigal*, p. 63.

8. Einstein, *Italian Madrigal*, p. 646.

9. The relevant excerpt from *Piangea Filli* can be found in ibid., pp. 651–52.

10. Wert's *Giunto alla tomba a5* (1581) was published in the same year as the first printed edition of the epic. Its singular style will be examined later in this chapter.

11. Einstein, *Italian Madrigal*, p. 624; and Lowinsky, "The Musical Avant-Garde of the Renaissance," p. 145.

12. Arnold, *Marenzio*, p. 23.

13. Newcomb, "Carlo Gesualdo and a Musical Correspondence of 1594." Watkins's book, *Gesualdo*, presents new insights into the composer's life, musical style, and influence.

14. This technique is explained in detail by Watkins; see, for example, his analysis of *Arde il mio cor a5* (1596). Ibid., pp. 162–63.

15. We should also mention Gesualdo's use of "dominant sevenths" in the final cadential phrase—a transitory one in third inversion and an obvious one in first inversion.

16. Einstein, *Italian Madrigal*, p. 684; and Arnold, *Marenzio*, pp. 35–36.

17. MacClintock, *Giaches de Wert*, p. 119. Note the contraposition of "mannered" and "baroque" in this scholar's comments. These words may be taken as indicators of the dual qualities present in Wert's *Mia benigna fortuna/ Crudel acerba inesorabil morte*, these qualities being intellectual preciosity on the one hand, and emotional communication on the other hand.

18. Einstein, *Italian Madrigal*, p. 687.

19. Arnold, *Marenzio*, p. 35.

20. Strictly speaking, the A is not a dissonance; however, its motion to the fifth above D—as if propelled by the magnetic force of the highest dissonant voice—creates a curiously empty and deliberately awkward sound.

21. Einstein, *Italian Madrigal*, p. 519; and MacClintock, *Giaches de Wert*, p. 108.

22. Einstein, *Italian Madrigal*, p. 732.

23. Ibid., p. 724.

24. *Ah dolente partita* is analyzed in detail by Pierluigi Petrobelli, who compares the settings by Marenzio, Wert, and Monteverdi in his article, "*Ah dolente partita.*" An encapsulated comparison also appears in Bianconi's article, "*Ah dolente partita.*" The latter scholar concludes that Marenzio's setting (1594) sets an individual precedent or model complete with its own *topoi* and *loci communes*, thereby suggesting connections between *musica poetica* and *maniera*. Ibid., pp. 110–12.

25. MacClintock, *Giaches de Wert*, p. 129.

26. Arnold, "Monteverdi and his Teachers," p. 105; MacClintock, *Giaches de Wert*, p. 127.

27. *Se tu dolce*, in Einstein, *Italian Madrigal*, p. 682.

28. As suggested by Engel, "Werden und Wesen des Madrigals," p. 51.

29. One notable exception from Marenzio's early works is *Scaldava il sol* (1582), where high ranges answer a specific need for mood evocation.

30. Einstein, *Italian Madrigal*, p. 501.

CHAPTER XXI

1. Redlich, article on Gesualdo in *Musik in Geschichte und Gegenwart*, 5:43.

2. *Censure* (1623). I cannot resist the idea that Effrem seeks to aggrandize himself by emulating Artusi; his imitation, however, amounts to a teapot tempest. Another interesting hypothesis is that Effrem, as a close associate of Gesualdo in Naples, shares his noble patron's belief that Gagliano, among other poachers, plagiarized from Gesualdo's chromatic compositions. Watkins, *Gesualdo*, p. 298.

3. *Cruda Amarilli, O Mirtillo, Ma se con la pietà*, and *Era l'anima mia*; all Guarini texts, the first three from *Il pastor fido*.

4. Three of the anonymous poems may also be by Guarini: *Amor se giusto sei, Questi vaghi concenti*, and *Che dar più*. Pirrotta, "Scelte poetiche di Monteverdi," p. 226, n. 66.

5. Einstein, *Italian Madrigal*, p. 851.

6. Pirrotta, "Scelte poetiche," pp. 226–27.

7. Wilhelm Weismann, "Ein verkannter Madrigal-Zyklus Monteverdis," pp. 45–46; and Leichtentritt, "Claudio Monteverdi als Madrigalkomponist," p. 228. The declamatory style of the cycle must not be underestimated; in fact, it exists in a manuscript version for two voices and continuo. See Pamela J. Willets, "A Neglected Source of Monody and Madrigal," p. 330.

8. This attribution is made by Pirrotta, "Scelte poetiche," p. 28.

9. The passage reappears in measures 46–47.

10. Einstein, *Italian Madrigal*, p. 710. The madrigal to which Einstein refers is *Mercè grido piangendo a5*, a work that features E♯ and B♯ accidentals as parts

of C♯ major and G♯ major chords on the words *Morrò* and *mora*, respectively.

11. Jackson, "On Frescobaldi's Chromaticism and its Background," pp. 265–66.

12. For example, *Tu m'uccidi o crudele* and *Mercè grido piangendo.*

13. This connection may emerge more clearly after the "Gesualdo school" of Neapolitan madrigalists has been studied in more detail. See Watkins, *Gesualdo*, pp. 228–42.

14. Jackson interprets this motive, E♮ D E♭ E♮, as an *inganno* variant, and notes that it is taken up by Girolamo Frescobaldi in his *Fantasia ottava* (1608). "On Frescobaldi's Chromaticism," pp. 262–63.

15. George R. Marshall, "The Harmonic Laws in the Madrigals of Carlo Gesualdo," p. 39; and Dahlhaus, "Zur chromatischen Technik Carlo Gesualdos," p. 91.

16. Einstein, *Italian Madrigal*, p. 715; Redlich, article on Gesualdo, p. 43; Dent, "The Sixteenth-Century Madrigal," p. 69; and Kerman, *The Elizabethan Madrigal*, p. 220.

17. Dent, "The Sixteenth-Century Madrigal," p. 68. Watkins considers this contrast to be the essentially mannerist aspect of his style. *Gesualdo*, p. 108.

18. Dahlhaus, "Zur chromatischen Technik Carlos Gesualdos," p. 90.

19. Ludwig Finscher, "Gesualdos 'Atonalität' und das Problem des musikalischen Manierismus," p. 77; and Rowland, *Mannerism—Style and Mood*, p. 23.

20. Shearman, *Mannerism*, p. 100. Watkins recognizes this twofold evaluation of Gesualdo in his historical context. *Gesualdo*, p. 212.

21. Arnold, "Monteverdi: some Colleagues and Pupils," p. 113.

22. They are reminiscent of the dissonant passage from Marenzio's *Così nel mio parlar* (1599), described in a previous chapter.

23. Palisca, *Baroque Music*, p. 12.

24. Petrobelli, *"Ah dolente partita,"* p. 372.

25. In addition to *Ah dolente partita*, *Anima mia perdona* (1603) and *O Mirtillo* (1605) can be cited.

26. Two scholars erroneously attribute this text to Boccaccio: Schrade, *Monteverdi*, p. 180; and Redlich, *Claudio Monteverdi: Das Madrigalwerk*, pp. 94–95. Actually, it is Linco's speech to Silvio from the first act.

27. Here I find echoes of Marenzio's *Scaldava il sol* (1582) and *Piangea Filli* (1585).

28. Arnold, *Monteverdi*, p. 64.

29. Salomone Rossi, bk. II (1602), Pompeo Signorucci, bk. I (1602), and Luzzasco Luzzaschi. *Madrigali per cantare et sonare* (1601).

30. Leichtentritt, "Claudio Monteverdi," p. 289.

31. Schrade, *Monteverdi*, p. 208.

32. The *quinto* voice, the second soprano, does not appear until the final seventeen measures of the piece.

33. Schrade, *Monteverdi*, p. 216; and Arnold, *Monteverdi*, pp. 76 and 78.

34. Bianconi, "Struttura poetica e struttura musicale nei madrigali di Monteverdi," p. 347.

35. This latter quality is linked with Mannerism by Fabbri, "Tasso, Guarini e il 'divino Claudio,'" p. 11.

36. Arnold, "Monteverdi: some Colleagues and Pupils," p. 122.

37. As does, for instance, Shearman, *Mannerism*, p. 101.

38. Humor, parody, and musical games characterize Orazio Vecchi's *Le veglie di Siena a5* (1604). In this case, Vecchi musicalizes the academic entertainments presented in Girolamo Bargagli's *Dialogo de'giuochi* (1572). The treatise describes the musical games played by the Sienese Accademia degli Introuati. For a discussion of these works and their relationship, see Haar, "On Musical Games in the Sixteenth Century."

CHAPTER XXII

1. Schrade, *Monteverdi*, pp. 277–78.
2. Pirrotta, "Early Opera and Aria," p. 45.
3. An instructive sample of such descriptions is the one provided by Vicenzo Giustiniani, *Discorso sopra la musica* (ca. 1628), American Institute of Musicology, 1962, p. 69.
4. Palisca, *Baroque Music*, p. 50.
5. Fortune, "Solo Song and Cantata," p. 181.
6. Pirrotta has identified Tasso's *Al lume delle stelle* and also has established that the text of *Tirsi e Clori* is not by Alessandro Striggio. "Scelte poetiche di Monteverdi," pp. 253 and 239.
7. *A quest'olmo a6* (Marino) and *Con che soavità a1* (Guarini). The latter solo work will be discussed later in this chapter.
8. Palisca, *Baroque Music*, p. 53.
9. Denis Stevens, "*Madrigali guerrieri, et amorosi*," p. 172.
10. The problematic designation *alla francese*, has not been definitively settled, although a number of theories have been put forward by different historians.
11. Two scholars evaluate it as such: Stevens, "*Madrigali guerrieri, et amorosi*," p. 182; and Redlich, *Claudio Monteverdi: Das Madrigalwerk*, p. 207.
12. Admiration for Monteverdi's composition encourages a budding tradition, and laments on ostinato patterns, specifically ones comprised of four descending notes, soon become a distinct convention in dramatic music—whether opera, cantata, or oratorio.
13. John H. Baron, "Monody: A Study in Terminology," pp. 462–63. The sole exception to this statement is found in the anonymous Besançon treatise, *De musica* (1571). Wilhelm Bäumker, "Über den Kontrapunkt," p. 64.
14. Einstein, *Italian Madrigal*, pp. 845–47.
15. Composers of solo madrigals still focus on the concettist lyrics of Tasso, Guarini, Marino, and their imitators, whereas the favorite poet of composers of strophic airs is Gabriello Chiabrera, one of the best exponents of lighthearted verse. His anacreontic poetry ranks far above that of other countless poetasters. In particular, Chiabrera's vivacious rhythmic configurations lend themselves to melodic invention.
16. Fortune, "Italian Secular Monody from 1600–1630," pp. 172, 176–77, and 181.
17. Bianconi, "Giulio Caccini e il manierismo musicale," pp. 27–29.
18. In the *Nuove musiche* of 1614, Caccini explores the solo aria. H. Wiley Hitchcock has proved that the *Fuggilotio musicale* (1613) is not by this composer. "Depriving Caccini of a Musical Pastime."
19. Hitchcock, "Vocal Ornamentation in Caccini's *Nuove musiche*," p. 183.

20. As does Fortune, "Italian Secular Monody," p. 183.

21. MacClintock, "The Monodies of Francesco Rasi." *Ahi fuggitivo ben*, a strophic aria on the *ruggiero* bass, and *Indarno Febo* (Chiabrera), both from his *Vaghezze di musica* (1608), exemplify the two types.

22. Schrade, *Monteverdi*, p. 288.

23. As does Redlich, *Claudio Monteverdi: Life and Works*, p. 82.

24. Fortune, "Monteverdi and the Seconda Prattica," p. 196.

25. The matter of the intermedio as a genre as well as its precise relationship to *Orfeo* will be examined in the next chapter.

26. Fortune, "Solo Song and Cantata," pp. 161–62. Aside from matters of aesthetic premises common to radical monodies and radical madrigals in the polyphonic tradition, there exists a continuity in the handling of certain technical elements, especially dissonances and chromatic inflections. For a detailed examination of the latter, see Dahlhaus, "Domenico Belli und der chromatische Kontrapunkt um 1600."

27. A less extreme, but still highly eccentric, monody is *Da te parto cor mio* (1620).

28. Fortune, "Solo Song and Cantata," p. 164.

29. Ibid., p. 170.

30. Eugen Schmitz, *Geschichte der weltlichen Solokantate*, pp. 45–46.

31. For example, in his *Folgarate a1* (1617). Fortune, "Solo Song and Cantata," pp. 176–77.

32. Jan Racek, "Die italienischen begleitete Monodie und das Problem der Entwicklung der italienischen Solokantata," p. 168.

33. Racek, "Die italienischen begleitete Monodie," p. 167; Bukofzer, *Music in the Baroque Era*, p. 32; and Palisca, *Baroque Music*, p. 103.

34. Palisca, *Baroque Music*, pp. 68–69.

35. The monodic version reappears as a *"Pianto della Madonna sopra il Lamento d'Arianna"* in Monteverdi's *Selva morale e spirituale* (1641).

36. Schrade, *Monteverdi*, p. 251; Stevens, "Where are the Vespers of Yesteryear"; and Stephen Bonta, "Liturgical Problems in Monteverdi's Marian Vespers."

CHAPTER XXIII

1. Osthoff, *Theatergesang und darstellende Musik in der Renaissance*.

2. Walter H. Rubsamen, *Literary Sources of Secular Music in Italy (ca. 1500)*, p. 32; Osthoff, *Theatergesang*, p. 10; and MacClintock, *Giaches de Wert*, p. 170.

3. Osthoff, *Theatergesang*, pp. 10, 144–47, and 150–51; Pirrotta, *Li due Orfei da Poliziano a Monteverdi*, pp. 77–96.

4. Osthoff, *Theatergesang*, p. 10.

5. Ibid., p. 9; Pirrotta, *Li due Orfei*, pp. 13–32; and André Pirro, "Leo X and Music," p. 2.

6. One scholar has traced portions of Peri's and Corsi's *Dafne* (1597) to this tradition. Porter, "Peri's and Corsi's *Dafne*."

7. Osthoff, *Theatergesang*, pp. 179–80, 220, and 223; and Slim, *A Gift of Madrigals and Motets*, pp. 92–104.

8. Einstein, *Italian Madrigal*, pp. 250–51; and Osthoff, *Theatergesang*, pp. 227–28.

9. Pirrotta, *Li due Orfei*, pp . 140–41; and MacClintock, *Giaches de Wert*, p. 162, and "New Light on Giaches de Wert," p. 597. According to MacClintock, Wert may have studied with Venafro and probably attended these performances.

10. The two works are *L'inconstantia che seco han* and *La giustizia immortale* (1548). Osthoff, *Theatergesang*, pp. 321–23.

11. Schrade, "L'Edipo tiranno d'Andrea Gabrieli et la renaissance de la tragédie grecque," and *La représentation d'Edipo tiranno au Teatro Olimpico (Vicence 1585)*; and Andrea della Corte, "Un capitolo nella preistoria dell'opera," pp. 96–97.

12. MacClintock, *Giaches de Wert*, p. 171. The music is lost.

13. Pirrotta, "Tragédie et comédie dans la Camerata fiorentina," p. 290 and "Temperaments and Tendencies in the Florentine Camerata," p. 178.

14. This method owes its conception to the courtly *Balletti della Duchesa* begun under Margherita Gonzaga (Ferrara, 1580). Cavicchi, "Teatro monteverdiano e tradizione teatrale ferrarese," p. 144.

15. Ibid., pp. 147–49. From these facts we can infer that other settings of the *Gioco della cieca* appearing in various publications by different composers were probably connected with staged productions of the pastoral.

16. Palisca, "Musical Asides in the Diplomatic Correspondence of Emilio de'Cavalieri," p. 348.

17. Shearman, *Mannerism*, p. 104.

18. Pirrotta, *Li due Orfei*, p. 214.

19. This production was given at the wedding of Cosimo de'Medici and Eleonora of Toledo. Corteccia's music as well as detailed descriptions of the intermedios are available in Andrew C. Minor and Bonner Mitchell, eds., *A Renaissance Entertainment*. Bronzino, among other artists, supplied several canvases for the presentation. Alois M. Nagler, *Theatre Festivals of the Medici 1539–1637*, p. 6.

20. The first person provided the text, the next three were involved with the visual aspects, and the last two, of course, provided the music: Intermedios I, II, and V (Striggio); Intermedios III, IV, and VI (Corteccia).

21. Pirrotta, *Li due Orfei*, pp. 230–34; and Federico Ghisi, *Feste musicali della Firenze Medicea (1480–1589)*, p. XXVI. The beginning of Striggio's *Fuggi speme mia* (Intermedio V) appears in a solo version in Vincenzo Galilei's *Fronimo* (1568). Striggio's double chorus, *A me che fatta a8*, has been reconstructed by Osthoff, *Theatergesang*, 2:122–31.

22. Fortune, "Solo Song and Cantata," p. 149; Pirrotta, *Li due Orfei*, p. 252; and Osthoff, *Theatergesang*, p. 347. In connection with solo singing and Caccini in particular, I mention here an interesting sidelight discovered by Pirrotta about the intermedios for Alessandro Piccolomini's *L'Alessandro* (Naples, 1558). Documents record that the third intermedio, whose text was by Luigi Tansillo, depicted Cleopatra on her barge singing a *canto sì novo e soave*. Pirrotta has found an anonymous composition setting the Tansillo text, *Che non può far*, and suggests that this piece—a kind of recitative—can be attributed to Scipione del Palla. Caccini, his pupil, is curiously silent on this subject; perhaps, as Pirrotta says, he did not wish to propagate another myth about a "Neapolitan Camerata." Pirrotta, *Li due Orfei*, pp. 247–48, and 250. See also, MacClintock, *Giaches de Wert*, pp. 167–68.

23. Angelo Solerti, *Musica, ballo e drammatica alla Corte Medicea dal 1600–1637*.

24. Pirrotta, *Li due Orfei*, p. 258.

25. Shearman, *Mannerism*, pp. 107–8; Pirrotta, *Li due Orfei*, p. 258; and Ghisi, *Feste musicali*, pp. XLII–XLIV.

26. All the extant music is edited by D. P. Walker, *Musique des intermèdes de "La Pellegrina,"* taken from Malvezzi's publication as well as the manuscript source of Caccini's monody. Descriptions of the intermedios can be found in the following additional works: Pirrotta, *Li due Orfei*, pp. 264–68, 276–79, and 281–83; and Flavio Testi, *La musica italiana nel seicento*; *Il Melodramma*, pp. 20, 22–25, and 26–41.

27. The patterned dance has always been seen as a dramatic symbol of harmony. The structure of the *ballo* suggests that someone—perhaps Cavalieri, who was an accomplished dancer—choreographed the steps; then Cavalieri wrote the music, and lastly, Guidiccioni supplied the words.

28. A detailed description of this event appears in Shearman, *Mannerism*, pp. 109–11.

29. The mannerist background of these productions is evident in the confusion surrounding Caccini's *Il rapimento* (Chiabrera), whose music is lost except for the final chorus. Some scholars consider it an opera (e.g. Testi, *Il Melodramma*, pp. 87–88; and Simon Towneley, "Early Italian Opera," p. 828) whereas another historian considers it to be a set of intermedios (Pirrotta, *Li due Orfei*, p. 284). This problem will be encountered again. Whichever the case may be, the production must have included several solo numbers, for we know that Peri, Francesco Rasi, and Melchior Palantrotti all sang. Nagler, *Theatre Festivals*, p. 100. All three names reappear in the cast of Peri's *Euridice*. Ibid., p. 95.

30. Other contributors to these intermedios were: Salomone Rossi, Marco da Gagliano, Giovanni Giacomo Gastoldi, and Paolo Biat. Testi, *Il Melodramma*, p. 47; and Schrade, *Monteverdi*, p. 239.

31. Schrade, *Monteverdi*, p. 240.

32. The 1590 production, text by Rinuccini, includes a monody sung by Margherita Caccini and, for this reason, attributed to her husband. Fortune, "Solo Song and Cantata," p. 150. The description of the 1611 production lists Gagliano, Peri, Vittoria Archilei, and Francesca and Settimia Caccini as participants. Nagler, *Theatre Festivals*, p. 116.

33. Towneley, "Early Italian Opera," p. 838. Monteverdi apparently wrote the music for another set of intermedios, texts by Ascanaio Pio, for a production that took place in Parma in 1608. Schrade, *Monteverdi*, pp. 311–12.

34. Monteverdi's disappointment with the text and the fact that Settimia Caccini sang in the performance are treated by Schrade, *Monteverdi*, p. 312.

35. Nagler, *Theatre Festivals*, p. 126.

36. The popularity of this kind of entertainment in Ferrara is recorded by Cavicchi, "Teatro monteverdiano," pp. 141–42. Pageantry by livestock disappears in early aristocratic operas. However, this form of mannerist ostentation returns in later grand opera.

37. Cavicchi, "Teatro monteverdiano," p. 152.

38. *La Dafne* (1608), "Preface."

39. Hellmuth C. Wolff, "Der Manierismus in der barocken und romantischen Oper," pp. 261 and 264; Bukofzer, *Music in the Baroque Era*, p. 395; Wolff, "Manierismus und Musikgeschichte," p. 247; and Fabbri, "Tasso, Guarini e il 'divino Claudio,'" p. 242.

40. Wolff, "Der Manierismus in der barocken und romantischen Oper," in reference to Bousquet, *La peinture maniériste*.

41. Fabbri, "Tasso, Guarini e il 'divino Claudio,'" pp. 233–35; and Wolff, "Manierismus und Musikgeschichte," p. 247.

42. Brown's statement to the effect that music in the intermedios is not genuinely dramatic must be reassessed in the total context of theatrical ideals in the mannerist period. Howard M. Brown, "Music—How Opera Began," p. 415. The same holds true, in my view, for Shearman's opinion. *Mannerism*, p. 111.

43. Einstein, *Italian Madrigal*, p. 766.

44. Pirrotta surmises that Cavalieri's *Il satiro* and *La disperazione di Fileno* (1590–91) qualify as operas. *Li due Orfei*, p. 290.

45. Porter, "Peri's and Corsi's *Dafne*," p. 196. See also, Pirrotta, "Temperaments and Tendencies," pp. 183–84.

46. *La Dafne*, "Preface."

47. Palisca, "Musical Asides," p. 351. The roster of singers includes Vittoria Archilei in the title role, Peri as Orfeo, Rasi as Aminta, and Palantrotti as Pluto. Nagler, *Theatre Festivals*, p. 95. Buontalenti staged the opera. Ibid., p. 94.

48. Anna Maria M. Vacchelli, "Elementi stilistici nell'*Euridice* di Jacopo Peri in rapporto all'*Orfeo* di Monteverdi," pp. 119–20.

49. One historian also notes elements derived from the madrigalian tradition —that is to say, third-related harmonies, evasion of cadences, and surprising changes in harmonic direction. Palisca, *Baroque Music*, p. 31.

50. Hanning, "The Influence of Humanist Thought and Italian Renaissance Poetry on the Formation of Opera," p. 3.

51. *Trattato della musica scenica* (ca. 1635). See Testi, *Il Melodramma*, p. 92.

52. Pirrotta, "Temperaments and Tendencies," p. 183.

53. Schrade, *Monteverdi*, pp. 224–26; Testi, *Il Melodramma*, p. 201.

54. Arnold, "Formal Design in Monteverdi's Church Music," p. 187.

55. Monteverdi's deployment of the ostinato bass in *Possente spirto* is especially sophisticated. During the first five variations, the actual bass line is hidden beneath subtle chordal variations. Only in the last strophe, a very simple setting for both voice and instruments, does the spine of the harmonic basis come to the foreground in an audible way. Instrumental ritornellos occur between the first four strophes where they act as buffers separating and diluting the force of Orfeo's sentiments. After the fourth strophe, which represents the emotional climax of the song, they disappear, allowing the remaining variations to gain momentum through an uninterrupted sequence.

The first four strophes feature virtuoso ornamentation that becomes more and more extravagant. In the first one, Orfeo addresses Charon, without whom no spirit can hope to enter Hades; here the singer's embellishments are echoed by two concerted string instruments. During the second strophe, Orfeo indulges in a typically mannerist pun—he too must be dead because his wife, who is his heart, has been deprived of life; two concerted cornetts. In the third one, Orfeo explains that he seeks her in Hades, a woman whose heavenly beauty is depicted by two concerted harps. Then in the fourth strophe, Orfeo, with his most beguiling virtuosity—accompanied by three string instruments—announces proudly: "I am Orfeo, who follows the steps of Euridice through dark places where no mortal man has dared to walk." His pride is reflected in his intricate ornaments.

Suddenly, the mood changes completely as Orfeo speaks to the entire assembly in tones of lyrical pathos: "O my serene lights, if only one glance from you could return me to life! Ah, who can deny comfort to my agony?" In this fifth strophe, Monteverdi switches to extremely passionate recitative accompanied only by the continuo, and the lyrical core of this strophe receives musical support in the form of the distinct ostinato pattern in the bass. In the final strophe, Orfeo once more pleads with Charon in words of nobility, but words that nonetheless contain a mannerist conceit (e.g. arming his harp with sweet strings). The three string instruments, forming a simple yet sensuous accompaniment, symbolize the harp.

56. Orfeo's *Ahi sventurato amante* (Act III), the celebrated recitatives of the Messagera, *Ahi caso acerbo* and *In un fiorito prato* (Act II), and Orfeo's lament, *Tu se'morta* (Act II).

57. Palisca, *Baroque Music*, p. 45.

58. The role of Arianna, originally written for Caterina Martinelli, was sung by Virginia Ramponi after Caterina's untimely death. Other singers in this production were Francesco Rasi and Settimia Caccini. Testi, *Il Melodramma*, p. 228.

59. Such was the case with *Le nozze di Peleo e Tetide* (Scipione Agnelli), a kind of intermedio-opera in 1617, *Andromeda* (Ercole Marigliani) in 1618, and *Licori finta pazza inamorata d'Aminta* (Giulio Strozzi) in 1627. Schrade, *Monteverdi*, pp. 303–13.

60. Monteverdi adapted the poem by changing the first few stanzas, omitting one altogether, and combining versions of others from the *Gerusalemme liberata* and the *Gerusalemme conquistata*. A detailed analysis of the text can be found in Pirrotta, *Li due Orfei*, p. 30, n. 37.

CHAPTER XXIV

1. For details on the history of music printing, see Alexander H. King, *Four Hundred Years of Music Printing*; and Guy A. Marco, *The Earliest Music Printers in Continental Europe*.

2. Richard L. Crocker, *A History of Musical Style*, p. 180.

3. MacClintock, *Giaches de Wert*, p. 21; and Einstein, "Aus der Frühzeit des Konzertlebens," pp. 14–16.

4. Einstein, "Aus den Frühzeit des Konzertlebens," p. 16; Giuseppe Turrini, *L'Accademia Filarmonica di Verona dalla fondazione (Maggio 1543) al 1600 e il suo patrimonio musicale antico*, pp. 14, 53, 73, and 86; and MacClintock, *Giaches de Wert*, p. 96.

5. The probability that the Accademia degli Rinnovati's *Il lauro secco* (1582) was also connected wtih Laura's impending marriage is investigated by Egon Kenton, "A Faded Laurel Wreath," p. 503.

6. Bruno Brunelli, "Francesco Portenari e le cantate degli accademie padovani," pp. 597–600; and Einstein, *Italian Madrigal*, pp. 471–73.

7. This society is still in existence today.

8. Einstein, *Italian Madrigal*, pp. 195–98; and Haar, "Notes on the 'Dialogo della Musica' of Antonfrancesco Doni." Adrian Willaert's activities in the musicales that took place in Polissena Pecorina's home, and her ownership of the *Musica Nova*, have been documented. See Newcomb, "Editions of Willaert's *Musica Nova*."

9. Lodovico Bellanda, an early monodist, belonged to this *ridotto*, and Pietro Ponzio's *Ragionamento di musica* (1588) was dedicated to Count Bevilacqua.

10. Lockwood, ed., *Pope Marcellus Mass*, pp. 10–16; Palisca, "The Beginnings of Baroque Music," pp. 93–96; and Shearman, *Mannerism*, pp. 167–68.

11. Lockwood, "Vincenzo Ruffo and Musical Reform after the Council of Trent," p. 342, as opposed to Palisca, "The Beginnings of Baroque Music," p. 97.

12. For detailed information on this topic, see Karl Weinmann, *Das Konzil von Trient und die Kirchenmusik*; Karl G. Fellerer, "Church Music and the Council of Trent"; and Lockwood, "Vincenzo Ruffo and Musical Reform."

13. Another collection of Masses by Ruffo is entitled *Messe a cinque voci seconda la forma del Concilio Tridentino* (1580).

14. Lockwood, "Vincenzo Ruffo and Musical Reform," pp. 346–48 and 353–54; and Paul D. Hilbrich, "The Aesthetics of the Counter-Reformation and Religious Painting and Music in Bologna 1565–1615," pp. 161 and 164–65.

15. One scholar finds this state of affairs to be "somewhat surprising." Hilbrich, "The Aesthetics of the Counter-Reformation," p. 165.

16. Arnold, "Formal Design in Monteverdi's Church Music," pp. 187–88. Reform of Gregorian Chant, ordered by the pope on the Council's recommendation, also attests to the negative aims of the movement, as does the final result, the notorious *Editio Medicea* (Rome, 1614).

17. For a history of the early Jesuit movement and the Collegium Romanum, see Thomas D. Culley, *Jesuits and Music*.

CHAPTER XXV

1. Hucke, "Das Problem des Manierismus in der Musik," p. 219; Palisca, "*Ut oratoria musica*," pp. 37–38; and Brown, *Music in the Renaissance*, p. 6.

2. Blume, *Renaissance and Baroque Music*, pp. 8, 36, and 38.

3. Haar, "Classicism and Mannerism in 16th-Century Music." This *desideratum* is also put forward by Palisca, a scholar who rejects the idea of Mannerism as a period in favor of Mannerism as a denotation for any specific amalgamations of affected mannerisms done in an eclectic way. "Towards an Intrinsically Musical Definition of Mannerism in the Sixteenth Century," p. 313.

4. A similar approach is advocated by Palisca, "*Ut oratoria musica*," p. 38.

5. Federhofer, "Zum Manierismus-Problem in der Musik," p. 117. This is only one argument among many supplied by Federhofer to support his denial of Mannerism as an historical period. See also, Enrico Fubini, "Il manierismo come categoria storiografica," pp. 7–8.

6. Bianconi, "Giulio Caccini e il manierismo musicale," p. 25; Shearman, *Mannerism*, p. 38; and Lockwood, "On 'Mannerism' and 'Renaissance' as Terms and Concepts in Music History," p. 95.

7. Kristeller, *Renaissance Thought*, pp. 92–93.

8. Haar, "Classicism and Mannerism," p. 61; Shearman, *Mannerism*, pp. 98–99; Watkins, *Gesualdo*, pp. 96–97.

9. Haar, "Classicism and Mannerism," p. 65.

10. Schrade, "Von der Maniera der Komposition in der Musik des 16. Jahrhunderts," p. 155.

11. Federhofer, "Zum Manierismus-Problem," pp. 114–15.

12. Clercx, *Le baroque et la musique*, p. 53. Two other scholars link the

Roman school with mannerist or baroque trends: Blume, *Renaissance and Baroque Music*, pp. 29–30; and Heinrich Besseler, "Das Renaissanceproblem in der Musik," p. 10.

13. Haar, "Classicism and Mannerism," p. 55; and Federhofer, "Zum Manierismus-Problem," pp. 112–13.

14. Federhofer, "Zum Manierismus-Problem," pp. 111–12, versus Blume, *Renaissance and Baroque Music*, p. 49; Lowinsky, "Music of the Renaissance as Viewed by Renaissance Musicians," p. 154; Cannon, Johnson, and Waite, *The Art of Music*, p. 182; and Wiora, "Der religiöse Grundzug im neuen Stil und Weg Josquin Des Prez."

15. Palisca, "The Beginnings of Baroque Music," p. 91. In this book, Palisca concentrates on early hints of baroque style, but in his later studies he equates new music of the sixteenth century with *musica reservata, musica poetica,* and Mannerism. "A Clarification of 'Musica Reservata' in Jean Taisnier's 'Astrologiae' 1559," and "*Ut oratoria musica.*"

16. Federhofer, "Zum Manierimus-Problem," p. 113; Bianconi, "Giulio Caccini," p. 26.

17. Palisca, "The Beginnings of Baroque Music," p. 91; Artz, *From the Renaissance to Romanticism*, p. 141; Wolf, "The Aesthetic Problem of the 'Renaissance,'" pp. 90–91.

18. Haar, "Classicism and Mannerism," p. 61.

19. Federhofer, "Zum Manierismus-Problem," pp. 112–13.

20. Blume, *Renaissance and Baroque Music*, p. 63; Shearman, *Mannerism*, p. 99; Harrán, "'Mannerism' in the Cinquecento Madrigal," pp. 525–28; and Roche, *The Madrigal*, p. 13.

21. Harrán, "'Mannerism,'" pp. 528–34 and 538–42; Haar, "Classicism and Mannerism," p. 67; Dean T. Mace, "Pietro Bembo and the Literary Origins of the Italian Madrigal," pp. 65, 67–69, 74, and 78; and Shearman, *Mannerism*, p. 99.

22. Cannon, Johnson, and Waite, *The Art of Music*, p. 188; Blume, *Renaissance and Baroque Music*, p. 64; Schrade, "Von der Maniera der Komposition," pp. 162–63; Harrán, "'Mannerism,'" pp. 528–34; Engel, "Werden und Wesen des Madrigals," p. 47; and Watkins, *Gesualdo*, p. 100. Palisca points out the presence of a similar aesthetic in the motets of Lasso. "*Ut oratoria musica,*" pp. 56–58.

23. Einstein, *Italian Madrigal*, p. 153, as opposed to Federhofer, "Zum Manierismus-Problem," p. 113.

24. Federhofer, "Zum Manierismus-Problem," p. 115.

25. Rowland's restriction of Mannerism to chromatic music, which he sees as the sole stylized deviation from classical norms, is a one-sided interpretation. *Mannerism—Style and Mood*. Furthermore, his emphasis on Gesualdo, a factor that leads him to evaluate musical Mannerism as a minor phenomenon compared to the visual arts, is a result of inadequate coverage of the history of chromaticism in the sixteenth century. In his monograph study, Watkins presents a more perspicacious assessment of Gesualdo and his relationship to the mannerist tradition.

Although Lowinsky, in his article "The Problem of Mannerism in Music," covers a much broader spectrum of chromatic music than does Rowland and, like Watkins, puts Gesualdo into historical perspective, his equation of Mannerism with chromaticism and "classical" or conventional renaissance music with diatonicism rests on an overly narrow interpretation of these phenomena, it seems to me. In fact, Lowinsky's general assessment of Mannerism directly opposes Shearman's—that is to say, Lowinsky excludes elegant and calculated *maniera*, and stresses instead experimental and avant-garde tendencies, tendencies which produce eccentric and grotesque works of art. See especially, ibid., pp. 140, 141, and 161.

26. Federhofer, "Zum Manierismus-Problem," p. 115.

27. Ibid., p. 114.

28. Shearman, *Mannerism*, pp. 99–100.

29. Ibid., p. 181; and Haar, "Classicism and Mannerism," pp. 65 and 67.

30. Harrán, "'Mannerism,'" p. 524.

31. Ibid., versus Fortune, "Italian Secular Monody from 1600–1635," p. 184. See also, Watkins, "Carlo Gesualdo and the Delimitations of Late Mannerist Style," pp. 16–17.

32. Dahlhaus, "'Neue Musik' als historische Kategorie," p. 36.

33. Kroyer, "Zwischen Renaissance und Barock," pp. 50–51.

34. This cultural interpretation goes contrary to the views of those scholars who deny the significance and even the existence of an intellectual framework for sixteenth-century music, a framework that could support any concept of Mannerism as a period. Lockwood, "On 'Mannerism' and 'Renaissance,'" pp. 89–90 and 94–95; and Federhofer, "Der Manierismus-Begriff in der Musikgeschichte," pp. 37–39; and Lowinsky, "The Problem of Mannerism in Music," p. 134.

৯৯৯

Bibliography

PRIMARY SOURCES

In order to facilitate use of this bibliography, the following features should be noted. All titles under individual names appear in chronological order wherever possible; when not possible, the titles are given in alphabetical order, as are titles for material appearing in the same year. Anonymous works are inserted in the general alphabetical list by title. In the case of individual musical pieces belonging to publications that have their own entries, the pieces appear after the publication in alphabetical order. This method allows easy reference to editions of the publications in question. Editions of specific compositions are added under the pertinent entries. The chronological listing in the bibliography is balanced by the alphabetical arrangement of titles and *capoversi* in the index.

In all cases, I give first printings with the addition of revised reprints whenever these represent substantial alterations or sources referred to in the footnotes. Generally, I list first any facsimiles, and then modern editions or translations. If two or more items appear in any one category, these are given in chronological order. Whenever such entries retain the original title, it is not repeated. Translated titles or other titles are given whenever necessary. Entries for artworks include the repository as well as books where reproductions can be found. Entries for theatrical material give the date and place of production, and information about publication, if the latter is known. Modern editions, if available, appear in the same way as in the case of treatises.

Although I have made no attempt to give comprehensive coverage, I have included all material discovered in standard library holdings. Precise references to pages and plates are omitted for the sake of brevity. Articles and books cited in this bibliography appear with full information in the Bibliography of secondary sources.

Aaron, Pietro. *Libri tres de institutione harmonica.* Bologna, 1516.
    Monuments of Music and Music Literature in Facsimile; Second Series—Music Literature, vol. 67. New York, 1976.

————. *Thoscanello della musica.* Venice, 1523. *Toscanello in musica.* Venice, 1529.

  Monuments of Music and Music Literature in Facsimile; Second Series—Music Literature, vol. 49. New York, 1969. (Venice, 1523).

  Toscanello in Music. Translated by P. Bergquist. Colorado College Music Press; Translations, vol. 4. Colorado Springs, 1970.

————. *Trattato della natura et cognitione di tutti gli tuoni di canto figurato.* Venice, 1525.

  Excerpts in O. Strunk, ed., *Source Readings in Music History.* New York, 1950.

————. *Lucidario in musica di alcune oppenioni antiche et moderne.* Venice, 1545.

  Bibliotheca Musica Bononiensis; sezione II, vol. 12. Bologna, 1969.

Abate, Niccolò dell'. *Conversion of St. Paul.* 1555. Vienna, Kunsthistorisches Museum.

  G. R. Hocke, *Die Welt als Labyrinth.* Hamburg, 1957.

  G. Briganti, *Le maniérisme italien.* Leipzig, 1962.

  A. Hauser, *Mannerism.* London, 1965.

Ad Herennium.

  Translated by H. Caplan. The Loeb Classical Library. Cambridge, Mass. and London, 1968.

Agostino, Ludovico. *Musica sopra le rime bizzarre di M. Andrea Calmo & altri autori a 4 voci.* Milan, 1567.

————. *Musica il primo libro de madrigali a cinque voci.* Venice, 1570.

Agricola, Martin. *Rudimenta musices.* Wittenberg, 1539.

  Monuments of Music and Music Literature in Facsimile; Second Series—Music Literature, vol. 34. New York, 1966.

Alberti, Leon B. *Della pittura.* Written ca. 1435–36. *Editio princeps,* Basel, 1540.

  Edited by L. Mallé. Florence, 1950.

  On Painting. Translated by J. R. Spenser. New Haven and London, 1966.

  De pictura and De statua. Translated by C. Grayson. London, 1972.

  Opere volgare. Vol. 3. Edited by C. Grayson. Scrittori d'Italia, vol. 254. Bari, 1973.

Alciati, Andrea. *Emblemata libellus.* N.p., 1531.

  Darmstadt, 1967.

Ambra, Francesco d'. *La Cofanaria.* Produced in Florence, 1565. Florence, 1566.

  Commedie. Biblioteca Classica Italiana Secolo XVI, vol. 7. Trieste, 1858.

Aquila, Serafino dell' (dei Ciminelli). *Rappresentazione allegorica.* Produced in Mantua, 1495.

  Le rime. Edited by M. Menghini. Bologna, 1894.

Arcadelt, Jacob. *Crudel acerba inesorabil morte a5.* F. Verdelot, *Le dotte et eccellente compositioni de i madrigali a cinque voci insieme con altri madrigali di varij autori.* Venice, 1538.
> *Opera Omnia.* Vol. 7. Edited by A. Seay. Corpus Mensurabilis Musicae, vol. 31. American Institute of Musicology, 1969.

―――. *Ecco pur che doppo sì lunghi affanni a4. Il terzo libro de i madrigali novissimi a quattro voci.* Venice, 1539.
> *Opera Omnia.* Vol. 4. Edited by A. Seay. Corpus Mensurabilis Musicae, vol. 31. American Institute of Musicology, 1968.
> W. Osthoff, *Theatergesang und darstellende Musik in der italienischen Renaissance.* Vol. 2. Tutzing, 1969.

―――. *Il bianco e dolce cigno a4. Il libro primo di madrigali a quatro.* Venice, 1539.
> C. Burney, *A General History of Music.* Bk. III. London, 1789. New York, 1975.
> *Trésor musicale: Musique profane.* Vol. 25. Edited by R. van Maldeghem. Brussels, 1889; 1965.
> *Das Chorwerk.* Vol. 5. Edited by W. Wiora. Wolfenbüttel, 1930.
> *Study Scores of Musical Styles.* Edited by E. R. Lerner. New York and St. Louis, 1968.
> *Opera Omnia.* Vol. 2. Edited by A. Seay. Corpus Mensurabilis Musicae, vol. 31. American Institute of Musicology, 1970.

―――. *Dov'ito son a4.* C. Veggio, *Madrigali a quattro voci.* Venice, 1540.
> *Opera Omnia.* Vol. 7. Edited by A. Seay. Corpus Mensurabilis Musicae, vol. 31. American Institute of Musicology, 1970.

Archilei, Antonio. *Dalle più alte sfere a5.* Intermedios for *La Pellegrina,* Florence, 1589. C. Malvezzi, *Intermedii and concerti fatti per la commedia rappresentata in Firenze nelle nozze del Serenissimo Don Ferdinando Medici e Madama Christiana di Lorena.* Venice, 1591.
> *Musique des intermèdes de "La Pellegrina."* Edited by D. P. Walker. Les fêtes de Florence, vol. 1. Paris, 1963.
> N. Pirrotta, *Li due Orfei da Poliziano a Monteverdi.* Turin, 1969; 1975.

Argenti, Agostino degli. *Lo sfortunato.* Produced in Ferrara, 1567.

Ariosto, Lodovico. *Orlando furioso.* Ferrara, 1516. Ferrara, 1537.
> *I quattri poeti italiani con una scelta di poesia italiana.* Edited by A. Buttura. Paris, 1836.
> *Orlando furioso e una scelta delle opere minori.* 2 vols. Edited by C. Muscetto and L. Lamberti. Turin, 1962.
> *Ludovico Ariosto's Orlando Furioso into English Heroical Verse by Sir Joshua Harington* (1591). Edited by R. McNulty. Oxford, 1972.

Aristotle (Aristoteles). *Peri poetikes.*
> *Introduction to Aristotle.* Edited by R. McKeon. New York, 1947.

Aristotle's Theory of Poetry and Fine Art. Edited by C. H. Butcher. New York, 1951.

Aristoxenos. *Harmonika stoichea.*

    Harmonicorum elementorum. Edited by A. Gogavino. Venice, 1562.

    The Harmonics of Aristoxenos. Edited by H. S. Macran. Oxford, 1902.

    Aristoxeni Elementa Harmonica. Edited by R. da Rios. Rome, 1954.

Artusi, Giovanni M. *L'arte del contraponto.* Venice, 1598; enlarged edition of Venice, 1586–89.

    Hildesheim and New York, 1969.

————. *L'Artusi overo delle imperfettioni della moderna musica.* Pt. I, Venice 1600; pt. II, Venice, 1603.

    Bibliotheca Musica Bononiensis; sezione II, vol. 36. Bologna, 1968.

    ————. *Considerationi musicali. L'Artusi.* . . . Pt. II. Venice, 1603. See above.

Avianus, Johannes. *Isagoge in libros musicae poeticae.* Erfurt, 1581.

Ballestra, Raimundo. "Petition to Archduke Ferdinand." Graz, ca. 13 January 1611.

    H. Federhofer, "Eine neue Quelle der musica reservata." *Acta Musicologica* 24 (1952).

Banchieri, Adriano. *La pazzia senile ragionamenti vaghi et dilettevoli libro secondo a tre voci.* Venice, 1598.

    L'arte musicale in Italia. Vol. 4. Edited by L. Torchi. Rome, n.d.

    Capolavori polifonici del secolo XVI. Vol. 6. Edited by B. Somma. Rome, 1960.

————. *Il zabaione musicale inventione boscareccia et primo libro di madrigali a cinque voci.* Milan, 1603.

————. *Barca di Venetia per Padova libro secondo de madrigali a cinque voci.* Venice, 1605.

    Capolavori polifonici del secolo XVI. Vol. 9. Edited by E. Piattelli. Rome, 1969.

————. *Festino nella sera del giovedi grasso avanti cena terzo libro madrigalesco con cinque voci.* Venice, 1608.

    Capolavori polifonici del secolo XVI. Vol. 1. Edited by B. Somma. Rome, 1956.

    "Preface."

    A. Einstein, *The Italian Madrigal.* Princeton, 1949; 1971.

    Excerpt in E. Vogel, *Bibliothek der gedruckten weltlichen Vocalmusik Italiens.* Hildesheim and New York, 1972.

————. *Cartella musicale nel canto figurato fermo & contrapunto.* Venice, 1614.

    Bibliotheca Musica Bononiensis; sezione II, vol. 26. Bologna, 1968.

Bardi, Giovanni de'. *L'amico fido.* Produced in Florence, 1567.

————. "Discorso mandato a Caccini sopra la musica antica." Ca. 1580.

Lyra Barberina. Vol. 2. Florence, 1763.

O. Strunk, ed., *Source Readings in Music History.* New York, 1950.

Bardi, Pietro de'. "Letter to G. B. Doni." 1634.

A. Solerti, *Le origini del melodramma.* Turin, 1903.

O. Strunk, ed., *Source Readings in Music History.* New York, 1950.

Bargagli, Girolamo. *Dialogo de'giuocchi.* Siena, 1572.

—————. *La Pellegrina.* Produced in Florence, 1589. Siena, 1589.

Edited by F. Cerreta. Biblioteca dell' "Archivum Romanicum"; serie 1, vol. 3. Florence, 1971.

Barre, Antonio. *Il primo libro delle muse a quattro voci madrigali ariosi di Ant. Barre et altri diversi autori.* Rome, 1555.

—————. *Dunque fia ver dicea a4.* Bk 1, Rome, 1555.

P. Wagner, "Das Madrigal und Palestrina." *Vierteljahrschrift für Musikwissenschaft* 8 (1892).

Bartoli, Cosimo. *Ragionamenti accademici . . . sopra alcuni luoghi difficili di Dante.* Venice, 1567.

Bassano, Giovanni. *Motetti madrigali et canzone francese di diversi eccellentissimi auttori a quattro cinque & sei voci diminuiti per sonar con ogni sorte di stromenti & anco per cantar con semplice voce.* Venice, 1591.

—————. *Ricercate passaggi et cadentie per potersi essercitar nel diminuire con ogni sorte d'istrumento et anco diversi passaggi per la semplice voce.* Venice, 1598.

Bati, Luca. Intermedios for *L'esaltazione della croce.* Produced in Florence, 1589.

Beccafumi, Domenico. *Last Judgment* or *St. Michael.* 1538. Siena, S. Maria del Carmine.

G. Briganti, *Le maniérisme italien.* Leipzig, 1962.

A. Hauser, *Mannerism.* London, 1965.

Beccari, Agostino. *Il sacrificio.* Produced in Ferrara, 1534. Ferrara, 1555.

Teatro antico, tragico, comico, pastorale, drammatico. Parnaso italiano ovvero raccolta de'poeti classici italiani, vol. 17. Venice, 1785.

Belli, Domenico. *Orfeo dolente.* Intermedios for *Aminta.* Florence, 1616.

Edited by A. Tirabassi. Brussels, 1927.

Bembo, Pietro. *Prose . . . nelle quali si ragione della volgar lingua.* Venice, 1525.

Benedetti, Giovanni B. "Letters to C. de Rore." Ca. 1563. *Diversarum speculationum mathematicorum & physicorum liber.* Turin, 1585.

J. Reiss, "Jo. Bapt. Benedictus, De intervallis musicis." *Zeitschrift für Musikwissenschaft* 7 (1924–25).

Excerpts in C. V. Palisca, "Scientific Empiricism in Musical Thought." In *Seventeenth Century Science and the Arts,* edited by H. H. Rhys. Princeton, 1961.

Berardi, Angelo. *Miscellanea musicale.* Bologna, 1689.

Bernhard, Christoph. *Tractatus compositionis augmentatus.* Ca. 1660.
　　J. Müller-Blattau, *Die Kompositioneslehre Heinrich Schützens in der Fassung eines Schülers Christoph Bernhard.* Leipzig, 1926. Kassel, 1963.
Bologna, Giovanni da. *Mercury.* Ca. 1575. Vienna, Kunsthistorisches Museum.
　　F. Würtenberger, *Mannerism.* New York, 1963. (Earlier version, ca. 1564.)
　　J. Shearman, *Mannerism.* Harmondsworth, 1967.
　　――――. *Apennine.* Ca. 1580. Villa Pratolino, now Villa Demidoff.
　　F. Würtenberger, *Mannerism.* New York, 1963.
　　R. E. Wolf and R. Millen, *Renaissance and Mannerist Art.* New York, 1968.
　　――――. *Rape of the Sabines.* 1582. Florence, Loggia dei Lanzi.
　　F. Würtenberger, *Mannerism.* New York, 1963.
　　L. Murray, *The Late Renaissance and Mannerism.* New York, 1967.
　　J. Shearman, *Mannerism.* Harmondsworth, 1967.
　　R. E. Wolf and R. Millen, *Renaissance and Mannerist Art.* New York, 1968.
　　A. Smart, *The Renaissance and Mannerism in Italy.* London, 1971.
Bonagionta de S. Genesi, Giulio, ed. *Corona della morte dell'illustre signore il Sig. Comendator Anibal Caro.* Venice, 1568.
　　"Preface."
　　　　Excerpt in E. Vogel, *Bibliothek der gedruckten weltlichen Vocalmusik Italiens.* Hildesheim and New York, 1972.
Bonini, Severo. *Madrigali e canzonette spirituali per cantare a una voce sola sopra il chitarrone o spinetto o altri stromenti.* Florence, 1607.
　　"Dedication" and "Preface."
　　　　Excerpts in E. Vogel, *Bibliothek der gedruckten weltlichen Vocalmusik Italiens.* Hildesheim and New York, 1972.
Borghini, Raffaele. *Il riposo.* Florence, 1584.
Borromeo, Carlo. *Instructiones fabricae et supellectis ecclesiasticae.* Milan, 1577.
　　Trattati d'arte del cinquecento fra manierismo e controriforma. Vol. 3. Edited by P. Barocchi. Scrittori d'Italia, vol. 222. Bari, 1962.
　　――――. "Letter to Niccolò Ormaneto." Rome, 10 March 1565.
　　　　Excerpt in L. Lockwood, ed., *Pope Marcellus Mass.* New York, 1975.
　　――――. "Letter to Niccolò Ormaneto." Rome, 31 March 1565.
　　See above.
Bottrigari, Ercole. *Il Patricio overo de'tetrachordi armonici di Aristosseno.* Bologna, 1593.
　　――――. *Il desiderio overo de'concerti di varii strumenti musicali.* Venice, 1594. Bologna, 1599.
　　Edited by K. Meyer. Veröffentlichungen der Musik-Bibliothek Paul

Hirsch, vol. 5. Berlin, 1924. (Facsimile of 1599 edition.)
Translated by C. MacClintock. Musicological Studies and Documents, vol. 9. American Institute of Musicology, 1962.
————. *Il Melone discorso armonico* and *Il Melone secondo*. Ferrara, 1602.
Bibliotheca Musica Bononiensis; sezione II, vol. 29. Bologna, 1969.
————. *Così mi sveglio a4. Il Melone discorso armonico*. Ferrara, 1602.
See above.
Bovicelli, Giovanni B. *Regole passaggi di musica madrigali e motetti passeggiati*. Venice, 1594.
Edited by N. Bridgman. Documenta Musicologica; Erste Reihe: Druckschriften-Faksimiles, vol. 12. Kassel, 1957.
Bronzino, Angelo. *A Young Man*. Ca. 1538. New York, Metropolitan Museum of Art.
A. Hauser, *Mannerism*. London, 1965.
J. Shearman, *Mannerism*. Harmondsworth, 1967.
————. *Eleanora of Toledo and her Son Don Giovanni*. Ca. 1545–46. Florence, Uffizi.
A. Smart, *The Renaissance and Mannerism in Italy*. London, 1971.
Brunelli, Antonio. *Regole et dichiaratione di alcuni contrappunti doppii utili alli studiosi della musica & maggioramente a quelli che vogliono far contrappunti all'improviso con diversi canoni sopra un solo canto fermo*. Florence, 1610.
"Preface."
Excerpt in H. Federhofer, "Monodie und musica reservata." *Deutsches Jahrbuch der Musikwissenschaft für 1957*. Leipzig, 1958.
Bruno, Giordano. *De gl'heroici furori*. Paris, 1585.
Scritti scelti di Giordano Bruno e di Tommaso Campanella. Edited by L. Firpo. Turin, 1949.
Opere di Giordano Bruno e di Tommaso Campanella. Edited by A. Guzzo and R. Amerio. Milan, 1956.
The Heroic Frenzies. Translated by P. E. Memmo, Jr. Chapel Hill, 1966.
————. *De vinculis in genere*. 1591–92.
Opere latine. Vol. 3. Edited by F. Tocco and H. Vitelli. Stuttgart, 1962. (Facsimile of Naples, 1879–91.)
Buonamici, Francesco. *Discorsi poetici nella Accademia Fiorentina in difesa d'Aristotele*. Florence, 1597.
Buontalenti, Bernardo. Altar Steps of S. Trinita. 1574–76. Florence, S. Stefano.
F. Würtenberger, *Mannerism*. New York, 1963.
J. Shearman, *Mannerism*. Harmondsworth, 1967.
Burmeister, Joachim. *Musica poetica*. Rostock, 1606.
Edited by M. Ruhnke. Documenta Musicologica; Erste Reihe:

Druckschriften-Faksimiles, vol. 10. Basel, 1955.

Burtius, Nicolaus. *Musices opusculum*. Bologna, 1487.

Bibliotheca Musica Bononiensis; sezione II, vol. 4. Bologna, 1969.

Caccini, Giulio. *Io che dal ciel cader a1*. Intermedios for *La Pellegrina*. Florence, 1589.

    Musique des intermèdes de "La Pellegrina." Edited by D. P. Walker. Les fêtes de Florence, vol. 1. Paris, 1963.

―――. *Euridice*. Florence, 1600.

Bibliotheca Musica Bononiensis; sezione IV, vol. 3. Bologna, 1968.

Publikation älterer praktischer und theoretischer Musikwerke. Vol. 10. Edited by R. Eitner. Leipzig, 1881.

"Dedication."

    A. Solerti, *Le origini del melodramma*. Turin, 1903.

    O. Strunk, ed., *Source Readings in Music History*. New York, 1950.

―――. *Il rapimento di Cefalo*. Produced in Florence, 1600.

―――. *Le nuove musiche*. Florence, 1601.

Monuments of Music and Music Literature in Facsimile; First Series—Music, vol. 29. New York, 1973.

Edited by F. Vatielli. Rome, 1934.

Edited by H. W. Hitchcock. Recent Researches in the Baroque Era, vol. 9. Madison, 1970.

"Preface."

    O. Strunk, ed., *Source Readings in Music History*. New York, 1950.

―――. *Amarilli a1. Le nuove musiche*. Florence, 1601.

Complete editions as above.

Geschichte der Musik in Beispielen. Edited by A. Schering. Leipzig, 1931; New York, 1950.

La Flora. Vol. 1. Edited by K. Jeppesen. Copenhagen, 1949.

―――. *Amor io parto a1. Le nuove musiche*. Florence, 1601.

Complete editions as above.

―――. *Ard'il mio petto a1. Le nuove musiche*. Florence, 1601.

Complete editions as above.

Geschichte der Musik in Beispielen. Edited by A. Schering. Leipzig, 1931; New York, 1950.

―――. *Cor mio deh non languire a1. Le nuove musiche*. Florence, 1601.

Complete editions as above.

―――. *Perfidissimo volto a1. Le nuove musiche*. Florence, 1601.

Complete editions as above.

R. Haas, *Die Musik des Barocks*. Potsdam, 1929. Handbuch der Musikwissenschaft.

―――. *Vedro'l mio sol a1. Le nuove musiche*. Florence, 1601.

Complete editions as above.

————. *Le nuove musiche e nuova maniera di scriverle con due arie particolari per tenere che richerchi le corde del basso.* Florence, 1614.

————. *Al fonte al prato a1. Le nuove musiche.* . . . Florence, 1614.

La Flora. Vol. 3. Edited by K. Jeppesen. Copenhagen, 1949.

————. *Amor ch'attendi? a1. Le nuove musiche.* . . . Florence, 1614.

La Flora. Vol. 3. Edited by K. Jeppesen. Copenhagen, 1949.

Caimo, Gioseppe. *Piangete valli a4. Il primo libro de madrigali a quattro voci.* Milan, 1564.

A. Einstein, *The Italian Madrigal.* Vol. 3. Princeton, 1949; 1971.

Calestani, Vincenzo. *Damigella tutta bella a1. Madrigali et arie per sonare et cantare nel chitarrone leuto o clavicembalo a una e due voci.* Venice, 1617.

N. Fortune, "Italian Secular Monody from 1600–1635: An Introductory Survey." *Musical Quarterly* 39 (1953).

————. *Folgarate a1. Madrigali et arie.* . . . Venice, 1617.

N. Fortune, "Solo Song and Cantata." In *The Age of Humanism 1540–1630,* edited by G. Abraham. New Oxford History of Music, vol. 4. London, 1968.

Calvisius, Sethus (Kalwitz). *Melopoiia sive melodia condendae ratio quam vulgo musicam poeticam vocant.* Erfurt, 1592.

Campanella, Tommaso. *Magia e grazia.* Ca. 1630.

Edited by R. Amerio. Edizione nazionale dei classici del pensiero italiano, vol. 5, ser. 2. Rome, 1957.

Cardano, Girolamo. *De subtilitate rerum.* Nuremberg, 1550.

Opera Omnia. Vol. 3. New York, 1967.

————. *De rerum varietate.* Basel, 1557.

Opera Omnia. Vol. 3. New York, 1967.

Carretto, Galeotto dal. *Beatrice.* Produced in Casale, 1499.

————. *Nozze di Psiche e Cupidino.* Produced in Casale, 1502. Venice, 1520.

Casa, Giovanni della. *Il galateo. Rime et prose.* Edited by E. Gemini. Venice, 1558.

Prose scelte e annotate. Edited by S. Ferrari. Florence, 1957.

Galateo: or the Book of Manners. Translated by R. S. Pine-Coffin. Harmondsworth, 1958.

Opere di Baldassare Castiglione, Giovanni della Casa, Benvenuto Cellini. Edited by C. Cordié. Milan, 1960.

Prose. Edited by A. di Benedetti. Turin, 1970.

————. *O Sonno. Rime et prose.* Edited by E. Gemini. Venice, 1558.

Lirici italiani del secolo decimosesto. Edited by L. Carrer. Venice, 1836.

Le rime. Edited by G. Mestica. Florence, 1896.

The Oxford Book of Italian Verse. Edited by St. John Lucas and C. Dionesotti. 2nd ed. Oxford, 1952.

Poesia del quattrocento e del cinquecento. Edited by C. Muscetta and D. Ponchiroli. Turin, 1959.

Rime e trionfi. Edited by F. Neri. Turin, 1960.

J. V. Mirollo, *The Poet of the Marvelous: Giambattista Marino.* New York, 1963.

Rime. Edited by D. Ponchiroli. Turin, 1967.

Rime. Edited by G. Bezzola and A. Zangetto. Milan, 1976.

Casa, Girolamo della. *Il vero modo di diminuir con tutti sorti di stromenti.* Venice, 1584.

Bibliotheca Musica Bononiensis; sezione II, vol. 23. Bologna, 1970.

Casentini, Marsilio. *La Cieca madrigali a cinque voci libro quarto.* Venice, 1609.

"Preface."

Excerpt in E. Vogel, *Bibliothek der gedruckten weltlichen Vocalmusik Italiens.* Hildesheim and New York, 1972.

Cassola, Luigi. *Altro non è il mio amor. Madrigali.* Venice, 1544.

Castiglione, Baldassare, and Gonzaga, Cesare. *Tirsi.* Produced in Urbino, 1506.

Poesie volgari e latine. Rome, 1760.

Cavalieri, Emilio. *Godi turba mortal a5.* Intermedios for *La Pellegrina,* Florence, 1589. C. Malvezzi, *Intermedii et concerti fatti per la commedia rappresentata in Firenze nelle nozze del Serenissimo Don Ferdinando Medici e Madama Christiana di Lorena.* Venice, 1591.

Musique des intermèdes de "La Pellegrina." Edited by D. P. Walker. Les fêtes de Florence, vol. 1. Paris, 1963.

―――. *O che nuovo miracolo a8.* Intermedios for *La Pellegrina,* Florence, 1589. C. Malvezzi, *Intermedii et concerti. . . .* Venice, 1591. See above.

―――. *La disperazione di Fileno.* Produced in Florence, 1590–91.

―――. *Il satiro.* Produced in Florence, 1590–91.

―――. *Lamentationes Hieremiae Prophetae.* Ca. 1599.

Lamentazioni di Geremia. Edited by G. Maselli. Zurich, 1950.

Lamentationes Jeremiae Prophetae. Edited by F. Màntica. Padua, 1960.

―――. Intermedios for *La contesa fra Giunone e Minerva.* Produced in Florence, 1600.

―――. *Rappresentatione di anima e di corpo.* Rome, 1600.

Bibliotheca Musica Bononiensis; sezione IV, vol. 1. Bologna, 1967. Farnborough, 1967.

I classici della musica italiana. Vol. 10. Edited by G. F. Malipiero. Milan, 1919.

"Dedication."

E. Vogel, *Bibliothek der gedruckten weltlichen Vocalmusik Italiens.* Hildesheim and New York, 1972.

Cellini, Benvenute. *Salt-Cellar of Francis I.* 1540–43. Vienna, Kunsthis-
torisches Museum.
    J. Shearman, *Mannerism*. Harmondsworth, 1967.
    R. E. Wolf and R. Millen, *Renaissance and Mannerist Art*. New
    York, 1968.
—————. *Narcissus.* 1546–47. Florence, Bargello.
    A. Hauser, *Mannerism*. London, 1965.
Cerreto, Scipione. *L'Amarillide a tre voci . . . con alcuni a due soprani il
terzo libro opera decima ottava*. Naples, 1621.
Cerone, Domenico P. *El melopeo y maestro*. Naples, 1613.
    Bibliotheca Musica Bononiensis; sezione II, vol. 25. Bologna, 1969.
Charles IX of France. "Letter to Duke Albrecht of Bavaria." 10 May
1571.
    W. Boetticher, *Aus Orlando di Lassos Wirkungskreis*. Kassel, 1963.
Cicero, Marcus T. *Rhetorici libri duo qui vocantur de inventione*.
    Translated by H. M. Hubbell. The Loeb Classical Library. Cam-
    bridge, Mass., and London, 1968.
Cirillo Franco, Bernardino. "Letter to Ugolino Guateruzzi." 1549.
    L. Lockwood, ed., *Pope Marcellus Mass*. New York, 1975.
Coclico, Adrianus P. *Compendium musices*. Nuremberg, 1552.
    Edited by M. Bukofzer. Documenta Musicologica; Erste Reihe:
    Druckschriften-Faksimiles, vol. 9. Kassel, 1954.
    Translated by A. Seay. Colorado College Music Press; Translations,
    vol. 5. Colorado Springs, 1973.
—————. *Musica reservata consolationes piae ex psalmis Davidicis.*
Nuremberg, 1552.
    Das erbe deutscher Musik. Vol. 42. Edited by M. Ruhnke. Leipzig,
    1958.
—————. *Non derelinquat Dominus a4. Musica reservata. . . .* Nuremberg, 1552.
    See above.
Conforto, Giovanni L. *Breve et facile maniera d'essercitarsi ad ogni sco-
laro non solamente a far passaggi sopra tutte le note si desidera per cantare a far la dispositione leggiadra et in diversi modi loro valore con le
cadenze ma ancore per potere da se senza maestro scrivere ogni opera
et arie passeggiata che voranno et come si notano*. Rome, 1593.
    Veröffentlichungen der Musik-Bibliothek Paul Hirsch. Berlin, 1922.
Copernicus, Nicolas. *De revolutionibus orbium coelestium*. Nuremberg,
1543.
    Turin, 1943.
    Complete Works. Vol. 1. London, 1972.
    Gesamtausgabe. Vol. 1. Hildesheim, 1974.
Cornazano, Antonio. *Il libro dell'arte del danzare*. 1455.
    Edited by C. Mazzi. *La Bibliofilia* (17), 1916.

Corteccia, Francesco. Intermedios for *Il Commodo*. Florence, 1539. *Apparato et feste nelle nozze dello Illustrissimo Signor Duca di Firenze e della Duchessa sua consorte con le stanze madriali comedia & intermedii in quelle recitati*. Florence, 1539.

> *A Renaissance Entertainment: Festivities for the Marriage of Cosimo I, Duke of Florence, in 1539*. Edited by A. C. Minor and B. Mitchell. Columbia, Miss., 1968.

————. *Quest'io tesseva a4. Libro primo de madrialo a quatro voci . . . con l'aggiunta d'alcuni madriali novamente fatti per la comedia del Furto*. Venice, 1547.

> A. Einstein, *The Italian Madrigal*. Vol. 3. Princeton, 1949; 1971.

Cortese, Giulio C. *Avvertimenti nel poetare*. Naples, 1591. *Rime del Sig. G. Cortese*. Naples, 1592.

> *Trattati di poetica e retorica del cinquecento*. Vol. 4. Edited by B. Weinberg. Scrittori d'Italia, vol. 258. Bari, 1974.

————. *Delle figure*. Naples, 1591. *Rime del Sig. G. Cortese*. Naples, 1592.

> See above.

————. *Dell'imitatione e dell'inventione*. Naples, 1591. *Rime del Sig. G. Cortese*, Naples, 1592.

> See above.

Danckerts, Ghiselin. *Trattado . . . sopra una differentia musicale*. Ca. 1556.

Dante Alighieri. *La divina commedia*.

> Turin, 1966.
> *The Divine Comedy*. Translated by G. L. Bickersteth. Cambridge, Mass., 1965.

De musica. Acts of the Synod of Besançon, 1571.

> *Concilia Germaniae*. Vol. 8. Edited by J. F. Schannat and J. Hartzheim. Cologne, 1759–75.
> Excerpt in W. Bäumker, "Über den Kontrapunkt." *Monatshefte für Musikgeschichte* 10 (1878).

Denores, Iason. *Apologia contra l'auttore del Verrato*. Padua, 1590.

> G. B. Guarini, *Il Verrato secondo*. Venice, 1593.

Dentice, Luigi. *Duo dialoghi della musica*. Naples, 1552.

Diruta, Girolamo. *Il transilvano*. Pt. II, Venice, 1609.

> Bibliotheca Musica Bononiensis; sezione II, vol. 132. Bologna, 1969.

Dolce, Lodovico. *Dialogo della pittura intitolato l'Aretino*. Venice, 1557.

> *Aretino, oder Dialog über Malerei*. Translated by C. Cerri. Quellenschriften für Kunstgeschichte, vol. 2. Vienna, 1871.
> *Trattati d'arte del cinquecento fra manierismo e controriforma*. Vol. 1. Edited by P. Barocchi. Scrittori d'Italia, vol. 219. Bari, 1960.
> *Aretin: A Dialogue on Painting*. Menston. 1970.

Doni, Anton F. *Dialogo della musica*. Venice, 1544.

L'opera musicale di Antonfrancesco Doni. Edited by A. M. Monterosso Vacchelli. Instituta et Monumenta; serie II: Instituta, vol. 1. Cremona, 1969.

————. *Disegno*. Venice, 1549.
Edited by M. Pepe. Milan, 1970.

Doni, Giovanni B. *Discorso sopra la perfettione delle melodie. Compendio del trattato de'generi e de'modi della musica*. Rome, 1635.

————. *Trattato della musica scenica*. Ca. 1635.
Lyra Barberina. Vol. 2. Edited by A. F. Gori and G. B. Passeri. Florence, 1763.

————. *Annotazione sopra il compendio de'generi e de'modi della musica*. Rome, 1640.

————. *De praestantia musica veteris libri tres*. Florence, 1647.
Lyra Barberina, Vol. 1. Edited by A. F. Gori and G. B. Passeri. Florence, 1763.
Bibliotheca Musica Bononiensis; sezione II, vol. 49. Bologna, 1970.

Dressler, Gallus. *Praecepta musicae poeticae*. Ca. 1564.
Edited by B. Engelke. *Geschichtsblätter für Stadt und Land Magdeburg*, 49–50 (1914–15).

Dürer, Albrecht. "Letter to W. Pirckheimer." Ca. 13 October 1506.
Dürers Briefe, Tagebücher und Reime. Edited by M. Thausing. Quellenschriften für Kunstgeschichte, vol. 3. Vienna, 1872.
Schriftlichen Nachlass. Vol. 1. Edited by H. Rupprich. Berlin, 1956.
Schriften, Tagebücher, Briefe. Edited by M. Steck. Stuttgart, 1961.
Schriftlichen Nachlass; eine Auswahl. Edited by H. Faensen. Darmstadt, 1963.

Ebreo, Guglielmo. *Trattato dell'arte del ballo*. 1463.
Edited by F. Zambrini. *Scelta di curiosità letterarie inedite o rare dal secolo XII al XVII* 131 (1873).

Effrem, Muzio. *Censure sopra il sesto libro de madrigali di M. Marco da Gagliano*. Venice, 1623.

Erasmus, Desiderius. *Adagiorum collectanea*. Paris, 1500. *Adagiorum chiliades*. Venice, 1508. *Adagiorum opus*. Basel, 1533.
The Adages of Erasmus: A Study and Translation. Edited by M. M. Phillips. Cambridge, 1964.
Proverbes or Adages. Translated by R. Taverner. (London, 1539.) Amsterdam, 1969.

Faber, Gregor. *Musices practicae erotematum*. Basel, 1553.
Faber, Heinrich. *Musica poetica*. 1548.
Festa, Costanzo. *Quanto più m'arde a4*. J. Arcadelt, *Il terzo libro de i madrigali novissimi a quattro voci*. Venice, 1539.
W. Osthoff, *Theatergesang und darstellende Musik in der italienischen Renaissance*. Vol. 2. Tutzing, 1969.
Fiesco, Giulio. *Il primo libro di madrigali a quattro voci*. Venice, 1554.

————. *Bacio soave a4. Il primo libro.* . . . Venice, 1554.

H. W. Kaufmann, "A 'Diatonic' and a 'Chromatic' Madrigal by Giulio Fiesco." In *Aspects of Medieval and Renaissance Music: A Birthday Offering to Gustave Reese.* New York, 1966.

E. E. Lowinsky, "The Problem of Mannerism in Music." *Studi Musicali* 3 (1974).

————. *Musica nova a cinque voci.* Venice, 1569.

"Dedication."

Excerpt in E. Vogel, *Bibliothek der gedruckten weltlichen Vocalmusik Italiens.* Hildesheim and New York, 1972.

Finck, Hermann. *Practica musica.* Wittenberg, 1556.

Hildesheim and New York, 1971.

Fogliano, Lodovico. *Musica theorica.* Venice, 1529.

Monuments of Music and Music Literature in Facsimile; Second Series—Music Literature, vol. 93. New York, 1969.

Francesco, Piero della. *De prospectiva pingendi.* Ca. 1482.

Edited by C. Winterberg. Strasbourg, 1899.

Edited by G. Nicco Fasola. Florence, 1942.

Frescobaldi, Girolamo. *Fantasia ottava. Il primo libro delle fantasie a quattro.* Milan, 1608.

Orgel- und Klavierwerke. Vol. 1. Edited by P. Pidoux. Kassel, 1949.

Gabrieli, Andrea. *Tirsi morir volea a7. Concerti continenti musica di chiesa madrigali & altro per voci & stromenti musicali a6, 7, 8, 10, 12 & 16 libro primo et secondo.* Venice, 1587.

A. Einstein, *The Italian Madrigal.* Vol. 3. Princeton, 1949; 1971.

————. *Chori in musica sopra li chori della tragedia di Edippo tiranno recitati in Vicenza l'anno MDLXXXV.* Venice, 1588.

La représentation d'Edipo Tiranno au Teatro Olimpico (Vicence 1585). Edited by L. Schrade. Paris, 1960.

Gaetano, Pietro. *Oratio de'origine et dignitate musices.* Ca. 1570.

Gafurius, Franchinus. *Practica musicae.* Milan, 1496.

Farnborough, 1967.

Translated by C. A. Miller. Musicological Studies and Documents, vol. 20. American Institute of Musicology, 1968.

Translated by I. Young. Madison, 1969.

Gagliano, Marco da. *O Sonno a5. Il primo libro de madrigali a cinque voci.* Venice, 1602.

A. Einstein, *The Italian Madrigal.* Vol. 3. Princeton, 1949; 1971.

————. *La Dafne.* Florence, 1608.

Bibliotheca Musica Bononiensis; sezione IV, vol. 4. Bologna, 1970.

Publikation älterer praktischer und theoretischer Musikwerke. Vol. 10. Edited by R. Eitner. Leipzig, 1881.

"Preface."

E. Vogel, *Bibliothek der gedruckten weltlichen Vocalmusik Italiens.* Hildesheim and New York, 1972.

————. *Mie speranze lusinghiere a1. Musiche a una dua e tre voci*. Venice, 1615.

La Flora. Vol. 2. Edited by K. Jeppesen. Copenhagen, 1949.

————. *Valli profondi a1. Musiche*. . . . Venice, 1615.

La Flora. Vol. 1. Edited by K. Jeppesen. Copenhagen, 1949.

Galilei, Galileo. *Considerazioni al Tasso*. 1589–1600. Rome, 1793.

T. Tasso, *Opere*. Vol. 23. Edited by G. Rosini. Pisa, 1828.

Le opere. Vol. 9. Edited by A. Favaro. Florence, 1933.

Scritti letterari. Edited by A. Chiara. Florence, 1970.

————. *Dialogo sopra i due massime sistemi del mondo Tolemaico e Copernico*. Florence, 1632.

Opere. Vol. 1. Edited by E. Alberti. Florence, 1842.

Le opere. Vol. 3. Edited by A. Favaro. Florence, 1933.

Opere. Edited by F. Flora. Milan and Naples, 1953.

Opere. Vol. 4. Edited by F. Brunetti. Turin, 1964.

Dialogue Concerning the Two Chief World Systems–Ptolemaic and Copernican. 2nd ed. Translated by S. Drake. Berkeley, 1967.

Edited by L. Sosio. Turin, 1970.

Galilei, Vincenzo. *Fronimo dialogo nel quale si contengono le vere et necessarie regole del intavolare la musica nel liuto*. Venice, 1568.

Bibliotheca Musica Bononiensis; sezione II, vol. 22. Bologna, 1969.

————. *Dialogo della musica antica e della moderna*. Florence, 1581.

Monuments of Music and Music Literature in Facsimile; Second Series—Music Literature, vol. 20. New York, 1967.

————. *Poi che'l mio largo pianto a4. Il secondo libro de madrigali a quattro et a cinque voci*. Venice, 1587.

A. Einstein, *The Italian Madrigal*. Vol. 3. Princeton, 1969; 1971.

————. *Discorso intorno all'opere di messer Gioseffo Zarlino da Chioggia*. Florence, 1589.

————. *L'arte et la pratica del moderno contrapunto*. 1591.

Gesualdo, Carlo. *Arde il mio cor. a5. Madrigali a cinque voci libro quarto*. Ferrara, 1596.

Istituto italiano per la storia della musica. Monumenti I, vol. 4. Edited by A. Bizzelli. Rome, 1957.

Sämtliche Werke. Vol. 4. Edited by W. Weismann. Hamburg, 1958.

————. *Moro e mentre sospiro a5. Madrigali . . . libro quarto*. Ferrara, 1596.

Complete editions as above.

R. G. Kiesewetter, *Schicksale und Beschaffenheit des weltlichen Gesanges*. Leipzig, 1841.

————. *Languisco al fin a5. Madrigali a cinque voci libro quinto*. Naples, 1611.

Sämtliche Werke. Vol. 5. Edited by W. Weismann. Hamburg, 1958.

————. *Mercè grido piangendo a5. Madrigali . . . libro quinto*. Naples, 1611.

Sämtliche Werke. Vol. 5. Edited by W. Weismann. Hamburg, 1958.
I Classici della musica italiana. Vol. 14. Edited by I. Pizzetti. Milan,
ca. 1919.
————. *Tu m'uccidi o crudele a5. Madrigali . . . libro quinto.* Naples,
1611.
See above (*Mercè grido piangendo*).
E. E. Lowinsky, "The Musical Avant-Garde of the Renaissance or:
The Peril and Profit of Foresight." In *Art, Science and History in
the Renaissance,* edited by C. S. Singleton. Baltimore, 1967.
————. *Moro lasso a5. Madrigali a cinque voci libro sesto.* Naples,
1611.
C. Burney, *A General History of Music.* Bk. 3. London, 1789. New
York, 1957.
Sämtliche Werke. Vol. 6. Edited by W. Weismann. Hamburg, 1957.
A Treasury of Early Music. Edited by C. Parrish. New York, 1958.
The Norton Scores. Vol. 1. Edited by R. Kamien. New York, 1970.
Giacomini, Lorenzo. *Sopra la purgazione della tragedia.* Lecture given to
the Accademia degli Alterati, 1586. *Orationi e discorsi.* Florence,
1597.
————. *Del furore poetico.* Lecture given to the Accademia degli Al-
terati, 1587.
Trattati di poetica e retorica. Vol. 3. Edited by B. Weinberg. Scrittori
d'Italia, vol. 253. Bari, 1972.
Gilio da Fabriano, Giovanni A. *Due dialoghi . . . nel secondo si ragione
degli errori de'pittori.* Camerino, 1564.
Trattati d'arte del cinquecento fra manierismo e controriforma. Vol.
2. Edited by P. Barocchi. Scrittori d'Italia, vol. 221. Bari, 1961.
Giovanelli, Ruggiero. *Il primo libro de madrigali a quatro voci.* Venice,
1587.
"Dedication."
Excerpt in E. Vogel, *Bibliothek der gedruckten weltlichen Vocal-
musik Italiens.* Hildesheim and New York, 1972.
Giraldi Cintio, Giambattista. *Discorso intorno al comporre de i romanzi
delle comedie e delle tragedie e di altre maniere di poesie.* Venice, 1554.
Giraldi Cintio on Romances. Translated by H. L. Snuggs. Lexington,
1968.
Scritti critici. Edited by C. G. Crocetti. Milan, 1973.
————. *Orbecche.* Produced in Ferrara, 1541. Venice, 1553.
Le tragedie. Venice, 1583.
————. *Selene.* Produced in Ferrara, 1548. Venice, 1583.
Le tragedie. Venice, 1583.
Giustiniani, Vicenzo. *Discorso sopra la musica.* Ca. 1628.
Translated by C. MacClintock. Musicological Studies and Docu-
ments, vol. 9. American Institute of Musicology, 1962.
Glareanus, Henricus. "Letter to J. Aal." 3 January 1540.

E. Tatarinoff, *Briefe Glareans an Joh. Aal aus den Jahren 1538–1550.* Solothurn, 1895.

Excerpt in W. Gurlitt, "Die Kompositionslehre des deutschen 16. und 17. Jahrhundert." *Musikgeschichte und Gegenwart.* Vol. 1. Wiesbaden, 1966.

———. *Dodecachordon.* Basel, 1547.

Monuments of Music and Music Literature in Facsimile; Second Series—Music Literature, vol. 65. New York, 1967.

Publikation älterer praktischer and theoretischer Musikwerke. Vol. 16. Translated by P. Bohn. Leipzig, 1888.

Translated by C. A. Miller, 2 vols. American Institute of Musicology, 1965.

Gracián y Morales, Baltasar. *Agudeza y arte de ingenio.* Madrid, 1642. Huesca, 1648.

Madrid, 1929. (Reprint of 1648 edition.)

The Art of Worldly Wisdom. Translated by J. Jacobs. London, 1904.

Edited by E. C. Calderón. 2 vols. Madrid, 1969.

Grammateus, Henricus (Schreiber). *Ayn new kunstlich Buech.* Nuremberg, 1518.

Grandi, Alessandro. *Cantade et arie a voce sola.* Venice, 1620.

Grazzini, Antonfrancesco ("Il Lasca"). *La commedia che si duol degli intermezzi.*

Commedie del cinquecento. Vol. 1. Edited by A. Borlenghi. Milan, 1969.

Greiter, Matthaeus. *Elementale musicum iuventati accommodum.* Strasbourg, 1544.

———. *Passibus ambiguis a4.* G. Faber, *Musices practicae erotematum.* Basel, 1553.

E. E. Lowinsky, "Matthaeus Greiter's *Fortuna*: An Experiment in Chromaticism and in Musical Iconography." *Musical Quarterly* 42 (1956).

Guarini, Alessandro. *Lezione nell'Accademia degl'Invaghiti in Mantua sopr'il sonnetto LIX.* Presented in Mantua, 1599.

G. della Casa, *Opere.* Vol. 1. Naples, 1733.

Guarini, Giovanni B. *A un giro sol. Rime.* Venice, 1621.

Opere. Edited by L. Fassò. Turin, 1950.

———. *Ardo sì ma non t'amo. Rime.* Venice, 1621. *Il pastor fido aggiontavi di nova le rime.* Venice, 1621.

———. *Tirsi morir volea.*

Opere. Edited by L. Fassò. Turin, 1950.

———. *Il Verrato.* Ferrara, 1588.

———. *Il Verrato secondo.* Ferrara, 1593.

———. *La contesa fra Giunone e Minerva.* Produced in Florence, 1600.

Dialogo fra Giunone e Minerva. Il pastor fido ... Rime. Venice, 1638.

————. *Il pastor Fido.* Venice, 1601. Venice, 1602.

     Opere. Edited by L. Fassò. Turin, 1950.

     A *Critical Edition of Sir Richard Fanshawe's 1647 Translation of Giovanni Battista Guarini's Il Pastor Fido.* Edited by W. F. Staton, Jr. and W. E. Simeone. Oxford, 1964.

————. *Compendio della poesia tragicomica.* Appended to *Il pastor fido.* Venice, 1601. Venice, 1602.

————. *L'Idropica.* Produced in Mantua, 1608. Venice, 1613.

     Commedie di vari autori. Vol. 1. Florence, 1619.

Herbst, Johann A. *Musica poetica sive compendium melopoeticum.* Nuremberg, 1643.

Hoffmann, Eucharius. *Doctrina de tonis seu modis musicis.* Greifswald, 1582.

Hunger, Wolfgang. *Emblematum libellus.* Paris, 1539.

India, Sigismondo d'. *Crud'Amarilli a5. Libro primo de madrigali a cinque voci.* Venice, 1607.

     I classici musicali italiani. Vol. 10. Edited by F. Mompellio. Rome, 1942.

————. *Le musiche da cantar solo nel clavichordo chitarone arpa doppia et altri istromenti simili.* Milan, 1609.

     Edited by F. Mompellio. Instituta et Monumenti; serie 1: Monumenti, vol. 4. Cremona, 1970.

     "Dedication" and "Letter."

     E. Vogel, *Bibliothek der gedruckten weltlichen Vocalmusik Italiens.* Hildesheim and New York, 1972.

————. *Là tra'l sangue a1. Le musiche. . . .* Milan, 1609.

     See above.

————. *Ma che squallido a1. Le musiche. . . .* Milan, 1609.

     See above.

————. *O dolcezze amarissime d'amore a1. Le musiche. . . .* Milan, 1609.

     See above.

Gl'ingannati. (Accademia Intronati di Siena.) Produced in Naples, 1545.

     Delle comedie elette libro primo. Venice, 1554.

     Commedie del cinquecento. Vol. 1. Edited by A. Borlenghi. Milan, 1969.

     Il teatro italiano II—2; *La commedia del cinquecento.* Edited by G. D. Bonino. Milan, 1977.

Ingegneri, Angelo. *Della poesia rappresentativa e del modo di rappresentare le favole sceniche.* Florence, 1598.

Kepler, Johannes. *Harmonice mundi.* Linz, 1619.

     Opera Omnia. Vol. 5. Edited by C. Frisch. Frankfurt am Main, 1864.

     Gesammelte Werke. Vol. 6. Edited by M. Caspar. Munich, 1940.

Landi, Antonio. *Il Commodo*. Produced in Florence, 1539. Florence, 1539. Florence, 1566.

Landi, Stefano. *Sant'Alessio*. Produced in Rome, 1632. *Il S. Alessio dramma musicale dall'eminentissimo et reverendissimo Signore Card. Barberino fatto rappresentare al serenissimo Prencipe Alessandro Carlo di Polonia*. Rome, 1634.

Bibliotheca Musica Bononiensis, vol. 11. Bologna, 1970.

Lanfranco, Giovanni M. *Scintille di musica*. Brescia, 1533.

B. Lee, "Giovanni Maria Lanfranco's *Scintille di musica* and its Relation to 16th-Century Music Theory." Ph.D. dissertation, Cornell University, 1961.

Lasso, Orlando di. *Il primo libro dove si contengono madrigali vilanesche canzoni francese e motetti e quattro voci*. Antwerp, 1555. "Dedication."

R. Eitner, "Chronologisches Verzeichnis des gedruckten Werke von Hans Leo Hassler und Orlandus Lassus." *Beilage zu den Monatshefte für Musikgeschichte V. und VI. Jahrgang*. Berlin, 1874.

Excerpt in H. W. Kaufmann, *The Life and Works of Nicola Vicentino*. American Institute of Musicology, 1966.

————. *Alma nemes a4. Le quatorsième livre à quatre parties*. Antwerp, 1555. *Il primo libro dove si contengono madrigali.*.... Antwerp, 1555.

C. Burney, *A General History of Music*. Bk. 3. London, 1789. New York, 1957.

Trésor musicale: Musique profane. Vol. 3. Edited by R. van Maldeghem. Brussels, 1867; 1965.

————. *Cantai hor piango a5. Il primo libro di madrigali a cinque voci*. Venice, 1555.

Sämtliche Werke. Vol. 2. Edited by F. X. Haberl and A. Sandberger. Leipzig, 1894.

————. *Crudel acerba inesorabil morte a5. Il primo libro di madrigali a cinque voci*. Venice, 1555.

See above.

————. *Tityre tu patulae a6*. 1559.

Sämtliche Werke. Vol. 19. Edited by F. X. Haberl. Leipzig, 1908.

Trésor musicale: Musique profane. Vol. 4. Edited by R. van Maldeghem. Brussels, 1868; 1965.

————. *Prophetiae Sibyllarum a4*. 1560.

Das Chorwerk. Vol. 48. Edited by H. J. Therstappen. Welfenbüttel, 1937.

————. *In me transierunt a5. Sacrae cantiones quinque vocum*. Nuremberg, 1562.

Sämtliche Werke. Vol. 9. Edited by F. X. Haberl and A. Sandberger. Leipzig, 1897.

C. V. Palisca, "*Ut oratoria musica*: the Rhetorical Basis of Musical Mannerism." In *The Meaning of Mannerism*. Hanover, N.H., 1972.

————. *Heremiae Prophetae Lamentationes et aliae piae cantiones*. Munich, 1585.

Collectio operum musicorum Batavorum saeculi XVI. Vol. 12. Edited by F. Commer. Berlin, 1858.

————. *Lagrime di S. Pietro a sette voci*. Monaco, 1595.

Das Chorwerk. Vols. 34, 37, and 41. Edited by H. J. Therstappen. Wolfenbüttel, 1935 and 1936.

Il lauro secco libro primo di madrigali a cinque voci di diversi autori. Ferrara, 1582.

Il lauro verde madrigali a sei voci di diversi autori. Ferrara, 1583.

Legname, Jacopo del. *Tragedia*. Produced in Treviso, 1517.

Leonardo da Vinci. *Paragone*. Ca. 1500. *Trattato della pittura*. Paris, 1651.

    Paragone: a Comparison of the Arts by Leonardo da Vinci. Edited by I. A. Richter. London, 1949.

    Treatise on Painting. Edited by A. P. McMahon. Princeton, 1956.

    The Literary Werks of Leonardo da Vinci. Vol. 1. Edited by J. P. Richter, London, 1970.

Le Roy, Adrien. "Letter to O. di Lasso." Paris, 14 January 1574.

    A. Sandberger, *Beiträge zur Geschichte der bayerische Hofkapelle unter Orlando di Lasso*. Vol. 3. Leipzig, 1895.

Listenius, Nicolaus. *Musica*. Wittenberg, 1537.

    Edited by G. Schünemann. Veröffentlichungen der Musik-Bibliothek Paul Hirsch, vol. 8. Berlin, 1927.

    Translated by A. Seay, Colorado College Music Press; Translations, vol. 6. Colorado Springs, 1975.

Lollio, Alberto. *L'Aretusa*. Produced in Ferrara, 1563. Ferrara, 1564.

Lomazzo, Giovanni P. *Trattato dell'arte della pittura scultura et architettura*. Milan, 1584.

    Hildesheim, 1967.

    A Tracte Containing the Artes of Curious Paintinge, Carvinge, Buildinge. Translated by R. Haydocke. (Oxford, 1598.) New York, 1969 (first five books only).

————. *L'idea del tempio della pittura*. Milan, 1590.

    Hildesheim, 1965.

Luzzaschi, Luzzasco. *Quivi sospiri a5. Secondo libro de madrigali a cinque voci*. Ferrara, 1576.

    A. Einstein, "Dante, on the Way to the Madrigal." *Musical Quarterly* 25 (1939).

    The Golden Age of the Madrigal. Edited by A. Einstein. New York, 1942.

————. *Sesto libro de'madrigali a cinque voci.* Ferrara, 1596.
  "Dedication."
  L. Bianconi, "Weitere Ergänzungen zu Emil Vogels 'Bibliothek der gedruckten weltlichen Vocalmusik Italiens, aus den Jahren 1500–1700' aus italienischen Bibliotheken." *Analecta Musicologica* 9 (1970).
————. *Madrigali per cantare et sonare a uno e doi e tre soprani.* Rome, 1601.
  Edited by A. Cavicchi. Monumenti di Musica Italiana; serie 2: Polifonia, vol. 2. Brescia, 1965.
————. *Cor mio deh non languire a2. Madrigali per cantare.* . . . Rome, 1601.
  Complete edition as above.
  Music of Earlier Times. Edited by J. Wolf. New York, 1942.
————. *O dolcezze amarissime d'amore a3. Madrigali per cantare.* . . . Rome, 1601.
  Complete edition as above.
  A. Einstein, *The Italian Madrigal.* Vol. 3. Princeton, 1949; 1971.
————. *O Primavera a1. Madrigali per cantare.* . . . Rome, 1601.
  Complete edition as above.
  Geschichte der Musik in Beispielen. Edited by A. Schering. Leipzig, 1931. New York, 1950.
Macchiavelli, Niccolò. *La Clizia.* Produced in Florence, 1525. Florence, 1525. Florence, 1537.
  Translated by O. Evans. Great Neck, N.Y., 1962.
Madrigali di diversi musici libro primo de la serena. Rome, 1530.
Maggi, Vincenzo and Lombardi, Bartolomeo. *In Aristotelis librum de poetica communes explanationes.* Venice, 1550.
Malvezzi, Cristofano. *Intermedii et concerti fatti per la commedia rappresentata in Firenze nelle nozze del Serenissimo Don Ferdinando Medici e Madama Christiana di Lorena.* Venice, 1591.
  Musique des intermèdes de "La Pellegrina." Edited by D. P. Walker. Les fêtes de Florence, vol. 1. Paris, 1963.
  "Dedication."
  E. Vogel, *Bibliothek der gedruckten weltlichen Vocalmusik Italiens.* Hildesheim and New York, 1972.
————. *Godi coppia reale a5.* Intermedios for *La Pellegrina.* Florence, 1589. *Intermedii et concerti.* . . . Venice, 1591.
  Complete edition as above.
————. *Io che l'onde raffreno a5.* Intermedios for *La Pellegrina.* Florence, 1589. *Intermedii et concerti.* . . . Venice, 1591.
  Complete edition as above.
Marenzio, Luca. *Dolorosi martir a5. Il primo libro de madrigali a cinque voci.* Venice, 1580.

Publikationen älterer Musik. Vol. 4:1. (*Luca Marenzio: Sämtliche Werke.*) Edited by A. Einstein. Leipzig, 1929. Hildesheim, 1967.

————. *O tu che fra le selve a8. Il primo libro.* . . . Venice, 1580.

See above.

————. *Partirò dunque a5. Il primo libro.* . . . Venice, 1580.

See above.

————. *Tirsi morir volea a5. Il primo libro.* . . . Venice, 1580.

See above.

————. *O voi che sospirate a5. Il secondo libro de madrigali a cinque voci.* Venice, 1581.

See above.

Music of Gabrieli and his Time. Edited by C. von Winterfeld. Ossining, N.Y., 1960.

E. E. Lowinsky, "The Musical Avant-Garde of the Renaissance or: The Peril and Profit of Foresight." In *Art, Science and History in the Renaissance,* edited by C. S. Singleton. Baltimore, 1967.

————. *O dolce anima mia a5. Il terzo libro de madrigali a cinque voci.* Venice, 1582.

Publikationen älterer Musik. Vol. 4:1. (*Luca Marenzio: Sämtliche Werke.*) Edited by A. Einstein. Leipzig, 1929. Hildesheim, 1967.

————. *Occhi lucenti e belli a5. Il terzo libro.* . . . Venice, 1582.

See above.

————. *Ohimè se tanto amate a5. Il terzo libro.* . . . Venice, 1582.

See above.

————. *Scaldava il sol a5. Il terzo libro.* . . . Venice, 1582.

See above.

Madrigali Italiani. Vol. 1. Edited by L. Virgili. Rome, 1952.

————. *Disdegno e gelosia a5. Il quarto libro de madrigali a cinque voci.* Venice, 1584.

Publikationen älterer Musik. Vol. 6. (*Luca Marenzio: Sämtliche Werke.*) Edited by A. Einstein. Leipzig, 1931. Hildesheim, 1967.

————. *Giunto a la tomba a5. Il quarto libro.* . . . Venice, 1584.

See above.

————. *O bella man a4. Madrigali a quatro voci libro primo.* Rome, 1585.

————. *Piangea Filli a6. Il terzo libro de madrigali a sei voci.* Venice, 1585.

Excerpt in A. Einstein, *The Italian Madrigal.* Vol. 2. Princeton, 1949; 1971.

————. *Madrigali a quatro cinque et sei voci.* Bk. 1. Venice, 1588.

The Secular Works. Vol. 7. Edited by S. Ledbetter and P. Myers. New York, 1978.

"Dedication."

Abridged version in E. Vogel, *Bibliothek der gedruckten welt-*

lichen Vocalmusik Italiens. Hildesheim and New York, 1972.

Ibid., in A. Einstein, *The Italian Madrigal.* Princeton, 1949; 1971.

———. *O fere stelle a6. Madrigali.* . . . Venice, 1588.

A. Einstein, *The Italian Madrigal.* Vol. 3. Princeton, 1949; 1971.

———. *"Moresca per combattimento" a5.* Intermedios for *La Pellegrina.* Florence, 1589.

———. *Ah dolente partita a5. Il sesto libro de madrigali a cinque voci.* Venice, 1594.

Publikationen älterer Musik. Vol. 6. (*Luca Marenzio: Sämtliche Werke.*) Edited by A. Einstein. Leipzig, 1931. Hildesheim, 1967.

———. *Udite lagrimosi spirti a5. Il sesto libro.* . . . Venice, 1594.

See above.

———. *Se tu dolce a5. L'ottavo libro de madrigali a cinque voci.* Venice, 1598.

Excerpt in A. Einstein, *The Italian Madrigal.* Vol. 2. Princeton, 1949; 1971.

———. *Così nel mio parlar a5. Il nono libro de madrigali a cinque voci.* Venice, 1599.

Le opere complete. Vol. 7. Edited by J. Steele. New York, 1975.

A. Einstein, "Dante im Madrigal." *Archiv für Musikwissenschaft* 3 (1921).

———. *Crudel acerba inesorabil morte a5. Il nono libro.* . . . Venice, 1599.

Marenzio: Ten Madrigals. Edited by D. Arnold. London, 1966.

———. *La bella man a5. Il nono libro.* . . . Venice, 1599.

Le opere complete. Vol. 7. Edited by J. Steele. New York, 1975.

L'arte musicale in Italia. Vol. 2. Edited by L. Torchi. Milan, 1897.

———. *Solo e pensoso a5. Il nono libro.* . . . Venice, 1599.

See above.

Geschichte der Musik in Beispielen. Edited by A. Schering. Leipzig, 1931; New York, 1950 (first part only).

Madrigali Italiani. Vol. 1. Edited by L. Virgili. Rome, 1952.

Mariconda, Giambattista. *La Filemia.* Produced in Naples, 1546.

"Marini, Biagio." "Court document." Neuberg, 1619.

W. Clark, "A Contribution to Sources of Musica Reservata." *Revue Belge de Musicologie* 11 (1957).

Marino, Giambattista. *A Dio Florida bella. Rime.* Venice, 1612. *Rime.* Venice, 1604. *La lira.* Venice, 1664.

———. *Dicerie sacre.* Turin, 1614.

Dicerie sacre e la strage degl'innocenti. Edited by G. Pozzi. Turin, 1960.

Opere. Edited by A. A. Rosa. Milan, 1967.

———. *Eccomi pronta ai baci. La lira.* Venice, 1664.

Poesie varie. Edited by B. Croce. Scrittori d'Italia, vol. 51. Bari, 1913.

Marino e i marinisti. Edited by G. G. Ferrero. Milan, 1954.

Opere. Edited by A. A. Rosa. Milan, 1967.

_____. *O del Silenzio figlio.*

See above.

The Oxford Book of Italian Verse. 2nd ed. Edited by St. John Lucas and C. Dionesotti. Oxford, 1952.

J. V. Mirollo, *The Poet of the Marvelous: Giambattista Marino.* New York, 1963.

_____. *Presso un fiume.*

Marino e i marinisti. Edited by G. G. Ferrero. Milan, 1954.

Opere. Edited by A. A. Rosa. Milan, 1967.

Mazzone, Marc A. *Il primo libro de madrigali a quattro voci.* Venice, 1569.

"Preface."

   E. Vogel, *Bibliothek der gedruckten weltlichen Vocalmusik Italiens.* Hildesheim and New York, 1972.

Mazzoni, Giacopo. *Della difesa della Comedia di Dante.* Cesena, 1587. Edited by M. Verdoni and D. D. Buccioli. Cesena, 1688.

Mei, Girolamo. "Letters to V. Galilei." 1572–99.

   C. V. Palisca, *Girolamo Mei: Letters on Ancient and Modern Music to Vincenzo Galilei and Giovanni Bardi.* American Institute of Musicology, 1960.

Mezzogorri, Giovanni N. *Il pastor fido armonico in due parti diviso.* Venice, 1617.

Michelangelo Buonarotti. *Sistine Ceiling.* 1508–12. Rome, Sistine Chapel, Vatican.

   F. Würtenberger, *Mannerism.* New York, 1963.

   A. Hauser, *Mannerism.* London, 1965.

   A. Smart, *The Renaissance and Mannerism in Italy.* London, 1971.

_____. Anteroom of the Biblioteca Laurenziana. 1524–55. Florence.

   W. Sypher, *Four Stages of Renaissance Style.* Garden City, N.Y., 1955.

   F. Würtenberger, *Mannerism.* New York, 1963.

   A. Hauser, *Mannerism.* London, 1965.

   R. E. Wolf and R. Millen, *Renaissance and Mannerist Art.* New York, 1968.

Michele, Agostino. *Discorso in cui contra l'opinione di tutti i più illustri scrittori dell'arte poetica chiaramente si dimostra come si possono scrivere con molta lode le comedie e le tragedie in prosa.* Venice, 1592.

Minturno, Antonio, S. *O Sonno.*

   Lirici misti del secolo XVI. Parnaso italiano ovvero raccolta de'poeti classici italiani, vol. 31. Venice, 1787.

Molanus, Johannes. *De historia ss. imaginum et picturarum pro vero earum usu contra abusus.* Louvain, 1594. (Enlarged edition of *De picturis et imaginibus sacris.* Louvain, 1570.)

Monte, Filippo di. *L'ottavo libro delli madrigali a cinque voci.* Venice, 1580.

"Dedication."

    Excerpt in E. Vogel, *Bibliothek der gedruckten weltlichen Vocalmusik Italiens.* Hildesheim and New York, 1972.

————. *Il decimo libro delli madrigali a cinque voci.* Venice, 1581.

"Dedication."

    See above.

————. *Musica sopra il pastor fido ove si contengono canzoni & madrigali vaghissimi libro secondo a sette voci.* Venice, 1600.

Monteverdi, Claudio. *Baci soavi a 5. Madrigali a cinque voci libro primo.* Venice, 1587.

    Tutte le opere. Vol. 1. Edited by G. F. Malipiero. Vienna, 1926.

————. *Dolcissimi legami a 5. Il secondo libro de madrigali a cinque voci.* Venice, 1590.

    Tutte le opere. Vol. 2. Edited by F. G. Malipiero. Vienna, 1927.

————. *Ecco mormorar l'onde a 5. Il secondo libro. . . .* Venice, 1590.

    See above.

————. *Mentre io miravo fiso a 5. Il secondo libro. . . .* Venice, 1590.

    See above.

————. *Non si levava ancor a 5. Il secondo libro. . . .* Venice, 1590.

    See above.

————. *Lumi miei cari lumi a 5. Il terzo libro de madrigali a cinque voci.* Venice, 1592.

    Tutte le opere. Vol. 3. Edited by G. F. Malipiero. Vienna, 1927.

————. *Perfidissimo volto a 5. Il terzo libro. . . .* Venice, 1592.

    See above.

————. *Vivrò fra i miei tormenti a 5. Il terzo libro. . . .* Venice, 1592.

    See above.

————. *Il quarto libro de madrigali a cinque voci.* Venice, 1603.

    Tutte le opere. Vol. 4. Edited by G. F. Malipiero. Vienna, 1927.

    Edited by E. Ferrari Barassi. Instituta et Monumenta; serie 1: Monumenti, vol. 5. Cremona, 1974.

————. *A un giro sol a 5. Il quarto libro. . . .* Venice, 1603.

    Complete editions as above.

————. *Ah dolente partita a 5. Il quarto libro. . . .* Venice, 1603.

    Complete editions as above.

————. *Anima mia perdona a 5. Il quarto libro. . . .* Venice, 1603.

    Complete editions as above.

————. *Non più guerra a 5. Il quarto libro. . . .* Venice, 1603.

    Complete editions as above.

Undici madrigali a 5 voci. Edited by J. P. Jacobsen. Copenhagen, 1968.

_____. *Ohimè se tanto amate a5. Il quarto libro.* . . . Venice, 1603.
Complete editions as above.

Historical Anthology of Music. Vol. 2. Edited by A. T. Davison and W. Apel. Cambridge, Mass., 1956.

Undici madrigali a 5 voci. Edited by J. P. Jacobsen. Copenhagen, 1968.

_____. *Piagne e sospira a5. Il quarto libro.* . . . Venice, 1603.
Complete editions as above.

_____. *Quel augellin che canta a5. Il quarto libro.* . . . Venice, 1603.
Complete editions as above.

_____. *Sfogava con le stelle a5. Il quarto libro.* . . . Venice, 1603.
Complete editions as above.

_____. *Il quinto libro de madrigali a cinque voci.* Venice, 1605.

Tutte le opere. Vol. 5. Edited by G. F. Malipiero. Vienna, 1927.
"Preface."
See above.

E. Vogel, *Bibliothek der gedruckten weltlichen Vocalmusik Italiens.* Hildesheim and New York, 1972.

_____. *Ahi come a un vago sol a5. Il quinto libro.* . . . Venice, 1605.
Complete edition as above.

_____. *Amor se giusto sei a5. Il quinto libro.* . . . Venice, 1605.
Complete edition as above.

_____. *Che dar più a5. Il quinto libro.* . . . Venice, 1605.
Complete edition as above.

_____. *Cruda Amarilli a5. Il quinto libro.* . . . Venice, 1605.
Complete edition as above.

R. G. Kiesewetter, *Schicksale und Beschaffenheit des weltlichen Gesanges.* Leipzig, 1841.

L'arte musicale in Italia. Vol. 4. Edited by L. Torchi. Milan, n.d.

_____. *E così a poco a poco a6. Il quinto libro.* . . . Venice, 1605.
Complete edition as above.

_____. *Ecco Silvio a5. Il quinto libro.* . . . Venice, 1605.
Complete edition as above.

_____. *Era l'anima mia a5. Il quinto libro.* . . . Venice, 1605.
Complete edition as above.

Edited by H. F. Redlich. London, 1967.

_____. *Ma se con la pietà a5. Il quinto libro.* . . . Venice, 1605.
Complete edition as above.

_____. *O Mirtillo a5. Il quinto libro.* . . . Venice, 1605.
Complete edition as above.

L'arte musicale in Italia. Vol. 4. Edited by L. Torchi. Milan, n.d.

_____. *Questi vaghi concenti a5. Il quinto libro.* . . . Venice, 1605.
Complete edition as above.

————. *T'amo mia vita a5. Il quinto libro.* . . . Venice, 1605.
Complete edition as above.

————. *Troppo ben può a5. Il quinto libro.* . . . Venice, 1605.
Complete edition as above.

————. *Orfeo.* Produced in Mantua, 1607. *L'Orfeo favola in musica rappresentata in Mantua l'anno 1607.* Venice, 1609.
Farnborough, 1972.
Publikation älterer praktischer und theoretischer Musikwerke. Vol. 10. Edited by R. Eitner. Leipzig, 1881.
Tutte le opere. Vol. 11. Edited by G. F. Malipiero. Vienna, 1930.
I classici musicali italiani. Vol. 9. Edited by G. Benvenuti. Milan, 1942.
Edited by D. Stevens. London, 1967.

————. *Scherzi musicali a tre voce.* Venice, 1607.
Tutte le opere. Vol. 10. Edited by G. F. Malipiero. Vienna, 1930.
"Dichiaratione" (glossed by G. C. Monteverdi).
Abridged version in E. Vogel, *Bibliothek der gedruckten weltlichen Vocalmusik Italiens.* Hildesheim and New York, 1972.
O. Strunk, ed. *Source Readings in Music History.* New York, 1950.

————. *I bei legami a3. Scherzi musicali.* . . . Venice, 1607.
Complete edition as above.

————. Intermedios for *L'Idropica*, Mantua, 1608. Collaborated with G. C. Monteverdi, S. Rossi, M. da Gagliano, G. G. Gastoldi, and P. Biat.

————. *Arianna.* Produced in Mantua, 1608.

————. "*Lamento d'Arianna*" a1. *Arianna,* 1608.
Tutte le opere. Vol. 11. Edited by G. F. Malipiero. Vienna, 1930.
Edited by R. Mingardo. Milan, 1970.

————. *Il ballo delle ingrate.* Produced in Mantua, 1608. *Madrigali guerrieri et amorosi con alcuni opusculi in genere rappresentativo libro ottavo.* Venice, 1638.
L'arte musicale in Italia. Vol. 6. Edited by L. Torchi. Milan, n.d.
Tutte le opere. Vol. 8. Edited by G. F. Malipiero. Vienna, 1929.
Edited by R. Leppard. London, 1967.

————. *Vespro della Beate Vergine.* Venice, 1610.
Tutte le opere. Vol. 14. Edited by G. F. Malipiero. Vienna, 1932.

————. *A Dio Florida bella a5. Il sesto libro de madrigali a cinque voci.* Venice, 1614.
Tutte le opere. Vol. 6. Edited by F. G. Malipiero. Vienna, 1927.

————. *Incenerite spoglie a5. Il sesto libro.* . . . Venice, 1614.
Complete edition as above.

————. *Lasciatemi morire a5. Il sesto libro.* . . . Venice, 1614.
Complete edition as above.

I classici della musica italiana. Vol. 19. Edited by C. Perinello. Milan, 1919.
————. *Misero Alceo a1. Il sesto libro.* . . . Venice, 1614.
Complete edition as above.
————. *Presso un fiume a7. Il sesto libro.* . . . Venice, 1614.
Complete edition as above.
————. *Qui rise o Tirsi a5. Il sesto libro.* . . . Venice, 1614.
Complete edition as above.
————. *Tirsi e Clori.* Produced in Mantua, 1616. *Concerto settimo libro de madrigali a1, 2, 3, 4 et sei voci con altri generi di canti.* Venice, 1619.
Tutte le opere. Vol. 7. Edited by G. F. Malipiero. Vienna, 1928.
Edited by K. Cooper. The Penn State Music Series, vol. 14. University Park and London, 1968.
————. *Le nozze di Peleo e Tetide.* (Mantua, 1617.)
————. *Andromeda.* (Mantua, 1618.)
————. *Concerto settimo libro de madrigali a1, 2, 3, 4 et sei voci con altri generi di canti.* Venice, 1619.
Tutte le opere. Vol. 7. Edited by G. F. Malipiero. Vienna, 1928.
————. *A quest'olmo a6. Concerto settimo libro.* . . . Venice, 1619.
Complete edition as above.
————. *Al lume delle stelle a4. Concerto settimo libro.* . . . Venice, 1619.
Complete edition as above.
————. *Chiome d'oro a2. Concerto settimo libro.* . . . Venice, 1619.
Complete edition as above.
————. *Con che soavità a1. Concerto settimo libro.* . . . Venice, 1619.
Complete edition as above.
————. *Dice la mia belissima Licori a2. Concerto settimo libro.* . . . Venice, 1619.
Complete edition as above.
————. *Ecco vicine o bella Tigre a2. Concerto settimo libro.* . . . Venice, 1619.
Complete edition as above.
————. *Interrotte speranze a2. Concerto settimo libro.* . . . Venice, 1619.
Complete edition as above.
La Flora. Vol. 3. Edited by K. Jeppesen. Copenhagen, 1949.
The Solo Song 1580–1730. Edited by C. MacClintock. New York, 1973.
————. *"Lettera amorosa" a1. Concerto settimo libro.* . . . Venice, 1619.
Complete edition as above.
R. Haas, *Die Musik des Barocks.* Potsdam, 1929. Handbuch der Musikwissenschaft.
————. *O come sei gentile a2. Concerto settimo libro.* . . . Venice, 1619.
Complete edition as above.

_____. *Ohimè dov'è il mio ben a2. Concerto settimo libro.* . . . Venice, 1619.

Complete edition as above.

_____. *Parlo miser o taccio a3. Concerto settimo libro.* . . . Venice, 1619.

Complete edition as above.

_____. *"Partenza amorosa" a1. Concerto settimo libro.* . . . Venice, 1619.

Complete edition as above.

Edited by R. Mingardo. Milan, 1970.

_____. *Tempro la cetra a1. Concerto settimo libro.* . . . Venice, 1619.

Complete edition as above.

Edited by R. Mingardo. Milan, 1970.

_____. *Combattimento di Tancredi e Clorinda.* Produced in Venice, 1624. *Madrigali guerrieri et amorosi con alcuni opusculi in genere rappresentativo libro ottavo.* Venice, 1638.

Tutte le opere. Vol. 8. Edited by G. F. Malipiero. Vienna, 1929.

L'arte musicale in Italia. Vol. 6. Edited by L. Torchi. Milan, n.d.

I classici della musica italiana. Vol. 19. Edited by C. Perinello. Milan, 1919.

Edited by D. Stevens. London, 1962.

Edited by L. Berio. London, 1968.

_____. *Licori finta pazza inamorata d'Aminta.* (Mantua, 1627.)

_____. *Mercurio e Marte.* Produced in Parma, 1627.

_____. *Proserpina rapita.* Produced in Venice, 1630.

_____. *Scherzi musicali coiè arie & madrigali in stil recitativo con una ciaccona a1 & 2 voci.* Venice, 1632.

Tutte le opere. Vol. 10. Edited by G. F. Malipiero. Vienna, 1930.

_____. *Armato il cor a2. Scherzi musicali.* . . . Venice, 1632.

Complete edition as above.

_____. *Ed è pur dunque vero a1. Scherzi musicali.* . . . Venice, 1632.

Complete edition as above.

Five Songs. Edited by G. Hunter and C. V. Palisca. Bryn Mawr, 1963.

_____. *Eri già tutta mia a1. Scherzi musicali.* . . . Venice, 1632.

See above.

_____. *Maledetto sia l'aspetto a1. Scherzi musicali.* . . . Venice, 1632.

Complete edition as above.

_____. *Quel sguardo sdegnosetto a1. Scherzi musicali.* . . . Venice, 1632.

Complete edition as above.

Five Songs. Edited by G. Hunter and C. V. Palisca. Bryn Mawr, 1963.

_____. *Zefiro torna a2. Scherzi musicali.* . . . Venice, 1632.

Complete edition as above.

The Norton Scores. Vol. 1. Edited by R. Kamien. New York, 1970.

————. *Madrigali guerrieri et amorosi con alcuni opusculi in genere rappresentativo libro ottavo.* Venice, 1638.

Tutte le opere. Vol. 8. Edited by G. F. Malipiero. Vienna, 1929.

"Preface."

Complete edition as above.

O. Strunk, ed., *Source Readings in Music History.* New York, 1950.

Abridged version in E. Vogel, *Bibliothek der gedruckten weltlichen Vocalmusik Italiens.* Hildesheim and New York, 1972.

————. *Altri canti d'Amor a6. Madrigali guerrieri et amorosi.* . . . Venice, 1638.

Complete edition as above.

————. *Ardo avvampo a2. Madrigali guerrieri et amorosi.* . . . Venice, 1638.

Complete edition as above.

————. *Chi vol haver felice a5. Madrigali guerrieri et amorosi.* . . . Venice, 1638.

Complete edition as above.

————. *Dolcissimo usignolo a5. Madrigali guerrieri et amorosi.* . . . Venice, 1638.

Complete edition as above.

————. *Hor che'l ciel a6. Madrigali guerrieri et amorosi.* . . . Venice, 1638.

Complete edition as above.

Edited by D. Stevens, University Park, 1965.

————. *Mentre vaga Angioletta a2. Madrigali guerrieri et amorosi.* . . . Venice, 1638.

Complete edition as above.

————. *Non havea Febo ancora a4. Madrigali guerrieri et amorosi.* . . . Venice, 1638.

Complete edition as above.

————. *Ogni amante è guerriero a3. Madrigali guerrieri et amorosi.* . . . Venice, 1638.

Complete edition as above.

————. *"Pianto della Madonna sopra il Lamento d'Arianna" a1. Selva morale e spirituale.* Venice, 1641.

Tutte le opere. Vol. 15. Edited by G. F. Malipiero. Vienna, 1941.

Morley, Thomas. *A Plaine and Easie Introduction to Practicall Musicke.* London, 1597.

Edited by R. A. Harman. New York, 1952.

Nucius, Johannes. *Musicae poeticae sive de compositionis cantus praeceptiones.* Neisse, 1613.

Ornitoparchus, Andreas (Vogelmeier). *Musicae activae micrologus.* Leipzig, 1517.

Andreas Ornitoparcus: His Micrologus or Introduction: Containing the Art of Singing. Translated by J. Dowland. (London, 1609.) New York, 1969.

Orso, Francesco. *Il primo libro de'madrigali con due madrigali cromatici nel fine.* Venice, 1567.

―――. *Il cantar novo a4. Il primo libro.* . . . Venice, 1567.

Excerpts in T. Kroyer, *Die Anfänge der Chromatik im italienischen Madrigal des XVI. Jahrhunderts.* Leipzig, 1902.

Othmayr, Caspar. *Symbola.* Nuremberg, 1547.

L'Ottuso Accademico. "Letter to G. M. Artusi." Ferrara, 1599.

G. M. Artusi, *L'Artusi overo delle imperfettioni della moderna musica.* Pt. II, Venice, 1603. (See separate entry.)

Pacioli, Luca. *Divina proportione.* Venice, 1509.

Edited by C. Winterberg. Quellenschriften für Kunstgeschichte; Neue Folge, vol. 2. Vienna, 1889.

Paleotti, Gabriele. *Discorso intorno alle imagini sacre e profane.* Bologna, 1582.

Trattati d'arte del cinquecento fra manierismo e controriforma. Vol. 2. Edited by P. Barocchi. Scrittori d'Italia, vol. 221. Bari, 1961.

Palla, Scipione del. *Che non può far a1. Intermedios for L'Alessandro,* Naples, 1558. *Due racolti insieme con altri bellissimi aggionti di diversi dove se cantano sonetti stanze & terze rime.* Naples, 1577.

N. Pirrotta, *Li due Orfei da Poliziano a Monteverdi.* Turin, 1969; 1975.

Palladio, Andrea. *Palazzo Chiericati.* Vicenza, 1550.

A. Hauser, *Mannerism.* London, 1965.

L. Murray, *The Late Renaissance and Mannerism.* New York, 1967.

―――. *Villa Rotunda.* Vicenza, 1550.

A. Hauser, *Mannerism.* London, 1965.

L. Murray, *The Late Renaissance and Mannerism.* New York, 1967.

―――. *Teatro Olimpico.* Vicenza, 1580–85.

F. Würtenberger, *Mannerism.* New York, 1963.

R. E. Wolf and R. Millen, *Renaissance and Mannerist Art.* New York, 1968.

Pallavicino, Benedetto. *Il quarto libro de madrigali a cinque voci.* Venice, 1588.

―――. *Cruda Amarilli a5. Il sesto libro de madrigali a cinque voci.* Venice, 1600.

Das Chorwerk. Vol. 80. Edited by D. Arnold. Wolfenbüttel, 1961.

Pallavicino, Sforza. *Considerazioni sopra l'arte dello stile e del dialogo.* Rome, 1646. Enlarged edition: *Trattato dello stile e del dialogo.* Rome, 1662.

Modena, 1819.

Opere edite ed inedite del Cardinal Sforza Pallavicino. Rome, 1845. *Trattatisti e narratori del seicento.* Edited by E. Raimondi. La letteratura Italiana; Storia e Testi, vol. 36. Milan and Naples, 1960 (six chapters only).

Pari, Claudio. *Il pastor fido secondo libro de'madrigali a cinque voci.* Palermo, 1611.

Parmigianino (Mazzola, Francesco). *Self-Portrait in a Convex Mirror.* Ca. 1524. Vienna, Kunsthistorisches Museum.

    G. R. Hocke, *Die Welt als Labyrinth.* Hamburg, 1957.

    F. Würtenberger, *Mannerism.* New York, 1963.

    J. Bousquet, *La peinture maniériste.* Neuchâtel, 1964.

    A. Hauser, *Mannerism.* London, 1965.

    R. E. Wolf and R. Millen, *Renaissance and Mannerist Art.* New York, 1968.

————. *Madonna of the Long Neck.* Ca. 1525. Florence, Uffizi.

    W. Sypher, *Four Stages of Renaissance Style.* Garden City, N.Y., 1955.

    G. R. Hocke, *Die Welt als Labyrinth.* Hamburg, 1957.

    G. Briganti, *Le maniérisme italien.* Leipzig, 1962.

    F. Würtenberger, *Mannerism.* New York, 1963.

    A. Hauser, *Mannerism.* London, 1965.

    L. Murray, *The Late Renaissance and Mannerism.* New York, 1967.

    J. Shearman, *Mannerism.* London, 1967.

    R. E. Wolf and R. Millen, *Renaissance and Mannerist Art.* New York, 1968.

    A. Smart, *The Renaissance and Mannerism in Italy.* London, 1971.

————. *Madonna of the Rose.* Ca. 1530. Dresden, Museum.

    G. R. Hocke, *Die Welt als Labyrinth.* Hamburg, 1957.

    G. Briganti, *Le maniérisme italien.* Leipzig, 1962.

    A. Hauser, *Mannerism.* London, 1965.

Partenio, Bernardino. *Della imitatione poetica.* Venice, 1560.

    Munich, 1969.

    Trattati di poetica e retorica del cinquecento. Vol. 2. Edited by B. Weinberg. Scrittori d'Italia, vol. 248. Bari, 1970.

Patrizi, Francesco. *Discorso della diversità de i furori poetici. Città felice.* Venice, 1553.

    Della poetica. Vol. 3. Edited by D. A. Barbagli. Florence, 1971.

————. *Parere in difesa dell'Ariosto.* T. Tasso, *Apologia.* Ferrara, 1585.

    T. Tasso, *Opere.* Vol. 10. Edited by G. Rosini. Pisa, 1824.

————. *Della poetica.* Ferrara, 1586.

    3 vols. Edited by D. A. Barbagli. Florence, 1969–71. (Includes *La deca istoriale, disputata, ammirabile, plastica, dogmatica universale, sacra,* and *semisacra.*)

————. *Nova de universis philosophia.* Ferrara, 1591.

Pecci, Tomaso. *Madrigali a cinque voci.* Siena, 1602.

    "Preface" by Mariano Tantucci.

Excerpt in E. Vogel, *Bibliothek der gedruckten weltlichen Vocal musik Italiens.* Hildesheim and New York, 1972.

Pellegrino, Camillo. *Il Caraffa overo dell'epica poesia.* Florence, 1584.

T. Tasso, *Opere.* Vol. 18. Edited by G. Rosini. Pisa, 1827.

Trattati di poetica e retorica. Vol. 3. Edited by B. Weinberg. Scrittori d'Italia, vol. 253. Bari, 1972.

_____. *Del concetto poetico.* Naples, 1598.

A. Borzelli, *Il Cavaliere Giovanbattista Marino 1569–1625.* Naples, 1898.

Peri, Jacopo. *Dunque fra torbid'onde a1.* Intermedios for *La Pellegrina.* Florence, 1589. C. Malvezzi, *Intermedii et concerti fatti per la commedia rappresentata in Firenze nelle nozze del Serenissimo Don Ferdinando Medici e Madama Christiana di Lorena.* Venice, 1589. *Musiques des intermèdes de "La Pellegrina."* Edited by D. P. Walker. Les fêtes de Florence, vol. 1. Paris, 1963.

_____. *Le musiche sopra l'Euridice.* Produced in Florence, 1600. Florence, 1601.

Bibliotheca Musica Bononiensis; sezione IV, vol. 2. Bologna, 1969.

Monuments of Music and Music Literature in Facsimile; First Series—Music, vol. 28. New York, 1973.

I classici della musica italiana. Vol. 24. Edited by C. Perinello. Milan, 1919.

L'arte musicale in Italia. Vol. 6. Edited by L. Torchi. Milan, n.d.

"Dedication."

Facsimile editions: Bologna, 1969 and New York, 1973.

A. Solerti, *Le origini del melodramma.* Turin, 1903.

O. Strunk, ed., *Source Readings in Music History.* New York, 1950.

E. Vogel, *Bibliothek der gedruckten weltlichen Vocalmusik Italiens.* Hildesheim and New York, 1972.

_____. *Tu dormi a1.* n.d.

R. Haas, *Die Musik des Barocks.* Potsdam, 1929. Handbuch der Musikwissenschaft.

The Solo Song 1580–1730. Edited by C. MacClintock. New York, 1973.

Peri, Jacopo, and Corsi, Jacopo. *Dafne.* Produced in Florence, 1594 and 1597.

M. Schneider, *Die Anfänge des Basso Continuo.* Leipzig, 1918.

F. Ghisi, *Alle fonti della monodia.* Milan, 1940.

W. V. Porter, "Peri's and Corsi's Dafne: Some Discoveries and Observations." *Journal of the American Musicological Society* 18 (1965).

Peruzzi, Baldassare. Palazzo Massimo alle Colonne. Ca. 1535. Rome.

W. Sypher, *Four Stages of Renaissance Style*. Garden City, N.Y., 1957.

M. Wackernagel, *Renaissance, Barock und Rokoko I*. West Berlin, 1963.

A. Hauser, *Mannerism*. London, 1965.

L. Murray, *The Late Renaissance and Mannerism*. New York, 1967.

R. E. Wolf and R. Millen, *Renaissance and Mannerist Art*. New York, 1968.

Petrarch (Petrarca, Francesco). *Rime in vita di Madonna Laura* and *Rime in morte di Madonna Laura*.

    I quattri poeti italiani con una scelta di poesie italiane. Edited by A. Buttura. Paris, 1836.

    Sonnets and Songs. Translated by A. M. Armi. New York, 1946.

    Le rime. Edited by L. Baldacci. Bologna, 1962.

    Le rime. Edited by N. Zingarelli. Bologna, 1964.

    Petrarch's Lyric Poems. Edited by R. M. Durling. Cambridge, Mass., 1976.

    Rime. Edited by G. Leopardi. Milan, 1976.

Piacenza, Domenico da. *De la arte di ballare et danzare*. Ca. 1450.

Piccioni, Giovanni (Pizzoni). *Il pastor fido musicale il sesto libro de madrigali a cinque voci*. Venice, 1602.

Piccolomini, Alessandro. *L'Alessandro*. Produced in Naples, 1558. Venice, 1550.

    Edited by F. Cerretta. Accademia Senese degli Intronati; Monografie di Storia e Letteratura Senese, vol. 6. Siena, 1966.

Pigna, Giovanni B. *I romanzi ne quali della poesia & della vita dell'Ariosto con nuovo modo si tratta*. Venice, 1554.

    Excerpt in *Scritti estetici*. Edited by G. Daelli. Milan, 1964.

Pino, Paolo. *Dialogo di pittura*. Venice, 1548.

    Edited by R. and A. Pallucchini. Venice, 1946.

    Edited by P. Nicodemi. Milan, 1954.

    Trattati d'arte del cinquecento fra manierismo e controriforma. Vol. 1. Edited by P. Barocchi. Scrittori d'Italia, vol. 219. Bari, 1960.

Plutarch ("Pseudo-Plutarch"). *Peri mousikes*.

    On Music. Translated by J. H. Bromby. Chiswick, 1822.

    Über die Musik. Edited by R. Westphal. Breslau, 1865.

    De la musique. Edited by F. Lasserre. Olten and Lausanne, 1954.

Poliziano, Angelo. *Favola d'Orfeo*. Produced in Mantua, 1480. Padua, 1749. Venice, 1776.

    Teatro antico, tragico, comico, pastorale, drammatico. Parnaso italiano ovvero raccolta de'poeti classici italiani, vol. 17. Venice, 1785.

    Orpheus und Eurydike. Edited by J. Schondorff. Munich, 1963.

    Il Poliziano, il Magnifico, lirici del quattrocento. Edited by M. Bontempelli. Florence, 1969.

Il teatro italiano I—2: Dalle origini al quattrocento. Edited by E. Faccioli. Turin, 1975.

Pomponazzi, Pietro. *De naturalium effectuum causis sive de incantationibus.* 1556. *Opera.* Basel, 1567.

Hildesheim, 1970.

Les causes des merveilles de la nature; ou, les enchantements. Translated by H. Busson. Paris, 1930.

Pontormo, Jacopo. *Visitation.* 1514–16. Carmignano, parochial church.

G. Briganti, *Le maniérisme italien.* Leipzig, 1962.

J. Bousquet, *La peinture maniériste.* Neuchâtel, 1964.

A. Hauser, *Mannerism.* London, 1965.

————. *Deposition.* 1525–28. Florence, S. Felicita, Capponi Chapel.

G. R. Hocke, *Die Welt als Labyrinth.* Hamburg, 1957.

G. Briganti, *Le maniérisme italien.* Leipzig, 1962.

D. P. Rowland, *Mannerism—Style and Mood.* New Haven, 1964.

L. Murray, *The Late Renaissance and Mannerism.* New York, 1967.

R. E. Wolf and R. Millen, *Renaissance and Mannerist Art.* New York, 1968.

A. Smart, *The Renaissance and Mannerism in Italy.* London, 1971.

Ponzio, Pietro (Pontio). *Ragionamento di musica.* Parma, 1588.

Edited by S. Clercx. Documenta Musicologica; Erste Reihe: Druckschriften-Faksimiles, vol. 16. Kassel, 1959.

————. *Dialogo ove si tratta della theorica e prattica di musica.* Parma, 1595.

Porta, Giovanni B. della. *Magia naturalis sive de miraculis rerum naturalium.* Naples, 1558; 1589.

Natural Magick. Edited by D. J. Price. New York, 1957 (reprint of London, 1658).

Praetorius, Michael. *Syntagma musicum.* Bks. II and III. Wolfenbüttel, 1619.

Documenta Musicologica; Erste Reihe: Druckschriften-Faksimiles, vols. 14 and 15. Kassel, 1958.

Prez, Josquin des. *Stabat mater a5.* 1474–79.

Trésor musicale: Musique religieuse. Vol. 3. Edited by R. van Maldeghem. Brussels, 1867; 1965.

A. W. Ambros, *Geschichte der Musik.* Vol. 5. Edited by O. Kade. Leipzig, 1882.

Werken van Josquin des Prés: Motetten. Vol. 2. Edited by A. Smijers. Amsterdam, 1942; 1971.

————. *Ave verum corpus a2–3.* Ca. 1486.

H. Glareanus, *Dodecachordon.* Basel, 1547. (See separate entry.)

Werken van Josquin des Prés: Motetten. Vol. 1. Edited by A. Smijers. Amsterdam, 1923; 1969.

————. *Factum est autem a4.* 1486–94.

Werken van Josquin des Prés: Motetten. Vol. 1. Edited by A. Smijers. Amsterdam, 1923; 1969.

————. *Ave Maria a4.* 1497.

H. Glareanus, *Dodecachordon.* Basel, 1547. (See separate entry.)

Trésor musicale: Musique religieuse. Vol. 2. Edited by R. van Maldeghem. Brussels, 1866; 1965.

Werken van Josquin des Prés: Motetten. Vol. 1. Edited by A. Smijers. Amsterdam, 1923; 1969.

Study Scores of Musical Styles. Edited by E. R. Lerner. New York, 1968.

————. *Absalon fili mi a4.* Ca. 1500. (1516–22) (1497).

Publikation älterer praktischer und theoretischer Musikwerke. Vol. 6. Edited by F. Commer, R. Schlecht, and R. Eitner. Berlin, 1877.

H. Osthoff, *Josquin Desprez.* Vol. 2. Tutzing, 1965.

An Anthology of Early Renaissance Music. Edited by N. Greenberg and P. Maynard. New York, 1975.

————. *Fortuna d'un gran tempo a3.* 1501. (1499).

O. Petrucci, *Harmonice musices Odhecaton A.* Venice, 1501. New York, 1973 (facsimile of 1504 edition). Edited by H. Hewitt. Cambridge, Mass., 1942.

E. E. Lowinsky, "The Goddess Fortuna in Music." *Musical Quarterly* 29 (1943).

————. *Dulces exuviae a4.* Ca. 1503. (1516–22).

Das Chorwerk. Vol. 54. Edited by H. Osthoff. Wolfenbüttel, 1955.

————. *Fama malum a4.* Ca. 1503. (1615–22) (1489). See above.

————. *Memor esto verbi tui a4.* 1501–1507.

Werken van Josquin des Prés: Motetten. Vol. 2. Edited by A. Smijers. Amsterdam, 1936.

————. *De profundis a4.* 1515.

H. Glareanus, *Dodecachordon.* Basel, 1547. (See separate entry.)

Publikation älterer praktischer und theoretischer Musikwerke. Vol. 6. Edited by F. Commer, R. Schlecht, and R. Eitner. Berlin, 1877.

Werken van Josquin des Prés: Motetten. Vol. 3. Edited by A. Smijers. Amsterdam, 1954; 1969.

Das Chorwerk. Vol. 57. Edited by H. Osthoff. Wolfenbüttel, 1956.

Werken van Josquin des Prés: Motetten. Vol. 5. Edited by M. Antonowycz. Amsterdam, 1963.

————. "Agnus Dei II" from *Missa Mater patris a4–6.*

H. Glareanus, *Dodecachordon.* Basel, 1547. (See separate entry.)

Werken van Josquin des Prés: Missen. Vol. 3. Edited by A. Smijers. Amsterdam, 1950.

Priuli, Giovanni. *Il terzo libro de madrigali a cinque voci di due maniere l'una per voci sole l'altre per voci & istromenti con partitura.* Venice, 1612.

Ptolemy (Ptolemaios, Klaudios). *Armonikon.*
> *Die Harmonielehre des Klaudios Ptolemaios.* Edited by I. Düring. *Göteborgs Högskolas Arsskrift* 36 (1930).
> *Ptolemaios und Porphyrios über die Musik.* Translated by I. Düring. *Göteborgs Högskolas Arsskrift* 40 (1932).

Quagliati, Paolo. *Il carro di fedeltà d'amore.* Produced in Rome, 1608. Rome, 1611.
> *La sfera armoniosa & Il Carro di fedeltà d'amore.* Edited by V. Gotwals and P. Keppler. Smith College Music Archives, vol. 13. Northampton, 1957.

————. *Il primo libro de'madrigali a quattro voci concertati per cantar con l'instrumento con un libro separato dove stà il basso seguito per sonarli.* Venice, 1608.
> "Preface."
>> E. Vogel, *Bibliothek der gedruckten weltlichen Vocalmusik Italiens.* Hildesheim and New York, 1972.

————. *Affetti amorosi spirituali.* Rome, 1617.

————. *La sfera armoniosa.* Rome, 1623.
> Edited by V. Gotwals and P. Keppler. Smith College Music Archives, vol. 13. Northampton, 1957.

————. *Come cantar poss'io a2. La sfera. . . .* Rome, 1623.
> See above.

————. *Felice chi vi mira a1. La sfera. . . .* Rome, 1623.
> See above.

Quickelberg, Samuel. "Commentary on O. di Lasso's *Psalmi Davidis poenitentiales.*" Munich, 1560.
> M. van Crevel, *Adrianus Petit Coclico.* The Hague, 1940.
> G. Reese, *Music in the Renaissance.* New York, 1954.
> W. Boetticher, *Orlando di Lasso und seine Zeit.* Kassel, 1958.
> C. V. Palisca, "A Clarification of 'Musica Reservata' in Jean Taisnier's 'Astrologiae' 1559." *Acta Musicologica* 31 (1959).

Quintilian, Marcus F. *Institutio oratoria.*
> 4 vols. Translated by H. E. Butler. The Loeb Classical Library. Cambridge, Mass., 1966–69.

Ramos de Pareja, Bartoloméo. *Musica practica.* Bologna, 1482.
> Edited by J. Wolf. Publikationen der Internationalen Musikgesellschaft; Beiheft, vol. 2. Leipzig, 1901.

Raphael (Sanzio, Raffaello). *School of Athens.* 1509–12. Rome, Vatican, Stanze della Signature.
> W. Sypher, *Four Stages of Renaissance Style.* Garden City, N.Y., 1955.
> A. Smart, *The Renaissance and Mannerism in Italy.* London, 1971.

————. *Fire in the Borgo.* 1512. Rome, Vatican.
> A. Hauser, *Mannerism.* London, 1965.

————. *Transfiguration.* After 1517. Rome, Vatican.

A. Hauser, *Mannerism*. London, 1965.
A. Smart, *The Renaissance and Mannerism in Italy*. London, 1971.
———. "Letter to Pope Leo X." 1519.
V. Golzio, ed., *Raffaello nei documenti*. Vatican City, 1936; 1971.
Rasi, Francesco. *Ahi fuggitivo ben a1. Vaghezze di musica per una voce sola*. Venice, 1608.
  The Solo Song 1580–1730. Edited by C. MacClintock. New York, 1973.
———. *Indarno Febo a1. Vaghezze di musica. . . .* Venice, 1608.
  See above.
———. *Dialoghi rappresentativi composti insieme con le parole*. Venice, 1620.
Ripa, Cesare. *Iconologia*. Rome, 1593. Rome, 1603.
  Hildesheim, 1970 (facsimile of 1603 edition).
  Baroque and Rococo Pictorial Imagery. Edited by E. A. Maser. New York, 1971 (based on Augsburg, ca. 1758–60 edition).
Robortello, Francesco. *In librum Aristotelis de arte poetica explicationes*. Florence, 1548.
Roggius, Nicolaus. *Musicae practicae sive artis canendi elementa*. Nuremberg, 1566.
Romano, Giulio. *Sala dei Giganti*. 1532–34. Mantua, Palazzo del Tè.
  F. Würtenberger, *Mannerism*. New York, 1963.
  J. Bousquet, *La peinture maniériste*. Neuchâtel, 1964.
  A. Hauser, *Mannerism*. London, 1965.
  L. Murray, *The Late Renaissance and Mannerism*. New York, 1967.
Rore, Cipriano de. *I madrigali a cinque voci*. Venice, 1542.
  Opera Omnia. Vol. 2. Edited by B. Meier. Corpus Mensurabilis Musicae, vol. 14. American Institute of Musicology, 1963.
———. *Hor che'l ciel e la terra a5. I madrigali. . . .* Venice, 1542.
  Complete edition as above.
———. *Per mezz'i boschi a5. I madrigali. . . .* Venice, 1542.
  Complete edition as above.
  A. Einstein, *The Italian Madrigal*. Vol. 3. Princeton, 1949; 1971.
———. *Il secondo libro de madrigali a cinque voci*. Venice, 1544.
  Opera Omnia. Vol. 2. Edited by B. Meier. Corpus Mensurabilis Musicae, vol. 14. American Institute of Musicology, 1963.
———. *Anchor che col partire a4*. P. Cambio, *Primo libro di madrigali a quatro voci con alcuni di Cipriano Rore*. Venice, 1547.
  F. de Monte, *Opera Omnia*. Vol. 8. Edited by C. van den Borren and J. van Nuffel. Bruges, 1829; 1965.
  R. G. Kiesewetter, *Schicksale und Beschaffenheit des weltlichen Gesanges*. Leipzig, 1841.
  Edited by G. P. Smith. Smith College Music Archives, vol. 6. Northampton, 1943.

A. Einstein, *The Italian Madrigal.* Vol. 3. Princeton, 1949; 1971.

Opera Omnia. Vol. 4. Edited by B. Meier. Corpus Mensurabilis Musicae, vol. 14. American Institute of Musicology, 1969.

———. *La giustizia immortale a4. La fama a quattro voce composti novamente da diversi eccellentissimi autori.* Venice, 1548. *Tutti i madrigali di Cipriano di Rore a quattro voci spartiti e accommodati per sonar d'ogni sorte d'istrumento perfetto & per qualunque studioso de contrapunti.* Venice, 1577.
Complete editions as above.

———. *L'inconstantia che seco han a4. La fama. . . .* Venice, 1548. *Tutti i madrigali. . . .* Venice, 1577.
Complete editions as above.

———. *Le Vergine canzone a5. Musica sopra le stanze del Petrarcha in laude della Madonna et altri madrigali a cinque voci libro terzo.* Venice, 1548. *Il terzo libro de madrigali dove si contengono Le Vergine & altri madrigali novamente con ogni diligenza ristampato a cinque voci.* Venice, 1552.

Opera Omnia. Vol. 3. Edited by B. Meier. Corpus Mensurabilis Musicae, vol. 14. American Institute of Musicology, 1961.

———. *Il primo libro de madrigali a quatro voci.* Venice, 1550.
Edited by G. P. Smith. Smith College Music Archives, vol. 6. Northampton, 1943.

Opera Omnia. Vol. 4. Edited by B. Meier. Corpus Mensurabilis Musicae, vol. 14. American Institute of Musicology, 1969.

———. *Calami sonum ferentes a4.* O. di Lasso, *Il primo libro dove si contengono madrigali vilanesche canzoni francesi e motetti a quattro voci.* Antwerp, 1555. O. di Lasso, *Le quatorsieme livre a quatre parties.* Antwerp, 1555.

C. Burney, *A General History of Music.* Bk. 3. London, 1789. New York, 1957.

Collectio operum musicorum Batavorum saeculi XVI. Vol. 12. Edited by F. Commer. Berlin, 1858.

Opera Omnia. Vol. 6. Edited by B. Meier. Corpus Mensurabilis Musicae, vol. 14. American Institute of Musicology, 1975.

———. *Il secondo libro de madrigali a quatro voci.* Venice, 1557.
Edited by G. P. Smith. Smith College Music Archives, vol. 6. Northampton, 1943.

Opera Omnia. Vol. 4. Edited by B. Meier. Corpus Mensurabilis Musicae, vol. 14. American Institute of Musicology, 1969.

———. *Beato mi direi a4. Il secondo libro. . . .* Venice, 1557.
Complete editions as above.

———. *Mia benigna fortuna / Crudel acerba inesorabil morte a4. Il secondo libro. . . .* Venice, 1557.
Complete editions as above.

A. Einstein, *The Italian Madrigal*. Vol. 3. Princeton, 1949; 1971 (pt. two only).

A. Harman and A. Milner, *Late Renaissance and Baroque Music*. Pt. two. New York, 1969 (pt. two only).

E. E. Lowinsky, "The Problem of Mannerism in Music." *Studi Musicali* 3 (1974). (Pt. one only).

————. *O Sonno a4. Il secondo libro.* . . . Venice, 1557.

Complete editions as above.

A. Einstein, *The Italian Madrigal*. Vol. 3. Princeton, 1949; 1971.

C. V. Palisca, *Baroque Music*. Englewood Cliffs, N.J., 1968.

————. *Schiet'arbuscel a4. Il secondo libro.* . . . Venice, 1557.

Complete editions as above.

————. *Un'altra volta la Germania strida a4. Il secondo libro.* . . . Venice, 1557.

Complete editions as above.

————. *Da le belle contrade a5. Il quinto libro di madrigali a cinque voci.* Venice, 1566.

Das Chorwerk. Vol. 5. Edited by W. Wiora. Wolfenbüttel, 1930.

Historical Anthology of Music. Vol. 1. Edited by A. T. Davison and W. Apel. Cambridge, Mass., 1959.

Opera Omnia. Vol. 5. Edited by B. Meier. Corpus Mensurabilis Musicae, vol. 14. American Institute of Musicology, 1971.

————. *Tutti i madrigali di Cipriano de Rore a quattro voci spartiti et accommodati per sonar d'ogni sorte d'istrumento perfetto & per qualunque studioso di contrapunti.* Venice, 1577.

Rossetti, Biagio. *Libellus de rudimentis musices.* Verona, 1529.

Monuments of Music and Music Literature in Facsimile: Second Series—Music Literature, vol. 136. New York, 1968.

Rossetti, Stefano. *Mentre ch'el cor a4. Il primo libro de madrigali a quattro voci.* Venice, 1560.

Il primo libro de madrigali a quattro voci. Edited by A. B. Skei. Recent Researches in the Music of the Renaissance, vol. 26. Madison, Wisc., 1977.

Excerpt in E. E. Lowinsky, "Matthaeus Greiter's *Fortuna*: An Experiment in Chromaticism and in Musical Iconography." *Musical Quarterly* 42 (1956).

Excerpt in E. E. Lowinsky, *Tonality and Atonality in Sixteenth-Century Music.* Berkeley, 1961.

Rossi, Michelangelo. *Erminia sul Giordano.* Produced in Rome, 1633. *Erminia sul Giordano dramma musicale rappresentato nel palazzo dell'illustrissimo et eccellentissimo Signore D. Taddeo Barberino.* Rome, 1637.

Bibliotheca Musica Bononiensis; sezione IV, vol. 12. Bologna, 1971.

Rossi, Salomone. *Il secondo libro de madrigali a cinque voci con il basso continuo per sonare in concerto.* Venice, 1602.

Rosso Fiorentino (Rosso, Giovanni B.). *Deposition*. 1521. Volterra, Pinacoteca.

    G. Briganti, *Le maniérisme italien*. Leipzig, 1962.

    D. P. Rowland, *Mannerism—Style and Mood*. New Haven, 1964.

    A. Hauser, *Mannerism*. London, 1965.

    L. Murray, *The Late Renaissance and Mannerism*. New York, 1967.

    A. Smart, *The Renaissance and Mannerism in Italy*. London, 1971.

————. *Moses Defending the Daughters of Jethro*. 1521. Florence, Uffizi.

    G. R. Hocke, *Die Welt als Labyrinth*. Hamburg, 1957.

    M. Wackernagel, *Renaissance, Barock, Rokoko I*. West Berlin, 1963.

    J. Bousquet, *La peinture maniériste*. Neuchâtel, 1964.

    A. Hauser, *Mannerism*. London, 1965.

    L. Murray, *The Late Renaissance and Mannerism*. New York, 1967.

    R. E. Wolf and R. Millen, *Renaissance and Mannerist Art*. New York, 1968.

————. *Dead Christ with Angels*. Ca. 1526. Boston, Museum of Fine Arts.

    A. Hauser, *Mannerism*. London, 1965.

    J. Shearman, *Mannerism*. London, 1967.

    A. Smart, *The Renaissance and Mannerism in Italy*. London, 1971.

Ruffo, Vincenzo. *Opera nuova di musica intitolata armonia celeste nella qualle si contengono 25 madrigali pieni d'ogni dolcezza et soavità musicale composti con dotta arte et reservato ordine libro quarto*. Venice, 1556.

————. *Missae quatuor concinate ad ritum concilii Mediolani*. Milan, 1570.

    "Preface."

    L. Lockwood, "Vincenzo Ruffo and Musical Reform after the Council of Trent." *Musical Quarterly* 43 (1957).

————. *Messe a cinque voci secondo la forma del Concilio Tridentino*. Brescia, 1580. (Reprint of an earlier publication whose date is unknown.)

    Excerpts in *L'arte musicale in Italia*. Vol. 1. Edited by L. Torchi. Milan, 1897.

    Missa Sine nomina a5. Edited by R. J. Snow. Musica Liturgica, vol. I/1. Cincinnati, 1958.

Salinas, Francisco de. *De musica libri septem*. Salamanca, 1577.

    Edited by M. S. Kastner. Documenta Musicologica; Erste Reihe: Druckschriften-Faksimiles, vol. 13. Kassel, 1958.

Salviati, Francesco. *Bathsheba Going to David*. 1552–54. Rome, Palazzo Sacchetti.

    G. Briganti, *Le maniérisme italien*. Leipzig, 1962.

————. *Charity*. 1554–58. Florence, Uffizi.

G. Briganti, *Le maniérisme italien*. Leipzig, 1962.

A. Hauser, *Mannerism*. London, 1965.

L. Murray, *The Late Renaissance and Mannerism*. New York, 1967.

Salviati, Lionardo. *Difesa dell'Orlando furioso dell'Ariosto contra'l Dialogo dell'epica poesia di Cammillo Pellegrino*. Florence, 1584.

Sannazaro, Jacopo. "*O fere stelle*," sixth stanza of *Spent'era nel mio cor*. *Rime*. Rome, 1530. *Le rime*. Venice, 1531. *Le rime*. Venice, 1536.
    Arcadia. Venice, 1638.
    L'Arcadia insieme colle rime. Naples, 1720.
    Opere volgari. Edited by A. Mauro. Bari, 1961.

Saracini, Claudio (Saraceni). *Christo smarrito a1*. (*Lamento della Madonna*.) *Le seconde musiche per cantar & sonar nel chitarrone arpicordo & altri stromenti*. Venice, 1620.
    Edited by G. Chigi-Saracini. Siena, 1930.
    Edited by V. Frazzi. Florence, 1937.

————. *Da te parto cor mio a1*. *Le seconde musiche*. . . . Venice, 1620.
    Edited by G. Chigi-Saracini. Siena, 1930.
    The Solo Song 1580–1730. Edited by C. MacClintock. New York, 1973.

————. *Lasso perchè mi fuggi a1*. *Le seconde musiche*. . . . Venice, 1620.
    Edited by G. Chigi-Saracini. Siena, 1930.
    R. Haas, *Die Musik des Barocks*. Potsdam, 1929. Handbuch der Musikwissenschaft.

————. *Stabat mater dolorosa a1*. (*Pianto della B.V.M.*) *Il terze musiche per cantar & sonar nel chitarrone arpicordo & altro stromenti e nel fine il Pianto della Beata V. M. in stile recitativo*. Venice, 1620.

Scacchi, Marco. *Breve discorso sopra la musica moderna*. Warsaw, 1649.
    C. V. Palisca, "Marco Scacchi's Defense of Modern Music." *Words and Music: A Scholar's View*. Cambridge, Mass., 1972.

Schütz, Heinrich. *Dunque addio care selve a5*. *Il primo libro de madrigali*. Venice, 1611.
    Sämtliche Werke. Vol. 9. Edited by P. Spitta. Leipzig, 1890.
    Neue Ausgabe sämtlicher Werke. Vol. 22. Edited by H. J. Moser. Kassel, 1962.

————. *Fuggi o mio core a5*. *Il primo libro*. . . . Venice, 1611.
    Complete editions as above.

————. *Selve beate a5*. *Il primo libro*. . . . Venice, 1611.
    Complete editions as above.

————. *Geistliche Chormusik*. Dresden, 1648.
    "Preface."
    Sämtliche Werke. Vol. 8. Edited by P. Spitta, A. Schering, and H. Spitta. Leipzig, 1889.
    Neue Ausgabe sämtlicher Werke. Vol. 5. Edited by H. J. Moser. Kassel, 1955.

Scialla, Alessandro. *Primo libro de'madrigali a cinque voci.* Naples, 1610.
    "Dedication."
    Excerpt in E. Vogel, *Bibliothek der gedruckten weltlichen Vocalmusik Italiens.* Hildesheim and New York, 1972.
Sdegnosi ardori musica di diversi auttori sopra un istesso soggetto di parole a cinque voci. Monaco, 1585.
Sebastiani, Claudius. *Bellum musicali inter plani et mensuralis cantus reges.* Strasbourg, 1563.
Segni, Agnolo. *Ragionamento sopra le cose pertinenti alla poetica.* Lectures given to the Accademia Fiorentina, 1573. Florence, 1581.
Seld, Dr. "Letter." Brussels, 28 April 1555.
    A. Sandberger, *Beiträge zur Geschichte der bayerische Hofkapelle unter Orlando di Lasso.* Vol. 3. Leipzig, 1895.
————. "Letter." Brussels, 1 July 1555.
    A. Sandberger, *Beiträge zur Geschichte der bayerische Hofkapelle unter Orlando di Lasso.* Vol. 1. Leipzig, 1894.
————. "Letter." Brussels, 22 September 1555.
    See above.
    M. van Crevel, *Adrianus Petit Coclico.* The Hague, 1940.
————. Appellation of O. di Lasso's *Tityre tu patulae* as *musica reservata.* Court document. Munich, 1559.
    H. W. Kaufmann, *Nicola Vicentino.* American Institute of Musicology, 1966.
Signorucci, Pompeo. *Concerti ecclesiastici a otto voci con il basso continuo per sonar nell'organo libro primo.* Venice, 1602.
Sigonio, Gandolfo. *Discorso intorno a'madrigali et a'libri dell'Antica musica ridutta alla moderna prattica da D. Nicola Vicentino.*
    E. Bottrigari, *Il Melone secondo.* Ferrara, 1602. (See separate entry.)
Sodoma, Il (Bazzi, Giovanni A.). *St. Sebastian.* 1525. Florence, Palazzo Pitti.
    R. E. Wolf and R. Millen, *Renaissance and Mannerist Art.* New York, 1968.
Spataro, Giovanni. *Honesta defensio in Nicolai Burtii parmensis opusculum.* Bologna, 1491.
    Opera Omnia. Vol. 1. Edited by G. Vecchi. Bologna, 1963.
————. *Dilucide et probatissime demonstratione contra certe frivole et vane excusatione da Franchino Gafurio (maestro de li errori).* Bologna, 1521.
    Edited by J. Wolf. Veröffentlichungen der Musik-Bibliothek Paul Hirsch. Berlin, 1925.
————. "Letter to P. Aaron." Bologna, 23 May 1524.
    S. S. Levitan, "Adrian Willaert's Famous Duo, 'Quidnam ebrietas.'" *Tijdschrift der Vereenigung voor Nederlandsche Muziekgeschiedenis* 25 (1938).

_____. "Letter to P. Aaron." 4 January 1529.

_____. "Letter to G. del Lago." 5 April 1529.

_____. "Letter to P. Aaron." 30 October 1533.

Speroni, Sperone. *Discorsi sopra Virgilio*. Ca. 1562.

    Opere. Vol. 4. Venice, 1740.

Stevin, Simon. *Music*.

    The Principal Works of Simon Stevin. Vol. 5. Edited by A. D. Fokker. Amsterdam, 1966.

Stomius, Johannes (Mulinus). *Prima ad musicen instructio*. Augsburg, 1537.

Stoquerus, Gaspar (Stocker). *De musica verbali*. Ca. 1570.

Striggio, Alessandro. *A me che fatta a8*. Intermedios for *La Cofanaria*, Florence, 1565. *Musica de diversi auttori illustri per cantare et sonar in concerti a sette otto nove dieci undeci & duodeci voci libro primo*. Venice, 1584.

    W. Osthoff, *Theatergesang und darstellende Musik in der italienischen Renaissance*. Vol. 2. Tutzing, 1969.

_____. *Fuggi speme mia a1*. Intermedios for *La Cofanaria*. Florence, 1565. V. Galilei, *Fronimo*. Venice, 1568. (See separate entry.)

    H. M. Brown, "Psyche's Lament: Some Music for the Medici Wedding in 1565." *Words and Music: The Scholar's View*. Cambridge, Mass., 1972.

_____. *Il cicalamento delle donne al bucato et la caccia*. Venice, 1567.

    A. Solerti and D. Alaleona, "Primi saggi del melodramma giocoso." *Rivista Musicale Italiana* 13 (1906).

    Capolavori polifonici del secolo XVI. Vol. 4. Edited by B. Somma. Rome, 1947.

_____. *Il gioco di primiera a5. Il cicalamento delle donne al bucato et la caccia con il gioco di primiera a cinque voci*. Venice, 1569.

    A. Einstein, *The Italian Madrigal*, Vol. 3. Princeton, 1949; 1971.

_____. *Non rumor di tamburi a6. Il secondo libro de madrigali a sei voci*. Venice, 1570.

Strozzi, Piero. *Fuor dell'humido nido a1*. Mascherata, Florence, 1579.

    F. Ghisi, *Feste musicali della Firenze medicea (1480–1589)*. Florence, 1939.

    F. Ghisi, *Alle fonti della monodia*, Milan, 1940.

    N. Pirrotta, *Li due Orfei da Poliziano a Monteverdi*. Turin, 1969; 1975.

Taglia, Pietro. *Il mal mi preme a4. Il primo libro de madrigali a quattro voci*. Milan, 1555.

    E. E. Lowinsky. "The Problem of Mannerism in Music." *Studi Musicali* 3 (1974).

Taisnier, Jean. *Astrologiae iudiciariae ysagoge*. Cologna, 1559.

    "Dedication."

C. V. Palisca, "A Clarification of 'Musica Reservata' in Jean Taisnier's 'Astrologiae' 1559." *Acta Musicologica* 31 (1959).
———. *Opus mathematicum.* Cologne, 1562.
"Dedication."
See above.
Tansillo, Luigi. *Lagrime di San Pietro. Nuova scelta di rime di diversi begli ingegni fra le quali sono molte del Tansillo.* Genoa, 1573.
Venice, 1592.
Edited by L. Marinella and T. Costo. Venice, 1738.
Tantucci, Mariano. See Pecci, Tomaso.
Tartaglia, Niccolò. *Euclide diligemente rassettato.* Venice, 1569.
Tasso, Torquato. *Considerazioni sopra tre canzoni di M. Gio. Battista Pigna intitolati Le tre sorelle.* 1568.
   Opere. Vol. 11. Edited by G. Rosini. Pisa, 1823.
———. *Aminta.* Produced in Ferrara, 1573. Cremona, 1580. Venice, 1581.
   Opere. Vol. 2. Edited by G. Rosini. Pisa, 1821.
   Edited by E. Grillo. London, 1924.
   Poesie. Edited by F. Flora. Milan, 1952.
   Opere. Vol. 2. Edited by B. T. Sozzi. Turin, 1956.
   Padua, 1957.
   Opere. Vol. 1. Edited by B. Maier. Milan, 1963.
   Edited by L. Fassò. Florence, 1967.
———. *Gerusalemme liberata.* Ferrara, 1581. Mantua, 1584.
   Opere. Vols. 14–16. Edited by G. Rosini. Pisa, 1830.
   I quattro poeti italiani con una scelta di poesie italiane. Edited by A. Buttura. Paris, 1836.
   Poesie. Edited by F. Flora. Milan, 1952.
   Opere. Vol. 1. Edited by B. T. Sozzi. Turin, 1955.
   Opere. Vol. 3. Edited by B. Maier. Milan, 1963.
   Edited by F. Chiapelli. Turin, 1968.
   Edited by L. Caretti. Turin, 1970.
   Opere. Vol. 1. Edited by E. Mazzali. Naples, 1970.
———. *Discorso sopra il Parere. Apologia.* Ferrara, 1585.
   Opere. Vol. 10. Edited by G. Rosini. Pisa, 1824.
———. *La Cavaletta overo della poesia toscana. Dialoghi e discorsi.* Venice, 1587.
   Opere. Vol. 7. Edited by G. Rosini. Pisa, 1822.
   Opere. Vol. 5. Edited by B. Maier. Milan, 1963.
———. *Ardi e gela a tua voglia.* "Riposta" to G. B. Guarini's *Ardo si ma non t'amo.* (See separate entry.) *Rime.* Ferrara, 1589. *Parte prima delle rime.* Mantua, 1591. G. B. Guarini, *Il pastor fido aggiontavi di novo le rime.* Venice, 1621. G. B. Guarini, *Rime.* Venice, 1621.
———. *Ecco mormorar l'onde. Rime.* Ferrara, 1589. *Parte prima delle rime.* Mantua, 1591.

Opere. Vol. 4. Edited by G. Rosini. Pisa, 1822.

Opere. Vol. 2. Edited by B. T. Sozzi. Turin, 1956.

The Penguin Book of Italian Verse. Edited by G. R. Kay. Harmondsworth, 1958.

Opere. Vol. 1. Edited by B. Maier. Milan, 1963.

Opere. Vol. 2. Edited by E. Mazzali. Naples, 1970.

Italian Poets of the Renaissance. Edited by J. Tusiani. Long Island City, N.Y., 1973.

————. *Sovra le verdi chiome. Rime*. Ferrara, 1589. *Parte prima delle rime*. Mantua, 1591.

Opere. Vol. 4. Edited by G. Rosini. Pisa, 1822.

Opere. Vol. 2. Edited by B. T. Sozzi. Turin, 1956.

The Penguin Book of Italian Verse. Edited by G. R. Kay. Harmondsworth, 1958.

Opere. Vol. 1. Edited by B. Maier. Milan, 1963.

Opere. Vol. 2. Edited by E. Mazzali. Naples, 1970.

————. *Gerusalemme conquistata*. Rome, 1593.

Opere. Vols. 18–19. Edited by G. Rosini. Pisa, 1822.

Opere. Vol. 1. Edited by B. T. Sozzi. Turin, 1955.

————. *Discorsi del poema eroico*. Naples, 1594. Revised version of *Discorsi dell'arte poetica*. Venice, 1587.

Opere. Vol. 12. Edited by G. Rosini. Pisa, 1823.

Opere. Vol. 1. Edited by B. T. Sozzi. Turin, 1955.

Prose. Edited by E. Mazzali. Naples, 1959.

Opere. Vol. 5. Edited by B. Maier. Milan, 1963.

Discorsi dell'arte poetica e del poema eroico. Edited by L. Poma. Scrittori d'Italia, vol. 228. Bari, 1964.

Discourses on the Heroic Poem. Translated by M. Cavalchini and I. Samuel. Oxford, 1970.

Opere. Vol. 1. Edited by E. Mazzali. Naples, 1970.

————. *Del giuditio sovra la Gerusalemme*. Ca. 1595.

Opere. Vol. 12. Edited by G. Rosini. Pisa, 1823.

Tesauro, Emanuele. *Il cannocchiale aristotelico*. Turin, 1654. Venice, 1663.

Thelamonius, Joachim. *Tractatus de compositione sive musica poetica*. Magdeburg, 1610.

Tibaldi, Pellegrino. *Dancing Spirits*. Ca. 1555. Bologna, Palazzo Poggi. G. Briganti, *Le maniérisme italien*. Leipzig, 1962.

Tigrini, Orazio. *Il compendio della musica*. Venice, 1588. Monuments of Music and Music Literature in Facsimile; Second Series—Music Literature, vol. 25. New York, 1966.

Tinctoris, Johannes. *De natura et proprietate tonorum*. Ca. 1470. *Scriptorum de musica medii aevi*. Vol. 4. Edited by E. de Coussemaker. Paris, 1876.

Translated by A. Seay. Colorado College Music Press; Translations, vol. 2. Colorado Springs, 1967.

————. *Proportionale musices*. Ca. 1474.

Scriptorum de musica medii aevi. Vol. 4. Edited by E. de Coussemaker. Paris, 1876.

A. Seay, "The *Proportionale musices* of Johannes Tinctoris." *Journal of Music Theory* 1 (1957).

"Dedication."

O. Strunk, *Source Readings in Music History*. New York, 1950.

————. *Liber de arte contrapuncti*. Naples, 1477.

Scriptorum de musica medii aevi. Vol. 4. Edited by E. de Coussemaker. Paris, 1876.

The Art of Counterpoint. Translated by A. Seay. American Institute of Musicology, 1961.

"Dedication."

O. Strunk, *Source Readings in Music History*. New York, 1950.

Tintoretto, Jacopo. *Removal of the Body of St. Mark*. Ca. 1562. Venice, Accademia de belle arti.

W. Sypher, *Four Stages of Renaissance Style*. Garden City, N.Y., 1955.

F. Würtenberger, *Mannerism*. New York, 1963.

A. Hauser, *Mannerism*. London, 1965.

Trabaci, Giovanni M. *Ricercate canzone francese capricci a quattro voci*. Naples, 1603.

"Preface."

Excerpt in A. Einstein, *The Italian Madrigal*. Princeton, 1949; 1971.

Trinumo. Produced in Mantua, 1499.

Tromboncino, Bartolomeo. *Queste lacrime a4. Frottole libro undecimo*. Fossombrone, 1514.

W. Osthoff, *Theatergesang und darstellende Musik in der italienischen Renaissance*. Vol. 2. Tutzing, 1969.

Tudino, Cesare. *Li madrigali a note bianche et negre cromatiche et napolitane a quatro*. Venice, 1554.

————. *Altro che lagrimar a4. Li madrigali. . . .* Venice, 1554.

T. Kroyer, *Die Anfänge der Chromatik im italienischen Madrigal des XVI. Jahrhunderts*. Leipzig, 1902.

————. *Chi desia di veder a4. Li madrigali. . . .* Venice, 1554.

Excerpt in T. Kroyer, *Die Anfänge der Chromatik im italienischen Madrigal des XVI. Jahrhunderts*. Leipzig, 1902.

Vanneo, Stephano. *Recanetum de musica aurea*. Rome, 1533.

Edited by S. Clercx. Documenta Musicologica; Erste Reihe: Druckschriften-Faksimiles, vol. 28. Kassel, 1959.

Varchi, Benedetto. *Lezzione*. (Pt. I, "Della maggioranza delle arti"; Pt. II,

"Qual sia più nobile o la scultura o la pittura"; Pt. III, "In che siano simili et in che differenti i poeti et i pittori." Florence, 1549. Lectures given to the Accademia Fiorentina, 1546.

   Trattati d'arte del cinquecento fra manierismo e controriforma. Vol. 1. Edited by P. Barocchi. Scrittori d'Italia, vol. 219. Bari, 1960.

————. *Lezzioni sopra diverse materie poetiche e filosophice.* ("Della poetica" and "Della poesia.") Florence, 1590. Lectures given to the Accademia Fiorentina, 1553.

Vasari, Giorgio. *Immaculate Conception.* 1540. Florence, SS. Apostoli.

   A. Hauser, *Mannerism.* London, 1965.

————. *Le vite de'più eccellenti architetti pittori et scultori italiani.* Florence, 1550; 1568.

   Lives of the Most Eminent Painters, Sculptors and Architects. 10 vols. Translated by G. du C. de Vere. London, 1912–15.

   Vasari on Technique. Edited by C. S. Maclehose. New York, 1960.

   Le vite de'più eccellenti pittori, scultori e architettori. 9 vols. Milan, 1962–66.

   The Lives of the Artists. Edited by G. Bull. Harmondsworth, 1965.

   Le vite de'più eccellenti pittori, scultori e architettori. 3 vols. Edited by R. Bettarini and P. Barocchi. Florence, 1966.

   Le vite de'più eccellenti pittori, scultori e architetti. 3 vols. Edited by L. and C. L. Ragghianti. Milan, 1971–76.

————. *Uffizi Colonnade.* 1560. Florence.

   F. Würtenberger, *Mannerism.* New York, 1963.

   A. Hauser, *Mannerism.* London, 1965.

————. *Perseus and Andromeda.* 1570. Florence, Studiolo del Palazzo Vecchio.

   G. Briganti, *Le maniérisme italien.* Leipzig, 1962.

   J. Bousquet, *La peinture maniériste.* Neuchâtel, 1964.

   J. Shearman, *Mannerism.* Harmondsworth, 1967.

Vecchi, Orazio. *Fa una canzone a4. Canzonette libro secondo a quattro voci.* Venice, 1580.

   A. Einstein, *The Italian Madrigal.* Vol. 3. Princeton, 1949; 1971.

————. *L'Amfiparnaso comedia harmonica.* Venice, 1597.

   L'arte musicale in Italia. Vol. 4. Edited by L. Torchi. Milan, n.d.

   Publikation älterer praktischer und theoretischer Musikwerke. Vol. 26. Edited by R. Eitner. Berlin, 1902. New York, 1966.

   Capolavori polifonici del secolo XVI. Vol. 5. Edited by B. Somma. Rome, 1953.

   Edited by C. Adkins. Early Musical Masterworks. Chapel Hill, N.C., 1976.

————. *Le veglie di Siena overo i varii humori della musica moderna a tre a 4 a 5 & a 6 voci.* Venice, 1604.

   Capolavori polifonici del secolo XVI. Vol. 2. Edited by B. Somma. Rome, 1958.

Veggio, Claudio. *Per quei begli occhi a4. Madrigali a quattro voci.* Venice, 1540.

Verdelot, Filippo. *Con lagrime et sospir a4. Madrigali novi di diversi excellentissimi musici libro primo de la serena.* Rome, 1533. Rearranged for solo and lute by Adrian Willaert, *Intavolatura de li madrigali di Verdelotto.* Venice, 1536.

    A. Einstein, *The Italian Madrigal.* Vol. 3. Princeton, 1949; 1971 (solo version).

————. *I vostri acuti dardi a4. Il secondo libro de madrigali.* Venice, 1536/37.

    Publikation älterer praktischer und theoretischer Musikwerke. Vol. 3. Edited by R. Eitner, L. Erk, and O. Kade. Berlin, 1875.

    H. C. Slim, *A Gift of Madrigals and Motets.* Vol. 2. Chicago, 1972.

————. *Madonna qual certezza a4. Il primo libro de madrigali.* Venice, 1537.

    A. Einstein, *The Italian Madrigal.* Vol. 3. Princeton, 1949; 1971.

    H. C. Slim, *A Gift of Madrigals and Motets.* Vol. 2. Chicago, 1972.

————. *Quanto sia lieto il giorno a4. Il primo libro. . . .* Venice, 1537.

    W. Osthoff, *Theatergesang und darstellende Musik in der italienischen Renaissance.* Vol. 2. Tutzing, 1969. (Original polyphonic version and solo version by A. Willaert, 1536.)

    N. Pirrotta, *Li due Orfei da Poliziano a Monteverdi.* Turin, 1969; 1975.

    H. C. Slim, *A Gift of Madrigals and Motets.* Vol. 2. Chicago, 1972.

Verdizotti, Giovanni M. *Genius sive de furore poetico.* Venice, 1575.

Vesalius, Andreas. *De humani corporis fabrica.* Basel, 1543.

    Brussels, 1964.

    The Illustrations from the Works of Andreas Vesalius of Brussels. Edited by J. B. de C. M. Saunders and C. D. O'Malley. Cleveland, 1950.

Vicentino, Nicola. *Madrigali a cinque voci per teorica et pratica composti al nuovo modo dal celeberrimo suo maestro ritrovato.* Venice, 1546.

    Opera Omnia. Edited by H. W. Kaufmann. Corpus Mensurabilis Musicae, vol. 26. American Institute of Musicology, 1963.

    "Dedication."

    Excerpt in E. Vogel, *Bibliothek der gedruckten weltlichen Vocalmusik Italiens.* Hildesheim and New York, 1972.

————. *L'antica musica ridotta alla moderna prattica.* Rome, 1555.

    Edited by E. E. Lowinsky. Documenta Musicologica; Erste Reihe: Druckschriften-Faksimiles, vol. 17. Kassel, 1959.

————. *Alleluia haec dies a4. L'antica musica. . . .* Rome, 1555.

    L'arte musicale in Italia. Vol. 1. Edited by L. Torchi. Milan, 1897.

    H. W. Kaufmann, *The Life and Works of Nicola Vicentino.* American Institute of Musicology, 1966.

————. "Diatonic composition without text" a4. L'antica musica. . . . Rome, 1555.

    H. W. Kaufmann, *The Life and Works of Nicola Vicentino*. American Institute of Musicology, 1966.

————. *Dolce mio ben a4. L'antica musica*. . . . Rome, 1555.

    See above.

    T. Kroyer, *Die Anfänge der Chromatik im italienischen Madrigal des XVI. Jahrhunderts*. Leipzig, 1902.

————. *Hierusalem convertere a4. L'antica musica*. . . . Rome, 1555.

L'arte musicale in Italia. Vol. 1. Edited by L. Torchi. Milan, 1897.

    E. E. Lowinsky, *Tonality and Atonality in Sixteenth-Century Music*. Berkeley, 1961.

    H. W. Kaufmann, *The Life and Works of Nicola Vicentino*. American Institute of Musicology, 1966.

    E. E. Lowinsky, "The Musical Avant-Garde of the Renaissance or: The Peril and Profit of Foresight." In *Art, Science and History in the Renaissance*, edited by C. S. Singleton. Baltimore, 1967.

————. *Madonna il poco dolce a4. L'antica musica*. . . . Rome, 1555.

    H. W. Kaufmann, *The Life and Works of Nicola Vicentino*. American Institute of Musicology, 1966.

————. *Musica prisca caput a4. L'antica musica*. . . . Rome, 1555.

    See above.

    E. E. Lowinsky, "The Musical Avant-Garde of the Renaissance or: The Peril and Profit of Foresight." In *Art, Science and History in the Renaissance*, edited by C. S. Singleton. Baltimore, 1967.

————. *Soav'e dolc'ardore a4. L'antica musica*. . . . Rome, 1555.

    H. W. Kaufmann, *The Life and Works of Nicola Vicentino*. American Institute of Musicology, 1966.

————. *Descrizione dell'arciorgano*. 1561.

    See above.

    H. W. Kaufmann, "Vicentino's *Arciorgano*: An Annotated Translation." *Journal of Music Theory* 5 (1961).

Vignola, Giacomo B. da. Palazzo Farnese. 1559–73. Caprarola.

    F. Würtenberger, *Mannerism*. New York, 1963.

    A. Hauser, *Mannerism*. London, 1965.

    L. Murray, *The Late Renaissance and Mannerism*. New York, 1967.

    J. Shearman, *Mannerism*. Harmondsworth, 1967.

Viola, Alfonso della. *In me cresce la voglia a4. Primo libro di madrigali*. Ferrara, 1539.

    Excerpt in A. Einstein, *The Italian Madrigal*. Princeton, 1949; 1971.

————. *O dei silvestri a4. Il sacricio*. Ferrara, 1555.

    W. Osthoff, *Theatergesang und darstellende Musik in der italienischen Renaissance*. Vol. 2. Tutzing, 1969.

————. *Tu ch'ai le corna a1. Il sacrificio*. Ferrara, 1555.

    See above.

A. Einstein, *The Italian Madrigal.* Princeton, 1949; 1971.

D. J. Grout, *A Short History of Opera.* New York, 1960.

Viola, Francesco della. *See* Willaert, Adrian, *Musica nova.*

Vitruvius, Marcus P. *De architectura libri decem.*

    I dieci libri dell'architettura. Translated by D. Barbaro. Venice, 1567.

    The Ten Books of Architecture. Translated by M. H. Morgan. New York, 1960.

    Zehn Bücher über Architektur. Translated by Dr. C. Fensterbusch. Darmstadt, 1964.

Vittoria, Alessandro. Fireplace. 1553. Vicenza, Palazzo Thiene.

    J. Shearman, *Mannerism.* Harmondsworth, 1967.

Wert, Giaches de. *Aspro cor'e selvaggio a5. Il primo libro de madrigali a cinque voci.* Venice, 1558.

    Opera Omnia. Vol. 1. Edited by C. MacClintock and M. Bernstein. Corpus Mensurabilis Musicae, vol. 24. American Institute of Musicology, 1961.

    ————. *Il primo libro de madrigali a quattro voci.* Venice, 1561.

    Opera Omnia. Vol. 15. Edited by C. MacClintock. Corpus Mensurabilis Musicae, vol. 24. American Institute of Musicology, 1972.

    ————. *Dolce spoglie a4. Il primo libro.* . . . Venice 1561.

    See above.

    ————. *Dunque baciar a4. Il primo libro.* . . . Venice, 1561.

    See above.

    ————. *Madrigali del fiore a cinque voci libro secondo.* Venice, 1561.

    Opera Omnia. Vol. 2. Edited by C. MacClintock and M. Bernstein. Corpus Mensurabilis Musicae, vol. 24. American Institute of Musicology, 1962.

    ————. *Amor io fallo a5. Madrigali del fiore.* . . . Venice, 1561.

    See above.

    ————. *Il terzo libro de madrigali a cinque voci.* Venice, 1563.

    Opera Omnia. Vol. 3. Edited by C. MacClintock. Corpus Mensurabilis Musicae, vol. 24. American Institute of Musicology, 1962.

    ————. *Nova amor nova fiamma a5. Il terzo libro.* . . . Venice, 1563.

    See above.

    ————. *Il quarto libro de madrigali a cinque voci.* Venice, 1567.

    Opera Omnia. Vol. 4. Edited by C. MacClintock and M. Bernstein. Corpus Mensurabilis Musicae, vol. 24. American Institute of Musicology, 1965.

    ————. *Qual nemica fortuna a5. Il quarto libro.* . . . Venice, 1567.

    See above.

    ————. *Il quinto libro de madrigali a cinque voci.* Venice, 1571.

    Opera Omnia. Vol. 5. Edited by C. MacClintock and M. Bernstein. Corpus Mensurabilis Musicae, vol. 24. American Institute of Musicology, 1969.

————. *Son animali al mondo a5. Il quinto libro.* . . . Venice, 1571.
See above.

————. *Il sesto libro de madrigali a cinque voci.* Venice, 1572.
Opera Omnia. Vol. 6. Edited by C. MacClintock. Corpus Mensurabilis Musicae, vol. 24. American Institute of Musicology, 1966.

————. *Era dunque ne'fatti a5. Il sesto libro.* . . . Venice, 1572.
See above.

————. *Se quel dolor a5. Il sesto libro.* . . . Venice, 1572.
See above.

————. *Il settimo libro de madrigali a cinque voci.* Venice, 1581.
Opera Omnia. Vol. 7. Edited by C. MacClintock and M. Bernstein. Corpus Mensurabilis Musicae, vol. 24. American Institute of Musicology, 1967.

————. *Giunto alla tomba a5. Il settimo libro.* . . . Venice, 1581.
Complete edition as above.
A. Einstein, *The Italian Madrigal.* Vol. 3. Princeton, 1949; 1971.

————. *Solo e pensoso a5. Il settimo libro.* . . . Venice, 1581.
Complete edition as above.
Das Chorwerk. Vol. 80. Edited by D. Arnold. Wolfenbüttel, 1961.

————. *Tirsi morir volea a7. Il settimo libro.* . . . Venice, 1581.
Complete edition as above.

————. *L'ottavo libro de madrigali a cinque voci.* Venice, 1586.
Opera Omnia. Vol. 8. Edited by C. MacClintock. Corpus Mensurabilis Musicae, vol. 24. American Institute of Musicology, 1968.

————. *Misera non credea a5. L'ottavo libro.* . . . Venice, 1586.
Complete edition as above.
A. Einstein, *The Italian Madrigal.* Vol. 3. Princeton, 1949; 1971.

————. *Non è sì denso velo a5. L'ottavo libro.* . . . Venice, 1586.
See above.

————. *Qual nemico gentil a5. L'ottavo libro.* . . . Venice, 1586.
Complete edition as above.

————. *Vezzosi augelli a5. L'ottavo libro.* . . . Venice, 1586.
Complete edition as above.

————. *Mia benigna fortuna/Crudel acerba inesorabil morte a5. Il nono libro de madrigali a cinque et sei voci.* Venice, 1588.
Opera Omnia. Vol. 9. Edited by C. MacClintock. Corpus Mensurabilis Musicae, vol. 24. American Institute of Musicology, 1970.

————. *Ah dolente partita a5. L'undecimo libro de madrigali a cinque voci.* Venice, 1595.
Opera Omnia. Vol. 12. Edited by C. MacClintock and M. Bernstein. Corpus Mensurabilis Musicae, vol. 24. American Institute of Musicology, 1972.

The Golden Age of the Madrigal. Edited by A. Einstein. New York, 1942.

———. *O Primavera a5. L'undecimo libro.* . . . Venice, 1595.
Complete edition as above.

———. *Udite lagrimosi spirti a5. L'undecimo libro.* . . . Venice, 1595.
Complete edition as above.

Willaert, Adrian. *Quid non ebrietas.* Ca. 1520.

    G. M. Artusi, *L'Artusi overo delle imperfettioni della moderna musica.* Pt. I, Venice, 1600. ("Ragionamento primo.") (See separate entry.)

    T. Kroyer, *Die Anfänge der Chromatik im italienischen Madrigal des XVI. Jahrhunderts.* Leipzig, 1902.

    J. S. Levitan, "Adrian Willaert's Famous Duo 'Quidnam ebrietas.'" *Tijdschrift der Vereenigung voor Nederlandsche Muziekgeschiedenis* 15 (1938–39).

    E. E. Lowinsky, "Adrian Willaert's Chromatic 'Duo' Re-Examined." *Tijdschrift voor Muziekwetenschap* 28 (1956).

———. *Amor mi fa morire a4.* F. Verdelot, *Il secondo libro de madrigali di Verdelot insieme con alcuni altri bellissimi madrigali di Adriano & Constantio Festa.* Venice, 1536.

    Opera Omnia. Vol. 14. Edited by H. Zenck, W. Gerstenberg, and B. and H. Meier. Corpus Mensurabilis Musicae, vol. 3. American Institute of Musicology, 1977.

    A. Einstein, *The Italian Madrigal.* Vol. 3. Princeton, 1949; 1971.

———. *Intavolatura de li madrigali di Verdelotto.* Venice, 1536.

———. *Qual dolcezza giammai a5.* F. Verdelot, *Le dotte et eccellente compositioni de i madrigali a cinque voci insieme con altri madrigali di varij autori.* Venice, 1538.
Complete edition as above.

    P. Wagner, "Das Madrigal und Palestrina." *Vierteljahrschrift für Musikwissenschaft* 8 (1892).

———. *Musica nova.* Venice, 1559.

    Opera Omnia. Vol. 13. Edited by H. Zenck and W. Gerstenberg. Corpus Mensurabilis Musicae, vol. 3. American Institute of Musicology, 1966.
"Preface" by Francesco della Viola.

    E. Vogel, *Bibliothek der gedruckten weltlichen Vocalmusik Italiens.* Hildesheim and New York, 1972.

———. *Liete e pensose a7. Musica nova.* Venice, 1559.
Complete edition as above.

    A. Einstein, *The Italian Madrigal.* Vol. 3. Princeton, 1949; 1971.

Zacconi, Lodovico. *Prattica di musica utile et necessaria al compositore per comporre i canti suoi regolatamente si anco al cantore per assicurarsi in tutte le cose cantabile.* Pt. I, Venice, 1592; pt. II, Venice, 1622.

Bibliotheca Musica Bononiensis; sezione II, vols. 1 and 2. Bologna, 1967.
————. *Canoni musicali proprii e di diversi autori.* Pesaro, n.d.
Zarlino, Gioseffo. *Dimostratione armoniche.* Venice, 1571.
Monuments of Music and Music Literature in Facsimile; Second Series—Music Literature, vol. 2. New York, 1965.
————. *Le istitutioni harmoniche.* Venice, 1558; 1562.
Monuments of Music and Music Literature in Facsimile; Second Series—Music Literature, vol. 1. New York, 1965.
The Art of Counterpoint. (Bk. III.) Edited by G. A. Marco and C. V. Palisca. New Haven, 1968.
————. *Sopplimenti musicali.* Venice, 1588.
Ridgewood, N.J., 1966.
Zuccaro, Federico. *Allegory of Design.* Ca. 1593. Rome, Palazzo Zuccaro.
L. Murray, *The Late Renaissance and Mannerism.* New York, 1967.
————. *L'idea de'pittori scultori e architetti.* Turin, 1607.
Scritti d'arte. Edited by D. Heikamp. Fonti per lo studia della storia dell'arte, vol. 1. Florence, 1961.

SECONDARY SOURCES

This bibliography does not contain citations of articles in the standard dictionaries.

Abert, Anna A. *Claudio Monteverdi und das musikalische Drama.* Lippstadt, 1954.
Accone, Frank d'. "Bernardo Pisano." *Report of the Tenth Congress of the International Musicological Society, Ljubljana 1967,* pp. 96–106. Kassel, 1970.
Ackerman, James S. "Architectural Principals in the Italian Renaissance." *Journal of the Society of Architectural Historians* 13 (1954): 3–11. Reprinted in *Renaissance Art,* edited by Creighton Gilbert, pp. 148–71. New York, 1973.
————. "Science and Visual Art." In *Seventeenth Century Science and the Arts,* edited by H. H. Rhys, pp. 63–90. Princeton, 1961.
Adler, Israel. "Une source hébraïque de 1602 relative à la musica reservata." *Fontes Artis Musicae* (1966): 9–15.
Albrecht, Hans. "Musik und Dichtkunst im 16. Jahrhundert." *Die Musikforschung* 8 (1955): 335–45.
Aldrich, Putnam. *Rhythm in Seventeenth Century Italian Monody.* New York, 1966.
Alessi, Giovanni d'. "Precursors of Adriano Willaert in the Practice of Coro Spezzato." *Journal of the American Musicological Society* 5 (1952): 187–210.

Antal, Friedrich. "Zum Problem des niederländischen Manierismus." *Kritische Berichte zur Kunstgeschichtlichen Literatur* 1–2 (1929): 207–56.

Anthon, Carl G. "Music and Musicians in Northern Italy during the Sixteenth Century." Ph.D. dissertation, Harvard University, 1943.

Apel, Willi. *Accidentien und Tonalität in der Musikdenkmälern des 15. und 16. Jahrhunderts.* Leipzig, 1937.

―――. "The Early Development of the Organ Ricercar." *Musica Disciplina* 3 (1939): 139–50.

―――. *French Secular Music of the Late Fourteenth Century.* Cambridge, Mass., 1949.

―――. *Geschichte der Orgel- und Klaviermusik bis 1700.* Kassel, 1967.

―――. "Solo Instrumental Music." In *The Age of Humanism 1540–1630,* edited by Gerald Abraham. New Oxford History of Music, vol. 4, pp. 602–708. London, 1968.

Argan, G. C. "Maniera e Manierismo." *Enciclopedia Italiana di Scienze, Lettere ed Arti* 22 (1934): 126.

Arnold, Denis. "Alessandro Grandi, Disciple of Monteverdi." *Musical Quarterly* 43 (1957): 171–86.

―――. "Andrea Gabrieli und die Entwicklung des 'cori-spezzati'-Technik." *Die Musikforschung* 12 (1959): 258–74.

―――. "Ceremonial Music in Venice at the Time of the Gabrielis." *Proceedings of the Royal Musical Association* 82 (1955–56): 47–59.

―――. "Formal Design in Monteverdi's Church Music." *Congresso Internazionale sul Tema Claudio Monteverdi e il suo Tempo,* pp. 187–216. Venice and Mantua, 1968.

―――. "Giovanni Croce and the *Concertato* Style." *Musical Quarterly* 39 (1953): 37–48.

―――. *Marenzio.* London, 1965.

―――. *Monteverdi.* London, 1963.

―――. "Monteverdi and his Teachers." In *The Monteverdi Companion,* edited by Denis Arnold and Nigel Fortune, pp. 91–109. London, 1968.

―――. "Monteverdi: some Colleagues and Pupils." In *The Monteverdi Companion,* edited by Denis Arnold and Nigel Fortune, pp. 110–30. London, 1968.

―――. "Music at the Scuola di San Rocco." *Music and Letters* 40 (1959): 229–41.

―――. "'Seconda pratica': A Background to Monteverdi's Madrigals." *Music and Letters* 38 (1957): 343–45.

―――. "The Significance of 'Cori spezzati.'" *Music and Letters* 40 (1959): 4–14.

Artz, Frederick B. *From the Renaissance to Romanticism: Trends in Art, Literature and Music, 1300–1830.* Chicago, 1962.

Baiardi, Giorgio. "Il dialogo *Del concetto poetico* di Camillo Pellegrino." *Rassegna della Letteratura Italiana* 62 (1958): 370–74.

Bainton, Roland H. "Man, God and the Church in the Age of the Renaissance." *The Renaissance: Six Essays*, pp. 77–96. New York, 1962.

Baldwin, Charles S. *Renaissance Literary Theory and Practice*. Gloucester, Mass., 1959.

Balmer, Lucie. *Orlando di Lassos Motetten*. Bern, 1938.

————. *Tonsystem und Kirchentöne bei Johannes Tinctoris*. Bern, 1935.

Baltrusaitis, Jurgis. *Anamorphoses ou perspectives curieuses*. Paris, 1955.

Bandmann, Günter. *Melankolie und Musik: Ikonographische Studien*. Cologne, 1960.

Barassi, Elena F. "Il madrigale spirituale nel cinquecento e la raccolta monteverdiana del 1583." *Congresso Internazionale sul Tema Claudio Monteverdi e il suo Tempo*, pp. 217–52. Venice and Mantua, 1968.

Barbéri-Squarcotti, Giorgio. "Per una descrizione e interpretazione della poetica di Giordano Bruno." *Studi Secenteschi*, 1:39–59. Florence, 1961.

Barbour, J. Murray. *Tuning and Temperament: A Historical Survey*. East Lansing, 1951.

Barocchi, Paola. "Sul Vasari pittore." *Studi Vasariani* 1950, pp. 186–91. Florence, 1952.

Baron, John H. "Monody: A Study in Terminology." *Musical Quarterly* 54 (1968): 462–74.

Battisti, Eugenio. *L'antirinascimento*. Milan, 1962.

————. "Le arti figurative nella cultura di Venezia e in quella di Firenze e Roma nel cinquecento." *Rinascimento e barocco*, pp. 157–74. Turin, 1960.

————. "Il concetto d'imitazione nel cinquecento italiano." *Rinascimento e barocco*, pp. 175–215. Turin, 1960.

————. "Sfortune del manierismo." *Rinascimento e barocco*, pp. 216–37. Turin, 1960.

————. "Lo spirito del manierismo." *Letteratura* 4 (1956): 3–10.

Bäumker, Wilhelm. *Das katholische deutsche Kirchenlied in seinem Singweisen von der frühesten Zeit bis gegen Ende des 17. Jahrhunderts*. 3 vols. Freiburg, 1883–91.

————. "Über den Kontrapunkt. Eine kurze Anweisung aus dem XVI. Jahrhundert." *Monatshefte für Musikgeschichte* 10 (1878): 63–65.

Baumgart, Fritz. *Renaissance und Kunst des Manierismus*. Cologne, 1963.

Bautier-Regnier, Anne-Marie. "Jacques de Wert." *Revue Belge de Musicologie* 4 (1950): 40–70.

Beat, Janet E. "Monteverdi and the Opera Orchestra of his Time." In *The Monteverdi Companion*, edited by Denis Arnold and Nigel Fortune, pp. 277–301. London, 1968.

Bedbrook, Gerold S. "The Genius of Giovanni Gabrieli (1557–1612):

The Quintessence of the Venetian School." *Music Review* 8 (1947): 91–101.

Béguin, Sylvie. *L'école de Fontainebleau: Le maniérisme à la cour de France*. Paris, 1960.

Bellingham, Bruce. "The *Bicinium* in the Lutheran Latin Schools during the Reformation Period." Ph.D. dissertation, University of Toronto, 1971.

Benesch, Otto. *The Art of the Renaissance in Northern Europe: Its Relation to the Contemporary Spiritual and Intellectual Movements*. London, 1965.

Bernal, J. D. *The Scientific and Industrial Revolution*. Science in History, vol. 2. Cambridge, Mass., 1965.

Bernet-Kempers, Karel P. *Jacobus Clemens non Papa und seine Motetten*. Augsburg, 1928.

Besseler, Heinrich. "Das Renaissanceproblem in der Musik." *Archiv für Musikwissenschaft* 23 (1966): 1–10.

Bethell, S. L. "Gracián, Tesauro and the Nature of Metaphysical Wit." *Northern Miscellany of Literary Criticism* 1 (1953): 19–40.

Bezdeck, Sister John J. "The Harmonic and Contrapuntal Style of Orlando Lasso." Ph.D. dissertation, University of Rochester, 1946.

Bianconi, Lorenzo. "'Ah dolente partita': espressione e artificio." *Studi Musicali* 3 (1974): 105–38.

⸻. "The Caccinian Workshop of Pietro Maria Marsolo." Preface to L. Bianconi's edition of P. M. Marsolo's *Madrigali quattro voci (1614)*. Musiche Rinascimentali Siciliani, vol. 4, pp. IX–LVIII. Rome, 1973.

⸻. "Giulio Caccini e il manierismo musicale." *Chigiana* 25 (1968): 21–38.

⸻. "Struttura poetica e struttura musicale nei madrigali di Monteverdi." *Congresso Internazionale sul Tema Claudio Monteverdi e il suo Tempo*, pp. 335–48. Venice and Mantua, 1968.

⸻. "Weitere Ergänzungen zu Emil Vogels 'Bibliothek der gedruckten weltlichen Vocalmusik Italiens, aus den Jahren 1500–1700' aus italienischen Bibliotheken." *Analecta Musicologica* 9 (1970): 142–202.

Birtner, Herbert. "Renaissance und Klassik in der Musik." *Theodor Kroyer Festschrift*, pp. 40–53. Regensburg, 1933.

Blume, Friedrich. "Begriff und Grenzen des Barock in der Musik." *Manierismo, Barocco, Rococò: Concetti e Termini*, pp. 377–84. Accademia Nazionale dei Lincei. Rome, 1962.

⸻. *Renaissance and Baroque Music: A Comprehensive Survey*. Translated by M. D. Herter Norton. New York, 1967.

Blunt, Anthony. *Artistic Theory in Italy, 1450–1600*. London, 1956.

Boas, George. "Philosophies of Science in Florentine Platonism." In *Art, Science and History in the Renaissance*, edited by Charles S. Singleton, pp. 239–54. Baltimore, 1967.

Boas, Marie. *The Scientific Renaissance 1540–1630.* New York, 1962.

Boetticher, Wolfgang. *Aus Orlando di Lassos Wirkungskreis.* Kassel, 1963.

————. "Neue Lasso-Funde." *Die Musikforschung* 8 (1955): 385–97.

————. "Orlando di Lasso als Demonstrationsobjekt in der Kompositionslehre des 16. und 17. Jahrhunderts." *Kongressbericht Bamberg 1953,* pp. 124–27. Kassel, 1954.

————. *Orlando di Lasso und seine Zeit, 1532–94.* Kassel, 1958.

————. "Über einige neue Werke aus Orlando di Lassos mittlerer Madrigal- und Motettenkomposition (1567–1569)." *Archiv für Musikwissenschaft* 22 (1965): 12–42.

————. "Zum problem der Übergangsperiode der Musik 1580–1620." *Kongressbericht Kassel 1962,* pp. 141–44. Kassel, 1963.

————. "Zum Spätstilsproblem im Schaffen Orlando di Lassos." *Bericht über den siebenten Kongress der Internationalen Gesellschaft für Musikwissenschaft, Köln 1958,* pp. 69–71. Kassel, 1959.

Böker-Heil, Norbert. "Die Motetten von Philippe Verdelot." Ph.D. dissertation, Johann Wolfgang Golth-Universität, Frankfurt am Main, 1967.

Bonaccorsi, Alfredo. "La dinamica nella storia." *Rassegna Musicale* 27 (1957): 290–95.

Bonta, Stephen. "Liturgical Problems in Monteverdi's Marian Vespers." *Journal of the American Musicological Society* 20 (1967): 87–106.

Bouleau, Charles. *The Painter's Secret Geometry.* New York, 1963.

Boulting, William. *Tasso and his Time.* London, 1907.

Bousquet, Jacques. *La peinture maniériste.* Neuchâtel, 1964.

Boyden, David. "When is a Concerto not a Concerto?" *Musical Quarterly* 43 (1957): 220–32.

Bragard, Anne-Marie. *Etude bio-bibliographique sur Philippe Verdelot, musicien français de la Renaissance.* Brussels, 1964.

Brand, C. P. *Torquato Tasso: A Study of the Poet and of His Contribution to English Literature.* Cambridge, 1965.

Brandes, Heinz. *Studien zur musikalischen Figurenlehre im 16. Jahrhundert.* Berlin, 1935.

Braudel, Fernand. *La méditerranée et le monde méditerranéen à l'époche de Philippe II.* Paris, 1949.

Brauner, Patricia B. "Giuseppe Caimo, 'Nobile Milenese.'" Ph.D. dissertation, Yale University.

Bray, René. *La préciosité et les précieux de Thibault de Champagne à Jean Giraudoux.* Paris, 1948.

Bridgeman, Nanie. "La frottola et la transition de la frottola au madrigal." In *Musique et poésie au XVIe siècle,* edited by Jean Jacquot, pp. 63–77. Paris, 1954.

Briganti, Giuliano. *Le maniérisme italien.* Leipzig, 1962.

Brown, Howard M. "Music—How Opera Began: An Introduction to

Jacopo Peri's *Euridice* 1600." In *The Late Italian Renaissance 1525–1630*, edited by Eric Cochrane, pp. 401–43. New York, 1970.

————. *Music in the Renaissance*. Englewood Cliffs, N.J., 1976.

————. "Psyche's Lament: Some Music for the Medici Wedding in 1565." *Words and Music: The Scholars View. (A Medley of Problems and Solutions Compiled in Honor of A. Tillman Merritt by Sundry Hands)*, pp. 1–27. Cambridge, Mass., 1972.

————. *Sixteenth-Century Instrumentation: The Music for the Florentine Intermedios*. American Institute of Musicology, 1973.

Brunelli, Bruno. "Francesco Portenari e le cantate degli accademie padovani." *Atti del Reale Istituto Veneto di Scienze, Lettere ed Arti* 79 (1919–20): 595–607.

Bukofzer, Manfred. *Music in the Baroque Era*. New York, 1947.

Butler, Gregory. "The Canonic Sequence in Theory and Practice: A Rhetorical-Musical Study of its Origins and Development in Keyboard Music to 1750." Ph.D. dissertation, University of Toronto, 1973.

Calcaterra, Carlo. *Poesia e canto: Studi sulla poesia melica italiana e sulle favole per musica*. Bologna, 1951.

Camilucci, Guido. "L'Amfiparnasso, comedia harmonica." *Rivista Musicale Italiana* 53 (1951): 42–60.

Cannon, Beekman, C.; Johnson, Alvin H.; and Waite, William G. *The Art of Music: A Short History of Musical Styles and Ideas*. New York, 1960.

Capua, A. G. de. "Baroque and Mannerism: Reassessment 1965." *Colloquia Germanica* 1 (1967): 101–10.

Carapetyan, Armen. "The Concept of *Imitazione della natura* in the Sixteenth Century." *Journal of Renaissance and Baroque Music* 1 (1946–47): 47–67.

————. "The *Musica Nova* of Adriano Willaert." Ph.D. dissertation, Harvard University, 1945.

Carapezza, Paolo E. "L'ultimo oltramontano o vero l'antimonteverdi: (Un essempio di musica reservata tra manierismo e barocco)." *Nuova Rivista Musicale Italiana* 4 (1970): 213–43 and 411–44.

Carozza, Davy A. "For a Definition of Mannerism: the Hatzfeldian Thesis." *Colloquia Germanica* 1 (1967): 66–77.

Cartwright, Julia. *Isabella d'Este Marchioness of Mantua 1474–1539*. 2 vols. London, 1932.

Castleman, Charles. "Three Musical *Virtuose di Ferrara*: Lucrezia Bendidio, Laura Peperara and Tarquinia Molza." *Anuario Musical* 23 (1968): 191–98.

Cavicchi, Adriano. "Preface" to A. Cavicchi's edition of L. Luzzaschi's *Madrigali per cantare et sonare*. Monumenti di Musica Italiana; serie 2: Polifonia, vol. 2, pp. 7–23. Brescia, 1965.

————. "Teatro monteverdiano e tradizione teatrale ferrarese." *Congresso Internazionale sul Tema Claudio Monteverdi e il suo Tempo*, pp. 139–56. Venice and Mantua, 1968.

Cazden, Norman. "Pythagoras and Aristoxenus Reconciled." *Journal of the American Musicological Society* 11 (1958): 97–105.

Cesari, Gaetano. *Die Entstehung des Madrigals im sechzehnten Jahrhundert.* Cremona, 1908.

————. "L'Orfeo di Claudio Monteverdi all'Associazione di Amici della Musica di Milano." *Rivista Musicale Italiana* 17 (1910): 132–78.

Chailley, Jacques. "Esprit et technique du chromatisme de la Renaissance." In *Musique et poésie au XVIe siècle,* edited by Jean Jacquot, pp. 225–39. Paris, 1954.

Chappell, Warren. *A Short History of the Printed Word.* New York, 1970.

Chastel, André. *Art et humanisme à Florence au temps du Laurent le Magnifique.* Paris, 1959.

Chastel, André and Klein, Robert. *The Age of Humanism.* New York, 1963.

Chiapelli, Fredi. "Tassos Stil im Übergang von Renaissance zu Barock." *Trivium* 7 (1949): 286–308.

Chrysander, Friedrich. "Lodovico Zacconi als Lehrer des Kunstgesanges." *Vierteljahrschrift für Musikwissenschaft* 7 (1891): 337–96; 9 (1893): 249–310; and 10 (1894): 531–67.

Chybinski, Adolf. "Zur Geschichte des Taktschlagens und des Kapellmeistersamtes in der Epoche der Mensuralmusik." *Sammelbände der Internationalen Musikgesellschaft* 10 (1908–1909): 385–95.

Cimbro, Attilio. "I madrigali di Claudio Monteverdi." *Musica* 2 (1943): 4–34.

Clark, Donald L. *Rhetoric and Poetry in the Renaissance.* New York, 1963.

Clark, Willene. "A Contribution to Sources of Musica Reservata." *Revue Belge de Musicologie* 11 (1957): 27–33.

Claro, Samuel. "Claudio Monteverdi—Giovanni Maria Artusi: una controversia musicale." *Revista Musical Chilena* 19 (1965): 86–94.

Clements, Robert J. *Michelangelo's Theory of Art.* New York, 1961.

————. *Picta Poesis: Literary and Humanistic Theory in Renaissance Emblem Books.* Rome, 1960.

Clercx, Susanne. *Le baroque et la musique: Essai d'esthétique musicale.* Brussels, 1948.

Cleugh, James. *The Divine Aretino.* New York, 1966.

Closson, Ernest. *Roland de Lassus.* Tournhout, 1919.

Coates, Henry and Abraham, Gerald. "VI Latin Church Music on the Continent—2; The Performance of the A Cappella Style." In *The Age of Humanism 1540–1630,* edited by Gerald Abraham. New Oxford History of Music, vol. 4, pp. 312–71. London, 1968.

Colie, Rosalie. *Paradoxia epidemica: the Renaissance Tradition of Paradox.* Princeton, 1966.

Collaer, Paul. "Lyrisme baroque et tradition populaire." *Studia Musicologica* 7 (1965): 25–40.

Corte, Andrea della. "Il barocco e la musica." *Manierismo, Barocco, Rococò: Concetti e Termini.* Accademia Nazionale dei Lincei. Rome, 1962, pp. 361–75.

———. "Un capitalo nella preistoria dell'opera." *Rassegna Musicale* 31 (1961): 93–98.

Cortellazzo, Angela T. "Il melodramma di Marco da Gagliano." *Congresso Internazionale sul Tema Claudio Monteverdi e il suo Tempo,* pp. 583–98. Venice and Mantua, 1968.

Crane, Thomas F. *Italian Social Customs of the Sixteenth Century.* New Haven, 1920.

Croce, Benedetto. "Franceso Patrizi e la critica della retorica antica." *Problemi di estetica e contributi alla storia dell'estetica italiana,* pp. 299–310. Bari, 1966.

———. "I trattatisti italiani del concettismo e Baltasar Gracián." *Problemi di estetica e contributi alla storia dell'estetica italiana,* pp. 311–46. Bari, 1966.

Crocker, Richard L. *A History of Musical Style.* New York, 1966.

Culcasi, Carlo. *Il petrarca e la musica.* Florence, 1911.

Culley, Thomas D. *Jesuits and Music: I.* Rome, 1970.

Curtius, Ernst R. *European Literature and the Latin Middle Ages.* Translated by Willard R. Trask. New York, 1963.

Dahlhaus, Carl. "Domenico Belli und der chromatische Kontrapunkt um 1600." *Die Musikforschung* 15 (1962): 315–40.

———. "Gesualdos manieristische Dissonanztechnik." *Convivium musicorum: Festschrift Wolfgang Boetticher,* pp. 34–43. Berlin, 1974.

———. "Musica poetica and musikalische Poesie." *Archiv für Musikwissenschaft* 28 (1966): 110–24.

———. "'Neue Musik' als historische Kategorie." In *Das musikalisch Neue und die neue Musik,* edited by Hans-Peter Reinecke, pp.26–39. Mainz, 1969.

———. "War Zarlino Dualist?" *Die Musikforschung* 10 (1957): 286–90.

———. "Zur chromatischen Technik Carlo Gesualdos." *Analecta Musicologica* 4 (1967): 77–96.

———. "Zur Theorie des Tactus im 16. Jahrhundert." *Archiv für Musikwissenschaft* 17 (1960): 22–39.

Dalfrati, Carlo. "Vecchio e nuovo nei madrigali di Adriano Banchieri." *Congresso Internazionale sul Tema Claudio Monteverdi e il suo Tempo,* pp. 599–610. Venice and Mantua, 1968.

Davidson, Colin. "Bomarzo I." *Architectural Review* (1954): 177–81.

Davies, J. H. Y. "The Sonnets of Michelangelo." *Nine* 7 (1951): 125–28.

Dent, Edward. "Music and Drama." In *The Age of Humanism 1540–*

1630, edited by Gerald Abraham. New Oxford History of Music, vol. 4, pp. 784–820. London, 1968.

————. "Notes on the 'Amfiparnasso' of Orazio Vecchi." *Sammelbände der Internationalen Musikgesellschaft* 12 (1910–11): 330–47.

————. "The Sixteenth-Century Madrigal." In *The Age of Humanism 1540–1630*, edited by Gerald Abraham. New Oxford History of Music, vol. 4, pp. 33–95. London, 1968.

Donington, Robert. "Monteverdi's First Opera." In *The Monteverdi Companion*, edited by Denis Arnold and Nigel Fortune, pp. 257–76. London, 1968.

Drake, Stillman. *Galileo Studies*. Ann Arbor, Mich., 1970.

————. "Renaissance Music and Experimental Science." *Journal of the History of Ideas* 31 (1970): 483–500.

————. "The Role of Music in Galileo's Experiments." *Scientific American* 232 (1975): 98–104.

Duhamel, P. Albert. "The Function of Rhetoric as Effective Expression." *Journal of the History of Ideas* 10 (1949): 344–56.

Dupont, Wilhelm. *Geschichte der musikalischen Temperatur*. Nördlingen, 1935.

Dvořák, Max. "El Greco and Mannerism." *Magazine of Art* 46 (1953): 14–23.

————. *Geschichte der italienischen Kunst im Zeitalter der Renaissance*. 2 vols. Munich, 1927–29.

Egen, Patricia. "'Poesia' and the 'fête Champetre.'" *Art Bulletin* 41 (1959): 303–13.

Eggebrecht, Hans H. *Heinrich Schütz: Musicus Poeticus*. Göttingen, 1959.

Einstein, Alfred. "Anfänge des Vokalkonzerts." *Acta Musicologica* 3 (1931): 8–13.

————. "Die Aria di Ruggiero." *Sammelbände der Internationalen Musikgesellschaft* 13 (1911–12): 444–54.

————. "Augenmusik im Madrigal." *Zeitschrift der Internationalen Musikgesellschaft* 14 (1912): 8–21.

————. "Aus der Frühzeit des Konzertlebens." *Nationale und Universale Musik*, pp. 11–22. Zurich, 1958.

————. "Eine Caccia im Cinquecento." *Festschrift Rochus Freiherrn von Liliencron*, pp. 72–80. Leipzig, 1910.

————. "Cipriano de Rore and the Madrigal." *Bulletin of the American Musicological Society* 6 (1942): 17.

————. "Dante im Madrigal." *Archiv für Musikwissenschaft* 3 (1921): 405–20.

————. "Dante on the Way to the Madrigal." *Musical Quarterly* 25 (1939): 142–55.

————. "Das elfte Buch der Frottole." *Zeitschrift für Musikwissenschaft* 10 (1927–28): 613–24.

————. "Filippo di Monte als Madrigalkomponist." *Report of the First Congress of the International Musicological Society, Liège 1930*, pp. 102–8. Burnham, 1930.

————. *The Italian Madrigal*. Translated by Alexander H. Krappe, Roger H. Sessions, and Oliver Strunk. Princeton, 1949; 1971.

————. "Das Madrigal." *Nationale und universale Musik*, pp. 23–34. Zurich. 1958.

————. "Das Madrigal und die Dichtung." *Nationale und universale Musik*, pp. 35–42. Zurich, 1958.

————. "Das Madrigal zum Doppelgebrauch." *Acta Musicologica* 6 (1934): 110–16.

————. "Ein Madrigaldialog von 1594." *Zeitschrift für Musikwissenschaft* 15 (1913–14): 202–12.

————. "Narrative Rhythm in the Madrigal." *Musical Quarterly* 29 (1943): 475–84.

————. "*Orlando furioso* and *La Gerusalemme Liberata* as set to music during the 16th and 17th centuries." *Notes* 8 (1950–51): 623–30.

————. "Ein unbekanntes Madrigal Palestrinas." *Zeitschrift für Musikwissenschaft* 7 (1925): 530–34.

————. "Vincenzo Ruffo's *Opera nova di musica*." *Journal of the American Musicological Society* 3 (1950): 233–35.

Eitner, Robert. "Cipriano Rore." *Monatshefte für Musikgeschichte* 21 (1889): 41–51, 57–66, and 73–80.

————. "Hermann Finck über die Kunst des Singens, 1556." *Monatshefte für Musikgeschichte* 11 (1879): 129–33, 135–41, and 151–66.

————. "Palestrina als Chromatiker." *Monatshefte für Musikgeschichte* 18 (1886): 77–82.

Elders, Willem. *Studien zur Symbolik in der Musik der alten Niederländer*. Bilthoven, 1968.

Engel, Hans. "Die Entstehung des italienischen Madrigals und die Niederländer." *Report of the Fifth Congress of the International Musicological Society, Utrecht 1952*, pp. 166–80. Amsterdam, 1953.

————. *Luca Marenzio*. Florence, 1956.

————. "Marenzios Madrigalen." *Zeitschrift für Musikwissenschaft* 17 (1935): 257–88.

————. "Marenzios Madrigalen und ihre dichterischen Grundlagen." *Acta Musicologica* 8 (1936): 129–39; 9 (1937): 11–12.

————. "Werden und Wesen des Madrigals." *Bericht über den siebenten Kongress der Internationalen Gesellschaft für Musikwissenschaft, Köln 1958*, pp. 39–52. Kassel, 1959.

Fabbri, Paolo. "Tasso, Guarini e il 'divino Claudio'; componenti manieristiche nella poetica di Monteverdi." *Studi Musicali* 3 (1974): 233–51.

Federhofer, Hellmut. "Die Dissonanzbehandlung im Monteverdis Kirchenmusikalischen Werken und die Figurenlehre von Christoph Bernhard." *Congresso Internazionale sul Tema Claudio Monteverdi e il suo Tempo*, pp. 435–78. Venice and Mantua, 1968.

————. "Eine neue Queelle der Musica Reservata." *Acta Musicologica* 24 (1952): 32–45.

————. "Graz Court Musicians and their Contributions to the Parnassus musicus Ferdinandaeus (1615)." *Musica Disciplina* 9 (1955): 167–214.

————. "Ist Palestrina ein Manierist?" *Convivium musicorum: Festschrift Wolfgang Boetticher*, pp. 44–51. Berlin, 1974.

————. "Der Manierismus-Begriff in der Musikgeschichte." *Studi Musicali* 3 (1974): 37–53. Also, *Archiv für Begriffsgeschichte* 17 (1973): 206–20.

————. "Monodie und musica reservata." *Deutsches Jahrbuch der Musikwissenschaft für 1957*, pp. 30–36. Leipzig, 1958.

————. "Zum Manierismus-Problem in der Musik." *Renaissance-Muziek 1400–1600: Donum Natalicium René Bernard Lenaerts*, pp. 105–19. Louvain, 1969.

Federhofer-Königs, Renate. *Johannes Oridryus und sein Musiktraktat*. Beiträge zur rheinischen Musikgeschichte, vol. 24. Cologne, 1957.

Feller, Marilyn. "The New Style of Giulio Caccini, Member of the Florentine Camerata." *Bericht über den siebenten Kongress der Internationalen Gesellschaft für Musikwissenschaft, Köln 1958*, pp. 102–4. Kassel, 1959.

Fellerer, Karl G. "Church Music and the Council of Trent." *Musical Quarterly* 39 (1953): 576–94.

————. *Die Deklamationsrhythik in der vokalen Polyphonie des 16. Jahrhunderts*. Düsseldorf, 1928.

————. "Zur Kontrapunktlehre im Zeitalter des Humanismus." *Festschrift Arnold Geering zum 70. Geburtstag: Beiträge zur Zeit und zum Begriff des Humanismus vorwiegend aus dem Bereich der Musik*, pp. 139–48. Bern, 1972.

Ferand, Ernst T. "*Anchor che col pertire*: Die Schicksale eines berühmten Madrigals." *Festschrift Karl Gustav Fellerer*, pp. 137–54. Regensburg, 1962.

————. "Didactic Embellishment Literature in the Late Renaissance: A Survey of Sources." *Aspects of Medieval and Renaissance Music: A Birthday Offering to Gustave Reese*, pp. 154–72. New York, 1966.

————. *Die Improvisation*. Das Musikwerk, vol. 12. Cologne, 1956.

————. *Die Improvisation in der Musik*. Zurich, 1938.

————. "Improvised Vocal Counterpoint in the Late Renaissance and Early Baroque." *Annales Musicologiques* 4 (1956): 129–74.

————. "What is *Res Facta*?" *Journal of the American Musicological Society* 10 (1957): 141–50.

————. "Zum Begrif der 'compositio' im 15. und 16. Jahrhundert." *Bericht über den seibenten Kongress der Internationalen Gesellschaft für Musikwissenschaft, Köln 1958*, pp. 104–7. Kassel, 1959.

Ferguson, Wallace K. *The Renaissance in Historical Thought*. Boston, 1948.

Ficker, Rudolf von. "Beiträge zur Chromatik des 14. bis 16. Jahrhunderts." *Studien zur Musikwissenschaft* 2 (1914): 5–33.

Finney, Gretchen L. "Music: a Book of Knowledge in Renaissance England." *Studies in the Renaissance* 6 (1959): 36–63.

————. *Musical Backgrounds for English Literature: 1580–1650*. New Brunswick, N.J., 1962.

Finscher, Ludwig. "Gesualdo's 'Atonalität' und das Problem des musikalisches Manierismus." *Archiv für Musikwissenschaft* 29 (1972): 1–16.

————. "Zur Problematik des Manierismus-Begriffes in der Musikgeschichtsschreibung." *Studi Musicali* 3 (1974): 75–81.

Fletcher, Angus. *Allegory: The Theory of a Symbolic Mode*. Ithaca, 1970.

Fletcher, Iain. "From Tasso to Marino." *Nine* 7 (1951): 129–38.

Fletcher, Jefferson B. *Literature in the Italian Renaissance*. Port Washington, N.Y., 1934.

Focillon, Henri. *The Life of Forms in Art*. New York, 1948.

Forster, Leonard. *The Icy Fire: Five Studies in European Petrarchism*. New York, 1969.

Fortune, Nigel. "A Florentine Manuscript and its Place in Italian Song." *Acta Musicologica* 23 (1951): 124–36.

————. "Italian Secular Monody from 1600–1630: An Introductory Survey." *Musical Quarterly* 39 (1953): 171–95.

————. "Monteverdi and the *Seconda Prattica*." In *The Monteverdi Companion*, edited by Gerald Abraham and Nigel Fortune, pp. 192–226. London, 1968.

————. "Sigismondo d'India: an Introduction to his Life and Works." *Proceedings of the Royal Musical Association* 81 (1954–55): 29–47.

————. "Solo Song and Cantata." In *The Age of Humanism 1540–1630*, edited by Gerald Abraham. New Oxford History of Music, vol. 4, pp. 125–217. London, 1968.

Fox, Charles W. "Non-Quartal Harmony in the Renaissance," *Musical Quarterly* 31 (1945): 33–53.

Frey, Dagobert. "Der Manierismus als europäische Stilerscheinung." *Kunstkronik* 5 (1952): 242–45.

Friedländer, Walter. *Mannerism and Anti-Mannerism in Italian Painting*. New York, 1965.

Fubini, Enrico. "Il manierismo come categoria storiografica." *Studi Musicali* 3 (1974): 3–11.

Gallico, Claudio. "Aspetti musicali fra disposizione manieristica ed età del barocco." *Studi Musicali* 3 (1974): 101–4.

Ghisi, Federico. "An Early Seventeenth Century Ms. with Unpublished Italian Monodic Music by Peri, Giulio Romano and Marco da Gagliano." *Acta Musicologica* 20 (1948): 46–60.

_____. *Feste musicali della Firenze Medicea (1480–1589)*. Florence, 1939.

_____. "L'orchestra in Monteverdi." *Festschrift Karl Gustav Fellerer*, pp. 187–92. Regensburg, 1962.

_____. "La tradition musicale des fêtes florentines et les origines de l'opéra." In *Musique des intermèdes de "La Pellegrina,"* edited by D. P. Walker. Les fêtes de Florence, vol. 1, pp. XI–XXII. Paris, 1963.

Gilbert, Allan H., ed. *Literary Criticism: Plato to Dryden*. New York, 1940.

Gilbert, Felix. "The Renaissance Interest in History." In *Art, Science and History in the Renaissance*, edited by Charles S. Singleton, pp. 373–87. Baltimore, 1967.

Goldron, Romain. *Music of the Renaissance*. New York, 1968.

Goldschmidt, Hugo. *Die italienische Gesangsmethode des XVII. Jahrhunderts und ihre Bedeutung für die Gegenwart*. Breslau, 1890.

_____. "Verzierungen, Veränderungen und Passaggien im 16. und 17. Jahrhundert, und ihre Bedeutungsbesprochen nach zwei bisher unbekannten Quellen." *Monatshefte für Musikgeschichte* 23 (1891): 111–26.

Gombrich, E. H. *Art and Illusion*. New York, 1962.

_____. "*Icones symbolicae*: The Visual Image in Neo-Platonic Thought." *Journal of Warburg and Courtauld Institute* 11 (1948): 163–92.

_____. "Introduction: the Historiographic Background." *The Renaissance and Mannerism: Studies in Western Art*. Acts of the Twentieth International Congress of the History of Art, vol. 2, pp. 163–73. Princeton, 1963.

_____. "The Leaven of Criticism in Renaissance Art." In *Art, Science and History of the Renaissance*, edited by Charles S. Singleton, pp. 3–42. Baltimore, 1967.

_____. *Norm and Form: Studies in the Art of the Renaissance*. London, 1966.

Gray, Cecil and Heseltine, Philip. *Carlo Gesualdo, Prince of Venosa: Musician and Murderer*. London, 1928.

Grendler, Paul F. *Critics of the Italian World (1530–1560)*. Madison, 1969.

Grillo, Giacomo. *Poets at the Court of Ferrara*. Boston, 1943.

Grout, Donald J. *A Short History of Opera*. New York, 1960.

Guerrieri Crocetti, Camillo. *G. B. Giraldi ed il pensiero critico del sec. XVI*. Milan and Genoa, 1932.

Gurlitt, Willibald. "Der Begriff der Sortisatio in der deutschen Kompositionslehre des 16. Jahrhunderts." *Musikgeschichte und Gegenwart*, vol. 1, pp. 93–104. Wiesbaden, 1966.

_____. "Die Kompositionslehre des deutschen 16. und 17. Jahrhundert." *Musikgeschichte und Gegenwart*, vol. 1, pp. 82–92. Wiesbaden, 1966.

Haar, James. "*Altro non è il mio amor.*" *Words and Music: The Scholar's View. (A Medley of Problems and Solutions Compiled in Honor of A. Tillman Merritt by Sundry Hands)*, pp. 93–114. Cambridge, Mass., 1972.

⸻. "Classicism and Mannerism in 16th-Century Music." *International Review of Music Aesthetics and Sociology* 1 (1970): 55–67.

⸻. "False Relations and Chromaticism in Sixteenth-Century Music." *Journal of the American Musicological Society* 30 (1977): 391–418.

⸻. "A Gift of Madrigals to Cosimo I: The MS. Florence, Bibl. Naz. Centrale, Magl. XIX. 130." *Rivista Italiana di Musicologia* 1 (1966): 167–89.

⸻. "Notes on the 'Dialogo della Musica' of Antonfrancesco Doni." *Music and Letters* 47 (1966): 198–224.

⸻. "On Musical Games in the Sixteenth Century." *Journal of the American Musicological Society* 15 (1962): 22–34.

⸻. "*Pace non trovo*: A Study in Literary and Musical Parody." *Musica Disciplina* 20 (1966): 95–149.

⸻. "Self-Consciousness about Style, Form and Genre in 16th-Century Music." *Studi Musicali* 3 (1974): 219–27.

⸻. "Zarlino's Definition of Fugue and Imitation." *Journal of the American Musicological Society* 24 (1971): 226–54.

Haas, Robert. *Die Musik des Barocks.* Handbuch der Musikwissenschaft. Potsdam, 1929.

Haberl, F. X. "Giovanni Maria Nanino." *Kirchenmusikalisches Jahrbuch* 6 (1891): 81–97.

Hager, Emanuela. *Übersetzungen und Nachdichtungen von Sonetten Petrarcas in der europäischen Lyrik des 16. Jahrhunderts.* Vienna, 1974.

Hager, Werner. "Zur Raumstruktur der Manierismus in der italienischen Architektur." *Festschrift Martin Wackernagel*, pp. 112–40. Cologne, 1958.

Hagstrum, Jean H. *The Sister Arts: The Tradition of Literary Pictorialism and English Poetry from Dryden to Gray.* Chicago, 1958.

Hall, Vernon, Jr. *Renaissance Literary Criticism: A Study of Its Social Content.* New York, 1945.

Hallmark, Rufus. "An Unknown English Treatise of the 16th Century." *Journal of the American Musicological Society* 22 (1969): 273–74.

Hamburger, Paul. "The Ornamentation in the Works of Palestrina." *Acta Musicologica* 22 (1950): 128–47.

Hanak, Miroslav J. "The Emergence of Baroque Mentality and its Cultural Impact on Western Europe after 1550." *Journal of Aesthetics and Art Criticism* 28 (1970): 315–26.

Hannas, Ruth. "Cerone, Philosopher and Teacher." *Musical Quarterly* 21 (1935): 408–22.

Hanning, Barbara R. "Apologia pro Ottavio Rinuccini." *Journal of the American Musicological Society* 26 (1973): 240–62.

―――――. "The Influence of Humanist Thought and Italian Renaissance Poetry on the Formation of Opera." Ph.D. dissertation, Yale University, 1969.

Harman, Alec, and Milner, Anthony. *Late Renaissance and Baroque Music.* Pt. II. New York, 1969.

Harrán, Don. "'Mannerism' in the Cinquecento Madrigal?" *Musical Quarterly* 55 (1969): 521–44.

―――――. "New Evidence for Musica Ficta: The Cautionary Sign." *Journal of the American Musicological Society* 29 (1976): 77–98.

―――――. "New Light on the Question of Text Underlay Prior to Zarlino." *Acta Musicologica* 45 (1973): 24–56.

―――――. "Rore and the Madrigale Cromatico." *Music Review* 34 (1973): 66–81.

―――――. "The 'Sack of Rome' Set to Music." *Renaissance Quarterly* 23 (1970): 412–21.

―――――. "Some Early Examples of the Madrigale Cromatico." *Acta Musicologica* 41 (1969): 240–46.

―――――. "Towards a Definition of the Early Secular Dialogue." *Music and Letters* 51 (1970): 37–50.

―――――. "Verse Types in the Early Madrigal." *Journal of the American Musicological Society* 22 (1969): 27–53.

―――――. "Vicentino and His Rules of Text Underlay." *Musical Quarterly* 59 (1973): 620–32.

Hartmann, Arnold, Jr. "Battista Guarini and *Il pastor fido.*" *Musical Quarterly* 39 (1953): 415–25.

Hartt, Frederick. "Power and the Individual in Mannerist Art." *The Renaissance and Mannerism: Studies in Western Art.* Acts of the Twentieth International Congress of the History of Art, vol. 2, pp. 222–38. Princeton, 1963.

Haskell, Francis. "The Moment of Mannerism." *Encounter* 35 (1970): 69–73.

Hathaway, Baxter. *The Age of Criticism: The Late Renaissance in Italy.* Ithaca, 1962.

―――――. *Marvels and Commonplaces: Renaissance Literary Criticism.* New York, 1968.

Hauser, Arnold. *Mannerism: The Crisis of the Renaissance and the Origin of Modern Art.* 2 vols. London, 1965.

―――――. *The Social History of Art.* Vol. 2, *Renaissance, Mannerism, Baroque.* London, 1962.

Hay, Denis. *The Italian Renaissance in its Historical Background.* Cambridge, 1966.

Haydn, Hiram. *The Counter-Renaissance.* New York, 1950.

Heartz, Daniel. "Les goûts réunis or the Worlds of the Madrigal and the

Chanson Confronted." In *Chanson and Madrigal 1480–1530*, edited by J. Haar, pp. 88–138. Cambridge, Mass., 1964.

Heer, Friedrich. *Europäische Geistesgeschichte*. Stuttgart, 1953.

Hermelinck, Siegfried. "Das rhythmische Gefüge in Monteverdis Ciaccona 'Zefiro torna.'" *Congresso Internazionale sul Tema Claudio Monteverdi e il suo Tempo*, pp. 323–34. Venice and Mantua, 1968.

Hersh, Donald L. (Harrán). "Verdelot and the Early Madrigal." Ph.D. dissertation, University of California at Berkeley, 1963.

Hertzmann, Erich. *Adrian Willaert in der weltlichen Vokalmusik seiner Zeit*. Leipzig, 1931.

Heuss, Alfred. "Ein Beitrag zu dem Thema: Monteverdi als Charakteristiker i seinen Madrigalen." *Festschrift Rochus Freiherrn von Liliencron*, pp. 93–109. Leipzig, 1910.

Heyl, Bernard C. "Meanings of Baroque." *Journal of Aesthetics and Art Criticism* 19 (1960–61): 275–85.

Hilbrich, Paul D. "The Aesthetics of the Counter-Reformation and Religious Painting and Music in Bologna 1565–1615." Ph.D. dissertation, Ohio University, 1969.

Hilmar, Ernst. "Ergänzungen zu Emil Vogels 'Bibliothek der gedruckten weltlichen Vocalmusik Italiens, aus den Jahren 1500–1700.'" *Analecta Musicologica* 4 (1967): 154–206.

————. "Weitere Ergänzungen zu Emil Vogels 'Bibliothek der gedruckten weltlichen Vocalmusik Italiens, aus den Jahren 1500–1700.'" *Analecta Musicologica* 5 (1968): 295–98.

Hitchcock, H. Wiley. "Caccini's 'Other' *Nuove Musiche*." *Journal of the American Musicological Society* 27 (1974): 438–60.

————. "Depriving Caccini of a Musical Pastime." *Journal of the American Musicological Society* 25 (1972): 58–78.

————. "Vocal Ornamentation in Caccini's *Nuove Musiche*." *Musical Quarterly* 56 (1970): 389–404.

Hocke, Gustav R. *Manierismus in der Literatur: Sprach-Alchemie und esoterische Kombinationskunst*. Hamburg, 1959.

————. *Der Neomanierismus: Malerei der Gegenwart*. Munich, 1975.

————. *Die Welt als Labyrinth: Manier und Manie in der europäischen Kunst*. Hamburg, 1957.

Hockley, Nancy. "Bartolomeo Barberino e i primordi della monodia." *Rivista Italiana di Musicologia* 7 (1972): 82–102.

Hoerner, Margarete. "Manierismus." *Zeitschrift für Ästhetik und allgemeine Kunstwissenschaft* 17 (1924): 262–68.

————. "Der Manierismus als künstlerische Anschauungsform." *Zeitschrift für Ästhetik und allgemeine Kunstwissenschaft* 22 (1928): 200–10.

Hoffmann, Hans. *Hochrenaissance, Manierismus, Frühbarock: Die italienischen Kunst des 16. Jahrhunderts*. Zurich, 1938.

Hol, Johannes. "L'Amfiparnasso e le veglie di Siena." *Rivista Musicale Italiana* 40 (1936): 3–22.

————. "Cipriano de Rore." *Festschrift Karl Nef*, pp. 139–49. Zurich, 1933.

————. "Horatio Vecchi." *Rivista Musicale Italiana* 37 (1930): 59–73.

————. *Horatio Vecchi als weltlicher Komponist*. Basel, 1917.

————. "Horatio Vecchi et l'évolution créatrice." *Gedenkboek aange-boden aan Dr. D. F. Scheurleer*, pp. 159–67. The Hague, 1925.

————. *Horatio Vecchi's weltlich Werke*. Strasbourg, 1934.

Hollander, John. *The Untuning of the Sky*. Princeton, 1961. New York, 1970.

Holst, Niels von. *Die deutsche Bildnismalerei zur Zeit des Manierismus*. Strasbourg, 1930.

Holt, Elizabeth G., ed. *A Documentary History of Art*. Vol. 2, *Michelangelo and the Mannerists: The Baroque and the Eighteenth Century*. Garden City, N.Y., 1958.

————. *Literary Sources of Art History*. Princeton, 1947.

Horsley, Imogene. "The Diminutions in Composition and Theory of Composition." *Acta Musicologica* 35 (1963): 124–53.

————. "Fugue and Mode in 16th-Century Vocal Polyphony." *Aspects of Medieval and Renaissance Music: A Birthday Offering to Gustave Reese*, pp. 406–22. New York, 1966.

————. "Improvised Embellishment in the Performance of Renaissance Polyphonic Music." *Journal of the American Musicological Society* 4 (1951): 3–19.

————. "The 16th-Century Variation: A New Historical Survey." *Journal of the American Musicological Society* 12 (1959): 118–22.

Huber, Kurt. *Ivo de Vento*. Lindenberg, 1918.

Hucke, Helmut. "Palestrina als Authorität und Vorbild im 17. Jahrhundert." *Congresso Internazionale sul Tema Claudio Monteverdi e il suo Tempo*, pp. 253–61. Venice and Mantua, 1968.

————. "Das Problem des Manierismus in der Musik." *Literaturwissenschaftliches Jahrbuch des Görres-Gesellschaft* 2 (1961): 219–38.

Huizinga, Johan. *Homo ludens*. Boston, 1955.

Hurstfield, Joel, ed. *The Reformation Crisis*. London, 1965.

Hutton, Edward. *Aretino, Scourge of Princes*. London, 1922.

Isgro, Robert M. "The First and Second Practices of Monteverdi: their Relation to Contemporary Theory." Ph.D. dissertation, University of Southern California, 1968.

Jackson, Roland. "On Frescobaldi's Chromaticism and its Background." *Musical Quarterly* 57 (1971): 255–69.

Jensen, H. James. *The Muses' Concord: Literature, Music, and the Visual Arts in the Baroque Age*. Bloomington, 1976.

Jeppesen, Knud. *Counterpoint*. New York, 1939.

————. "A Forgotten Master of the Early 16th Century: Gaspar de Albertis." *Musical Quarterly* 44 (1958): 311–28.

————. "Eine musikhistorische Korrespondenz des frühesten Cinquecento." *Acta Musicologica* 13 (1941): 13–38.

_____. "Some Remarks to 'The Ornamentation in the Works of Palestrina' by Paul Hamburger." *Acta Musicologica* 22 (1950): 148–52.

Johnson, Margaret F. "Agazzari's *Eumelio*, a 'dramma pastorale.'" *Musical Quarterly* 57 (1971): 491–505.

Kaufmann, Henry W. "Art for the Wedding of Cosimo de'Medici and Eleanora of Toledo (1539)." *Paragone* 243 (1970): 52–67.

_____. "A 'Diatonic' and a 'Chromatic' Madrigal by Giulio Fiesco." *Aspects of Medieval and Renaissance Music: A Birthday Offering to Gustave Reese*, pp. 474–88. New York, 1966.

_____. *The Life and Works of Nicola Vicentino*. American Institute of Musicology, 1966.

_____. "More on the Tuning of the Archicembalo." *Journal of the American Musicological Society* 23 (1970): 84–94.

_____. "Music for a Noble Florentine Wedding (1539)." *Words and Music: The Scholar's View. (A Medley of Problems and Solutions Compiled in Honor of A. Tillman Merritt by Sundry Hands)*, pp. 161–88. Cambridge, Mass., 1972.

_____. "Vicentino's *Arciorgano*: An Annotated Translation." *Journal of Music Theory* 5 (1961): 32–53.

Keiner, Ferdinand. *Die Madrigale Gesualdos von Venosa*. Leipzig, 1914.

Kenton, Egon. "A Faded Laurel Wreath." *Aspects of Medieval and Renaissance Music: A Birthday Offering to Gustave Reese*, pp. 500–18. New York, 1966.

_____. "The Instrumental Works of Giovanni Gabrieli's Late Period." *Journal of the American Musicological Society* 9 (1956): 234–36.

_____. "The Late Style of Giovanni Gabrieli." *Musical Quarterly* 48 (1962): 427–43.

_____. *Life and Works of Giovanni Gabrieli*. American Institute of Musicology, 1967.

_____. "A Note of the Classification of 16th-Century Music." *Musical Quarterly* 38 (1952): 202–14.

Kerman, Joseph. *The Elizabethan Madrigal: A Comparative Study*. New York, 1962.

Kermode, Frank. *Romantic Image*. London, 1957.

King, Alexander H. *Four Hundred Years of Music Printing*. London, 1964.

Kinkeldey, Otto. *A Jewish Dancing Master of the Renaissance: Guglielmo Ebreo*. Brooklyn, N.Y., 1966.

_____. "Luzzasco Luzzaschi's Solo-Madrigale mir Klavierbegleitung." *Sammelbände der Internationalen Musikgesellschaft* 9 (1908): 538–65.

_____. *Orgel und Klavier in der Musik des 16. Jahrhunderts*. Leipzig, 1910.

Kirby, Frank E. "Hermann Finck on Methods of Performance." *Music and Letters* 42 (1961): 212–20.

_____. "Hermann Finck's *Practica musica*: A Comparative Study in

16th-Century Musical Theory." Ph.D. dissertation, Yale University, 1957.

Kiwi, Edith. *Studien zur Geschichte des italienischen Liedmadrigals im XVI. Jahrhundert*. Berlin, 1937.

Klein, Robert and Zerner, Henri, eds. *Italian Art 1500–1600: Sources and Documents*. Englewood Cliffs, N.J., 1966.

Kramer, Margarethe. *Beiträge zu einer Geschichte des Affektbegriffs in der Musik von 1550–1700*. Halle, 1924.

Krebs, Carl. "Girolamo Diruta's Transilvano." *Vierteljahrschrift für Musikwissenschaft* 8 (1892):307–88.

Kristeller, Paul O. *Eight Philosophers of the Italian Renaissance*. Stanford, 1964.

———. "The Modern System of the Arts." *Renaissance Thought II: Papers on Humanism and the Arts*, pp. 163–227. New York, 1965.

———. "Music and Learning in the Early Italian Renaissance." *Journal of Renaissance and Baroque Music* 1 (1947):255–74. Reprinted in *Renaissance Thought II: Papers on Humanism and the Arts*, pp. 142–62. New York, 1965.

———. "Philosophy and Humanism in Renaissance Perspective." In *The Renaissance Image of Man and the World*, edited by Bernard O'Kelley, pp. 29–51. Columbus, 1966.

———. *Renaissance Thought: The Classic, Scholastic and Humanistic Strains*. New York, 1961.

Kroyer, Theodor. *Die Anfänge der Chromatik im italienischen Madrigal des XVI. Jahrhunderts*. Leipzig, 1902.

———. "Dialog und Echo in der alten Chormusik." *Jahrbuch Musikbibliothek Peters* 16 (1909): 13–32.

———. "Die threnodische Bedeutung der Quart in der Mensuralmusik." *Kongressbericht Basel 1924*, pp. 231–42. Leipzig, 1925.

———. "Von der Musica Reservata des 16. Jahrhunderts." *Festschrift Heinrich Wölfflin zum siebzigsten Geburtstag*, pp. 127–44. Dresden, 1935.

———. "Zwischen Renaissance und Barock." *Jahrbuch Musikbibliothek Peters* 34 (1927): 45–54.

Kuhn, Max. *Die Verzierungs-Kunst in der Gesangs-Musik des XVI. und XVII. Jahrhunderts (1535–1650)*. Leipzig, 1902.

Kunze, Stefan. "Die Entstehung des Concertoprinzips im Spätwerk Giovanni Gabrielis." *Archiv für Musikwissenschaft* 21 (1964): 81–110.

———. *Die Instrumentalmusik Giovanni Gabrielis*. Tutzing, 1963.

Lang, Paul H. *Music in Western Civilization*. New York, 1941.

Lange, Klaus-Peter. *Theoretiker des literarischen Manierismus*. Munich, 1968.

Lanham, Richard S. *The Motives of Eloquence: Literary Rhetoric in the Renaissance*. New Haven, 1976.

Le Coat, Gerard. *The Rhetoric of the Arts, 1550–1650*. Comparative Literature Series XVIII, vol. 3. Frankfurt am Main, 1975.

Ledda, Primarosa. "Giovanni Battista Doni: il *De praestantia musicae veteris.*" *Congresso Internazionale sul Tema Claudio Monteverdi e il suo Tempo*, pp. 409–20. Venice and Mantua, 1968.

Lee, Barbara. "Giovanni Maria Lanfranco's *Scintille di musica* and its Relation to 16th-Century Music Theory." Ph.D. dissertation, Cornell University, 1961.

Lee, M. Owen. "'Orpheus and Euridice': Blueprint for Opera." *Canadian Music Journal* 6 (1962): 23–36.

Lee, Rensselaer W. "*Ut pictura poesis*: the Humanistic Theory of Painting." *Art Bulletin* 22 (1940): 197–269.

Legrand, Jacques. "A la découverte du maniérisme européen." *Critique* 152 (1960): 34–47.

Leichtentritt, Hugo. "Claudio Monteverdi als Madrigalkomponist." *Sammelbände der Internationalen Musikgesellschaft* 11 (1910): 255–91.

_____. "Musica riservata." *Bulletin of the American Musicological Society* 6 (1942): 18–19.

Lenaerts, Réne B. "Parodia, Reservata-Kunst en muzikaal symbolisme." *Liber amicorum Charles van den Borren*, pp. 107–12. Antwerp, 1964.

Leuchtmann, Horst. *Die musikalische Wertausdeutung in den Motetten des Magnum Opus Musicum von Orlando di Lasso*. Strasbourg, 1959.

Levitan, Joseph S. "Adrian Willaert's Famous Duo 'Quidnam ebrietas.'" *Tijdschrift voor Nederlandsche Musikgeschiedenis* 15 (1937): 166–233.

Levy, Kenneth J. "Costeley's Chromatic Chansons." *Annales Musicologiques* 3 (1955): 213–33.

Lichtenhahn, Ernst. "'Ars perfecta'—zu Glareans Auffassung der Musikgeschichte." *Festschrift Arnold Geering zum 70. Geburtstag: Beiträge zur Zeit und zum Begriff des Humanismus vorwiegend aus dem Bereich der Musik*, pp. 129–38. Bern, 1972.

Lockwood, Lewis H. "On 'Mannerism' and 'Renaissance' as Terms and Concepts in Music History." *Studi Musicali* 3 (1974): 85–96.

_____. "On 'Parody' as Term and Concept in 16th-Century Music." *Aspects of Medieval and Renaissance Music: A Birthday Offering to Gustave Reese*, pp. 560–75. New York, 1966.

_____. "A Sample Problem of *Musica Ficta*: Willaert's *Pater noster.*" *Studies in Music History: Essays for Oliver Strunk*, pp. 161–81. Princeton, 1968.

_____. "Vincenzo Ruffo and Musical Reform after the Council of Trent." *Musical Quarterly* 43 (1957): 342–71.

_____. "Vincenzo Ruffo and Two Patrons of Music at Milan: Alfonso d'Avalos and Cardinal Carlo Borromeo." *Il duomo di Milano: Congresso Internazionale*. Atti, vol. 2, pp. 23–34. Milan, 1969.

_____, ed. *Pope Marcellus Mass*. New York, 1975.

Longhi, Roberto. "Comprimarij spagnoli della maniera italiana." *Paragone* 4 (1953): 3–15.

Lotz, Wolfgang. "Mannerism in Architecture: Changing Aspects." *The Renaissance and Mannerism: Studies in Western Art*. Acts of the Twentieth International Congress of the History of Art, vol. 2, pp. 239–46. Princeton, 1963.

Lowinsky, Edward E. "Adrian Willaert's Chromatic 'Duo' Reexamined." *Tijdschrift voor Muziekwetenschap* 18 (1956): 1–36.

―――――. "Das Antwerper Motettenbuch Orlando di Lasso's und seine Beziehungen zum Motettenschaffen der niederländischen Zeitgenossen." *Tijdschrift der Vereenigung voor Nederlandsche Muziekgeschiedenis* 14 (1935): 185–229.

―――――. "Ascanio Sforza's Life. A Key to Josquin's Biography and an Aid to the Chronology of his Works." In *Josquin des Prez: Proceedings of the International Josquin Festival-Conference 1971*, edited by Edward E. Lowinsky and Bonnie J. Blackburn, pp. 31–75. London, 1976.

―――――. "The Concept of Physical and Musical Space in the Renaissance." *Papers Read by Members of the American Musicological Society* (1941): 57–84.

―――――. "Early Scores in Manuscript." *Journal of the American Musicological Society* 13 (1960): 126–73.

―――――. "Echoes of Adrian Willaert's Chromatic 'Duo' in Sixteenth- and Seventeenth-Century Compositions." *Studies in Music History: Essays for Oliver Strunk*, pp. 183–238. Princeton, 1968.

―――――. "The Function of Conflicting Signatures in Early Polyphonic Music." *Musical Quarterly* 31 (1945): 227–60.

―――――. "The Goddess Fortuna in Music." *Musical Quarterly* 29 (1943): 45–77.

―――――. "Josquin Des Prez and Ascanio Sforza." *Il duomo di Milano: Congresso Internazionale*. Atti, vol. 2, pp. 17–22. Milan, 1969.

―――――. "Matthaeus Greiter's *Fortuna*: An Experiment in Chromaticism and in Musical Iconography." *Musical Quarterly* 42 (1956): 500–19; 43 (1957): 68–85.

―――――. "Music of the Renaissance as Viewed by Renaissance Musicians." In *The Renaissance Image of Man and the World*, edited by Bernard O'Kelley, pp. 129–77. Columbus, 1966.

―――――. "The Musical Avant-Garde of the Renaissance or: The Peril and Profit of Foresight." In *Art, Science and History in the Renaissance*, edited by Charles S. Singleton, pp. 113–62. Baltimore, 1967.

―――――. "Musical Genius—Evolution and Origins of a Concept." *Musical Quarterly* 50 (1964): 321–40 and 476–95.

―――――. "The Problem of Mannerism in Music: An Attempt at a Definition." *Studi Musicali* 3 (1974): 131–218.

―――――. "Problems in Adrian Willaert's Iconography." *Aspects of Medieval and Renaissance Music: A Birthday Offering to Gustave Reese*, pp. 376–94. New York, 1966.

————. "Renaissance Writings on Music Theory (1964)." *Renaissance News* 18 (1964): 358–70.

————. *Secret Chromatic Art in the Netherlands Motet*. New York, 1946; 1967.

————. *Tonality and Atonality in Sixteenth-Century Music*. Berkeley, 1961.

————. "Towards a New Interpretation of 'Musica Reservata.'" *Bulletin of the American Musicological Society* 7 (1943): 4–5.

————. "A Treatise on Text Underlay by a German Disciple of Francisco de Salinas." *Festschrift Heinrich Besseler*, pp. 231–51. Leipzig, 1961.

————. "The Use of Scores by Sixteenth Century Musicians." *Journal of the American Musicological Society* 1 (1948): 17–23.

————. "Zur Frage der Deklamationsrhythmik in der a cappella-Musik des 16. Jahrhunderts." *Acta Musicologica* 7 (1935): 62–67.

MacClintock, Carol. *Giaches de Wert: Life and Works*. American Institute of Musicology, 1966.

————. "Giaches de Wert: virtuoso raro." *Journal of the American Musicological Society* 7 (1954): 248.

————. "The Monodies of Francesco Rasi." *Journal of the American Musicological Society* 14 (1961): 31–36.

————. "New Light on Giaches de Wert." *Aspects of Medieval and Renaissance Music: A Birthday Offering to Gustave Reese*, pp. 595–602. New York, 1966.

————. "Some Notes on the Secular Music of Giaches de Wert." *Musica Disciplina* 10 (1956): 106–41.

Mace, Dean T. "Pietro Bembo and the Literary Origins of the Italian Madrigal." *Musical Quarterly* 55 (1969): 65–86.

Mahood, Molly M. *Poetry and Humanism*. London, 1950.

Maione, Italo. "Tasso-Monteverdi: *Il Combattimento di Tancredi e Clorinda*." *Rassegna Musicale* 3 (1930): 206–15.

Malipiero, Gian F. *Antonfrancesco Doni musico*. Venice, 1946.

Maniates, Maria R. "Maniera: The Central Issue in 16th-Century Musical Controversy." *Journal of the Canadian Association of University Schools of Music* 7 (1977): 1–30.

————. "Mannerist Composition in Franco-Flemish Polyphony." *Musical Quarterly* 42 (1966): 17–36.

————. "Musical Mannerism: Effeteness or Virility?" *Musical Quarterly* 57 (1971): 270–93.

————. Review of W. Elders, *Studien zue Symbolik in der Musik der Alten Niederländer*. *Musical Quarterly* 58 (1972): 482–95.

————. "The Sacred Music of Nicolas Gombert." *Canadian Music Journal* 6 (1962): 25–38.

————. "Vicentino's 'Incerta et Occulta Scientia' Re-examined." *Journal of the American Musicological Society* 28 (1975): 335–51.

Marco, Guy A. *The Earliest Music Printers of Continental Europe*. Bibliographical Society of the University of Virginia, 1962.

Marco, Guy A. and Palisca, Claude V., eds. *The Art of Counterpoint: Gioseffo Zarlino.* New Haven, 1968.

Marshall, George R. "The Harmonic Laws in the Madrigals of Carlo Gesualdo." Ph.D. dissertation, New York University, 1956.

Massera, Giuseppe. "Dalle 'imperfezioni' alle 'perfezioni' della moderna musica." *Congresso Internazionale sul Tema Claudio Monteverdi e il suo Tempo,* pp. 397–408. Venice and Mantua, 1968.

———. *De Musica* (G. Anselmo). Florence, 1961.

———. *La "mano musicale perfetto" di Fra Francesco de Brugis.* Florence, 1963.

Mattingly, Garrett. *Renaissance Diplomacy.* Boston, 1971.

Maze, Nancy. "Tenbury Ms. 1018: A Way to Caccini's Art of Embellishment." *Journal of the American Musicological Society* 9 (1956): 61–63.

Mazzeo, Joseph A. "Metaphysical Poetry and the Poetic of Correspondence." *Journal of the History of Ideas* 14 (1953): 221–34.

Mazzoli, Ettore. "Literature—Torquato Tasso: An Introduction." In *The Late Italian Renaissance,* edited by Eric Cochran, pp. 134–48. New York, 1970.

McLuhan, Marshall. *The Gutenberg Galaxy.* Toronto, 1962.

Meier, Bernhard. "Alter und neuer Stil in lateinisch textierten Werken von Orlando di Lasso." *Archiv für Musikwissenschaft* 15 (1958): 151–61.

———. "Eine weitere Quelle der Musica Reservata." *Die Musikforschung* 8 (1955): 83–85.

———. "Hieroglyphisches in der Musik des 16. Jahrhunderts." *Kongressbericht Kassel 1962,* pp. 127–29. Kassel, 1963.

———. "Melodie-zitate in der Musik des 16. Jahrhunderts." *Tijdschrift der Vereeniging voor Nederlandsche Muziekgeschiedenis* 20 (1967–68): 1–19.

———. "The Musica Reservata of Adrianus Petit Coclico and its Relationship to Josquin." *Musica Disciplina* 10 (1956): 67–105.

———. "Musiktheorie und Musik im 16. Jahrhundert." *Kongressbericht Kassel 1962,* pp. 356–59. Kassel, 1963.

———. "Reservata-Probleme, ein Bericht." *Acta Musicologica* 30 (1958): 77–89.

———. *Die Tonarten der klassischen Vokalpolyphonie.* Utrecht, 1974.

———. "Wortausdeutung und Tonalität bei Orlando di Lasso." *Kirchenmusikalisches Jahrbuch* 47 (1963): 75–104.

Melchiori, Giorgio. *The Tightrope Walkers: Studies in Mannerism in Modern English Literature.* London, 1956.

Menapace Brisca, Lidia. "L'arguta et ingegnosa elocuzione." *Aevum* 28 (1954): 45–60.

Meyer, Ernst H. "Concerted Instrumental Music." In *The Age of*

Humanism 1540–1630, edited by Gerald Abraham. New Oxford History of Music, vol. 4, pp. 550–601. London, 1968.

Meyer-Baer, Kathi. "Nicholas of Cusa on the Meaning of Music." *Journal of Aesthetics and Art Criticism* 5 (1946–47): 301–8.

Michel, Artur. "The Earliest Dance Manuals." *Medievalia et Humanistica* 3 (1945): 117–31.

Millon, Henry. "The Architectural Theory of Francesco di Giorgio." *Art Bulletin* 40 (1958): 275–61. Reprinted in *Renaissance Art*, edited by Creighton Gilbert, pp. 133–47. New York, 1973.

Milner, Anthony. *The Musical Aesthetics of the Baroque*. Hull, 1960.

Minor, Andrew C. and Mitchell, Bonner, eds. *A Renaissance Entertainment: Festivities for the Marriage of Cosimo I, Duke of Florence, in 1539*. Columbia, 1968.

Mirollo, James V. "The Mannered and the Mannerist in Late Renaissance Literature." *The Meaning of Mannerism*, pp. 7–24. Hanover, N.H., 1972.

————. *The Poet of the Marvelous: Giambattista Marino*. New York, 1963.

Miskimin, Harry E. *The Economy of Later Renaissance Europe 1460–1600*. Cambridge, 1977.

Mompellio, Federico. " 'Opere recitative, balletti et inventioni' di Sigismondo d'India per la corte del Savioa." *Collectanea Historiae Musicae*, vol. 2, pp. 291–96. Florence, 1957.

————. "Sigismondo d'India e il suo primo libro de musiche da cantar solo." *Collectanea Historiae Musicae*, vol. 1, pp. 113–34. Florence, 1953.

————, ed. *Sigismondo d'India: Madrigale a cinque voci libro I*. I Classici Musicali Italiani, vol. 10. Milan, 1942.

Monterosso, Raffaello. "Claudio Monteverdi e il suo tempo." *Congresso Internazionale sul Tema Claudio Monteverdi e il suo Tempo*, pp. 17–32. Venice and Mantua, 1968.

————. "L'estetica di Gioseffo Zarlino." *Chigiana* 24 (1967): 13–28.

————. "Strutture ritmiche nel madrigale cinquecentesco." *Studi Musicali* (1974): 287–308.

Mourgues, Odette de. *Metaphysical, Baroque, and Précieux Poetry*. Oxford, 1953.

Müller, Karl F. *Die Technik der Ausdrucksdarstellung in Monteverdis monodischen Frühwerken*. Berlin, 1931.

Murphy, Richard M. "Fantasia and Ricercare in the Sixteenth Century." Ph.D. dissertation, Yale University, 1954.

Murray, Linda. *The Late Renaissance and Mannerism*. New York, 1967.

Musiol, Josef. *Cyprian de Rore, ein Meister der venezianischen Schule*. Breslau, 1932.

Nagler, Alois. *Theatre Festivals of the Medici 1539–1637*. New Haven, 1964.

Newcomb, Anthony. "Carlo Gesualdo and a Musical Correspondence of 1594." *Musical Quarterly* 54 (1968): 409–36.

———. "Editions of Willaert's *Musica Nova*: New Evidence, New Speculations." *Journal of the American Musicological Society* 26 (1973): 132–45.

———. Review of A. Cavicchi, ed., *Madrigali per cantare et sonare*. *Journal of the American Musicological Society* 21 (1968): 222–26.

———. "The Three Anthologies for Laura Peverara." *Rivista Italiana di Musicologia* 10 (1975): 329–45.

———. "The 'Three Ladies of Ferrara' in the Early 1580's." *Abstracts of Papers Read at the Thirty-Fifth Annual Meeting of the American Musicological Society*, pp. 17–18. St. Louis, 1967.

Nicco Fasola, Giusta. "Manierismo e architettura." *Studi Vasariani* 1950, pp. 175–80. Florence, 1952.

———. "Storiografica del manierismo." *Scritti e storia dell'arte in onore di Lionello Venturi*, vol. 1, pp. 429–77. Rome, 1956.

Nicolson, Margery H. *The Breaking of the Circle*. New York, 1960.

Nuernberger, Louis D. "The Five-Voiced Madrigals of Cipriano de Rore." Ph.D. dissertation, University of Michigan, 1963.

Obortello, Alfredo. *Madrigali italiani in Inghilterra*. Milan, 1949.

Olschki, Leonardo. *Bildung und Wissenschaft im Zeitalter der Renaissance in Italien*. Geschichte der neusprachlichen wissenschaftlichen Literatur, vol. 2. Leipzig, 1922.

Osthoff, Helmut. "Domenico Mazzochis Vergil-Kompositionen." *Festschrift Karl Gustav Fellerer*, pp. 407–16. Regensburg, 1962.

———. "Einwirkungen der Gegenreformation auf die Musik des 16. Jahrhunderts." *Jahrbuch Musikbibliothek Peters* 41 (1934): 32–50.

———. *Josquin Desprez*. 2 vols. Tutzing, 1962.

———. *Die Niederländer und das deutsche Lied (1400–1640)*. Berlin, 1938.

———. "Vergils Aeneis in der Musik von Josquin des Prez bis Orlando di Lasso." *Archiv für Musikwissenschaft* 11 (1954): 85–102.

Osthoff, Wolfgang. *Das dramatische Spätwerk Claudio Monteverdis*. Munich, 1959.

———. *Theatergesang und darstellende Musik in der italienischen Renaissance (15. und 16. Jahrhundert)*. 2 vols. Tutzing, 1969.

Palisca, Claude V. "The Alterati of Florence: Pioneers in the Theory of Dramatic Music." *New Looks at Italian Opera: Essays in Honor of Donald J. Grout*, pp. 9–38. Ithaca, 1968.

———. "The Artusi-Monteverdi Controversy." In *The Monteverdi Companion*, edited by Denis Arnold and Nigel Fortune, pp. 133–66. London, 1968.

———. *Baroque Music*. Englewood Cliffs, N.J., 1968.

———. "The Beginnings of Baroque Music: Its Roots in Sixteenth-Century Theory and Polemics." Ph.D. dissertation, Harvard University, 1953.

———. "A Clarification of 'Musica Reservata' in Jean Taisnier's 'Astrologiae' 1559." *Acta Musicologica* 31 (1959): 133–61.

———. "Girolamo Mei, Mentor to the Florentine Camerata." *Musical Quarterly* 40 (1954): 1–20.

———. *Girolamo Mei: Letters on Ancient and Modern Music to Vincenzo Galilei and Giovanni Bardi.* American Institute of Musicology, 1960.

———. "Marco Scacchi's Defense of Modern Music (1649)." *Words and Music: The Scholar's View. (A Medley of Problems and Solutions Compiled in Honor of A. Tillman Merritt by Sundry Hands)*, pp. 189–235. Cambridge, Mass., 1972.

———. "The *Musica* of Erasmus of Höritz." *Aspects of Medieval and Renaissance Music: A Birthday Offering to Gustave Reese*, pp. 628–48. New York, 1966.

———. "Musica Reservata and Osservata: A Critical Review." *Journal of the American Musicological Society* 7 (1954): 168–69.

———. "Musical Asides in the Diplomatic Correspondence of Emilio de'Cavalieri." *Musical Quarterly* 49 (1963): 339–55.

———. "Scientific Empiricism in Musical Thought." In *Seventeenth Century Science and the Arts*, edited by H. H. Rhys, pp. 91–137. Princeton, 1961.

———. "Towards an Intrinsically Musical Definition of Mannerism in the Sixteenth Century." *Studi Musicali* 3 (1974): 313–46.

———. "*Ut oratoria musica*: the Rhetorical Basis of Musical Mannerism." *The Meaning of Mannerism*, pp. 37–65. Hanover, N.H., 1972.

———. "Vincenzo Galilei and Some Links between Pseudo-Monody and Monody." *Musical Quarterly* 46 (1960): 344–60.

———. "Vincenzo Galilei's Counterpoint Treatise: A Code for the *Seconda Pratica*." *Journal of the American Musicological Society* 9 (1956): 81–96.

Panofsky, Erwin. "Artist, Scientist, Genius: Notes on the 'Renaissance-Dämmerung.'" *The Renaissance: Six Essays*, pp. 123–82. New York, 1962.

———. *Galileo as Critic of the Arts.* The Hague, 1954.

———. *Idea: A Concept in Art History.* Columbia, 1968.

———. "Renaissance and Renascences." *Kenyon Review* 6 (1944): 201–36.

———. *Studies in Iconology: Humanistic Themes in the Art of the Renaissance.* New York, 1962.

Parrish, Carl. "A Renaissance Music Manual for Choir Boys." *Aspects of Medieval and Renaissance Music: A Birthday Offering to Gustave Reese*, pp. 649–64. New York, 1966.

Patterson, Annabel. *Hermogenes and the Renaissance.* Princeton, 1970.

Perella, Nicolas J. *The Critical Fortune of Battista Guarini's "Il Pastor Fido."* Florence, 1973.

Perkins, Leeman L. "Mode and Structure in the Masses of Josquin." *Journal of the American Musicological Society* 26 (1973): 189–239.

Pestelli, Giorgio. "Le poesie per la musica monteverdiana: il gusto poetico di Monteverdi." *Congresso Internazionale sul Tema Claudio Monteverdi e il suo Tempo*, pp. 349–60. Venice and Mantua, 1968.

Petrobelli, Pierluigi. "'Ah dolente partita': Marenzio, Wert, Monteverdi." *Congresso Internazionale sul Tema Claudio Monteverdi e il suo Tempo*, pp. 361–76. Venice and Mantua, 1968.

Pevsner, Nicolaus. *Academies of Art Past and Present.* Cambridge, 1940.

————. "The Architecture of Mannerism." In *The Mint*, edited by G. Grigson, pp. 116–38. London, 1946.

————. "Gegenreformation und Manierismus." *Repertorium für Kunstwissenschaft* 46 (1925): 243–62.

————. *An Outline of European Architecture.* Harmondsworth, 1960.

Piel, Friedrich. "Zum Problem des Manierismus in der Kunstgeschichte." *Literaturwissenschaftliches Jahrbuch des Görres-Gesellschaft* 2 (1961): 207–18.

Pinder, Wilhelm. "Zur Physiognomik des Manierismus." *Die Wissenschaft am Scheidewege von Leben und Geist: Festschrift Ludwig Klagen*, pp. 148–56. Leipzig, 1932.

Pirro, André. "Leo X and Music." *Musical Quarterly* 21 (1935): 1–16.

Pirrotta, Nino. *Li due Orfei da Poliziano a Monteverdi.* Turin, 1969; 1975.

————. "Early Opera and Aria." *New Looks at Italian Opera: Essays in Honor of Donald J. Grout*, pp. 39–107. Ithaca, 1968.

————. "Novelty and Renewal in Italy: 1300–1600." *Studien zur Tradition in der Musik: Kurt von Fischer zum 60. Geburtstag*, pp. 49–63. Munich, 1973.

————. "Scelte poetiche di Monteverdi." *Nuova Rivista Musicale Italiana* 2 (1968): 10–42 and 226–54.

————. "Teatro, scene e musica nelle opere di Monteverdi." *Congresso Internazionale sul Tema Claudio Monteverdi e il suo Tempo*, pp. 45–67. Venice and Mantua, 1968.

————. "Temperaments and Tendencies in the Florentine Camerata." *Musical Quarterly* 40 (1954): 169–89.

————. "Tragédie et comédie dans la Camerata fiorentina." In *Musique et poésie au XVIe siècle*, edited by Jean Jacquot, pp. 287–97. Paris, 1954.

Poggioli, Renato. *The Theory of the Avant-Garde.* Translated by G. Fitzgerland. Cambridge, Mass., 1968.

Pope-Hennessy, John. "Nicolas Hilliard and Mannerist Art Theory." *Journal of the Warburg and Courtauld Institute* 6 (1943): 89–100.

Porter, William V. "The Origins of the Baroque Solo Song: A Study of Italian MSS and Prints from 1590–1610." Ph.D. dissertation, Yale University, 1962; Ann Arbor, 1971.

————. "Peri's and Corsi's *Dafne*: Some New Discoveries and Observations." *Journal of the American Musicological Society* 18 (1965): 170–96.

Praz, Mario. *Bellezza e bizzarria*. Milan, 1960.

————. "Maniérisme et anti-maniérisme." *Critique* 137 (1958): 819–31.

————. *Mnemosyne: The Parallel between Literature and the Visual Arts*. Princeton, 1970.

Racek, Jan. "Die italienischen begleitete Monodie und das Problem der Entwicklung der italienischen Solokantata." *Liber amicorum Charles van den Borren*, pp. 160–91. Antwerp, 1964.

————. "Les madrigaux à voix seule de Luzzasco Luzzaschi." *Revue Musicale* 13 (1932): 11–23.

————. *Stilprobleme der italienischen Monodie*. Prague, 1965.

Raimondi, Ezio. *Letteratura barocca: Studi sul seicento italiano.* Florence, 1961.

————. "Per la nozione di manierismo letterario." *Manierismo, Barocco, Rococò: Concetti e Termini*, pp. 57–79. Accademia Nazionale dei Lincei. Rome, 1962.

Rastelli, Dario. "Tancredi e Clorinda 'al paragone.'" *Congresso Internazionale sul Tema Claudio Monteverdi e il suo Tempo*, pp. 557–69. Venice and Mantua, 1968.

Redlich, Hans F. *Claudio Monteverdi: Life and Works*. London, 1952.

————. *Claudio Monteverdi: Das Madrigalwerk*. Berlin, 1932.

————. "Early Baroque Church Music." In *The Age of Humanism 1540–1630*, edited by Gerald Abraham. New Oxford History of Music, vol. 4, pp. 520–49. London, 1968.

————. "Latin Church Music on the Continent-1; (d) The Venetian School." In *The Age of Humanism 1540–1630*, edited by Gerald Abraham. New Oxford History of Music, vol. 4, pp. 275–300. London, 1968.

————. "Das Orchester Claudio Monteverdis: Instrumentalpraxis in Monteverdis Madrigalwerk." *Musica Viva* 1 (1936): 55–64.

Reese, Gustave. *Fourscore Classics of Music Literature*. New York, 1957.

————. *Music in the Renaissance*. New York, 1959.

————. "The Repertoire of Book II of Ortiz's Tratado." *The Commonwealth of Music: in Honor of Curt Sachs*, pp. 201–7. New York, 1965.

Reiss, Josef. "J. Bapt. Benedictus, De intervallis musicis." *Zeitschrift für Musikwissenschaft* 7 (1924–25): 13–20.

Richter, Irma A., ed. *Paragone*. London, 1949.

Riemann, Hugo. *History of Music Theory: Books I and II, Polyphonic Theory to the Sixteenth Century*. Translated by Raymond H. Haggh, Lincoln, Nebraska, 1962.

Riemschneider-Hoerner, Margarete. "Holbein, Erasmus und der frühe Manierismus des XVI. Jahrhunderts." *Zeitschrift für Ästhetik und allgemeine Kunstwissenschaft* 33 (1939): 27–40.

Roche, Jerome. *The Madrigal.* London, 1972.

―――. "Monteverdi and the *Prima Prattica*." In *The Monteverdi Companion*, edited by Denis Arnold and Nigel Fortune, pp. 167–91. London, 1968.

Rogerson, Brewster. "The Art of Painting the Passions." *Journal of the History of Ideas* 14 (1953): 68–94.

Rolland, Romain. *Musiciens d'autrefois.* Paris, 1927.

Ronga, Luigi. "Tasso e la musica." *Torquato Tasso*, pp. 187–202. Milan, 1957.

Rose, Gloria. "Agazzari and the Improvising Orchestra." *Journal of the American Musicological Society* 18 (1965): 382–93.

―――. "Polyphonic Italian Madrigals of the Seventeenth Century." *Music and Letters* 47 (1966): 153–59.

Roskill, Mark W. *Dolce's 'Aretino' and Venetian Art Theory of the Cinquecento.* New York, 1968.

Rossi, Umberto. *Lettere di Cipriano de Rore, musico del secolo XVI.* Reggio-Emilia, 1890.

Rowland, Daniel P. *Mannerism—Style and Mood.* New Haven, 1964.

Rubsamen, Walter H. "From Frottola to Madrigal: The Changing Pattern of Secular Italian Vocal Music." In *Chanson and Madrigal 1480–1530*, edited by James Haar, pp. 51–87. Cambridge, Mass., 1964.

―――. *Literary Sources of Secular Music in Italy (ca. 1500).* Berkeley, 1943.

―――. "Sebastian Festa and the Early Madrigal." *Kongressbericht Kassel 1962*, pp. 122–26. Kassel, 1963.

Rüegge, Raimund. *Orazio Vecchis geistliche Werke.* Bern, 1967.

Ruhnke, Martin. *Joachim Burmeister: Ein Beitrag zur Musiklehre um 1600.* Kassel, 1955.

Sachs, Curt. "Barocksmusik." *Jahrbuch Musikbibliothek Peters* 26 (1919): 7–15.

―――. *The Rise of Music in the Ancient World.* New York, 1943.

Salop, Arnold. "On Stylistic Unity in Renaissance-Baroque Distinctions." *Essays in Musicology—A Birthday Offering to Willi Apel*, pp. 107–21. Bloomington, 1968.

Samuels, Richard S. "Benedetto Varchi, the *Accademia degli Infiammati*, and the Origins of the Italian Academic Movement." *Renaissance Quarterly* 29 (1976): 599–633.

Sandberger, Adolf. *Beiträge zur Geschichte der bayerische Hofkapelle unter Orlando di Lasso.* 2 vols. Leipzig, 1894 and 1895.

―――. "Roland Lassus' Beziehungen zur italienischen Literatur." *Sammelbände der Internationalen Musikgesellschaft* 5 (1903–1904): 402–41.

Santillana, Giorgio de. *The Age of Adventure: The Renaissance Philosophers.* Boston, 1957.

Sarton, George. "The Quest for Truth: Scientific Progress during the Renaissance." *The Renaissance: Six Essays*, pp. 55–76. New York, 1962.
_____. *Six Wings: Men of Science in the Renaissance*. Bloomington, 1957.
Schenk, Erich. "Über Begriff und Wesen des musikalischen Barock." *Zeitschrift für Musikwissenschaft* 17 (1935): 377–92.
Schmitz, Eugen. *Geschichte der weltlichen Solokantate*. Leipzig, 1914; 1955.
_____. "Zur Frühgeschichte der lyrischen Monodie des 17. Jahrhunderts." *Jahrbuch Musikbibliothek Peters* 18 (1911): 35–48.
_____. "Zur Geschichte der italienischen Continuo-Madrigals im siebzehnten Jahrhundert." *Sammelbände der Internationalen Musikgesellschaft* 11 (1910): 509–18.
_____. "Zur Geschichte des italienischen Kammerduetts." *Jahrbuch Musikbibliothek Peters* 23 (1916): 43–60.
Schrade, Leo. "L'Edipo tiranno' d'Andrea Gabrieli et la renaissance de la tragédie grecque." In *Musique et poésie au XVIe siècle*, edited by Jean Jacquot, pp. 276–85. Paris, 1954.
_____. *Monteverdi: Creator of Modern Music*. New York, 1950.
_____. "Renaissance: the Historical Conception of an Epoch." *Kongressbericht Utrecht 1952*, pp. 19–32. Amsterdam, 1953.
_____. *La représentation d'Edippo Tiranno au Teatro Olimpico (Vicence 1585)*. Paris, 1960.
_____. "Von der Maniera der Komposition in der Musik des 16. Jahrhunderts." *Zeitschrift für Musikwissenschaft* 16 (1934): 3–20, 98–117, and 152–70.
Schwartz, Rudolf. "Hans Leo Hassler unter dem Einfluss der italienischen Madrigalisten." *Vierteljahrschrift für Musikwissenschaft* 9 (1893): 1–61.
_____. "Zu den Texten der ersten fünf Bücher der Madrigale Monteverdis." *Festschrift Hermann Kretschmar*, pp. 147–48. Leipzig, 1918.
_____. "Zu den Texten der weltlichen Madrigale Palestrinas." *Jahrbuch Musikbibliothek Peters* 13 (1906): 95–97.
Scrivano, Riccardo. *Cultura e letteratura nel cinquecento*. Rome, 1966.
_____. *Il manierismo nella letteratura del cinquecento*. Padua, 1959.
Seay, Albert. "The Dialogus of Johannes Ottobi Anglici in arte musici." *Journal of the American Musicological Society* 8 (1955): 86–100.
_____. "The *Expositio Manus* of Johannes Tinctoris." *Journal of Music Theory* 9 (1965): 194–232.
_____. "The 15th Century *Coniuncta*: A Preliminary Study." *Aspects of Medieval and Renaissance Music: A Birthday Offering to Gustave Reese*, pp. 723–37. New York, 1966.
_____. "The 'Liber Musices' of Florentius de Faxolis." *Musik und Geschichte. (Leo Schrade zum sechzigsten Geburtstag)*, pp. 71–95. Cologne, 1963.

————. "Paolo Orlandini's *La musica in istanze vulgari.*" *Journal of the American Musicological Society* 22 (1969): 261–73.

Segre, Cesare. "Edonismo linguistico del cinquecento." *Giornale Storico della Letteratura Italiana* 130 (1958): 145–77.

Seldmayr, Hans. "Zur Revision der Renaissance." *Epochen und Werken,* vol. 1, pp. 202–34. Vienna, 1959.

Senn, Walter. *Musik und Theater am Hof zu Innsbruck.* Innsbruck, 1954.

Seznec, Jean. *The Survival of the Pagan Gods.* Princeton, 1972.

Shearman, John. "*Maniera* as an Aesthetic Ideal." *The Renaissance and Mannerism: Studies in Western Art.* Acts of the Twentieth International Congress of the History of Art, vol. 2, pp. 200–21. Princeton, 1963. Reprinted in *Renaissance Art*, edited by Creighton Gilbert, pp. 182–221. New York, 1973.

————. *Mannerism.* Harmondsworth, 1967.

Sholund, Edgar R. "The *Compendium Musices* of Adrianus Petit Coclico." Ph.D. dissertation, Harvard University, 1951.

Shumaker, Wayne. *The Occult Sciences in the Renaissance.* Berkeley, 1972.

Silverman, Faye-Ellen. "Gesualdo: Misguided or Inspired." *Current Musicology* 16 (1973): 49–54.

Slim, H. Colin. *A Gift of Madrigals and Motets.* Chicago, 1972.

Smart, Alastair. *The Renaissance and Mannerism in Italy.* London, 1971.

————. *The Renaissance and Mannerism in Northern Europe and Spain.* London, 1972.

Smyth, Craig H. *Mannerism and Maniera.* Locust Valley, N.Y., 1962.

————. "Mannerism and Maniera." *The Renaissance and Mannerism: Studies in Western Art.* Acts of the Twentieth International Congress of the History of Art, vol. 2, pp. 174–99. Princeton, 1963.

Solerti, Angelo. *Musica, ballo e drammatica alla Corte Medicea dal 1600–1637.* Florence, 1905.

————. *Le origini del melodramma.* Turin, 1903.

————. "La rappresentazioni musicali di Venezia dal 1571–1605." *Rivista Musicale Italiana* 9 (1902): 503–58.

Sphau, Blake L. "Baroque and Mannerism: Epoch and Style." *Colloquia Germanica* 1 (1967): 77–100.

Spiro, Arthur G. "The Five-Part Madrigals of Luzzasco Luzzaschi." Ph.D. dissertation, Boston University, 1961.

Spitzer, Leo. *Classical and Christian Ideas of World Harmony.* Baltimore, 1963.

Stark, James. "Giulio Caccini and the 'Noble Manner of Singing.'" *Journal of the Canadian Association of University Schools of Music* 1 (1971): 39–53.

Stechow, Wolfgang, ed. *Northern Renaissance Art 1400–1600: Sources and Documents.* Englewood Cliffs, N.J., 1966.

Steele, John. "The Later Madrigals of Luca Marenzio." *Studies in Music* 3 (1969): 17–24.

Stevens, Denis. "Gesualdo in a New Light." *Musical Times* 103 (1962): 332–33.

————. "*Madrigali guerrieri, et amorosi*: A Reappraisal for the Quartercentenary." *Musical Quarterly* 53 (1967): 161–87. Reprinted in *The Monteverdi Companion*, edited by Denis Arnold and Nigel Fortune, pp. 227–54. London, 1968.

————. "Music in Mantua." *Musical Times* 102 (1961): 360–61.

————. "Where are the Vespers of Yesteryear?" *Musical Quarterly* 47 (1961): 315–30.

Stevenson, Robert. *Juan Bermudo.* The Hague, 1960.

————. "Vicente Lusitano: New Light on his Career." *Journal of the American Musicological Society* 15 (1962): 72–77.

Strainchamps, Edmond. "New Light on the Accademia degli Elevati of Florence." *Musical Quarterly* 62 (1976): 507–35.

Strinati, Claudio M. "Sulla storia del concetto di manierismo." *Studi Musicali* 3 (1974): 13–32.

Strunk, Oliver. "Vergil in Music." *Musical Quarterly* 16 (1930): 482–97.

————, ed. *Source Readings in Music History.* New York, 1950.

Sypher, Wylie. *Four Stages of Renaissance Style: Transformations in Art and Literature 1400–1700.* Garden City, N.Y., 1955.

————. *Rococo to Cubism in Art and Literature.* New York, 1960.

Terza, Dante della. "Manierismo nella letteratura del cinquecento." *Belfazor* 15 (1960): 462–64.

Testi, Flavio. *La musica italiana nel seicento: Il melodramma.* Milan, 1970.

Thalmann, Marianne. *Romantik und Manierismus.* Stuttgart, 1963.

Torri, Luigi. "Vincenzo Ruffo, madrigalista e compositore di musica sacra del secolo XVI." *Rivista Musicale Italiana* 3 (1896): 635–83; 4 (1897): 233–51.

Toulmin, Stephen and Goodfield, June. *The Fabric of the Heavens.* New York, 1961.

Towneley, Simon. "Early Italian Opera." In *The Age of Humanism 1540–1630*, edited by Gerald Abraham. New Oxford History of Music, vol. 4, pp. 821–43. London, 1968.

Treves, Marco. "*Maniera*, the History of a Word." *Marsyas* 1 (1941): 69–88.

Turrell, Frances B. "The *Isagoge Musicen* of Henry Glarean." *Journal of Music Theory* 3 (1959): 97–139.

Turrini, Giuseppe. *L'Accademia Filarmonica di Verona dalla fondazione (Maggio 1543) al 1600 e il suo patrimonio musicale antico.* Verona, 1941.

Tusiani, Joseph, ed. *Italian Poets of the Renaissance.* Long Island City, N.Y., 1971.

Ulivi, Ferruccio. *L'imitazione nella poetica del rinascimento.* Milan, 1959.

————. *Il manierismo del Tasso e altri studi.* Florence, 1966.

Unger, Hans-Heinrich. *Die Beziehungen zwischen Musik und Rhetorik im 16.–18. Jahrhundert.* Würzburg, 1941.

Ursprung, Otto. "Der vokale Grundcharakter des diskantbetonten figurierte Stils." *Kongressbericht Basel 1924,* pp. 364–74. Leipzig, 1925.

Vacchelli, Anna Maria M. "Elementi stilistici nell'*Euridice* de Jacopo Peri in rapporto all'*Orfeo* di Monteverdi." *Congresso Internazionale sul Tema Claudio Monteverdi e il suo Tempo,* pp. 117–26. Venice and Mantua, 1968.

Van Crevel, Marius. *Adrianus Petit Coclico: Leben und Beziehungen eines nach Deutschland emigrierten Josquinschülers.* The Hague, 1940.

Van den Borren, Charles. "Le madrigalisme avant le madrigal." *Studien zur Musikgeschichte: Festschrift Guido Adler,* pp. 78–83. Vienna, 1930.

————. *Orlande de Lassus.* Paris, 1930.

————. "Philippe de Monte." *Revue Musicale* 15 (1934): 97–103.

————. *Roland de Lassus.* Brussels, 1944.

————. "Der Universalist des seicento: Roland de Lassus, der Meister aus Mons." *Musica* 10 (1956): 311–14.

————. "Y avait-il une pratique musicale ésotérique au temps de Roland de Lassus?" *Revue Belge de Musicologie* 2 (1948): 38–43.

Van Doorslaer, G. "Die Musikkapelle Kaiser Rudolphe II im Jahre 1582, unter der Leitung von Ph. de Monte." *Zeitschrift für Musikwissenschaft* 13 (1931): 481–91.

————. *La vie et les oeuvres de Philippe de Monte.* Brussels, 1921.

Van Regteren Altena. J. Q. "Two Sixteenth-Century Exhibitions in Holland." *Burlington Magazine* 97 (1955): 315–19.

Vatelli, Francesco. "Il madrigale drammatico e Adriano Banchieri." *Arte e vita musicale a Bologna,* pp. 57–115. Bologna, 1927.

————. *Un musicista pesarese nel secolo XVI (Ludovico Zacconi).* Bologna, 1904.

Vecchi, Giuseppe. "L'opera didattico-teorico di Adriano Banchieri in rapporto alla 'nuova prattica.'" *Congresso Internazionale sul Tema Claudio Monteverdi e il suo Tempo,* pp. 385–95. Venice and Mantua, 1968.

Venturini, Giuseppe. *Saggi critici. (Cinquecento minori: O Ariosti, G. M. Verdizotti e il loro influsso nella vita e nell'opere del Tasso.)* Biblioteca di Lettere e Arti, vol. 31. Ravenna, 1970.

Vogel, Emil. *Bibliothek der gedruckten weltlichen Vocalmusik Italiens. (Aus den Jahren 1500–1700.)* Hildesheim and New York, 1972.

————. *Marco da Gagliano: Zur Geschichte des Florentiner Musikleben von 1570–1650.* Leipzig, 1889.

Volpe, Galvano della "Poetica del cinquecento." *Opere*, vol. 5, pp. 103–90. Rome, 1972.

Wagner, Peter. "Das Madrigal und Palestrina." *Vierteljahrschrift für Musikwissenschaft* 8 (1892): 423–98.

————. *Palestrina als weltlicher Komponist*. Strasbourg, 1890.

Walker, D. P. "Musical Humanism in the Sixteenth and Early Seventeenth Centuries." *Music Review* 2 (1941): 1–13, 111–31, 220–27, and 288–308; 3 (1942): 55–71.

————. "La musique des intermèdes florentines de 1589 et l'humanisme." In *Musique des intermèdes de "La Pellegrina,"* edited by D. P. Walker. Les fêtes de Florence, vol. 1, pp. XXIII–XXXI. Paris, 1963.

————. "Orpheus as Theologian and Renaissance Platonists." *Journal of Warburg and Courtauld Institutes* 16 (1953): 100–20.

————. *Spiritual and Demonic Magic from Ficino to Campanella*. Notre Dame, 1975.

Wangermée, Robert. *Flemish Musical Society in the Fifteenth and Sixteenth Centuries*. New York, 1968.

Ward, John M. "Parody Technique in 16th-Century Instrumental Music." *The Commonwealth of Music: in Honor of Curt Sachs*, pp. 208–28. New York, 1965.

Watkins, Glenn. "Carlo Gesualdo and the Delimitations of Late Mannerist Style." *Studi Musicali* 3 (1973): 55–74.

————. *Gesualdo: The Man and His Music*. London, 1973.

Weaver, Robert L. "The Orchestra in Early Italian Opera." *Journal of the American Musicological Society* 17 (1964): 83–89.

————. "Sixteenth-Century Instrumentation." *Musical Quarterly* 47 (1961): 363–78.

Weinberg, Bernard. *A History of Literary Criticism in the Italian Renaissance*. 2 vols. Chicago, 1961.

Weinmann, Karl. *Das Konzil von Trient und die Kirchenmusik*. Leipzig, 1919.

Weisbach, Werner. *Der Barock als Kunst der Gegenreformation*. Berlin, 1921.

————. "Gegenreformation—Manierismus—Barock." *Repertorium für Kunstwissenschaft* 49 (1928): 16–28.

————. "Der Manierismus." *Zeitschrift für bildene Kunst* 30 (1918–1919): 161–83.

————. "Zum Problem des Manierismus." *Studien zur deutschen Kunstgeschichte*, pp. 15–20. Strasbourg, 1934.

Weise, Georg. "La doppia origine del concetto di manierismo." *Studi Vasariani 1950*, pp. 181–85. Florence, 1952.

————. "Maniera und pellegrino: zwei Lieblingswörter der italienischen Literatur der Zeit der Manierismus." *Romanistisches Jahrbuch* 3 (1950): 321–402.

————. "Manierismo e letteratura." *Rivista de Letterature Moderne e Comparate* 13 (1960): 5–52.

————. "Manieristiche und frühbarocke Elemente in der religiosen Schriften des Pietro Aretino." *Bibliothèque d'Humanisme et Renaissance* 19 (1957): 170–207.

————. "Storia del termine 'Manierismo.'" *Manierismo, Barocco, Rococò: Concetti e Termini*, pp. 27–38. Accademia Nazionale dei Lincei. Rome, 1962.

Weismann, Wilhelm. "Ein verkannter Madrigalzyklus Monteverdis." *Deutsches Jahrbuch der Musikwissenschaft für 1957*, pp. 37–51. Leipzig, 1958.

Wescher, Paul. "The 'Idea' in Giuseppe Arcimboldo's Art." *Magazine of Art* 43 (1950): 3–8.

Westrup, Jack A. "Monteverdi's 'Lamento d'Arianna.'" *Music Review* 1 (1940): 144–54.

————. "The Originality of Monteverdi." *Proceedings of the Royal Musical Association* 60 (1933–34): 1–25.

White, John. "Paragone: Aspects of the Relationships between Sculpture and Painting." In *Art, Science and History in the Renaissance*, edited by Charles S. Singleton, pp. 43–109. Baltimore, 1967.

Wienpahl, Robert W. "Zarlino, the Senario and Tonality." *Journal of the American Musicological Society* 12 (1959): 27–41.

Willets, Pamela J. "A Neglected Source of Monody and Madrigal." *Music and Letters* 43 (1962): 329–39.

Wilson, Harold S. "Some Meanings of 'Nature' in Renaissance Literary Theory." *Journal of the History of Ideas* 2 (1941): 430–48.

Wind, Edgar. *Pagan Mysteries in the Renaissance*. New York, 1968.

Winter, Carl. *Ruggiero Giovanelli (c. 1560–1625)*. Munich, 1935.

Wiora, Walter. "Musica poetica und musikalisches Kunstwerk." *Festschrift Karl Gustav Fellerer*, pp. 579–89. Regensburg, 1962.

————. "Der religiöse Grundzug im neuen Stil und Weg Josquin des Prez." *Die Musikforschung* 6 (1953): 23–37.

Wittkower, Rudolf. *Architectural Principles in the Age of Humanism*. New York, 1971.

Wittkower, Rudolf and Margot. *Born under Saturn: The Character and Conduct of Artists*. London, 1963.

Wlassics, Tibor. *Galilei critico letterario*. Ravenna, 1974.

Wölfflin, Heinrich. *Principles of Art History*. New York, 1932.

Wolf, Robert E. "The Aesthetic Problem of the 'Renaissance.'" *Revue Belge de Musicologie* 9 (1955): 83–102.

————. "Renaissance, Mannerism, Baroque: Three Styles, Three Periods." *Les Colloques de Wégimont IV (1957)*, pp. 35–80. Paris, 1963.

————, and Millen, Ronald. *Renaissance and Mannerist Art*. New York, 1968.

Wolff, Hellmuth C. "Der Manierismus in der barocken und romantischen Oper." *Die Musikforschung* 19 (1966): 261–69.

————. "Manierismus und Musikgeschichte." *Die Musikforschung* 24 (1971): 245–50.

————. "Der Stilbegriff der 'Renaissance' in der Musik der alten Nieder-länder." *Report of the Fifth Congress of the International Musicological Society, Utrecht 1952*, pp. 450–55. Amsterdam, 1953.

Würtengerber, Franzsepp. *Mannerism: The European Style of the Sixteenth Century.* New York, 1963.

Yates, Frances A. *The Art of Memory.* London, 1966.

————. *Giordano Bruno and the Hermetic Tradition.* London, 1964.

————. "The Hermetic Tradition in Renaissance Science." In *Art, Science and History in the Renaissance*, edited by Charles S. Singleton, pp. 255–74. Baltimore, 1967.

————. *Theater of the World.* Chicago, 1970.

Zenck, Hermann. "Nicola Vicentino's 'L'antica musica' (1555)." *Theodor Kroyer Festschrift*, pp. 86–101. Regensburg, 1933.

————. "Zarlinos 'Istitutioni harmoniche' als Quelle zur Musikanschauung der italienischen Renaissance." *Zeitschrift für Musikwissenschaft* 12 (1930): 540–78.

Zupnick, Irving L. "The 'Aesthetics' of the Early Mannerists." *Art Bulletin* 35 (1953): 302–6.

Addenda

PRIMARY SOURCES

Luzzaschi, Luzzasco. *Dolorosi martir a5. Il quarto libro de madrigali a cinque voci.* Ferrara, 1594.
   A. Einstein, *The Italian Madrigal.* Vol. 3. Princeton, 1949; 1971.

Michelangelo Buonarotti. *Last Judgment.* 1536. Rome, Sistine Chapel, Vatican.
   F. Würtenberger, *Mannerism.* New York, 1963.
   A. Hauser, *Mannerism.* London, 1965.
   L. Murray, *The Late Renaissance and Mannerism.* New York, 1967.
   R. E. Wolf and R. Millen, *Renaissance and Mannerist Art.* New York, 1968.

Index of Names

A

Aaron, Pietro, 145, 186, 286, 545 (n. 7); on genius, 130–31, 209, 240–41; on tuning, 136–37; on modes, 156–57; on counterpoint, 159–60, 235, 264, 537 (n. 28); on mutation, 184–85; on cosmology, 536 (n. 35); on genera, 548 (n. 24)
Abate, Niccolò dell', 43, 46
Achillini, Claudio, 417, 418, 434, 465
Ad Herennium, anonymous of, 268
Affanni, Federigo, 328
Agnelli, Scipione, 416, 562 (n. 59)
Agostino, Lodovico, 302, 329, 527 (n. 5)
Agricola, Martin, 180, 184, 539 (n. 23)
Agrippa von Nettesheim, Cornelius, 98
Alammani, Luigi, 333
Alberti, Leon Battista, 11, 13, 14, 16, 52, 518 (n. 3)
Albrecht V (duke of Bavaria), 272, 310
Alciati, Andrea, 30
Alexander VI (pope), 551 (n. 3)
Ambra, Francesco d', 457
Aquila, Serafino dell', 454
Arcadelt, Jacob, 68, 124, 291, 293–95, 302, 510, 552 (n. 25)
Archilei, Antonio, 462
Archilei, Vittoria, 214, 231, 232, 252, 451, 460, 462, 463, 560 (n. 32), 561 (n. 47)
Arcimboldo, Giuseppe, 18
Aretino, Pietro, 19, 20, 89–90, 237, 488, 519 (nn. 41, 45), 527 (n. 5)
Argenti, Agostino degli, 456
Ariosto, Lodovico, 67, 90, 226, 325, 329, 410, 528 (n. 22)
Aristotle, 23, 31, 194, 229, 519–20 (n. 3), 521 (n. 36)
Aristoxenos, 139, 140, 142, 488, 533 (n. 20)
Arnold, Denis, 408, 473

Arpa, Giovanni Leopardo dell', 455, 488
Artusi, Giovanni Maria, 131, 139, 146, 151, 167, 171, 205, 206, 207, 216, 256, 267, 354, 398, 555 (n. 2); attack on Monteverdi and novel style, 127–28, 135, 169–70, 373, 394, 396, 531 (n. 41); on dissonance treatment, 199; quarrel with Bottrigari, 520 (n. 13); on tuning, 533 (n. 6); on counterpoint, 535 (n. 8); on ornamentation, 543 (n. 23)
Avalos, Alfonso d', 68, 294, 297
Avianus, Johannes, 541 (n. 33)

B

Baccusi, Ippolito, 367
Ballestra, Raimundo, 263, 269, 272
Banchieri, Adriano, 175, 549 (n. 33); on counterpoint, 126, 169, 208, 541 (n. 28); on ornamentation, 217; on gratiosa maniera, 257; madrigal-comedies, 368, 408–9; his academy, 487
Barberini family, 466, 479
Barbour, J. Murray, 135, 533 (n. 15)
Bardi, Giovanni de': his Camerata, 217, 230, 412, 427, 431, 489; on old and new music, 220–21, 543 (n. 25); intermedio texts, 460–61, 462
Bardi, Pietro de', 230
Bargagli, Girolamo, 461, 557 (n. 38)
Barre, Antonio, 291, 325, 326, 327, 329, 358, 553 (n. 16)
Bartoli, Cosimo, 118, 291, 530 (n. 2)
Bassano, Giovanni, 216
Bati, Luca, 461
Battisti, Eugenio, 8
Baudelaire, Charles, 7
Baumgart, Fritz, 8, 34, 104
Beccafumi, Domenico, 35

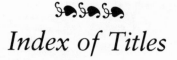

Index of Titles

In this index names of authors and artists appear in parentheses to distinguish them from those of composers. Initials are used to identify persons with identical surnames, with the following exceptions—(Torquato) Tasso, (Giovanni Battista) Guarini, (Vincenzo) Galilei, and (Claudio) Monteverdi. In these instances, initials indicate persons other than those named above (e.g., Bernardo Tasso or Giulio Cesare Monteverdi). Page numbers in boldface type refer to examples of poems, art works, and music.

Abbreviations

C.	La Clizia		O.F.	Orlando furioso
D.C.	Divine Comedy		P.F.	Il pastor fido
E.	Euridice		S.	Selene
G.C.	Gerusalemme conquistata		Sa.	Il sacrificio
G.L.	Gerusalemme liberata		T.	Tirsi
O.	Orfeo		V.	Vespers

A

A Dio Florida bella (Marino), **76**, 589
—Monteverdi, 76, 416, 593
A me che fatta (Cini), Striggio, 559 (n. 21), 610
A Plaine and Easie Introduction to Practicall Musicke (Morley), 534 (nn. 47, 2), 536 (n. 11), 537 (nn. 41, 43), 596
A quest'olmo (Marino), Monteverdi, 421, 557 (n. 7), 594
A un giro sol (Guarini), 73, 583
—Monteverdi, 401, **402–4**, 405, 591
A Young Man (Bronzino), 522 (n. 15), 573
Absalon fili mi, des Prez, 285, 602
Acuity and the Art of Wit (Gracián), 30. See Agudeza y arte del ingenio
Ad Herennium, 268, 568
Adages (Erasmus), 535 (n. 29), 579
Aeneid (Virgil), 284

Affetti amorosi spirituali, Quagliati, 451, 603
Affetti spirituali, 494
Agudeza y arte del ingenio (Gracián), 30, 521 (nn. 20, 24), 522 (n. 41), 583
Ah dolente partita (Guarini, P.F.), **78**, 555 (n. 24)
—Monteverdi, 399, **400**, 555 (n. 24), 556 (n. 25), 591
—Marenzio, 555 (n. 24), 589
—Wert, 555 (n. 24), 618–19
Ahi caso acerbo (Striggio, O.), Monteverdi, 474, 562 (n. 56), 593
Ahi come a un vago sol (Guarini), Monteverdi, 406–7, 417, 592
Ahi fuggitivo ben, Rasi, 558 (n. 21), 604
Ahi sventurato amante (Striggio, O.), Monteverdi, 562 (n. 56), 593
Al fonte al prato (Chiabrera), Caccini, 446, 575

The Author

Maria Rika Maniates is professor of musicology
at the University of Toronto.

The Book

Composition by The University of
North Carolina Press

Text set in Mergenthaler V-I-P Sabon

Music engraving by
Pisces Press, London

Printed on sixty-pound 1854
by S. D. Warren Company

Cover stock, Roxite Vellum C 56548
by The Holliston Mills, Incorporated

Printing and binding
by Braun-Brumfield, Incorporated

Design by Dariel Mayer

Published by The University of
North Carolina Press

091613